Studies in American
Historical Demography

STUDIES IN POPULATION

Under the Editorship of: H. H. WINSBOROUGH

Department of Sociology
University of Wisconsin
Madison, Wisconsin

Studies in American Historical Demography

edited by

Maris A. Vinovskis

Department of History
and
Center for Political Studies
   of the Institute for
   Social Research
University of Michigan
Ann Arbor, Michigan

ACADEMIC PRESS   1979

A Subsidiary of Harcourt Brace Jovanovich, Publishers

New York   London   Toronto   Sydney   San Francisco

ACADEMIC PRESS, INC.
111 Fifth Avenue, New York, New York 10003

United Kingdom Edition published by
ACADEMIC PRESS, INC. (LONDON) LTD.
24/28 Oval Road, London NW1 7DX

Library of Congress Cataloging in Publication Data
Main entry under title:

Studies in American historical demography.

(Studies in population)
1. United States—Population—History—Addresses,
essays, lectures. I. Vinovskis, Maris. II. Series.
HB3505.S79   301.32'9'73   78-25611
ISBN 0-12-722050-X

PRINTED IN THE UNITED STATES OF AMERICA

79 80 81 82   9 8 7 6 5 4 3 2 1

To

John Demos, Philip Greven, Jr., Ken Lockridge

whose pioneering efforts and personal friendships have made the field of historical demography more meaningful for the rest of us.

Contents

Contributors

WENDELL H. BASH

EDWIN S. DETHLEFSEN

JOHN DEMOS

RICHARD EASTERLIN

JACK EBLEN

JOHN FULTON

PHILIP J. GREVEN, JR.

TAMARA K. HAREVEN

IRENE HECHT

MICHAEL S. HINDUS

RUSSELL R. MENARD

JOHN MODELL

SUSAN L. NORTON

NANCY OSTERUD

ELIZABETH H. PLECK

ANITA H. RUTMAN

DARRETT B. RUTMAN

DANIEL SCOTT SMITH

PETER UHLENBERG

MARIS A. VINOVSKIS

ROBERT V. WELLS

Preface

The past fifteen years have witnessed a dramatic increase in interest in American demographic development. Stimulated by the work of European historical demographers such as Louis Henry and E. A. Wrigley, American scholars have tried to reconstruct the population of the United States in the past. As a result, the number of studies in American demographic history have greatly increased.

One of the most healthy things about American historical demography is that it has attracted scholars from a variety of different disciplines. Not only have historians and demographers participated in this effort, but also scholars from anthropology, economics, and sociology. This interdisciplinary approach to the study of population has been very useful because it has produced analyses from very different perspectives.

Most of the work in American historical demography has been in the form of articles and essays rather than books. Unfortunately, the interdisciplinary nature of this undertaking has meant that these articles and essays are scattered throughout a variety of different journals—many of which are often inaccessible to scholars in the different disciplines. Thus, historians are often unaware of the work published in such journals as the *Milbank Memorial Fund Quarterly,* while their counterparts in demography probably are not familiar with articles published in the *Proceedings of the American Antiquarian Society.*

In order to bring together some of the best studies in American historical demography, I have selected twenty-five articles from thirteen different journals. Though this is not a comprehensive collection of the recent efforts in American historical demography, it does represent a large proportion of the existing literature and should be of use to practitioners in the field as well as to more general readers who simply want to follow recent developments in this area. The selection of materials for this volume was significantly improved by the willingness of many of my colleagues in American historical demography to make suggestions at various stages of this undertaking.

I am grateful to the authors of these contributions as well as to the journals for permission to reprint these articles. Without their cooperation and support, this volume would not have been possible.

RECENT TRENDS IN AMERICAN HISTORICAL DEMOGRAPHY: Some Methodological and Conceptual Considerations

Maris A. Vinovskis

Department of History, and Center for Political Studies, Institute for Social Research, University of Michigan, Ann Arbor, Michigan 48104

There is an increased interest in the role of demographic factors in American development. During the last 15 years, scholars from a variety of disciplines have explored the impact of demographic changes on American society in the past. A collection of 26 of the major articles from diverse journals has just been published (Vinovskis 1978c).

Whereas most of the demographic studies of colonial America have been done by historians, the demographic analysis of nineteenth century America has been carried out to a large extent by demographers and economists. While studies of colonial demography have relied very heavily on reconstituting families from the vital records, those of nineteenth century America usually have been based on the federal censuses. Finally, scholars of colonial history tend to be less well trained in statistics and demography than their counterparts in nineteenth century demographic history.

This essay does not analyze or even mention most of the work in American historical demography, rather it suggests some of the major issues and problems of this field. In the section on colonial demographic history, I emphasize some of the methodological and conceptual problems of the current studies, since most scholars have accepted these efforts rather uncritically. In the discussion of nineteenth century demographic history, I analyze the works on fertility and mortality patterns and trends in the antebellum period.

603

Reprinted from *Annual Reviews in Sociology*
4, 603–627. Copyright © 1978 by permission
of the publisher.

COLONIAL DEMOGRAPHIC HISTORY

Most of the recent interest in American demographic history has been focused on the colonial period—due largely to the excitement generated by the publication of the first wave of demographic analyses of colonial communities (Demos 1970; Greven 1970; Lockridge 1970). These studies were largely concerned with the nature of the colonial family and how it was affected by demographic events such as births, marriages, and deaths. Understandably, scholars from many different disciplines have relied upon these demographic studies for information about the colonial family. Most of the efforts to integrate the findings from these analyses with other information about colonial society have simply assumed that it is possible to infer the demographic characteristics of colonial America from these existing studies. In reviewing some of the basic studies, I focus on the methodological and conceptual problems that need to be considered before we can interpret American colonial development from the perspective of the recent work in the field of demographic history.[1]

Representativeness of the Groups Analyzed

The lack of readily available data discouraged historians until recently from studying the demographic development of early America. A few crude efforts were made to estimate the population size of the colonies (Greene & Harrington 1932); almost no attempts were made to estimate demographic indices such as birth, marriage, or death rates. Meanwhile, French and English scholars made impressive strides during the 1950s and early 1960s in analyzing the preindustrial population trends in their countries. Using the technique of family reconstitution that was developed by Henry (1956), historians could estimate vital events in the past from the nominal lists of births, marriages, and deaths that had been recorded by local parish priests.

American colonial historians were quick to adopt these new ways of analyzing past populations, (Lockridge 1977). By the mid 1960s studies of colonial America based on family reconstitution techniques began to appear in the scholarly journals (Demos 1965; Greven 1966; Lockridge 1966). With the publication of these studies in monograph form (Demos 1970; Greven 1970; Lockridge 1970), the field of colonial demographic history was well established. Unfortunately, most scholars who used these studies were unaware of the methodological limitations inherent in analyses based on family reconstitution.

---

[1]The section on colonial demographic history is an expansion and updating of an earlier article on the study of early American family life (Vinovskis 1974).

MARIS A. VINOVSKIS

One of the problems in using family reconstitution techniques to extract demographic indices from nominal lists of births, marriages, and deaths is that the process is very time consuming. Some recent innovations have been made in the use of computers to initially reconstruct the vital events into family groups (Winchester 1970; Wrigley 1973), but most of these procedures are still quite primitive. All of the colonial family reconstitution studies so far have been linked by hand. Scholars usually do not reconstitute more than 2000–3000 individuals in such studies. As a result, the only American communities that have been reconstituted are small, agricultural villages such as Andover (Greven 1970), Dedham (Lockridge 1970), Deerfield (Swedlund et al 1976), Hingham (Smith 1975), or Windsor (Bissell 1973). There has been some work on small urban areas such as Salem, but most of this focused on only a part of the total population (Farber 1972; Somerville 1969). Large urban centers such as Boston, New York, or Philadelphia have not been analyzed.

Because most colonists lived in small communities in the seventeenth and eighteenth centuries, this bias in the selection of towns has not been perceived as very serious. However, historians are often interested in the impact of urban life on the family. Furthermore, there were large rural-urban differences in demographic events such as mortality during the colonial period (Vinovskis 1972). Therefore, the almost exclusive focus on rural areas makes it impossible to analyze the nature of the family in different social settings in colonial America.

Sometimes the process by which data are collected results in a biased sample of towns. For example, Wigglesworth's life table of 1789 is based on 62 bills of mortality that he obtained from members of the newly founded American Academy of Arts and Sciences in Boston. Demographers and economists who relied on the Wigglesworth life table incorrectly assumed that it was representative of the New England area. An overrepresentation of large communities in the Wigglesworth sample of morality partly helps to explain why Wigglesworth's estimate of the colonial death rate was higher than those found from more recent demographic analyses of small, agricultural communities (Demos 1970; Greven 1970; Vinovskis 1971a).

We must not only consider the sizes of the towns, but also their stage of economic and social development. The demographic characteristics of families are affected by when the town was settled and by the type and extent of resources available to the population. Demos (1968) found a much younger population in Bristol, Rhode Island, in 1689 than in 1774. In addition, there was a surplus of women in Bristol by 1774, which resulted in a small increase in the age at first marriage as well as in the proportion of women married. Similarly, Bissell (1974) found that rates of geographic mobility were significantly affected by the general economic and social developments within Windsor.

A major hypothesis from studies of nineteenth century fertility is that declining availability of farmland spurs fertility declines as areas become older and more densely settled. Just how important the variations in fertility are among towns in different stages of development in the seventeenth and eighteenth century is yet to be settled.[2] Some argue that marital fertility varied only slightly on a geographic basis and attribute differences in child-woman ratios among towns mainly to differences in the age structure of adults as well as differences in mortality levels. Smith (1972) uses the marital fertility rates from the town of Hingham for women who married in the two decades from 1761 to 1780 as being reasonably representative of all eighteenth century New England women. An analysis of child-woman ratios among Massachusetts townships in 1765 and 1790 (Vinovskis 1978e) suggests the importance of geographic and socioeconomic factors in predicting the levels of fertility. The point worth reemphasizing is that historians must at least consider the possible impact of different stages of economic and social development on the demographic characteristics of families in early America.

Another way in which the sample selected for study affects the representativeness of the results is that complete data on births, marriages, and deaths are available only for certain families. Family reconstitution studies usually are able only to reconstitute completely 10–50% of the population due to the inadequacy of the vital records. European historians have begun to consider the implications of using a method of analysis that deals with only a small proportion of the total population (Dupaquier 1972; Levine 1976; Schofield 1972). Unfortunately, most American historians neglect the issue of which particular group has been studied and how this might affect the results of the analysis.

Farber's (1972) study of Salem families in 1800 was based on the members and relatives of William Bentley's East Parish Church. Farber assumes that the members of this particular church were typical of the town as a whole and generalizes about Salem families in 1800 from these data. The 1790 members of Bentley's church and their families constituted about 16% of the total population of Salem. The question that needs to be resolved is whether there were any significant socioeconomic differences between these

---

[2]Though the land availability theory of fertility decline is one of the most interesting efforts to develop an explanation for the decline in rural fertility, colonial historians have not made much use of it. This is somewhat surprising, because colonial historians have done considerable work on the diminishing amount of farmland available in the seventeenth and eighteenth centuries (Lockridge 1968).

church members and the rest of the community. Even if there were no major socioeconomic differences, there is a definite religious bias in the data. Farber found Puritan religious ideals still important in the lives of the residents of Salem in 1800, perhaps because he concentrated so much of his investigation on the families in Salem who were religious enough to belong to Bentley's church.

Another example of how the subgroup of the population selected for study affects the conclusions drawn from the investigation is illustrated by the analysis of families in colonial Ipswich, Massachusetts (Norton 1971). Though Ipswich was a commercial seaport in the eighteenth century, its mortality rates seem to be closer to agrarian communities such as Andover and Plymouth than to urban areas such as Boston and Salem. The deaths of single men engaged in the particularly hazardous occupation of seamen were excluded from the calculations. As a result, the estimated mortality rates may not reflect the mortality of Ipswich as a whole.

Many historians used the data gathered by Greven (1970) in his analysis of Andover, Massachusetts, in the seventeenth and eighteenth centuries. Usually they assumed that the demographic characteristics of the population described in the book were representative of the entire Andover community. Yet Greven reconstituted only the descendants of the first settlers of Andover. As a result, he did not provide much information on the families of latecomers who, by the eighteenth century, constituted between one half and three quarters of the town's population. It is likely that the descendants of the settlers remaining in Andover were generally more affluent than the latecomers (Vinovskis 1971b). Consequently, the demographic characteristics of the population in Greven's sample may be only representative of the wealthier segments of that society.

Besides biases introduced by the selection of the towns or the groups studied within them, there is also a serious regional distortion. Almost all of the detailed family reconstitution studies now available focused on New England—and particularly on Massachusetts. Yet there are reasons to suspect that this regional concentration does not provide a very accurate picture of the colonial family elsewhere; many of the most interesting efforts in early American demographic history are now being done on the South. There was a much greater excess of males in the South than in New England in the seventeenth and eighteenth centuries (Craven 1971; Hecht 1973; Menard 1973; Moller 1945; Wells 1975a). As a result, it was more difficult for men in the South to establish their own families than for their counterparts in the North. Because of this imbalance in sex ratios, natural increase played a much smaller role in the population growth of the South than of the North.

Mortality rates in colonial New England were significantly lower than in the South. Throughout the colonial period, New England was relatively healthy compared to England at that time or other American colonies (Demos 1970; Greven 1970; Smith 1972; Vinovskis 1971a, 1972). The South was characterized by very high mortality in the seventeenth and eighteenth centuries (Craven 1971; Hecht 1973; Morgan 1975; Rutman & Rutman 1976; Walsh & Menard 1974).

Finally, there is a bias in the racial and ethnic groups selected for demographic analysis. Demographic data are much more abundant and more accurately recorded for the white population than for blacks or Indians. Most of the early efforts focused exclusively on the white settlers. Recently, some studies of blacks in colonial America have been produced—particularly on slaves in the South (Menard 1975; Wood 1974). But relatively little is known about the demographic characteristics of the black population in the North. An area even more neglected by most demographic historians has been the study of American Indians. Though there have been some very useful attempts to study native American demography by scholars of Latin America (Borah 1969), much less effort has been devoted to North American Indians (Dobyns 1976). It is likely that there will be a significant increase in studies of blacks and native Americans in the colonial period, even though the demographic sources for these populations are considerably worse than those for the white population.

Problems of Data Analysis

One of the major strengths of the recent work in American demographic history is its quantitative orientation. Rather than relying solely on the generalizations made by contemporaries about the characteristics of the colonial population, historians have calculated various demographic indices from the registration of births, deaths, and marriages in the local communities. Since most historians using quantitative data have not had extensive formal training in statistics and research design, some of their studies are marred by incorrect data processing or analysis.

One of the most common problems in using data is that historians may not choose the most appropriate indices for their analyses. Farber (1972:45) found that the median age at death for laborers, mariners, and fishermen was 63.8 years, while the median age at death for artisans was 72.0 years. But the median age at death is not a very useful index of mortality differentials, because it may simply reflect differences in the age structure of the populations rather than differences in the conditions of life each group encountered. A more useful measure would be the life expectancy of each group using age-specific mortality rates.

The importance of using life-table methods for the analysis of mortality data can be seen in the study of Andover.[3] Using the ratio of births to deaths from the town vital records as well as the infant and adult death rates based on the reconstitution of the families of the first settlers and their descendants, Greven (1970) reported an increasing death rate in eighteenth century Andover. If Greven's mortality data are converted into life expectancies, there does not appear to be any clear-cut decrease in the expectation of life at age twenty from the seventeenth to the eighteenth century (Vinovskis 1971b). Furthermore, Greven's use of cohort analysis was misapplied to measure mortality changes from the seventeenth to the eighteenth centuries. Though Greven treats the death rates of those born between 1670 and 1699 as seventeenth century mortality rates, a large proportion of that birth cohort was actually experiencing the conditions of life in the eighteenth century. Although Greven's data on the mortality experiences of various birth cohorts give very useful information on the lives of these individuals, they do not really tell us much about the different conditions of life in the seventeenth and eighteenth centuries.

Since we do not have adequate demographic data for many areas of colonial America, such as the South, historians have tried to use other indices of population development such as militia rolls, poll taxes, and headrights. Though the use of indirect measures of population size and growth are necessary when we do not have adequate demographic data, we must be aware of the possibility of biases in such information due to the manner in which the data were generated. Craven (1971) studied immigration to seventeenth century Virginia by using data on the number of headrights (grants of land made to new immigrants or their sponsors). He assumed that the number of headrights granted were an appropriate index of the relative levels of immigration into Virginia. Using these data, Craven found that the bulk of immigration to seventeenth century Virginia came in the period 1650–1675 rather than in the earlier decades. Unfortunately, the system of granting headrights probably did not reflect the actual or even relative levels of population immigration to seventeenth century Virginia. Settlers often obtained the rights to acquire land without immediately regis-

---

[3]A few scholars (Dethlefsen 1969; Sharlin 1978) used or advocated the use of life tables based on the distribution of deaths in an area (in which they assumed the appropriateness of using a stationary life-table model) rather than a life table constructed from age-specific mortality data for that area. There are often significant differences between the two approaches. Thus, whereas a stationary-population model would yield a male life expectancy of 29.5 years at birth in Salem between 1818 and 1822, a life table constructed from the age-specific death rates for that community would yield a life expectancy at birth for males of 39.7 years (Vinovskis 1972:194).

tering their headright (Morgan 1972). The great increase in headrights after 1650 might reflect to a large degree the efforts of land speculators to acquire and to register the unused headrights of earlier immigrants. Though this issue is quite complicated and has not been satisfactorily resolved, it does point to the danger of using indices of population development without thoroughly considering how those data were generated.

Most scholars of American colonial demography lack any formal training in demography. Many historians have devised their own demographic measures or indices rather than relying on more established and standardized ways of handling their data. It is very difficult to make comparisons among studies that do not use the same framework for ordering their demographic data. For example, data on marriages have been presented in several different ways. Wells (1972) grouped data according to the date of birth of the wives. Farber (1972) categorized data on the basis of the date of marriage. Greven (1970) arranged material on marriages according to generations rather than any specific chronological time period. Consequently, when one is using information from all of these studies, it is difficult to find comparable time periods or categories.[4]

Some colonial historians claim that geographic mobility was significantly less in New England than in England (Greven 1967, 1970; Lockridge 1966, 1970; Murrin 1972), but measurement differences render such comparisons tenuous. Whereas Lockridge (1966) measured the geographic mobility of the adult population in Dedham, Laslett & Harrison (1963) estimated the geographic mobility of the entire population of Clayworth and Cogenhoe in England. Prest (1976) recalculated the rates of geographic mobility for Clayworth, duplicating the procedures used by Lockridge. Prest found that Dedham was a somewhat more demographically stable community than Clayworth, but this was due largely to the differences in mortality levels rather than to variations in emigration rates in those two communities.

The small number of cases is a pervasive problem in historical demography. For example, Wells (1971) investigated the fertility of 271 Quaker families to see if and when married women tried to control their fertility. To determine exactly when the Quaker families began to employ birth control, Wells subdivided his sample into three cohorts (wives born by 1730, 1731–1755, and 1756–1785), subdivided each cohort by whether the wives were married before or after age 25, and then calculated five-year age-specific fertility rates. His conclusion that deliberate family limitation among Quaker women occurred at the end of the eighteenth century must

---

[4]The best procedure for organizing data on families is the use of life-course analysis—a framework that has been developed and advocated by family sociologists (Elder 1974, 1975, 1978). Historians are just now becoming aware of the advantages as well as the limitations of a life-course approach (Vinovskis 1978d).

be treated with caution, for the total number of cases in each of the final subdivisions was too small to provide reliable estimates.[5]

Some Conceptual Issues in Colonial Demographic History

Much of the early effort in American demographic history was focused on ascertaining simple demographic indices such as birth rates, death rates, and marriage rates. Relatively little attention was paid to the interaction of demographic and socioeconomic factors in shaping colonial society. Attempts to interpret the impact of demographic factors on colonial life were limited by the few socioeconomic variables considered, as well as by the conceptual framework employed.

Some demographic research on colonial America concerned the interaction of demographic and economic factors. Greven (1970) analyzed the transmission of land from one generation to another to see how this process affected the relationship between fathers and sons. He claims that the first settlers of Andover wanted to continue to control their sons even after they had become adult members of the community (just as the fathers had already used their authority to delay the marriage of their sons until their mid or late twenties). Hence, the first settlers did not grant their sons full rights to the land on which they settled them.

Greven's analysis of the interaction of demographic (the age at marriage) and economic (the inheritance of land) factors is a very imaginative and useful effort. There is no reason to doubt his evidence that the first-generation fathers deliberately delayed the transmission of land to their sons. Greven does not make a convincing case, however, that the fear of losing their inheritance was the primary reason for the late age at marriage for the second-generation sons. His analysis is not designed to test such a proposition; he did not calculate separately the age at marriage of sons who immediately received land from their fathers as opposed to those who received full title to their land several years after they had settled upon it (Vinovskis 1971b).

One of the most interesting and sophisticated efforts to study the interaction between demographic and economic factors is an analysis of parental power and marriage patterns in Hingham, Massachusetts (Smith 1973). Smith used marriage order as an index of parental control and found that an erosion and collapse of the traditional family patterns in Hingham

---

[5]The problems of using a small or an unrepresentative sample are by no means confined to demographic historians. In fact, traditional historians have been committing the same errors for years, but most scholars simply have not noticed the problem. For example, Miller's (1939) analysis of the New England mind is heavily based on the writings of only six Puritan ministers, even though the book tries to give the impression of a much broader and a more comprehensive coverage (Selement 1974).

occurred in the middle and late eighteenth century. Two less satisfactory efforts to study demographic and economic factors are Farber's (1972) investigation of Salem families in 1800 and Hall's (1977) analysis of Massachusetts merchant families from 1700 to 1850. Farber studied Salem families in order to see the influence of "the Protestant ethic" on economic development and family life in early America. But his knowledge of Puritanism is limited and incorrect. His description of Salem approximates more closely the town in 1700 than in 1800 (Gildrie 1975; Vinovskis 1973). Although Hall's analysis of merchant families in Massachusetts is quite provocative, it is much too simplistic in its efforts to demonstrate that marriage patterns among merchants shifted primarily to suit the needs of the changing capitalist system in Massachusetts in the eighteenth and nineteenth centuries. Both statistical rigor and breadth of historical knowledge are necessary to properly incorporate economic and demographic interaction into an analysis of colonial society.

Another exciting and fruitful area of research is the demographic analysis of church membership in colonial America. Rather than relying only on the writings of Puritan ministers, several scholars have analyzed the demographic and socioeconomic characteristics of those who joined the colonial churches (Bumstead 1971; Cowing 1968; Greven 1972; Moran 1972). These studies found that the age of conversion dropped as teenagers flocked to the churches during the Great Awakening of the early 1740s. In addition, it appears that a disproportionate number of women joined the New England churches during the late seventeenth and early eighteenth centuries.

One recent approach to the demographic study of colonial religion is to compare those who joined these churches with those who did not. Moran's (1978) study of religion and society in seventeenth century Milford, Connecticut, nicely illustrates the value of analyzing the demographic and socioeconomic characteristics of members and nonmembers of a local church. Almost all of the first settlers of Milford joined the church, whereas those who arrived later were much less likely to do so—especially if they were to remain in that community only for a short period of time. Furthermore, the new arrivals to Milford took longer to become church members than the original settlers. By comparing the experiences of those who joined the Milford church with those who did not, Moran was able to provide a much richer and a more balanced account of Puritan religious development than those based only on the literary sources generated by the ministers.

The study of the interaction of political and demographic factors has attracted considerable effort—particularly the analysis of the effect of demographic and social changes on the political leadership. In a classic essay on the relationship between politics and the social structure, Bailyn (1959) traces the struggle in Virginia between a newly emerging colonial elite and the royal governor, which led to Bacon's Rebellion. Similarly,

Lockridge & Kreider (1966) argued that the deaths of the leading settlers of Dedham and Watertown in the late seventeenth century contributed significantly to the increasing role of the town meeting rather than the town selectmen in determining policies at the local level.

Most of the early efforts to study the interaction of demographic and political factors focused on one or two communities because of the logistical difficulties of obtaining such information on the community level. But Cook's (1976) analysis of leadership and community structure in eighteenth century New England demonstrates the possibility as well as the benefits of studying more than one community. Cook analyzed 74 towns in four New England colonies. Particularly interesting is his attempt to study the role of families in local politics—an issue that has been pursued in many of the local community studies without being placed within the broader context of colonial development. Though some of Cook's interpretations of his data have already been challenged, his book is a decided improvement on generalizations about colonial politics based on only one or two communities.

Finally, we need to integrate attitudinal and demographic variables in our analyses. We should consider not only how people behaved, but also how they perceived their behavior. Unfortunately, most of the recent demographic studies of colonial America only analyzed the behavioral characteristics of the population without considering whether the colonists interpreted their own experiences and opportunities accurately. For example, we now know that death rates in colonial New England were quite low —especially for those who managed to survive infancy. Yet most New Englanders thought that their own chances of dying were considerably higher than suggested by our revised life tables. An interesting problem is why these individuals misperceived their environment and how this affected their behavior. Vinovskis (1976a) argued that the cultural emphasis placed on death in early New England, particularly by the Puritan Church, misled colonists into believing that adult mortality rates were significantly higher than the actual mortality rates suggest. If colonial historical demography is to go beyond simply ascertaining levels and trends of vital events, it should turn to the issue of the interaction of attitudinal and demographic factors and avoid an unnecessary and undesirable split between a social science approach to the study of history and the more traditional, humanistic effort to recapture the essence of the past.

NINETEENTH CENTURY DEMOGRAPHIC HISTORY

Two aspects of nineteenth century demographic development have attracted the most attention and effort—antebellum fertility and mortality. Studies of differentials and trends in fertility and mortality illustrate the problems and opportunities in that field facing nineteenth century demographic historians.

Fertility Differentials and Trends

The population explosion has led to a wide ranging debate among policy analysts on means for curtailing fertility in the developing countries today. The introduction of modern contraceptive devices is not sufficient to reduce fertility levels (Revelle et al 1971). Attention has shifted to the problems of motivating the child-bearing population to have smaller families. Inevitably, new interest has developed in an assessment of the causes of the historic decline in fertility in the United States and Western Europe.

The case of the United States is particularly relevant, because American fertility levels in the eighteenth and early nineteenth centuries were much higher than those of Western Europe and close to the levels observed in many developing countries today. A sustained decline in birth rates began in some parts of the United States before the nineteenth century—well before a comparable decline in most West European countries and before modern contraceptive devices were available (Easterlin 1971; Vinovskis 1976b; Wells 1971). Reductions in the birth rates in nineteenth century America reflect shifts in attitudes and circumstances favoring small families rather than the introduction of better contraceptives. Because industrialization in America in the first half of the nineteenth century occurred in the countryside rather than in the existing urban centers, it is possible to separate analytically the effects of urbanization and industrialization on fertility differentials and trends.

In the absence of effective birth registration systems in most states, it is necessary to devise some other means of measuring fertility. The most commonly used index is a ratio of the number of children under 5 years old (or under 10 years old) per woman aged 15–25 years (or 20–50 years), calculated from federal census data.

The child-woman ratio (more commonly referred to as the fertility ratio) does not measure actual fertility levels, but the number of surviving young children per woman in the child-bearing ages. Though the child-woman ratio is not an ideal measure of fertility, it is a useful approximation of actual fertility levels—especially for the white population in areas where mortality differentials are not particularly great. Several studies have already considered the methodological problems of using child-woman ratios, but more work still needs to be done on this matter (Vinovskis 1978e; Hareven & Vinovskis 1975; Hareven & Vinovskis 1978; Yasuba 1961).[6]

[6]For a critical assessment discussion of the use of child-woman ratios in American historical demography, see the recent essay by Sharlin (1978). Though Sharlin's points are well taken, he is too pessimistic and appears to be unaware that various American historical demographers have considered the biases in the use of child-woman ratios as an index of fertility.

One of the recurring explanations advanced to account for fertility differentials and trends in nineteenth century America is that fertility in America declined as the result of urban and industrial development. Potter (1965:678) argued, for example, that urbanization and industrialization played a key role in the decline in fertility in the United States:

> The findings have to remain inconclusive. But the evidence still seems to support the view that industrialization and urbanization with the accompaniment of higher living standards and greater social expectations (but possibly also higher infant mortality), were the main reasons for the declining rate of population growth either through the postponement of marriage or the restriction of family size.

An urban-industrial explanation of the decline in American fertility has some appealing features. First, there was a definite rural-urban difference in fertility in nineteenth century America (Bash 1955; Easterlin 1976a,b; Forster & Tucker 1972; Hareven & Vinovskis 1978; Leet 1975; Potter 1965; Vinovskis 1967b,c, 1978e,f; Yasuba 1961). Secondly, many scholars have already used such an explanation for accounting for fertility differentials and declines in the developing countries today (Abu-Lughod 1964; Jaffe 1942; Robinson 1961, 1963).

Most demographic historians are skeptical of an urban-industrial explanation of fertility declines in nineteenth century America. Only a small proportion of the population lived in urban areas. Even if one defines urban as towns of 2500 or more persons, only 19.8% of the population was in urban communities by 1860. Although the proportion of nonagricultural workers in America rose from 28.1% in 1820 to 41.0% in 1860, the majority of antebellum Americans were still engaged in agricultural activities. Thus, it would be impossible to account for the overall decline in fertility in America by any urban-industrial explanation. In fact, Forster & Tucker (1972) estimated that of the absolute decline in fertility ratio for the period 1810–1840, 78% was due to a decline in rural birth rates, 11% to a decline in urban birth rates, and another 11% to a population shift from rural to urban areas.

Among economic historians the most common explanation of fertility differentials and trends in the late eighteenth and early nineteenth centuries is the availability of readily accessible farmland (Yasuba 1961; Easterlin 1971, 1976a,b, 1977; Easterlin et al 1978; Forster & Tucker 1972; Leet 1975). Since the United States was predominantly an agricultural society during these years, access to land constituted a major source of economic opportunity. Any decrease in the availability of farmland might lead to lower fertility through higher ages at first marriage or a decline in marital fertility. As marriages were closely tied to the ability to support a family, a decrease in the availability of farmland would increase the difficulty of establishing a new household and discourage early marriages. In addition, marital fertility would decrease as parents reacted to the decrease in the value of their children's labor, to the dangers of the fragmentation of the family farm, and to the increased cost of eventually providing their children with sufficient land to establish their own households. The overall result of the increase in the age at first marriage and the decline in marital fertility would be a sizable drop in the total fertility rate of that population.

Much of the current debate about the decline in rural fertility centers around the definition of land availability. Modell (1971) used population density as a measure of agricultural opportunity. Population density, however, does not take into consideration the quality of the land or the degree of agricultural settlement of the area. Furthermore, population density not only measures the number of farmers in a given locality, but also the number of persons living in villages and towns.

Yasuba (1961) tried to avoid these problems by defining agricultural opportunity as the number of persons per 1000 arable acres. The population estimates were obtained from the nineteenth century federal censuses, while the data on arable acres came from 1949 figures on cropland. Yasuba used the latter data because he wanted some measure of the potentially arable land rather than the amount of land actually being cultivated in the antebellum period. Because twentieth century farming technology and practices are considerably different than those in the nineteenth century, other analysts believe the cropland figures from 1949 are not likely to reflect actual or even relative levels of potential farming areas in the nineteenth century (Forster & Tucker 1972; Leet 1975; Vinovskis 1976c, 1978e).

A more recent effort by Forster & Tucker (1972) relied on the number of white adults per farm, using the white adult population in the census year under investigation and the number of farms in 1850, 1860, or 1880. Their index has the advantage of reflecting nineteenth century farming conditions and practices more accurately than either Modell's or Yasuba's measures. However, even Forster & Tucker's index of land availability leaves much to be desired. At the state level, an index of white adults per farm is highly correlated with the percentage of the population engaged in nonagricultural occupations and with the percentage of the population in urban areas. Therefore, we cannot be sure whether the high correlation between the white adult–farm ratio and the white refined-fertility ratio is due to the availability of farms, to the percentage of the population in nonagricultural occupations, or to the percentage of the population living in urban areas.

When economists speak of the availability of farms, they are in effect considering the relative costs of establishing a farm. Ideally, we would like to have information on the cost of establishing new farm households. Unfortunately, that information is not available for the nineteenth century. Instead, we must rely on a crude approximation—the average value of a farm.

Using this measure, it becomes evident that there was wide geographic variation in the costs of farming in antebellum America. To take an extreme example, in 1860 the average value of a farm in Kansas was $1179, whereas the average value of a farm in Louisiana was $11,818 (Vinovskis 1976c).

Many of the earlier studies display statistical and methodological short-comings. For example, Yasuba (1961) was interested in examining the effects of a series of independent variables on his white refined-fertility ratios, but he did not use the appropriate multivariate techniques to investigate this problem. Forster & Tucker (1972) included in their analysis of 1860 the Dakota Territory, which had a very high and unusual sex ratio (171) and a very small white population (2576). They should have either omitted all of the territories, since they were quite undeveloped at that time or they should have weighted their variables by population size in order to minimize the impact of a sparsely settled territory on their overall analysis (Vinovskis 1977). When the appropriate corrections are made in Yasuba's (1961) or Forster & Tucker's (1972) analysis, a very different picture emerges (Vinovskis 1976c). The availability of land (as measured by the average value of a farm) is still strongly negatively related to the white refined-fertility ratio in 1850, but it is less important than the percentage of the population in urban areas or the percentage of white adults who are illiterate. In 1860 the value of the average farm remains negatively related to fertility, but it becomes quite unimportant in terms of strength.

At the aggregate level, this debate will undoubtedly continue. Some studies continue to show the importance of land availability in explaining fertility differentials at the county level (Leet 1975), while others at the county (Vinovskis 1976b) and township (Vinovskis 1978e,f) levels do not. However, the entire debate is quickly shifting away from aggregate studies to those at the household level. Here again the results to date are mixed. The results from an extensive analysis of northern farm households in 1860 suggest the importance of land availability (Easterlin et al 1978), while the results from an analysis of households in early nineteenth century Weston, Massachusetts (Notzon 1973), or households in Washtenaw County (Michigan) in 1850 (Trierweiler 1976) do not find a strong relationship between fertility and the availability of farmland.

The entire debate about the relationship of land availability to fertility still needs to be clarified conceptually. The model in its present form is quite crude and does not pursue all of the ramifications of a decrease in farmland. For example, though the decreasing availability of farmland makes it more expensive for sons to acquire farm households, it also raises the value of their father's farm—thus giving him more capital with which to assist his children. The entire debate has been focused so much on the contradictory empirical results from these various studies that relatively little effort has been made to think through the implications of this model for farm life and behavior in nineteenth century America (Bogue 1976; Vinovskis 1976c, 1978e). Nevertheless, this is certainly one of the more exciting areas of demographic history today and has attracted considerable attention from both economists and historians.

Another explanation for the decline in fertility in nineteenth century America is the changes in the ratio of males to females. The sex ratio is presumed to be an important determinant of fertility differentials and trends, because it reflects the availability of marriage partners in a given area. T'ien (1959) asserted that the sex ratio of the population at the state level was very important for explaining fertility differentials and trends in the first half of the nineteenth century. But Yasuba (1961) minimized the significance of the sex ratio, seeing it as a reflection of the crucial explanatory variables; availability of land, migration, and urbanization.

Yasuba was correct that the change in the sex ratio in antebellum America was not sufficiently large to account for the decline in fertility. He was wrong, however, to argue that the sex ratio would not be an important predictor of fertility differentials after the influence of other variables such as urbanization, land availability, or industrialization was controlled. In most of the studies that analyzed fertility differentials using multiple regression analysis, the sex ratio remained an important predictor variable (Vinovskis 1978e; Leet 1975; Forster & Tucker 1972). Furthermore, in a detailed analysis of the relationship between the sex ratio and the percentage of the population that is married, it does appear that the two items are strongly related—just as T'ien had suggested (Vinovskis 1978a). Unfortunately, very little attention has been paid to the entire issue of marriage in the nineteenth century—especially from the perspective of fertility levels. A recent effort to relate the changes in fertility to changes in marriage patterns and the control of fertility within marriages is the analysis of the decline in fertility in Sturbridge, Massachusetts, from 1730 to 1850 (Osterud & Fulton 1976).

Ethnicity has been cited as a determinant of fertility differentials in nineteenth century America. Almost everyone has assumed that the foreign-born population had larger families than the native population. Recent studies, however, challenged this interpretation. Both Katz's (1975) analysis of Hamilton, Ontario, and Blumin's (1975) study of Kingston, New York, found little difference in fertility among women of different ethnic or religious backgrounds. Though these two studies are among the best nineteenth century community analyses that we have, their treatment of fertility differentials is weakened by the indices they constructed. Katz (1975) calculated the number of children under age 15 years to women ages 15–45 years without adjusting his data for differences in the age distribution of the women in the different ethnic groups. Blumin (1975) estimated the number of all children in the household per married woman (calculated separately for the different age groups of the women), but did not consider the possibility that his index would be affected by the selective out-migration of young children. The authors should have calculated the age-specific child-woman ratios for the married women and then standardized the results for the differences in the age distribution of the women from the different ethnic groups (Hareven & Vinovskis 1975, 1978; Trierweiler 1976). Thus, one of the apparent new discoveries of nineteenth century demographic history may have been only the result of errors in the way fertility levels were computed.

Some scholars (Vinovskis 1976b,c, 1978e; Wells 1975b) argued that the demographic and socioeconomic variables that have been surveyed above are inadequate by themselves to account for the fertility decline in nineteenth century America. They have noted the parallel decline in rural and urban fertility and have questioned whether both areas might have been affected by some broad social changes occurring in that society. Although these changes have been categorized in a variety of different ways, they are commonly summarized under the heading of "modernization." Several demographic studies of developing countries found a strong inverse relationship between fertility and modernization (Clifford 1971; Fawcett & Bornstein 1973; Kahl 1968; Miller & Inkeles 1974; Rosen & Simmons 1971; Williamson 1970). Furthermore, several recent studies argued that American society was in the process of modernization during the nineteenth century (Brown 1972, 1976; Vinovskis 1978e; Wells 1975b).

The hypothesis of modernization as a determinant of fertility trends is not without its legitimate critics. In fact, use of the term in the other social sciences has been severely criticized (Bendix 1967; Smelser 1968). The lack of a precise definition of modernization is one of the chief complaints. Critics see the term being used so loosely that it has become meaningless. Furthermore, modernization has often been improperly identified with urbanization and industrialization, even though it is quite clear now that some rural and preindustrial societies in the past have been quite modern by other standards. Finally, the concept of modernization has sometimes been mistakenly linked with the notion of progress, overlooking the severe hardships and turmoil endured by many individuals.

Careless use of modernization theory among sociologists has been properly discredited, and modernization theory can be effectively utilized as a research tool (e.g. Inkeles & Smith 1974). Historians are relative latecomers to the use of modernization theory, and they have avoided some of the simplistic notions of the earlier sociological literature. However, one of the continued weaknesses in the use of modernization theory by historians is that most of them are simply unaware of the recent sociological writings in this area. As a result, historians tend to debate the modernization issue in terms of the sociological literature of the 1950s and 1960s rather than in terms of the recent refinements by sociologists.

Though demographers and economists have been very reluctant to look beyond socioeconomic explanations of the fertility decline in nineteenth century America, it is important that we also consider some of the broader attitudinal and cultural shifts that were occurring in that society. The fact that the concept of modernization has been badly misused by some scholars in the past should not deter us from analyzing the possibility that American society in the late eighteenth and early nineteenth centuries experienced major changes that could be appropriately summarized under the caption of modernization. I suspect that there will be more efforts in this direction in the future as economic historians move beyond a narrow focus on the land availability theory of fertility decline and as more historians enter this debate who are more willing to consider the possible importance of attitudinal and cultural shifts in nineteenth century American society.

Mortality Differentials and Trends

The study of nineteenth century mortality patterns has been less frequently pursued than the analysis of fertility patterns. Most scholars have been content to estimate mortality levels at a particular time and place, and only a few serious efforts have been made to ascertain long-term trends. Methodological weaknesses are common. Particularly lacking are attempts to estimate the possible biases introduced by the reliance on quite different sources of mortality data. Until recently most of the information about nineteenth century mortality was based only on Massachusetts data, and the question festered of whether the Massachusetts estimates were appropriate for the rest of the country.

The standard interpretation of mortality levels and trends in antebellum America was set forth by Thompson & Whelpton (1933), who saw a steady improvement in life expectancy during the first half of the nineteenth century. They cited the life tables of Wigglesworth for 1789 and of Elliott for 1855 as their evidence. A more recent analysis of antebellum mortality rates by Yasuba (1961) reverses the Thompson & Whelpton interpretation by arguing that death rates were increasing just prior to the Civil War because of the unhealthy conditions associated with the increase in urban and industrial development.

Several recent studies suggested that nineteenth century mortality levels remained relatively constant before 1880—particularly in the rural areas of the country (Meeker 1972, 1978; Vinovskis 1972, 1978b). Challenging the validity of the life tables relied upon by Thompson & Whelpton (1933) or by Yasuba (1961), Vinovskis (1972) showed how mortality levels and trends in Massachusetts remained relatively constant in the first half of the nineteenth century. Furthermore, he argued that urban and industrial development in that state was not as unhealthy as the earlier scholars suggested.

Easterlin (1977) argues that there was a significant increase in life expectancy in the first half of the nineteenth century. His argument, however, rests very heavily on two life tables that have been thoroughly discredited —the Wigglesworth life table of 1789 (Vinovskis 1971a, 1972) and the Jacobson life table of 1850 (Vinovskis 1978b).

Thus, the debate on whether conditions of life improved in the first half of the nineteenth century continues. We do not have enough national or even regional mortality data to be reasonably certain of mortality trends. The bulk of the existing evidence for the New England area, however, does not point to any dramatic increases in life expectancy during that period— particularly in the rural areas. Perhaps there were major improvements in nineteenth century life expectancy in the South—especially since that area was so unhealthy in the seventeenth and eighteenth centuries (Craven 1971; Hecht 1973; Morgan 1975; Rutman & Rutman 1976; Walsh & Menard 1974). The level of mortality in the South during the first half of the nineteenth century still remains to be established. Recent efforts to calculate mortality of slaves in antebellum America (Evans 1962; Fogel & Engerman 1974) found that the life expectancy of slaves was considerably higher than had been previously suspected. Fogel & Engerman (1974) argue that the life expectancy of slaves was higher than that of urban workers in the North. Other scholars feel that these estimates of the life expectancy of slaves are too high (Eblen 1974; Vinovskis 1975). In any case, it is apparent that the debate on nineteenth century mortality levels and trends will attract even more attention in the next decade than it has during the past ten years.

Very little effort has been made by demographers and economists to evaluate the reliability or the representativeness of mortality data in the nineteenth century federal censuses. Yasuba (1961) claims that even if census mortality data are underenumerated, the relative underenumeration is about the same for all subgroups, so that these data are still appropriate for comparative purposes. But there is reason to believe that mortality data were not enumerated at the same rate throughout the country or among different segments of the population. The superintendent of the census (DeBow 1855) as well as other nineteenth century scholars, argued that the mortality returns were so badly and unevenly underenumerated that they were of little value even for comparative purposes. No matter how sophisticated the statistical analysis, it is of little use without evaluation of the possible biases in the data. One simply cannot use nineteenth-century census materials as if they were as accurate as those produced by the US Bureau of the Census today (Vinovskis 1977).

Even if the decennial census data are accurate, it does not mean that they are typical or representative of that decade. Almost none of the studies using census data have adequately tested the possibility that the year in which the census was taken was atypical in terms of the variable being investigated. This is particularly hazardous for historical data, since there were much larger and more frequent fluctuations in demographic and socio-economic variables in the past than today.

Again, let me illustrate this point by using mortality data from the federal census. One of the major life tables for nineteenth century America is the Jacobson life table (Jacobson 1957). It is based on census mortality data for Massachusetts and Maryland in 1850. The data were originally assembled and converted to life expectancies by L. W. Meech and then recalculated by Jacobson a hundred years later. The Jacobson life table has been accepted by virtually all scholars as the definitive estimate of life expectancy in mid nineteenth century America (Easterlin 1977; Fischer 1977; Fogel & Engerman 1974; Higgs 1973; Jacobson 1964; Meeker 1972; Uhlenberg 1969; Yasuba 1961).

The question we need to ask is whether the period June 1, 1849–June 1, 1850, was a typical year in terms of mortality. Naturally, since the census itself covers only one year, it is not of much help in answering this question. Fortunately, Massachusetts established a state vital registration system in 1843, so we have annual mortality information.

It happens that 1849 was a very unusual year in terms of mortality because of the outbreak of cholera, which greatly inflated death rates. The expectation of life for Massachusetts males at birth was 39.4 years in 1849, 46.0 years in 1850, and 43.0 years in 1851 (Vinovskis 1978b). Clearly, the Jacobson life table is based on census data from an unusually unhealthy year. Perhaps the exaggeration of mortality due to the cholera epidemic was compensated by the underenumeration of the mortality data. Though this is plausible, it does not appear to be true. When we analyze the Massachusetts mortality data in more detail, it still appears that the Jacobson life table for 1850 greatly exaggerates the extent of mortality in the state for most years during the antebellum period (Vinovskis 1978b).

CONCLUSION

This brief review of the field of American historical demography has indicated some of the strengths and weaknesses of this area of scholarship. Most of the work in this field has been done during the past 15 years and is still unfamiliar to large segments of the scholarly world. It is an area of research that is attracting new scholars and will undoubtedly continue to be exciting and challenging.

One of the major attractions of historical demography is that it has allowed scholars to see American development from a very different perspective, while at the same time providing valuable information about the relationship between social structure and demographic changes for contemporary demographers. The quality of the work in American historical demography, however, is rather uneven—especially since many of its practitioners have had no formal training in either statistics or demography. But given the current interest in this field as well as the general increase in the statistical sophistication among young historians, the next generation of historical demographers should be able to avoid many of the earlier mistakes.

The real challenge in the future will probably be in the efforts to use demographic analyses to explore areas of American development that have hitherto been ignored by historical demographers. Some of these new areas will involve the use of demographic techniques and information to study religious and political behavior. But the most interesting as well as the most difficult task ahead will be to analyze the interrelationship between behavioral and attitudinal development in early America. Historians as well as other scholars must avoid studying separately either the behavioral or attitudinal aspects of American life in order to develop a more dynamic and balanced social history that takes into account not only the actions of Americans in the past, but also their perceptions.

Literature Cited

Abu-Lughod, J. 1964. Urban-rural differences as a function of the demographic transition: Egyptian data and an analytical model. *Am. J. Sociol.* 69:476–90

Archdeacon, T., Vinovskis, M. A. 1974. *Ideology and the social structure: a critique of the Bailyn thesis.* Paper presented at OAH meeting, Denver

Bailyn, B. 1967. *The Ideological Origins of the American Revolution.* Cambridge, Mass.: Harvard Univ. Press. 335 pp.

Bailyn, B. 1959. Politics and social structure in Virginia. In *Seventeenth-Century Colonial America: Essays in Colonial History,* ed. J. M. Smith, pp. 90–115. Chapel Hill: Univ. North Carolina Press. 238 pp.

Bash, W. H. 1955. Differential fertility in Madison county, New York, 1865. *Milbank Mem. Fund Q.* 33:161–86

Bendix, R. 1967. The comparative analysis of historical change. In *Social Theory and Economic Change,* ed. T. Burns, S. B. Saul, pp. 67–86. London: Tavistock 104 pp.

Berkhofer, R. F. 1973. Clio and the culture concept: some impressions of a changing relationship in American historiography. In *The Idea of Culture in the Social Sciences,* ed. L. Schneider, C. Bonjean, pp. 77–100. Cambridge, England: Cambridge Univ. Press. 149 pp.

Bissell, L. A. 1974. From one generation to another: mobility in seventeenth-century Windsor, Connecticut. *William Mary Q.* 3rd series. 31:79–110

Bissell, L. A. 1973. Family, friends, and neighbors: social interaction in seventeenth-century Windsor, Connecticut. PhD thesis, Brandeis Univ. 246 pp.

Blumin, S. M. 1975. Rip Van Winkle's grandchildren: family and household in the Hudson Valley, 1800–1860. *J. Urban Hist.* 1:293–315

Bogue, A. 1976. Comment on paper by Easterlin. *J. Econ. Hist.* 36:76–81

Borah, W. W. 1969. Conquest and population: a demographic approach to Mexican history. *Am. Philos. Proc.* 113:117–83

Brown, R. D. 1976. *Modernization: The Transformation of American Life, 1600–1865.* New York: Hill & Wang. 229 pp.

Brown, R. D. 1972. Modernization and the modern personality in early America, 1600–1865: a sketch of a synthesis. *J. Interdisc. Hist.* 2:201–28

Bumstead, J. M. 1971. Religion, finance, and democracy in Massachusetts: the town of Norton as a case study. *J. Am. Hist.* 67:817–31

Clifford, W. B. 1971. Modern and traditional value orientations and fertility behavior: a social-demographic study. *Demography* 8:37–48

Cook, E. M. Jr. 1976. *The Fathers of the Towns: Leadership and Community Structure in Eighteenth-Century New England.* Baltimore: Johns Hopkins Univ. Press 273 pp.

Cowing, C. 1968. Sex and preaching in the Great Awakening. *Am. Q.* 20:624–44

Craven, W. F. 1971. *White, Red, and Black.* Charlottesville: Univ. Va. Press 114 pp.

DeBow, J. D. 1855. *Mortality Statistics of the Seventh Census of the United States, House Executive Documents No. 98, 33rd Congress, 2nd Session.* Washington DC

Demos, J. 1970. *A Little Commonwealth: Family Life in Plymouth Colony.* New York: Oxford Univ. Press. 201 pp.

Demos, J. 1968. Families in colonial Bristol, Rhode Island: an exercise in historical demography. *William Mary Q.* 3rd series. 25:40–57

Demos, J. 1965. Notes on life in Plymouth Colony. *William Mary Q.* 3rd series. 22:264–86

Dethlefsen, E. 1969. Colonial gravestones and demography. *Am. J. Physic. Anthropol.* 31:321–33

Dobyns, H. F. 1976. *Native American Historical Demography: A Critical Bibliography.* Bloomington: Ind. Univ. Press. 95 pp.

Dupaquier, J. 1972. Problems de representativite dans les etudes fondees sur la reconstitution des familles. *Ann. Demogr. Hist.* 1972:83–92

Easterlin, R. A. 1977. Population issues in American economic history: a survey and critique. In *Research in Economic History,* ed. P. J. Uselding, Suppl. 1, pp. 133–58. Greenwich, Conn.: Johnson 450 pp.

Easterlin, R. A. 1976a. Factors in the decline of farm family fertility in the United States: some preliminary research results. *J. Am. Hist.* 63:600–14

Easterlin, R. A. 1976b. Population change and farm settlement in the northern United States. *J. Econ. Hist.* 36:45–83

Easterlin, R. A. 1971. Does human fertility adjust to the environment? *Pap. Proc. Am. Econ. Assoc.* 61:399–407

Easterlin, R. A., Alter, G., Condran, G. A. 1978. Farms and farm families in old and new areas: the northern states in 1860. In *Demographic Processes and Family Organization in Nineteenth-Century American Society,* ed. T. K. Hareven, M. A. Vinovskis. Princeton, NJ: Princeton Univ. Press. In press

Eblen, J. E. 1974. New estimates of the vital rates of the United States black population during the nineteenth century. *Demography* 9:301–19

Elder, G. H. Jr. 1978. Family history and the life course. In *Family Transitions and the Life Course,* ed. T. K. Hareven. New York: Academic. In press

Elder, G. H. Jr. 1975. Age differentiation and the life course. *Ann. Rev. Sociol.* 1:165–90

Elder, G. H. Jr. 1974. *Children of the Great Depression.* Univ. Chicago Press, Ill. 400 pp.

Evans, R. Jr. 1962. The economics of American Negro slavery. In *Aspects of Labor Economics,* ed. Universities-National Bureau Committee for Economic Research, pp. 185–243. Princeton, NJ: Princeton Univ. Press. 349 pp.

Farber, B. 1972. *Guardians of Virtue: Salem Families in 1800.* New York: Basic. 228 pp.

Fawcett, J. T., Bornstein, M. H. 1973. Modernization, individual modernity, and fertility. In *Psychological Perspectives on Population,* ed. J. T. Fawcett, pp. 106–31. New York: Basic. 522 pp.

Fischer, D. H. 1977. *Growing Old in America,* Chester Bland-Dwight E. Lee Lectures in History. New York: Oxford Univ. Press. 242 pp.

Fogel, R. W., Engerman, S. L. 1974. *Time on the Cross: The Economics of American Negro Slavery.* Vols. 1, 2. Boston: Little, Brown. 286 pp., 267 pp.

Forster, C., Tucker, G. S. L. 1972. *Economic Opportunity and White American Fertility Ratios, 1800–1860.* New Haven: Yale Univ. Press. 121 pp.

Gildrie, R. P. 1975. *Salem, Massachusetts, 1626–1683: A Covenant Community.* Charlottesville: Univ. Va. Press. 187 pp.

Greene, E. B., Harrington, V. D. 1932. *American Population Before the Federal Census of 1790.* New York: Columbia Univ. Press. 228 pp.

Greven, P. J. Jr. 1972. Youth, maturity, and religious conversion: a note on the ages of converts in Andover, Massachusetts, 1711–49. *Essex Inst. Hist. Collect.* 108:119–34

Greven, P. J. Jr. 1970. *Four Generations: Population, Land, and Family in Colonial Andover, Massachusetts.* Ithaca, NY: Cornell Univ. Press. 329 pp.

Greven, P. J. Jr. 1967. Historical demography and colonial America. *William Mary Q.* 3rd series. 24:438–54

Greven, P. J. Jr. 1966. Family structure in seventeenth-century Andover, Massachusetts. *William Mary Q.* 3rd series. 23:234–56

Gross, R. A. 1976. *The Minutemen and Their World.* New York: Hill & Wang. 242 pp.

Hall, P. D. 1977. Family structure and economic organization: Massachusetts merchants, 1700–1850. In *Family and Kin in Urban Communities, 1700–1930,* ed. T. K. Hareven, pp. 38–61. New York: New Viewpoints. 214 pp.

Hareven, T. K., Vinovskis, M. A. 1978. Childbearing in five Essex county towns in 1880. See Easterlin et al 1978

Hareven, T. K., Vinovskis, M. A. 1975. Marital fertility, ethnicity, and occupation in urban families: an analysis of South Boston and the South End in 1880. *J. Soc. Hist.* 9:69–93

Hecht, I. 1973. The Virginia muster of 1624–25 as a source for demographic history. *William Mary Q.* 3rd series. 30:65–92

Henry, L. 1956. *Anciennes familles genevoises. Etude demographique XVI–XXe siecles.* Paris: Presses Universitaires de France. 232 pp.

Higgs, R. 1973. Mortality in rural America, 1870–1920: estimates and conjectures. *Explor. Econ. Hist.* 10:177–95

Inkeles, A., Smith, D. H. 1974. *Becoming Modern: Individual Change in Six Developing Countries.* Cambridge, Mass.: Harvard Univ. Press. 436 pp.

Jaffe, A. J. 1942. Urbanization and fertility. *Am. J. Sociol.* 48:48–60

Jacobson, P. H. 1964. Cohort survival for generations since 1840. *Milbank Mem. Fund Q.* 42:36–53

Jacobson, P. H. 1957. An estimate of the expectation of life in the United States in 1850. *Milbank Mem. Fund Q.* 35:197–202

Kahl, J. A. 1968. *The Measurement of Modernism: A Study of Values in Brazil and Mexico.* Austin: Univ. Tex. Press. 210 pp.

Katz, M. B. 1975. *The People of Hamilton, Canada West: Family and Class in a Mid-Nineteenth-Century City.* Cambridge, Mass.: Harvard Univ. Press 381 pp.

Laslett, P., Harrison, J. 1963. Clayworth and Cogenhoe. In *Historical Essays 1600–1750 Presented to David Ogg,* ed. H. E. Bell, R. L. Ollard, pp. 157–84. London: Barnes & Noble. 274 pp.

Leet, D. R. 1975. Human fertility and agricultural opportunities in Ohio counties: from frontier to maturity, 1810–60. In *Essays in Nineteenth-Century Economic History: The Old Northwest,* ed. D. C. Klingaman, R. K. Vedder, pp. 138–58. Athens: Ohio Univ. Press. 356 pp.

Levine, D. 1976. The reliability of parochial registration and the representativeness of family reconstitution. *Popul. Stud.* 30:107–22

Lockridge, K. A. 1977. Historical demography. In *The Future of History,* ed. C. F. Delzell, pp. 53–64. Nashville, Tenn.: Vanderbilt Univ. Press. 263 pp.

Lockridge, K. A. 1973. Social change and the meaning of the American Revolution. *J. Soc. Hist.* 6:403–39

Lockridge, K. A. 1970. *A New England Town: The First Hundred Years, Dedham, Massachusetts, 1636–1736.* New York: Norton. 208 pp.

Lockridge, K. A. 1968. Land, population, and the evolution of New England society, 1630–1790. *Past Present* 39:62–80

Lockridge, K. A. 1966. The population of Dedham, Massachusetts, 1636–1736. *Econ. Hist. Rev.* 19:318–44

Lockridge, K. A., Kreider, A. 1966. The evolution of Massachusetts town government, 1640 to 1740. *William Mary Q.* 3rd series. 23:549–74

Meeker, E. 1978. Public health and medicine. In *Dictionary of American Economic History.* New York: Scribner's. In press

Meeker, E. 1972. The improving health of the United States, 1850–1915. *Explor. Econ. Hist.* 9:353–74

Menard, R. R. 1975. The Maryland slave population, 1658–1730: a demographic profile of blacks in four counties. *William Mary Q.* 3rd series. 32:29–54

Menard, R. R. 1973. Immigration to the Chesapeake colonies in the seventeenth century: a review essay. *Maryland Hist. Mag.* 68:323–29

Miller, K. A., Inkeles, A. 1974. Modernity and acceptance of family limitation in four developing countries. *J. Soc. Issues* 30:167–88

Miller, P. 1939. *The New England Mind: The*

Seventeenth Century. New York: Macmillan. 528 pp.

Modell, J. 1971. Family and fertility on the Indiana frontier, 1820. *Am. Q.* 23: 615–34

Moller, H. 1945. Sex composition and correlated culture patterns of colonial America. *William Mary Q.* 3rd series. 2:113–53

Moran, G. F. 1978. Religion and society in seventeenth-century New England: the town of Milford, Connecticut as a case study. *William Mary Q.* 3rd series. In press

Moran, G. F. 1972. Conditions of religious conversion in the first society of Norwich, Connecticut, 1718–1744. *J. Soc. Hist.* 5:331–43

Morgan, E. S. 1975. *American Slavery, American Freedom: The Ordeal of Colonial Virginia.* New York: Norton. 454 pp.

Morgan, E. S. 1972. Head rights and head counts. *Va. Mag. Hist. Biogr.* 59:5–29

Murrin, J. M. 1972. Review essay. *Hist. Theory* 11:226–75

Norton, S. L. 1971. Population growth in colonial America: a study of Ipswich, Massachusetts. *Popul. Stud.* 25:433–52

Notzon, F. 1973. Fertility and farmland in Weston, Massachusetts, 1800–1820. MA thesis, Univ. Wisc., Madison

Osterud, N., Fulton, J. 1976. Family limitation and age at marriage: fertility decline in Sturbridge, Massachusetts, 1730–1850. *Popul. Stud.* 30:481–94

Potter, J. 1965. The growth of population in America, 1700–1860. In *Population in History: Essays in Historical Demography,* ed. D. V. Glass, D. E. C. Eversley, pp. 631–88. London: Arnold. 692 pp.

Prest, W. R. 1976. Stability and change in old and New England: Clayworth and Dedham. *J. Interdisc. Hist.* 6:359–74

Revelle, R., Vinovskis, M. A., Khosla, A., eds. 1971. *The Survival Equation: Man, Resources, and the Environment.* Boston: Houghton Mifflin. 508 pp.

Robinson, W. C. 1963. Urbanization and fertility: the non-western experience. *Milbank Mem. Fund Q.* 41:291–308

Robinson, W. C. 1961. Urban-rural differences in Indian fertility. *Popul. Stud.* 14:218–34

Rosen, B. C., Simmons, A. B. 1971. Industrialization, family, and fertility: a structural-psychological analysis of the Brazilian case. *Demography* 8:49–69

Rutman, D. B., Rutman, A. H. 1976. Of agues and fevers: malaria in the early Chesapeake. *William Mary Q.* 3rd series. 33:31–60

Schofield, R. S. 1972. Representativeness and family reconstitution. *Ann. Demogr. Hist.* 1972:121–25

Selement, G. 1974. Perry Miller: a note on his sources in the *New England Mind: The Seventeenth Century. William Mary Q.* 3rd series. 31:453–64

Sharlin, A. N. 1978. Historical demography as history and demography. *Am. Behav. Sci.* In press

Smelser, N. J. 1968. *Essays in Sociological Explanation.* Englewood Cliffs, NJ: Prentice-Hall. 280 pp.

Smith, D. 1975. Population, family, and society in Hingham, Massachusetts, 1635–1880. PhD thesis, Univ. Calif., Berkeley. 387 pp.

Smith, D. 1973. Parental power and marriage patterns: an analysis of historical trends in Hingham, Massachusetts. *J. Marriage Fam.* 35:419–28

Smith, D. 1972. The demographic history of New England. *J. Econ. Hist.* 32:165–83

Somerville, J. 1969. *A demographic profile of the Salem family, 1660–1770.* Presented at Conf. Soc. Hist., Stony Brook, NY, 1969

Swedlund, A., Temkin, H., Meindl, R. 1976. Population studies in the Connecticut Valley: prospectus. *J. Hum. Evol.* 5:75–93

Thompson, W. S., Whelpton, P. K. 1933. *Population Trends in the United States.* New York: McGraw Hill. 415 pp.

T'ien, H. Y. 1959. A demographic aspect of interstate variation in American fertility, 1800–1860. *Milbank Mem. Fund Q.* 37:49–59

Trierweiler, W. C. 1976. *The differential child-woman ratios in Washtenaw county, Michigan in 1850: an investigation into the patterns of fertility decline in antebellum America.* Honors thesis, Univ. Mich.

Uhlenberg, P. R. 1969. A study of cohort life cycles: cohorts of native born Massachusetts women, 1830–1920. *Popul. Stud.* 23:407–20

Vinovskis, M. A. 1978a. Marriage patterns in mid-nineteenth-century New York State: a multivariate analysis. *J. Fam. Hist.* In press

Vinovskis, M. A. 1978b. The Jacobson life table of 1850: a critical re-examination from a Massachusetts perspective. *J. Interdisc. History.* In press

Vinovskis, M. A., ed. 1978c. *Studies in American Historical Demography.* New York: Academic. In press

Vinovskis, M. A. 1978d. From household size to the life course: some observations on recent trends in family history. *Am. Behav. Sci.* In press

Vinovskis, M. A. 1978e. *Demographic Changes in America from the Revolution to the Civil War: An Analysis of the Socio-Economic Determinants of Fertility Differentials and Trends in Massachusetts from 1765 to 1860.* New York: Academic. In press

Vinovskis, M. A. 1978f. A multivariate regression analysis of fertility differentials among Massachusetts towns and regions in 1860. In *Historical Studies of Changing Fertility,* ed. C. Tilly. Princeton, NJ: Princeton Univ. Press. In press

Vinovskis, M. A. 1977. *Problems and opportunities in the use of individual and aggregate level census data.* Presented at Conf. Quantification Methods Soc. Sci. Res., Cologne, Germany, 1977

Vinovskis, M. A. 1976a. Angels' heads and weeping willows: death in early America. *Proc. Am. Antiquarian Soc.* 86: 273–302

Vinovskis, M. A. 1976b. *Demographic History and the World Population Crisis.* Chester Bland-Dwight E. Lee Lectures in History. Worcester, Mass.: Clark Univ. Press. 94 pp.

Vinovskis, M. A. 1976c. Socio-economic determinants of interstate fertility differentials in the United States in 1850 and 1860. *J. Interdisc. Hist.* 6:375–96

Vinovskis, M. A. 1975. The demography of the slave population in antebellum America: a critique of *Time on the Cross. J. Interdisc. Hist.* 5:459–67

Vinovskis, M. A. 1974. The field of early American history: a methodological critique. *Fam. Hist. Perspect.* 7:2–8

Vinovskis, M. A. 1973. Review of *Guardians of Virtue. Fam. Hist. Perspect.* 3:2–5

Vinovskis, M. A. 1972. Mortality rates and trends in Massachusetts before 1860. *J. Econ. Hist.* 32:184–213

Vinoskis, M. A. 1971a. The 1789 life table of Edward Wigglesworth. *J. Econ. Hist.* 31:570–90

Vinovskis, M. A. 1971b. American historical demography: a review essay. *Hist. Methods Newslett.* 4:141–48

Walsh, L. S., Menard, R. R. 1974. Death in the Chesapeake: two life tables for men in early colonial Maryland. *Maryland Hist. Mag.* 69:211–17

Wells, R. V. 1975a. *The Population of the British Colonies in America before 1776: A Survey of Census Data.* Princeton, NY: Princeton Univ. Press. 342 pp.

Wells, R. V. 1975b. Family history and demographic transition. *J. Soc. Hist.* 9:1–20

Wells, R. V. 1972. Quaker marriage patterns in a colonial perspective. *William Mary Q.* 3rd series. 29:415–42

Wells, R. V. 1971. Family size and fertility control in eighteenth-century America: a study of Quaker families. *Popul. Stud.* 25:73–82

Williamson, J. B. 1970. Subjective efficacy and ideal family size as predictors of favorability toward birth control. *Demography* 7:329–39

Winchester, I. 1970. The linkage of historical records by man and computer: techniques and problems. *J. Interdisc. Hist.* 1:107–24.

Wood, P. H. 1974. *Black Majority: Negroes in Colonial South Carolina from 1670 through the Stono Rebellion.* New York: Knopf. 352 pp.

Wrigley, E. A., ed. 1973. *Identifying People in the Past.* London: Arnold. 159 pp.

Yasuba, Y. 1961. *Birth Rates of the White Population in the United States, 1800–1860: An Economic Study.* Baltimore: Johns Hopkins Univ. Press. 198 pp.

The Demographic History of Colonial New England

T HE central fact of the demographic history of early North America is rapid growth. Both Canada and the white population of the English colonies experienced increases of 2½ percent per year during the eighteenth century. Seventeenth-century rates, beginning from a low base and more influenced by immigration, were even higher. In contrast, the expansion of population in early modern Europe rarely exceeded 1 percent per annum over an extended period.[1] Since Franklin and Malthus, interpretations of early American demography have centered on the high fertility associated with near universal marriage for women at a low average age. The extremely youthful population, high dependency ratio, and one of the largest mean census family sizes ever recorded all follow from the high level of fertility.[2]

Because the high growth and its explanation have been long recognized and virtually unquestioned, until recently very little scholarly research has focused on the estimation of the components of population increase or on the analysis of the socio-economic context of the colonial demographic experience. Interpretive consensus and an absence of reliable data have also hindered the construction of precise distinctions over time and space within the

[1] For data on colonial and contemporary European population growth rates, see J. Potter, "The Growth of Population in America, 1700-1860," in D. V. Glass and and D. E. C. Eversley, eds., *Population in History* (London: Edward Arnold, 1965), pp. 639-43; and J. T. Krause, "Some Implications of Recent Work in Historical Demography," *Comparative Studies in Society and History*, I, No. 2 (June 1959), 173.

[2] Forty-nine percent of the American population was under age sixteen in 1790 and the mean white family size was 5.7. In New York in 1771 there were 105 males under sixteen and over sixty per 100 males sixteen to fifty-nine. Data are taken from W. S. Rossiter, *A Century of Population Growth* (New York: Johnson Reprint Corporation, 1966; orig. pub. 1909), pp. 94, 96, 183. Only three of sixty-four nations over 100,000 population in censuses from 1955 to 1963 had mean family sizes above 5.7. See Thomas K. Burch, "The Size and Structure of Families: A Comparative Analysis of Census Data," *American Sociological Review*, 32, No. 3 (June 1967), p. 353. Mean English family size was nearly one person less than the 1790 American figure over three centuries of stability from 1574 to 1911. See Peter Laslett, "Size and Structure of the Household in England over Three Centuries, Part I, Mean Household Size in England since the Sixteenth Century," *Population Studies*, XXIII, No. 2 (July 1969), 199-223.

Reprinted from *Journal of Economic History*, No. 1, 165–183. Copyright © 1972 by permission of the publisher.

150 years of colonial population history. By integrating knowledge of population trends on the colony-wide level with findings forthcoming from recent intensive demographic analyses of New England communities, generalizations are possible about three central issues: (1) the demographic sources of the higher colonial growth rate compared to a reliably documented European society;(2) decadal variation in the pattern of population growth, particularly the central role of lower fertility in the apparent pause in rapid growth around 1700; and (3) the determinants of the level of marital fertility, especially evidence for the conscious limitation of family size before the "demographic transition" of the first half of the nineteenth century.

A COMPARATIVE PERSPECTIVE ON NEW ENGLAND GROWTH

Since the net reproduction rate (NRR) summarizes fertility, mortality, and marital patterns and is also algebraically related to the intrinsic growth rate of the population, it is a particularly useful measure for contrasting the demographic structures of two societies. Very simply the NRR is the ratio of the size of the female population one generation later to its size at a given point in time; mathematically it is related to the intrinsic growth rate(r) and the mean age of women at childbearing(T) by the expression, $NRR = e^{rT}$. Although data on immigration do not exist for the colonial period, the contribution of net migration to the region may be inferred from the difference between the crude and intrinsic growth rates. The crude growth rate can be calculated from two series of total population estimates at decadal intervals.[3] Although England would be the most relevant country for comparative purposes, Sweden is the only eighteenth-century European society for which the necessary parameters for the estimation of a net reproduction rate exist.[4] The contrast in Table 1 rests on the Swedish mortality experience of 1751-1800, the marital fertility of 1776-1800, and the marital structure in 1800; estimates for New England are drawn

[3] Two series of colonial population totals at decadal intervals have been constructed: by Rossiter, *A Century . . .* , pp. 9-10 and by Stella H. Sutherland in U.S. Bureau of the Census, *Historical Statistics of United States, Colonial Times to 1957* (Washington, D.C.: GPO, 1960), Series Z1-19, p. 756. Potter, "The Growth of Population . . ." uses the Rossiter estimates.

[4] H. Gille, "The Demographic History of the Northern European Countries in the Eighteenth Century," *Population Studies*, III, No. 1 (June 1949), 3-65, was the source for the Swedish data.

TABLE 1

ANALYSIS OF THE COMPONENTS OF THE DIFFERENCE BETWEEN LATE EIGHTEENTH-CENTURY SWEDISH AND NEW ENGLAND FEMALE LEGITIMATE NET REPRODUCTION RATES

Component	ADJUSTED MODEL		RECORDED MODEL	
	Contribution to difference in NRR (1)	Percentage of total difference (2)	Contribution to difference in NRR (3)	Percentage of total difference (4)
(1) New England NRR	1.991		2.285	
(2) Lower New England mortality				
(a) Begin with Swedish GRR	0.140	15.2%	0.432	35.4%
(b) With marital structure	0.062	6.7	0.190	15.6
(c) With marital fertility	0.020	2.2	0.026	2.1
(d) Combination of (b) & (c)	0.006	0.6	0.001	0.1
(e) Begin with New England GRR	0.228	24.7	0.650	53.3
(3) Higher N.E. proportion married				
(a) New England mortality	0.535	58.0	0.668	54.8
(b) Swedish mortality	0.473	51.2	0.478	39.2
(c) Difference (a) − (b) = (2b)	0.062	6.7	0.190	15.6
(4) Higher N.E. marital fertility				
(a) New England mortality	0.178	19.3	0.093	7.6
(b) Swedish mortality	0.158	17.1	0.068	5.6
(c) Difference (a) − (b) = (2c)	0.020	2.2	0.026	2.1
(5) Interaction of proportions married and marital fertility				
(a) New England mortality	0.052	5.6	0.008	0.7
(b) Swedish mortality	0.046	5.0	0.006	0.5
(c) Difference (a) − (b) = (2d)	0.006	0.6	0.002	0.2
(6) Lower N.E. mean age at childbearing (with Swedish NRR)	0.018	1.9	0.018	1.5
(7) Swedish NRR	1.068	100.0%	1.068	100.0%

Calculation:

(A) $NRR = 1/2.05(TFR)(U')(l_T/l_0)$, where $1/2.05$ is the proportion of females among all births, TFR is the total fertility rate, U' is the correction factor for under-registration, and l_T/l_0 is the proportion of females surviving from birth to T, the mean age of women at childbirth.

(B) Total fertility rate, New England:

	15-19	20-24	25-29	30-34	35-39	40-44	45-49
(i) Pct. married, Conn., 1774[a]	.070	.545	.733	.816	.871	.840	.819
(ii) Hingham marital fertility, marriages of 1761-1780	.513	.454	.407	.320	.279	.138	.012
(iii) TFR = 5Σ(i)(ii) =	.036	.247	.298	.261	.235	.116	.009 = 6.01

(iv) GRR = (6.01)/2.05 = 2.93

(v) U' = (No. of births in reconstituted marriages, 1761-1780) + (No. of births necessary to raise infant mortality in first month to 60% of total)[b] + (No. of births omitted, estimated by unusual variance in birth intervals)[c]/(No. of births in reconstituted families) = (886 + 45 + 25.7)/(886) = 1.079.

(vi) Adjusted TFR = (6.01)(1.079) = 6.48; adjusted GRR = 3.16

(C) Total fertility rate, Sweden[d]:

	15-19	20-24	25-29	30-34	35-39	40-44	45-49
(i) Pct. married, 1800	.027	.194	.507	.675	.747	.767	.739
(ii) Marital fertility, 1776-1800	.522	.467	.387	.323	.229	.121	.029
(iii) TFR = 5Σ(i)(ii)	.014	.091	.194	.218	.167	.093	.021 = 3.99

(iv) GRR = (3.99)/(2.05) = 1.946

(D) Mortality, l_T/l_0, estimated by projecting l_{20}/l_0 for both sexes to age 30 for females by use of model life tables:

(i) Adjusted model: $l_{20}/l_0 = 0.672$; $l_{30}/l_0 = 0.63$ (Model West, Level 10).[e] Included as dying before age 20 are all recorded deaths (142) plus all children whose survival to maturity is unknown (101) plus additional deaths of children whose births were not recorded but whose existence was detected by large intervals between recorded births (25.7) and by the absence of deaths in the first month of life (45). This procedure yields a maximum estimate of mortality.

(ii) Recorded model: $l_{20}/l_0 = 0.811$; $l_{30}/l_0 = 0.78$ (Model West, Level 15).[e] Included as dying before age 20 are the recorded deaths plus the additional deaths produced by the assumption that the "unknowns" die in the same proportion as the known population

(E) Interaction of age-specific proportions married and marital fertility:

	15-19	20-24	25-29	30-34	35-39	40-44	45-49
(i) Difference in pct. married	.053	.351	.226	.141	.094	.073	.080
(ii) Difference in marital fertility	.032	.023	.057	.077	.022	.028	-.016
(iii) Interaction = 5Σ(i)(ii)	.0017	.0081	.0130	.0031	.0072	.0020	-.0013 = .169

(F) Mean age of mothers at birth, T:

    (i) New England: Estimated as age 30 from assumption that the New England mean age at first marriage was 22.0 years; Watertown women who married at this age in 1761-1800 had a mean age at childbirth of 29.98 years.

    (ii) Sweden: Mean age at marriage assumed to be 25.0; hence T would be 31.5; this rough estimate probably understates the difference in mean marriage age and hence the mean age at birth.[f]

Sources:

[a] Yasukichi Yasuba, *Birth Rates of the White Population of the United States 1800 to 1860* (Baltimore: Johns Hopkins Press, 1961), p. 114.

[b] For a convenient summary of pre-industrial west-European data on the distribution of deaths within the first year, see E. A. Wrigley, "Mortality in Pre-Industrial England: The Example of Colyton, Devon, over three Centuries," *Daedalus*, 97, No. 2 (Spring 1969), Table 14, p. 568.

[c] Method adopted from Louis Henry, "Interval between confinements in the absence of birth control," *Eugenics Quarterly*, VIII, No. 2 (June 1961), 200-11. Two-thirds of the families whose variance of birth intervals exceeded 150 were assumed to have had a child not recorded.

[d] H. Gille, "The Demographic History of the Northern European Countries in the Eighteenth Century," *Population Studies*, III, No. 1 (June 1949), 27, 31.

[e] Ansley J. Coale and Paul Demeny, *Regional Model Life Tables and Stable Populations* (Princeton: Princeton University Press, 1966), pp. 11, 16.

[f] H. Gille, "The Demographic History of the Northern European Countries in the Eighteenth Century," *Population Studies*, III, No. 1 (June 1949), Table 7, p. 28.

169

from a colonial census and a local community. From the reconstitution of the civil and religious vital records of Hingham, Massachusetts, adjusted estimates of mortality and marital fertility were calculated. Since the marital structure of the town was quite atypical by the middle of the eighteenth century, the age-specific proportions of women married estimated by Yasuba from the Connecticut census of 1774 provide the final parameter needed to calculate a reasonable approximation of a net reproduction rate.[5] Since no reasonably accurate estimate of illegitimacy in New England could be made, its contribution to population growth in each society is ignored in the calculation.

By interchanging Swedish and New England parameters in the calculation of the net reproduction rate, the quantitative importance of each may be assessed. The proportion of the difference in NRR's that can be attributed to lower New England mortality depends on the assumptions simultaneously made about the fertility and marriage variables. In the adjusted estimates (left columns of Table 1) mortality accounts for only 0.140 points in the differential between NRR's if the Swedish gross reproduction rate (GRR) serves as the initial point in the calculation. Beginning with the New England GRR, on the other hand, mortality differences are responsible for 0.228 points in the NRR or a quarter of the gap between the rates. In the adjusted model between one-half and three-fifths of the difference in NRR's may be attributed to the higher proportion of women married in New England. The third major component, higher marital fertility in the colonies, explains from a fifth to a sixth of the difference.

While the conclusions for the adjusted data do not conflict with the conventional wisdom concerning New England population growth in the colonial period, the calculation does suggest a more complex and pluralistic pattern of causation than is usually conceived. More importantly the contrast specifies the quantitative importance of each component; instead of a list of causes of higher growth in New England, the procedure provides something better than a rank-ordering of the demographic mechanisms involved. Before these conclusions can be accepted, the reliability of the order

---

[5] Yasukichi Yasuba, *Birth Rates of the White Population of the United States, 1800-1860* (Baltimore: The Johns Hopkins Press, 1960), p. 114. With heavy male outmigration in Hingham, nearly 15 percent of all women born to reconstituted marriages of 1721 to 1760 survived to age forty-five as spinsters.

DANIEL SCOTT SMITH

of magnitude of the NRR estimate must be assessed, the assumptions underlying the calculation must be justified, the representativeness of the Hingham data and the Swedish contrast must be defended and the problem of under-registration in the colonial data must be considered. With thirty as the mean age at childbirth the estimated adjusted New England NRR of 1.99 implies an intrinsic growth rate of 22.4 per 1,000, slightly below the crude long-term eighteenth century rate of 24.6 per 1,000. Thus *net* migration into New England has but a minor role in eighteenth century growth. During the eighteenth century the middle and southern colonies absorbed most of the European immigration. Furthermore, the last three decades of the century were almost certainly characterized by net migration from New England.

With unadjusted fertility and mortality data the identical calculation substantially increases the significance of lower mortality in the explanation of the more rapid growth rate of New England. The unadjusted NRR of 2.28 implies an intrinsic growth rate of 27.6 per 1,000, well above the crude long-term increase. If we assume that the registered fertility and mortality rates are correct, then Yasuba's method overstates the proportions married in the 1774 Connecticut census. Under-registered or not, the fertility and mortality pattern for all of New England has been estimated from the demographic experience of a single town. Are the data for Hingham both reliable and representative?

(A) Mortality.—The proportion of females dying before the mean age at childbirth was estimated by projecting, by means of model life tables, the adjusted mortality of both sexes before age twenty. Adjusted mortality before twenty (328 per 1,000) was more than twice the registered rate (160 per 1,000). Even with this radical upward adjustment (see notes to Table 1), life expectation at birth was forty-one years for both sexes. On the other hand, the recorded childhood mortality figure implies an expectation at birth in excess of fifty-five years. In the overlapping Wigglesworth and McKean collections of late eighteenth-century New England mortality data, the age pattern of deaths more nearly approximates the adjusted model than the recorded. In the Wigglesworth table (4,893 deaths), 66.5 percent of persons dying over five died over age thirty while in the McKean collection (6,756 deaths) the comparable figure is 67.6 percent. In the stable population with the parameters of the adjusted estimate (Model West, Mortality Level 10, GRR = 3.00),

67 percent of the population dying over age five, die over age thirty, but in the stable population corresponding to the recorded data (Model West, Mortality Level 15, GRR = 3.00), the figure is 71 percent. Even though less (34 percent) of the living population over age five is over age thirty in the recorded model than in the adjusted (36 percent), a higher proportion of deaths occur at advanced ages in the low mortality life table.[6]

(B) Marital fertility and proportions married.—Was the fertility experience of 155 Hingham women married in the two decades from 1761 to 1780 reasonably representative of all eighteenth-century New England women? Total unadjusted fertility for women marrying at exact age twenty was already 9 percent below the peak Hingham cohort of 1721-1740; the secular trend toward low fertility within marriage had already begun in the town by the end of the colonial period. Still, marital fertility probably varied only slightly on a geographic basis. Child-woman ratios, lowest in the densely settled areas of eastern New England, reflect adult age-structure and mortality as well as fertility. For example, the coefficient of variation of the ratio of children under ten per woman aged twenty to sixty-nine among Connecticut counties in 1774 was 8.2 percent; for children per married woman, the ratio was only 4.7 percent.[7] Age-structure, if known in detail for adults, would probably account for still more of the inter-county variation in the child-woman ratio. Although marital fertility was high in eighteenth-century New England, it was not extraordinary by contemporary west European standards. Unadjusted total fertility for women marrying at exact age twenty in Hingham between 1761 and 1780

---

[6] The stable population and ratios of deaths by age are from Ansley J. Coale and Paul Demeny, *Regional Model Life Tables and Stable Populations* (Princeton: Princeton University Press, 1966), pp. 92-3, 188-89 and 102-03, 198-99. Edward Wigglesworth, "A Table Showing the Probability of the Duration, the Decrement, and the Expectation of Life, in the States of Massachusetts and New Hampshire, formed from sixty-two Bills of Mortality on the files of the American Academy of Arts and Sciences, in the year 1789," *Memoirs of the American Academy of Arts and Sciences*, II, pt. I (1793), 132. Reverend Joseph McKean, "Synopsis of Several Bills of Mortality," *Memoirs of the American Academy of Arts and Sciences*, II, pt. II (1804), 65. For the deficiencies of the Wigglesworth material, see Maris A. Vinovskis, "The 1789 Life Table of Edward Wigglesworth," THE JOURNAL OF ECONOMIC HISTORY, XXXI, No. 3 (Sept. 1971), 570-90. Some 1,113 of the 4,893 deaths in the Wigglesworth sample were taken from the records of Ebenezer Gay, minister of the first parish in Hingham.

[7] Calculated from the census data for Connecticut counties in Rossiter, *A Century . . .* , pp. 166-69. For state variations in child-woman ratios within New England in 1800, see Yasuba, *Birth Rates . . .* , p. 61.

was only 4 percent above the 1776-1800 Swedish level, below that found in most reconstituted French parishes, and considerably lower than the marital fertility rates of early eighteenth-century French Canada. Even with extreme assumptions about under-regis-tration (7.9 percent for the 1761-1780 cohort), the marital fertility of Hingham still was not unusual by west European standards.[8]

The proportion of adult women who were married in New England approaches what Hajnal has defined as the non-European pattern. In Connecticut in 1774, 73.5 percent of women aged twenty to sixty-nine were married, while two-thirds of New Hampshire females in 1767 and 1773 were wed.[9] In order to use the census data on marital status in the calculation of the NRR, age-specific propor-tions must be estimated. Yasuba's method basically assumes that the percentage non-married changed proportionately in the various age groups between 1890 and 1774.[10]

(C) Age-Structure in the Recorded Model.—If we assume that Yasuba's method overstates the proportion married, particularly in the crucial high fertility decade from twenty to twenty-nine, and that the true NRR for New England was 2.00, then the correspond-ing gross reproduction rate would be slightly over 2.50. With the above parameters and mortality level 15 in the Coale-Demeny "West" tables only 28.9 percent of the population would be under ten years of age. However, in the Connecticut census of 1774, 32.1 percent of the population was under ten, and for New England as a whole in 1800 the percentage was 32.2. The extremely low mor-tality of the unadjusted estimate is incompatible with the rate of population growth, if we assume that the marital and fertility pat-terns have been estimated accurately. If the calculated NRR is approximately correct, then the unadjusted estimate is incongruent

---

[8] Gille, "The Demographic History . . .", p. 31. For a summary of age-specific fertility data from reconstitutions of French parishes and French-Canadian gene-alogies, see A. Chamoux and C. Douphin, "La contraception avant la Revolution française: L'exemple de Châtillon-sur Seine," *Annales, Economies, Sociétés, Civili-sations*, 24, No. 3 (May-June 1969), 668-69. Yasuba, *Birth Rates . . .*, *p.* 115, calcu-lated that marital fertility was 26 percent higher in Connecticut in 1774 and New Hampshire in 1773 than in Sweden from 1776 to 1800.

[9] Generalizing from European censuses from 1850 to 1910 Hajnal concluded that, "On the European pattern, the percentage of women over 15 who were married in a country as a whole was below 55 and usually below 50 in the nineteenth century." J. Hajnal, "European Marriage Patterns in Perspective," in *Population in History*, p. 119. Only 50.3 percent in 1750 and 50.1 percent in 1800 of the female popula-tion over 15 in Sweden was married. Gille, "The Demographic History . . .", p. 25.

[10] For details of Yasuba's method, see *Birth Rates . . .*, pp. 111-15.

with the extremely youthful age composition of the population. Although precision is not possible with the limited data available on the demographic structure of New England, the adjusted model obviously approximates reality more perfectly than the recorded estimate. In addition it should be noted that the choice of the Swedish contrast influences the relative magnitude of the differences in the components of the NRR. If national data existed for eighteenth-century France, characterized by somewhat higher mortality and lower marriage ages than Sweden, the French contrast with New England would naturally show mortality of greater importance and marital structure of lesser significance in explaining the differences in the net reproduction rates.

THE PATTERN OF NEW ENGLAND GROWTH, 1670-1790

To some extent the decadal estimates of total population in New England in Table 2 exhibit the consistently high rates of increase corresponding to a stable population interpretation of constant birth and age-specific death rates. To be sure, the assumptions of stable population theory do not conform precisely to the annual experience of pre-modern populations.[11] Following the initial extreme growth rates of the period of original settlement in New England, the decadal growth rate from 1670/80 to 1780/90 averaged 26.6 percent in the Rossiter series and 27.4 percent in the Sutherland estimates. Both series were constructed by aggregating estimates for each colony and each total is independent of the preceding and following figures. Since high growth rates tended to follow increases below the trend, some of the variation is doubtless due to the imprecision of the estimates of total population. The necessarily inexact sources available to Rossiter and Sutherland render it impossible either to accept or reject the notion that the rate of growth was constant.

Decades of more rapid growth also tended, inasmuch as impressionistic evidence permits a conclusion, to be periods of rela-

---

[11] The average annual net reproduction rate from 1751 to 1800 in Sweden was 1.172; however, there was considerable variation from year to year with a standard deviation of 0.1719 and thus a coefficient of variation of 14.7 percent. Calculated from Hannes Hyrennius, "Reproduction and Replacement: A Methodological Study of Swedish Population Changes during 200 Years," *Population Studies*, IV, No. 4 (March 1951), Table 2, 424.

TABLE 2

ESTIMATED TOTAL POPULATION AND DECADAL GROWTH RATES FOR NEW ENGLAND, 1650 TO 1790

Year	Estimated population in New England		Decadal growth rates		Percent change in succeeding decades	
	Rossiter (1)	Sutherland (2)	Rossiter (3)	Sutherland (4)	Rossiter (5)	Sutherland (6)
1650	21,800	22,832				
1660	36,800	33,136	68.8%	45.1%		
1670	45,500	51,896	23.6	56.6		
1680	61,000	68,462	34.1	31.9	+ 0.3%	− 4.0%
1690	82,000	86,961	34.4	27.0	− 5.1	−20.3
1700	106,000	92,763	29.3	6.7	−10.1	+17.4
1710	126,500	115,094	19.3	24.1	+ 1.2	+24.4
1720	152,500	170,893	20.5	48.5	+18.5	−21.3
1730	208,950	217,351	37.0	27.2	− 5.9	+ 6.1
1740	274,000	289,707	31.1	33.3	− 4.8	− 9.0
1750	346,000	360,009	26.3	24.3	+ 6.3	+ 0.6
1760	459,000	449,634	32.6	24.9	+ 1.2	+ 4.4
1770	614,000	581,308	33.8	29.3	−13.0	− 6.7
1780	742,000	712,959	20.8	22.6	+ 3.7	+ 7.0
1790	923,865	923,865	24.5	29.6		
Mean: 1670-80 to 1780-90			28.6%	27.4%		
Standard deviation			5.91	9.07		

Sources: W. S. Rossiter, *A Century of Population Growth* (New York: Johnson Reprint Corporation, 1966, orig. pub. 1909), pp. 9-10. U. S. Bureau of the Census, *Historical Statistics of the United States, Colonial Times to 1957* (Washington, D.C.: GPO, 1960), Series Z1-19, p. 756.

tively high immigration to the colonies.[12] From the existing evidence on colonial mortality, no conclusions connecting high or low decadal growth rates to periods of lesser or greater mortality can be made. Reconstitution studies of towns and genealogies, the chief source of colonial mortality data, typically include so few families that their authors do not disaggregate their data into periods as short as a decade. Extensive under-registration and the probability of significant local and regional variation in death rates make the subject the most unknown and difficult area of colonial demographic history. Finally there may be generational cycles in population growth disturbing the generally smooth pattern of increase. In the absence of detailed age-structure in eighteenth-century censuses, this hypothesis is probably unverifiable above the local level. New settlements contained an unusually large number of persons in the young adult ages which potentially could produce an "echo" a generation later.[13] Natural population growth (births minus deaths) was undoubtedly more even than the crude decadal growth rates indicate. Despite these qualifications concerning the reliability of the total population estimates, two successive decades in each series stand out as a distinct period of less rapid growth, that is, 1690-1710 in the Sutherland totals and 1700-1720 in the Rossiter estimates.

The turn of the eighteenth century marks an interlude between two eras of very rapid growth and a watershed in the evolution of the traditional demographic structure of New England. The first decades of settlement were characterized by a low age at first marriage for women and a high or essentially European marriage age for men. This differential, originally generated by the high sex ratio among the original settlers, narrowed considerably by the end of the seventeenth century and the beginning of the eighteenth by an increase in marriage age for females.[14] In Hingham the age at

[12] Potter notes that the decades of most rapid growth in all the colonies (the 1720's, 1740's and 1780's) were also periods of heavier immigration. "The Growth of Population . . .," pp. 638-39.

[13] For recent suggestive approaches using generational hypotheses in colonial studies, see Kenneth A. Lockridge, "The Population of Dedham, Massachusetts, 1636-1736," *Economic History Review*, 2d ser., XIX (Aug. 1966), 328, 341-42; Philip J. Greven, Jr., *Four Generations: Population, Land and Family in Colonial Andover, Massachusetts* (Ithaca: Cornell University Press, 1970), esp. pp. 17-18, 180-81, 205-06; and P.M.G. Harris, "The Social Origins of American Leaders: The Demographic Foundations," *Perspectives in American History*, III (1969), pp. 220-34, 311-33.

[14] There were 157 males per 100 females among the passengers to New England from 1620 to 1640. See Herbert Moller, "Sex Composition and Correlated Culture

TABLE 3
AGE AT FIRST MARRIAGE IN ALL RECONSTITUTED FAMILIES, AGE AT
LAST BIRTH AND NUMBER OF CHILDREN PER COMPLETE FAMILY IN
HINGHAM, MASS., 1641-1800

| Marriage cohort | Age at first marriage | | Age at last birth | | Children per complete family |
	Men (1)	Women (2)	M<25 (3)	M25+ (4)	Mean (5)
Before 1691	27.4(77)	22.0(97)	39.6	41.3	7.59(69)
1691-1715	28.4(76)	24.7(84)	36.5	39.7	4.61(52)
1716-1740	27.0(125)	23.8(157)	40.3	41.1	6.74(91)
1741-1760	26.0(117)	22.8(135)	39.1	41.5	7.16(94)
1761-1780	24.6(126)	23.5(155)	39.6	40.0	6.39(104)
1781-1800	26.4(159)	23.7(188)	38.4	40.1	6.23(119)

Note: Sample sizes in parentheses.
Source: Daniel Scott Smith, "Population, Family and Society in Hingham, Massa-
chusetts, 1635-1880" (Unpublished Dissertation, University of California,
Berkeley, 1972).

marriage for both sexes increased between 1680 and 1720 before
declining in the eighteenth century (Table 3).

More surprising than the increase in age at first marriage is
the behavior of total fertility during this interlude. Hingham women
marrying from 1691 to 1715 who survived, still married, to age
forty-five had only 4.6 children in contrast to the 7.6 in the previous
cohort and 6.7 and 7.2 in the succeeding marriage groups. The increase in female marriage age explains less than half of the decline in

Patterns of Colonial America," *William and Mary Quarterly*, 3d ser., II (1945), 115-
17. In a sample of Plymouth Colony couples the age at marriage converged from 27.0
and 20.6 for men and women respectively born 1600-25 to 24.6 and 22.3 for those
born 1675-1700 (sample size of 650 persons in five birth cohorts). John Demos, *A
Little Commonwealth, Family Life in Plymouth Colony* (New York: Oxford University Press, 1970), p. 193. In Andover, the male age at first marriage did not
decline until after 1730; averages for the second, third, and fourth generation male
descendants of the original settlers are 26.7 (104), 27.1 (224) and 25.3 (294). For
Andover women the corresponding generational averages are 22.3 (81), 24.5 (210)
and 23.2 (282), with the increase coming after 1704. Greven, *Four Generations*, pp.
188-90, 206-10. In Ipswich, a larger, more commercial town near Andover, marriage
ages were 27.2 (34), 26.5 (73) and 24.0 (88) for men and 21.7 (17), 23.6 (70) and,
23.3 (98) for women marrying in the periods 1652-1700, 1701-1725 and 1726-1750.
Susan L. Norton, "Population Growth in Colonial America: A Study of Ipswich, Massachusetts," *Population Studies*, XXV, 3 (Nov. 1971), p. 445. Older studies based on
family genealogies confirm these trends. In Jones' sample, male age dropped from
27.0 to 24.8 while female age at marriage increased from 21.4 to 22.2 between 1651-
1700 and 1701-50 (27 and 176 marriages respectively). Carl E. Jones, "A Genealogical Study of Population," *Publications of the American Statistical Association*, XVI
(1918), p. 208. In the genealogical study by Frederick S. Crum, "The Decadence
of the Native American Stock: A Statistical Study," *Publications of the American
Statistical Association*, XIV (1914), 220, the age at first marriage increased from 21.4
(30) before 1700 to 21.7 (147) for women married from 1700 to 1749.

completed fertility.[15] As would be expected in the case of deliberate family limitation, the drop in fertility was greater for those marrying young; the difference in the mean age at last birth, significant at the 0.05 level, for women marrying before and after age twenty-five was not surpassed until the Hingham cohort marrying from 1821 to 1840, a group well-advanced into the transition to a modern level of low fertility. Overall the fall in age-specific fertility over age thirty for women marrying between 1691 and 1715 compared to the cohort wed before 1691 is statistically significant at the 0.005 level.[16] In addition there is a marked differential in marital fertility rates after thirty between women marrying before and after age twenty-five in the 1691-1715 cohort, although both marriage groups had lower fertility than preceding and succeeding cohorts (Table 4).

Evidence from other New England population groups suggests that the decline in total fertility in Hingham was not unique to that community. There is a less dramatic but substantial decrease

TABLE 4

RECORDED AGE-SPECIFIC MARITAL FERTILITY FOR HINGHAM WOMEN IN COMPLETED FAMILIES MARRYING BEFORE AND AFTER AGE TWENTY-FIVE

Marriage cohort	Age-specific marital fertility				
	25-29	30-34	35-39	40-44	45-49
Before 1691					
(a) married < 25	415(272)	389(272)	290(279)	157(274)	012(255)
(b) married 25+	250(16)	509(55)	350(60)	204(64)	024(83)
(c) ratio b/a	———	1.31	1.21	1.31	2.00
1691-1715					
(a) married < 25	333(120)	233(120)	150(120)	083(120)	000(105)
(b) married 25+	366(60)	371(102)	290(124)	133(135)	008(126)
(c) ratio b/a	1.10	1.59	1.93	1.60	
1721-1780					
(a) married < 25	414(951)	352(944)	283(944)	138(951)	016(910)
(b) married 25+	492(94)	449(222)	304(920)	161(304)	022(318)
(c) ratio b/a	1.19	1.27	1.07	1.17	1.37

Note: Women-years of experience in parentheses.
Source: See Table 3.

[15] Using pre-1691 marital fertility rates for women aged 20-24, the increase of 2.76 years in the average age at first marriage for women can account for only 1.29 of the total decline of 2.98 children (43.3 percent) per complete family in the 1691-1715 cohort compared to the women married before 1691.

[16] Marital fertility over age thirty was tested by the same analysis of variance method used by E. A. Wrigley, "Family Limitation in Pre-Industrial England," *Economic History Review*, 2d ser. XIX, No. 1 (April 1966), pp. 90-91. The test yielded a F of 20.38 with 1 and 430 degrees of freedom.

DANIEL SCOTT SMITH

in fertility among New England college graduates, third-generation residents of Andover, and the descendants of the early settlers of Watertown.[17] The decline in fertility in Hingham was not the result of worsening conditions on the immediate local level. Although little is known of the economic situation in the town during this period, the last of its proprietary lands were not distributed until the 1730's. A land shortage for sons could have been met either by the allotment of these undivided lands or by increased outmigration of the excess members of the younger generation. However, from King Philip's War in 1675 to the Peace of Utrecht in 1713, the geographic expansion of settlement in New England was extremely limited. Some new towns were formed within the periphery of existing settlement. Although military danger from the Indians and French during this period was a significant element in the limitation of expansion, perhaps the major impact of these external pressures was their feedback on the marital patterns and fertility behavior of the population.[18]

The relative shutting off of the frontier in conjunction with the equalization of the sex ratio among young adults kept the age at marriage for men high and thereby increased the female age at marriage. An alternative scenario of population change can easily by constructed. Without the narrowing of opportunities for geographical expansion, the age at marriage for men might have dropped, with that for women remaining low at the mid-seventeenth

[17] The average number of births per Harvard or Yale alumnus declined from 5.96 (186) for graduates aged 34 in 1656 to 1698 to 5.21 (289) for graduates aged 34 in 1699-1722, before rebounding to 5.98 (1,153) for alumni aged 34 in 1723-1758. Harris, "The Social Origins . . .", Table 14, p. 317. In Andover there was a drop from 8.7 (37) children per complete family, 1685-1704, to 7.4 (67) for families formed from 1705 to 1724; a very small sample of those married from 1725 to 1744 averaged 7.5 (17) children per complete family. Greven, *Four Generations*, Table 21, p. 202. The increase in marriage age in Andover between 1685-1704 and 1705-24 explains between 69 percent and 83 percent of the total decrease in mean family size. The number of children per complete family among the descendants of the original settlers of Watertown, was 8.85 (20), 7.48 (105), 8.63 (150) and 7.84 (168) respectively for marriages formed before 1670, 1671-1720, 1721-1760 and 1761-1800. Calculated from Henry Bond, *Genealogies of the Families and Descendants of the early Settlers of Watertown, Massachusetts* (Boston: N.E. Historic-Genealogical Society, 2d ed., 1860). Internal evidence suggests a substantial upward bias in these figures with the author concentrating on the ancestors of his mid-nineteenth century generation.

[18] On the halt to New England expansion from 1675 to 1713, see Lois Kimball Matthews, *The Expansion of New England* (New York: Russell and Russell, Inc., 1962), pp. 43-75, and Douglas Edward Leach, *The Northern Colonial Frontier* (New York: Holt, Rinehart and Winston, 1966), pp. 109-25. Both Matthews and Leach emphasize the direct security impediments to frontier expansion.

century level. Instead of limitation of fertility through higher marriage ages for females and restraint within marriage, population and land could have been maintained at the social equilibrium by a combination of more outmigration and the greater use of primogeniture. With the addition of higher mortality in the immediate decades after 1715 this particular demographic drama was in fact enacted in the next half century in Hingham. The temporary "fertility solution" to the population problem at the turn of the eighteenth century was the product of a unique conjunction of external constraints on migration, the continuation of a marriage pattern established in an era of male surplus, and a family structure in which fathers had considerable control over the demographically important decision of when their children could marry. As the eighteenth century progressed, fathers increasingly lost control of the marriage process.[19]

DEMOGRAPHIC DETERMINANTS OF MARITAL FERTILITY

In all three cohorts in Table 4 women in marriages of shorter duration exhibited higher fertility over the age of thirty than women who married before the age of twenty-five. The 1691-1715 cohort is particularly unusual both for its higher marriage ages and its extreme differential in fertility between early- and late-marrying women. The higher fertility of late-marrying women is partially a spurious product of the relatively short interval between marriage and first birth, which inflates the age-specific fertility of women marrying over age twenty-five. This effect can be removed by contrasting the fertility after age thirty of women marrying before age twenty-five with those marrying from twenty-five to twenty-nine. Furthermore, late-marrying women are more likely to have younger husbands than women who marry at a younger age. Nearly one-third of all women marrying between twenty-five and twenty-nine from 1721 to 1800 had younger husbands in contrast to 6 percent of women marrying before the age of twenty-five (Table 5). The lower coital frequency in marriages with older hus-

---

[19] The complex socio-demographic evolution uncovered in post-1715 Hingham can only be hinted at here. Premarital pregnancy, outmigration, daughters not marrying in order of birth, and primogeniture are among the indicators which show increases in frequency as the eighteenth century progresses. Tension between generations probably increased as fathers were unable to maintain their dominance on the old seventeenth century basis; however, it is not until after the Revolution that marriage was established as a "free" act of the couple being wed.

DANIEL SCOTT SMITH

bands has a substantial effect on the fertility of wives over age thirty.[20] Nevertheless, this unconscious mechanism does not completely erase the differential in fertility in Table 5. If the women marrying before twenty-five in the period from 1721 to 1800 had husbands whose ages were distributed the same as the husbands of the twenty-five to twenty-nine marriage group, the increase in the fertility of the early-marrying women would be only 35.4 percent of the difference between the recorded post-thirty means of 3.78 and 4.26. If advancing age of the husband lowers coital frequency,

TABLE 5

EFFECT OF THE RELATIVE AGE OF THE HUSBAND ON
THE AVERAGE NUMBER OF CHILDREN BORN TO
HINGHAM WOMEN AFTER AGE THIRTY IN COMPLETE FAMILIES

	Period married						
	Before 1691		1691-1715		1721-1800		
Wife's marriage age	<25	25-29	<25	25-29	<25	25-29	All
Age of husband relative to wife:							
Husband younger	4.75	6.33	0.00	4.14	4.56	4.37	4.46
	(4)	(3)	(1)	(7)	(16)	(19)	(50)
Husband same age or 1-4 years older	4.47	4.75	2.82	4.50	3.94	4.85	4.03
	(15)	(4)	(12)	(4)	(141)	(20)	(196)
Husband 5-9 years older	4.23	—	1.50	3.00	3.55	3.89	3.50
	(13)	(0)	(8)	(1)	(80)	(9)	(111)
Husband 10 or more years older	3.92	6.00	2.50	2.75	3.16	3.20	3.34
	(13)	(1)	(2)	(4)	(25)	(10)	(55)
Totals	4.27	5.50	2.22	3.81	3.78	4.26	3.85
	(45)	(8)	(23)	(16)	(262)	(58)	(412)

Note: Sample sizes in parentheses.
Source: See Table 3.

[20] It may appear highly speculative to conclude that the effect of husband's age on the fertility of the wife operates through coital frequency. Between the ages of 20 and 45 at least, the fecundity of the male does not decline. See John MacLeod and Ruth Z. Gold, "The Male Factor in Fertility and Infertility. VII. Semen Quality in Relation to Age and Sexual Activity," *Fertility and Sterility*, 4, No. 3 (1953), 194-209. Furthermore, modern studies indicate a marked decrease with age in rates of sexual intercourse. John MacLeod and Ruth Z. Gold, "The Male Factors in Fertility and Infertility. VI. Semen Quality and Certain Other Factors in Relation to Ease of Conception," *Fertility and Sterility*, 4, No. 1 (1953), 10-33; and Alfred C. Kinsey, Wardell B. Pomeroy, Clyde V. Martin and Paul H. Gebhard, *Sexual Behavior in the Human Female* (New York: Pocket Books ed., 1965), pp 392-94. Finally empirical data confirm a strong relationship between frequency of intercourse and the probability of conception. MacLeod and Gold, "Semen Quality and Certain other Factors . . . ," Table 19, p. 29; John C. Barrett and John Marshall, "The Risk of Conception on Different Days of the Menstrual Cycle," *Population Studies*, XXIII, 3 (Nov. 1969), 455-61. Barrett and Marshall calculate, for example, that the probability of conception during a given menstrual cycle increases from 0.24 to 0.68 for coital patterns of every fourth day and every day respectively.

then marriages of longer duration presumably could also be characterized by reduced levels of sexual activity compared to more recently formed marriages. The apparent statistical evidence for the conscious control of marital fertility (the higher age-specific rates in marriages of shorter duration) may derive instead from non-fertility related differences in sexual behavior.

Additional data confirm the interpretation of the absence of family limitation for eighteenth-century Hingham women. If couples had rationally aimed for a given family size, then the death of a child would presumably cause them to increase their fertility to make up the loss. The so-called "replacement hypothesis," recently advanced for colonial New England in a study of the diptheria epidemic of the 1730's,[21] is not supported by the comparison of the fertility behavior of couples who had lost a child before the wife reached age thirty and the couples without a known death in their family (Table 6). More surprising is the fact that women with more children by age thirty had still more births in their remaining fertile life than women with fewer children at age thirty (Columns 4 & 5 of Table 6). The positive correlation of early and late fertility may result from substantial variation in fecundity among women or from non-fertility related behavioral differences in nursing practices or coital frequency. It is compatible with the existence of conscious family limitation only under the hypothesis that some of the couples had small target family sizes from the inception of marriage that were achieved by the deliberate prolongation of the interval between births. Increases in child spacing, certainly consciously attained, were more important in the nineteenth-century decline in marital fertility in Hingham than the concomitant trend toward an earlier completion of childbearing. Long and irregular intervals between births would be expected if a partially effective means of contraception, such as coitus interruptus, were employed by couples seeking to limit their ultimate family size.[22]

[21] H. Louis Stettler, "The New England Throat Distemper and Family Size," in H. Klarman, ed., *Empirical Studies in Health Economics* (Baltimore: Johns Hopkins University Press, 1970), pp 17-27. Stettler's conclusions may be questioned since he failed to compare the post-epidemic record of families of the same size or women of the same age at the time of the outbreak. His data (Table 2, p. 23) merely confirm the probabilistic point that the chance a family will lose a child increases with the number of children already born.

[22] For emphasis on spacing as an important means in the control of marital fertility and a critique of the classic tests for the existence of family limitation, see J. J. Dupaquier and M. Lechiver, "Sur les débuts de la contraception en France ou

TABLE 6
EFFECT OF THE MORTALITY OF CHILDREN DYING BEFORE THE
MOTHER REACHES AGE 30 ON FERTILITY BETWEEN AGE 30 AND THE
TERMINATION OF CHILDBEARING (HINGHAM WOMEN IN COMPLETE
FAMILIES WHO MARRIED BEFORE AGE 25 IN THE PERIOD
FROM 1721 TO 1780)

| Number of children born before age 30 | No. (1) | Women with child dying before she reached age 30 | | Mean number of children born after age 30 No. deaths < 30 | | Difference (5) − (4) |
		No. (2)	Pct. (3)	Zero (4)	1 or more (5)	(6)
0	8	—	—	0.12	—	—
1	4	0	0.0%	2.25	—	—
2	27	7	25.9	2.80	3.86	+1.06
3	40	13	32.5	3.41	3.31	−0.10
4	42	14	33.3	4.85	3.93	−0.92
5	43	25	58.1	4.56	4.48	−0.08
6	19	10	52.6	5.11	5.60	+0.49
7	5	4	80.0	5.00	4.75	−0.25
8	1	1	100.0	—	7.00	—
9	0	—	—	—	—	—
10	1	1	100.0	—	11.00	—
Totals	190	75	39.5%	3.37	4.73	+1.16
Weighted average of differences (parity 2 to 7)						→ (−0.05)
Total born before age 30				3.71	4.33	
All children born				7.08	8.86	

Source: See Table 3.

Although there are significant reasons to doubt the existence of conscious limitation of fertility within marriage during most of the colonial period, the experience of the 1691-1715 cohort demonstrates the potential of an early modern population to respond to a perceived disequilibrium between numbers and resources. The threat of relative deprivation can be as powerful a motivating force as the impending reality of subsistence or starvation. The discovery of the influence of relative age of the husband on the fertility of the wife confirms again, as if anyone needed a reminder, the subtlety and complexity of the historical behavior of human populations.[23]

DANIEL SCOTT SMITH, *University of Connecticut*

les deus malthusianismes," *Annales, E. S. C.*, XXIV, No. 6 (Nov.-Dec. 1969), 1391-406.

[23] For the complexity of the map of pre-demographic transition European fertility, see Ansley J. Coale, "The Decline in Fertility in Europe from the French Revolution to World War II," in S. J. Behrman, Leslie Corsa, Jr., and Ronald Freedman, eds., *Fertility and Family Planning. A World View* (Ann Arbor: University of Michigan Press, 1969), pp. 3-19.

Notes on Life in Plymouth Colony

John Demos*

OUR traditional picture of the earliest New England communities is essentially a still life. By emphasizing the themes of steadfast piety, the practice of the old-fashioned virtues, measured forms of civil government, and a closely-ordered social life, it suggests a placid, almost static kind of existence. We take for granted the moral and religious aims which inspired the founding of many of these communities; and we accept the assumption of the colonists themselves, that success in these aims depended on maintaining a high degree of compactness and closeness of settlement.

Yet, in the case of the Plymouth Colony at least, this picture is seriously misleading. It has served to obscure certain striking elements of movement and change—indeed, a kind of fluidity that is commonly associated with a much later phase of our national history. Individuals frequently transferred their residence from one house, or one town, to another. Land titles changed hands with astonishing rapidity. Families were rearranged by a wide variety of circumstances.[1]

These tendencies can be traced back to the first years of the settlement at Plymouth. Some of the original townspeople began to take up lots across the river in Duxbury even before 1630; among them were such prominent figures as John Alden, Myles Standish, Jonathan Brewster, and Thomas Prence. The process was accelerated by the arrival to the

---

* Mr. Demos is a Ph.D. candidate at Harvard.

[1] Such conclusions, and the observations which follow, are based upon an examination of several sorts of records. Town and church records have been useful for determining certain vital statistics such as dates of birth, marriages, and deaths. Nathaniel B. Shurtleff and David Pulsifer, eds., *Records of the Colony of New Plymouth, in New England* (Boston, 1855-61), offers a broad picture of laws and lawbreaking, and, less directly, of deeper social and economic forces at work in 17th-century Plymouth. Numerous genealogical studies provide many relevant dates and places, and are obviously indispensable for establishing family relationships. Land deeds reveal much about the economic and geographic layout of the colony; there are also other deeds relating to such things as marriage and apprenticeship. Finally, of particular importance are the wills, perhaps the prime source of information about family and community organization.

Reprinted from *William and Mary Quarterly*, 3rd Series, **XXII**, 264–286. Copyright © 1965 by permission of the author.

north of the settlers at Massachusetts Bay. An important new market for cattle and corn was thereby opened up, and the compact town of Plymouth was not large enough to meet the demand for increased production.[2] But the profits to be made from farming were probably not the only, or even the major, stimulus to expansion. The land beckoned because it was empty; the colonists were excited simply by the prospect of ownership for its own sake.

In any case, by the mid-1630's this pattern of geographical expansion had become well established. In 1636 the town of Scituate was officially incorporated and began to send its own representatives to the General Court. Duxbury achieved a similar status the following year; and by 1646 seven other new towns had been established. The direction of the earliest expansion was north and south along the coast; then a westerly thrust began, which led to the founding of such towns as Taunton, Rehoboth, Bridgewater, and Middleborough, all well inland. Still other groups of people pushed onto Cape Cod; indeed, in the early 1640's there was a move to abandon the original settlement at Plymouth altogether and relocate the town on the outer cape. This proposal was finally defeated after much discussion in the meetings of the freemen, but some families went anyway, on their own, and founded the town of Eastham. By 1691, the year that Plymouth ended its independent existence and joined with Massachusetts Bay, it contained no less than twenty-one recognized townships, and many smaller communities as well.[3]

This steady dispersion of settlement caused considerable anxiety to some of the leaders of the colony, and sporadic efforts were made to keep it under control. On several occasions when new land was parceled out, the General Court directed that it be used only for actual settlement by the grantees themselves.[4] Also, the Court criticized the unrestrained way

[2] See William Bradford, *Of Plymouth Plantation, 1620-1647,* ed. Samuel E. Morison (New York, 1952), 252-253.

[3] Plymouth, 1620; Scituate, 1636; Duxbury, 1637; Barnstable, 1639; Sandwich, 1639; Taunton, 1639; Yarmouth, 1639; Marshfield, 1641; Rehoboth, 1645; Eastham, 1646; Bridgewater, 1656; Dartmouth, 1664; Swansea, 1667; Middleborough, 1669; Edgartown, 1671; Tisbury, 1671; Little Compton, 1682; Freetown, 1683; Rochester, 1686; Falmouth, 1686; Nantucket, 1687.

[4] See the terms of the grant to Charles Chauncey, John Atwood, and Thomas Cushman at Mattapoisett, in *Plym. Col. Recs.,* II, 9. Also Bradford, *Of Plymouth Plantation,* ed. Morison, 253-254, where another kind of attempt to control expansion is described: "Special lands were granted at a place general called Green's Harbor" to "special persons that would promise to live at Plymouth, and likely to be helpful to the church or commonwealth and so [to] tie the lands to Plymouth as farms for

in which lands were distributed by the freemen in certain of the newer townships. Grants were no longer confined to upright, religious-minded settlers. Towns accepted, with no questions asked, almost anyone who proposed to move in. Such was the charge leveled against the people of Sandwich, for example, in 1639. A similar situation seems to have prevailed in Yarmouth, for in 1640 the Court specifically directed the town elders there to require of each new arrival a "certificate from the places whence they come . . . of their religious and honest carriage."[5]

William Bradford was one of those to whom the process of dispersion came as a great disappointment; it runs through much of his famous history of Plymouth as a kind of tragic refrain. "This I fear will be the ruin of New England, at least of the churches of God there," he wrote at one point, "and will provoke the Lord's displeasure against them." When the plan for moving the town to Eastham was debated, Bradford, and others of like mind, discerned the real motive behind the proposal: "Some were still for staying together in this place, alleging men might here live if they would be content with their condition, and that it was not for want or necessity so much that they removed as for the enriching of themselves." Finally, near the end of his work, with more and more of the original stock moving away, Bradford described Plymouth as being "like an ancient mother grown old and forsaken of her children, though not in their affections yet in regard of their bodily presence and personal helpfulness; her ancient members being most of them worn away by death, and these of later time being like children translated into other families, and she like a widow left only to trust in God. Thus, she that had made many rich became herself poor."[6] He could hardly have chosen a better metaphor. It is extremely telling as a literary device, and—more than that —is highly suggestive from a historical standpoint. It describes an experience that must have been quite real, and quite painful, for many Plymouth settlers. The whole process of expansion had as one of its chief effects the scattering of families, to an extent probably inconceivable in the Old World communities from which the colonists had come. This was particularly hard upon elderly people; their anxiety that they should be

---

the same; and there they might keep their cattle and tillage by some servants and retain their dwellings here." No sooner was the plan put into effect, however, than its beneficiaries demanded permission to move directly onto their new farms. "Alas," concludes Bradford, "this remedy proved worse than the disease."

[5] *Plym. Col. Recs.,* I, 131, 142.
[6] Bradford, *Of Plymouth Plantation,* ed. Morison, 254, 333-334.

properly cared for in their old age is readily apparent in the wills they wrote. The flow of men into new areas was inexorable, but it took a profound psychological toll, even among those who were most willingly a part of it.

Nearly every category of person—young and old, rich and poor, immigrant and old settler—was involved in the expansion of the Plymouth community. The careers of the four Winslow brothers who arrived at various times during the early years of the colony may be regarded as more or less typical.[7] Kenelm Winslow came from England to Plymouth in 1629 and moved to Marshfield in 1641; Edward came in 1620 from Leyden and returned to England in 1646; John went from England to Leyden, to Plymouth, and in 1656 to Boston; and Josiah Winslow arrived in Plymouth from England in 1631, moved to Scituate in 1637, and then went from there to Marshfield. Although two of the sons of Kenelm Winslow remained in Marshfield on land that he bequeathed to them, another son moved to Yarmouth and the fourth one moved three times, to Swansea in 1666, to Rochester in 1678, and to Freetown in 1685. And third-generation Winslows could be found scattered among many different towns of Massachusetts and in other colonies as well. Nor did William Bradford's strong convictions on the matter of expansion prevent his own children from leaving Plymouth. His daughter married a Boston man; two sons moved to the neighboring settlement of Kingston; and a third led a large Bradford migration, mostly third generation, to Connecticut.[8]

The movers were often young men, but not invariably so. Indeed there were many who moved in middle age and with a large family. Experience Mitchell and William Bassett, both of whom arrived in the early 1620's, were among the original proprietors—and residents—of three different towns. After several years in Plymouth they resettled in Duxbury (each one, by this time, with a wife and young children), and in the 1650's they went to Bridgewater.

For the most part, removals were arranged and carried out by individuals; they were not affairs of large groups and elaborate organization. Family ties were sometimes a factor, as in the case of the Connecticut Bradfords, but even here the pattern was rather loose. It was usually a

---

[7] See David-Parsons Holton, *Winslow Memorial . . .* , I (New York, 1877).
[8] See Ruth Gardiner Hall, *Descendants of Governor William Bradford* (Ann Arbor, 1951).

matter of one man moving to a new community, and then several other members of his family following, separately and later on.

An obvious concomitant of such general mobility was a rapid rate of turnover in the ownership of land. In this connection the land deeds and proprietary lists that survive from the period become an important source. For example, there are two lists of proprietors for the town of Bridgewater, one made in 1645 at the time of its incorporation, and the other in 1682 when additional grants of land were being debated.[9] Of the fifty-six names on the first list only twelve reappear thirty-seven years later. To the latter group should be added five sons of original proprietors who had died in the meantime, making a grand total of seventeen men who retained their interest in Bridgewater. But this means that thirty-nine relinquished their holdings altogether, fully 70 per cent of the initial group. It is probable that some of them never lived in Bridgewater at all, acquiring rights there only in order to sell.

This pattern of land turnover is further exemplified by the varied transactions of certain individuals, as noted in the *Colony Records*. Samuel Eddy, a good case in point, came to Plymouth in 1630 as a young man of twenty-two. In the next fifty years he was involved in at least eighteen transactions for land and housing.[10] Presumably there were still more, of which no record remains, as in some cases we find him selling lands not previously identified as being in his possession. At least three times he seems to have moved his residence within Plymouth (selling one house in order to buy another), and as an old man he left the town altogether and went to Swansea in the western part of the colony. Two of his sons had already settled there, and he probably wished to be near them. A third son had gone to Martha's Vineyard; and a fourth, who seems to have been particularly restless, moved from Plymouth to Sandwich, to Middleborough, back to Plymouth, back to Middleborough, back to Plymouth, to Taunton, and back once more to Middleborough, over a period of some forty years.

Seven of Samuel Eddy's land transactions seem to have been directly connected with his changes of residence; the rest were for the purpose of enlarging his estate, or for profit. Eddy, incidentally, was a tailor by trade and not a rich man; most of the business in which he engaged was for

[9] "A Description of Bridgewater, 1818," in Massachusetts Historical Society, *Collections*, 2d Ser., VII (Boston, 1826), 137-176.

[10] Byron B. Horton, *The Ancestors and Descendants of Zachariah Eddy of Warren, Pa.* (Rutland, Vt., 1930), 29-31.

relatively small amounts of land and money. The profit motive was equally clear in the dealings of many other Plymouth residents. Perhaps one more example will suffice. In June 1639 John Barnes bought four acres of meadowland from John Winslow for eight pounds and a month later resold them to Robert Hicks for nine pounds, fifteen shillings. Soon afterwards he made a similar deal in which he bought a parcel of land for twelve pounds and sold it within a few months for eighteen.[11]

It would be interesting to know more about the lives of these people, and the lives of their ancestors, before their migration to America. Perhaps there was more mobility among inhabitants of the English countryside than is commonly supposed.[12] Perhaps the first colonists at Plymouth were conditioned for change by their prior attempt to establish themselves in Holland. It is hard to say. In any case, the settlers were doubtless predisposed to conceive of wealth in terms of land, and the circumstances of Plymouth, where currency was so scarce and land so plentiful, probably strengthened this instinct. It is clear from the wills they left that their desire to possess and to expand was usually satisfied. Even a man of relatively moderate means usually had several plots of land to deed away, and wealthy ones had as many as twelve, fifteen, or even twenty.[13] In some cases these holdings were located in a number of different townships—showing that their owners could not always have thought in terms of actual settlement at the time of acquisition.

It would be interesting to know how many people lived in Plymouth Colony during these years. Three scholars have offered guesses based on varying kinds of evidence.[14] Their findings do not agree, but suggest, when averaged together, that the total number of Plymouth residents was probably around 300 in 1630, and did not exceed 1,000 before the early 1640's. It had passed 3,000 by 1660, 5,000 by 1675, and by the time the colony had merged with Massachusetts probably stood somewhere between

[11] *Plym. Col. Recs.*, XII, 45, 64-65, 69.

[12] For recent works directed to this point, see E.E. Rich, "The Population of Elizabethan England," *Economic History Review*, 2d Ser., II (1949-50), 247-265; and Peter Laslett and John Harrison, "Clayworth and Coggenhoe," in H. E. Bell and R. L. Ollard, eds., *Historical Essays, 1600-1750, Presented to David Ogg* (London, 1963), 157-184.

[13] See, for example, the wills of Samuel Fuller (Barnstable, 1683) and Thomas Cushman (Plymouth, 1690) in *Mayflower Descendant*, II (1900), 237-241; IV (1902), 37-42.

[14] See Richard LeBaron Bowen, *Early Rehoboth . . .*, I (Rehoboth, 1945), 15-24; Joseph B. Feet, "Population of Plymouth Colony," in American Statistical Association, *Collections*, I, Pt. ii (Boston, 1845), 143-144; and Bradford, *Of Plymouth Plantation*, ed. Morison, xi.

12,000 and 15,000. The rate of growth, if not spectacular, was steady and fairly sharp; the population seems to have doubled about every fifteen years.

This growth was due, in part, to immigration but perhaps even more to certain characteristics of the people within the colony itself. For example, the popular impression today that colonial families were extremely large finds the strongest possible confirmation in the case of Plymouth. A sample of some ninety families about whom there is fairly reliable information, suggests that there was an average of seven to eight children per family who actually grew to adulthood. The number of live births was undoubtedly higher, although exactly how much higher we cannot be sure because no trace exists today of many who died in infancy and early childhood.[15]

SIZE OF FAMILIES IN PLYMOUTH

TABLE I

	Average Number of Children Born	Average Number Lived to Age 21
Sixteen First-Generation Families	7.8	7.2
Forty-seven Second-Generation Families	8.6	7.5
Thirty-three Third-Generation Families	9.3	7.9

Even allowing for the obvious likelihood that errors in the figures for the number born are somewhat greater than in the figures for those who grew to maturity, the rate of infant mortality in Plymouth seems to have

[15] Various attempts to subject evidence to quantitative analysis have been an important part of my "method," such as it is. It is not possible to achieve anything approaching total accuracy in these computations; the sources simply are not that exact. I have not knowingly employed doubtful figures, but probably a small portion of those that I have used are incorrect. In certain cases I have accepted an approximate date (e.g. 1671, when it might as well be 1670 or 1672), but only where it would not prejudice the over-all result. In general, the numerical data that I shall present should be regarded as suggestive rather than conclusive in any sense. Above all, I have sought to keep my focus on individual lives and to build up my story from there. The people about whom I have assembled information total roughly 2,000. (It is very difficult even to estimate the total number of people who lived in Plymouth Colony between 1620-91, but it was probably between 25,000 and 50,000.) Only a part of these could be employed in the treatment of any particular question, since the data for most individuals are not complete. But a sample of several hundred should still be enough at least to outline certain general patterns.

With respect to the data on family size (Table I), I have used only families in which both parents lived at least to age 50, or else if one parent died, the other quickly remarried. That is, in all these families there were parents who lived up to, and past, the prime years for childbearing.

been relatively low. In the case of a few families for which there are un-usually complete records, only about one in five children seems to have died before the age of twenty-one. Furthermore, births in the sample come for the most part at roughly two-year intervals[16] with relatively few "gaps" which might indicate a baby who did not survive. All things considered, it appears that the rate of infant and child mortality in Ply-mouth was no more than 25 per cent[17]—less than half the rate in many parts of the world today.

These figures seem to indicate a suprising standard of health and physical vigor among Plymouth residents, and a study of their longevity—the average life expectancy in the colony—confirms this impression. The following tables (II and III) are based on a sample of more than six hundred people, who lived at least to the age of twenty-one and for whom the age at death was ascertainable.

LIFE EXPECTANCY IN PLYMOUTH

TABLE II

(The figures in the left-hand column are the control points, i.e., a 21-year-old man might expect to live to age 69.2, a 30-year-old to 70.0, and so forth.)

TABLE III

(The figures in columns two and three represent the percentages of the men and women in the sample who died between the ages indicated in column one.)

Age	Men	Women	Age group	Men (percentages)	Women (percentages)
21	69.2	62.4	22–29	1.6	5.9
30	70.0	64.7	30–39	3.6	12.0
40	71.2	69.7	40–49	7.8	12.0
50	73.7	73.4	50–59	10.2	10.9
60	76.3	76.8	60–69	18.0	14.9
70	79.9	80.7	70–79	30.5	20.7
80	85.1	86.7	80–89	22.4	16.0
			90 or over	5.9	7.6

[16] This spacing is quite interesting in itself, for it immediately raises questions as to how Plymouth parents avoided having even higher numbers of children. Prob-ably the mothers nursed their babies for at least one year, but—contrary to popular belief—there is no proved biological impediment in this to further conception. Since effective contraceptive methods are a fairly recent development, it seems likely that Plymouth couples simply eschewed sexual contact over long periods of time. In many less advanced cultures of the world today there are taboos on sexual relations be-tween husband and wife for one year or more following the birth of a child. It is just possible that a similar custom prevailed in Plymouth.

[17] It is impossible to estimate what proportion of these were infants (less than one year old) and what proportion were young children, for in most cases the re-cords say only "died young."

The figures in II are really astonishingly high. Indeed, in the case of the men, they compare quite favorably with what obtains in this country today. (The life expectancy of an American male of twenty-one is now a fraction over seventy, and for a female of the same age, is approximately seventy-six.) It is at least possible that some selective bias, built into the data, may have distorted the results. For example, as between two men one of whom died at thirty and the other at ninety, it is more likely that the latter should leave some traces for the genealogist and historian to follow up. Still, I do not believe that this has been a serious problem in the above sample. A good part of the information on longevity has come from a few especially well-preserved graveyards in the Plymouth area, and presumably these offer a fairly random selection of the adults in the community. Moreover, those families for which information is relatively complete—where we know the age at death of all the members—present a picture not very different from that of the total sample. And even if we do allow for a certain inflation of the figures, the outcome is still striking.

The difference in the results for men and women is mainly due to the dangers attendant on childbirth. A young woman's life expectancy was seven years less than a man's, whereas today, with childbirth hazards virtually eliminated by modern medicine, it is six years longer. The second table shows that 30 per cent of the women and only 12 per cent of the men in the sample died between ages twenty and fifty, the normal years of child bearing. If a woman survived these middle years, her prospects for long life became at least as good as those of a man, and indeed a little better. A majority of those who lived to a really very old age (ninety or more) seem to have been women.

The records which reveal this pattern of growth and dispersion in the colony of Plymouth also provide much information about courtship, marriage, and family life. Courtships were usually initiated by the young people themselves, but as a relationship progressed toward something more permanent, the parents became directly involved. In fact, a requirement of parental consent was written into the colony's laws on marriage: "If any shall make any motion of marriage to any mans daughter . . . not having first obtayned leave and consent of the parents or master so to doe [he] shall be punished either by fine or corporall punishment or both, at the discretion of the bench and according to the nature of the offence."[18] The attitude of parents toward a proposed match depended on a variety of spiritual and material considerations. Speaking very generally, it was desirable that both parties be of good moral and religious character. Beyond that, the couple would hopefully have enough land and possessions, given to them by both sets of parents, to establish a reasonably secure household.

But in a community as fluid as Plymouth it is unlikely that parental control over courtship and marriage could have been fully preserved. A few surviving pieces of evidence suggest that it was possibly quite an issue. In 1692 the widow Abigail Young died without leaving a will. The court moved to settle her estate on the basis of her intentions as revealed in several conversations held before her death. Two sons, Robert and Henry, were the prime candidates for the inheritance. Witnesses testified that "when shee dyed [she said] shee would Leave all the estate that shee had with Henry, if Robart had that gierl that there was a discourse about: but if he had her not I understood that the estate should be devided betwix them." A third son, Nathaniel, confirmed this. "My mother young," he reported, "told me that if Robirt had that gierl which there was a talke about shee would not give him a peny."[19]

The first official step toward marriage was normally the betrothal or "pre-contract"—a ceremony before two witnesses at which the couple exchanged formal promises to wed in due time. A period of several weeks or months followed, during which these intentions were "published." A betrothed couple was considered to have a special status, not married but no longer unmarried either. They were required to be completely loyal each to the other; the adultery laws treated them no differently from husbands and wives. Sexual contact between them was forbidden; but the penalty for it was only a quarter of what was prescribed for single people.[20] It may be that this actually encouraged premarital relations

---

[18] *Plym. Col. Recs.*, XI, 29, 108, 190. Occasionally there were prosecutions under this statute, the most notorious of which involved Elizabeth Prence, the daughter of a governor of the colony, and Arthur Howland, Jr., who belonged to another of Plymouth's leading families. Many of the Howlands had become Quakers, young Arthur among them; the Governor, on the other hand, was firmly opposed to this new and "foreign" religious movement. Twice he brought Howland before the General Court for having "disorderly and unrighteously endeavored to obtain the affections of Mistress Elizabeth Prence." But the story had a happy ending: after seven long years the Governor relented, and the couple were finally married in the spring of 1668. *Ibid.*, IV, 140, 158-159. For another case of this kind, see *ibid.*, III, 5.

[19] *Mayflower Descendant*, XV (1913), 79-80.

[20] *Plym. Col. Recs.*, XI, 172.

JOHN DEMOS

among betrothed couples because of its implication that fornication was much less reprehensible in their case than otherwise.[21] The Court records show sixty-five convictions for misconduct of this kind, over a forty-five year period. (Note that this total comprises only those who were *caught,* and whose cases were recorded.) In some instances members of the most prominent families were involved: for example, Peregrine White, Thomas Delano, and Thomas Cushman, Jr. Occasionally the basis for conviction was the arrival of a child less than nine months after the wedding ceremony. Perhaps innocent couples were sometimes punished under this system; but the number of "early" babies was, in any event, extremely high.[22]

Once the betrothal was formalized, considerable thought had to be given to the economic future of the couple. In all but the poorest families each child could expect to receive from its parents a "portion"—a certain quantity of property or money with which to make an independent start in life. In most cases this occurred at the time of marriage, and its purpose was everywhere the same. A man was to use it to "be for himself" (in the graphic little phrase of the time); a woman would transfer it to her husband for the greater good of the household which they were starting together. To make special provision for the possibility that he might die while his children were still young, a man usually directed in his will that his "overseers" hold part of his estate intact to be distributed later as portions, at the appropriate time.

There was no set formula governing the actual substance of these portions. More often than not, however, a male child was given land, cattle, tools, and a house or a promise of help in the building of a house; a woman, for her part, usually received movable property, such as furniture or clothing and money. Occasionally the terms of these bequests were officially recorded in a "deed of gift";[23] more often they seem to have been arranged informally. Most parents hoped to have accumulated sufficient property by the time their children came of age to make these

[21] This point is argued at greater length in George Elliott Howard, *A History of Matrimonial Institutions* . . . , II (Chicago, 1904), 169-200. Howard's discussion of marriage customs in colonial New England is, in general, quite helpful.

[22] For example, a random sampling of fourth-generation Bradfords turned up nine couples whose first child arrived within eight months of their wedding and all but two of these within six months. Also, it appears that Thomas Cushman's first baby was not only conceived, but actually born, before his marriage.

[23] As on the occasion of the marriage of Jacob Cook and Damaris Hopkins in 1646. *Mayflower Descendant,* II, 27-28.

gifts without suffering undue hardship. Some had to buy land specifically for this purpose;[24] others petitioned the Court "to accommodate them for theire posterities," i.e., to give them a free grant.[25] It appears that fathers sometimes retained the title to the lands which they gave as portions: there are many Plymouth wills which direct that a son shall inherit "the land wherein he now dwells," or use words to this effect.[26] Perhaps this practice served to maintain some degree of parental authority beyond the years of childhood.

It is widely supposed that people married early in the colonial period. For Plymouth, however—and I suspect for most other communities of that time—this impression cannot be sustained. Indeed, the average age of both men and women at the time of their first marriage was considerably higher then than it is today—and quite possibly has never been exceeded at any subsequent point in our history.

TABLE IV

FIRST MARRIAGES IN PLYMOUTH
(Based on a sample of some 650 men and women)

	Born Before 1600	Born 1600–25	Born 1625–50	Born 1650–75	Born 1675–1700
Mean age of men at time of 1st marriage	27.0	27.0	26.1	25.4	24.6
Mean age of women at time of 1st marriage	—*	20.6	20.2	21.3	22.3
Percentage of men married at age 23 or over	25%	18%	25%	26%	38%
Percentage of men married at age 30 or over	44%	23%	27%	18%	14%
Percentage of women married at age 25 or over	—*	9%	10%	20%	28%

*Insufficient data for women born before 1600.

This table is largely self-explanatory. Only one point requires additional comment: the steady, if unspectacular, narrowing of the age gap between the sexes at the time of marriage. At the start this gap averaged

[24] In 1653, for instance, John Brown of Rehoboth bought land from Capt. Thomas Willet, which he immediately deeded over to his sons, John and James. *Ibid.*, IV, 84.

[25] *Plym. Col. Recs.*, III, 164.

[26] See, for examples, the wills of John Thompson and Ephraim Tinkham, *Mayflower Descendant*, IV, 22-29, 122-125.

JOHN DEMOS

six and one-half years; by the end it was verging on two. Men were marrying earlier and women later. During the early years of the colony there was certainly a shortage of women; spinsters were a rarity, and marriageable girls, of whatever charm and property, must have received plenty of offers. At some point, however, new factors began to come into play, and this imbalance in the sex ratio was gradually corrected. Above all, the process of expansion removed substantial numbers of young men from the areas that had been settled first, and by the end of the century some towns may well have held a surplus of females. Wherever women outnumbered men, there were some who did not find husbands until relatively late and at least a few who never married at all. Conversely, the men had a larger and larger group to choose from and tended to marry somewhat earlier. By 1700 there were occasional marriages in which the woman was older than her husband, and for the first time the number of spinsters had become noticeable. The earliest official count of males and females in Plymouth that still survives comes from a census taken for all Massachusetts in 1765. At that time all of the eastern counties showed a substantial majority of women over men; the reverse was true for the western counties. In the towns which formerly belonged to Plymouth Colony the figures were 53.2 per cent female as against 46.8 per cent male. It is my guess that this surplus began as much as a century earlier.[27]

Marriage was conceived to be the normal estate for adults in colonial New England. When one spouse died, the other usually remarried within a year or two. Most were in their thirties and forties at the time of their remarriage, but some were much older. Robert Cushman, Jr., for instance,

---

[27] See J. H. Benton, Jr., *Early Census Making in Massachusetts, 1643-1765* . . . (Boston, 1905). The dimensions of the problem, for Plymouth, can be further refined. The findings in the 1765 census are divided into two parts: people under 16, and people 16 and over. The 53.2 to 46.8 ratio, quoted above, is for the 16-and-over group. But, as almost all males remained single until age 21, a more significant ratio would be one for only those males and females who were 21 or over. We can assume, from a breakdown of other parts of the census, that the 16-21 grouping composed about 10 per cent of the total over 16. We also know from the census that the ratio of males under 16 to females under 16 was 51.2 males to 48.8 females. If this ratio of 51.2 to 48.8 is projected to the 16-21 age group for the purpose of eliminating those under 21 from the final ratio, we discover that the ratio of men 21 or older to women 21 or older becomes approximately 53.8 to 46.2. This means that for one out of every seven girls there was no man, at least in her own home area. In a few individual towns the situation was worse—as high as one in four.

took a new wife at eighty! This pattern affected a very considerable portion of the community, as the following table shows.

TABLE V

RATES OF REMARRIAGE IN PLYMOUTH COLONY

(The figures for men and women are separate, and in each case there is a percentage for all those who lived to be fifty or more, and another for those who lived to be seventy or more. The sample, comprising over seven hundred people, does not include anyone who died before the age of fifty.)

Number of Marriages	Men		Women	
	Over 50	Over 70	Over 50	Over 70
1	60%	55%	74%	69%
2	34%	36%	25%	30%
3	6%	8%	1%	1%
4	—*	.5%	—	—
5	—*	.5%	—	—
Total married more than once	40%	45%	26%	31%

*Less than one half of one per cent.

Generally speaking, the property of husband and wife was not merged in a second marriage to the extent customary for a first one. The main reason for this, of course, was to preserve the claims of the children by the first marriage to a just inheritance. In fact, wills were always framed with this point in mind. Often the bulk of a man's estate was transmitted at his death directly to his children, or if to his wife, only until she married again. The part that remained to herself alone was usually one third of the estate, and sometimes less. Widows in Plymouth did not control a large amount of property.

When a marriage between a widow and widower was planned it was customary to make an explicit agreement as to terms. The man pledged a certain sum to his (new) wife in the event of his death, but it was often only a token amount, much less than the "thirds" that a first wife might expect. The woman, for her part, retained the right of "sole disposition" of any property she might possess; it never became part of her husband's estate.[28]

A widow's children were placed in a doubtful position when their

[28] See, for example, the agreement between Ephraim Morton and Mary Harlow, widow. *Mayflower Descendant*, XVII (1915), 49. There were, admittedly, some exceptions to the pattern. When William Sherman died in 1680, he left six small children and no will. His widow remarried soon afterwards. When her new husband agreed to provide for the children, the courts ordered Sherman's estate made over to him, because of the obvious expenses he would have to meet. *Ibid.*, IV, 171 ff.

mother remarried. Sometimes the new husband agreed to take them into his household, but more often they were placed elsewhere. Occasionally the first husband had anticipated this problem before his death. Anthony Besse's will provided that should his widow remarry, "the five bigest [children] to bee put forth and theire Cattle with them according to the Descretion of the overseers." Another father,

Lawrance Lichfeild lying on his Death bedd sent for John Allin and Ann his wife and Desired to give and bequeath unto them his youngest son Josias Lichfeild if they would accept of him and take him as theire Child; then they Desired to know how long they should have him and the said Lawrance said for ever; but the mother of the child was not willing then; but in a short time after willingly Concented to her husbands will in the thinge; if the said John and Ann would take the Child for theire adopted Child; whereunto they Assented . . . [The boy too] being asked by his owne mother . . . if hee Did Concent and Chuse to live with the said John and Ann as hitherto by the space of about nine yeares hee had Done; Willingly answered yea.

No doubt the boy was deeply attached to the Allens after having lived with them for so long. The agreement, then, imposed no particular hardship on anyone involved; it simply continued, and formalized, a previous arrangement.[29]

If children did remain with their mother after her remarriage, their stepfather was not supposed to exercise normal parental authority over them. Although at the time of his marriage to the widow, Mary Foster, Jonathan Morey contracted to "bring up" her son Benjamin at his own expense, he also agreed not to interfere in any future plans for binding the boy out. A fairly common solution to the problem of stepchildren was to keep them with their mother for a few years and then as they grew older to "put them out." Ultimate responsibility for such children passed to some persons specially designated in their father's will—often to his overseers, occasionally to his own parents. When Jacob Mitchell and his wife were killed by Indians at Rehoboth in 1675, their small children went to live with Mitchell's father in Bridgewater. John Brown of Swansea wrote in his will: "Conserning all my five Children I Doe wholly leave them all to the ordering and Disposeing of my owne father . . . for him to bring them up not once questioning but that his love and Care

[29] Ibid., XIV (1912), 152; XII (1910), 134.

for them wilbee as it hath bine for my selfe." Brown's wife survived him, and the children probably remained in her day-to-day care, or else were "bound out"; but over-all direction of their lives was henceforth in the hands of their grandfather.[30]

It has been widely assumed that the "extended family" was character-istic of Western society everywhere until at least the eighteenth century, and that the change to our own "nuclear" pattern came only with the Industrial Revolution.[31] The term "extended family" in its strict sense means a household consisting of several couples, related as siblings or cousins, and their children, and perhaps their children's children. This pattern, of course, still prevails in many parts of the world. Its most striking results are a diffusion of affections and authority within the whole, or extended, family, and a sharing of economic responsibilities. The term is also applied, somewhat more loosely, to situations where the various family members do not form one household in the sense of living "under one roof" but still live close together and share loyalties and re-sponsibilities which go beyond their own offspring or parents.

In colonial Plymouth, there were no extended families at all, in the sense of "under one roof." The wills show, beyond any doubt, that married brothers and sisters never lived together in the same house. As soon as a young man became betrothed, plans were made for the build-ing, or purchase, of his own house. For example, when Joseph Buckland of Rehoboth married his father promised "to build the said Joseph a Convenient house for his Comfortable liveing with three score of acrees of land ajoyning to it."[32] Some young men moved out of the family even before marrying, either to join in the expansion toward the interior or simply to "be for themselves" while remaining nearby. Girls stayed with their parents until they found a husband, but never beyond that time. I know of only one case in which there is documentary evidence suggesting that two couples shared a house, and it is truly the exception that proves the rule. The will of Thomas Bliss (Plymouth, 1647) contained this

[30] *Ibid.*, XIV, 15-16; XXI (1919), 185; XVIII (1916), 14-15.

[31] However, a few very recent studies have thrown some doubt on this idea. See Laslett and Harrison, "Clayworth and Coggenhoe," for evidence implying very small families indeed in rural English villages of the late 17th century.

[32] *Mayflower Descendant*, XVI (1914), 82. When Thomas Little of Taunton died leaving two teenage sons, his will directed that £10 be paid to each toward the building of houses "when they shall have occation." *Ibid.*, IV, 162.

clause: "I give unto my soon Jonathan my house and home lot Condition-
ally that hee shall give unto my sonninlaw Thomas Willmore his lot
which hee now hath and allso the one half of my broken up ground for
two yeares and shall healp him to build him an house and let him peac-
ably and quietly live in the house with him untell they shall bee able to
set up an house for him."[33]

In a true extended family the death of the father, or even of both
parents, causes no radical change in living arrangements. The widow or
the children, or both, continue their lives much as before, and the functions of the deceased are assumed by other relatives (uncles or cousins or
grandparents). When a man died in Plymouth, however, his household
usually broke up. If the children were still young, some might remain
with their mother, but others were likely to be placed in new families. If
the children were adult, the "homestead" was given to a certain designated
one of them, who was then obliged to pay to each of his brothers and
sisters an amount equivalent to some fair proportion of the property's
value.[34]

An unusually wealthy man in Plymouth Colony, and especially one
who participated directly in the founding of new towns, could accumulate
enough land to provide his sons with lots near or adjoining his own. Wills
and land deeds show, for example, that John Washburn divided up his
very large estate in Bridgewater with three sons, and that John Turner
did the same kind of thing in Scituate.[35] This sort of arrangement comes
as close to being an extended family as anything found in and around
Plymouth—and it is not very close at all. There is no evidence of shared
economic activity, no mention in the wills of profits or crops to be divided
up. Moreover, in both the Washburn and the Turner families there were
other sons who do not seem to have remained nearby.

Among those who were less wealthy, the drive to expand and to increase their property proved more powerful than the bonds which might
have held families together. Children left, when they came of age, to
take up new holdings several towns and many miles away. The process
of dispersion was, in fact, sometimes encouraged by the very system of
portions described earlier. Often a father simply had no land to spare in

---

[33] *Ibid.*, VIII (1906), 85.
[34] See, for example, the will of David Linnell (Barnstable, 1688), *ibid.*, X (1908),
100-101.
[35] *Ibid.*, XV, 248-253; V (1903), 41-46.

the immediate vicinity of his own farm. He might, however, own property in one, or two, or three, of the newer townships; and this was what he passed on to his children. The will of William Bradford, Jr., shows that he had sons living in Connecticut (on land which he had given them); and he made additional bequests, to his youngest children, in Plymouth and Duxbury. Similarly, when Benjamin Bartlett died he left his children a wide variety of lots in Duxbury, Middleborough, Little Compton, and Rochester.[36] In some cases the recipients may have sold these gifts soon afterwards, but at least as often they went to make their homes on them.

What we would most like to know is something of the effect of this dispersion on a whole range of more intimate aspects of family life. A court case at Plymouth in 1679 throws some light on such matters. An elderly man named Samuel Ryder had just died and left his whole estate to two sons, Benjamin and John. A third son, Joseph, had been left nothing. What made this especially hard was the fact that Joseph had already built a house on a piece of land belonging to his father and had expected to receive title to it in the father's will. The Court approached the problem by taking a number of depositions from friends and family. Elizabeth Mathews was called first and gave the following testimony: "I being att the Raising of Joseph Riyders house; Joseph Ryders Mother Came into the house Joseph then lived in and Cryed and wrong her hands fearing that Joseph would Goe away; Josephs Mother then said that if you would beleive a woman beleive mee that youer father saith that you shall never be Molested; and you shall Never be Molested." Samuel Mathews verified this report and supplied additional details: "In the Morning before wee Raised the house old Goodman Ryder Joseph Ryders father Came out and marked out the Ground with his stick; and bid the said Joseph sett his house where it Now stands . . . the occation of the womans Lamenting as above said was fearing her son would Goe away; for shee said if hee went shee would Goe too."[37]

There are several striking things about this episode: the mother's distress at the thought that her son might leave (even to the point of suggesting that she would follow him); the hint of hostility between father and son; the threat to go away used by the son as a means of forcing a

[36] *Ibid.*, IV, 143-147; VI (1904), 44-49.
[37] *Ibid.*, XI (1909), 50-53. In this context to "molest" means to make trouble about the ownership of something.

gift from his father; and the implication that parents could, and did, use gifts of land to induce their children to stay nearby. Evidence bearing directly on the human dimension of life in Plymouth is extremely hard to come by, but something like the Ryder case does offer a glimpse of the enormous strain that the whole pattern of geographic mobility must have placed upon family ties and sanctions.

Land and property represented one advantage still possessed by most parents when they wished to rearrange their own lives and the lives of their children. They tried to use it in a variety of ways. Bequests to children were often hedged by a requirement of good behavior: "I give [my estate to] my two sonnes Daniell and Samuell [ages 15 and 17] upon this proviso that they bee Obeidient unto theire mother and carrye themselves as they ought . . . but if the one or both live otherwise then they ought and undewtyfully and unquietly with theire Mother . . . then hee that soe carryeth himselfe shall Disinherit himselfe of his parte of this land." Another legacy, this one to a daughter, was made conditional on her "pleas[ing] her mother in her match." In still another case a man left his widow to judge their child's behavior and reward him accordingly from out of his estate. And the reasoning behind this was made explicit: "I would have the boy beholding to my wife; and not my wife to the boy."[38] Sometimes portions were shaped in the same way. One of the rare letters that survives from seventeenth-century Plymouth describes a father bestowing upon his son "the full of his porshon except upon his sons better behaver [he] should desarve more."[39]

It is likely, then, that rewards in the form of property were held out as an inducement to all sorts of "better behavior." But this was especially true in regard to the care of elderly couples and widows. Virtually every man who left a widow directed in his will that she be looked after by one of their children, and made a large bequest contingent thereupon. Usually the family homestead went to a particular child, with one room or more reserved for the widow. Often the instructions were spelled out in great detail: She would have full rights to the use of the "garden" and "orchard"; yearly payments of a certain specified amount must be made to

[38] Will of Thomas Hicks (Scituate, 1652), will of Samuel Newman (Rehoboth, 1661), and depositions concerning the estate of John Allen (Scituate, 1662), *ibid.*, XI, 160; XV, 234-236; XVII, 218.
[39] Benjamin Brewster to Daniel Wetherell, date not known, *ibid.*, II, 113.

her, wood must be brought to her door in wintertime, her cows milked, etc.[40]

Some men made arrangements of this kind even before their deaths. John and Deborah Hurd of Barnstable, for example, deeded "all that our hom sted" to their daughter and son-in-law in exchange for "the whole and sole Care and charge of us . . . for and during the tarm of our Natural Lives." And Robert Sprout of Middleborough gave his farm to his sons Ebenezer and James, on condition that they "pay yearly for my support . . . the sum of forty pounds to that child which I live with and provides for me and looks after me."[41] These conditions are nailed down so tightly in so many wills (and similar deeds) that it is tempting to infer some particular anxiety behind them.[42] It clearly was the general custom for aged parents to live with one of their children who would provide the care and support they needed. Probably in the majority of cases this was managed without too much difficulty; but in a society as fluid as Plymouth there must have been some elderly fathers and mothers who were more or less neglected. One recalls Bradford's vivid image of the "ancient mother, grown old and forsaken of her children, though not in their affections, yet in regard of their bodily presence and personal helpfulness."

Although one set of parents with their own children always formed the core of a Plymouth household, this nuclear pattern was, as we have seen, sometimes modified by the inclusion of one or more aged grandparents. It was often further modified by servants and apprentices, who lived in the houses of their masters. Among such people were at least a few Negroes and Indians whose service was normally for life.[43] The vast majority, however, were young boys and girls, "bound out" for a specified term of years. Some of them were orphans but many others had both parents living. Often, in fact, the parents had made all the arrangements and signed a formal contract with the couple whom their child served. In

[40] See, for examples, the wills of Thomas King, Sr., of Scituate and of Robert Hicks of Plymouth, *ibid.*, XXXI (1933), 101; VIII, 144-146.

[41] *Ibid.*, XVI, 219; VI, 9-10.

[42] One eldest son who inherited his father's homestead complained that the conditions attached to the bequest, especially with regard to his father's widow, were such as to make him virtually "a servant for life." *Ibid.*, XII, 106.

[43] The inventory of the property of John Gorham of Yarmouth in 1675 included the item "1 Negro man." *Ibid.*, IV, 156. For similar treatment of Indian servants, see the wills of Samuel Fuller and Anthony Snow, *ibid.*, II, 237-241; V, 1-5.

JOHN DEMOS

1660 "An agreement appointed to bee Recorded" stated that "Richard Berry of yarmouth with his wifes Concent; and other frinds; hath given unto Gorge Crispe of Eastham and his; wife theire son Samuell Berry; to bee att the ordering and Disposing of the said Gorge and his wife as if hee were theire owne Child, untill hee shall accomplish the age of twenty one yeares; and in the meane time to provide for the said Samuell in all thinges as theire owne Child; and afterwards if hee live to marry or to goe away from them; to Doe for him as if hee were theire own Child."[44] It is noteworthy that the Crispes took full responsibility for young Samuel —even to the point of promising him a portion. This is, then, a virtual deed of adoption.

No age was indicated for Samuel Berry, but it is clear from other cases that the children involved were often very young. John Smith and his wife gave their four-year-old son to Thomas Whitney "to have the full and sole disposing of him . . . without annoyance or disturbance from the said John Smith or Bennit his wife."[45] Samuel Eddy arranged apprenticeships for three of his sons, at ages six, seven, and nine. Two of them went to the same man, Mr. John Brown of Rehoboth. Upon reaching maturity, they both received property from Brown, and, in addition, were given modest portions by their father. It appears from this that Eddy continued to take a direct interest in his children even after they had left his household.

The most difficult question these arrangements raise is, what purpose lay behind them? No answer that would serve in all cases suggests itself. In some, poverty was obviously a factor. For example, Samuel Eddy, in the apprenticeship papers for his sons, pleaded his "many children" and "many wants." On the other hand, George Soule of Duxbury bound out his daughter to John Winslow, and Soule was a wealthy man. In certain cases, learning a trade was mentioned, but in a perfunctory manner. When young Benjamin Savory was bound out to Jonathan Shaw in 1653, the papers directed that he be taught "whatsoever trad[e] the said Jonathan Shaw can Doe." Something must have gone amiss with this arrangement, because four years later the child was placed with still another family. The terms were only slightly less vague: his new master, Stephen Bryant, was to "teach him in learning that is to say to read and write and to Intruct him in husbandry."[46]

[44] Ibid., XV, 34.
[45] Plym. Col. Recs., XII, 181-182.
[46] Mayflower Descendant, II, 30; V, 90; XII, 133.

Another possible motive was to improve a child's educational opportunities. Instruction in reading and writing was often included among the conditions of the contract, as in the case of Benjamin Savory above. Finally, Edmund Morgan has suggested in his *The Puritan Family* that "Puritan parents did not trust themselves with their own children . . . and were afraid of spoiling them by too great affection";[47] it was for this reason, he argues, that so many children were placed in families other than their own. It is an interesting thought, but there is simply no explicit proof for it. At least Morgan found none, and I have had no better luck with the materials for Plymouth.

The household of Samuel Fuller seems to have been about as varied as any in Plymouth, and is worth mentioning in this connection. When Fuller died in 1633 it included nine people, six of whom were not of his own immediate family. There were, beside himself, his wife, and his son, a nephew, two servants, a ward, and two "additional children." The last of these had been sent to him for education, from families in Charlestown and Sagos. The ward was the daughter of a close friend who had died some years before. Meanwhile, Fuller's own daughter was living with "goodwife Wallen." Fuller was obliged to leave instructions about all these people in his will.[48] His daughter was to continue where she was for the time being. The children from Charlestown and Sagos should be returned to their former homes. The ward was committed to his brother-in-law, and passed thereby into her third family. Fuller's son should continue to live in the "homestead" and one day would inherit it; but the same brother-in-law was to take charge of his education. Fuller's wife would have the day-to-day care of the youth until she died or remarried. She would also take charge of the servants for the remainder of their contracted term.

Fuller's household was hardly typical, however. A close reading of hundreds of Plymouth wills has turned up no other family as complicated as this one. In many there were one or two people not of the immediate family—aged grandparents, servants, wards, or additional children—but rarely more. The basic unit remained one set of parents and their children or stepchildren, living apart from all other relatives.

Clearly children in seventeenth-century Plymouth often found themselves growing up in a household other than that of their parents. The

[47] Edmund S. Morgan, *The Puritan Family* . . . (Boston, 1956), 38.
[48] *Mayflower Descendant,* I (1899), 24-28.

records are so scattered that it is impossible to calculate how many this category actually included. It must, however, have been a considerable number; my own guess is somewhere between a third and a half of all the children. This figure does not seem too high when it is remembered that one in three of the parents in the colony married twice or more, and that some children were placed in new homes even when their own father and mother were living.

The impact of these situations on the children cannot be proved—only imagined. But a hint of what they could mean comes to us in the story of a rather sad little episode, which by a lucky chance has been preserved in the *Colony Records*. Christian (Penn) Eaton and Francis Billington, widow and widower, were married in Plymouth in 1635. Christian's son, Benjamin Eaton, was "put forth" into another family immediately thereafter. The couple began to have children of their own: first, Elizabeth, and then, Joseph—both of whom were also placed in other families. But little Joseph apparently did not take to this arrangement very well, for in 1643 the Court was obliged to issue the following order:

Whereas Joseph, the sonn of Francis Billington . . . was . . . placed with John Cooke the younger, and hath since beene inveagled, and did oft departe his said masters service, the Court, upon longe heareing of all that can be said or alleadged by his parents, doth order and appoynt that the said Joseph shalbe returned to his said master againe immediately, and shall so remaine with him during his terme; and that if either the said Francis, or Christian, his wyfe, do receive him, if he shall againe depart from his said master without his lycence, that the said Francis, and Christian, his wyfe, shalbe sett in the stocks . . . as often as he or shee shall so receive him, untill the Court shall take a further course with them.[49]

Joseph Billington was five years old.

[49] *Plym. Col. Recs.*, II, 58-59.

Family Structure in Seventeenth-Century Andover, Massachusetts

Philip J. Greven, Jr.*

S URPRISINGLY little is known at present about family life and family structure in the seventeenth-century American colonies. The generalizations about colonial family life embedded in textbooks are seldom the result of studies of the extant source materials, which historians until recently have tended to ignore.[1] Genealogists long have been using records preserved in county archives, town halls, churches, and graveyards as well as personal documents to compile detailed information on successive generations of early American families. In addition to the work of local genealogists, many communities possess probate records and deeds for the colonial period. A study of these last testaments and deeds together with the vital statistics of family genealogies can provide the answers to such questions as how many children people had, how long people lived, at what ages did they marry, how much control did fathers have over their children, and to what extent and under what conditions did children remain in their parents' community. The answers to such questions enable an historian to reconstruct to some extent the basic characteristics of family life for specific families in specific communities. This essay is a study of a single seventeenth-century New England town, Andover, Massachusetts, during the lifetimes of its first and second generations —the pioneers who carved the community out of the wilderness, and their children who settled upon the lands which their fathers had acquired. A consideration of their births, marriages, and deaths, together with the disposition of land and property within the town from one generation to the next reveals some of the most important aspects of family life and family structure in early Andover.

The development of a particular type of family structure in seven-

* Mr. Greven is a member of the Department of History, The University of British Columbia.

[1] Two notable exceptions to this generalization are Edmund S. Morgan, *The Puritan Family* . . . (Boston, 1956), and John Demos, "Notes on Life in Plymouth Colony," *William and Mary Quarterly*, 3d Ser., XXII (1965), 264-286.

Reprinted from *William and Mary Quarterly*, 3rd Series, **XXIII** (1966), 234–256. By permission of the William and Mary Quarterly. This essay has been incorporated into "Four Generations" ("Population, Land, and Family in Colonial Andover, Massachusetts," pub. 1970 by Cornell Univ. Press, Ithaca, New York).

teenth-century Andover was dependent in part upon the economic development of the community during the same period. Andover, settled by a group of about eighteen men during the early 1640's and incorporated in 1646, was patterned at the outset after the English open field villages familiar to many of the early settlers. The inhabitants resided on house lots adjacent to each other in the village center, with their individual holdings of land being distributed in small plots within two large fields beyond the village center. House lots ranged in size from four to twenty acres, and subsequent divisions of land within the town were proportionate to the size of the house lots. By the early 1660's, about forty-two men had arrived to settle in Andover, of whom thirty-six became permanent residents. During the first decade and a half, four major divisions of the arable land in the town were granted. The first two divisions established two open fields, in which land was granted to the inhabitants on the basis of one acre of land for each acre of house lot. The third division, which provided four acres of land for each acre of house lot, evidently did not form another open field, but was scattered about the town. The fourth and final division of land during the seventeenth century occurred in 1662, and gave land to the householders at the rate of twenty acres for each acre of their house lots. Each householder thus obtained a minimum division allotment of about eighty acres and a maximum allotment of about four hundred acres. Cumulatively, these four successive divisions of town land, together with additional divisions of meadow and swampland, provided each of the inhabitants with at least one hundred acres of land for farming, and as much as six hundred acres. During the years following these substantial grants of land, many of the families in the town removed their habitations from the house lots in the town center onto their distant, and extensive, farm lands, thus altering the character of the community through the establishment of independent family farms and scattered residences. By the 1680's, more than half the families in Andover lived outside the original center of the town on their own ample farms. The transformation of the earlier open field village effectively recast the basis for family life within the community.[2]

2 For a full discussion of the transformation of 17th-century Andover, see my article, "Old Patterns in the New World: The Distribution of Land in 17th Century Andover," *Essex Institute Historical Collections,* CI (April 1965), 133-148. See also the study of Sudbury, Mass., in Sumner Chilton Powell, *Puritan Village: The Formation of a New England Town* (Middletown, Conn., 1963).

PHILIP J. GREVEN, JR.

An examination of the number of children whose births are recorded in the Andover town records between 1651 and 1699 reveals a steady increase in the number of children being born throughout the period. (See Table I.[8]) Between 1651 and 1654, 28 births are recorded, followed by 32 between 1655 and 1659, 43 between 1660 and 1664, 44 between 1665 and 1669, 78 between 1670 and 1674, and 90 between 1675 and 1679. After 1680, the figures rise to more than one hundred births every five years.

TABLE I

THE NUMBER OF SONS AND DAUGHTERS LIVING AT THE AGE OF 21
IN TWENTY-NINE FIRST-GENERATION FAMILIES

Sons	0	1	2	3	4	5	6	7	8	9	10
Families	1	2	7	1	6	6	3	3	0	0	0
Daughters	0	1	2	3	4	5	6	7	8	9	10
Families	0	2	7	6	11	2	0	0	0	1	0

The entire picture of population growth in Andover, however, cannot be formed from a study of the town records alone since these records do not reflect the pattern of generations within the town. Looked at from the point of view of the births of the children of the first generation of settlers who arrived in Andover between the first settlement in the mid-1640's and 1660, a very different picture emerges, hidden within the entries of the town records and genealogies.[4] The majority of the second-generation children were born during the two decades of the 1650's and the 1660's. The births of 159 second-generation children were distributed in decades as follows: 10 were born during the 1630's, either in England

[8] The figures in Table I were compiled from the first MS book of Andover vital records, A Record of Births, Deaths, and Marriages, Begun 1651 Ended 1700, located in the vault of the Town Clerk's office, Town Hall, Andover, Mass. For a suggestive comparison of population growth in a small village, see W. G. Hoskins, "The Population of an English Village, 1086-1801: A Study of Wigston Magna," *Provincial England: Essays in Social and Economic History* (London, 1963), 195-200.

[4] The most important collection of unpublished genealogies of early Andover families are the typed MSS of Charlotte Helen Abbott, which are located in the Memorial Library, Andover. The two vols. of *Vital Records of Andover, Massachusetts, to the End of the Year 1849* (Topsfield, Mass., 1912) provide an invaluable and exceptionally reliable reference for vital statistics of births, marriages, and deaths.

or in the towns along the Massachusetts' coast where their parents first settled; 28 were born during the 1640's; 49 were born during the 1650's; 43 were born during the 1660's; declining to 21 during the 1670's, and falling to only 8 during the 1680's. Because of this pattern of births, the second generation of Andover children, born largely during the 1650's and the 1660's, would mature during the late 1670's and the 1680's. Many of the developments of the second half of the seventeenth century in Andover, both within the town itself and within the families residing there, were the result of the problems posed by a maturing second generation.

From the records which remain, it is not possible to determine the size of the first-generation family with complete accuracy, since a number of children were undoubtedly stillborn, or died almost immediately after birth without ever being recorded in the town records. It is possible, however, to determine the number of children surviving childhood and adolescence with considerable accuracy, in part because of the greater likelihood of their names being recorded among the children born in the town, and in part because other records, such as church records, marriage records, tax lists, and wills, also note their presence. Evidence from all of these sources indicates that the families of Andover's first settlers were large, even without taking into account the numbers of children who may have been born but died unrecorded. An examination of the families of twenty-nine men who settled in Andover between 1645 and 1660 reveals that a total of 247 children are known to have been born to these particular families. Of these 247 children whose births may be ascertained, thirty-nine, or 15.7 per cent, are known to have died before reaching the age of 21 years.[5] A total of 208 children or 84.3 per cent of the number of children known to be born thus reached the age of 21 years, having survived the hazards both of infancy and of adolescence. This suggests that the number of deaths among children and adolescents during the middle of the seventeenth century in Andover was lower than might have been expected.

In terms of their actual sizes, the twenty-nine first-generation families

[5] While this figure is low, it should not be discounted entirely. Thomas Jefferson Wertenbaker, *The First Americans, 1607-1690* (New York, 1929), 185-186, found that, "Of the eight hundred and eight children of Harvard graduates for the years from 1658 to 1690, one hundred and sixty-two died before maturity. This gives a recorded child mortality among this selected group of *twenty* per cent." Italics added.

PHILIP J. GREVEN, JR.

varied considerably, as one might expect. Ten of these twenty-nine families had between 0 and 3 sons who survived to the age of 21 years; twelve families had either 4 or 5 sons surviving, and six families had either 6 or 7 sons living to be 21. Eighteen of these families thus had four or more sons to provide with land or a trade when they reached maturity and wished to marry, a fact of considerable significance in terms of the development of family life in Andover during the years prior to 1690. Fewer of these twenty-nine families had large numbers of daughters. Fifteen families had between 0 and 3 daughters who reached adulthood, eleven families had 4 daughters surviving, and three families had 5 or more daughters reaching the age of 21. In terms of the total number of their children born and surviving to the age of 21 or more, four of these twenty-nine first-generation families had between 2 and 4 children (13.8 per cent), eleven families had between 5 and 7 children (37.9 per cent), and fourteen families had between 8 and 11 children (48.3 per cent). Well over half of the first-generation families thus had 6 or more children who are known to have survived adolescence and to have reached the age of 21. The average number of children known to have been born to these twenty-nine first-generation families was 8.5, with an average of 7.2 children in these families being known to have reached the age of 21 years.[6] The size of the family, and particularly the number of sons who survived adolescence, was a matter of great importance in terms of the problems which would arise later over the settlement of the second generation upon land in Andover and the division of the estates of the first generation among their surviving children. The development of a particular type of family structure within Andover during the first two generations depended in part upon the number of children born and surviving in particular families.

Longevity was a second factor of considerable importance in the development of the family in Andover. For the first forty years following the settlement of the town in 1645, relatively few deaths were recorded among the inhabitants of the town. Unlike Boston, which evidently

[6] Comparative figures for the size of families in other rural New England villages are very rare. Wertenbaker, *First Americans*, 182-185, suggested that families were extremely large, with 10 to 20 children being common, but his data for Hingham, Mass., where he found that 105 women had "five or more children," with a total of 818 children "giving an average of 7.8 for each family," is in line with the data for Andover. The figures for seventeenth-century Plymouth are also remarkably similar. See Demos, "Notes on Life in Plymouth Colony," 270-271.

suffered from smallpox epidemics throughout the seventeenth century, there is no evidence to suggest the presence of smallpox or other epidemical diseases in Andover prior to 1690. With relatively few people, many of whom by the 1670's were scattered about the town upon their own farms, Andover appears to have been a remarkably healthy community during its early years. Lacking virulent epidemics, the principal hazards to health and to life were birth, accidents, non-epidemical diseases, and Indians. Death, consequently, visited relatively few of Andover's inhabitants during the first four decades following its settlement. This is evident in the fact that the first generation of Andover's settlers was very long lived. Prior to 1680, only five of the original settlers who came to Andover before 1660 and established permanent residence there had died; in 1690, fifteen of the first settlers (more than half of the original group) were still alive, forty-five years after the establishment of their town. The age at death of thirty men who settled in Andover prior to 1660 can be determined with a relative degree of accuracy. Their average age at the time of their deaths was 71.8 years. Six of the thirty settlers died while in their fifties, 11 in their sixties, 3 in their seventies, 6 in their eighties, 3 in their nineties, and 1 at the advanced age of 106 years.[7] The longevity of the first-generation fathers was to have great influence on the lives of their children, for the authority of the first generation was maintained far longer than would have been possible if death had struck them down at an early age. The second generation, in turn, was almost as long lived as the first generation had been. The average age of 138 second-generation men at the time of their deaths was 65.2 years, and the average age of sixty-six second-generation women at the time of their deaths was 64.0 years. (See Table 2.[8]) Of the 138 second-generation men who reached the

[7] The town of Hingham, according to the evidence in Wertenbaker, *First Americans,* 181-186, was remarkably similar to Andover, since the life expectancy of its inhabitants during the 17th century was very high. "Of the eight hundred and twenty-seven persons mentioned as belonging to this period [17th century] and whose length of life is recorded, one hundred and five reached the age of eighty or over, nineteen lived to be ninety or over and three . . . attained the century mark."

[8] Since the size of the sample for the age of women at the time of their death is only half that of the sample for men, the average age of 64.0 may not be too reliable. However, the evidence for Hingham does suggest that the figures for Andover ought not to be dismissed too lightly. "The average life of the married women of Hingham during the seventeenth century," Wertenbaker noted, "seems to have been 61.4 years." He also found that for their 818 children, the average age at the time of death was 65.5 years. "These figures," he added, "apply to one little

age of 21 years and whose lifespan is known, only twenty-five or 18.1 per cent, died between the ages of 20 and 49. Forty-two (30.3 per cent) of these 138 men died between the ages of 50 and 69; seventy-one (51.6 per cent) died after reaching the age of 70. Twenty-five second-generation men died in their eighties, and four died in their nineties. Longevity was characteristic of men living in seventeenth-century Andover.

TABLE 2

SECOND-GENERATION AGES AT DEATH

Ages	Males		Females	
	Numbers	Percentages	Numbers	Percentages
20–29	10	7.3	4	6.1
30–39	9	6.5	4	6.1
40–49	6	4.3	6	9.1
50–59	16	11.5	10	15.2
60–69	26	18.8	13	19.7
70–79	42	30.4	16	24.2
80–89	25	18.1	8	12.1
90–99	4	3.1	5	7.5
Total	138	100.0%	66	100.0%

The age of marriage often provides significant clues to circumstances affecting family life and to patterns of family relationships which might otherwise remain elusive.[9] Since marriages throughout the seventeenth

town only, and cannot be accepted as conclusive for conditions throughout the colonies, yet they permit of the strong presumption that much which has been written concerning the short expectation of life for women of large families is based upon insufficient evidence." *Ibid.*, 184. The observation remains cogent. For the longevity of Plymouth's settlers, see Demos, "Notes on Life in Plymouth Colony," 271.

[9] The most sophisticated analyses of marriage ages and their relationship to the social structure, family life, and economic conditions of various communities have been made by sociologists. Two exceptionally useful models are the studies of two contemporary English villages by W. M. Williams: *Gosforth: The Sociology of an English Village* (Glencoe, Ill., 1956), esp. pp. 45-49, and *A West Country Village, Ashworthy: Family, Kinship, and Land* (London, 1963), esp. pp. 85-91. Another useful study is Conrad M. Arensberg and Solon T. Kimball, *Family and Community in Ireland* (Cambridge, Mass., 1940). For the fullest statistical and historiographical account of marriage ages in the United States, see Thomas P. Monahan, *The Pattern of Age at Marriage in the United States*, 2 vols. (Philadelphia, 1951).

century and the early part of the eighteenth century were rarely fortuitous, parental authority and concern, family interests, and economic considerations played into the decisions determining when particular men and women could and would marry for the first time. And during the seventeenth century in Andover, factors such as these frequently dictated delays of appreciable duration before young men, especially, might marry. The age of marriage both of men and of women in the second generation proved to be much higher than most historians hitherto have suspected.[10]

Traditionally in America women have married younger than men, and this was generally true for the second generation in Andover. Although the assertion is sometimes made that daughters of colonial families frequently married while in their early teens, the average age of sixty-six second-generation daughters of Andover families at the time of their first marriage was 22.8 years. (See Table 3.) Only two girls are known to have married at 14 years, none at 15, and two more at 16. Four married at the age of 17, with a total of twenty-two of the sixty-six girls marrying before attaining the age of 21 years (33.3 per cent). The largest percentage of women married between the ages of 21 and 24, with twenty-four or 36.4 per cent being married during these years, making a total of 69.7 per cent of the second-generation daughters married before reaching the age of 25. Between the ages of 25 and 29 years, fourteen women (21.2 per cent) married, with six others marrying at the age of 30 or more (9.1 per cent).

TABLE 3

SECOND-GENERATION FEMALE MARRIAGE AGES

Age	Numbers	Percentages	
under 21	22	33.3	24 & under = 69.7%
21–24	24	36.4	25 & over = 30.3%
25–29	14	21.2	29 & under = 90.9%
30–34	4	6.1	30 & over = 9.1%
35–39	1	1.5	
40 & over	1	1.5	
	—	———	Average age = 22.8 years
	66	100.0%	

[10] In Plymouth colony during the seventeenth century, the age of marriage also was higher than expected. See Demos, "Notes on Life in Plymouth Colony," 275. For a discussion of various historians' views on marriage ages during the colonial period, see Monahan, *Pattern of Age at Marriage,* I, 99-104.

PHILIP J. GREVEN, JR.

Relatively few second-generation women thus married before the age of 17, and nearly 70 per cent married before the age of 25. They were not as young in most instances as one might have expected if very early marriages had prevailed, but they were relatively young nonetheless.

The age of marriage for second-generation men reveals a very different picture, for instead of marrying young, as they so often are said to have done, they frequently married quite late. (See Table 4.) The average age for ninety-four second-generation sons of Andover families at the time of their first marriages was 27.1 years. No son is known to have married before the age of 18, and only one actually married then. None of the ninety-four second-generation men whose marriage ages could be determined married at the age of 19, and only three married at the age of 20. The contrast with the marriages of the women of the same generation is evident, since only 4.3 per cent of the men married before the age of 21 compared to 33.3 per cent of the women. The majority of second-generation men married while in their twenties, with thirty-three of the ninety-four men marrying between the ages of 21 and 24 (35.1 per cent), and thirty-four men marrying between the ages of 25 and 29 (36.2 per cent). Nearly one quarter of the second-generation men married at the age of 30 or later, however, since twenty-three men or 24.4 per cent delayed their marriages until after their thirtieth year. In sharp contrast with the women of this generation, an appreciable majority of the second-generation men married at the age of 25 or more, with 60.6 per cent marrying after that age. This tendency to delay marriages by men until after the age of 25, with the average age being about 27 years, proved to be charac-

TABLE 4

SECOND-GENERATION MALE MARRIAGE AGES

Age	Numbers	Percentages	
Under 21	4	4.3	24 & under = 39.4%
21–24	33	35.1	25 & over = 60.6%
25–29	34	36.2	
30–34	16	17.2	29 & under = 75.6%
35–39	4	4.3	30 & over = 24.4%
40 & over	3	2.9	
	—	———	Average age = 27.1 years
	94	100.0%	

teristic of male marriage ages in Andover throughout the seventeenth century.

Averages can sometimes obscure significant variations in patterns of behavior, and it is worth noting that in the second generation the age at which particular sons might marry depended in part upon which son was being married. Eldest sons tended to marry earlier than younger sons in many families, which suggests variations in their roles within their families, and differences in the attitudes of their fathers towards them compared to their younger brothers. For twenty-six eldest second-generation sons, the average age at their first marriage was 25.6 years. Second sons in the family often met with greater difficulties and married at an average age of 27.5 years, roughly two years later than their elder brothers. Youngest sons tended to marry later still, with the average age of twenty-two youngest sons being 27.9 years. In their marriages as in their inheritances, eldest sons often proved to be favored by their families; and family interests and paternal wishes were major factors in deciding which son should marry and when. More often than not, a son's marriage depended upon the willingness of his father to allow it and the ability of his father to provide the means for the couple's economic independence. Until a second-generation son had been given the means to support a wife—which in Andover during the seventeenth century generally meant land—marriage was virtually impossible.

Marriage negotiations between the parents of couples proposing marriage and the frequent agreement by the father of a suitor to provide a house and land for the settlement of his son and new bride are familiar facts.[11] But the significance of this seventeenth-century custom is much greater than is sometimes realized. It generally meant that the marriages of the second generation were dependent upon their fathers' willingness to let them leave their families and to establish themselves in separate households elsewhere. The late age at which so many sons married during this period indicates that the majority of first-generation parents were unwilling

[11] See especially Morgan, *Puritan Family*, 39-44. For one example of marriage negotiations in Andover during this period, see the agreement between widow Hannah Osgood of Andover and Samuel Archard, Sr., of Salem, about 1660 in the *Records and Files of the Quarterly Courts of Essex County, Massachusetts* (Salem, 1912-21), III, 463, cited hereafter as *Essex Quarterly Court*. Also see the negotiations of Simon Bradstreet of Andover and Nathaniel Wade of Ipswich, *New England Historical and Genealogical Register*, XIII, 204, quoted in Morgan, *Puritan Family*, 41.

PHILIP J. GREVEN, JR.

to see their sons married and settled in their own families until long after they had passed the age of 21. The usual age of adulthood, marked by marriage and the establishment of another family, was often 24 or later. Since 60 per cent of the second-generation sons were 25 or over at the time of their marriage and nearly one quarter of them were 30 or over, one wonders what made the first generation so reluctant to part with its sons?

At least part of the answer seems to lie in the fact that Andover was largely a farming community during the seventeenth century, structured, by the time that the second generation was maturing, around the family farm which stood isolated from its neighbors and which functioned independently. The family farm required all the labor it could obtain from its own members, and the sons evidently were expected to assist their fathers on their family farms as long as their fathers felt that it was necessary for them to provide their labor. In return for this essential, but prolonged, contribution to their family's economic security, the sons must have been promised land by their fathers when they married, established their own families, and wished to begin their own farms. But this meant that the sons were fully dependent upon their fathers as long as they remained at home. Even if they wanted to leave, they still needed paternal assistance and money in order to purchase land elsewhere. The delayed marriages of second-generation men thus indicates their prolonged attachment to their families, and the continuation of paternal authority over second-generation sons until they had reached their mid-twenties, at least. In effect, it appears, the maturity of this generation was appreciably later than has been suspected hitherto. The psychological consequences of this prolonged dependence of sons are difficult to assess, but they must have been significant.

Even more significant of the type of family relationships emerging with the maturing of the second generation than their late age of marriage is the fact that paternal authority over sons did not cease with marriage. In this community, at least, paternal authority was exercised by the first generation not only prior to their sons' marriages, while the second generation continued to reside under the same roof with their parents and to work on the family farm, and not only at the time of marriage, when fathers generally provided the economic means for their sons' establishment in separate households, but also *after* marriage, by the further step of the father's withholding legal control of the land from the sons who had settled upon it.[12]

[12] Similar delays in the handing over of control of the land from one generation to the next are discussed by W. M. Williams in his study of Ashworthy, *West*

The majority of first-generation fathers continued to own the land which they settled their sons upon from the time the older men received it from the town to the day of their deaths. All of the first-generation fathers were willing to allow their sons to build houses upon their land, and to live apart from the paternal house after their marriage, but few were willing to permit their sons to become fully independent as long as they were still alive. By withholding deeds to the land which they had settled their sons upon, and which presumably would be theirs to inherit someday, the first generation successfully assured the continuity of their authority over their families long after their sons had become adults and had gained a nominal independence.[18] Since the second generation, with a few exceptions, lacked clear legal titles to the land which they lived upon and farmed, they were prohibited from selling the land which their fathers had settled them upon, or from alienating the land in any other way without the consent of their fathers, who continued to own it. Being unable to sell the land which they expected to inherit, second-generation sons could not even depart from Andover without their fathers' consent, since few had sufficient capital of their own with which to purchase land for themselves outside of Andover. The family thus was held together not only by settling sons upon family land in Andover, but also by refusing to relinquish control of the land until long after the second generation had established its nominal independence following their marriages and the establishment of separate households. In a majority of cases, the dependence of the

---

Country Village, 84-98. Williams noted (p. 91) that "the length of time which the transference of control takes is broadly a reflection of the degree of patriarchalism within the family: the more authoritarian the father, the longer the son has to wait to become master."

[13] The use of inheritances as a covert threat by the older generation to control the younger generation is revealed only occasionally in their wills, but must have been a factor in their authority over their sons. One suggestive example of a threat to cut off children from their anticipated inheritances is to be found in the will of George Abbot, Sr., who died in 1681 at 64 years old. Prior to his death, his two eldest sons and one daughter had married, leaving at home five unmarried sons and two unmarried daughters with his widow after his death. Abbot left his entire estate to his wife except for the land which he had already given to his eldest son. At her death, he instructed, his wife was to divide the estate with the advice of her sons and friends, and all the children, except the eldest, who had already received a double portion, were to be treated equally unless "by their disobedient carige" towards her "there be rasen to cut them short." Widow Abbot thus had an effective means for controlling her children, the oldest of whom was 24 in 1681. George Abbot, MS will, Dec. 12, 1681, Probate File 43, Probate Record Office, Registry of Deeds and Probate Court Building, Salem, Mass.

PHILIP J. GREVEN, JR.

second-generation sons continued until the deaths of their fathers. And most of the first generation of settlers was very long lived.

The first generations' reluctance to hand over the control of their property to their second-generation sons is evident in their actions.[14] Only three first-generation fathers divided their land among all of their sons before their deaths and gave them deeds of gift for their portions of the paternal estate. All three, however, waited until late in their lives to give their sons legal title to their portions of the family lands. Eleven first-generation fathers settled all of their sons upon their family estates in Andover, but gave a deed of gift for the land to only one of their sons; the rest of their sons had to await their fathers' deaths before inheriting the land which they had been settled upon. Ten of the settlers retained the title to all of their land until their deaths, handing over control to their sons only by means of their last wills and testaments. For the great majority of the second generation, inheritances constituted the principal means of transferring the ownership of land from one generation to the next.[15] The use of partible inheritances in Andover is evident in the division of the estates of the first generation.[16] Twenty-one of twenty-two first-generation fami-

---

[14] For deeds of gift of first generation Andover fathers to their second-generation sons, see the following deeds, located in the MSS volumes of Essex Deeds, Registry of Deeds and Probate Court Building, Salem, Mass.: Richard Barker, v. 29, pp. 115-116; Hannah Dane (widow of George Abbot), v.94, pp. 140-141; Edmund Faulkner, v.39, p. 250; John Frye, v.9, pp. 287-288; Nicholas Holt, v.6, pp. 722-723, 814-821; v.7, pp. 292-296; v.9, p. 12; v.32, pp. 130-131; v.34, pp. 255-256; Henry Ingalls, v. 14, pp. 40-41; John Lovejoy, v.33, pp. 40-41.

[15] The intimate relationship between inheritance patterns and family structure has been noted and examined by several historians and numerous sociologists. George C. Homans, in his study of *English Villagers of the Thirteenth Century* (New York, 1960), 26, pointed out that "differences in customs of inheritance are sensitive signs of differences in traditional types of family organization." See Homans' discussions of inheritance in England, chs. VIII and IX. H. J. Habakkuk, in his article, "Family Structure and Economic Change in Nineteenth-Century Europe," *The Journal of Economic History*, XV (1955), 4, wrote that "inheritance systems exerted an influence on the structure of the family, that is, on the size of the family, on the relations of parents to children and between the children . . . ." Very little, however, has been written about the role of inheritance in American life, or of its impact upon the development of the American family. One of the few observers to perceive the importance and impact of inheritance customs upon American family life was the shrewd visitor, Alexis de Tocqueville. See, for instance, his discussion of partible inheritance in *Democracy in America,* ed. Phillips Bradley (New York, 1956), I, 47-51.

[16] For further details, see the following wills: George Abbot, Probate File 43; Andrew Allen, Probate File 370; John Aslett, *Essex Quarterly Court,* IV, 409;

lies which had two or more sons divided all of their land among all of their surviving sons. Out of seventy-seven sons who were alive at the time their fathers either wrote their wills or gave them deeds to the land, seventy-two sons received some land from their fathers. Out of a total of sixty-six sons whose inheritances can be determined from their fathers' wills, sixty-one or 92.4 per cent received land from their fathers' estates in Andover. Often the land bequeathed to them by will was already in their possession, but without legal conveyances having been given. Thus although the great majority of second-generation sons were settled upon their fathers' lands while their fathers were still alive, few actually owned the land which they lived upon until after their fathers' deaths. With their inheritances came ownership; and with ownership came independence. Many waited a long time.

The characteristic delays in the handing over of control of the land from the first to the second generation may be illustrated by the lives and actions of several Andover families. Like most of the men who wrested their farms and their community from the wilderness, William Ballard was reluctant to part with the control over his land. When Ballard died intestate in 1689, aged about 72 years, his three sons, Joseph, William, and John, agreed to divide their father's estate among themselves "as Equally as they could."[17] They also agreed to give their elderly mother, Grace Ballard, a room in their father's house and to care for her as long as she remained a widow, thus adhering voluntarily to a common practice for the provision

---

William Ballard, Administration of Estate, Probate Record, Old Series, Book 4, vol. 304, pp. 388-389; Richard Barker, Probate File 1708; Samuel Blanchard, Probate File 2612; William Blunt, Probate File 2658; Thomas Chandler, Probate File 4974; William Chandler, Probate File 4979; Rev. Francis Dane, Probate File 7086; John Farnum, Probate File 9244; Thomas Farnum, Probate File 9254; Edmund Faulkner, Probate File 9305; Andrew Foster, Probate Record, Old Series, Book 2, vol. 302, pp. 136-137 (photostat copy); John Frye, Probate File 10301; Henry Ingalls, Probate File 14505; John Lovejoy, Probate File 17068; John Marston, Probate File 17847; Joseph Parker, *Essex Quarterly Court*, VII, 142-144; Andrew Peters, Probate File 21550; Daniel Poor, Probate Record, vol. 302, pp. 196-197; John Russ, Probate File 24365; John Stevens, *Essex Quarterly Court*, II, 414-416; and Walter Wright, Probate File 30733. The Probate Files of manuscript wills, inventories, and administrations of estates, and the bound Probate Records, are located in the Probate Record Office, Registry of Deeds and Probate Court Building, Salem, Mass.

[17] MS Articles of Agreement, Oct. 23, 1689, Probate Records, Old Series, Book 4, vol. 304, pp. 388-389 (photostat copy). For genealogical details of the Ballard family, see Abbott's Ballard genealogy, typed MSS, in the Memorial Library, Andover.

of the widow. The eldest son, Joseph, had married in 1665/6, almost certainly a rather young man, whereas his two brothers did not marry until the early 1680's, when their father was in his mid-sixties. William, Jr., must have been well over 30 by then, and John was 28. Both Joseph and William received as part of their division of their father's estate in Andover the land where their houses already stood, as well as more than 75 acres of land apiece. The youngest son, John, got all the housing, land, and meadow "his father lived upon except the land and meadow his father gave William Blunt upon the marriage with his daughter," which had taken place in 1668. It is unclear whether John lived with his wife and their four children in the same house as his parents, but there is a strong likelihood that this was the case in view of his assuming control of it after his father's death. His two older brothers had been given land to build upon by their father before his death, but no deeds of gift had been granted to them, thus preventing their full independence so long as he remained alive. Their family remained closely knit both by their establishment of residences near their paternal home on family land and by the prolonged control by William Ballard over the land he had received as one of the first settlers in Andover. It was a pattern repeated in many families.

There were variations, however, such as those exemplified by the Holt family, one of the most prominent in Andover during the seventeenth century. Nicholas Holt, originally a tanner by trade, had settled in Newbury, Massachusetts, for nearly a decade before joining the group of men planting the new town of Andover during the 1640's. Once established in the wilderness community, Holt ranked third among the householders, with an estate which eventually included at least 400 acres of land in Andover as a result of successive divisions of the common land.[18] At some time prior to 1675, he removed his family from the village, where all the original house lots had been located, and built a dwelling house on his third division of land. Although a small portion of his land still lay to the north and west of the old village center, the greatest part of his estate lay in a reasonably compact farm south of his new house. Holt owned no land outside of Andover, and he acquired very little besides the original di-

---

[18] For Nicholas Holt's land grants in Andover, see the MS volume, A Record of Town Roads and Town Bounds, 18-19, located in the vault of the Town Clerk's office, Andover, Mass. For genealogical information on the Holt family, see Daniel S. Durrie, *A Genealogical History of the Holt Family in the United States . . .* (Albany, N. Y., 1864), 9-16.

vision grants from the town. It was upon this land that he eventually settled all his sons. In 1662, however, when Nicholas Holt received the fourth division grant of 300 acres from the town, his eldest son, Samuel, was 21 years old, and his three other sons were 18, 15, and 11. The fifth son was yet unborn. His four sons were thus still adolescents, and at ages at which they could provide the physical labor needed to cultivate the land already cleared about the house, and to clear and break up the land which their father had just received. The family probably provided most of the labor, since there is no evidence to indicate that servants or hired laborers were numerous in Andover at the time. With the exception of two daughters who married in the late 1650's, the Holt family remained together on their farm until 1669, when the two oldest sons and the eldest daughter married.

By 1669, when Holt's eldest son, Samuel, finally married at the age of 28, the only possible means of obtaining land to settle upon from the town was to purchase one of the twenty-acre lots which were offered for sale. House-lot grants with accommodation land had long since been abandoned by the town, and Samuel's marriage and independence therefore depended upon his father's willingness to provide him with sufficient land to build upon and to farm for himself. Evidently his father had proved unwilling for many years, but when Samuel did at last marry, he was allowed to build a house for himself and his wife upon his father's "Three-score Acres of upland," known otherwise as his third division.[19] Soon afterwards, his second brother, Henry, married and also was given land to build upon in the third division. Neither Samuel nor Henry was given a deed to their land by their father at the time they settled upon it. Their marriages and their establishment of separate households left their three younger brothers still living with their aging father and step-mother. Five years passed before the next son married. James, the fourth of the five sons, married in 1675, at the age of 24, whereupon he, too, was provided with a part of his father's farm to build a house upon.[20] The third son, Nicholas, Jr., continued to live with his father, waiting until 1680 to marry at the late age of 32. His willingness to delay even a token independence so long suggests that personal factors must have played an important part in his continued assistance to his father, who was then about 77 years old.[21] John Holt, the youngest of the sons, married at the age of 21, shortly before his father's death.

[19] Essex Deeds, v. 32, p. 130.
[20] Ibid., v. 7, pp. 292-296.
[21] See ibid., v. 6, pp. 814-815.

PHILIP J. GREVEN, JR.

For Nicholas Holt's four oldest sons, full economic independence was delayed for many years. Although all had withdrawn from their father's house and had established separate residences of their own, they nonetheless were settled upon their father's land not too far distant from their family homestead, and none had yet been given a legal title to the land where they lived. Until Nicholas Holt was willing to give his sons deeds of gift for the lands where he had allowed them to build and to farm, he retained all legal rights to his estate and could still dispose of it in any way he chose. Without his consent, therefore, none of his sons could sell or mortgage the land where they lived since none of them owned it. In the Holt family, paternal authority rested upon firm economic foundations, a situation characteristic of the majority of Andover families of this period and these two generations.

Eventually, Nicholas Holt decided to relinquish his control over his Andover property by giving to his sons, after many years, legal titles to the lands which they lived upon. In a deed of gift, dated February 14, 1680/1, he conveyed to his eldest son, Samuel, who had been married almost twelve years, one half of his third division land, "the Said land on which the said Samuels House now Stands," which had the land of his brother, Henry, adjoining on the west, as well as an additional 130 acres of upland from the fourth division of land, several parcels of meadow, and all privileges accompanying these grants of land.[22] In return for this gift, Samuel, then forty years old, promised to pay his father for his maintenance so long as his "naturall life Shall Continue," the sum of twenty shillings a year. Ten months later, December 15, 1681, Nicholas Holt conveyed almost exactly the same amount of land to his second son, Henry, and also obligated him to pay twenty shillings yearly for his maintenance.[23] Prior to this gift, Nicholas had given his fourth son, James, his portion, which consisted of one-third part of "my farme" including "the land where his house now stands," some upland, a third of the great meadow, and other small parcels. In return, James promised to pay his father three pounds a year for life (three times the sum his two elder brothers were to pay), and to pay his mother-in-law forty shillings a year when she should become a widow.[24] The farm which James received was shared by his two other brothers, Nicholas and John, as well. Nicholas, in a deed of June 16, 1682, received "one third part

[22] *Ibid.*, v. 32, pp. 130-131.
[23] *Ibid.*, v. 34, pp. 255-256.
[24] *Ibid.*, v. 7, pp. 292-296.

of the farme where he now dwells," some meadow, and, most importantly, his father's own dwelling house, including the cellar, orchard, and barn, which constituted the principal homestead and house of Nicholas Holt, Sr.[25] In "consideration of this my fathers gift . . . to me his sone," Nicholas, Junior, wrote, "I doe promise and engage to pay yearly" the sum of three pounds for his father's maintenance. Thus Nicholas, Junior, in return for his labors and sacrifices as a son who stayed with his father until the age of 32, received not only a share in the family farm equal to that of his two younger brothers, but in addition received the paternal house and homestead. The youngest of the five Holt sons, John, was the only one to receive his inheritance from his father by deed prior to his marriage. On June 19, 1685, Nicholas Holt, Sr., at the age of 83, gave his "Lovinge" son a parcel of land lying on the easterly side of "my now Dwelling house," some meadow, and fifteen acres of upland "as yett unlaid out."[26] One month later, John married, having already built himself a house upon the land which his father promised to give him. Unlike his older brothers, John Holt thus gained his complete independence as an exceptionally young man. His brothers, however, still were not completely free from obligations to their father since each had agreed to the yearly payment of money to their father in return for full ownership of their farms. Not until Nicholas Holt's death at the end of January 1685/6 could his sons consider themselves fully independent of their aged father. He must have died content in the knowledge that all of his sons had been established on farms fashioned out of his own ample estate in Andover, all enjoying as a result of his patriarchal hand the rewards of his venture into the wilderness.[27]

Some Andover families were less reluctant than Nicholas Holt to let their sons marry early and to establish separate households, although the control of the land in most instances still rested in the father's hands. The Lovejoy family, with seven sons, enabled the four oldest sons to marry at the ages of 22 and 23. John Lovejoy, Sr., who originally emigrated from Eng-

---

[25] Ibid., v. 6, pp. 814-816.

[26] Ibid., v. 9, p. 12.

[27] For an example of a first-generation father who gave a deed of gift to his eldest son only, letting his five younger sons inherit their land, see the MS will of Richard Barker, dated Apr. 27, 1688, Probate File 1708. The deed to his eldest son is found in the Essex Deeds, v. 29, pp. 115-116. All of Barker's sons married late (27, 31, 35, 28, 28, and 25), and all but the eldest continued to be under the control of their father during his long life.

land as a young indentured servant, acquired a seven-acre house lot after his settlement in Andover during the mid-1640's, and eventually possessed an estate of over 200 acres in the town.[28] At his death in 1690, at the age of 68, he left an estate worth a total of £327.11.6, with housing and land valued at £260.00.0, a substantial sum at the time.[29] Although he himself had waited until the age of 29 to marry, his sons married earlier. His eldest son, John, Jr., married on March 23, 1677/8, aged 22, and built a house and began to raise crops on land which his father gave him for that purpose. He did not receive a deed of gift for his land, however; his inventory, taken in 1680 after his premature death, showed his major possessions to consist of "one house and a crope of corn" worth only twenty pounds. His entire estate, both real and personal, was valued at only £45.15.0, and was encumbered with £29.14.7 in debts.[30] Three years later, on April 6, 1683, the land which he had farmed without owning was given to his three year old son by his father, John Lovejoy, Sr. In a deed of gift, the elder Lovejoy gave his grandson, as a token of the love and affection he felt for his deceased son, the land which John, Junior, had had, consisting of fifty acres of upland, a piece of meadow, and a small parcel of another meadow, all of which lay in Andover.[31] Of the surviving Lovejoy sons only the second, William, received a deed of gift from the elder Lovejoy for the land which he had given them.[32] The others had to await their inheritances to come into full possession of their land. In his will dated September 1, 1690, shortly before his death, Lovejoy distributed his estate among his five surviving sons: Christopher received thirty acres together with other unstated amounts of land, and Nathaniel received the land which his father had originally intended to give to his brother, Benjamin, who had been killed in 1689. Benjamin was 25 years old and unmarried at the time of his death, and left an

[28] For John Lovejoy's Andover land grants, see the MS volume, A Record of Town Roads and Town Bounds, 96-98.

[29] See John Lovejoy's MS inventory in Probate File 17068.

[30] For the inventory of the estate of John Lovejoy, Jr., see *Essex Quarterly Court*, VIII, 56.

[31] Essex Deeds, v.33, pp. 40-41.

[32] This deed from John Lovejoy, Sr., to his son, William, is not recorded in the Essex Deeds at the Registry of Deeds, Salem, Mass. The deed, however, is mentioned in his will, Probate File 17068, wherein he bequeathed to William the lands which he already had conveyed to his son by deed. It was customary for such deeds to be mentioned in wills, since they usually represented much or all of a son's portion of a father's estate.

estate worth only £ 1.02.8, his wages as a soldier.[33] Without their father's land, sons were penniless. The youngest of the Lovejoy sons, Ebenezer, received his father's homestead, with the house and lands, in return for fulfilling his father's wish that his mother should "be made comfortable while she Continues in this world."[34] His mother inherited the east end of the house, and elaborate provisions in the will ensured her comfort. With all the surviving sons settled upon their father's land in Andover, with the residence of the widow in the son's house, and with the fact that only one of the sons actually received a deed for his land during their father's lifetime, the Lovejoys also epitomized some of the principal characteristics of family life in seventeenth-century Andover.

Exceptions to the general pattern of prolonged paternal control over sons were rare. The actions taken by Edmund Faulkner to settle his eldest son in Andover are instructive precisely because they were so exceptional. The first sign that Faulkner was planning ahead for his son came with his purchase of a twenty-acre lot from the town at the annual town meeting of March 22, 1669/70.[35] He was the only first-generation settler to purchase such a lot, all of the other purchasers being either second-generation sons or newcomers, and it was evident that he did not buy it for himself since he already had a six-acre house lot and more than one hundred acres of land in Andover.[36] The town voted that "in case the said Edmond shall at any time put such to live upon it as the town shall approve, or have no just matter against them, he is to be admitted to be a townsman." The eldest of his two sons, Francis, was then a youth of about nineteen years. Five years later, January 4, 1674/5, Francis was admitted as a townsman of Andover "upon the account of the land he now enjoyeth," almost certainly his

[33] For the inventory to Benjamin Lovejoy's estate, see the Probate File 17048.

[34] *Ibid.*, 17068. Provision for the widow was customary, and is to be found in all the wills of first-generation settlers who left their wives still alive. Generally, the son who inherited the paternal homestead was obligated to fulfill most of the necessary services for his mother, usually including the provision of firewood and other essentials of daily living. Provision also was made in most instances for the mother to reside in one or two rooms of the paternal house, or to have one end of the house, sometimes with a garden attached. Accommodations thus were written into wills to ensure that the mother would be cared for in her old age and would retain legal grounds for demanding such provisions.

[35] Andover, MS volume of Ancient Town Records, located in the Town Clerk's office, Andover.

[36] For Edmund Faulkner's land grants in Andover, see the MS Record of Town Roads and Town Bounds, 52-53.

father's twenty acres.[37] The following October, aged about 24, Francis married the minister's daughter. A year and a half later, in a deed dated February 1, 1676/7, Edmund Faulkner freely gave his eldest son "one halfe of my Living here at home" to be "Equally Divided between us both."[38] Francis was to pay the town rates on his half, and was to have half the barn, half the orchard, and half the land about his father's house, and both he and his father were to divide the meadows. Significantly, Edmund added that "all my Sixscore acres over Shawshinne river I wholly give unto him," thus handing over, at the relatively young age of 52, most of his upland and half of the remainder of his estate to his eldest son. The control of most of his estate thereby was transferred legally and completely from the first to the second generation, Edmund's second and youngest son, John, was still unmarried at the time Francis received his gift, and waited until 1682 before marrying at the age of 28. Eventually he received some land by his father's will, but his inheritance was small compared to his brother's. Edmund Faulkner's eagerness to hand over the control of his estate to his eldest son is notable for its rarity and accentuates the fact that almost none of his friends and neighbors chose to do likewise.[39] It is just possible that Faulkner, himself a younger son of an English gentry family, sought to preserve most of his Andover estate intact by giving it to his eldest son. If so, it would only emphasize his distinctiveness from his neighbors. For the great majority of the first-generation settlers in Andover, partible inheritances and delayed control by the first generation over the land were the rule. Faulkner was the exception which proved it.

Embedded in the reconstructions of particular family histories is a general pattern of family structure unlike any which are known or suspected to have existed either in England or its American colonies during the seventeenth century. It is evident that the family structure which developed during the lifetimes of the first two generations in Andover cannot

[37] Town meeting of Jan. 4, 1674/5, Andover, Ancient Town Records.

[38] Essex Deeds, v. 39, p. 250. Only one other instance of the co-partnership of father and son is to be found in the wills of seventeenth-century Andover, but not among the men who founded the town. See the MS will of Andrew Peters, Probate File 21550.

[39] The only instance of impartible inheritance, or primogeniture, to be found in the first generation of Andover's settlers occurred within the first decade of its settlement, before the extensive land grants of 1662 had been voted by the town. See John Osgood's will, dated Apr. 12, 1650, in *Essex Quarterly Court*, I, 239. Osgood left his entire Andover estate to the eldest of his two sons.

be classified satisfactorily according to any of the more recent definitions applied to types of family life in the seventeenth century. It was not simply a "patrilineal group of extended kinship gathered into a single household,"[40] nor was it simply a "nuclear independent family, that is man, wife, and children living apart from relatives."[41] The characteristic family structure which emerged in Andover with the maturing of the second generation during the 1670's and 1680's was a combination of both the classical extended family and the nuclear family. This distinctive form of family structure is best described as a *modified extended family*—defined as a kinship group of two or more generations living within a single community in which the dependence of the children upon their parents continues after the children have married and are living under a separate roof. This family structure is a *modified* extended family because all members of the family are not "gathered into a single household," but it is still an *extended* family because the newly created conjugal unit of husband and wife live in separate households in close proximity to their parents and siblings and continue to be economically dependent in some respects upon their parents. And because of the continuing dependence of the second generation upon their first-generation fathers, who continued to own most of the family land throughout the better part of their lives, the family in seventeenth-century Andover was *patriarchal* as well. The men who first settled the town long

[40] Bernard Bailyn, *Education in the Forming of American Society: Needs and Opportunities for Study* (Chapel Hill, 1960), 15-16. "Besides children, who often remained in the home well into maturity," Bailyn adds, the family "included a wide range of other dependents: nieces and nephews, cousins, and, except for families at the lowest rung of society, servants in filial discipline. In the Elizabethan family the conjugal unit was only the nucleus of a broad kinship community whose outer edges merges almost imperceptibly into the society at large." For further discussions of the extended family in England, see Peter Laslett, "The Gentry of Kent in 1640," *Cambridge Historical Journal,* IX (1948), 148-164; and Peter Laslett's introduction to his edition of *Patriarcha and Other Political Works of Sir Robert Filmer* (Oxford, 1949), esp. 22-26.

[41] Peter Laslett and John Harrison, "Clayworth and Cogenhoe," in H. E. Bell and R. L. Ollard, eds., *Historical Essays, 1660-1750, Presented to David Ogg* (London, 1963), 168. See also H. J. Habakkuk, "Population Growth and Economic Development," in *Lectures on Economic Development* (Istanbul, 1958), 23, who asserts that "from very early in European history, the social unit was the nuclear family—the husband and wife and their children—as opposed to the extended family or kinship group." See also Robin M. Williams, Jr., *American Society: A Sociological Interpretation,* 2d ed. rev. (New York, 1963), 50-57. For a contrasting interpretation of family structure in other 17th-century New England towns, see Demos, "Notes on Life in Plymouth Colony," 279-280.

remained the dominant figures both in their families and their community. It was their decisions and their actions which produced the family characteristic of seventeenth-century Andover.

One of the most significant consequences of the development of the modified extended family characteristic of Andover during this period was the fact that remarkably few second-generation sons moved away from their families and their community. More than four fifths of the second-generation sons lived their entire lives in the town which their fathers had wrested from the wilderness.[42] The first generation evidently was intent upon guaranteeing the future of the community and of their families within it through the settlement of all of their sons upon the lands originally granted to them by the town. Since it was quite true that the second generation could not expect to acquire as much land by staying in Andover as their fathers had by undergoing the perils of founding a new town on the frontier, it is quite possible that their reluctance to hand over the control of the land to their sons when young is not only a reflection of their patriarchalism, justified both by custom and by theology, but also of the fact that they could not be sure that their sons would stay, given a free choice. Through a series of delays, however, particularly those involving marriages and economic independence, the second generation continued to be closely tied to their paternal families. By keeping their sons in positions of prolonged dependence, the first generation successfully managed to keep them in Andover during those years in which their youth and energy might have led them to seek their fortunes elsewhere. Later generations achieved their independence earlier and moved more. It remains to be seen to what extent the family life characteristic of seventeenth-century Andover was the exception or the rule in the American colonies.

[42] Out of a total of 103 second generation sons whose residences are known, only seventeen or 16.5 per cent, departed from Andover. Five left before 1690, and twelve left after 1690. The majority of families in 17th-century Andover remained closely knit and remarkably immobile.

Families in Colonial Bristol, Rhode Island: An Exercise in Historical Demography

John Demos*

NO aspect of early American history has been more badly served by unsystematic, impressionistic methods of handling source materials than the whole vast area of family life. Our understanding of the subject has begun from a set of assumptions sustained chiefly by the force of a venerable popular folklore. Many of them can be tested in quite simple numerical terms, yet only very recently has the effort to do so even been started. Perhaps the best way to illustrate the seriousness of the situation is to list some of the most prominent of these assumptions, together with the verdict that present and future research seems likely to render upon them: (1) The colonial family was, initially at least, "extended" rather than "nuclear." (This is almost certainly false.) (2) The normal age of marriage was extremely early by our own standards. (Wrong again.) (3) The average number of children per family was very high. (True, but with some qualifications.) (4) Life expectancy was generally quite low, though a few people who managed to escape the manifold hazards of the day survived to a prodigiously old age. (Largely false.) (5) The mortality rate for infants, and for mothers in childbirth, was particularly high. (Much exaggerated.) (6) Many men and women were married two or more times, owing to the death of their first spouses. (Somewhat exaggerated.)[1]

---

* Mr. Demos is a Teaching Fellow in the Department of History, Harvard University. This article is part of a broader investigation of family life in Plymouth Colony, sponsored by Plimoth Plantation, Inc.

[1] This summation is based partly on my own work with various towns in Plymouth Colony. See John Demos, "Notes on Life in Plymouth Colony," *William and Mary Quarterly,* 3d Ser., XXII (1965), 264-286. But see also Philip J. Greven, Jr., "Family Structure in Seventeenth-Century Andover, Massachusetts," *ibid.,* XXIII (1966), 234-256, for another set of findings closely approximating most of the results for Plymouth. Note that my use of the term "extended family" is a rather formal one, comprising simply common residence "under the same roof." Greven's model of the "modified extended family," which he regards as applicable to Andover, does not then conflict with my first conclusion above. For he is referring to families in which the various conjugal units lived apart, while retaining significant economic and emotional ties to one another.

Reprinted from *William and Mary Quarterly,* 3rd Series, XXV, 40–57. Copyright © 1968 by permission of the publisher.

But if the need for precise information on these matters is urgent, the *opportunity* to make a fresh approach has never been more promising. For some years past, in England and France, a small group of scholars has been engaged in applying new methods of demographic analysis to certain key problems of European social history. This important development has recently been accorded its first real American exposure in a long review article by Philip J. Greven, Jr., and my own task is thereby simplified considerably.[2] The reader who wishes a general initiation into the mysteries of historical demography can do no better than consult the essay by Greven. My purpose here is to offer a concrete instance of this kind of analysis within the context of a single colonial town. For a variety of reasons, chiefly reflecting deficiencies in the source materials, certain of the more significant results obtained for England and France cannot be duplicated here. Still, it may be useful to rehearse at least some of the procedures that are central to this discipline, as much to show the difficulties involved as to communicate new findings.

Before concluding these introductory comments let me try to outline in advance the basic direction in which the argument will proceed, since in a study with an underlying methodological focus there is some danger that the end product may seem somewhat spotty and disjointed. An initial set of questions will concern the membership of households in colonial Bristol. Then, in order to establish the degree to which these results are "representative," Bristol will be examined in terms of the over-all age-structure of its populace. This, in turn, will suggest certain broader conclusions about the comparative demographic profiles of "old" versus "new" towns. Finally, after treating Bristol in this fashion at two different points in time, the analysis will move briefly into a somewhat different area of family life. An investigation of "birth intervals" will be attempted —with results which, while disappointing alongside comparable European studies, will at least suggest some intriguing possibilities with regard to the sexual mores of the time.

The story of the town of Bristol reaches back to the last quarter of the seventeenth century.[3] The site had been the home of the Indian chief

[2] Philip J. Greven, Jr., "Historical Demography and Colonial America," *ibid.*, XXIV (1967), 438-454.
[3] There is no recent scholarly study of Bristol, but the main outlines of the story can be found in George L. Howe, *Mount Hope; a New England Chronicle* (New York, 1959). Certain 19th-century compilations are useful: for instance, Wilfred H. Munro, *The History of Bristol, R. I. . . . .* (Providence, 1880); Wilfred

Ousamequin (Massasoit) and later of his son Philip, the Indian leader in King Philip's War. Settlers in adjacent parts of New England knew it as the Mount Hope Lands. With the defeat of King Philip, it fell by right of conquest into the hands of the English, who subsequently added it to the territory of Plymouth Colony. The General Court at Plymouth then conveyed the land to a group of four Boston merchants who undertook to perform the functions of town proprietors. The proprietors readily procured settlers, the majority coming from the adjoining towns of Rehoboth and Swansea; and by the fall of 1681 Bristol seems to have been a going concern. In 1692 Plymouth Colony was absorbed by Massachusetts Bay, the settlement at Bristol included. In 1747, however, it was one of five towns transferred to the jurisdiction of Rhode Island; there, of course, it has remained ever since.

Bristol was initially laid out as a farming community, and presumably agriculture remained a central pursuit for many of its inhabitants throughout the colonial period. However, the site offered strong possibilities as a seaport that were clearly apparent from the very beginning.[4] By the middle of the eighteenth century Bristol had become an important center of commerce, and most of its leading citizens were engaged in some form of mercantile activity. Trade with the West Indies followed lines long known to historians of early New England. The outward cargo comprised various sorts of produce, horses, and fish; these goods were exchanged for coffee, molasses, sugar, and tropical fruits. Distilleries were soon established in the town for converting molasses into rum, which became, in turn, the key item in an expanding slave trade with the coast of West Africa. Whaling was another important industry for the town's seagoing populace; and at least a few captains made a fortune at privateering. These aspects of the history of Bristol are important for the demographic profile that I shall attempt to establish. The commercial orientation of the town may well impose limitations on the opportunity to generalize from the Bristol findings. Indeed, the possibility that the demographic structure of colonial settlements varied markedly among different regions,

---

H. Munro, *Tales of an Old Seaport* (Princeton, 1917); and James P. Lane, *Historical Sketches of the First Congregational Church, Bristol, R. I., 1689–1872* (Providence, 1872). See also Richard LeBaron Bowen, *Early Rehoboth* (Rehoboth, Mass., 1945–48), I, which contains a chapter of notes on the early years of Bristol.

[4] Indeed, according to local traditions, it was this prospect which induced the settlers to name their town after the great English seaport of Bristol. See Munro, *History of Bristol,* 78.

FAMILIES IN COLONIAL BRISTOL, RHODE ISLAND   97

or between town and country, should constitute a major focus in future research of this type.

The demographic data for Bristol are of two kinds. There are, first of all, the same sort of vital records that can be found for nearly every New England town—long listings of births, "intentions" to be married, marriages, and deaths.[5] Their accuracy and completeness seem to have varied considerably over time. For some periods they are rather sketchy, while for others they seem quite full and careful. It is my impression, however, that there was no time in the history of colonial Bristol when all of the pertinent events were officially recorded. One must, therefore, be reconciled from the start to working with partial data.

The second type of material, census listings, is much less common. Indeed, the complete census of Bristol residents made in 1689 may possibly be unique: I at least have never seen another such document for the seventeenth century.[6] It provides a rare opportunity to view the population structure of an early New England community in a kind of cross section and at one given point in time. The vital records, by contrast, permit us to construct a *running picture* of the same developments, but a picture, as already mentioned, that is never complete or wholly reliable. The possibility of using these different sources to supplement each other is what makes Bristol a particularly hopeful demographic prospect.

Unfortunately the original census has long since been lost, and we have no idea for what purpose it was compiled. The material survives thanks to a copy made by George T. Paine from the records in the "Church of Christ" in Bristol, which was published in 1880 in the *Register* of the New England Historic and Genealogical Society.[7] The document begins: "1688-9. Feb. 11. All the families in New Bristol and children and servants." There follows, in a vertical column at the left, a list of names which clearly comprises all the heads-of-household in the town. Three adjacent columns, headed "Wife," "Children," and "Servants," provide the relevant figures for each family. The census shows a total population of 421 persons, distributed through 70 families. There are 68 husbands, 68 wives, 1 man without wife or child but listed with the heads-of-family,

[5] See James N. Arnold, *Vital Records of Rhode Island,* VI (Providence, 1894).

[6] Lists compiled for military or tax purposes are, of course, common enough, but these normally include only male citizens above the age of 16.

[7] See "Census of Bristol in Plymouth Colony, now in Rhode Island, 1689," *New-England Historical and Genealogical Register,* XXXIV (1880), 404-405. The census has been republished in Bowen, *Early Rehoboth,* I, 75-76.

226 children, 56 servants (of whom 1 is identified as "black" and listed separately), and 2 unclassified men (added at the end as "Jacob Mason 1 more Zachary Cary 1 more"[8]).

The census permits a precise analysis of several important aspects of family structure. There is, first of all, the simple matter of the over-all size of Bristol households, for which the relevant data are gathered in the following table:

TABLE I

SIZE OF HOUSEHOLDS

Number of Persons in Household	1	2	3	4	5	6	7	8	9	10	11	12	13	14	15
Number of Families	1	6	5	11	9	13	5	7	6	3	2	1	0	0	1

The evidence on this point seems fairly clear-cut. Households of four, five, and six persons were most common, comprising almost half of the total sample, though there were many units both smaller and larger. The mean figure for these seventy households is 5.99, and the median is 5.72. It is important to anticipate one possible objection to these conclusions. The term "household" has been treated as equivalent to the "families" listed in the census, but can we be sure that some domestic units did not in fact include several families? Such households would be "extended" in the formal sense of the term. There is no *prima facie* way of eliminating this possibility, but the sum total of the evidence against it seems virtually overwhelming. First, careful study of the wills and land deeds of Plymouth Colony strongly suggests that married adults normally lived with their children and *apart* from all other relatives.[9] The sole exception was the occasional residence of aged parents in the family of some one of their children. Moreover, the census itself seems to imply the same pattern.

[8] The instance of the man without wife or child—one Eliaship Adams—suggests that in rare cases a single person might live alone and maintain his own domestic establishment. The vital records show that Adams was married later during the year 1689 and began to have children soon thereafter. The fact that he is listed among the original inhabitants of Bristol, in 1681, suggests that he must have been at least 30 when the census was taken. The case of the two men that I have referred to as "unclassified" is more mysterious. Clearly without wife or children, they do *not* seem to have been regarded as heads-of-family. Yet they are not likely to have been servants in the usual sense of the term—else they would have been listed in the appropriate space, as part of some other family.

[9] See Demos, "Notes on Life in Plymouth Colony," 279-280.

There are, among the heads-of-family, a few sets of individuals bearing the same surname for whom we can establish a definite relationship, either as brothers or as father and sons. The respective positions on the list of the men within a given set are seemingly quite random. But if they had in fact shared the same household, there is some probability that their names would have followed one after the other. This, of course, begs the whole question of the reasons for the order in which all the families were recorded. There is no ready answer, but some possibilities can at least be ruled out. For example, the order is not alphabetical, nor does it reflect any rankings in terms of wealth or social prestige. The most likely guess, I think, would make spatial proximity the determining factor, and would assume that the census-taker moved from one house to the next until he had covered all the families in town. If this was the case, the "extended family" alternative is clearly set aside.

The category of children, which included some 54 per cent of the total population of the town, can be broken down in a similar manner:

TABLE II

CHILDREN PER FAMILY

Number of Children in Family	0	1	2	3	4	5	6	7	8	9	10
Number of Families	7	10	11	12	9	8	6	4	1	0	1

The mean in this case is 3.27 and the median, 3.04. Nearly half of the families listed had one, two, or three children, though the "tail" of the distribution toward the higher brackets is fairly substantial. If these results seem rather on the low side, certain additional factors must be considered. The average parents produced children at roughly two-year intervals, beginning from the time of their marriage in their early or mid-twenties.[10] Birth intervals tended gradually to increase as the wife grew older and the last child would usually arrive sometime between her fortieth and forty-fifth birthday. (These regularities obviously do *not* represent those families in which one spouse died before the childbearing years were over.) Families, in short, grew slowly. This means that at any given time only those parents in a certain limited age-range, about thirty-

[10] *Ibid.*, 271, 275. I am assuming here that Bristol conformed to the general pattern for age-at-marriage which obtained in other parts of Plymouth Colony. The comment on birth intervals is left somewhat imprecise, but its general validity can be sustained by even a cursory perusal of the vital records.

five to fifty, would be likely to show really large numbers of children. Younger couples would not yet have produced their full complement of children, whereas in the case of elderly parents some or all of the children would have reached maturity and started their own independent lives. The census listings for Bristol, therefore, do not invalidate the common notion that colonial parents usually raised many children, at least in comparison to the norm for our own day.

It remains to consider the fifty-six servants in the town. Their distribution can best be described with another simple table:

TABLE III

SERVANTS PER FAMILY

Number of Servants	0	1	2	3	4	8	11
Number of Families	48	8	8	3	1	1	1

Thus twenty-two Bristol families (31.5 per cent) had one or more servants. Only two men, however, possessed a really large group of servants: Captain Nathaniel Byfield, who was the first Bristol resident to cut a substantial figure in the larger affairs of Massachusetts Bay, and John Saffin, Esq. To the Byfield household was also attributed the single Negro in the town.

The analysis will now shift somewhat in order to meet certain possible difficulties bearing on the question of whether or not these findings for Bristol can be regarded as "representative" of a wider picture. It could, for example, be argued that since the town was still quite new in 1689, its demographic profile may in some respects have been atypical. In particular, there is the possibility that most of its inhabitants were quite young and that its families might therefore have been smaller than the norm for most other towns, or for Bristol itself some years later. In short, the next task is to form some impression, if possible, of the structure of Bristol's population in 1689 by age-groups.

Here the method which the European demographers call "family reconstitution" suggests itself.[11] It must be said at once, however, that the

---

[11] The basic elements of family reconstitution are simple enough. The prime requisite is some reliable and reasonably complete data about the dates of birth, marriage, and death of all the residents in a given village or town; and fortunately in both France and England there are parish registers which meet these specifications quite nicely. This information is then arranged so as to dovetail *by families,* and the outcome is a large body of vital statistics, hopefully extending

data for early Bristol are far too scanty to permit extensive work along these lines. The origins of many of its citizens cannot definitely be traced, and the sum total of precise and reliable information about dates of birth, marriage, and death is disappointingly small. Partial reconstruction of many families is possible, but for very few is the picture anywhere near complete.

The situation is not, however, wholly without possibilities. One can obtain at least a general picture of the structure of the population by age-groups through a careful study of the women of the town. The importance of women in this connection stems from the more or less definite limits that nature has set upon their childbearing years. Thus if one can determine the ages of at least some of a given couple's children, it is possible to make a rough guess as to the wife's own birth date. The word "rough" should be stressed here; in my own efforts with the Bristol materials I have tried only to classify women in one or another ten-year age-group. Moreover, because of the approximate nature of these estimates, the categories have been made to overlap: they are 20-30, 25-35, 30-40, 35-45, 40-50, 45-55, and over 55. An individual woman has been placed in whichever one of these seemed the most likely in her particular case. Some concrete examples may be helpful. The census reports that the family of Jabez Gorham contained in 1689 six persons—himself, his wife Hannah, and four children. The vital records attribute nine births to this family, spanning a period from April 1682 to October 1701. Since virtually no woman in seventeenth-century New England had her first child before the age of 19, one can assume that Hannah Gorham was not born later than 1663. Similarly, since nearly every woman had ceased to bear children by the age of 45, the earliest likely birth year in this instance is 1656. This means that Hannah Gorham was somewhere between 26 and 33 years of age when the census was taken, and in the sample analyzed below (Table IV) she has been included in the 25-35 category. Mary Throop, wife of William, was a somewhat older woman. The census describes her family as containing five children; but the only one of these whose arrival was noted in the vital records was a daughter born in July

---

over a considerable span of time. The method has even been standardized by the use of Family Reconstitution Forms ("FRFs" to the initiated), which contain a set of spaces for recording each of the pertinent bits of data. A complete account of the method can be found in E. A. Wrigley, ed., *An Introduction to English Historical Demography from the Sixteenth to the Nineteenth Century* (New York, 1966), chap. IV. See also Greven, "Historical Demography and Colonial America," 440-442.

1686. However, two bits of data help to establish a terminus at the *other* end of her childbearing span: a listing in the records of Barnstable, where the Throops lived before migrating to Bristol, of their marriage in 1666; and a notation in the Bristol records of the birth of the couple's first grandchild in November 1688. Thus a birth year between 1641 and 1647 can be inferred for Goodwife Throop, which places her in the 40-50 age-category.

Similar procedures have been employed for forty-seven other Bristol women. A few of the estimates may possibly be in error, owing to special circumstances of which no hint remains today, but I feel reasonably certain that the great majority are right. The final results are as follows:

TABLE IV

AGE OF WIVES

Age-group	20–30	25–35	30–40	35–45	40–50	45–55	Over 55
Number of Women	12	10	12	11	3	1	0

(*Note:* This sample comprises 49 of the 68 wives in the town. There are no data for adult female servants, if indeed there were any.)

The mean age here is 33.6 years. What is immediately striking about this outcome is the relative youth of the town's adult women. The table suggests that there was a fairly even distribution between the ages of 20 and 45, but very few women older than this. There remains, however, the question of nineteen Bristol women whom the sample does *not* include. In their case the data are so scanty as not to permit classification even in the ten-year groupings; but in most instances it is possible at least to infer that they fall on the younger side of 50. There are only two women among all the Bristol families for whom some shred of evidence exists that suggests a more advanced age.

These data for the women will not sustain deductions about the ages of their husbands in specific cases, for there may have been some men who were considerably older than their spouses. Still, it does seem possible to make the general inference that the great majority of the men were comparably young. There are some other pieces of information with which to fill out this picture. In the first place, it is striking that there should be in a town of over four hundred people only one widow and one widower. Of course, in the case of some Bristol couples one or both spouses may have been previously married and widowed; but I have been able to discover this for a fact in only a single instance.[12] Second, there is the matter of those couples who are listed with less than the average complement of children. As mentioned earlier, this could indicate either youth and a very recent marriage, or old age with most or all of the children grown up and on their own. But the evidence for Bristol in 1689 is heavily weighted toward the former alternative. Five of the seven couples without children and nine of the ten with only a single child seem likely to have been people in their twenties and recently married. For the remaining three cases there is simply no evidence one way or the other.

The various materials bearing on the age structure of the Bristol population may, then, be summarized as follows: (1) A majority of those listed in the census fall under the heading "children." (2) An additional category of "servants" (13 per cent of the whole) comprises persons who are likely also to have been quite youthful. (3) Nearly all of the fully adult residents, heads-of-family and their wives, were contained within a range whose upper limit seems to have been "middle age." What are the implications of all this for the question of the "representativeness" of the earlier findings about families? It seems clear that the Bristol citizenry was quite youthful; but can we assume, then, that its households will therefore prove to be smaller than in the average town? I would argue strongly *against* making any such inference. For if perhaps the considerable number of young couples (say, those under 30) created some bias in favor of small families, this effect was more than offset by the nearly complete absence of elderly couples. Moreover, the Bristol population in 1689 does seem to have included quite a number of couples at or near middle age, and, hence, most likely to show large households. Thus any distortion in the sample may conceivably be in the direction of families slightly *larger* than the average for other towns.

The question of the age-structure of Bristol in 1689 is also pertinent in one other context; for it serves to call attention to a kind of demographic model for the process of settlement which, while not inherently new or startling, seems worth an explicit statement. The settlers of new towns were generally young people, presumably because the opportunities for gaining wealth and prestige were greater there than in the more established communities of their birth and also because the problems of town building required a youthful strength, imagination, and resourcefulness.[13]

[12] That is, in the course of "reconstituting" the various families on the basis of the vital records.

[13] This conclusion is in no way modified by the presence in Bristol in 1689 of

We may suspect, in addition, that when a young man left his place of origin to make an independent start in a newer settlement, he did not always take a bride with him. This can be demonstrated for about a dozen of the firstcomers to Bristol, but the most striking evidence is to be found in certain materials from the eighteenth century. The census taken for the whole colony of Massachusetts in 1765 provides a good case in point. It shows virtually all the towns of the eastern section—the older ones—with an appreciable surplus of women, while in the "frontier" parts to the west the ratio is largely reversed.[14]

Thus, in sum, the older towns were gradually left with a disproportionate number of elderly people and women. These kinds of imbalance may well have important implications for many aspects of the social history of the colonies. For example, the growth of schools in the older towns of New England may have been related to the rise of a substantial class of spinsters, who would serve as teachers. The problem of caring for elderly persons whose children had gone elsewhere may have stimulated fresh approaches in the area of welfare services. Almost certainly rates of marriage and remarriage were affected. But for the present these matters can be raised only in a speculative way.

In 1774 an official census was ordered for the whole colony of Rhode Island; and this permits us to restudy Bristol nearly a century after the compilation of the initial set of data.[15] While it is appropriate to ask the same basic questions a second time, a somewhat different set of arrangements for the later materials complicates the situation. Adjoining a list of all the heads-of-family are seven columns. Four appear under the major heading "Whites": "Males Above 16," "Males Under 16," "Females Above 16," "Females Under 16." There are separate categories for both "Indians" and "Blacks" without distinctions of age or sex, and finally there is a column marked "Total" that provides the sum of all the members in each household.

The picture for the town as a whole can be quickly summarized. In an over-all population of 1209, there were 1079 whites, 114 Negroes, and 16

a significant number of middle-aged couples. Most of these people had come when the town was founded—that is, when they were eight years younger than at the time of the census.

[14] See J. H. Benton, Jr., *Early Census Making in Massachusetts, 1643-1765* (Boston, 1905).

[15] The listings for Bristol are printed in full, Munro, *History of Bristol,* 188-191.

Indians. Among the whites 504 were men, 575 were women. By age, 591 people were "Above 16," and 488 "Under 16." Two changes since 1689 are immediately apparent. First, the growth of Bristol as a seaport and its development of substantial trading connections with the West Indies and Africa have brought a significant nonwhite population into the town. Nearly all of these people appear as part of white households and are presumably slaves. The exceptions are 1 independent family of 3 Negroes and 1 family of 7 Indians. Second, there is among the whites a substantial preponderance of female residents. This, I believe, reflects the impact on the sex ratio of the process of settlement—a matter already discussed above. Bristol had by this time become itself an "older town"; and it is not unreasonable to infer the regular loss of some portion of its young men.

The figures for the size of the individual households in 1774 are as follows:

TABLE V

SIZE OF HOUSEHOLDS, 1774

Total Number of Persons in Family	Total Number of Families		Total Number of Persons in Family	Total Number of Families	
	All-inclusive	Whites Only		All-inclusive	Whites Only
1	4	4	9	10	11
2	18	25	10	12	13
3	21	28	11	6	4
4	28	28	12	5	1
5	22	19	13	1	3
6	28	23	14	3	0
7	19	22	15	2	0
8	16	16	16	2	0

Table V provides separate listings for entire households, including Negroes and Indians, and for whites only in order to facilitate comparisons with the data for 1689. Unfortunately, such comparisons are problematical at best, but in order to examine all possibilities the relevant material for both periods has been reorganized in two further tables, with all the figures expressed as percentages of the whole sample:

TABLE VI

COMPARATIVE SIZE OF HOUSEHOLDS IN 1689 AND 1774

Number of Persons Per Household	Percentage of Total Number of Households			
	1689 All-inclusive	1774 All-inclusive	1689 Without Servants	1774 Whites Only
1–3	17.1%	21.8%	25.7%	28.9%
4–6	47.1%	39.6%	45.7%	35.5%
7–9	25.7%	22.8%	25.7%	24.9%
10–12	8.6%	11.7%	2.9%	9.2%
13 and over	1.5%	4.1%	0%	1.5%

TABLE VII

MEAN AND MEDIAN NUMBER OF PERSONS PER
HOUSEHOLD IN 1689 AND 1774

	1689 All-inclusive	1774 All-inclusive	1689 Without Servants	1774 Whites Only
Mean	5.99	6.14	5.21	5.53
Median	5.72	5.70	4.95	5.21

It seems at first sight most natural to set the first against the second column and the third against the fourth, but certain distortions are inherent in this tactic. First, the all-inclusive listings for the two dates effectively conceal the addition of the non-white segment of the population during the eighteenth century. One must recognize that a Negro slave was probably a member of a 1774 household in quite a different sense from what had obtained for a white servant in 1689. Moreover, there still were some white servants in Bristol in 1774, a fact which tends to blur the possibilities of comparing the other two columns in the tables.[16] In short, the figures for "1689 Without Servants" comprise only blood-members of families, whereas those for "1774 Whites Only" include some servants as well. When this factor is taken into account, the slightly larger average for

[16] Further discussion of the question of white servants in Bristol in 1774 appears below, p. 55.

the later period shrinks to virtually nothing. Thus the following general conclusions emerge: (1) The mean and median size of Bristol families in terms of blood-members changed very little between 1689 and 1774. (2) The same observation applies for the category of all-inclusive households comprising servants and slaves too. (3) There is, however, one noticeable and interesting difference between the figures for the two periods, namely, the greater concentration of 1689 households in the middle ranges, especially the 4-6 person units, and of the 1774 households at both the lower and higher extremes. In short, the distribution of sizes of households widened considerably as time passed.

In order to be able to understand these patterns more clearly, a second effort at family reconstitution seems advisable. Fortunately the data for 1774 are somewhat more amenable to this procedure than were the earlier materials. The vital records, for example, show the year of birth of many of the white persons reported in the 1774 census. This permits construction of the following table depicting the age structure of the population at the time:

TABLE VIII
AGE-STRUCTURE OF BRISTOL, 1774
VS. UNITED STATES, 1960

| | Percentage of Total Population | | | |
| | Bristol, 1774 | | United States, 1960[17] | |
Age-group	Men	Women	Men	Women
Under 10	27.6%	26.9%	21.7%	20.3%
10–19	21.8%	19.8%	17.0%	15.9%
20–29	15.2%	18.7%	12.0%	11.9%
30–39	10.9%	13.4%	13.6%	13.5%
40–49	10.6%	9.9%	12.7%	12.7%
50–59	7.5%	6.5%	10.2%	10.1%
60–69	3.2%	3.1%	7.4%	8.7%
70 and over	3.2%	1.7%	5.4%	6.9%

(Size of sample for Bristol, 1774: 348 men and 353 women.)

[17] The figures for the American population in 1960 are based on tables in U. S. Bureau of the Census, *Statistical Abstract of the United States, 1965* (Washington, 1965), 23.

The sample on which these percentages are based comprises almost two-thirds of all the white residents of Bristol. This is a sufficiently large majority to give some credibility to the results, but the chance remains that certain age-groups are a little underrepresented, owing to possible defects in the vital records, etc. A partial check can be attempted by dividing the above sample at age 16 and comparing the outcome with the similar breakdown in the census itself. Thus, whereas the census shows 46.1 per cent of the men to be under 16, the sample yields a figure of 44.8 per cent; for women the comparable percentages are 44.5 and 42.5. This suggests that the sample may be slightly biased against the younger categories, but *only* slightly.

In general terms, then, the predominance of youth is still striking in the Bristol of 1774. The comparable breakdown for our own day serves only to highlight this pattern. Nonetheless there is by 1774 a significant group of older people in the town, in contrast to the situation that had obtained nearly a century earlier. This matter relates, I think, to the change mentioned previously with regard to the pattern of household sizes, that is, the shrinking of the distribution in the middle ranges, with a corresponding gain at both the lower and higher extremes. In brief, the presence of elderly couples would add to the proportion of *small* households in the town as a whole. It is also worth noting that the list of heads-of-family included no less than twenty-five widows and two widowers.

The gain in large households is more difficult to interpret. However, one possible factor immediately suggests itself, namely, the presence in many families of single people over the age of 16. Indeed, this category comprises 224 people, some 23 per cent of the town's total white population. Who were they? In many specific instances, the vital records reveal them to be older, but as yet unmarried, sons and daughters of the head of the household. But it is also worth demonstrating that some of them were probably servants—witness the following very crude "proof." The various families in Bristol can be divided with regard to the possession of nonwhite servants or slaves. There are 147 families recorded as being without such slaves; of these, 54 per cent have at least one white member over 16 who cannot be identified as a parent. But the comparable figure is 75 per cent for those families which had some nonwhite membership. In short, as between families which did and did not own Negro or Indian slaves, the former were more likely also to have *white* servants. These comparisons show only that some portion of the whites over 16 living as subordinate members of larger families, were servants. Unfortunately there is no way to determine exactly *what* portion, but very probably it was less than one-half. If so, the slaves in Bristol had by this time become a larger group than the white servants.

But there yet remains a considerable number of people who were apparently older children living at home. This suggests a new question: did the average age of first marriage rise during the latter part of the eighteenth century? Table IX offers an answer by comparing samples of marriages made before and after 1750.

TABLE IX

AGES OF FIRST MARRIAGE

Time of Marriage	Age of Men		Number in Sample	Age of Women		Number in Sample
	Mean	Median		Mean	Median	
Before 1750	23.9	23.4	(37)	20.5	20.3	(32)
After 1750	24.3	23.8	(71)	21.1	20.8	(54)

The change, while in the expected direction, is very small indeed, and its utility as an explanation for the size of the "Over 16" group seems correspondingly limited. There is, however, an additional factor that may be relevant here, the imbalance in the sex ratio. As previously noted, Bristol had joined those "older" towns which showed an appreciable surplus of females, and perhaps in some families there were daughters for whom husbands were simply not available. It seems significant that in the "Over 16" group 98 were men and 126 were women. There is the further likelihood that the "white servant" category included more men than women; if so, the preponderance of unmarried daughters as against sons would be even greater. Such a pattern would have the obvious effect of adding to the total membership of at least some Bristol households.

One final set of questions will now be raised relating to the matter of "birth intervals." As the European historical demographers have shown, careful analysis of the time periods that elapsed between the births of children permits definite inferences about the practice, in certain communities, of some form of birth control.[18] It might be interesting to apply the

[18] See, for example, Louis Henry, *Anciennes familles genevoises* (Paris, 1956); and E. A. Wrigley, "Family Limitation in Pre-Industrial England," *Economic History Review*, 2d Ser., XIX (1966), 82-109.

same models to the study of Bristol. Unfortunately, however, the absence of full and precise data presents major obstacles here. One needs very exact information on the births of *all* the children in each family to be included in the sample, and the Bristol records fall badly short of this standard. The general conclusion that births occurred at roughly two-year intervals is the extent of our findings on this point.[19]

But I do want to point out one other use for information about dates of birth, which throws some light on a very different area of a people's life. I have tried with as many Bristol couples as possible to check the date of marriage against the date recorded for the birth of the first child. The purpose is to discover how many babies may have been conceived *before* a formal ceremony of marriage, and thus to develop some impression of possible changes in the sexual mores of the community. Consider, then, the following table for Bristol, which summarizes data for over one hundred cases broken down into five twenty-year time periods:

TABLE X

INTERVALS BETWEEN MARRIAGE AND BIRTH OF FIRST CHILD

Time of Marriage	Total Number of Couples	Number With First Child Within 8 Months	Percentage With First Child Within 8 Months
1680–1700	19	0	0%
1700–1720	8	0	0%
1720–1740	42	4	10%
1740–1760	35	17	49%
1760–1780	23	10	44%

The variance of these figures over time is really quite dramatic. It would seem to indicate some significant loosening of sexual prohibitions as the eighteenth century wore on, but its specific meaning in the lives of the people directly involved is hidden from us.[20] For example, in the cases

[19] See above, p. 45. The pattern did not visibly change between 1689 and 1774.

[20] One point with regard to changing legal practice seems relevant here. Throughout the 17th century in all the New England colonies fornication was a punishable offense, and court records for the period contain a large number of such cases. The standard "proof" of guilt was the arrival of a baby within eight months of marriage. The usual penalty was a fine and, in some instances, a whipping. In the 18th century, however, such prosecutions seem to have become steadily more rare and finally to have ceased altogether. This too, therefore, suggests a falling away from

where conception seems to have occurred before the marriage, what was the precise relation between these two events? Did the discovery of a pregnancy *force* a hasty wedding on the model of the "shotgun weddings" of our own day? Or were the couples in question "engaged" (or "going steady") when conception occurred? Did the community come to condone sexual relations in such cases? Is it even possible to infer here a kind of "trial marriage," an effort to establish that both partners were fertile before the actual wedding ceremony?

In short, there are many ways to interpret these results, but it is worth hoping that further research may begin to suggest some answers. The history of sexual behavior and mores is still largely unwritten, yet in our own post-Freudian era its immense significance can scarcely be questioned. The problem of data is something else again: it is clear that new source materials, and new methods of analyzing the *old* materials, will be required. All of this will call for extraordinary patience and ingenuity. Yet the effort must be made, and in the end demographic study may prove to be one of the more fruitful lines of approach.

---

restrictive standards of sexual morality. It is my own guess that when the subject of American sexual behavior is more fully explored, the middle and late 18th century may prove to have been the most "free" period in our history. But much more research is necessary before such hypotheses can be offered with confidence. The only useful study in this whole area is one by Edmund Morgan, "The Puritans and Sex," *New England Quarterly,* XV (1942), 591-607.

Daniel Scott Smith and Michael S. Hindus

Premarital Pregnancy in America 1640-1971:
An Overview and Interpretation

Sexual expression is a basic human drive and its control, a ubiquitous feature of all societies. Although all cultures prescribe sexual intercourse within marriage, in Western and especially American society sex has been proscribed without. Since behavior obviously does not always conform to norms, essential to uncovering the history of sex is some objective measure of the extent of non-marital intercourse. As Schumpeter once put it, "we need statistics not only for explaining things but also in order to know precisely what there is to explain." [1] Since children are a measurable, if not inevitable, result of intercourse, premarital pregnancy—operationally defined as the conception, before marriage, of the first post-maritally born child—provides an index of change in sexual behavior. This measure has the advantages of coverage (since nearly all adults marry), reliability (since the births are legitimate and more likely to be recorded than illegitimate births), objectivity (since its measurement depends on the matching of records collected for other purposes), and sensitivity to change in the underlying phenomenon (since premarital pregnancy is a relatively minor violation of the prevailing ban on non-marital intercourse).

What has to be explained in the white American premarital pregnancy record is the cyclical pattern of troughs in the seventeenth century (under 10 percent of first births) and mid-nineteenth century (about 10 percent) and peaks in the second half of the eighteenth century (about 30 percent) and in contemporary America (between 20 and 25 percent) (Fig. 1). This cycle cannot be explained away by changes in the variables intermediate between premarital coitus and

Daniel Scott Smith is Assistant Professor of History at the University of Illinois, Chicago Circle, and Associate Director of the Family History Program at the Newberry Library. Michael S. Hindus is a Fellow at the Center for the Study of Law and Society, University of California, Berkeley.

An earlier version of this analysis was presented to the annual meeting of the American Historical Association in 1971. We are indebted to John Demos, Michael Gordon, Kenneth Lockridge, Susan Norton, Edward Shorter, and Etienne van de Walle for criticism of the original paper.

1 Joseph A. Schumpeter, *History of Economic Analysis* (New York, 1954), 14. For a general introduction to the sociology of sex, see Kingsley Davis, "Sexual Behavior," in Robert K. Merton and Robert A. Nisbet (eds.), *Contemporary Social Problems* (New York, 1966; 2nd ed.), 322–372.

Reprinted from *The Journal of Interdisciplinary History* V, 537-570 (1975). By permission of The Journal of Interdisciplinary History and The M.I.T. Press, Cambridge, Massachusetts.

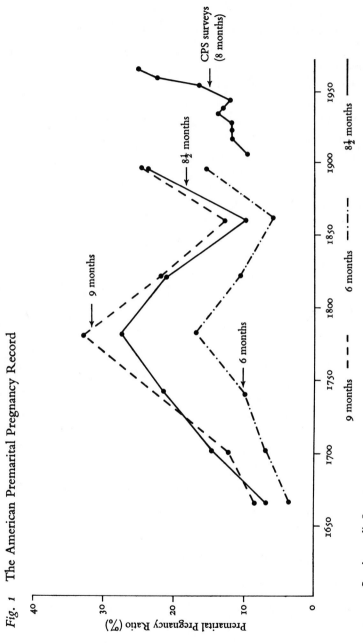

Fig. 1   The American Premarital Pregnancy Record

SOURCE: See Appendix I.

post-marital birth—fecundability and pregnancy wastage, contraceptive usage, induced abortion, and illegitimacy. Although these variables influence the level, we are concerned with the direction of the trend. It is unlikely that the underlying biological bases of American reproduction have varied enough to account for the magnitude and timing of the fluctuations in the premarital pregnancy ratio. Although contraceptive use obviously lowers fertility, since World War II both illegitimacy and premarital pregnancy have increased. Historically the trend in premarital pregnancy has paralleled that in illegitimacy.[2] Although the proportion of bridal pregnancies in all non-maritally conceived births is not constant over time and space, it appears to be a rule that when the overall level of non-marital conception increases, the proportion of non-marital pregnancies born outside of wedlock also rises.[3] To explain the major swings in premarital pregnancy, primary emphasis must rest on an analysis of the variation in the proportion of women who have engaged in premarital coitus. A similar long cycle also exists in West European illegitimacy and premarital pregnancy data (Fig. 2). Superficially at least the cyclical variation in premarital pregnancy is a striking regularity of early modern and modern social history.[4]

The basic strategy of this analysis is to distinguish between the periods with high ratios by comparing differentials in premarital

2   These are international phenomena; see Sidney Goldstein, "Premarital Pregnancies and Out-of-Wedlock Births in Denmark, 1950–1965," *Demography*, IV (1967), 925–936; K. G. Basavarajappa, "Pre-marital Pregnancies and Ex-Nuptial Births in Australia, 1911–66," *Australian and New Zealand Journal of Sociology*, IV (1968), 126–145; Shirley M. Hartley, "The Amazing Rise of Illegitimacy in Great Britain," *Social Forces*, XLIV (1966), 533–545; Daniel Scott Smith, "The Dating of the American Sexual Revolution: Evidence and Interpretation," in Michael Gordon (ed.), *The American Family in Social-Historical Perspective* (New York, 1973), 321–335. For the long-run European pattern see Edward Shorter, "Illegitimacy, Sexual Revolution, and Social Change in Modern Europe," *Journal of Interdisciplinary History*, II (1971), 237–272; Shorter, John Knodel, and Etienne van de Walle, "The Decline of Non-Marital Fertility in Europe, 1880–1940," *Population Studies*, XXV (1971), 375–393.
3   This rule is derived from the postwar experience of Great Britain (Hartley, "Amazing Rise," 540, Table 3), Denmark (Goldstein, "Premarital Pregnancies," 930), Australia (Basavarajappa, "Pre-marital Pregnancies," 141), and the cross-national relationship in Phillips Cutright, "Illegitimacy in the United States, 1920–1968," in Charles F. Westoff and Robert Parke, Jr. (eds.), *Demographic and Social Aspects of Population Growth* (Washington, D.C., 1972), 405.
4   The American and West European cycles are not identical. The early nineteenth-century American decline occurred a half-century or more before the corresponding downturn in Western Europe. Although a reduced incidence of premarital coitus seems central to the American decline, the use of contraception is the principal variable in the European decrease.

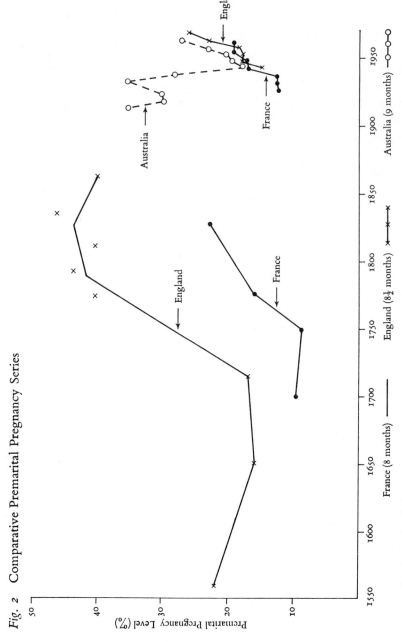

Fig. 2   Comparative Premarital Pregnancy Series

SOURCE: See Appendix II.

pregnancy between groups, and then to assess eras with lower ratios by focusing on differences in the social control of sexuality. The social relationships underlying similar premarital pregnancy levels are strikingly dissimilar. The analysis of the transitions thus concentrates on the changing relationships between sexual behavior and the social mechanisms controlling it. Throughout we will be concerned with individual behavior, the role of the family as the principal regulator of sexual expression, and the larger societal context.

PERIODS WITH HIGH RATIOS   The family of orientation (family of birth) played a much more direct role in the high premarital pregnancy level of the late eighteenth century than it does in the modern peak. This contrast is apparent in the incidence of premarital pregnancy by age; the incidence by class; the relative incidence among interclass unions; and the transmission and support of the tendency toward premarital pregnancy.

Age   In contrast to the relatively constant age-specific pattern among pre-industrial women, modern premarital pregnancy is increasingly concentrated among teen-agers (Table 1). Although the low teen-age rates for seventeenth-century Hingham, Massachusetts and pre-industrial West European samples may be attributed to adolescent subfecundity, the relative stability after age 20 can best be explained by the absence of a clear demarcation between youth and maturity in pre-industrial society.[5] Couples in their late 20s entered into marriage in the same social context as those marrying at an earlier age. In contemporary populations, by contrast, teen-agers do not employ contraceptives as often and as effectively as women in their 20s. Aging in modern society from 15 to 25 involves qualitative changes in the context of behavior which did not occur two centuries earlier.

Economic strata   Although family income had little impact on the incidence of premarital coitus of white 15–19 year-old unmarried females surveyed in 1971, parental economic status was inversely related to the frequency of premarital pregnancy in the eighteenth-century case (Table 2). Based on a Detroit sample of 1960, parental

5   Since a low age at menarche is related to diet, particularly protein consumption, the American age historically may have been below that in Europe. For this suggestion see Peter Laslett, "Age at Menarche in Europe since the Eighteenth Century," *Journal of Interdisciplinary History*, II (1971), 236.

Table 1 Relationship of Female Age at First Marriage to Premarital Pregnancy

DESCRIPTION OF SAMPLE PLACE AND PERIOD OF MARRIAGE	AGE AT MARRIAGE OF WOMAN				
	15–19	20–24	25–29	30–34	35 AND OVER
Hingham, Mass. (rate)					
−1720	2.4 (100)	11.4 (475)	3.9 (162)[a]		
1721–1800	40.9 (100)	23.8 (58)	21.6 (53)		
1801–1840	23.9 (100)	15.5 (65)	13.5 (56)		
1841–1880	15.4 (100)	11.0 (71)	2.7 (17)		
Andover, Mass. (ratio)[1]					
1685–1744	19.0 (100)	15.8 (83)	6.7 (35)[a]		
United States (ratio)[2]					
1964–1966	29.8 (100)	14.7 (49)	5.9 (20)[a]		
Northwest France (ratio)[3]					
1670–1769	3.7 (100)	6.4 (175)	6.8 (184)	6.3 (171)	6.5 (177)
France (rate)[4]					
1925–1929	18.4 (100)	11.9 (65)	8.6 (47)	7.1 (39)	6.0 (33)
1955–1959	33.0 (100)	18.2 (55)	14.4 (44)	11.3 (34)	3.7 (11)
Australia (rate)[5]					
1911	58.8 (100)	34.5 (59)	20.3 (34)	15.2 (26)	6.8 (12)
1965	44.6 (100)	16.2 (36)	13.5 (30)	10.8 (24)	3.9 (9)

a 25 or more.

SOURCES:

1 We are indebted to Philip J. Greven, Jr. for these unpublished data.

2 Mary Grace Kovar, "Interval from First Marriage to First Birth: United States, 1964–66 Births," unpub. paper, (1970), Table A.

3 Louis Henry, "Intervalle entre le mariage," 277, Table 9.

4 Jean-Claude DeVille, *Structure*, 91, Table 35.

5 K. G. Basavarajappa, "Pre-marital Pregnancies," 143, Table A.

Table 2 Economic Status, Premarital Pregnancy in Eighteenth-Century Hingham, Mass., The United States, 1964–66, and Premarital Coital Incidence for White American 15–19 Year-Olds, 1971

DESCRIPTION OF SAMPLE	WEALTH CRITERION AND INCIDENCE OF PREMARITAL PREGNANCY IN QUINTILES					
	TOP 20%	U–M 20%	M 20%	L–M 20%	POOR 20%	TOTAL
WEALTH OF HUSBAND, HINGHAM RECONSTITUTED FAMILIES OF 1721–1800	19.8% (91)	22.5% (89)	29.1% (103)	43.8% (105)	29.2% (130)	29.3% (518)
Children of taxpayers on 1767 first parish list						
Sons	24.7% (81)	35.2% (54)	34.6% (26)	47.9% (48)	50.0% (34)	36.2% (243)
Daughters	16.4% (67)	37.3% (67)	44.2% (43)	37.8% (45)	22.2% (27)	31.3% (249)
	FAMILY INCOME (IN THOUSANDS OF DOLLARS)					
United States, 1964–66[1]	$10+ 8.2%	7–9.9 11.5%	5–6.9 17.6%	3–4.9 23.3%	<3 37.5%	21.6%
	FAMILY INCOME (IN THOUSANDS OF DOLLARS)					
Premarital coital experience of unmarried white 15–19 year old females, 1971[2]	$15+ 25.6%	10–14.9 23.6%	6–9.9 22.1%	3–5.9 23.4%	<3 28.5%	23.4%

SOURCES:
1 Kovar, "Interval from first Marriage," Table F.
2 John F. Kantner and Melvin Zelnik, "Sexual Experience of Young Unmarried Women in the United States," Family Planning Perspectives, IV (1972), 10–11, Tables 1, 2.

119

status also has relatively little effect on the frequency of premarital pregnancy.[6] Higher economic status no longer provides parents with leverage over the sexual behavior of their children.

Heterogamy   In the Detroit sample, premarital pregnancy ratios were markedly higher when the wife's father was of higher status than the husband's father; pregnancies in which the male's family had higher status presumably ended in illegitimate births. Interclass marriages in Hingham show the same lower pattern of premarital pregnancy exhibited by marriages within the wealthier 40 percent of the population (Table 3). Since behavior followed the pattern of the higher status partner, parental control is more evident. The absence of a differential in interclass marriages suggests that community coercion overcame the more serious consequences of pregnancy for women. Further suggestive detail on the roles of parental and community authority is available for the reconstituted Hingham families established between 1761 and 1780. Men who married daughters of wealthier parents were penalized most by premarital pregnancy, implying that there was no necessity for the girl's father to contribute economically to a marriage that had been made inevitable by pregnancy.[7] For the children of poorer parents, premarital pregnancy seemed to have involved no economic setback. Lacking economic resources, less wealthy fathers could not restrain the sexual activity of their unmarried children.[8]

Sexually Restrictive and Permissive Groups   Continuity is apparent in the institutional basis of the sexually more restrictive subculture. In both eras, religious involvement is associated with lower levels of pre-

6 Lolagene C. Coombs, Ronald Freedman, Judith Friedman, and William F. Pratt, "Premarital Pregnancy and Status before and after Marriage," *American Journal of Sociology*, LXXV (1970), 810, Table 3.
7 Premaritally pregnant couples, whose fathers both ranked in the upper 40 percent by wealth, were 1.9 quintiles lower in wealth with respect to the husband's father than couples of similar status who were not pregnant at marriage. When the husband's father was wealthy and the wife's father less so, the difference was 0.6 quintiles; in the reverse case, the premaritally pregnant were 1.5 quintiles poorer on the average. Finally, if both fathers ranked in the poorer 60 percent of the population, the premaritally pregnant were 0.4 quintiles higher in comparison with the husbands' fathers than the non-premaritally pregnant.
8 In both the eighteenth century and today, couples who had a child on the way at the wedding have lower subsequent economic status than those not pregnant at marriage (see the first and fourth row of Table 2). Curtailment of education is the major reason for the modern differential.

Table 3 Proportions Pregnant at Marriage by Status of Parents

DESCRIPTION OF SAMPLE	STATUS OF WIFE'S FATHER	STATUS OF HUSBAND'S FATHER		
		%		
		GRADE SCHOOL	HIGH SCHOOL	COLLEGE
Detroit marriages of 1960 (father's education)[1]	Grade school	16.0	16.7	16.1
	High school	17.5	20.7	16.9
	College	31.3	24.5	15.9
		WEALTHIER 40%	POORER 60%	TOTAL
Hingham reconstituted families of 1761–1780 (father's wealth)	Wealthier 40%	31.0 (29)	35.7 (14)	32.6 (43)
	Poorer 60%	33.3 (18)	50.0 (38)	44.6 (56)
	Total	31.9% (47)	44.6% (52)	39.4% (99)

[1] Coombs et al., "Premarital Pregnancy and Status," 810.

Table 4 Church Membership (1717–1786), Wealth,[1] Premarital Pregnancy Status of Parents, and Premarital Pregnancy Status of Children

CATEGORY	WEALTH STATUS		
	WEALTHIER 40%	POORER 60%	TOTAL
Persons taxed in 1767			
One or both spouses members	9.4% (53)	32.3% (34)	18.4% (87)
Neither spouse member	27.3 (33)	35.3 (68)	32.7 (101)
Parents pregnant at marriage			
Sons			
Both or spouse member	36.4% (11)	0.0% (2)	30.8% (13)
Neither church member	25.0 (12)	46.9 (32)	40.9 (44)
Daughters			
Both or spouse member	50.0% (4)	50.0% (12)	50.0% (16)
Neither church member	40.0 (20)	69.2 (13)	51.5 (33)
Parents not pregnant at marriage			
Sons			
Both or spouse member	25.4% (63)	50.0% (20)	31.3% (83)
Neither church member	23.1 (39)	44.7 (38)	33.8 (77)
Daughters			
Both or spouse member	23.8% (63)	36.0% (25)	27.3% (88)
Neither church member	28.6 (28)	33.3 (48)	31.6 (76)

[1] Hingham first parish list of 1767.

marital sexual activity, On the Hingham first parish tax list of 1767, only 18.4 percent of the cases where the property holder or his spouse were church members involved premarital conceptions; in 30.3 percent of the cases where neither spouse was identified as a church member, there was a premarital pregnancy (Table 4, top two rows). This relationship holds, however, only for the wealthier stratum.[9] In the 1971 survey of teen-age sexual experience, females who attended church on less than three occasions in the previous month were, depending on denomination, two to three times more likely to be non-virgins than those who attended four or more times. Active religious participation is also closely related to restrictive sexual attitudes.[10]

The association of religiosity and premarital sexual restrictiveness does not automatically imply a causal relationship. In more than 80 percent of the Hingham cases from the 1767 list, church membership followed marriage, often by five or more years. Arguing from chronology, premarital pregnancy deterred religious affiliation among the wealthier rather than vice versa. Although the children of Hingham church members were less likely to be pregnant at marriage, this minor effect disappears when one controls for wealth (Table 4). Since beginning sexual intercourse and abandoning church attendance are part of a general change in life style of maturing teen-agers, the association of religiosity and premarital sexual restrictiveness in cross-sectional surveys may be largely spurious. Religion can be said to have an impact on the overall incidence of premarital sex only when it is an encompassing and controlling force in the lives of the young and not merely an option.

The more impressive relationship in Table 4 is the consistent difference between the daughters whose mothers were pregnant at marriage and those whose mothers were not. Inasmuch as there existed a sexually permissive subculture in eighteenth-century Hingham, its continuity depended on the female line and on the less wealthy section of the population. The former relationship did not pass unnoticed by

9 In the town of Groton only 11.3 percent of persons admitted to full communion between 1761 and 1775 confessed to premarital fornication while 33 percent of those owning the baptismal covenant did so. Since formal church membership is probably related to wealth, the causation here is uncertain. For the Groton figures see Henry Reed Stiles, *Bundling: Its Origins, Progress and Decline in America* (Albany, 1871), 78.
10 Kantner and Zelnik, "Sexual Experience," 16, Table 11; Ira L. Reiss, *The Social Context of Premarital Sexual Permissiveness* (New York, 1967), 42–44, 99–100.

contemporaries, as is evidenced by the subtitle and following lines of an anonymous poem published around 1785:

> Some maidens say, if through the nation,
> Bundling should quite go out of fashion,
> Courtship would lose its sweets; and they
> Could have no fun till wedding day.
> It shant be so, they rage and storm,
> And country girls in clusters swarm,
> And fly and buz like angry bees,
> And vow they'll bundle when they please.
> Some mothers too, will plead their cause,
> And give their daughters great applause,
> And tell them 'tis no sin nor shame,
> For we, your mothers did the same.[11]

In summary, intergenerational family relationships are deeply involved in the great boom of premarital pregnancy in the eighteenth century.

Premarital sexual activity in modern society is structured through the peer group and more broadly through a youth subculture, which is reinforced by age-stratified institutions such as schools and promoted by other forces such as marketing and the mass media. Although objective family background characteristics such as income, education, or religious preference have little impact on the incidence of teen-age intercourse, higher familiar status, especially parental education, is associated with the more frequent use of contraception by sexually active teen-agers.[12] Modern parents generally lack the power to be oppressive in an effective way. This absence of parental control and influence is strikingly demonstrated by the low correspondence between the political opinions of parents and children.[13] If teen-agers are not controlled by their parents, neither are they autonomous. The adolescent way station between dependent childhood and independent adulthood is characterized by an alienation but not a separation from

11 Anon., "A New Bundling Song; Or a reproof to those Young Country Women, who follow that reproachful Practice, and to their Mothers for upholding them therein," in Stiles, *Bundling*, 81–82.
12 Reiss, *Social Context*, 171–180; James J. Teevan, Jr., "Reference Groups and Premarital Sexual Behavior," *Journal of Marriage and the Family*, XXXIV (1972), 283–291; Kantner and Zelnik, "Sexual Experience," Tables 2, 3, 4, 10; "Contraception and Pregnancy: Experience of Young Unmarried Women in the United States," *Family Planning Perspectives*, V (1973), 21–35, esp. Tables 2, 3, 9.
13 See the summary article by R. W. Connell, "Political Socialization in the American Family: The Evidence Re-Examined," *Public Opinion Quarterly*, XXXVI (1972), 322–333. The median correlation in a range of studies was only 0.2.

parental values and culture. Survey research suggests that premarital coitus is directly related to the extent of this estrangement.[14] Although the modern family fails to restrict successfully the sexual activity of children, it and the other institutions involving youth limit the possibilities of a rational separation of sex and procreation.

PERIODS WITH LOW RATIOS   Just as the peaks in premarital pregnancy when examined in detail reflect quite different underlying patterns, so the troughs of the seventeenth and nineteenth centuries result from different systems of control. Although a sexually repressive ideology characterized both centuries, the emphasis in the Puritan seventeenth century was on external controls, while internal control or self-repression was the central feature of Victorian morality. Premarital sexual restraint was possible both in the seventeenth-century community and in nineteenth-century society, but not during the transition. Maintenance of morality, however, shifted from direct to indirect, from being based primarily on social control to resting principally on socialization.

The importance of external controls in the seventeenth century may be readily demonstrated. Premarital pregnancy ratios were low not just in North America but in England and France as well. English premarital pregnancy, for example, was 26 percent below the sixteenth-century figure, and illegitimacy ratios between 1651 and 1720 were less than half of those prevailing between 1581 and 1630 and from 1741 to 1820. English North America shared the organized religious intensity that pervaded Western Europe during the seventeenth century.[15] With a premarital pregnancy level less than half that of England, mid-seventeenth-century New England, as Governor Bradford of Plymouth was "verily persuaded," was a society "with not more evils in this kind [sexual deviation], nor nothing near so many by proportion as in other places; but they are here more discovered and seen and made public by due search, inquisition and due punishment; for the churches look narrowly to their members, and the magistrates over all, more

14 For example, 43.4 percent of white 15–19 year-old females who "strongly agreed" with the statement, "I don't confide very much in my parents," had had intercourse, while only 13.5 percent of those who strongly disagreed were not virgins (Kantner and Zelnik, "Sexual Experience," 15, Table 9).

15 For English bridal pregnancy data, see Appendix II. For illegitimacy trends see Peter Laslett, *The World We Have Lost* (London, 1971; 2nd ed.), 142. John Bossy, "The Counter-Reformation and the People of Catholic Europe," *Past & Present*, XLVII (1970), 51–70.

strictly than in other places."[16] Instead of the Puritans becoming "inured to sexual offenses, because there were so many," as Morgan puts it, they prosecuted their comparatively few sexual offenders vigorously. Morgan was right in his now classic reading of the court records, however, when he emphasized the calm, matter-of-fact approach of the Puritans toward even the most extreme manifestations of sexual deviance. Although this composure had its roots in the theological belief in original sin, the elaborate structure of social repression maintained by the Puritans suggests that they did not expect the population at large to have internalized sexual control. Broadly speaking, Puritanism may be characterized as a communal response to the strains accompanying the disintegration of the bases of medieval society.[17]

Nineteenth-century morality was forged in a new social matrix and constructed with different materials. The reappearance of premarital sexual restraint in the nineteenth century was based on the autonomy of the young adult and the incorporation of the groups tending toward premarital pregnancy into a new social order. By the early nineteenth century, people were generally independent in life at a younger age than ever before.[18] Although there were objective changes, such as the economic shift from the apprentice to the wage system and the substitution of boarding for service as the transitional living arrangement for young people, most significant was the social acceptance of youthful autonomy.

The new independence of nineteenth-century youth was recognized in various ways. The practical impact of the introduction of universal male suffrage was not so much the enfranchisement of a permanent proletariat as the granting of political rights to young adults. Proponents of manhood suffrage presented their arguments in terms of the reality of allowing young men the political autonomy commensurate with their social and economic status.[19] During and after the

16 William Bradford (ed. Samuel Eliot Morison), *Of Plymouth Plantation, 1620–1647* (New York, 1959), 317.

17 Edmund S. Morgan, "The Puritans and Sex," *New England Quarterly*, XV (1942), 595; Michael Walzer, "Puritanism as a Revolutionary Ideology," *History and Theory*, III (1961), 59–90.

18 Joseph F. Kett, "Growing Up in Rural New England, 1800–1840," in Tamara K. Hareven (ed.), *Anonymous Americans* (Englewood Cliffs, N.J., 1971), 9–10. For the comments of European travelers on the freedom of antebellum youth, see Frank F. Furstenberg, Jr., "Industrialization and the American Family: A Look Backward," *American Sociological Review*, XXXI (1966), 329–330, 335.

19 For examples of this argument, see Chilton Williamson, *American Suffrage from Property to Democracy* (Princeton, 1960), 139, 147, 171, 177, 187–188, 195.

Second Great Awakening, religious conversion became a common experience for teen-agers. Not unrelated to early religious involvement is the fact that youths began to play important roles in reform movements.[20]

The early nineteenth century also witnessed the social incorporation of the groups previously prone to premarital pregnancy. The erosion of the social base of the sexually permissive segment of the population was partly the result of a dramatic expansion of religious participation. Estimated formal church membership in America tripled from 7 to 23 percent between 1800 and 1860.[21] With younger conversion, religion could have a more effective impact on premarital sexual choices. The concomitant splintering of American Protestantism meant that each stratum had one or more denominations tailored to its particular condition and needs. Although denominations differed in social base and religious style, the regulation of individual morality was a central concern of nineteenth-century Protestantism.[22] Although seventeenth-century Puritanism stressed external controls, antebellum religious enthusiasm rejected Calvinist determinism in favor of free will doctrines. The basic social support of nineteenth-century sexual restraint—religion—rested on the centrality of autonomy and individual choice. Finally, nineteenth-century Protestantism incorporated women, the apparent source of the intergenerational transmission of premarital pregnancy in the eighteenth century, into the social order. If women did not entirely dominate religion symbolically and organizationally in the nineteenth century, the churches did provide an important outlet for a wide range of female needs.[23] A more active part of the churches, nineteenth-century women absorbed the message of sexual restraint more completely.

Since the supporting social restraints involved voluntary action, the new anti-sexual ideology of the nineteenth century was necessarily more total than the Puritan hostility to non-marital sexual expression.

20 Joseph F. Kett, "Adolescence and Youth in Nineteenth-Century America, "*Journal of Interdisciplinary History*, II (1971), 289–291; Lois W. Banner, "Religion and Reform in the Early Republic: The Role of Youth," *American Quarterly*, XXIII (1971), 677–695.
21 N. J. Demerath III, "Trends and Anti-Trends in Religious Change," in Eleanor B. Sheldon and Wilbert E. Moore (eds.), *Indicators of Social Change: Concepts and Measurements* (New York, 1968), 353.
22 Timothy L. Smith, *Revivalism and Social Reform* (New York, 1965), esp. 33–44, 148–162. See also Alexis de Tocqueville (ed. Phillips Bradley), *Democracy in America* (New York, 1945), I, 313–318.
23 Barbara Welter, "The Feminization of American Religion: 1800–1860," in William L. O'Neill (ed.), *Insights and Parallels: Problems and Issues of American Social History* (Minneapolis, 1973), 305–332.

Intellectually intertwined with the entire system of liberal bourgeois ideology, Victorian morality was more than a functional system for the control of premarital sexual behavior. The exaggerated aversion to masturbation, for example, is inexplicable if the system were merely designed to prevent premarital pregnancy.[24] Victorian morality was relevant to the immediate needs and social position of both young men and women. Tocqueville emphasized the free marriage market as the structural determinant of the high degree of sexual restraint among young American women. "No girl," observed the aristocratic visitor, "then believes that she cannot become the wife of the man who loves her, and this renders all breaches of morality before marriage very uncommon."[25] Since women were on their own in the marriage market but lacked economic resources thereafter, Victorian morality raised the price of sex and thus substantially increased the bargaining power of both single and married women.[26]

Because sexual restraint was compatible with the norms of thrift and abstinence required of the upwardly striving young capitalist, the morality advantageous to women also appealed to the rationality, if not the passion, of males. The early age of independence from the family of orientation prepared young middle-class men not for early marriage but for a period of capital accumulation and entry into a career, the two prerequisites to marriage. Having internalized the mechanism of deferred gratification in terms of his economic life, the nineteenth-century American male would not risk the consequences of a marriage precipitated by a premarital pregnancy. Although not every man was making it in nineteenth-century America, more and more were caught up in the competition. Most importantly, the obstacles to advancement in society were seen as within the capacity of the individual to overcome.

THE TRANSITIONS AND THEIR IMPLICATIONS   Have basic American institutions changed gradually and easily? Have the external forms

24 Peter Cominos, "Late Victorian Sexual Respectability and the Social System," *International Review of Social History*, VIII (1963), 18–48, 216–250; Steven Willner Nissenbaum, "Careful Love: Sylvester Graham and the Emergence of Victorian Sexual Theory in America, 1830–1840," unpub. Ph.D. diss. (University of Wisconsin, 1968), 3–32.

25 Tocqueville, *Democracy*, II, 216; generally, 215–221.

26 For a more extended discussion of the role of nineteenth-century women in promoting Victorian morality, see Daniel Scott Smith, "Family Limitation, Sexual Control and Domestic Feminism in Victorian America," *Feminist Studies*, I (1973), 40–57.

of control been painlessly modified to conform to new or more freely expressed desires of individuals? Or did "crises" arise in the older social arrangements before new patterns of behavior appeared? With more than three centuries of data on the key aspect of human behavior which is under examination here, some insights are possible concerning this fundamental problem in American history. Since two thirds of white women were not pregnant at marriage throughout the course of American history, continuity in the efficacy of control is obviously apparent. Yet, since premarital pregnancy is at least a mild form of deviancy, the magnitude of the cyclical fluctuation is impressive. Our contention is that rising premarital pregnancy is a manifestation of a collision between an unchanging and increasingly antiquated family structure and a pattern of individual behavior which is more a part of the past than a harbinger of the future. The downturn in premarital pregnancy follows as a necessary but not sufficient consequence of a transformation in the family's role as a regulator of the sexual behavior of the young. Neither the old institutional pattern of control nor the rebellion against it can predict the subsequent sexual behavior of the young. The sexual revolutionaries of the eighteenth century, if the premarital procreators may be so labeled, were obviously not the vanguard of a sexually liberated nineteenth century.

The increase in premarital pregnancy in late seventeenth-century New England provides empirical evidence for the notion of the declension of Puritanism from a "golden age." At first the authorities attempted to maintain their vigilance in the face of increased sexual deviance (Table 5). As late as the 1670s, at least by a rough estimate of the number of premarital pregnancies in Essex County, well over half of the guilty couples were being convicted.[27] Before any marked socio-economic change occurred in New England, cracks surfaced in the sexually repressive order. During the last third of the century punishment declined from corporal to monetary, and individuals were given the choice between fines or whippings.[28] Although illegitimacy

27 Direct matching of premarital pregnancy cases from the vital records to prosecutions in court records yields a similar estimate. Three of five couples in Ipswich (1657–1682), and three of five in Hingham (1670–1682) with a birth within six complete months of marriage were found in the published court records.

28 See Table 5. Even with this amelioration in penalties, punishment and prosecution were more severe in New England than in English church courts. See Ronald A. Marchant, *The Church under the Law: Justice, Administration and Discipline in the Diocese of York, 1560–1640* (Cambridge, 1969), 27, 215–219, 240–243; George Elliott Howard, *A History of Matrimonial Institutions* (Chicago, 1904), II, 180–200.

Table 5. Crime and Punishment for Fornication in Essex County, Massachusetts, 1643–1682

CONVICTIONS	1643–1652	1653–1667	1668–1682	TOTAL
Married couples	4	19	85	108
(known early birth)	3	3	13	19
Women only	6	30	69	105
(known pregnancy)	2	18	38	58
Men only	4	22	46	72
(bastardy cases)	2	7	26	35
Total incidences[a]	11	54	161	226
Mean population[b]	4,100	6,000	11,000	
Incidence rate (per 1000 per decade)	2.7	6.0	9.8	
KNOWN PUNISHMENTS				
fine	5	22	66	93
whipping	4	27	17	48
whipping or fine	2	8	95	105
child support only	1	22	17	40
other	2	2	1	5
Total known	14	81	196	291

ESTIMATE OF PERCENTAGE OF PREMARITAL PREGNANCIES CONVICTED:

MARRIED COUPLES CONVICTED, 1671–80	POPULATION ESTIMATE	MARRIAGE RATE[c]	PREGNANCIES EXPECTED[d]	PERCENT CONVICTED
65	11,000	12/1000	106	61%

a   The total of incidences is obtained by adding the number of married couples convicted, the number of single women convicted, and the small number of single men (thirteen for the forty year period) who were prosecuted without a partner being arraigned.
b   From William I. Davisson, "Essex County Wealth Trends," *Essex Institute Historical Collections*, CIII (1967), 292.
c   From Susan Norton, "Population Growth in Colonial America: A Study of Ipswich, Massachusetts," *Population Studies*, XXV (1971), 451.
d   Premarital pregnancy ratio of 8% based on three Essex County towns—Ipswich (7.3% before 1700), Salem (8.2%, 1671–1700), and Topsfield (7.7%, 1660–1679). To be conservative, a nine-month standard was used.

prosecutions continued after 1700, civil punishment for premarital pregnancy gradually disappeared. Although the churches then picked up the burden of repression by requiring confessions for baptism and admission, individuals, typically, were ready to join only after their premarital experience had passed. As premarital pregnancy continued to increase during the eighteenth century, the churches dropped or diluted the confession requirement.[29] In short, the severity of active social repression is inversely related over time to the level of premarital pregnancy.

The removal of the communal controls of Puritanism left exposed a set of traditional relationships. Although pressures in the direction of the substantive autonomy of youth may have been inherent in the American wilderness from the beginning, environmental forces were more than blunted by traditional familial, social, and ideological arrangements. Nearly a century passed before the customary high male age at marriage was lowered. Other indices of traditionalism in family patterns persisted well past the middle of the eighteenth century.[30] Even the modernity of the influential *Some Thoughts Concerning Education* may be questioned.[31] Although Locke stressed affection between mature sons and their fathers (who handily reserved the right to disinherit), the psychological basis for this rational relationship developed in the context of a severe, but not total, crushing of the son's will as an infant. "Fear and awe," proclaimed Locke to fathers, "ought to give you the first power over their minds," and thus compliance "will seem natural to them."[32]

Alternative explanations do not account adequately for the transition to higher premarital pregnancy levels in the eighteenth century. Premarital sex was never normatively approved, even during engagement. Most premaritally pregnant couples (from two thirds to three fourths of those marrying in Hingham between 1741 and 1780) were also pregnant at the time of legal engagement—the filing of the intention to marry.[33] On the other hand, over 40 percent of women not

29 Emil Oberholzer, Jr., *Delinquent Saints: Disciplinary Action in the Early Congregational Churches of Massachusetts* (New York, 1956), 136.

30 Philip J. Greven, Jr., *Four Generations: Population, Land, and Family in Colonial Andover, Massachusetts* (Ithaca, 1970); Daniel Scott Smith, "The Demographic History of Colonial New England," *Journal of Economic History*, XXXII (1972), 176–180; *idem*, "Parental Power and Marriage Patterns: An Analysis of Historical Trends in Hingham, Massachusetts," *Journal of Marriage and the Family*, XXXV (1973), 419–428.

31 For the mixture of patriarchalism and consent in Locke, see Gordon J. Schochet, "The Family and the Origins of the State," in John W. Yolton (ed.), *John Locke: Problems and Perspectives* (Cambridge, 1969), 81–98; M. Seliger, *The Liberal Politics of John Locke* (New York, 1968), 209–226.

32 John Locke, *Some Thoughts Concerning Education* in James E. Axtell (ed.), *The Educational Writings of John Locke* (Cambridge, 1968), 146–147. In the introduction to his recent documentary collection (*Childrearing Concepts, 1620–1860* [Itasca, Ill., 1973], 1–6), Greven stresses the continuity of repressive ideas until the 1820s and 1830s.

33 Of the thirty-six children born within 4 complete months of marriage, thirty-three (91.7%) were born within 8½ months of the intention to marry; of the thirty-seven born in the fifth and sixth month after marriage, twenty-nine (78.4%) were born within

pregnant at marriage had been legally engaged for three months or longer. If betrothal licence is an unsatisfactory explanation, the custom of bundling is even less adequate. Although an environmental explanation (cold weather and poorly heated houses) has been seriously advanced, the low seventeenth-century incidence of premarital pregnancy and its seasonal pattern contradict this argument. Premarital conceptions occurred year-round with a slight bulge during the warmer months.[34] Bundling was an eighteenth-century compromise between persistent parental control and the pressures of the young to subvert traditional familial authority.

As a system with contradictory elements, eighteenth-century courtship was not dominated by the newer theme of romantic love. If interpersonal affection and attraction—resulting in premarital pregnancy—had been replacing the old criteria of property and status in mate selection, then one would expect that "love matches" would be more heterogamous than "property matches." To the contrary, however, premaritally pregnant couples were as similar in wealth origins as non-pregnant couples.[35] The eighteenth-century surge in premarital pregnancy did involve a revolt of the young, but it was constrained within the framework of traditional motivation. The generational interpretation is not, of course, new. Eilert Sundt, the most astute observer of courtship practices in nineteenth-century rural Europe, saw the phenomenon as "a form of protest against inordinate parental authority; its decline was in part explained by the moderating of familial controls which young people sought to subvert."[36] And an

---

$8\frac{1}{4}$ months of the intention; of the thirty-eight born between the beginning of the seventh and $8\frac{1}{4}$ months of marriage, only thirteen (34.2%) were born within $8\frac{1}{4}$ months of the intention. Overall, 67.6% of the births within $8\frac{1}{4}$ months of marriage came within $8\frac{1}{4}$ months of the intention, and 73.9% were born within 9 months of the intention.

34 Stiles, *Bundling*, 53. Of premarital conceptions in Hingham between 1721 and 1800, 27.2%, 26.5%, 23.1%, and 23.1% (N = 147) occurred respectively in the quarters April–June, July–Sept., Oct.–Dec., and Jan.–March. Post-marital first conceptions (N = 363) were distributed in the same quarters as follows—19.0%, 21.5%, 26.7%, and 32.8%.

35 Comparing the wealth of the wife's father and the husband's father in Hingham reconstituted marriages between 1761 and 1780, we find no difference between the relative origins of the pregnant and nonpregnant couples. (Gamma for the pregnant couples was 0.70 (N = 39) and 0.69 (N = 60) for the nonpregnant).

36 Arthur Hillman, "Eilert Sundt: Pioneer Student of Family and Culture," in Thomas D. Eliot et al. (eds.), *Norway's Families* (Philadelphia, 1960), 40. On the work of Sundt, see Michael Drake, *Population and Society in Norway, 1735–1865* (Cambridge, 1969), 19–29.

Anglican polemicist in 1763 anticipated Sundt's conclusion. "Among dissenters, when a married pair happen to have a child born too soon after marriage," he noted, "they do not repent but if they were again in the same circumstances, they would do the same again, because otherwise they could not obtain their parent's consent to marry." [37]

The transference of this generational conflict to the political domain during the pre-Revolutionary crisis with Great Britain was not, as two scholars have recently maintained, because the contractual, Lockean, and republican nature of the family was a settled issue in everyday experience. Rather, power relationships within the family were being challenged, and the very ambiguity of the relationship between parents and children heightened the salience of the familial analogy for the parallel struggle that was developing between the colonies and the mother country. [38] Nor did the leaders of the resistance to England wish to incite a revolution in the family. For example, among the other evils which Jefferson cited in the preamble to the Virginia bill to abolish entail was that this custom "sometimes does injury to the morals of youth, by rendering them independent of, and disobedient to their parents." [39] The Revolution did signal, however, a general shift from passive to active consent on the part of the people; although an analogy is necessarily vague, it is not unreasonable to assume that a similar shift occurred in intergenerational relations. By the 1830s this new republican consensus on the family was firmly established. The father, according to Tocqueville, "exercised no other power than that which is granted to the affection and experience of age. . . . . The master and the constituted ruler have vanished, the father remains." [40] The sexual expression underlying the eighteenth-century peak in premarital pregnancy was a product of a situation of profound social disequilibrium, not an end in itself. Once the familial and social context had altered, sexual restrictiveness reappeared.

37 John Beach, *A Friendly Expostulation with all persons concern'd in publishing a late Pamphlet, Entitled, The real Advantages which Ministers and People may enjoy, especially in the Colonies, by conforming to the Church of England* (New York, 1763), 38. (We are indebted to Samuel Haber for this reference.)

38 Edwin G. Burrows and Michael Wallace, "The American Revolution: The Ideology and Psychology of National Liberation," *Perspectives in American History*, VI (1972), 167–306, esp. 255–267.

39 Paul Leicester Ford (ed.), *The Works of Thomas Jefferson* (New York, 1904), II, 269.

40 Tocqueville, *Democracy*, II, 205–206, and generally Ch. 8 "Influence of Democracy on the Family," 202–208

The crisis in traditional family structure was resolved by a republican solution—the acceptance of the maturity of young adults. Men and women in the nineteenth century responded to the risks of premarital freedom by constraining their sexual drives. Yet, the ideology of the participant-run courtship system emphasized romantic affection and love. Although elaborate dichotomies between pure love and evil sex were developed, the potential for premarital sexual intimacy was built into the Victorian system of courtship. As the Victorian cultural synthesis collapsed in the late nineteenth and twentieth centuries, the dominant themes in premarital sexuality continued to be commitment, love, and marriage. For the young adults who had become autonomous as a result of the transformation in age roles in the family a century earlier, higher rates of sexual intercourse did not produce proportional increases in premarital pregnancy. Contraception made possible the temporary separation of sex and procreation. Teen-agers, on the other hand, remained psychologically enmeshed in but not controlled by their families of orientation. With the extension of schooling in the twentieth century, the trend toward youthful autonomy perhaps has been reversed.

The dependence-independence ambivalence is crucial in the explanation of the high premarital pregnancy ratios of contemporary teen-agers. With an estimated decline in the age of menarche of 2.5 to 3.3 years during the twentieth century, American females are biologically mature earlier but socially immature as long or longer than in the nineteenth century.[41] Not independent in society (and therefore not responsible for the consequences of their actions), teen-aged girls accept the risk of pregnancy rather than consciously separate sexual intercourse from procreation. The rational use of contraception requires a teen-aged girl to adopt a self-definition inconsistent with her own assumptions.[42] The "problem," then, is not an absence of "morality" among teen-agers, but rather the persistence of a morality based on the sexual restraint of women presumed to be independent and responsible. In modern America, teen-age sexual behavior is

41 J. M. Tanner, "Earlier Maturation in Man," *Scientific American*, CCXVIII (Jan. 1968), 24–27.

42 For example, roughly two thirds of 13–19 year olds agreed with statement, "If a girl uses birth control pills or other methods of contraception, it makes it seem as if she were *planning* to have sex" (Robert C. Sorenson, *Adolescent Sexuality in Contemporary America* [New York, 1973], 408, Table 185). Both the responses and the use of italics in the question convey the implicit values.

guided neither by the old standard of prohibition nor by a new one of rational expressiveness.[43]

SUMMARY   The historical variation in premarital pregnancy in America suggests a notable absence of a Malthusian constancy of passion. Sexual restraint before marriage typified eras in which inter-generational relationships were well defined, in which extrafamilial institutions reinforced familial controls, and in which the population was relatively well integrated into the central structure of values. Conversely, premarital sexual activity has been more prevalent when there was more ambiguity and uncertainty in the parent-child relation-ship, when the social supports of morality were weakened or not appropriate to the current realities of coming of age, and when there emerged a segment of the population outside the mainstream of the culture. Discontinuity is the central fact of the premarital pregnancy record. In this important area of behavior, American history has not been a "seamless web." The transitions, furthermore, have not in-volved the simple triumph of new behavioral patterns over outmoded institutions of control. During the crisis periods the actions of the "rebels" appear, ironically, to be well integrated into the old regime of sexuality and its control.

Perhaps the cycle in premarital pregnancy should not surprise social historians. It fits two well-known models of the discontinuities of modern history—the cultural and the structural stages. The first perspective is the familiar Puritan-Enlightenment-Victorian-Post-modern organization of the four centuries of American cultural history. The latter and more interesting model involves a sequence of equilibrium-shock-adjustment-new equilibrium. In this perspective, the eighteenth-century surge in premarital pregnancy is related to the disintegration of the traditional, well-integrated rural community and to the beginnings of economic and social modernization. Once the crisis of transition to modern society had passed, premarital pregnancy began to decrease. Expectations among individuals and groups were once again predictable, and the various parts of the social system

---

43   The sex education debate is revealing in this context. Both sides in the con-troversy oppose sexual autonomy for teen-agers. Although the opponents see it as a threat to parental authority, the supporters perceive it as a supplement to parental authority by presenting sex in a wider matrix of adult values. For an amusing and perceptive account of the struggle, see Mary Breasted, *Oh! Sex Education* (New York, 1970).

meshed together.[44] Contemporary Western societies also appear to be in a similar transitional phase. The proliferation of transitional terms, e.g., post-industrial, post-modern, post-Protestant, suggests an awareness that a social order is dead but a new one is not yet definable.

What, then, of the future of premarital pregnancy and sexuality? If sexuality and procreation do become separated in the future through the universal acceptance and use of contraception and abortion in premarital relations, and if teen-agers emerge as an autonomous age group in society, then premarital pregnancy will obviously decline. Whether sexuality will continue within the romantic boundaries of love and relatively permanent commitment between individuals or jump to the utopian sexuality envisioned by Herbert Marcuse and Wilhelm Reich is more problematic. Alterations in the social control of sexuality historically have had unanticipated consequences for sexual behavior. Thus the future qualitative meaning of sexuality cannot be categorized as either romantic or utopian. Evidence exists that the structural basis for such an option is being constructed at present. The eighteen-year-olds' vote, for example, is a symbolic recognition of a younger age at maturity. Less symbolic but more to the point at issue here is the sharp drop from 68 percent of Americans in 1969 to only 48 percent in 1973 who think that "it is wrong for people to have sex relations before marriage."[45] If the analysis in this essay has validity, such a redefinition of the family and age groups in society has a clear historical precedent.

44 Examples of the use of this model are numerous. See Charles Tilly, "Collective Violence in European Perspective," in Hugh Davis Graham and Ted Robert Gurr (eds.), *The History of Violence in America* (New York, 1969), 4–44, esp. 21–33; E. J. Hobsbawm, "Economic Fluctuations and Some Social Movements since 1800," in his *Laboring Men* (New York, 1967), 148–184, esp. 153–157. For the framework applied to the family, see Shorter, "Illegitimacy, Sexual Revolution, and Social Change"; Neil Smelser, *Social Change in the Industrial Revolution* (Chicago, 1959); Smith, "Parental Power and Marriage Patterns."

45 Gallup poll for national sample reported in the *Hartford Courant*, 12 Aug. 1973, 24. The trend toward a complete separation of premarital sex and conception is apparent in Western Europe. Between the mid-1960s and c. 1970 the premarital pregnancy rate increased in only one of nine countries examined in a recent study; during the first half of the 1960s, however, the rate increased in seven of the nine countries. See France Prioux-Marchal, "Les Conceptions Prénuptiales en Europe Occidentale Depuis 1955," *Population*, XXIX (1974), 63, Table 1.

APPENDIX I

Summary

PERIOD	UNDER 6 MONTHS		UNDER $8\frac{1}{2}$ MONTHS		UNDER 9 MONTHS	
	%	N	%	N	%	N
–1680	3.3	511	6.8	511	8.1	663
1681–1720	6.7	445	14.1	518	12.1	1156
1721–1760	9.9	881	21.2	1146	22.5	1442
1761–1800	16.7	970	27.2	1266	33.0	1097
1801–1840	10.3	573	17.7	815	23.7	616
1841–1880	5.8	572	9.6	467	12.6	572
1881–1910	15.1	119	23.3	232	24.4	119

Individual Studies: For the efficient display of the maximum detail, the data are reported in the following order: sample description, marriage period, percent of marriages linked to first births, number matched, percentage born under 6, $8\frac{1}{2}$, and 9 months.

Hingham, Massachusetts: reconstitution study (non-native-born excluded in the nineteenth century).

	%		%	%	%
1641–1660	n.a.	33	0.0	0.0	0.0
1661–1680	n.a.	80	5.0	11.2	11.2
1681–1700	n.a.	86	3.5	12.8	18.6
1701–1720	69	109	7.3	13.8	17.4
1721–1740	67	172	11.6	22.7	27.3
1741–1760	65	212	13.2	31.2	38.2
1761–1780	64	200	19.0	33.5	36.5
1781–1800	55	204	21.0	32.8	39.1
1801–1820	58	215	14.9	24.6	28.4
1821–1840	61	276	7.3	16.0	20.3
1841–1860	n.a.	235	4.7	8.5	10.2
1861–1880	n.a.	145	9.0	16.0	16.5

Watertown, Massachusetts: genealogy.

	%		%	%	%
–1660	n.a.	9	0.0	11.1	11.1
1661–1680	n.a.	35	0.0	8.6	8.6
1681–1700	n.a.	44	6.8	9.1	13.6
1701–1720	n.a.	76	7.9	19.8	25.1
1721–1740	n.a.	96	4.2	18.7	25.8
1741–1760	n.a.	110	10.9	21.8	23.6
1761–1780	n.a.	112	15.2	24.1	29.4
1781–1800	n.a.	111	15.3	26.1	32.5

Dedham, Massachusetts: vital record study.

	%		%	%	%
1662–1669	84	21	4.8	4.8	4.8
1671–1680	67	36	2.8	8.5	11.1
1760–1770	43	73	19.2	30.1	32.9

Topsfield, Massachusetts: vital record study.

	%		%	%	%
1660–1679	n.a.	13	7.7	7.7	7.7
1680–1699	n.a.	44	2.3	4.5	6.8
1738–1740	n.a.	25	12.0	24.0	24.0

Andover, Massachusetts: Greven, *Four Generations,* 113. (The figure for 1731–1749 comes from unpublished data kindly furnished by Greven.)

	%				%
1655–1674	41	21	—	—	0.0
1675–1699	55	64	—	—	12.5
1700–1730	41	115	—	—	11.5
1731–1749	8	29	—	—	17.3

Hollis, New Hampshire: vital record study.

	%		%	%	%
1741–1760	n.a.	39	2.6	12.8	17.9
1761–1780	n.a.	84	13.1	26.2	29.8
1781–1800	n.a.	57	10.5	31.6	35.1

Coventry, Connecticut: vital record study; Cheryl Krajcik, "The Trend in Premarital Pregnancy Ratios in Mansfield 1700–1849 and Coventry, 1711–1840," unpub. undergraduate sociology paper (University of Connecticut, 1972). We are indebted to the author and to Michael Gordon for this reference.

	%				%
1711–1740	n.a.	84	—	—	20.2
1741–1770	n.a.	179	—	—	23.5
1771–1800	n.a.	104	—	—	25.0
1801–1840	n.a.	43	—	—	4.6

Mansfield, Connecticut: vital record study; Phyllis Schneider, "Premarital Pregnancy in Mansfield, Connecticut, 1700–1849," unpub. undergraduate sociology paper (University of Connecticut, 1972.) We are indebted to the author and to Michael Gordon for this reference.

	%				%
1700–1739	n.a.	73	—	—	12.3
1740–1769	n.a.	265	—	—	19.2

	%				%
1770–1799	n.a.	296	—	—	20.6
1800–1819	n.a.	154	—	—	12.3
1820–1849	n.a.	88	—	—	5.7

Christ Church Parish, Middlesex County, Virginia: vital record study of marriages and baptisms.

	%		%	%	%
1720–1736	64	191	9.4	15.2	16.8

Kingston Parish, Gloucester County, Virginia: vital record study of marriages and baptisms, letters A–I.

	%		%	%	%
1749–1760	n.a.	36	2.8	13.9	13.9
1761–1770	n.a.	66	12.1	22.7	24.2
1771–1780	n.a.	63	12.7	25.4	30.1
1749–1780	64	165	10.3	21.8	24.2

Bergen, New Jersey: Reformed Dutch Church, vital record study of marriages and baptisms.

	%		%	%	%
1665–1680	64	18	0.0	5.6	5.6
1681–1700	55	31	19.4	19.4	19.4
1701–1720	47	16	18.7	25.0	25.0

New Paltz, New York: Reformed Dutch Church, vital record study of marriages and baptisms.

	%		%	%	%
1801–1803 ⎱ 1808–1812 ⎰	37	82	8.5	28.0	33.0

Boston, Massachusetts: vital record study.

	%		%	%	%
1651–1655	62	84	3.6	6.0	14.3
1690, 1692	52	39	0.0	17.9	23.1

Ipswich, Massachusetts: reconstitution; Susan Norton, "Population Growth in Colonial America: A Study of Ipswich, Massachusetts," *Population Studies,* XXV (1971), 636; (1650–1687 from our own study).

	%		%	%	%
–1700	n.a.	68	—	—	7.3
1701–1725	n.a.	143	—	—	5.6
1726–1750	n.a.	100	—	—	6.3
1650–1687	76	182	3.8	6.0	8.2

Bristol, Rhode Island: vital record study; John Demos, "Families in Colonial Bristol, Rhode Island: An Exercise in Historical Demography," *William and Mary Quarterly*, XXV (1968), 56.

	%				%
1680–1700	c.33	19	—	—	0.0
1700–1720	c.14	8	—	—	0.0
1720–1740	c.40	42	—	—	10.0
1740–1760	c.23	35	—	—	49.0
1760–1780	c.14	23	—	—	44.0

Salem, Massachusetts: reconstitution (based on unpublished data kindly supplied by James Somerville).

	%				%
1651–1670	n.a.	131	—	—	5.3
1671–1700	n.a.	123	—	—	8.2
1701–1730	n.a.	239	—	—	5.8
1731–1770	n.a.	176	—	—	12.5

Lexington, Massachusetts: vital record study.

	%		%	%	%
1854–1866	n.a.	56	3.6	3.6	12.5
1885–1895	n.a.	119	15.1	19.3	24.4

Willimantic, Connecticut: vital record study; John P. Sade, "Premarital Conception and Social Change in Willimantic, Connecticut, 1850–1910," unpub. undergraduate history paper (University of Connecticut, 1973). We are indebted to Sade for these data.

	%				%
1850, 1870	26	31	—	—	19.3
1890	48	41	—	—	31.7
1910	46	72	—	—	25.0

Washentaw County, Michigan: vital record study. Data for 1867–1870 and 1886–1890 include Ann Arbor and Ypsilanti only. Overall, 34.2% of marriages were linked to births (Samuel Gorsline and Harold Smith, "A Study of Premarital Pregnancy in Washentaw County, 1867–1900," unpub. undergraduate history paper [University of Michigan, 1972]). We are indebted to the authors and to Kenneth Lockridge for these data.)

			%		%
1867–1870 } 1876–1880 }	—	136	5.1	—	11.8
1886–1890 } 1896–1900 }	—	162	8.0	—	16.0

Utah County, Utah, vital record study. Percent born within 196 and 251 days of all first births coming in first 48 months of marriage; 1670 cases. Harold T. Christensen, "The Time between Marriage of Parents and the Birth of Their First Children: Utah County, Utah," *American Journal of Sociology,* XLIV (1939), 521.

	196 days (%)	251 days (%)
1905–1907	11.9	20.1
1913–1915	14.8	29.1
1921–1923	9.6	20.4
1929–1931	8.0	19.3

Tippecanoe County, Indiana: vital record study. Percent born within 196 and 251 days of all first births coming within the first 48 months of marriage. Harold T. Christensen and Olive P. Bowden, "Studies in Child-Spacing, II: The Time-Interval between Marriage of Parents and Birth of Their First Child, Tippecanoe County, Indiana," *Social Forces,* XXXI (1953), 348.

	%		196 days (%)	251 days (%)
1919–1921	39	487	11.9	19.6
1929–1931	28	352	14.8	28.2
1939–1941	37	692	9.8	20.0

Defiance County, Ohio: vital record study. Percent born within 196 days of marriage of those births coming within first 48 months of marriage. Harold T. Christensen, "Child-Spacing Analysis via Record Linkage: New Data plus a Summing Up from Earlier Reports," *Marriage and Family Living,* XXXV (1963), 275.

	%
1918–1922	10.9
1929–1931	14.1
1939–1942	6.9

Wood County, Ohio: vital record study; Samuel H. Lowrie, "Early Marriage, Premarital Pregnancy and Associated Factors," *Journal of Marriage and the Family,* XXVII (1965), 50.

		195 days (%)	265 days (%)
1957–1962	1,850	9.3	18.8

Massachusetts: vital record study. Elizabeth Murphy Whelan, "The Temporal Relationship of Marriage, Conception, and Birth in Massachusetts," *Demography,* IX (1972), 404.

	196 days (%)	265 days (%)
1966–1968	17.8	29.0

National surveys: See the discussion and data in Smith, "Dating of the American Sexual Revolution," 323–327.

APPENDIX II

I. *France* (within 7 complete months of marriage):

PLACE	SOURCE	PERIOD	RATIO (%)
A. *Before the second half of the eighteenth century:*			
Sainghin-en-Mélantois	5	1690–1769	15.2
Boulay	15	before 1749	9.1
Boulay (7 surrounding villages)	16	before 1760	8.6
Crulai	11	1674–1742	2.8
Meulan	19	1660–1739	7.7
Troarn	2	1661–1740	12.0
Tamerville	28	1624–1740	10.1
Tourouvre	4	before 1750	3.0
Bayeux	8	1600–1699	8.3
Lourmarin	24	1681–1750	15.1
Sérignan	22	1716–1750	20.0
Northwest France	13	1670–1769	5.8
Southwest France	14	1720–1769	6.4
Total of 13 samples			**9.5**
B. *Encompassing the mid-eighteenth century:*			
Saint-Méen	1	1720–1792	8.9
Bayeux	8	1700–1780	11.3
Blere	20	1677–1788	4.0
Bessin, three villages	8	1686–1792	17.1
Bas-Quercy	27	1700–1792	4.8
Saint-Agnan	17	1730–1792	9.1
Ingouville	26	1730–1770	14.7
Rumont	23	1720–1790	9.0
Tonnerrois	7	1720–1800	7.8
Villedieu-les Poëles	18	1711–1790	2.6
Saint-Pierre-Eglise	21	1657–1790	9.0
Total of 11 samples			**8.9**
C. *Second half of the eighteenth century:*			
Tamerville	28	1741–1790	20.0
Tourouvre	4	after 1750	10.0
Meulan	19	1740–1789	11.8
Lourmarin	24	1751–1800	18.1
Boulay	15	1750–1809	12.3
Boulay (7 surrounding villages)	16	1760–1799	7.4

PLACE	SOURCE	PERIOD	RATIO (%)
C. *Second half of the eighteenth century* (continued):			
Sainghin-en-Mélantois	5	1770–1799	15.8
Troarn	2	1741–1780	13.7
Saint-Auban	1	1749–1789	4.3
Bilhères	9	1740–1819	10.3
Ile-de-France	10	1740–1799	14.0
Sotteville-les-Rouen	12	1760–1790	30.2
Châtillon-sur-Seine	3	1772–1805	15.8
Southwest France	14	1770–1789	12.1
Serignan	22	1751–1792	40.9
Total of 15 samples			17.4
D. *First half of the nineteenth century:*			
Sainghin-en-Mélantois	5	1800–1849	50.5
Boulay	15	1810–	28.5
Boulay (7 surrounding villages)	16	1800–1862	18.3
Meulan	19	1790–1839	23.6
Bilhères	9	1820–1859	2.8
Lourmarin	24	1801–1830	23.9
Southwest France	14	1790–1819	11.2
Total of 7 samples			22.7

E. *Twentieth Century* (within 7 complete months per 100 marriages; sample of 240,000 families in the 1962 census):

France	6	1925–1929	12.3
		1930–1934	12.6
		1935–1939	12.6
		1940–1944	17.0
		1945–1949	17.2
		1950–1954	19.4
		1955–1959	19.5
		1960–1961	19.3

SOURCES

(1) Yves Blayo, "Trois paroisses d'Ille-et-Villaine," *Annales de démographic historique*, VI (1969), 206.

(2) Michel Bouvet and Pierre-Marie Bourdin, "A travers la Normandie des XVIIe et XVIIIe siècles," *Cahier des Annales de Normandie*, VI (1968), 191–202.

(3) Antoinette Chamoux and Cécile Dauphin, "La Contraception avant la Révolution francaise: L'exemple de Châtillon-sur-Seine," *Annales: E.S.C.*, XXIV (1969), 680.

(4) Hubert Charbonneau, *Tourouvre-au-Perche aux XVIIe et XVIIIe siècles: Etude de démographie historique* (Paris, 1969), 142.

(5) Raymond Deniel and Louis Henry, "La population d'un village du Nord de la France, Sainghin-en-Mélantois, de 1665 a 1851," *Population*, XX (1965), 581.

(6) Jean-Claude Deville, *Structure des Familles* (Paris, 1972), 91.

(7) D. Dinet, "Quatre paroisses du Tonnerrois," *Annales de démographie historique*, VI (1969), 80.

(8) Mohamed El Kordi, *Bayeux aux XVIIe et XVIIIe siècles: Contribution à l'histoire urbaine de la France* (Paris, 1970), 91.

(9) Michel Fresel-Lozey, *Histoire démographique d'un village en Béarn: Bilheres-d'Ossau* (Bordeaux, 1969), 142.

(10) Jean Ganiage, *Trois villages d'Ile-de-France au XVIIIe siècle* (Paris, 1963), 92.

(11) Etienne Gautier and Louis Henry, *La population de Crulai, paroisse normande* (Paris, 1958), 257–264.

(12) Pierre Girard, "Aperçus de la démographie de Sotteville-les-Rouen vers la fin du XVIIIe siècle," *Population*, XIV (1959), 494.

(13) Louis Henry, "Intervalle entre le mariage et la première naissance. Erreurs et corrections," *ibid.*, XXVIII (1973), 263.

(14) Louis Henry, "La fécondité des mariages dans le quart sud-ouest de la France de 1720 a 1829," *Annales: E.S.C.*, XXVII (1972), 998.

(15) J. Houdaille, "La population de Boulay (Moselle) avant 1850," *Population*, XXII (1967), 1075.

(16) Jacques Houdaille, "La population de sept villages des environs de Boulay (Moselle) aux XVIIIe et XIXe siècles," *ibid.*, XXVI (1971), 1063.

(17) Jacques Houdaille, "Un village du Morvan: Saint-Agnan," *ibid.*, XVI (1961), 304.

(18) Marie-Hélène Jouan, "Les originalités démographiques d'un bourg artisan normand au XVIIIe siècle: Villedieu-les-Poeles (1711–1790)," *Annales de démographie historique*, VI (1969), 107.

(19) Marcel Lachiver, *La population de Meulan du XVIIe au XIXe siècle (vers 1600–1850)* (Paris, 1969), 175.

(20) Marcel Lachiver, "Une étude et quelques equisses," *Annales de démographie historique*, VI (1969), 220.

(21) Jacques Lelong, "Saint-Pierre-Eglise, 1657–1790," *ibid.*, 131.

(22) Alain Molinier, "Une paroisse du Bas-Languedoc, Sérignan, 1650–1792," *Mémoires de la société archéologique de Montpellier*, XII (1968), 164.

(23) Patrice Robert, "Rumont (1720–1790)," *Annales de démographie historique*, VI (1969), 36.

(24) Thomas F. Sheppard, *Lourmarin in the Eighteenth Century: A Study of a French Village* (Baltimore, 1971), 41.

(25) Edward Shorter, "Female Emancipation, Birth Control, and Fertility

in European History," *American Historical Review*, LXXVIII (1973), 638–639.
(26) Michel Terrisse, "Un faubourg du Havre: Ingouville," *Population*, XVI (1961), 286.
(27) Pierre Valmary, *Familles paysannes au XVIIIe siècle en Bas-Quercy* (Paris, 1965), 93.
(28) Phillipe Wiel, "Une grosse paroisse du Cotentin aux XVIIe et XVIIIe siècles," *Annales de démographie historique*, VI (1969), 161.

II. *Australia* (nine-month standard):

MARRIAGE PERIOD	PREMARITAL PREGNANCY INDEX	
	% OF MARRIAGES	% OF FIRST BIRTHS
1911–1915	29.1	35.0
1916–1920	25.2	29.9
1921–1925	25.0	29.8
1926–1930	26.7	32.5
1931–1935	26.4	35.1
1936–1940	19.3	27.7
1941–1945	13.8	17.9
1946–1950	16.7	19.2
1951–1955	18.1	20.2
1956–1960	21.9	23.2
1961–1965	23.6	28.3

SOURCE: Basavarajappa, "Pre-marital Pregnancies," 143, Table A; 145, Table C.

III. *Great Britain*

A. *England:* non-random sample of printed parish records; marriages traced to birth or baptism within $8\frac{1}{2}$ months.

PERIOD	% MATCHED	NO. MATCHED	% PREGNANT
1500s	46	164	22.6
1600s	44	275	15.6
Late 1600s to 1749	50	199	17.6
1750 to c. 1800	50	713	40.2
1800 to 1819	43	388	40.2
1820 to 1843	45	95	46.3

SOURCE: P. E. H. Hair, "Bridal Pregnancy in Rural England in Earlier Centuries," *Population Studies*, XX (1966), 241–242.

III. (continued):

B. *England:* same description as above.

PERIOD	% MATCHED	NO. MATCHED	% PREGNANT
1500s	52	301	21.3
1600s	41	328	16.5
Late 1600s to 1749	42	79	16.5
1750 to 1836	48	288	43.4
1837 to 1887	52	50	40.0

SOURCE: P. E. H. Hair, "Bridal Pregnancy in Earlier Rural England Further Examined," *Population Studies*, XXIV (1970), 60.

C. *England and Wales:* To 1951, an interval of 8½ months was used; after 1951, 8 months.

MARRIAGE PERIOD	PREMARITAL PREGNANCY INDEX	
	% OF MARRIAGES	% OF LEGITIMATE FIRST BIRTHS
1941–1945	11.7	14.5
1946–1950	14.5	18.0
1951–1955	12.9	18.0
1956–1960	14.6	18.8
1961–1965	18.3	23.0
1966–1968	18.6	26.0

SOURCE: Great Britain, General Register Office, *The Registrar General's Statistical Review of England and Wales for the year 1968*, Part II (London, 1969), 192, Table UU; 12, Table Cl.

Marital Migration in Essex County, Massachusetts, in the Colonial and Early Federal Periods

SUSAN L. NORTON

Department of Anthropology,
University of Michigan

Marriage records from six towns in Essex County, Massachusetts, have been analyzed, to determine the extent of migration at the time of marriage. Records have been considered for three periods, 1701-1720, 1751-1770, and 1801-1820. Rates of endogamous marriage were determined, and the geographical extent of migration considered.

Records indicating the extent of migration at the time of marriage are available for many societies, covering a substantial chronological and geographical range. Marriage records are generally found as part of a more or less complete system of vital records kept by clerical or civil authorities or individual families; such records often indicate the town of residence of the partners to the marriage. In Essex County, Massachusetts, marriage records of this type have been kept by civil law since early in the seventeenth century; records from six towns in this county have been considered for six decades in the colonial and early federal periods. The analysis offered here is a fairly simple and straightforward tabulation of the data, suggesting that migration at the time of marriage was common enough to be an important social phenomenon. It seems reasonable to suggest that the further study of marital migration would make a considerable contribution to the more sophisticated study of some complex and important issues in demographic and social history. Migration at the time of marriage seems to be a significant proportion of general internal migration in both pre-industrial and modern societies, and so a study of marital migration would be useful for the consideration of this broader topic, which has been particularly difficult to approach in historical situations. Also, the study of marital migration may make a contribution to the study of social and familial history, by suggesting factors involved in the choice of a marriage partner and the formation of the family.

American social historians have long realized the importance of migration to the history of the country. American history could almost be written in terms of the several massive movements of people that have marked out distinctive periods: the original settlement of the land by those coming from Asia via the Bering Strait, the first European migration and colonization in the seventeenth and eighteenth centuries, the movement of Americans from East to West across the continent, the great, largely European immigrations to United States cities in the late nineteenth and early twentieth centuries, the dispersal of blacks from the South to urban areas of the North and Midwest, and the rural to urban migration that has marked industrialization whenever and wherever it has occurred. Other, less dramatic forms of migration have received less attention. For instance, we know virtually nothing about moderate and short distance migration within and between the American colonies in the seventeenth, eighteenth, and early nineteenth centuries. We probably have a better idea of the extent of migration between Boston and London in the eighteenth century than between Boston and Salem.

One obvious reason for the lack of a substantial body of information about internal migration in early America is the difficulty of the development of appropriate methods and sources for its study. Historical demography as a whole has really only in the last fifteen years or so made remarkable progress and begun to be a sophisticated discipline. Even within historical demography, the study of internal migration is particularly difficult and peculiarly underdeveloped. Because of the nature of the sources, usually parish registers or tax lists or some similarly local documents, it is often easier to obtain a fairly good estimate of fertility or even mortality within a town than it is to obtain reasonable information on the

Reprinted from *Journal of Marriage and the Family* XXXV, No. 3, 419–428. Copyright © 1973 by permission of the publisher.

147

migration of individuals to and from that town.

A number of ingenious approaches to migration have been suggested (see, for example, Buckatzsch, 1951), with the data from various European populations, but relatively few American studies have been attempted so far. Kenneth Lockridge (1966), in a study of Dedham, Massachusetts, estimated mobility by comparing names on a series of local tax lists; while such a method provides an estimate of the constancy of the local population, it gives no information on the locations involved in the migration. Another study, by Philip J. Greven, Jr. (1970), attempts particularly to detail the social and economic circumstances under which some residents left Andover, Massachusetts, for other areas, and to compare these men with those who remained. Greven's method, a sophisticated one involving family reconstitution and such legal documents as wills, yields great amounts of information about the population of the town, but it is not primarily a tool for the study of migration per se. There is a substantial literature on the spread of settlements in New England in the seventeenth and eighteenth centuries, which is an important contribution to the study of one aspect of internal migration (Leach, 1966).

This study admittedly focuses on a rather narrow range of migratory activity, migration at the time of marriage. However, sociologists have long known that a great deal of migration occurs at particular stages in the life cycle: at graduation from college, at marriage, or perhaps at retirement, for example, for modern Americans (see Shryock, 1964; Jansen, 1969; Lee, 1969). There is not a great deal of detailed information about migration in pre-industrial societies, but it seems reasonable to expect that marital migration would constitute a higher proportion of general internal migration than it does today (see Cavalli-Sforza, 1962a; Shryock, 1964). Even if this were not the case, we would expect that variations in marital migration over time and between areas would be meaningful as an index of migration in general, and as a specific case of an important type of movement.

Records of many towns in Massachusetts seem particularly promising for the study of marital migration. In this state records of vital events have been kept by civil authorities since 1639, in accordance with civil law (Cassedy, 1969:29-30). The marriage records include a notation of the town of residence or origin of the partners to the marriage. These records, along with those for births and deaths, have been collected for many towns, for the period to 1850, and have been published in a series by the New England Historical and Geneological Society. This publication makes the records easily accessible and practical to use for purposes (*e.g.,* scanning and sampling) for which consultation of the originals would undoubtedly be too laborious. Also, and of particular benefit to a study of migration, the records for the many towns have been published in a very similar format. This means that the same type of information can easily be gained for various towns.[1] In the present study, the marriage records for six towns in Essex County (Beverly, Boxford, Ipswich, including Hamilton and Essex in the later periods, Manchester, Topsfield, and Wenham) were considered (see NEHGS references), for three sample periods, 1701-1720, 1751-1770, and 1801-1820. The area is shown in Figure 1. The first period chosen appeared to be the earliest that might yield a reasonable sample size; the other intervals were chosen more or less arbitrarily, to study changes over time.

The published *Vital Records* include a variety of entries from town, church, and private sources; nearly all the information about marriages, however, comes from official town documents. The performance of marriage was, for the Puritans, a civil and not a religious function; the clergy were authorized after 1692 to perform the ceremony, but marriage remained in essence a civil act and was not regarded as a sacrament (Powell, 1928; Cassedy, 1969; Morgan, 1966; Howard, 1904). The records are thus civil rather than ecclesiastical, as they are in most European countries. The records extend from the founding of the towns (all in the present study were established in the seventeenth century) to 1850. The marriage records alone do not allow a distinction to be made between first and subsequent marriages, useful though this information would be. In some cases the brides are identified as widows, but this notation does not always seem to appear for such cases, and no indication is ever given of any previous marriage of the groom. Therefore, it was decided to treat all marriages together, including those known to be of widows. All of the marriages in each town in each sample period have been used.

The procedures for Puritan marriage were adopted from the medieval church, via the

---

[1] Since the records are arranged alphabetically by surname, it is even possible to trace individuals and families to various towns within Massachusetts. While laborious, this would be an almost invaluable and unique method for the study of migration in preindustrial societies.

SUSAN L. NORTON

Church of England, and involved five steps: a private engagement (*i.e., spousals de futuro*), the publication of the banns, the civil ceremony including the marriage vows, a social gathering to celebrate the marriage, and consummation of the union (Powell, 1928). All these were generally performed by the Puritans, but they laid extraordinary stress on the publication of intentions to marry, in an attempt to eliminate all sorts of irregular marriages. The custom of separate publication of intentions continued into the nineteenth century. In the *Vital Records* the details of the marriage ceremony itself are recorded if available, but a notation of the existence of the intention record is also made, and any additional information appearing on the intention record is included. In some cases we have records of the intention to marry, but no record of the marriage ceremony. In this study, these intentions have been disregarded, and only the record of the marriage ceremony, when available, has been used. It seems likely that the majority of couples for whom only intentions are recorded did in fact marry; at least in the early part of this period the betrothed couple was legally bound, and the union could not be casually broken, even before the marriage ceremony. The lack of a marriage record, then, would seem to be more often a failure of registration than of the ceremony itself. In a study involving individuals from different towns, however, it is impossible to use the available intention records. Intentions to marry are generally recorded in both towns if the partners are from different localities, so a single or even both intentions give no indication of the location of the marriage. In many cases we have both intentions, from different towns, but no record of marriage. All of the figures in this paper refer to the actual marriage ceremonies.

The lack of marriage records to follow some published intentions suggests a certain amount of underregistration of marriages. It is difficult to estimate the extent of this phenomenon. There is no obvious reason, however, for the unrecorded marriages to be systematically different from those registered, although there is of course always the possibility that some socioeconomic factors that influenced migration also affected the probability of registration. Marriage records do seem to be more complete than birth records, and are certainly more adequate than death records. By linking records from the six towns considered here, it is possible to get an estimate of the accuracy of registration in a given town of the marriages of the inhabitants of that town who married

outside the town; this information is included below in discussing such marriages.

The utility of the present records comes from their notation of place of residence of the marriage partners. Unfortunately, we have little idea of the precise meaning of these locations. It is not clear if they indicate the birthplaces of the marriage partners or, as might seem more likely, the most recent reasonably permanent residence. We cannot say how long a person would be required to live in a town before the records-keeper would see fit to classify him or her as a resident, although an estimate of at least several years would seem reasonable. If there were not a great amount of general migration internally, these residences (at least for first marriages) would most often be birthplaces. If a person moved before marriage, living in a town other than his or her birthplace and other than the town in which he or she was married, the use of these "intermediate" residences in the marriage records might give a sort of minimal estimate of migration between birth and marriage, since most often the move from the birthplace would be in the direction of the ultimate marriage location (see Cavalli-Sforza, 1962b, for a good discussion of the relationship between marital and general migration).

Also of interest, but not directly available from the marriage records, is the pattern of migration after marriage; we would like to know the relationship between the location of the ceremony itself and the ultimate residence of the couple. The majority of marriages occur in the town of the bride. This is a common phenomenon, seen in data from England and the United States for various time periods (Boyce *et al.,* 1968; Buckatzsch, 1951; Spuhler and Clark, 1961). This means that the location of the marriage ceremony itself is not an adequate indicator of the ultimate residence of the couple. Commonly it is assumed that the marriage occurs in the town of the bride and that the couple then assumes residence in the town of the groom, at least in England (Boyce *et al.,* 1968). For a sample of marriages of Ipswich residents who chose partners from elsewhere, in the colonial period, this assumption was tested by matching children to the couple, and noting whether the children were born in Ipswich or in the town of the other partner. The marriage could have occurred either in Ipswich or in the town of the other partner. Of the 115 couples whose residence could be unambiguously determined when they bore children, 36.5 per cent had settled where they had been married, while 77.4 per cent settled in the home town of the husband.[2] Since Ipswich was in many ways not a typical town with respect to marital migration, as will be seen below, these results should be interpreted carefully. However, they do suggest the degree of the accuracy of commonly held assumptions.

Even in the best of circumstances and with the best of records, the measurement of migration in any meaningful way is not a simple matter. The most basic general demographic measure, used in the study of fertility and mortality and many other phenomena, is the rate in which the number of cases of a certain event is related to the total population at risk of this event. Usually this calculation is more or less straightforward. In migration work, however, there is difficulty in determining the appropriate population at risk, the base population. For out-migration the base is the population of the town or area considered. For in-migration the base should be the population of the entire area from which migrants could come, but such a rate is very rarely used (Shryock *et al.*, 1971:619). More commonly, the number of in-migrants is related to the population of the town to which they have moved. In marital migration, there is a similar problem in determining the population to which migrants should be related. The data may be approached in two ways. Marriages in a town can be studied and divided into those involving both partners from the town (endogamous marriages) and those involving one or two nonresidents (exogamous marriages). Alternatively, the people from one town could be followed, to determine where they married. In either case, only the marriages of a given time period are used. The two approaches differ in geographical focus much as period and cohort fertility measures differ in time perspective. The first takes a cross-section of all marriages in a town, regardless of the origin of partners, in a way analagous to the period measure's delineation of births, regardless of age of mother; the second works from a point of origin and traces dispersal the way cohort fertility analysis works from a group of births and traces subsequent pregnancies within this group.

The first measurement of marital migration used here is of the former type; percentages of

various types of marriages in each town, for each period, are calculated. The results are presented in Table 1. Each marriage was classified as one of four types: an endogamous marriage in which both partners are from the town, a marriage in which the husband comes from another town and the wife is from the given town, a marriage in which the wife is from another town and the husband is from the given town, and a marriage in which neither partner is from the given town (the partners may be from the same or different towns).

A number of immediate observations may be made from this table. The percentage of endogamous marriages varies widely, from 35 to 91. Of the exogamous marriages, most result from the migration of men into the town to marry. The percentage of women coming to the town to marry is in almost all cases substantially smaller than the percentage of men, and is often less than one-fourth the figure for men; this would be expected from the custom of marriage in the bride's home town. The higher figures for men might also of course represent a real phenomenon and not just be an artifact of marriage customs; male servants, for example, might well be more mobile than female ones. The percentage of marriages in which both partners are from out of town is almost negligible, less than three per cent in most cases.

In looking at the results for the towns within a given time period, we find wide variation. For 1701-1720, for example, the endogamy rates, *i.e.*, percentages of endogamous marriages, range from 36 to 91 per cent, while in the last period the rates range from 36 to 79 per cent. We might reasonably expect to find that endogamy rates, as an indicator of marital migration, would vary with the population and/or geographical size of the town, as rates of internal mobility have been shown to vary with the size and shape of the unit considered (Shryock *et al.*, 1971:665). We know that mate selection is not a simple matter; the partner chosen must fulfill various personal and socioeconomic criteria. (For a discussion of the sociological theory of mate selection in relation to marital migration see Katz and Hill, 1962.) For instance, to the Puritans it was particularly important to marry within one's social class (Morgan, 1966). If one lives in a town of relatively few people, no or few partners of suitable sex, age, religion, socioeconomic status, etc., may be available, and one will have to look elsewhere. Sometimes this decision is consciously made. For example, Thomas Walley in 1675 decided to marry and planned on going to

[2] The marriages were a sample from two periods, 1691-1715 and 1766-1790. The couples were linked to children born later to them, either in Ipswich or in the town from which the other partner came, by reference to the *Vital Records* for the various towns. For the later period, these records have been supplemented by reference to the returns from the first federal census, conducted in 1790 (United States, 1909).

TABLE 1. RESIDENTIAL ORIGIN OF PARTNERS TO MARRIAGES IN SIX ESSEX COUNTY, MASSACHUSETTS, TOWNS

		Both from town	Husband migrant, wife from town	Wife migrant, husband from town	Both migrant	Total
Beverly						
1701-1720	N	135	40	22	35	232
	%	58.2	17.2	9.5	15.1	100.0
1751-1770	N	285	84	17	4	390
	%	73.1	21.5	4.4	1.0	100.0
1801-1820	N	516	97	34	6	653
	%	79.0	14.8	5.2	0.9	99.9
Total	N	936	221	73	45	1275
	%	73.4	17.3	5.7	3.5	99.9
Boxford						
1701-1720	N	37	6	3	0	46
	%	80.4	13.0	6.5	0.0	99.9
1751-1770	N	67	49	24	1	141
	%	47.5	34.8	17.0	0.7	100.0
1801-1820	N	68	63	27	2	160
	%	42.5	39.4	16.8	1.2	99.9
Total	N	172	118	54	3	347
	%	49.6	34.0	15.6	0.9	100.1
Ipswich						
1701-1720	N	114	18	9	2	143
	%	79.7	12.6	6.3	1.4	100.0
1751-1770	N	339	107	24	1	471
	%	72.0	22.7	5.1	0.2	100.0
1801-1820	N	439	179	19	26	663
	%	66.2	27.0	2.9	3.9	100.0
Total	N	892	304	52	29	1247
	%	69.8	23.8	4.1	2.3	100.0
Manchester						
1701-1720	N	21	1	1	0	23
	%	91.3	4.4	4.4	0.0	100.1
1751-1770	N	104	26	4	0	134
	%	77.6	19.4	3.0	0.0	100.0
1801-1820	N	116	25	8	6	152
	%	74.8	16.1	5.2	3.9	100.0
Total	N	241	52	13	6	312
	%	77.2	16.7	4.2	1.9	100.0
Topsfield						
1701-1720	N	55	31	9	3	98
	%	56.1	31.6	9.2	3.1	100.0
1751-1770	N	88	43	9	1	141
	%	62.4	30.5	6.4	0.7	100.0
1801-1820	N	73	24	5	2	104
	%	70.2	23.1	4.8	1.9	100.0
Total	N	216	98	23	6	343
	%	63.0	28.6	6.7	1.8	100.1
Wenham						
1701-1720	N	4	7	0	0	11
	%	36.4	63.6	0.0	0.0	100.0
1751-1770	N	49	62	11	3	125
	%	39.2	49.6	8.8	2.4	100.0
1801-1820	N	19	29	5	1	54
	%	35.2	53.7	9.3	1.8	100.0
Total	N	72	98	16	4	190
	%	37.9	51.6	8.4	2.1	100.0

Boston to find a wife. Shortly after he had made this decision, he wrote in a letter, "As for my Journey to Boston, it is spoiled. god [sic] hath sent me a wife home to me and saved m[e] the labor of a tediouse Journey" (Morgan, 1966:54-55).

If the town is geographically small, or of a certain shape, one may in the course of one's normal activities be more inclined to go outside one's town to neighboring towns, so higher migration will result. In this study, no attempt has been made to relate endogamy rates to geographical size or shape of towns. The population size of the towns, however, can be briefly considered.

One of the problems of historical demography is that there are few readily available data to use; almost every piece of information must be developed specifically for use in each particular study. For example, determining the population of the towns accurately is not, except in the last period, a matter of looking up the census figures, as it would probably be for a modern population. For the earlier two periods, it would be unnecessarily laborious for our purposes to attempt to obtain the best possible estimate of the population at, say, the midpoint of the periods considered. We will use two simple sources as they stand, the militia list of 1690 (Greene and Harrington, 1932:20) and the state census of 1765 (Benton, 1905).

For the first period we have only the militia list of 1690, reporting the number of men from each town eligible for militia service. There are obvious problems in determining the relationship between the size of the militia and the general population, and there is no report for Manchester, town with the highest endogamy rate. There is no apparent connection between the five other militia reports and the endogamy rates for these towns. For example, the next two highest endogamy rates belong to the largest and smallest towns.

For 1765 (see Table 2) there is a clearer relationship between size of town and endogamy rate, with the two largest towns having the highest rates and the smallest town having the lowest rate. The rates, however, do not vary directly with population size, and again Manchester seems to have an extraordinarily high percentage of endogamous marriages. It should be noted that the 1765 census was probably not very accurate, as it was taken against the will of most of the population by a colonial administration (Benton, 1905), and the differential accuracy of the reports from the various towns could affect an analysis such as the one considered here.

For the last period, the population data are best, from the United States Censuses. The censuses of 1810 and 1820 yield similar results, as does the use of the population of marriageable age (over 16) rather than the total population. Again, the larger towns tend to have the higher endogamy rates, although the relationship is far from perfect.

TABLE 2. RELATIONSHIP BETWEEN ENDOGAMY RATE AND POPULATION SIZE IN SIX ESSEX COUNTY, MASSACHUSETTS, TOWNS

	Endogamy, 1751-1770	1765 Census, Total Whites	
	%	N	
Beverly	73.1	2091	
Boxford	47.5	841	
Ipswich	72.0	3670	
Manchester	77.6	715	
Topsfield	62.4	703	
Wenham	39.2	531	
	Endogamy 1801-1820	1810 Census, Total Whites	1820 Census, Total Whites
	%	N	N
Beverly	79.0	4547	4269
Boxford	42.5	879	906
Ipswich*	66.2	4278	4406
Manchester	76.3	1135	1198
Topsfield	70.2	808	862
Wenham	35.2	549	568

Sources: Benton (1905); United States Census Office (1811, 1821).
*The town of Ipswich here includes Essex and Hamilton, formerly parts of Ipswich, which have been treated as parts of Ipswich throughout.

It is also possible that endogamy rates may be influenced not only by the population of the town, but also by the availability of mates outside the town, *i.e.,* by the population of nearby towns. In an attempt to study this, the endogamy rates for each town were related to the population within a five-mile radius of the center of the town. This is a fairly crude measure whose use was necessitated by the population data. Since population figures are available only for whole towns, any analysis must consider towns as points, and no attempt can be made to consider the true distribution of population within the area. The association between the endogamy rates of the towns and the population within a five-mile radius of them is no more satisfactory than the association using population sizes for the single towns. Of course with a sample of only six towns and with population data only by large units (towns), it would be difficult to demonstrate an association between endogamy rates and population size unless it were a very strong one. More sophisticated models of population and distance relationships may be useful to consider when more detailed data are available (see for instance the theoretical approaches discussed in Haggett, 1965:31-60, and the data and sociological theory offered in Katz and Hill, 1962:53-56).

It is important to note that any relationship between endogamy rates and population size seems to rest on a consideration of the relative sizes of towns in the area, not on absolute population size. If the latter were true, we would expect more dramatic changes in endogamy rates over the full period studied, as the population of all the towns rose considerably in this period. Population size is not the only variable to be considered; high rates in the first period probably resulted from the relative geographical and perhaps social isolation of the towns. The improvement of transportation networks in time has been shown to have a dramatic effect on marital migration (see Boyce *et al.,* 1968, on the consequences of the introduction of the railroad in England; note also the secular changes over the twentieth century in Spuhler and Clark, 1961).

In variation over time within each town there is little consistent pattern. Considering how widely endogamy rates vary between towns in each period, there seems a surprising constancy of rates for each town. Wenham, for instance, maintained an endogamy rate of between 35 and 40 per cent for all periods. The higher rates varied more, but still didn't fluctuate wildly. Ipswich, for instance, varied between 66 and 80 per cent. Beverly ranged from 58 to 79 per cent, and the first rate is strongly affected by the relatively large number of marriages in Beverly in that period in which both partners came from out of town. Boxford and Manchester had extraordinarily high endogamy rates in the first period, but the rates were relatively constant over the last two periods. Rates for Topsfield rose consistently over the three periods.

To the degree that the rates for a town remain constant over time, we can suggest that factors influencing such rates also remained more or less constant. It might be plausible to suggest for example that geographical position might be one determinant. Also, while the population of the entire area grew considerably over the period considered, the populations of the various towns did not change dramatically relative to each other, at least in rank order.

Several other minor observations may be made from Table 1. Women seem to have accounted for more migration in most towns in the first period than in the latter two. Boxford has the highest proportion of exogamous marriages due to the migration of women into the town. The extraordinarily high number of marriages in Beverly in 1701-1720 in which both partners were from out of town is not explained, although almost one-third of these were of couples in which both partners were from Manchester.

It is possible to compare these endogamy rates from Essex County with other roughly contemporaneous rates from Massachusetts. Swedlund (1971) reported rates for Deerfield, a more western town, in the Connecticut River Valley. For the period we have considered, the rates range from 89 to 38 per cent. There seems to be a rather sharp drop in the rates about 1785. Rates before that are generally above 70, and after that they are below 50. Greven (1970:211) has published an analysis of marriages in Andover, not far from the area we have considered, for 1650-1749. The endogamy rates are 48.1 per cent, 66.5 per cent, and 56.0 per cent, respectively, for marriages in the periods 1650-1699, 1700-1719, and 1720-1749. These rates are within the range of those found in this study. Surprisingly, Greven finds that substantially more women than men migrated to marry in Andover in the first two periods; in the third period about twice as many men as women came to marry in Andover. Greven notes this last as a period of high out-migration of young males from Andover, and he suggests that they are being replaced by men from other towns. Greven's seventeenth-century figures are particularly interesting in view of the observation in the six towns of this study that female migration seemed to be more significant in the first period than it later was. Perhaps in the earlier periods of settlement there was a greater tendency for the marriage to take place in the town of the groom, if the couple was going to settle there. This plan would generally be less expensive, by involving less travel, than marriage in the bride's town; it would be fascinating to know if various patterns of marriage and migration were differential by socioeconomic status, as one might expect.

Endogamy rates and other considerations of marriages within a town are of course not the only possible approaches to marital migration. Since the records of a town usually include records of marriages of residents that occurred outside the town, it would theoretically be possible to analyze out-migration from the town to marry, as well as in-migration. The problem with this approach is that the records of such marriages outside the town are patently incomplete. In this study it was possible to cross-match records from the six towns to determine accuracy of registration of such marriages. The results are presented in Table 3. From the table, it is clear that registration was most complete between 1751 and 1770, when about 80 per cent of the marriages in the five other towns were properly recorded in the towns from which the partners came. More than 50 per cent of such records were made in the first period. From 1801 to 1820, registration of out-of-town marriages is no longer

attempted, and only intentions for such marriages are recorded. In this study, marriages involving the six towns can be assigned back to the town of residence of the partner(s), regardless of the lack of registration in that town, but this procedure gives only a partial picture of marital migration, since it deals with marriages occurring in only a few of the towns to which partners might have migrated. The registration problem with this approach of course affects the studies of men from a town more than studies of women, since more men than women would probably marry out of town. In view of these difficulties, the analysis of marriages in this format is difficult to interpret, and is not presented.

Endogamy rates and rates for various types of exogamous marriages clearly give an indication of the amount of marital migration, but a more detailed analysis is required to determine the geographical range of such migration. In this study, for exogamous marriages, distances were determined between the residence of the migrant partner and the location of the marriage. The analysis was conducted separately for men and women, for each town and period. Distances were measured on standard maps, as a straight line between two points. Undoubtedly, there is a considerable margin of error in these distances, partly because not all locations mentioned could be identified on a single map. Moreover, there is some ambiguity in determining locations when only the name of the town, not the state, is given, as often several New England states have same-named towns. In this case, it was assumed that the town was in

TABLE 3. REGISTRATION OF MARRIAGE IN TOWN OF RESIDENCE OF MIGRANT MARRIAGE PARTNERS; COMBINED FIGURES FOR SIX TOWNS IN ESSEX COUNTY, MASSACHUSETTS

		1701-1720	1751-1770	1801-1820	Total
Migrant husband					
Intention only recorded	N	6	19	91	116
	%	14.0	13.1	87.5	39.7
Marriage recorded	N	33	117	0	150
	%	76.7	80.7	0.0	51.4
No record	N	4	9	13	26
	%	9.3	6.2	12.5	8.9
Total	N	43	145	104	292
	%	100.0	100.0	100.0	100.0
Migrant wife					
Intention only recorded	N	6	6	40	52
	%	18.8	14.6	76.9	41.6
Marriage recorded	N	22	33	0	55
	%	68.8	80.5	0.0	44.0
No record	N	4	2	12	18
	%	12.5	4.9	23.1	14.4
Total	N	32	41	52	125
	%	100.1	100.0	100.0	100.0

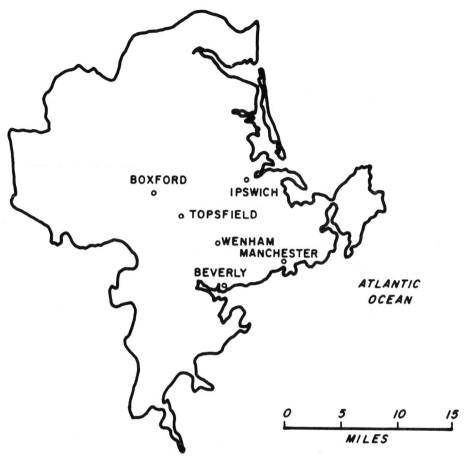

Massachusetts or, failing that, the closest town of that name from another state was used. To exclude such cases would have introduced a downward bias into the results, for such locations would generally be further away than the nearby towns which could be readily identified. Finally, a very few locations could not be found, and were excluded, probably introducing a slight downward bias.

The distributions of the migration distances have a distinctive shape, and a characteristic one is given in Figure 2. Most migrations are over quite short distances (say, under ten miles), but, if there are very many migrants at all, a few will be from quite far away. Thus, the mode of the distribution is at a fairly low value, but there is a long tail to the right. In such a situation, the mean is greater than the median value, and the standard deviation or variance may be quite large.

Table 4 presents the means, standard deviations, and number of cases for migrating men and women. The most remarkable observation is that the distances travelled by men are much greater than those covered by women. Thus, women not only marry less often away from their home towns, but when they do it is over shorter distances. These facts may not be unrelated; conceivably a marriage ceremony might be more likely to take place in the man's home if the woman's home were not too far away. There is really no evidence on this point. Beyond this observation, there is even less consistency of pattern in these distributions than there is in the exogamy rates. For men, mean distances vary from below 8 to almost 30

FIGURE 2. DISTRIBUTION OF DISTANCES OF MARITAL MIGRATIONS OF MEN IN BEVERLY, 1751-1770.

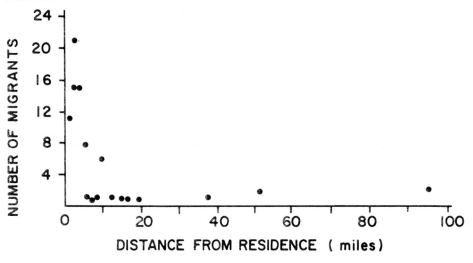

TABLE 4. MEANS AND STANDARD DEVIATIONS (IN MILES) OF DISTANCES TRAVELLED BY MIGRANTS MARRYING IN SIX ESSEX COUNTY, MASSACHUSETTS, TOWNS

| | 1701-1720 | | 1751-1770 | | 1801-1820 | |
	Men	Women	Men	Women	Men	Women
Beverly						
Mean	7.97	4.83	7.80	5.43	29.80	6.69
S.D.	7.64	2.72	15.81	3.21	64.58	6.70
N	75	57	88	21	102	40
Boxford						
Mean	22.28	9.77	12.98	11.04	23.55	11.72
S.D.	27.75	1.66	14.06	8.18	40.10	10.68
N	6	3	50	25	64	29
Ipswich						
Mean	28.23	15.38	26.82	11.59	22.81	10.18
S.D.	39.06	21.82	87.10	12.12	28.92	15.83
N	20	11	107	25	203	45
Manchester						
Mean	6.09	7.39	11.62	6.08	25.55	6.06
S.D.	---	---	17.07	0.87	38.56	0.77
N	1	1	26	4	31	14
Topsfield						
Mean	23.84	6.66	7.84	5.09	14.58	5.13
S.D.	27.36	2.99	9.06	5.74	26.97	1.88
N	32	11	44	10	25	7
Wenham						
Mean	10.47	---	8.73	5.71	19.70	5.69
S.D.	10.71	---	10.65	5.13	31.09	2.95
N	7	0	65	14	30	6

miles. Within a town, over different periods, only Ipswich shows a fair degree of consistency; rates for the other towns vary considerably from period to period. For all towns but Ipswich, the lowest mean values are for the 1751-1770 period. Men are migrating to Ipswich in this period from a greater distance than to any other town and, as the high standard deviation shows, from an extreme range of distances. In the first period, there are three towns with means over 20 miles—Boxford, Ipswich, and Topsfield—and two nearer 10—Beverly and Wenham. (Manchester has only one male migrant in this period.) In the last period, means rise dramatically for every town except Ipswich, which has a high mean for the middle period. Standard deviations, not surprisingly, rise too, reflecting the range of distances from which migrants are now coming.

The observed pattern of chronological change suggests perhaps two different sorts of marital migration for men. In the first period, communities were relatively small. People tried to marry within the town (rates of endogamy are high), but if they had to marry elsewhere, they might have to travel a considerable distance in the sparsely-settled country to find a mate. By the nineteenth century, the towns were larger, and endogamy was still the norm for most towns. Probably there was, however, by this time a more general movement of goods and people in the area, as transportation improved and the commercial nexus of a growing industrialization emerged. In the middle period there may have been less of the general commerce than in the early nineteenth century, but the country was more populated than in the early eighteenth century, so it might have been less necessary to travel long distances to find suitable mates. It is also possible that the French and Indian War affected marital migration; a change in marital patterns after the First and Second World Wars was seen in Italy, France, and the United States (see "Discussion"

following Boyce et al., 1968:318-319; Spuhler and Clark, 1961:226-227).

For women, mean distances range from almost 5 to about 15 miles. The means for women vary less sharply from period to period for a single town than do the men's, and they do not follow the same pattern. The groups, however, are small, and random fluctuations may be involved. Two towns, Beverly and Boxford, show a gradual increase in each of the periods, while the other four have their highest means in the first period (or, in the case of Manchester and Wenham, second period) and lowest in the last. Differentials between the sexes are lowest in the middle period, when men's distances were shortest. Women consistently travelled further into Boxford and Ipswich than the other towns.

There is no apparent connection between endogamy rates for a town and the mean distance of either men or women migrating to marry in the town.

The advantage of using the median rather than the mean in comparing distributions is that extreme values are not considered. The disadvantage in using this measure in this situation would seem to be that the median is almost always chosen from a small number of possible values, the distances from the given town to the several closest towns. Since the distance to nearby towns varies for each town, the exact value of the median would seem to be almost as much a function of geography as of migration, and comparisons between towns may be risky because of this. The medians are presented in Table 5. The range of values, from 3.0 to 12.3 miles, is fairly small. As with the means, women's medians are smaller than men's for almost all groups. It is interesting to note that in general the lowest values for both men and women are found in the 1751-1770 period. This suggests a closer relationship between the distances travelled by men and women than was seen in the analysis based on the means. The

TABLE 5. MEDIANS (IN MILES) OF DISTANCES TRAVELLED BY MIGRANTS MARRYING IN SIX ESSEX COUNTY, MASSACHUSETTS, TOWNS*

	1701-1720		1751-1770		1801-1820	
	Men	Women	Men	Women	Men	Women
Beverly	5.65	3.70	3.04	3.70	5.65	4.68
Boxford	10.21	10.00	7.83	7.39	10.32	8.00
Ipswich	12.38	6.52	9.57	7.83	9.57	6.52
Manchester	---	---	6.09	5.65	7.83	5.65
Topsfield	10.22	6.52	5.87	3.70	6.52	4.35
Wenham	5.87	---	5.87	3.70	5.87	4.78

*Sample sizes are the same as in Table 4.

lowest medians for all periods are found in Beverly, although in the last period the mean was very high. This, along with the high standard deviation, indicates that some very long-distance movers entered Beverly at that time, while most marriages were still contracted over a small area.

Comparative data on distances of marriage migration are available for areas of England and Italy since the seventeenth century. The English data show consistently lower means than the Massachusetts sample; the mean marriage distance is roughly from four to eight miles between 1601 and 1850 (Boyce *et al.*, 1968). Similarly, a sample of Italian mountain villages studied for a period of 300 years indicates that the mean distance over which migrating mates travelled was only about five miles (Cavalli-Sforza, 1957).

No detailed analysis of the geographical pattern of migration has been attempted, to determine directions from which migrants came. A consideration of population density and topography would have to be included. However, a strong tendency is readily apparent to draw migrants from the north, from New Hampshire and Maine. This is not surprising since Essex County is near these states, and the marked sparsity of population in them may have led many people to go south to marry. Areas to the south and southwest of Essex County were far more densely settled. There is a fair amount of movement from the Boston area, but a relative paucity of migrants from other areas to the south and west.

CONCLUSION

This study has demonstrated the possibility of obtaining, fairly simply, a great deal of detailed information about migration in early Massachusetts. It has demonstrated that many (in some towns, most) marriages involved one or both partners who had come from another town; while most of this migration was over distances of less than 10 miles, a significant proportion involved journeys of 50 to 100 miles. But we cannot stop with the simple observation that there was apparently quite a lot of geographical mobility. To provide the maximum yield for social historians, the study of marital migration should be integrated into the consideration of more general social questions. Greven, for example, demonstrated the utility of examining migration in studying the histories of families in Andover; Harris (1969) suggested that internal migration must be considered in studies of social origins of American leaders. Certainly geographical and social mobil-

ity are related, and internal migration is also an important question for economic historians. In more detailed and revealing studies of marital migration, it should be possible to consider for example age, social class, wealth, and occupational differentials. The study of all sorts of marital mobility, including but not limited to geographical mobility, is one possible approach to the general study of mobility in American society, and this remains an important task for social historians.

REFERENCES

Benton, J. H.
  1905 Early Census Making in Massachusetts, 1643-1763, with a Reproduction of the Lost Census of 1765. Boston:Charles E. Goodspeed.
Boyce, A. J., C. F. Küchemann, and G. A. Harrison
  1968 "The reconstruction of historical movement patterns." Pp. 303-319 in E. D. Acheson (ed.), Record Linkage in Medicine. Edinburgh:E. and S. Livingstone.
Buckatzsch, E. J.
  1951 "The constancy of local populations and migration in England before 1800." Population Studies 5 (July:62-69).
Cassedy, James H.
  1969 Demography in Early America. Cambridge: Harvard University Press.
Cavalli-Sforza, L. L.
  1957 "Some notes on the breeding patterns of human populations." Acta Genetica et Statistica Medica 6:395-399.
  1962a "Demographic attacks on genetic problems: some possibilities and results." Pp. 221-231 in The Use of Vital and Health Statistics for Genetic and Radiation Studies. New York: United Nations.
  1962b "The distribution of migration distances: models, and applications to genetics." Pp. 139-158 in J. Sutter (ed.), Les déplacements humains, Entretiens de Monaco en Sciences Humaines. No place.
Greene, E. B. and V. D. Harrington
  1932 American Population before the Federal Census of 1790. New York:Columbia University Press.
Greven, Philip J., Jr.
  1970 Four Generations: Population, Land and Family in Colonial Andover, Mass. Ithaca: Cornell University Press.
Haggett, Peter
  1965 Locational Analysis in Human Geography. London:Edward Arnold.
Harris, P. M. G.
  1969 "The social origins of American leaders: the demographic foundations." Perspectives in American History 3:157-344.
Howard, G. F.
  1904 A History of Matrimonial Institutions. Chicago:University of Chicago Press.

Jansen, Clifford
  1969 "Some sociological aspects of migration."
        Pp. 60-73 in J. A. Jackson (ed.), Migration.
        Cambridge:University Press.
Katz, Alvin M. and Reuben Hill
  1962 "Residential propinquity and marital selec-
        tion: a review of theory, method, and fact."
        Pp. 41-60 in J. Sutter (ed.), Les déplace-
        ments humains, Entretiens de Monaco en
        Sciences Humaines.
Leach, Douglas Edward
  1966 The Northern Colonial Frontier 1607-1763.
        New York:Holt, Rinehart and Winston.
Lee, Everett S.
  1969 "A theory of migration." Pp. 282-297 in J.
        A. Jackson (ed.), Migration. Cambridge:Uni-
        versity Press.
Lockridge, Kenneth
  1966 "The population of Dedham, Massachusetts,
        1536-1736." Economic History Review 19
        (August):318-344.
Morgan, Edmund S.
  1966 The Puritan Family. New York:Harper and
        Row.
New England Historical and Geneological Society
  1903a Vital Records of Manchester, Massachusetts.
         Salem:Essex Institute.
  1903b Vital Records of Topsfield, Massachusetts.
         Topsfield:Topsfield Historical Society.
  1904   Vital Records of Wenham, Massachusetts.
         Salem:Essex Institue.
  1905   Vital Records of Boxford, Massachusetts.
         Topsfield:Topsfield Historical Society.
  1906   Vital Records of Beverly, Massachusetts.
         Topsfield:Topsfield Historical Society.
  1908a Vital Records of Essex, Massachusetts.
         Salem:Essex Institute.

  1908b Vital Records of Hamilton, Massachusetts.
         Salem:Essex Institute.
  1910   Vital Records of Ipswich, Massachusetts.
         Salem:Essex Institute.
Powell, Chilton L.
  1928 "Marriage in early New England." New
        England Quarterly 1 (July):323-334.
Shryock, Henry S., Jr.
  1964 Population Mobility within the United
        States. Chicago: Universtiy of Chicago,
        Community and Family Study Center.
Shryock, Henry S., Jr., Jacob S. Siegel, and Associates
  1971 The Methods and Materials of Demography.
        Washington:Government Printing Office.
Spuhler, J. N. and P. J. Clark
  1961 "Migration into the human breeding popula-
        tion of Ann Arbor, Michigan, 1900-1951."
        Human Biology 33 (September):223-236.
Swedlund, Alan C.
  1971 The Genetical Structure of an Historical
        Population: A Study of Marriage and Fertil-
        ity in Old Deerfield, Massachusetts. Re-
        search Reports Number 7, Department of
        Anthropology, University of Massachusetts,
        Amherst.

United States Census Office
  1811 Aggregate Amount of Persons within the
        United States in the Year 1810. Washington.
  1821 Census for 1820. Washington:Gales and
        Seaton.

United States, Bureau of the Census
  1909 Heads of Families at the First Census of the
        United States Taken in the Year 1790:
        Massachusetts. Washington:Government
        Printing Office.

Parental Power and Marriage Patterns: An Analysis of Historical Trends in Hingham, Massachusetts

DANIEL SCOTT SMITH
Department of History,
University of Connecticut, Storrs

Few of the changes in the family suggested by modernization theory have been empirically documented with historical evidence. Through a reconstitution analysis of the families of Hingham, Massachusetts, from the mid-seventeenth through the mid-nineteenth century, important changes, consistent with theoretical expectations, in the extent of parental control over marriage formation are documented and analyzed. Changes are apparent in measures which reflect the structuring of marriage on both the individual and social level. The shift from the centrality of the family of orientation to the dominance of the family of procreation was not linear but concentrated in the late eighteenth and early nineteenth centuries.

Perhaps the central conceptual issue in the sociology of the family is the relationship of modernization to family structure. Paradoxically the theoretical significance of this problem has not engendered an empirical preoccupation with the details of the transition from "traditional" to "modern" family structure. For sociologists, as Abrams (1972:28) puts it, "the point after all was not to know the past but to establish an idea of the past which could be used as a comparative base for the understanding of the present." While historians often implicitly use a conception of the modern family as a baseline for their researches into the past, formally at least they attempt to relate the family to the culture and other institutions of an historical period. Only rarely have either group of scholars actually measured the dimensions of change by analyzing data over a long time interval. Thus the element of change in family structure has been more usually assumed or inferred from casual comparisons of past and present than consciously measured and analyzed. A great chasm persists between the theoretical perspective on the family and moderization (see Smelser, 1966:115-117, for a concise summary) and a limited body of empirical evidence more often qualifying or denying these relationships (for example, Furstenberg, 1966; Lantz et al., 1968; and Laslett and Wall, 1972) than supporting or extending them.

The problem of the connections between modernization and family structure may be conveniently divided into three analytically

distinct areas—the relevance of the family for the structuring of other institutions, the role of the family in shaping individual lives, and finally the significance to the individual of the family he is born into (family of orientation) for the one he creates by marriage (family of procreation). Since the historical trends in the first two areas have presumably seemed so obvious, systematic empirical data have not been collected and analyzed to establish the precise dimensions and timing of change. In the first instance the modern family is not as quantitatively important for the organization of other structures—economic, political, and social.[1] What influence the modern family

[1] While it is undoubtedly true, for example, that more members of the Virginia House of Burgesses in 1773 had fathers who served in that body than United States Congressmen of 1973 whose fathers were also congressmen, no quantitative evidence exists to determine the magnitude of these changes. Perhaps more importantly, it is not certain how family status "worked" to get men into office in the colonial period—whether through deference to the family name or through arrangement by the class of elite families. Nor has the relative importance of wealth and family status in political recruitment been determined. Determination of the timing of the shift away from family domination of office would be of considerable historical importance. Trends in this area are not necessarily linear. Harvard students, for example, were ranked by their ability in the seventeenth century, but their family status counted in the eighteenth (Shipton, 1954). The fathers of 16 per cent of the U.S. Senators of 1820 had held political office, 8 per cent in 1860, 12 per cent in 1900 and 19 per cent in 1940 (Hoogenbloom, 1968:60). Although the numbers involved are very small to be sure, perhaps the final phase of the system in which office was a concomitant of social prestige and the emergence of politics as a specialized profession is reflected in this cycle. In the

Reprinted from *Journal of Marriage and the Family* XXXV, No. 3, 406–418. Copyright © 1973 by permission of the publisher.

exerts in these areas is indirect, exerted either through early socialization and personality formation or mediated by intervening institutions. Male occupational status in modern America, for example, is related to the family of orientation mainly through the provision of education, not by direct parental placement. Few families today control jobs which can be given to their children (Blau and Duncan, 1967:131-133). Having less of an instrumental role, the family is now a specialized institution providing nurture and affection for both children and adults. Perhaps the best historical study of the transformation in this second area is the impressionistic classic of Aries (1962) which delineates the social separation of the family from the community and the emergence of the psychological centrality of the child in the conjugal family. Since this interpretation now rests on changes in ideals and lacks adequate behavioral support, more historical analysis is required to determine the extent of this shift. It is possible, for example, that emotional or expressive ties between parents and children have been essentially invariant over the course of American history. These affective relationships may appear to have increased historically only because of the separation of instrumental activities from the family.

Although not necessarily more significant than the changes in the first two areas, the relationship between the family of orientation and the family of procreation has often been considered to be the central issue in the modernization of the family. Davis (1949:414-418), in fact, has argued that this distinction is the most adequate key to understanding other variations in family structure. If the family newly created by marriage is dominated by pre-existing families of birth, then households are more likely to be extended in structure, marriages are more likely to be arranged and will take place at earlier ages, intrafamilial relationships will tend to be authoritarian, etc. Despite Parsons later disclaimer that his well-known analysis (Parsons, 1943) was mainly concerned with the isolation of the family from other social structures and his acceptance of the Litwack-Seeman critique as complementary not contradictory, he was not deterred from elaborating his earlier argument. The substance of the debate on extended

kinship in modern American society continues precisely on the quantity and nature of interaction between married couples and their parents (Parson, 1965). Historians as well have concentrated on this question, usually employing the classic extended-nuclear dichotomy to summarize their findings. Greven (1970) has argued that by withholding land fathers in seventeenth century Andover, Massachusetts, were able to exercise considerable power over their adult sons. Once land had become relatively scarce in the early eighteenth century, they found it more difficult or less desirable to do so. More recently an entire volume of papers has been devoted to crushing the proposition that extended *households* ever were a significant element in western society, at least since the middle ages (Laslett and Wall, 1972).[2]

THE HISTORICAL PROBLEM

In a decade review of research on modern American kinship, Adams (1970) has suggested that the most recent work is moving beyond debate and description to the more significant tasks of specification, interrelation, and comparison. This change of emphasis is as important for historical as for contemporary studies, even though an adequate, empirically based, systematic description of the historical evolution of the relationship between the family of orientation and the family of procreation does not presently exist. Despite the fact that it is always easier to decry than to remedy scholarly failures, this absence should be a challenge rather than an obstacle for historians. Much of the critical evidence regarding the extent and kind of interaction between parents and adult children is, of course, unwritten. Despite their interest in the same substantive issues, historians inevitably are forced to employ different methods than sociologists. Yet there are serious problems in the interpretation of historical evidence on the family. While a body of literary comment on ideal family relationships does exist, it becomes progressively more biased toward higher social strata as one moves farther back into the past (Berkner, 1973). Furthermore, the relating of historical information about ideals to actual behavior is not easily

---

[2] The relevance of household composition data to the nuclear-extended dichotomy pertains only to three-generation households. Although servants were an important addition to pre-industrial western households and lodgers to nineteenth century urban-industrial households, these nonkin additions were *in* but not *of* the family. Other kin also resided in households but their presence is probably chiefly due to demographic failure elsewhere—orphanhood, widowhood, and spinsterhood.

---

economic area nineteenth century entrepreneurial capitalism may be closer in terms of the linkage between family and property to medieval feudalism than to twentieth century corporate capitalism (Bell, 1961:39-45).

accomplished (Goode, 1968:311-313). Since literary sources are available, relatively inexpensive to exploit, and suggestive concerning the more subtle aspects of family interaction, it would be foolish to dismiss them as biased and unreliable. It would be equally risky to base the entire history of the American family on these sources. What appears to be crucial at this point for a reliable descriptive history of the American family is the development of series of quantitative indicators for various aspects of family behavior.

On both theoretical and historical grounds the idea that a shift from the centrality of the family of orientation to the family of procreation has occurred within the time span of American history may be questioned. American history, it is often argued, lacks a "traditional" or "premodern" period. If modernization and the transformation of the family from extended to nuclear are related, one would not expect to find evidence for it within the three and one-half centuries of American history. The classic polarities of sociological theory are often used by historians to contrast America with England or as a literary device to highlight rather small shifts over time. Still, the dominant theme in American historiography is "uniqueness" and this peculiar quality of the American experience is linked to the various characteristics of modernity. Ideal types, of course, describe no particular empirical realities. Since these classic dichotomies emerged from the attempt to understand the transformation of western society in the nineteenth century, their empirical relevance surely ought to be as much in the analysis of the history of western development as in the explanation of cross-cultural differences. If the discussion of historical change in the family is to progress, the selection of terms is less important than the precise specification of the extent of change along the theoretical continuum.

Some important aspects of the nuclear, conjugal, or family-of-procreation-dominant family system such as neolocal residence, undoubtedly have been dominant since the earliest American settlement in the seventeenth century (Goode, 1970a:xvi). Other significant historical continuities such as the priority given to nuclear as against extended kin (Demos, 1970:181) may also be present. If change is to be detected in an area of known continuity, a specific, well-defined problem and subtle and discriminating measures of change are required. The relative centrality of the family of orientation versus the family of procreation can be examined from various angles. Marriage forma-

tion, however, is probably the most crucial since it is the point of transition for the individual. Transitions involving decisions are inevitably problematic. Furthermore, marriages produce records for nearly the entire population, not just for atypical elites. Thus a substantial data base exists for historical analysis. If the American family has undergone substantial historical change, it should be reflected in the conditions of marriage formation. Were, in fact, the marriages of a significant segment of the American population ever controlled by parents at any point in our history? Parents today are, of course, not irrelevant in the courtship and marriage formation process. The earlier, "traditional," pattern of control should be direct rather than indirect, involve material rather than psychological relationships, and involve power exercised by parents in their own interest at the expense of the children.

A shift in the control of marriage formation is clearly to be expected by the sociological theory of family modernization.[3] Confident, if vague, statements exist describing the emergence of a non-parentally controlled, participant-run courtship system within the time span encompassed by American history (Reiss, 1964:57-58; Stone, 1964:181-182).[4] Yet Reiss presumably relies on literary evidence in his broad summary and Stone on the decidedly atypical experience of the English aristocracy. Furthermore, the shift specified is subtle—from a parental choice, child veto system in the seventeenth century to its converse by the late nineteenth or early twentieth century. Given the particularistic relationship between parents and children, choosing and vetoing choices may not be a constitutional system but instead an ongoing process of action and reaction.

METHOD AND SAMPLE

The dead, of course, cannot be subjected to

[3] According to Smelser (1966:117), for example, "In many traditional settings, marriage is closely regulated by elders; the tastes and sentiments of the couple to be married are relatively unimportant . . . . With the decay of extended kinship ties and the redefinition of parental authority, youth becomes emancipated with respect to choosing a spouse."

[4] The necessary imprecision of Reiss' succinct summary reflects the dearth of hard historical evidence: "The seventeenth century saw the working out of a solution. Romantic love had spread to much of the populace (but) almost exclusively among couples who were engaged. . . . The parents were still choosing mates. . . . By the eighteenth century the revolt had secured many adherents and was increasingly successful, so that by the end of the nineteenth century, in many parts of Europe and especially in America, young people were choosing their own mates and love was a key basis for marriage. The revolution had been won!" (Reiss, 1964:57-58).

surveys. The extent of parental power in courtship and marriage formation cannot be directly measured. Inherently the concept has a certain diffuseness and multidimensionality. Parents, for example, could determine the actual choice of spouse, they could determine the age at marriage but not name the partner, or they could merely structure indirectly the range of acceptable spouses. The actual process of decision making and bargaining is forever lost to the historian of ordinary people. If the dead cannot be interviewed, they can be made to answer questions if various consequences of the larger issue of parental control over marriage can be explicitly formulated. This is possible through the construction of long-term series of indices which are logically associated with the operational existence of parental control. Unlike the possibilities available in direct interaction with respondents, these indices inevitably lack meaning in an absolute, substantive sense. Conclusions must rest not just on one measure but on the conformity of various indicators to some pattern. Quantitative measures, whatever their limitations, have the great advantage of providing consistent information about change over time—the great question in the sociological history of the family and the most severe limitation of literary source materials.

Since the expected transition to a participant-run courtship system allegedly occurred between the seventeenth and late nineteenth century, either comparable data sets separated by more than a century or a long continuous series seem appropriate. For sociological purposes the former would be sufficient since a test of the change is all that is required. For historical analysis the time-series approach is better suited since the timing and pace of the transition are equally interesting. If the change did occur, was it gradual or concentrated in a few decades as a result, say, of the American revolution or the inception of rapid economic growth.

The larger study from which the ensuing data derive covers the social and demographic experience of the population of one Massachusetts town over a quarter-millienium (Smith, 1973). Economically, this period—1635 to 1880—encompasses the shift, mainly after 1800, from agriculture to commerce and industry. Demographically, it includes the transition from a fertility level which was high by west European standards to the below replacement reproduction rates of the mid-nineteenth century (Smith, 1972a; Uhlenberg, 1969). The basic methodological technique of the larger

study was family reconstitution—essentially statistical genealogy (Wrigley, 1966). Records of births, deaths, intentions to marry, marriages, and wealth data from tax lists were combined into family units for analysis. Various series of comparable data extending over the two centuries were constructed to measure change in demographic, familial, and social behavior. By examining differences in the timing of changes in these indicators, the history of the evolution of the population and social structure can be interpreted (Furet, 1971). Every decision about research design necessarily involves a price. Although long-term trends and change can be studied by this approach, the conclusions strictly must be limited to the population of the town of Hingham. Furthermore, primarily because of migration, nearly one-half of the families could not be fully reconstituted. Although wealth is inversely related to outmigration after marriage, this distortion only marginally affects most indictors. Since the wealth-bias is fairly consistent over time, trends are affected to a lesser degree than levels for any particular cohort.

EVIDENCE

In early New England, as in the pre-industrial West generally, marriage was intimately linked to economic independence (Wrigley, 1969:117-118). As a result, age at marriage and proportions never-marrying were higher in western Europe than in other cultural areas (Hajnal, 1965). Since the late marriage pattern tended to reduce fertility, European societies had less of a dependency burden from non-productive children; the easy mobility of the young, unmarried adult population may also have facilitated the transition to modern economic growth. Arguing in theoretical terms, one historical demographer has suggested that mortality level was also an important mechanism in the determination of marriage age. Higher mortality would open up opportunities for sons who then could marry earlier than if their fathers survived longer. The growth of population was thus controlled by the countervailing forces of mortality and marriage age (Ohlin, 1961).

These central demographic characteristics of west European societies can be used to formulate a test of the extent of paternal economic power. Since newly married sons were not incorporated into the paternal economic or living unit, marriage meant a definite transfer of power intergenerationally. The transfer might be eased by custom, limited by paternal retention of formal title to the land, and

Period of Fathers' Marriage Cohort	Age at marriage of sons by age at death of fathers:		
	Under 60	60 and over	Difference
1641-1700	26.8 (64)	28.4 (142)	+1.6
1701-1720	24.3 (30)	25.9 (130)	+1.6
1721-1740	24.7 (38)	26.7 (104)	+2.0
1741-1760	26.1 (43)	26.5 (145)	+0.4
1761-1780	25.7 (42)	26.8 (143)	+1.1
1781-1800	26.0 (71)	25.8 (150)	−0.2
1801-1820	25.7 (93)	26.5 (190)	+0.8
1821-1840	26.0 (42)	25.9 (126)	−0.1
1641-1780	25.73(217)	26.89(664)	+1.16
1781-1840	25.86(206)	26.11(466)	+0.25

Note: Sample size of sons whose marriage ages are known in parentheses.

moderated by continuing relations along non-instrumental lines. However, fathers inevitably had something to lose—either economic resources or unpaid labor services—by the early marriage of their sons.[5] One might expect, therefore, that sons of men who die early would be able to marry before sons of men who survive into old age. By law male orphans inherited at age twenty-one and were thus economically free to marry. On the other hand, if fathers either could not or would not exercise such control, no differential in marriage age should exist between these two groups of sons.

Over two centuries of the study 60 years was the approximate mean age of fathers at the time of marriage of their sons. For the three cohorts of sons born to marriages up to 1740, Table 1 shows a differential of 1.6, 1.6, and 2.0 years in the predicted direction between sons whose fathers died before age 60 and sons whose fathers survived that age. For sons born to marriages formed after 1740 and especially after 1780, the "paternal power" effect is greatly diminished. While one and one-half to two years may appear to be a small difference, this gap is wider than that between the marriage ages of first and younger sons or between sons of wealthy and less wealthy parents (Smith, 1973). Nor should an extreme differential be expected. Fathers had a cultural obligation to see their children married although it was not in their short-run self-interest. The most meaningful interpretation of the magnitude of the differential depends on comparison with results

[5] John Winthrop, the leader of the great Puritan migration of 1630, was partially influenced to leave England by his declining economic status resulting from launching three of his sons with substantial gifts of land that cut his own holdings in half (Morgan, 1958:43).

obtained from reconstitution studies of English population samples.

Since the meaning of this differential is inferential, this index cannot by itself confirm the argument that parents significantly controlled the marriage of their sons. An additional aspect of the relative centrality of the family of orientation in a society is a concern for the preservation of the line at the expense of a coexistent desire to provide for all children in the family. Inasmuch as the number and sex composition of surviving children are not completely certain and economic circumstances are not perfectly forecast, this tension is essentially insoluble for individual families (Goode, 1970b:125-126). By favoring only one son, families could help to maintain the social continuity of the family line. Although strict primogeniture did not obtain in Massachusetts, the eldest son was granted a double share in intestacy cases before the egalitarian modification of the law in 1789. Fathers, however, were not legally required to favor the eldest son. They had a free choice between an emphasis on the lineage or giving each child an equal start in life. If common, this limited form of primogeniture should have an influence on the social origins of the spouses of first and younger sons. Having more resources eldest sons should be able, on the average, to marry daughters of wealthier men. In seventeenth century marriage contracts the wife's parents provided half as much as the husband's for launching the couple into marriage (Morgan, 1966:82). In order to test the influence of birth order on marriage chances, Table 2 compares the quintile wealth status of fathers and fathers-in-law who were living in Hingham at the earlier date to men who were taxed by the town at the later date. While these nonmigratory requirements limit

TABLE 2. RELATIONSHIP OF WEALTH STATUS OF FATHERS AND FATHERS-IN-LAW OF FIRST AND YOUNGER SONS

Tax list date for:		Percentage of men whose fathers-in-law were in:						
		Same quintile as father		Higher quintile than father		Lower quintile than father		
Fathers and fathers-in-law	Sons	1st	younger	1st	younger	1st	younger	
		%	%	%	%	%	%	N
1647--1680		25	29	58	29	17	43	26
1749--1779		30	33	44	26	25	41	94
1779--1810		26	30	55	27	18	43	117
1810--1830		36	27	30	36	34	37	139
1830--1860		34	35	34	30	32	34	138

and perhaps bias the sample, the differences are quite dramatic. First sons taxed on the 1680, 1779, and 1810 property lists were roughly twice as likely as younger sons to have a father-in-law who was in a higher wealth quintile than their own father. They were similarly only half as likely as younger sons to have a father-in-law who was poorer than their own father. Birth order was thus an important determinant of the economic status of the future spouse and influential in determining the life chances of men during the colonial period.[6]

A radical change is apparent for men on the town tax lists of 1830 and 1860. Birth order in the nineteenth century exerted no significant effect on the relationship between the relative wealth of father and father-in-law. Instead of a gradual dimunition in paternal power, as was apparent in the effect of father's survival on the marriage age of sons, a decisive break is apparent.[7] While the measure in Table 1

---

[6] This empirical conclusion contradicts the conventional interpretation of the social insignificance of primogeniture in colonial America (Bailyn, 1962:345; Keim, 1968:545-586). Earlier studies, however, have only shown that all sons generally got some property, not *how much* each one actually received. Wills lack a monetary value for the bequests making direct measurement impossible. In Virginia younger sons often received land in less-developed (and presumably land of less value) frontier areas while first sons got the home plantation. More generally historians who have analyzed inequality in colonial America have thought in- terms of industrial society and have thus ignored sources of *intrafamilial* inequality. No published studies exist comparing the actual life experiences of first and younger sons in early America. In England, of course, the differential treatment accorded to first and younger sons was of considerable economic, social, and political importance (Thirsk, 1969).

[7] The use of primogeniture may actually have increased in the early and mid-eighteenth century as the supply of land within settled areas declined. This trend has been documented for the town of Andover, Massachusetts (Greven, 1970:131-132), and on a broader cross-cultural basis the relationship between land scarcity and impartible inheritance has been suggested (Goldschmidt and Kunkel, 1971).

involves the operation of paternal power on the individual level, primogeniture reflected in Table 2 is more a social constraint on the "freeness" of marriage choice. Apparently it was easier for all fathers to discriminate automatically against younger sons than it was for individual fathers, after the middle of the eighteenth century, to postpone the age at marriage of their own sons. The change evident in both indicators relating to the marriage process of sons is consistent with the larger hypothesis of a shift away from the dominance of the family of orientation in the family system.

The distinction between individual and social aspects of parental control is also apparent for daughters as well as sons. Traditionally in western society women have been more subject than men to parental control, particularly in the area of sexual behavior. Although penalties for premarital fornication were assessed equally against both parties, colonial New England did not escape this patriarchal bias. As a symbolic example geographically-mixed marriages usually occurred in the hometown of the bride, suggesting that the husband had to receive his wife from her father. Post-marital residence in these cases, however, was more often in the husband's town. Although the Puritan conception of marriage as a free act allowed women veto power over the parental choice of husband, marriages in the upper social strata were arranged through extensive negotiations by the parents (Morgan, 1966:79-86). In short the existing evidence points to a pattern intermediate between total control of young women by their parents and substantive premarital autonomy for women. The historical question, once again, is not either-or but how much? Were women, in fact, "married off," and was there any change over time in the incidence of this practice? Direct evidence does not exist to chart a trend, but a hypothetical pattern

JOURNAL OF MARRIAGE AND THE FAMILY

DANIEL SCOTT SMITH

may be suggested. If parents did decide when their daughters could and should marry, one might expect them to procede on the basis of the eldest first and so on. Passing over a daughter to allow a younger sister to marry first might advertise some deficiency in the elder and consequently make it more difficult for the parents to find a suitable husband for her. If, on the other hand, women decided on the basis of personal considerations when (and perhaps who) they should marry, more irregularity in the sequence of sisters' marriages should be expected.

Table 3 demonstrates a marked increase in the proportions of daughters who fail to marry in order of sibling position after the middle of the eighteenth century. Because of the age difference among sisters most will marry in order of birth. Since women may remain single for reasons independent of parental choice, *e.g.*, the unfavorable sex ratio in eastern Massachusetts in the second half of the eighteenth century, the measure which omits these cases (left column of Table 3) is a more precise indicator of the trend. However, the increasing tendency in the eighteenth and particularly the nineteenth century for women to remain permanently single is certainly consistent with an increasing absence of strong parental involvement in the marriage process of their

children. More and more women in the late eighteenth and early nineteenth century were obviously not being "married off." Suggesting the obvious point that their marriages were controlled more indirectly through the power fathers had over economic resources, a similar index of sons marrying out of birth order shows no secular trend.

Just as primogeniture relates to the intergenerational transmission of economic resources, so too does the relationship of parental wealth to the marriage age of daughters. If wealth transmission by marriage were important in the society, than parents obviously would have greater direct control over their daughters than if women were expected to provide no resources to their future husbands. If daughters brought economic resources to the marriage, then one would expect that daughters of wealthier men would naturally be sought after by other families as being the more desirable marriage partners for their sons. The higher level of demand should mean that daughters of the wealthier would marry at a younger age than daughters of the less wealthy. If, on the contrary, property transfer and marriage were not intimately connected, then the class pattern of female marriage age would conform to male class career patterns. Market conditions rather than the behavior of individual actors can be assessed by examining the differential by wealth in the female age at first marriage. For daughters born to marriages formed in Hingham between 1721 and 1780 there is a perfect inverse relationship between paternal wealth and marriage age. Once more there is evidence for a significant role of the family of orientation in structuring marriage patterns. This wealth pattern is dramatically reversed for daughters born to marriages between 1781 and 1840. The stability in the mean marriage age (bottom row of Table 4) masks the divergent class trends. Daughters of the wealthy married later in the nineteenth century, while daughters of the less wealthy married at a younger age than before.[8] The slight positive relationship between wealth and male marriage age becomes much stronger during the nineteenth century as well. Nothing could be more suggestive of the severing of direct property considerations from marriage.

TABLE 3. PERCENTAGE OF DAUGHTERS NOT MARRYING IN BIRTH ORDER IN RELATIONSHIP TO THOSE AT RISK

Periods when daughters are marriageable	Spinsters excluded		Spinsters included	
	%	N	%	N
1651-1650 to 1691-1710	8.1	86	11.2	89
1701-1720 to 1731-1750	11.6	138	18.4	147
1741-1760 to 1771-1790	18.2	176	25.1	191
1781-1800 to 1811-1830	14.9	214	24.9	245
1821-1840 to 1861-1880	18.4	298	24.7	320

Note: In a family with n known adult sisters, there are n-1 possibilities for not marrying in birth order, *e.g.*, an only daughter cannot marry out of birth order, two daughters can marry out of order in only one way, etc. The interpretation of this measure is dependent, of course, on the assumption (true until the early nineteenth century) that the mean interval separating living sisters remains constant. With the fall in marital fertility during the nineteenth century, the gap between sisters increases. Since daughters who never marry obviously do not marry in order of birth, the left column excludes and right column includes these women.

[8] Although the data are unreliable because of an absence of information on the marital status of many daughters, the shame shift occurred in the class incidence of permanent spinsterhood. In the eighteenth century the daughters of the wealthier strata were most likely to marry; in the 1781-1840 period, daughters of the wealthier were most likely to remain spinsters.

TABLE 4. AGE AT MARRIAGE OF DAUGHTERS BY WEALTH QUINTILE OF FATHERS

Wealth quintile class of father	Daughters born to marriages of				Change in mean age
	1721-1780		1781-1840		
	Age	N	Age	N	
Richest 20 per cent	23.3	99	24.5	114	+1.31
Upper-middle 20 per cent	23.5	98	24.4	179	+0.96
Middle 20 per cent	23.6	110	22.1	172	−1.47
Lower-middle 20 per cent	24.5	92	23.1	159	−1.37
Poorest 20 per cent	24.5	57	22.9	135	−1.63
Fathers not present on extant tax list	22.7	37	23.0	96	+0.30
Totals	23.7	493	23.3	855	−0.37

During the nineteenth century, then, daughters were not property exchanged between families. Nineteenth century marriage, in contrast to the preceeding two centuries, was between individuals rather than families. Parents, of course, continue to play an important role in structuring the premarital environment of their children (Sussman, 1953). Their role today is presumably more indirect and their influence is more psychological than instrumental. What may be conceded in principle may be denied in practice. The extent of parental resources and the age of the children are key determinants of the efficacy of parental power. One could argue that the historical shift has been not the disappearance of parental power but its limitation to the earlier phases of the life cycle of the child. On the symbolic-ideological level the shift, albeit incomplete, toward the recognition of the child's independence from his family of orientation is apparent in child-naming patterns.[9]

The decline of parental involvement in marriage formation is also suggested by the decrease in the proportion of marriages involving couples who were both residents of the town. One may presume that parents were more knowledgeable about, and hence more influential in, marriages to children of other families in the town. Between 59.6 per cent and 71.8 per cent of all marriages in decades between 1701-1710 and 1791-1800 involved two residents of Hingham; by 1850-1853, only 48.2 per cent of all marriages, by 1900-1902 only 32.0 per cent and finally by 1950-1954, a mere 25.8 per cent were both residents of the town. Improved transportation and communication in the nineteenth and twentieth centuries, of course, modify the magnitude of this trend. Once again, the shift is in the predicted direction and it occurs at the time—the first half of the nineteenth century—consistent with changes in the other indices.

CONCLUSIONS

At least in the area of parental control over marriage, significant, documentable historical change has occurred in American family behavior. There are difficulties, of course, in extending the findings of a local study to the entire American population. The trend in the family parameter which has been best-documented on the national level, fertility, is consistent with the more detailed evidence on the families of Hingham. From the early nineteenth century onward American marital fertility has been declining. With a level of fertility lower than the national average in 1800, New England was the leader in the American fertility transition (Grabill et al., 1958:14-16; Yasuba, 1962:50-69). What the sequence of change in the Hingham indicators suggests is an erosion and collapse of traditional family patterns in the middle and late eighteenth century before the sharp decline in marital fertility began. In the seventeenth and early eighteenth century there existed a stable, parental-run marriage system, in the nineteenth century a stable, participant-run system. Separating these two eras of stability was a period of change and crisis, manifested most notably in the American Revolution itself—a political upheaval not un-

[9] Some 94.4 per cent of families formed before 1700 with three or more sons and 98.5 per cent with three or more daughters named a child for the parent of the same sex. For families formed between 1841 and 1880 with the same number of boys or girls (to control for declining fertility), the respective figures are 67.8 per cent and 53.2 per cent. The decline in parent-child name sharing and especially the more rapid decrease in mother-daughter name sharing reflects the symbolic fact of the ultimate separation of children, especially girls, from their family of birth. The persistence of kin-naming in the nineteenth and twentieth centuries simultaneously confirms the continuing importance of kinship in modern American society (Rossi, 1966; Smith, 1972b).

connected to the family (Burrows and Wallace, 1972).[10]

Articles which begin with a capsule or caricature of a theoretical perspective and then procede to a narrow body of empirical evidence typically conclude that the theory fails to explain the data adequately. Only criticism and revisionism represent *real* scholarly contributions. Only covertly does this study follow that format. Substantively, the empirical measures presented above for the population of Hingham, Massachusetts, confirm, if more precisely define and elaborate, the conclusions and interpretations of Smelser, Goode, Reiss, and Stone. It is perhaps revisionist in the sense that the current state of the field is confused because of the great gap separating a bold and sweeping theory of change and the evidence which would support it. A systematic history of the American family can be reconstructed if sociological theory, long-run series of quantitative data, and historical imagination in devising subtle measures of change are combined. The vulgar notion of a drastic shift from "extended" to "nuclear" families had to be exposed and rejected in order to generate historical research. The equally simple-minded opposite extreme of the historical continuity of the conjugal family is just as fallacious both on historical as well as the better-known sociological grounds. American *households* may always have been overwhelmingly nuclear in structure, but household composition is a measure of family structure—not the structure of the family itself. Historians love complexity—the tension between change and continuity over time. Unravelling this complexity is the particularly challenging task for scholars working in the history of the family.

REFERENCES

Abrams, Philip
1972 "The sense of the past and the origins of sociology." Past and Present 55 (May): 18-32.
Adams, Bert N.
1970 "Isolation, function, and beyond: American kinship in the 1960's." Journal of Marriage and the Family 32 (November):575-597.
Aries, Phillipe
1962 Centuries of Childhood. A Social History of Family Life. Tr. by Robert Baldwick. New York:Knopf.

Bailyn, Bernard
1962 "Political experience and enlightenment ideas in eighteenth-century America." American Historical Review 67 (January): 339-351.
Bell, Daniel
1961 "The breakup of family capitalism: on changes of class in America." Pp. 39-45 in Daniel Bell, The End of Ideology. New York:Collier.
Berkner, Lutz K.
1973 "Recent research on the history of the family in Western Europe." Journal of Marriage and the Family 35 (August).
Blau, Peter and Otis Dudley Duncan
1967 The American Occupational Structure. New York:Wiley.
Burrows, Edwin G. and Michael Wallace
1972 "The American Revolution: the ideology and practice of national liberation." Perspectives in American History 6:167-306.
Davis, Kingsley
1949 Human Society. New York:Macmillan.
Demos, John
1970 A Little Commonwealth: Family Life in Plymouth Colony. New York:Oxford.
Furet, Francois
1971 "Quantitative history." Daedalus 100 (Winter):151-167.
Furstenberg, Frank F., Jr.
1966 "Industrialization and the American family: a look backward." American Sociological Review 31 (June):326-337.
Goldschmidt, Walter and Evalyn Jacobson Kunkel
1971 "The structure of the peasant family." American Anthropologist 73 (October): 1058-1076.
Goode, William J.
1968 "The theory and measurement of family change." Pp. 295-348 in Eleanor Bernert Sheldon and Wilbert E. Moore (eds.), Indicators of Social Change. New York:Russell Sage Foundation.
1970a World Revolution and Family Patterns. New York:Free Press Paperback.
1970b "Family systems and social mobility." Pp. 120-136 in Reuben Hill and Rene Konig (eds.), Families in East and West. Paris: Mouton.
Grabill, Wilson H., Clyde V. Kiser, and Pascal K. Whelpton
1958 The Fertility of American Women. New York:Wiley.
Greven, Philip J., Jr.
1970 Four Generations: Population, Land, and Family in Colonial Andover, Massachusetts. Ithaca:Cornell.
Hajnal, J.
1965 "European marriage patterns in perspective." Pp. 101-143 in D. V. Glass and D. E. C. Eversley (eds.), Population in History. London:Edward Arnold.
Hoogenbloom, Ari
1968 "Industrialism and political leadership: a

[10] Trends in premarital pregnancy—very low mid-seventeenth and mid-nineteenth century levels, high mid- and late eighteenth century rates—support this periodization of family change (Smith and Hindus, 1971).

case study of the United States Senate." Pp. 49-78 in Frederic Cople Jaher (ed.), The Age of Industrialism in America. New York:Free Press.

Keim, C. Ray
1968 "Primogeniture and entail in colonial Virginia." William and Mary Quarterly 25 (October):545-586.

Lantz, Herman R., Margaret Britton, Raymond Schmitt, and Eloise C. Snyder
1968 "Pre-industrial patterns in the colonial family in America: a content analysis of colonial magazines." American Sociological Review 33 (June):413-426.

Laslett, Peter and Richard Wall (eds.)
1972 Household and Family in Past Time Cambridge:Cambridge University Press.

Morgan, Edmund S.
1958 The Puritan Dilemma: The Story of John Winthrop. Boston:Little, Brown.
1966 The Puritan Family: New York:Harper Torchbooks.

Ohlin, G.
1961 "Mortality, marriage, and growth in pre-industrial populations." Population Studies 14 (March):190-197.

Parsons, Talcott
1943 "The kinship system of the contemporary United States." American Anthropologist 45 (January-March):22-38.
1965 "The normal American family." Pp. 31-50 in Seymour Farber, Piero Mustacchi, and Roger H. Wilson (eds.), Man and Civilization: The Family's Search for Survival. New York:McGraw-Hill.

Reiss, Ira L.
1964 Premarital Sexual Standards in America. New York:Free Press Paperback.

Rossi, Alice S.
1965 "Naming children in middle class families." American Sociological Review 30 (August): 499-513.

Shipton, Clifford K.
1954 "Ye mystery of ye ages solved, or, how placing worked at colonial Harvard and Yale." Harvard Alumni Bulletin 57 (December 11): 258-263.

Smelser, Neil J.
1966 "The modernization of social relations." Pp.

110-122 in Myron Weiner (ed.), Modernization: The Dynamics of Growth. New York: Basic Books.

Smith, Daniel Scott
1972a "The demographic history of colonial New England." Journal of Economic History 32 (March):165-183.
1972b "Child-naming patterns and family structure change: Hingham, Massachusetts, 1640-1880." Unpublished paper presented at the Clark University conference on the family, social structure, and social change.
1973 "Population, family and society in Hingham, Massachusetts, 1635-1880." Unpublished Ph. D. dissertation, University of California.

Smith, Daniel Scott and Michael S. Hindus
1971 "Premarital pregnancy in America, 1640-1966: an overview and interpretation." Unpublished paper presented at the annual meeting of the American Historical Association.

Stone, Lawrence
1964 "Marriage among the English nobility." Pp. 153-183 in Rose Laub Coser (ed.), The Family: Its Structure and Functions. New York:St. Martin's Press.

Sussman, M. B.
1953 "Parental participation in mate selection and its effects upon family continuity." Social Forces 32 (October):76-81.

Thirsk, Joan
1969 "Younger sons in the seventeenth century." History 54 (October):358-377.

Uhlenberg, Peter R.
1969 "A study of cohort life cycles: cohorts of native born Massachusetts women, 1830-1920." Population Studies 23 (November):407-420.

Wrigley, E. A.
1966 "Family reconstitution." Pp. 96-159 in E. A. Wrigley (ed.), An Introduction to English Historical Demography. New York:Basic Books.
1969 Population and History. New York: McGraw-Hill.

Yasuba, Yasukichi
1962 Birth Rates of the White Population of the United States, 1800-1860. Baltimore:Johns Hopkins.

Family Size and Fertility Control in Eighteenth-Century America: A Study of Quaker Families

ROBERT V. WELLS

(i)

It has long been assumed, on the basis of the information provided by the colonial and early national censuses, that the birth rate in eighteenth-century America must have been very high to account both for the rapid rate of growth and the high proportion of the population under the age of sixteen. Employing several methods of analysis, a number of experts have agreed in estimating that the birth rate at the end of the eighteenth and in the early nineteenth century was about 50, or a little higher.[1] At the same time, the evidence in the decennial censuses is sufficient to indicate that the birth rate of the American population had begun a long-term decline by the early nineteenth century and that this lasted until the 1930's.[2] It would obviously be of interest to know when and why the reduction in the level of childbearing began, but the limitations of the early census data make it unlikely that such information ever will be available for the population of the United States as a whole.

For the first time, however, it is possible to indicate when the reduction in fertility began for one segment of the American population, and to explore the reasons for the changes in the patterns of childbearing of this particular group. The group in question, whose story is the main concern of this paper, is composed of 276 Quaker families who belonged to the monthly meetings of New York City, Flushing, Jericho, and Westbury in New York; Plainfield and Rahway, Salem, and Burlington in New Jersey; and Falls, and Philadelphia in Pennsylvania.[3] Quaker families were selected for study here primarily because the quality of records kept by the Friends allowed families to be reconstructed from the lists of births, marriages and deaths with greater ease and in larger numbers than from any other set of records in the middle colonies.[4]

Because of the interest in change over time, the date of birth of the wife was used to divide the 276 families included in this study into three chronological groups. A desire to identify any demographic patterns that might be associated with the American Revolution and a concern to avoid groups with very small numbers were the principal determinants of the division. The first grouping of families included all those in which the wife was born no later than 1730. Because it is extremely rare for a woman who has reached the age of 45 to bear children, it could be assumed that all the children in this grouping of families would have been born by 1775, and such was the fact. This group of families will be described as 'pre-revolutionary'. The second group of families

---

[1] A. J. Lotka, 'The size of American families in the eighteenth century', *Journal of the American Statistical Association*, 22 (1927), p. 165; J. Potter, 'The growth of population in America: 1700–1860', in D. V. Glass and D. E. C. Eversley (Eds.), *Population in History* (London, 1965), pp. 646, 672; Warren S. Thompson and P. K. Whelpton, *Population Trends in the United States* (New York, 1933), p. 263; Yasukichi Yasuba, *Birth Rates of the White Population in the United States, 1800–1860* (Baltimore, 1962), p. 99.

[2] Ansley J. Coale and Melvin Zelnik, *New Estimates of Fertility and Population in the United States* (Princeton, 1963), p. 39; Thompson and Whelpton, *op. cit.*, p. 263.

[3] The records are to be found in: *Genealogical Magazine of New Jersey*, 27–28 (1952–1953); William Wade Hinshaw (Ed.), *Encyclopedia of American Quaker Genealogy*, 6 vols. (Ann Arbor, 1936–1950); New York Genealogical and Biographical Society, *Record*, 8–11 (1877–1880); *Rahway and Plainfield Monthly Meeting Register*, MS. in the Genealogical Society of Pennsylvania in Philadelphia.

[4] Families were reconstructed according to the method presented in E. A. Wrigley (Ed.), *An Introduction to English Historical Demography* (London, 1966), pp. 96–159.

73

Reprinted from *Population Studies* XXV, 1, 73–82. Copyright © 1971 by permission of the publisher.

was defined by wives who were born from 1731 to 1755; and, as was expected, their childbearing had ended by 1800. Because these women experienced their more fertile years during the half century which included the American Revolution, this group can be referred to as the 'revolutionary' group. A final group, which can be designated as 'post-revolutionary', was determined by wives born from 1756 to 1785. Most of the children of this last group of families would have been born after the Revolution, and all of the children were born by 1830. It was considered undesirable to include any families in this study which might have had children after 1830, because the Hicksite separation which split the Quakers in 1827 had a disastrous effect on the quality of their records.

The principal story we are concerned with here involves changes in the demographic patterns of these Quakers and the reasons for those changes. Most of what follows is true only for the 276 families under study here, and cannot be assumed to apply to any wider segment of the population. However, the last part of the paper will be devoted to a consideration of how 'representative' these Quakers may have been of the American population in general at the end of the eighteenth century, especially with regard to changes in childbearing patterns.

(ii)

The average size of the Quaker family will be considered first, principally because it is helpful in exploring other questions to be discussed later. The term 'family' can be used in a number of different ways, but for the purposes of this study it will be defined as a man, his wife, and any children born to that particular union. 'Family size' will refer to the number of children born to a given couple.

Out of the 276 Quaker families included in this study, 271 couples were married at a time when the bride's age fell within the normal limits of the childbearing stage of life – which is to say, between 15 and 45. In the five remaining couples the bride was 45 or older at the time of her wedding, and in none of these cases were there children. Accordingly, the total of 271 couples has been used in computing the average size of the family.

The figures in Table 1 indicate an average size for the Quaker family of 5·69 children. This figure, which is lower than the traditional estimate of the size of colonial families, reflects the fact that relatively few couples had very large families. While families of eight were the most common, it is also true that no more than 97 of the 271 families had as many as eight or more children, that the families having ten or more children numbered 40, and that no couple had more than 14 children. Small families, on the other hand, occurred more often than might be expected. Of the 271 families, 109 had fewer than five children, families of two or less numbered 54, while 22 couples were childless.

Interestingly, the evidence on the difference in the size of complete and incomplete families indicates that, at least among these Quakers, mortality among parents had a surprisingly small effect on family size. Complete families are defined in this study as unions which lasted until the wife reached her 45th birthday and, hence, normally had completed her childbearing; incomplete families include those unions in which the family might have been larger had not the marriage ended by the death of one spouse before the wife was 45.[5] Whereas complete families averaged 6·04 children, the average for incomplete families was only 4·93. The difference in the average of just over one child is surprisingly small.

When the data are grouped chronologically, as in Table 2, significant differences in the size of the family appear. From a high of 6·68 children for the 'pre-revolutionary' families, in which the last child was born by 1775, the average number of children declined to 5·02 in the 'post-revolutionary' group in which childbearing was finished by 1830. The decline in average family size was well under way with the middle group of mothers, those of the revolutionary era. Their families already averaged 5·67 children, one less than those of the mothers of the colonial period.

[5] Of the 271 unions used in the analysis of family size, 267 were first marriages for the wife. Thus, virtually all complete families were first marriages for the wife which lasted until she had reached the age of 45.

TABLE 1. *Family size*

Number of children	All families Number	%	Completed families Number	%	Incomplete families Number	%
0	22	8·12	14	7·57	8	9·30
1	14	5·17	6	3·24	8	9·30
2	18	6·64	9	4·86	9	10·47
3	27	9·96	19	10·27	8	9·30
4	28	10·33	20	10·81	8	9·30
5	22	8·12	16	8·65	6	6·98
6	28	10·33	19	10·27	9	10·47
7	15	5·54	11	5·95	4	4·65
8	36	13·28	23	12·43	13	15·12
9	21	7·75	13	7·03	8	9·30
10	18	6·64	16	8·65	2	2·33
11	9	3·32	7	3·78	2	2·33
12	10	3·69	9	4·86	1	1·16
13	2	0·74	2	1·08	—	—
14	1	0·37	1	0·54	—	—
Total	271	100·00	185	100·00	86	100·00
Children per family	5·69		6·04		4·93	

TABLE 2. *Changes in family size*

Wives born	By 1730	1731–1755	1756–1785	All wives
Last child born by	1775	1800	1830	
All families	6·68	5·67	5·02	5·69
Completed families	7·51	6·23	5·12	6·04
Incomplete families	5·39	4·45	4·76	4·93
Percentage of all families which were complete	61%	69%	73%	68%

It is of special interest to note that the greatest change came in complete families. The size of the average complete family was reduced between 1775 and 1830 by almost 2·4 children from 7·51 to 5·12 children. On the other hand, incomplete families decreased from 5·39 to 4·76 children over the same period, an average reduction of less than two-thirds of a child. Indeed, the decline in the size of completed families was so great that the last group of complete families actually showed a smaller average size than the incomplete families of the first group. Equally impressive is the fact that the overall size of the family would have fallen still lower than it did, had not the proportion of complete families risen with time from 61% to 73%.

(iii)

In seeking an explanation for the striking decline in the average family size of these Quakers, one thinks first of the possibility that women began to marry at later ages. Since a woman is seldom able to bear children for more than the 30 years between ages 15 and 45, the age at which she marries plays an obvious role in determining how many of those years may be spent in childbearing.

In this instance, the average age at marriage for the 271 brides whose families are being considered here rose from 22·14 to 22·94 between the 'pre-revolutionary' and the 'post-revolutionary' groups, a difference of only 0·8 of a year – hardly enough to explain a decline in family size of 1·66 children between the same two groups. In fact, at the highest rate of reproduction observed for these Quakers, this shift in the age of marriage would account for only a little more than 22% of the decline in the number of children born to an average couple.[6] Clearly, shifting patterns in the age at marriage explain only a small part of the decline in family size discussed above.

The duration of the marriage also plays an important role in determining the amount of time which may be spent in childbearing. Thus, it is possible that the decrease in family size could be attributed to increased mortality among parents which led, in turn, to shorter marriages. However, the available evidence indicates that, if anything, the duration of marriage increased over time. The average duration of marriage rose steadily from a low of 28·7 years for the families defined as 'pre-revolutionary' to 29·6 and 32·8 years among the 'revolutionary' and 'post-revolutionary' families respectively. The effects of this change can be seen in the rise in the proportion of complete families from 61% in the first group to 73% in the last group. Thus, what changes there were in mortality seem to have favoured larger, rather than smaller, families.

The explanation for the decline in family size among these Quakers lies in the fact that the reproductive patterns of these Friends were altered so as to reduce the level of childbearing within marriage. This change is best illustrated by the differences in the age-specific marital fertility rates of the three chronological groups. In calculating these rates, the first step was to establish certain age intervals for the wives of the various groups (this study uses the common five-year intervals of 15–19, 20–24, 25–29, and so forth up to ages 40–44). Then, to obtain the age-specific marital fertility rate for a particular age interval, the number of births within the specified age limits to the women under study was divided by the total years lived within the same interval by the same group of women while they were married. The result indicates the average number of children born per year to a married woman of a given group while of a particular age.

When the age-specific fertility rates of these Quakers are computed for the wives born by 1730, 1731 to 1755, and 1756 to 1785, a steady decrease with time is evident, as is shown in Table 3. Except for the middle, or 'revolutionary' group of women whose rates are slightly above those of the preceding group at ages 15–19 and 40–44, the age-specific fertility rates are lower at every age for each successive group. When the evidence from Table 3 is presented graphically in Chart I,

TABLE 3. *Age-specific fertility by time*

| Wives born | Age interval | | | | | |
	15–19	20–24	25–29	30–34	35–39	40–44
By 1730	0·443*	0·466	0·423	0·402	0·324	0·147
	(56·4)	(242·6)	(324·3)	(345·7)	(324·0)	(278·4)
1731–1755	0·446	0·408	0·410	0·326	0·228	0·171
	(49·3)	(183·7)	(231·4)	(239·4)	(232·8)	(222·3)
1756–1785	0·347	0·351	0·346	0·275	0·215	0·101
	(69·2)	(336·3)	(491·9)	(515·5)	(506·1)	(467·0)

NOTE: The total number of years of married life of the group is given in the brackets.

* When substantial proportions of the brides at the youngest ages are pregnant at the time of their marriage, it is generally wise to eliminate the figures for age-specific marital fertility in the interval 15–19 from consideration. The figures for that interval have been presented here because bridal pregnancy was virtually the same for women married before 20, as at that age or older.　In any case, both bridal pregnancy and illegitimacy were rare among these Quakers.

[6] Mothers aged 20–24, who were born by 1730, averaged 0·466 births each year (see Table 3). At this rate a shift in age at marriage of 0·8 years would have reduced the total family size by 0·37 children if changing marriage patterns alone were causing the change in family size. As it was, this was only 0·37/1·66 or 22·1% of the total change.

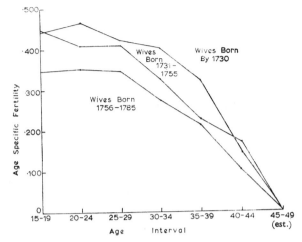

CHART I *(Information from Table 3). Age Specific Fertility by Time.*

the decline in the fertility of the successive groups is quite evident. The 'pre-revolutionary' wives had the highest overall level of fertility, while the line representing the fertility level of the 'post-revolutionary' group of wives is obviously the lowest of the lot.

(iv)

The explanation for the reduction in fertility among these Quakers is of obvious interest. Studies have indicated that births were being voluntarily limited in France and England by the eighteenth century, and as we shall see, these Quaker couples were just as capable of controlling their fertility.[7] At the same time, involuntary reductions in fertility may have occurred as the result of changes in environment or customs. Quite possibly both voluntary and involuntary reductions were responsible for the smaller average family size among these Quakers. However, most of the attention below will be directed towards the voluntary limitation of births, in part because the presence of deliberate family limitation in eighteenth-century America is somewhat surprising, but also because the evidence is more conclusive on that subject than for an involuntary decline in fertility.

When family limitation results from deliberate action on the part of husbands and wives to control the number of children they may have, differences appear between the fertility patterns of women who marry relatively early and women who marry at a later age. Couples who limit the size of their family tend to have most of their children in the first years of the marriage. As duration of marriage increases, presumably more attention is paid to the prevention or delaying of conception. Thus, at age 35, for example, women who married early will tend to have fewer children on the average than women who married later, simply because they have been married longer and are paying more attention to limiting births as they near their desired family size. By examining the childbearing patterns of women of equal ages who married at different ages, it is possible to determine whether differences exist which indicate the presence of family limitation. If family

[7] The following analysis of the practice of deliberate family limitation uses as models Louis Henry, *Anciennes Familles Genèvoises* (Paris, 1956), Chapters iv and v; and E. A. Wrigley, 'Family limitation in pre-industrial England'. *Economic History Review*, 2nd Ser., **19** (1966), pp. 82–109.

limitation were being practised, then the women who married early should have lower age-specific fertility rates at comparable ages, should cease bearing children at an earlier age, and should have a longer interval between the penultimate and the last birth than do women who married late and so achieve their desired family size at a later age.

The age-specific fertility rates of women who married early and of women who married late in each of the three chronological groups are presented in Table 4. For the purposes of this study, an early marriage has been defined as one in which the bride was under 25 years old; late marriage,

TABLE 4. *Age-specific fertility by age of marriage*

Age interval

Wives	15–19	20–24	25–29	30–34	35–39	40–44
			Wives born by 1730			
Married						
before 25	0·443	0·466	0·419	0·400	0·309	0·145
25 or older	—	—	0·462	0·409	0·373	0·154
			Wives born 1731–1755			
Married						
before 25	0·446	0·408	0·410	0·322	0·182	0·159
25 or older	—	—	0·412	0·344	0·354	0·196
			Wives born 1756–1785			
Married						
before 25	0·347	0·351	0·340	0·265	0·180	0·086
25 or older	—	—	0·383	0·315	0·316	0·139

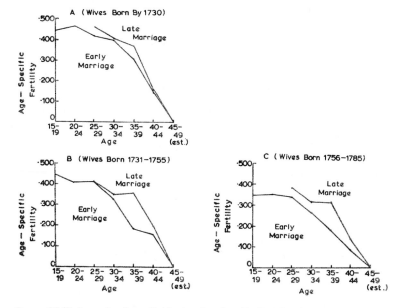

CHART II (*Information from Table 4*). *Age-Specific Fertility by Age of Marriage.*

on the other hand, refers to unions in which the bride was 25 or older. In each group and at every comparable age women who married at 25 or older have higher fertility rates than do the women who married before that age. The difference becomes more apparent after the early marriages have lasted at least ten years, and it is consistently greatest in the age group 35–39. This is precisely the pattern which would emerge from the practice of deliberate family limitation.

Chart II presents graphically the information from Table 4 on the fertility patterns of the three successive groups, when the age of marriage of the mother is taken into account. If the individual parts of the chart are considered separately, it becomes possible to suggest when these particular Quakers began to practise family limitation. The fertility rates for women born in 1730 or before (Chart II-A), and who finished childbearing by 1775, do not seem to have been influenced by the age at which the wife married. The differences that are apparent in the age groups 25–29 and 35–39 are not to be ignored, but the overall agreement between the two fertility patterns suggests that family limitation may have been rare in the 'pre-revolutionary' group. The experience of the women born between 1731 and 1755, who had their children during the Revolutionary period, was different. Although the fertility patterns in Chart II-B are close in the first years, a wide gap between the two lines appears in the 35–39 age group. This is, perhaps, the most likely interval in which first to perceive a difference in fertility patterns, since the women who married early would be nearing their desired family size and so would pay attention to limiting births, while the wives who married late would be less interested in preventing births, and at the same time would still be physically able to have children. Thus, the gap between the two lines at ages 35–39 may well indicate that family limitation first became common among these Quakers about the time of the Revolution. The last part of the Chart (II-C) leaves little doubt that deliberate limitation of births was successfully practised among the Quakers after the Revolution. The fertility patterns of the women born between 1756 and 1785 show a wide gap at every comparable age between those who married early and those who married late. Furthermore, the gap exists despite the fact that the fertility of the women who married late in this last group had declined considerably from that of their counterparts in the group born in 1730 or earlier.

Evidence based on the average age of the mother at the birth of her last child supports the main conclusions reached above, namely that these Quakers were deliberately limiting the size of their families, and that this practice first became apparent among the families defined as 'revolutionary'. This evidence is based on the assumption that mothers would cease childbearing at younger ages among the couples most interested in techniques of family limitation. The figures for age of mother at the birth of her last child, presented in Table 5, are based upon the experience of completed families only, in order to eliminate those women who ceased childbearing because of death.

TABLE 5. *Age of mother at last birth (completed families)*

Wives born	All wives	Wife married under 25	Wife married at 25 or older
By 1730	38·93	38·89	39·06
1731–1755	38·54	37·29	41·14
1756–1785	38·32	37·55	40·24

The first point to note is that the average age of the mother at the birth of her last child declined in each successive grouping from 38·93 in the 'pre-revolutionary' group to 38·32 among the 'post-revolutionary' women. Although the difference is not large, it is the kind of change which would occur as family limitation became common. Apparently family limitation was not common among the 'pre-revolutionary' families, for in that group wives who married early ceased bearing children at virtually the same age as wives who married late, the averages being 38·89 and 39·06 respectively. However, among the wives of the last two groups, mothers who married before the age of 25 were on average significantly younger when they had their last child than mothers who married at a later age. Among the women born between 1731 and 1755, wives who married early had their last child when they were 37·29 years old, almost four years younger than the women who married late whose last child was born when they were aged 41·14 on average. This certainly suggests that family limitation was consciously practised by the wives of the 'revolutionary' group and their husbands. The difference in the 'post-revolutionary' group is not as large, with those married early ceasing to bear children at an average age of 37·55 compared with 40·24 for those married late, but it is still large enough to suggest the presence of family limitation.

The length of the last birth interval is the third index which may reflect the practice of family limitation as a conscious policy. When there is no attempt to curtail the size of the family, all women will presumably continue to have children until they are physically unable to do so. Only the natural loss of reproductive power with increasing age will determine the time between a woman's penultimate and last child. However, when family limitation is consciously practised in a population, a noticeable increase in the length of the last birth interval should occur, as biological limits are no longer the sole determinant of the time of the last birth. Without modern contraceptives, the husbands and wives of the eighteenth century were certainly able to delay conceptions so as to reduce the total number of children they might have. They were less able, short of total abstinence from sexual relations, to determine the number of children they wanted and have no more. Those couples who knew how to avoid having children might, after several years, have one more child, either by accident or by design. Both delayed births and births which were the reversal of an earlier decision to have no more children may have lengthened the last birth interval for the women who were deliberately trying to limit the size of their families.

The length of the last birth interval for mothers of completed families has been given in Table 6. No important difference was noticeable in the length of the last birth interval of the first two groups of wives. The group defined as 'pre-revolutionary' had their last child on average 39·61 months after the preceding child, while the 'revolutionary' group had an average interval of 39·96 months. Differences do appear between the wives who married early and late, but they are not large enough to be statistically significant. But, among the wives born between 1756 and 1785 the average length of the last birth interval of 49·48 months was almost ten months longer than that of either of the earlier two groups. This increase, moreover, occurred where it logically should have if family limitation was practised. The women of the 'post-revolutionary' group who married early, and who presumably were the most concerned with limiting their families, had by far the longest last birth intervals, with an average of 54·33 months. In contrast, the length of the last birth interval of the women of that group who married at a relatively late age, and who were presumably not as interested in limiting their families, was only 37·25 months on average. Thus, the evidence from the length of the last birth interval points to deliberate family limitation among the wives born between 1756 and 1785, but there is no support for the conclusion, based on the age-specific fertility rates and the age of the mother at the birth of her last child, that couples of the 'revolutionary' group were also limiting the size of their families.

TABLE 6. *Length of last birth interval in months (completed families)*

Wives born	All wives	Wife married under 25	Wife married at 25 or older
By 1730	39·61	40·66	36·38
1731–1755	39·96	40·10	36·69
1756–1785	49·48	54·33	37·25

It seems apparent that at least part of the fall in age-specific fertility rates and the decline in family size among these Quakers at the end of the eighteenth century can be attributed to some form of deliberate family limitation. Each of the three reproductive patterns considered is indicative of the conscious control of fertility; together they offer consistent evidence that such a practice became common among the couples in which the wife was born between 1756 and 1785. It is possible, though less certain, that the wives born between 1731 and 1755 and their husbands were the first group of these Quakers to practise deliberate family limitation. In all probability, women born by 1730 made no attempt to control the sizes of their families.

It is important to keep in mind that this evidence for family limitation explains only part of the fall in fertility. We noted above that fertility declined at every age in each successive group, and among women who married both early and late. Deliberate family limitation can account for the decline at the older ages among wives who married early, but it does not necessarily explain why fertility also fell in the younger age groups and among the wives marrying late. Individual family histories indicate a series of factors which could have resulted in a general and involuntary decline in fertility (among them are declining health, changes in nursing customs, or separation of husband and wife because of missionary activities or migration). On the other hand, if these Quakers were particularly conscious about the size of their families, childbearing might have been reduced among women not normally expected to be deliberately limiting births. Certainly, plausible explanations exist for the decline in fertility in the younger age groups and among wives who married late, but, at present, it is not possible to determine which explanation is correct.

(v)

In view of the fact that declining fertility, attributable in part to deliberate family limitation, seems to have characterized the reproductive behaviour of the Quakers studied here about the time of the American Revolution, it is of interest to know whether their fertility patterns were similar to those of other Americans at the end of the eighteenth century. In the absence of fuller historical study, a recent work by Ansley J. Coale and Melvin Zelnik, which provides an estimate of total fertility for the year of 1800, offers us the means for making some interesting comparisons between the reproductive behaviour of these Quakers and the larger population of which they were a part.[8]

Total fertility is a measure of reproduction which indicates the average total number of children born per woman in the population under study (regardless of marital status), according to the prevailing average rates of childbearing at each age. Total fertility can be determined by summing the age-specific fertility rates calculated by single years of age. By computing the age-specific marital fertility rates for all three groups of Quaker wives together, and by converting those rates into estimated age-specific fertility for women at each age without regard to marital status, it is possible to obtain the information necessary for estimating the total fertility of the Quakers in this study.[9] Such an estimate makes it possible to compare the reproductive patterns of these Quakers with those of the general population of the United States in the period under study.

The results indicate that the Quakers had a level of reproduction well below that of all American women at the end of the eighteenth century. There is no possibility that a difference as large as that between the total fertility of 5·3 among these Friends and the 7·0 estimated by Coale and Zelnik for the United States as a whole in 1800 is a result of different techniques of estimation.[10] Furthermore, the fertility of the country as a whole did not decline to a level as low as 5·3 until after 1850. Thus, our study of a small part of the American population in the eighteenth and nineteenth centuries has uncovered a group with a fertility remarkably different from that of the larger population of which they were a part.

This finding lends added interest to the decline in the average size of the Quaker families and to the evidence of the initiation and increasing use of family limitation. It is, therefore, worth while

---

[8] Coale and Zelnik, *op. cit.*

[9] All figures below for Quaker total fertility are based on calculations given in Robert V. Wells, 'A Demographic Analysis of Some Middle Colony Quaker Families of the Eighteenth Century' (unpublished Ph.D. dissertation, Princeton University, 1969), pp. 143–148.

[10] The figures for total fertility of the U.S. population here and below are from Coale and Zelnik, *op. cit.*, p. 36.

to make estimates of the total fertility of Quaker wives born in 1730 or before, and of those born between 1756 and 1785. The results give a figure of 7·1 for the total fertility of the former group and 4·0 for the latter group. The fertility of the 'pre-revolutionary' group is essentially identical with the estimate of 7·0 for American women in 1800 made by Coale and Zelnik. On the other hand, the total fertility of 4·0 of the 'post-revolutionary' Friends is less than 60% of the estimated national average in 1800. The fertility of the white population of the United States as a whole did not fall to this level until 1889.

It is of special interest to find a group within the American colonies whose fertility was strikingly reduced before there had been a substantial decline in the overall national figure. It is also of interest that the decline resulted not only because of changing marriage patterns, but also because of a decline in fertility within marriage which was, in part, the result of the deliberate limitation of births. Although, of course, we cannot be sure, it seems plausible that the Quakers that we have studied were the vanguard in a pattern of changing behaviour that spread through the remainder of the American population during the ensuing 130 years. The implication seems clear that the reduction in fertility which was noticeable on a national level at the start of the nineteenth century was not a movement which began in every place at the same time, but rather the result of different groups experiencing changes in their childbearing patterns at various times.

ROBERT V. WELLS

Angels' Heads and Weeping Willows: Death in Early America

MARIS A. VINOVSKIS

M OST RECENT studies of America's past can be placed into one of two distinct and sometimes hostile camps. Traditional historians have continued to rely almost exclusively on literary sources of information. As a result, their work has focused on the ideology and attitudes of early Americans. On the other hand, a small group of historians, borrowing heavily from the other social sciences, have undertaken to re-create the behavioral patterns of American society in the past. Though these two approaches are potentially complementary to each other, there has been very little effort made to integrate them.

This bifurcation of approaches to the study of American history is quite evident in the recent efforts to analyze the role of death in America. Traditional historians have begun to examine the writings of early Americans in order to re-create their attitudes and images of death. Historical demographers have exploited the censuses and vital records to calculate the incidence and timing of death in early America.

This paper was presented as a public lecture at the American Antiquarian Society on May 22, 1974, while the author was the Rockefeller Fellow in the History of the Family Program at Clark University and AAS. The author is deeply indebted to Andrew Achenbaum, Georgia Bumgardner, Ronald Formisano, Tamara Hareven, John Hench, Kathryn Sklar, Mary Vinovskis, and John Zeugner for their helpful comments and suggestions.

273

But no one has attempted to explore systematically the relationship between attitudes toward death and the actual levels and trends in mortality in early America. In part, this is the result of the assumption by most historians that the attitudes toward and the incidence of death in America were identical.

In this essay we will demonstrate that most colonists did not accurately perceive the extent of mortality in their society. We will suggest some of the reasons for their misperception. Hopefully this essay will encourage other scholars to integrate attitudinal and behavioral approaches to the study of American history.

Most of us have certain preconceived notions about death in colonial America. We envision the early settlers of our country facing such a multitude of hazards that death at a fairly early age was practically inevitable. We also imagine that persons surviving to old age were quite rare and extremely fortunate in having escaped the continuous waves of famine and pestilence which swept through the population. The idea that high mortality rates prevailed in colonial America has been reinforced by the numerous instances of entire families or communities perishing in the hostile environment of the New World.

Nearly all of us are familiar with the tragic experiences of the Pilgrims who landed at Plymouth on November 11, 1620. Though only one of the 102 passengers aboard the *Mayflower* perished at sea, the eleven-week journey had left the rest of them weak, exhausted, and unprepared for the coming winter. Bradford noted their ordeal in his diary: '. . . But that which was most sadd & lamentable was, that in 2. or 3. moneths time halfe of their company dyed, espetialy in Jan: & February, being the depth of winter, and wanting houses & other comforts; being infected with the scurvie & other diseases, which this long vioage & their inacomodate condition had brought upon them; so as ther dyed some times 2. or 3.

of a day, in the foresaid time; that of 100 & odd persons, scarce 50 remained. . . .'[1]

Even those settlers who survived the rigors of the first year in the New World faced unforeseen epidemics which took very heavy tolls of the inhabitants—especially in urban areas such as Boston and Salem. In 1721 there was an outbreak of smallpox in Boston in which over fifty percent of its eleven thousand inhabitants contracted the disease. In that year the Boston death rate soared to an incredible 103 deaths per thousand population. Thus, over ten percent of the city's population died within the space of one year.[2] Only the very small percentage of the people daring enough to try the new technique of inoculation managed to escape the high death rate among those who had smallpox.[3]

Smaller communities were not safe from the terrors of epidemics. For example, in the parish of Hampton Falls in New Hampshire the 'sore-throat distemper' in 1735 nearly decimated the population. This epidemic, later identified as diphtheria, resulted in the deaths of 210 persons—or over one-sixth of the entire population of that parish. The outbreak of diphtheria caused fatalities particularly among young people—ninety-five percent of those who died in Hampton Falls were under the age of twenty. Nearly twenty families buried all of their children that year.[4]

Any person still skeptical of the existence of high mortality in early America would certainly be convinced by one of the

[1] William Bradford, *Of Plymouth Plantation*, Harvey Wish, ed. (New York, 1962), p. 70. For a more detailed discussion of the experiences of the Pilgrims, see George D. Langdon, Jr., *Pilgrim Colony: A History of New Plymouth, 1620–1691* (New Haven, 1966).

[2] On the extent of mortality in Boston, see John B. Blake, *Public Health in the Town of Boston, 1630–1882* (Cambridge, Mass., 1952).

[3] Blake, *Public Health*, pp. 74–98; John Duffy, *Epidemics in Colonial America* (Baton Rouge, 1953), pp. 16–112.

[4] Duffy, *Epidemics*, pp. 117–18; Ernest Caulfield, 'A History of the Terrible Epidemic, Vulgarly Called the Throat Distemper, as It Occurred in His Majesty's New England Colonies between 1735 and 1740,' *Yale Journal of Biology and Medicine* 11(1938–39),219–72, 277–335.

few extant life tables for that period—the Wigglesworth Life Table of 1789. Edward Wigglesworth, Hollis Professor of Divinity at Harvard, became interested in life tables when he was advising the Massachusetts Congregational Charitable Society on how to establish an annuity fund for the widows of ministers. At that time there were no life tables available for the United States from which to estimate the life expectancies of the ministers and their wives. Therefore, Wigglesworth collected bills of mortality from various New England towns with the active cooperation of the newly established Academy of Arts and Sciences in Boston. From the sixty-two bills of mortality returned, Wigglesworth constructed a life table in 1789. He calculated that the average person in New England could expect to live only 35.5 years— thus reinforcing our grim image of health conditions in early America.[5]

Most writers have argued that death rates in seventeenth- and eighteenth-century New England were very high, and there is also a consensus that life expectancy improved significantly in the first half of the nineteenth century. This interpretation is based on a comparison of Wigglesworth's Life Table of 1789 and Elliott's table of 1855 for Massachusetts. On the basis of these two tables, it appears that the average person in the Commonwealth could expect to live an additional 4.3 years by 1855.[6]

[5] Edward Wigglesworth, 'A Table Shewing the Probability of the Duration, the Decrement, and the Expectation of Life, in the States of Massachusetts and New Hampshire, formed from sixty two Bills of Mortality on the files of the American Academy of Arts and Sciences, in the Year 1789,' *Memoirs of the American Academy of Arts and Sciences*, 2, pt. 1(1793):131–35. For an analysis of the gathering of that data as well as its utilization, see Maris A. Vinovskis, 'The 1789 Life Table of Edward Wigglesworth,' *Journal of Economic History* 31(1971):570–90.

[6] Warren S. Thompson and P. K. Whelpton, *Population Trends in the United States* (New York, 1933), pp. 228–40. A more recent interpretation of mortality trends by Yasukichi Yasuba argues that death rates probably were increasing just prior to the Civil War because of the increase in urbanization and industrialization. Yasukichi Yasuba, *Birth Rates of the White Population in the United States, 1800–1860: An Economic Study*, The Johns Hopkins University Studies in Historical and Political Science, vol. 79, no. 2 (Baltimore, 1962), pp. 86–96.

Thus, the traditional picture of mortality in early America is one of high death rates in the seventeenth and eighteenth centuries followed by a marked improvement in the nineteenth century. A sociologist has recently summarized the extent of mortality in early America as follows:

> Although precise statistical evidence is lacking, the little that scientists have been able to compile from various anthropological and archaeological sources indicates that throughout most of his existence man has had to contend with an extremely high death rate. The brutally harsh conditions of life in the pre-industrial world made human survival very much a touch-and-go affair. A newborn infant had no more than a fifty-fifty chance of surviving to adulthood; the average life expectancy of primitive man was probably not much in excess of twenty-five or thirty years. Even more significant, the survival situation was not a great deal better as recently as the middle of the eighteenth century. Early records for the state of Massachusetts, for example, indicate that average life expectancy in colonial America was still somewhat less than forty years.[7]

Most studies of Puritan attitudes toward death have accepted the notion that death rates in early New England were very high. In fact, the imminence of death in Puritan society is often used by historians to explain the preoccupation of early Americans with the process of dying.

Recent work in historical demography, however, raises serious questions about the validity of the traditional view of death in early America. During the last ten years historical demographers have used family reconstitution techniques to provide a very different interpretation of mortality levels in New England.[8]

[7] Edward G. Stockwell, *Population and People* (Chicago, 1968), p. 26.

[8] Philip Greven, Jr., *Four Generations: Population, Land, and Family in Colonial Andover, Massachusetts* (Ithaca, N.Y., 1970); John Demos, *A Little Commonwealth: Family Life in Plymouth Colony* (New York, 1970); Susan L. Norton, 'Population Growth in Colonial America: A Study of Ipswich, Massachusetts,' *Population Studies* 25(1971):433–52; Kenneth A. Lockridge, 'The Population of Dedham, Massachusetts, 1636–1736,' *Economic History Review*, 2d ser. 19(1966):318–44; Daniel Scott

This recent work verifies that death rates were very high in urban areas in colonial New England. Boston deaths averaged thirty to forty per thousand population during the years 1701 to 1774. Furthermore, there were large fluctuations in the death rates in Boston. Most of the sudden rises in the death rate in 1702, 1721, 1730, and 1752 were the result of epidemics that ravaged that busy seaport (see fig. 1).

The newer work also shows that death rates in urban areas such as Boston or Salem were not typical of the rest of the population. In most rural communities, the settlers who managed to survive the hardships of the early years could look forward to many more years of life in the New World. Though data on mortality levels are very scarce for the colonial period, historical demographers have been able to provide some estimates by relying on the reconstitution of families from the vital records of the community. On the basis of detailed investigations of Andover, Dedham, Hingham, Ipswich, and Plymouth, it now appears that life expectancy was much higher in rural New England than was previously believed. These communities experienced death rates of fifteen to twenty-five per thousand rather than the higher mortality rates in Boston or Salem. Since most people in America in the seventeenth and eighteenth centuries lived in small, rural communities, not unlike these five Massachusetts towns, it is likely that most Americans did not have the same frequent encounter with death that residents of commercial centers did.

Since most seventeenth- and eighteenth-century Americans

Smith, 'The Demographic History of New England,' *Journal of Economic History* 32(1972):165–83; Maris A. Vinovskis, 'American Historical Demography: A Review Essay' *Historical Methods Newsletter* 4(1971):141–48; Maris A. Vinovskis, 'Mortality Rates and Trends in Massachusetts before 1860,' *Journal of Economic History* 32(1972):184–213.

These generalizations only apply to the New England area. Mortality rates in the colonial South were considerably higher according to some of the recent work in that area. Irene Hecht, 'The Virginia Muster of 1624/5 as a Source for Demographic History,' *William and Mary Quarterly*, 3d ser. 30(1973):65–92; Lorena S. Walsh and Russell R. Menard, 'Death in the Chesapeake: Two Life Tables for Men in Early Colonial Maryland,' *Maryland Historical Magazine* 69(1974):211–27.

Figure 1

NUMBER OF DEATHS PER THOUSAND
POPULATION IN BOSTON, 1701–74

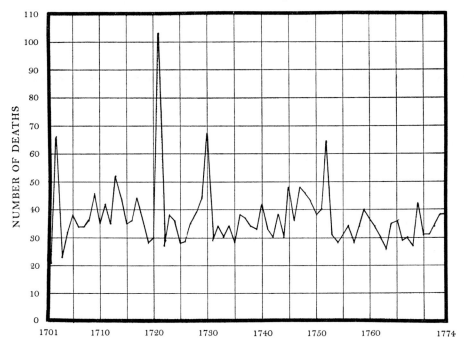

SOURCE: John B. Blake, *Public Health in the Town of Boston* (Cambridge, Mass., 1959), pp. 247–49.

were English or were at least influenced by an English heritage, it is useful to compare the death rates in the New and Old Worlds. Generally, death rates in America were lower than in Europe. Death rates for infants in Andover and Ipswich were significantly lower than those in Europe, while infant mortality rates in Salem were comparable to those in Europe. Similarly, death rates after the age of twenty were lower in most Massachusetts communities than in Europe.

These findings appear to be in direct contradiction to the expectation of life according to the Wigglesworth Life Table of 1789. A detailed examination of that life table, however, reveals serious methodological flaws in its construction and coverage. Wigglesworth's table is based only on the ages at death obtained from bills of mortality. Since he did not have data available on the population who were liable to die in that period, he was forced to assume that the age-distribution of the deaths in the bills of mortality approximated the actual age-distribution of the entire population. Though Wigglesworth realized that this crucial assumption was incorrect, his attempts to adjust his stationary population model must be viewed as intelligent guessing at best. Furthermore, his sample of towns was not representative of the entire region. Most of his data came from towns which were more urban than the area as a whole and consequently probably exaggerated the extent of colonial mortality. As a result, his estimate of life expectancy in colonial New England is probably too low and therefore does not invalidate the results from the family reconstitution studies.[9]

Another problem with many of the interpretations of living conditions in colonial America is that they are based on a faulty understanding of life tables. If the expectation of life at birth is 40.0 years, it means that the average person could expect to live that long. It does not mean, however, that once this average person had reached age twenty-one that he had only nineteen years remaining. When an individual had survived the perils of early childhood and the rigors of early adulthood, his or her chances of continuing to live were actually increased.[10] For example, the average male at age twenty-one in seventeenth-century Plymouth could expect another

[9] Vinovskis, 'The 1789 Life Table of Edward Wigglesworth.'

[10] For an introduction to the use and interpretation of life tables, see Louis I. Dublin, Alfred J. Lotka, ánd ·Mortimer Spiegelman, *Length of Life: A Study of the Life Table* (New York, 1949).

Figure 2

LIFE EXPECTANCY OF ADULTS
IN SEVENTEENTH-CENTURY PLYMOUTH

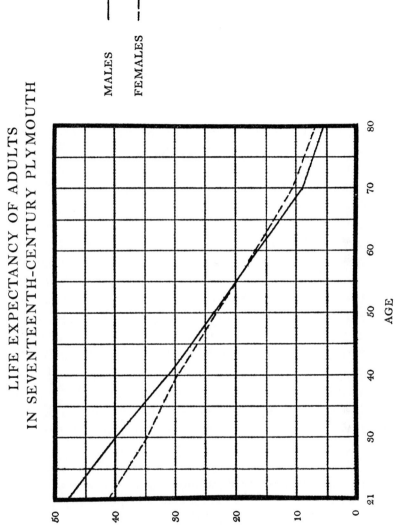

MALES

FEMALES

SOURCE: John Demos, *A Little Commonwealth: Family Life in Plymouth Colony* (New York, 1970), p. 192.

48.2 years of life and the average female at the same age another 41.4 years (see fig. 2).

Most of the differences in life expectancy between colonial Americans and Americans of today are due to the much higher rate of infant and child mortality in the past. Adults in colonial New England often could anticipate lives almost as long as each one of us today—especially if they were male. The average male at age twenty-one in seventeenth-century Plymouth had a life expectancy only one year less than the typical American male today. The average female at age twenty-one in seventeenth-century Plymouth, however, could expect to live 14.6 years less than her counterpart today—in large measure because maternal mortality rates in colonial America were very high.

Death rates in early America did not remain constant. In the seventeenth century there were large rural-urban differences in mortality in Massachusetts since small agricultural communities such as Dedham, Plymouth, Andover, Hingham, and Ipswich had relatively high life expectancies whereas Boston and Salem had much lower ones. The eighteenth century witnessed the convergence of these rates as mortality rose slightly in some of the smaller towns while death rates fell in Salem. Boston continued to have very high death rates throughout the eighteenth century. In the early nineteenth century there was a further convergence as Boston death rates dropped to around twenty per thousand while mortality in rural areas remained fairly steady.[11]

In order to analyze the level of mortality in nineteenth-century America in more detail and to look especially at the rural-urban differences, life tables for various Massachusetts towns in 1860 have been calculated from the federal census and the state vital records. Since the only previous life table for this period that might be of use to us, Elliott's Life Table of 1855, is inadequate because of several methodological short-

[11] Vinovskis, 'Mortality Rates and Trends.'

Figure 3

LIFE EXPECTANCY AT BIRTH IN MASSACHUSETTS TOWNS IN 1860

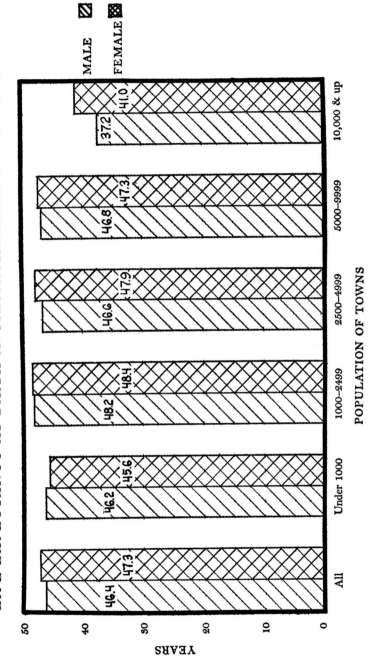

SOURCE: Maris A. Vinovskis, 'Mortality Rates and Trends in Massachusetts before 1860,' *Journal of Economic History* 32(1972):211.

comings, these tables provide an unusual opportunity to assess the presence of death in mid-nineteenth-century society.[12]

Life expectancy at birth in Massachusetts in 1860 was relatively high compared to most European countries. The average male at birth had a life expectancy of 46.4 years while the average female could look forward to 47.3 years of life (see fig. 3).

Contrary to the assertions of most other scholars, there was very little difference in mortality between rural and urban areas in Massachusetts. The major difference according to town size was between towns with populations under 10,000 and those with populations over 10,000. Furthermore, socioeconomic differences among these towns could not account for a large proportion of the differences in mortality. In a multiple regression analysis where the age-standardized death rate was the dependent variable and a variety of socioeconomic characteristics of those towns were the independent variables, the resultant equation for the state accounted for less than fifteen percent of the variance in the death rates. Put more simply, our detailed statistical analysis of mortality levels among Massachusetts towns in 1860 displayed a remarkable similarity amongst themselves.[13]

Compared to England and Wales in 1838–54, life expectancy in Massachusetts in 1860 was significantly higher for both males and females (see fig. 4). It is interesting to observe the generally similar pattern in life expectancy for both areas. If an American, English, or Welsh child survived the

---

[12] Ibid.

[13] Ibid. The results of this regression analysis have not been published yet. However, the use of the 1860 standardized mortality in a regression analysis of fertility differentials in Massachusetts is reported in Maris A. Vinovskis, 'A Multivariate Regression Analysis of Fertility Differentials among Massachusetts Towns and Regions in 1860,' a paper presented at the Conference on Early Industrialization, Shifts in Fertility, and Changes in the Family Structure at Princeton University, June 18 – July 10, 1972 (forthcoming in a volume of the conference proceedings to be edited by Charles Tilly).

Figure 4

LIFE EXPECTANCY IN MASSACHUSETTS IN 1860
AND IN ENGLAND AND WALES IN 1838-54

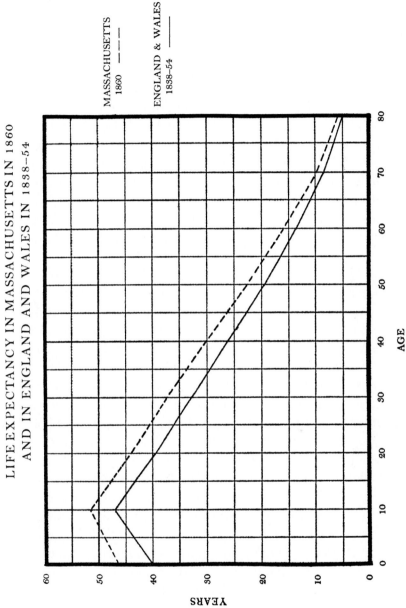

MASSACHUSETTS
1860

ENGLAND & WALES
1838-54

Sources: Maris A. Vinovskis, 'Mortality Rates and Trends in Massachusetts before 1860,' *Journal of Economic History* 32(1972):211; Louis I. Dublin, Alfred J. Lotka, and Mortimer Spiegelman, *Length of Life* (New York, 1949), p. 346.

high levels of infant and child mortality, his life expectancy increased dramatically.

Though the overall level of mortality in colonial New England was probably much lower than previously estimated, it does not mean that death was not a serious problem—particularly for the young. Adults in rural New England could anticipate reasonably long lives but their children faced much worse odds. Infant mortality rates in colonial America ranged from 115 per thousand births in seventeenth-century Andover to 313 per thousand for females and 202 per thousand for males in seventeenth-century Salem. In other words, ten to thirty percent of the children never survived for the first year of life. In the United States in 1974, on the other hand, the infant mortality rate was 16.5 per thousand—or almost ten times less than that of the colonial period.

The higher mortality rate among children in the past can be illustrated by comparing the expectation ot life for males in Massachusetts in 1860 with those of males in the United States in 1969 (see fig. 5). At the later ages the expectation of life for both groups is very similar, but there is a very substantial difference at birth. The average male child at birth today can expect to live to age 67.8; if he survives to age ten, he increases his total life expectation by only 1.8 years. On the other hand, the average male child in Massachusetts born in 1860 could anticipate 46.4 years of life; if he survived to age ten, his total life expectancy would increase by 16.6 years.

In addition, since the average family in colonial New England usually had three times as many children as we have today, there was a high probability that most families would experience the loss of at least one child during their lifetimes. The combination of high infant mortality rates and high birth rates increased the likelihood that the typical family in early America would have had to deal with the death of a member of their nuclear family.

Figure 5

LIFE EXPECTANCY IN MASSACHUSETTS IN 1860 AND IN U.S. IN 1969

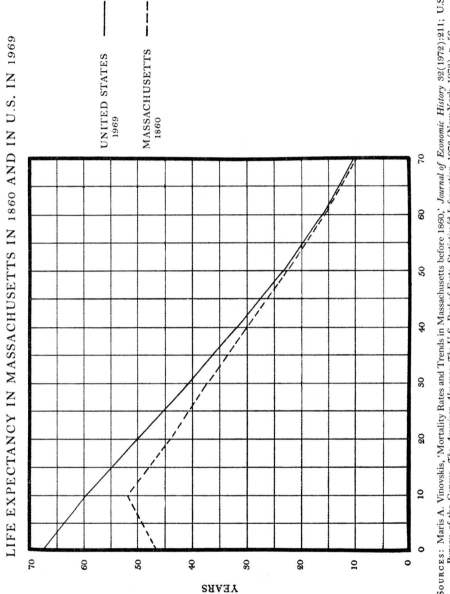

SOURCES: Maris A. Vinovskis, 'Mortality Rates and Trends in Massachusetts before 1860,' *Journal of Economic History* 32(1972):211; U.S. Bureau of the Census, *The American Almanac: The U.S. Book of Facts, Statistics & Information, 1973* (New York, 1973), p. 56.

Our analysis of mortality levels and trends in New England before 1860 suggests that most individuals, especially those who had survived the dangers of early childhood, could look forward to reasonably long lives. Therefore, we might expect that our Puritan ancestors would not have been very concerned or worried about mortality—especially about deaths among adults. Yet New England society seemed obsessed with death despite the moderate mortality rates for that period. Even more astonishing is the fact that most people in those days greatly overestimated the extent of mortality in their society.

Some colonists, such as Edward Wigglesworth, did realize that death rates in the New World were somewhat lower than in England. But even Wigglesworth, the foremost expert on colonial mortality, seriously underestimated the expectation of life in early New England. The general populace seemed convinced that death rates were very high. Anyone reading through the diaries of these people is immediately struck by the fascination and concern with death. The image of early American society one receives from these writings is that of a very unhealthy environment in which each individual anticipates his demise at any moment.[14]

For example, Samuel Rodman began to keep a diary at age twenty-nine in 1821. He was a very scientifically oriented man who collected weather data from 1812 to 1876 and was generally calm about discussions of death throughout his diary during the next thirty-eight years. But it is very interesting to observe how he misperceived the dangers to his life even well into the nineteenth century.

Rodman often mentions how he should devote more attention to his spiritual needs because he anticipates he may die

---

[14] Various scholars have commented on the preoccupation of early Americans with the issue of death in their writings. For example, see Charles Allen Shively, 'A History of the Conception of Death in America, 1650–1860,' (Ph.D. diss., Harvard University, 1969); Lewis O. Saum, 'Death in the Popular Mind of Pre–Civil War America,' *American Quarterly* 26(1974):477–95.

at any moment. In 1838 he celebrates his birthday by noting in his diary that 'this is the 46th anniversary of my birth. I have lived therefore already considerably beyond the average of human life.'[15] Three years later, he repeats the general theme: 'I should not conclude this note without attesting to the fact that this is my 49th anniversary, and that I have entered on my 50th year. It seems a matter of surprise that I have lived so long, and without yet any material change. I have actually passed beyond the period of youth and middle age and may justly be classed among the old.'[16]

If Rodman had had the benefit of our life tables for 1860, he could have taken comfort in the fact that he was likely to survive at least another twenty years at age fifty. The intriguing question is why Rodman, an unusually intelligent and perceptive man, should have underestimated so greatly the extent of longevity in his society. Why did he and so many other diarists of the period feel that death was imminent when in fact the death rates for adults in their communities were not very high?

Perhaps the misperceptions of the extent of mortality in New England society were due to the unusual life experiences of those individuals who kept diaries. Maybe they were less healthy and/or came from families which had experienced higher mortality than the rest of the population. Keeping a diary might be part of an attempt to introduce order and stability in a life that was constantly overshadowed by the presence of death.

In the case of Samuel Rodman, this interpretation does not appear to be valid. Despite his frequent anticipations of dying, he managed to survive to age eighty-four and his wife lived to be eighty-two. Though two of their eight children did die early, at ages one and three, the remaining six lived to

---

[15] Zepharriah Pease, ed., *The Diary of Samuel Rodman: A New Bedford Chronicle of Thirty-Seven Years: 1821–1859* (New Bedford, Mass., 1927), p. 180.

[16] Ibid., p. 218.

the ages of twenty-three, sixty-one, seventy-seven, seventy-eight, eighty-seven, and ninety-one. One might properly object that these figures are misleading because Samuel Rodman had no way of knowing how long he or his offspring would survive. Perhaps he was merely reacting to the much higher mortality of his parents and siblings. Yet his father lived to age eighty-two and his mother to age ninety-five. Furthermore, his sisters survived to the ages of thirty-one, sixty, seventy-eight, and eighty-one while his brothers died at ages twenty-four, sixty-eight, and eighty-one.[17] In other words, whatever indications of low life expectancy that Rodman had, they probably did not come mainly from the experiences of his immediate family.

Though our analysis of Rodman's own longevity suggests that his anticipation of imminent death probably was not based on his own physical frailty, we should be careful not to generalize about the relationship between personal health and preoccupation with death among diarists on the basis of just one individual. Kathryn Kish Sklar has coded data from published diaries of seventy-one American women who lived in the eighteenth and early nineteenth centuries. These data are of particular interest to us because many historians have remarked on the preoccupation of women with items about health and death in their diaries. We already know that women who kept diaries were more educated than the rest of the population and probably came from more affluent backgrounds. Using her data, it is possible to calculate age at death for forty of these women.[18] Therefore, one is now able to estimate the life expectancy of these women who kept diaries.

Of the forty women, the average age at death was 56.4 years. This compares very favorably with the expectation of

---

[17] Ibid.

[18] I am deeply indebted to Kathryn Kish Sklar of the University of California, Los Angeles, for allowing me to use her data for these calculations.

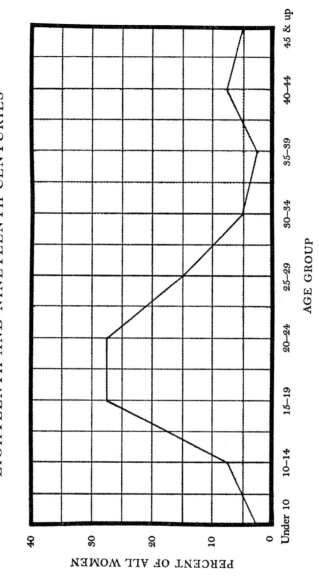

Figure 6

DISTRIBUTION OF AGES AT WHICH WOMEN
BEGAN TO KEEP THEIR DIARIES IN THE
EIGHTEENTH AND NINETEENTH CENTURIES

SOURCE: Calculated from data on American diaries collected by Kathryn Kish
Sklar of the University of California, Los Angeles.

life at birth for Massachusetts women in 1860 of 47.3 years. This is a very misleading comparison, however, because most women did not begin to keep diaries until they had already survived the perils of early childhood (see fig. 6).

Instead, we need to take into consideration the ages at which these women began their diaries before calculating their life expectancies. Now we can compare their expectation of life to that of women in the general public (see fig. 7).

The results indicate that women who kept diaries were in fact less healthy than Massachusetts women in 1860—particularly at ages twenty and thirty. Though this does reinforce the argument that unhealthy people were more likely to keep diaries, it is important to bear in mind that the average woman who kept a diary at age twenty could expect to live another 35.5 years. Thus, most women who kept these diaries were actually quite healthy and their own prospect of dying in the very near future was not very likely despite their utterances to the contrary in those diaries.

Since we cannot account for the misperceptions of the level of mortality in early New England in terms of the colonists' personal encounters with death, we need to look at the general context of life in that period to see what factors encouraged people to imagine such high death rates—especially among the adult population. Though death is a biological phenomenon, the reactions of people to it are largely defined by the manner in which society handles its dying. It is my contention that the great emphasis placed on death in early New England led people to overestimate the extent of its occurrence in their communities and lives.

Americans today are remarkably unwilling to discuss death. Our society refuses to face the issue of death openly—thus, death has replaced sex as the major taboo. Geoffrey Gorer in a very insightful essay has argued that 'In the 20th century there seems to have been an unremarked shift in prudery;

Figure 7

LIFE EXPECTANCY OF MASSACHUSETTS
FEMALES IN 1860 AND EIGHTEENTH- AND
NINETEENTH-CENTURY FEMALE DIARISTS

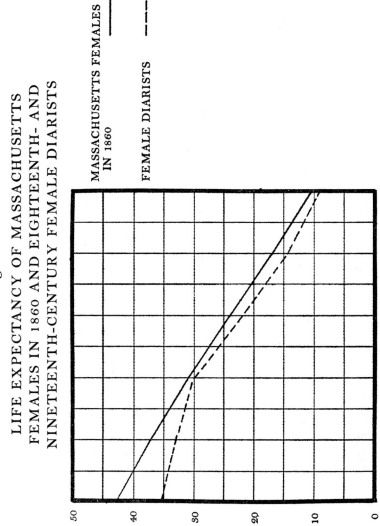

MASSACHUSETTS FEMALES
IN 1860

FEMALE DIARISTS

SOURCE: Calculated from data on American diaries collected by Kathryn Kish Sklar
of the University of California, Los Angeles.

whereas copulation has become more and more mentionable, particularly in the Anglo-Saxon societies, death has become more and more unmentionable as a natural process.'[19]

Puritan society had a very different attitude toward death —there was a great fascination and interest in that subject and people were encouraged to discuss it amongst themselves. Furthermore, the very process of dying in early New England forced people to come to terms with death rather than being able to pretend that death did not really exist.[20]

The location in which an individual dies is important because it determines the access his relatives and friends will have to him during that time. In addition, the place where a person dies also influences the amount of exposure the rest of society will have to the process of dying.

Today there is a debate over whether it is better to die at home or in a hospital. Some elderly actually prefer to die away from home in order to avoid becoming burdens to their families. Yet when one dies at home he or she is in familiar surroundings and among friends. A patient who is hospitalized is largely removed from the help and care of his family.

Public opinion in America has gradually shifted away from the idea of dying at home. Less than a third of the public now would prefer to have someone die at home. In 1968 a public opinion poll asked: 'Do you feel that if an individual is dying and is beyond any available medical aid, that it is more desirable to remove the person to a hospital or other institution, rather than have them remain at home?' The replies were as follows:[21]

---

[19] Geoffrey Gorer, *Death, Grief, and Mourning* (Garden City, N.Y., 1965), pp. 192–99.

[20] For analyses of the reactions of Puritans to death, see David E. Stannard, 'Death and Dying in Puritan New England,' *American Historical Review* 78(1973):1305–30; Shively, 'History of the Conception of Death.'

[21] Glen M. Vernon, *Sociology of Death: An Analysis of Death-Related Behavior* (New York, 1970), p. 110. For a more general discussion of American attitudes toward death, see Richard G. Dumont and Dennis C. Foss, *The American View of Death: Acceptance or Denial?* (Cambridge, Mass., 1972).

	N	*Percent*
Yes, this is best for all concerned	669	34.1
No, death should be at home if at all possible	553	28.2
Undecided	692	35.3
No answer	47	2.4

This change in attitudes has been accompanied by a shift in the actual location of dying. In 1963, fifty-three percent of all deaths occurred in a hospital and many others in nursing homes or as a result of accidents outside the home.[22] As a result, most Americans today do not often see the process of dying firsthand. This isolation from death is compounded by the development of 'retirement cities' in the United States where the elderly are in effect segregated from the rest of society. As Robert Fulton has so aptly put it, 'Here for the first time modern man is able to avoid almost entirely the grief and anguish of death. By encouraging the aged members of the society to congregate in segregated communities, familial and friendship commitments are made fewer by time and distance, and emotional and social bonds are loosened. Physically and emotionally separated from those most likely to die, the modern individual is freed of the shock he would otherwise experience from their death. Herein may lie a form of man's "conquest" of death.'[23]

The colonists died mainly in their own homes since there were few hospitals or other institutions in which the aged could be placed. In the absence of a specialized nursing profession, relatives and neighbors attended to the needs of the dying—thus increasing the amount of contact between the living and the dying.

The homes of the early colonists were very small com-

[22] Robert L. Fulton, 'Death and the Self,' *Journal of Religion and Health* 3(1964): 354.
[23] Ibid., p. 367.

pared to today—especially those built in the early years of settlement. According to the probate inventories, the average number of rooms per house in rural Suffolk County, Massachusetts, rose from 4.3 in 1675–99, to 5.7 in 1700–19, and to 6.0 in 1750–75.[24] Thus, there was relatively little privacy available in these homes to shield the dying person from the rest of the family even if the colonists had desired to isolate him.

Finally, since there were no funeral homes in the seventeenth and eighteenth centuries, the dead person remained in his own home where friends and neighbors could view him. As the art of embalming was still in its infancy in colonial America, very little effort was made to preserve or repair the dead body. People were forced to see the dead persons as they were rather than having them cosmetically preserved or improved to enhance their appearance in death.[25]

The funeral itself encouraged people to come into intimate contact with death. At first funerals in colonial America were simple affairs since there was an effort to avoid the excesses of English funeral practices. One contemporary observer of early colonial funerals described them: 'At Burials nothing is read, nor any funeral sermon made, but all the neighborhood or a goodly company of them come together by tolling of the bell, and carry the dead solemnly to his grave, and then stand by him while he is buried. The ministers are most commonly present.'[26]

Gradually funerals became more elaborate and expensive. The practice of distributing gifts of gloves, rings, or scarfs to participants at funerals was a custom brought over from Eng-

[24] For a description of the development of embalming in America, see Robert W. Habenstein and William M. Lamers, *The History of American Funeral Directing* (Milwaukee, 1955).

[25] David H. Flaherty, *Privacy in Colonial New England* (Charlottesville, Va., 1972), p. 39.

[26] Thomas Lechford, *Plain Dealing or News from New England*, ed. J. Hammond Trumbull (Boston, 1867), pp. 87–88.

land and which flourished in New England in the late seventeenth and eighteenth centuries. The practice quickly became excessive as the quality of the gifts distributed was supposed to reflect the social status of the deceased. At the funeral of Governor Belcher's wife in 1736, over 1,000 pairs of gloves were distributed. Ministers, who usually received gifts at all the funerals they attended, often accumulated large quantities of such items. For example, Andrew Eliot, minister of the North Church in Boston received 2,940 pairs of funeral gloves in his thirty-two years in the pulpit. Rather than allow such gifts to overwhelm his household, Reverend Eliot sold them to supplement his modest salary.[27]

As the costs of these funeral items rose, there were numerous attempts by the General Court as well as individual citizens to curtail funeral expenses. None of the proposed measures, however, succeeded because our colonial ancestors were just as determined to have extravagant funerals then as we are today.[28]

But these social aspects of funerals provided still greater encouragement for people to attend them. It was expected in the small rural communities of New England that everyone would attend the funerals of any of their townsmen. Given the death rate of that period, it was likely that in a small village of a thousand inhabitants, there would be at least ten to twenty-five funerals each year. Since most burials were handled by the neighbors and friends rather than by a professional undertaker, the significance of each funeral became even more important to the living. Thus, there was a constant reminder to the entire community of the presence of

---

[27] For a description of the extravagant expenditures on early funerals, see Alice Morse Earle, *Customs and Fashions in Old New England* (New York, 1894).

[28] Though Jessica Mitford argues that the excesses in funeral expenditures are only a recent phenomena, there is ample evidence that often the colonists also spent large sums on their funerals. Jessica Mitford, *The American Way of Death*, paperback ed. (Greenwich, Conn., 1963).

death whereas today most of us are not affected by the deaths of anyone except very close friends or relatives.

Finally, the practice of giving funeral sermons became established by the early eighteenth century. Ministers now used the occasion of the gathering at the grave to preach to the living the importance of coming to terms with the inevitability of death. Increasingly these sermons were published and distributed to the congregation as a remembrance of the departed and a reminder of the frailty of life.[29]

The awareness of death by an individual in colonial America did not end with the lowering of the body into the grave. The grave as well as the burial place continued to further the notion of the shortness of life on earth for the survivors. Scholars such as Harriette Forbes, Allan Ludwig, and Dickran and Ann Tashjian have already explored the artistic and symbolic implications of the early gravestones that are dotted throughout the countryside. Rather than simply repeat their insightful analyses of the meaning of these early artifacts, we will try only to reconstruct how these images of death might have influenced the perceptions of our ancestors about the extent of mortality in their communities.[30]

Before 1660, graveyards in New England were quite plain. Often people were buried in convenient locations near their homes rather than being interred in burial grounds near the churches. We can understand this casual attitude toward the burial site better if we recall that in England the common practice had been to bury many different individuals on the same plot of land. No effort was made to keep a separate spot for each person who died—rather bodies were buried with the expectation that someone else would share that same

---

[29] On the evolution of Puritan attitudes and practices at funerals, see Shively, 'History of the Conception of Death.'

[30] Harriette Merrifield Forbes, *Gravestones of Early New England and the Men Who Made Them, 1653–1800* (New York, 1927); Allan I. Ludwig, *Graven Images: New England Stonecarving and Its Symbols, 1650–1815* (Middletown, Conn., 1966); Dickran and Ann Tashjian, *Memorials for Children of Change: The Art of Early New England Stonecarving* (Middletown, Conn., 1974).

area as soon as the previous occupant had been decomposed sufficiently. Thus, the church of St. John the Baptist in Widford, Hertfordshire, buried nearly 5,000 people in a plot of less than half an acre in area. Usually these early English burials did not include even placing the deceased in a coffin.[31]

Gradually the burial places became more important to the Puritans as a reminder of the presence of death. As efforts were made to preserve the memory of those who had departed, gravestones were used to identify the bodily remains as well as to provide inspiration for the living. Partly for ornamental reasons but mainly for instructing the living, colonial gravestones began to depict the reality of death.

These symbolic illustrations of death were significant reminders of the frailty of life in a society in which many of its citizens were illiterate and therefore unable to read the messages about death from the inscriptions on the gravestones. These grim symbols of death were meant to remind the living that the day of judgment was coming and that all would be called upon to account for their lives.[32]

The symbolic messages of the early New England gravestones were usually simpler and plainer than those on the religious art works of Europe at that time. The Puritans were very anxious to avoid duplication of symbols that were commonly identified with the Roman Catholic Church. The imagery of the early New England gravestones ranged across a wide variety of themes—from emblems of death to symbols of resurrection. Furthermore, there was an evolution in gravestone imagery over time—from the vivid and often harsh depiction of death by the use of death's heads to the more cheerful and subtle representations of death by winged cherubs and weeping willows in the late eighteenth and early nineteenth centuries.[33]

[31] Habenstein and Lamers, *History of American Funeral Directing*, pp. 91–191.

[32] On the extent of illiteracy in early New England, see Kenneth A. Lockridge, *Literacy in Colonial New England* (New York, 1974).

[33] Ludwig, *Graven Images*; Tashjian, *Memorials for Children of Change*.

Probably the single most important factor in reminding early New Englanders of the presence of death was their religion which placed such great emphasis on death and an afterlife for those who had been saved. Ministers preached with great frequency about death and the demise of any member of the congregation was seen as an opportunity to remind the living of the proper ways of serving God.[34]

Ministers tried to encourage everyone in their congregations to think about the meaning of death. Thus, Cotton Mather in his work *A Christian Funeral* advises the survivors that 'when any Person known to me *Dies*, I would set my self particularly to consider; *What lesson of goodness or Wisdom I may learn from any thing that I may observe in the Life of that Person.*'[35] And in his *Death Made Easie & Happy*, Mather implores his readers to remind themselves each day that 'he is to die shortly. Let us look upon everything as a sort of Death's-Head set before us, with a *Memento mortis* written upon it.'[36]

In the early decades of settlement, church leaders were relatively matter-of-fact about the presence and inevitability of death. But as the children of the original settlers gradually turned away from the church, there was a widespread fear that their errand in the wilderness might fail. Ministers now seized upon the terrors of death to persuade their sinful townsmen to return to God's way. Thus, Solomon Stoddard in his *The Efficacy of the Fear of Hell to Restrain Men from Sin* wrote, 'Many seem to be Incorrigible and Obstinate in their Pride and Luxury and Profaness . . . they are afraid of Poverty, and afraid of Sickness, but not afraid of Hell; that

[34] On the importance of religion during this period, see John Higham, 'Hanging Together: Divergent Unities in American History,' *Journal of American History* 61(1974):5–29. For a very useful analysis of the role of liberal clergymen in emphasizing death in the mid-nineteenth century, see Ann Douglass, 'Heaven Our Home: Consolation Literature in the Northern United States, 1830–1880,' *American Quarterly* 26(1974):496–515.

[35] Cotton Mather, *A Christian Funeral* (Boston, 1713), p. 27.

[36] Cotton Mather, *Death Made Easie & Happy* (London, 1701), p. 94.

MARIS A. VINOVSKIS

would restrain them from sinful Practices, Destruction from God would be a Terrour to them.'[37]

Increasingly these ministers directed their message to young children. From a very early age, Puritan children were admonished to think of their impending doom in hell unless they were saved by God's grace.[38] This message can be seen in an anonymous broadside of that period:

> My Cry's to you, my Children . . .
> Be wise before it be too late.
> Think on your latter end.
> Though you are young and yet you must die,
>   and hasten to the Pit.[39]

People were also encouraged to keep diaries in which they recorded their spiritual progress and failings. There seems to have been much emphasis on continually thinking about the shortness of one's own life. Therefore, it is not surprising that the death of anyone in the community often stimulated these diarists to reflect on their own precarious situation even though the actual conditions of life in that society were much healthier than they imagined.

Perhaps now we are in a better position to account for the misperceptions of early New Englanders of the level of mortality in their society. They came from England where mortality rates were very high. Their expectations of continued high mortality in the New World were reinforced by the difficulties of the early years of settlement, the uncertainty of life due to the presence of periodic epidemics, and the particularly high mortality of their children. Though their chances of survival in America were actually much better than those of

[37] Solomon Stoddard, *The Efficacy of the Fear of Hell to Restrain Men from Sin* (Boston, 1713), p. 10.

[38] The best account of death and young children in early American society is by David E. Stannard, 'Death and the Puritan Child,' *American Quarterly* 26(1974): 456–76.

[39] Quoted in Shively, 'History of the Conception of Death,' p. 52.

their relatives and friends in the old country, they usually did not realize this fact because of the great emphasis that was placed on death by their religion. The continued reminder of the shortness of their lives whenever anyone died made it difficult for the average person to comprehend the changes in the overall mortality level that had occurred. Furthermore, their incessant preoccupation with death helps to explain why most scholars of colonial history thought that there was such a high death rate in the seventeenth and eighteenth centuries. Since most of these historians relied only on literary evidence, there was no reason for them to suspect that the colonists had incorrectly assessed the living conditions in early New England.

Colonial Gravestones and Demography

EDWIN S. DETHLEFSEN

Anthropology Department, Harvard University, Cambridge, Massachusetts 02238

ABSTRACT   This paper discusses in a general way the range and use of demographic data that are, or may be, retrieved from colonial New England gravestones. In particular it examines some limitations of the usefulness of these data. The uses of gravestone data are also discussed in conjunction with those of published vital records and of early census figures. An optimistic view is expressed of the feasability of using such data in bridging the "credibility gap" between paleo and modern demography, with particular reference to possible studies of average age at death and of population composition and change.

The cemeteries of colonial New England promise to be of interest in demographic research because:

1. the colonization of New England represents a well-documented case of transfer of an established culture into a new and essentially unoccupied niche; since there have been a number of other such instances in recorded history it is of interest here to examine the available details of culture and population change;

2. intrinsic limitations on paleodemographic data have created a sizeable methodological gap between its procedures and those of modern demography.

I hope that experimentation with colonial cemetery data may offer opportunities to bridge this gap. The volume and reliability of the data to be described lie somewhere between those of pre-literate paleo and modern demographic data, so it may be possible, by judicious use of these data, to extend backwards our knowledge and understanding of human demographic change.

THE DATA

The primary data consist of inscriptions on gravestones in colonial cemeteries located in or near most cities and towns of New England. Most of these graveyards, with their stones often dating from the late seventeenth century, are in a remarkably good state of preservation, the majority of headstones still standing and legible.

Most of the earliest stones are of slate and are extremely durable, although durability varies to some extent with the re-gion. Black and reddish slate stones even of the seventeenth century have borne the climate well and are still easily legible, while some of the more schisty sorts of greenish slate used in Plymouth County, Massachusetts, have survived poorly and are difficult to read. In some areas around the mid-eighteenth century many gravestones were made of a coarse red sandstone which has not survived very well, especially along the coast. Marble stones had begun to be produced by 1810 in many regions and by 1850 were in the majority as memorial choices in New England, but marble is perhaps the least durable of gravestone material.

Every headstone bears the full name of the deceased. If the deceased is a married female her name is accompanied by that of her husband. In a small percentage of cases her name is also accompanied by those of her parents, or at least that of her father, where the parents were people of importance. In the case of a deceased child, or of an unmarried female aged less than about forty, the parents' names are included.

All seventeenth and eighteenth century stones bear inscribed the date of death to the day. Age at death is always given to the year, frequently to the day and hour.

Marital and familial status is determinable usually by inference in the case of a female, and in the case of males whose wives and/or children are represented elsewhere in the same sample. Otherwise there is usually no indication of the family status of adult males. Sex is easy to determine from the given name. In the rela-

From *American Journal of Physical Anthropology.*
"Colonial Gravestones and Demography," **31**, No. 3, 321–333 (1969). Reprinted by permission of Johnson Reprint Corporation.

tively rare occurrences of infant burials where parents' names only are given the child's sex cannot be determined except for frequent cases designating "Infant son of . . .", etc.

Epitaphs occasionally give cause of death and, where the stone is a cenotaph, indicate the place of death. But the number of such references is too small to be of statistical use.

VITAL RECORDS

Two kinds of occasional supplementary data sources may turn out to be of some consequence. According to an entry made in 1646 to the *Laws of the Colony of New Plymouth*, it was enacted

> ". . . by the Court That there Shalbe in every Towne within this Government a Cleark or some one appoynted and ordayned to keepe a register of the day & yeare of the marriage, birth and buriall of every man woeman and child within their townshippe." (Brigham, 1836, p86)

All persons having children or being married or closely related to anyone deceased were required to report these events to the Town Clerk, the penalty for failure to do so being a fine of three shillings.

> "And the Clearke, or register keeper of each Townshippe shall exhibite a true & perfect Copy fairely written annually at March Courte unto the said Courte of all birthes, marriages and burialls of the yeare past." (Brigham, 1836, p87)

Unfortunately such records, however carefully they may have been kept, have for the most part long since disappeared. But many local New England historical societies have compiled sets of vital records gleaned from a variety of sources, notably the cemeteries but including church records, family bibles, town records, and whatever else the investigators were able to find; hence for a given town the available periodic mortality sample is likely to be quite a bit greater than that offered by the graveyard alone. This provides conditions for comparing the probable degrees of randomness of representation at least in selected cemeteries. The published or written records, where available, bear the added advantage of containing information on births and marriages as well as deaths. Even these records, however, contain relatively few statistics pertaining to times be-

fore the mid-eighteenth century, while the graveyard data generally begin to be statistically useful shortly after 1700, and sometimes earlier.

CENSUS DATA

Another set of demographic data which can be useful in checking the validity of the kinds already discussed are census figures, available for parts of Massachusetts for the years 1765 (Benton, '05) and 1776 (scattered sources), and for all of the United States beginning with the first official census of 1790 (Bureau of the Census, '67). These are certainly not of a precision to make a modern demographer jump for joy, but they are far superior to what is usually available to the paleodemographer.

While the reporting method varied somewhat from census to census, one can in general discover from each the: population of a given town; number of households; number of individuals by sex and by some measure of age. These data on population composition are such that it may be possible to make good and dependable tests of the cemetery data through the construction of life tables and other, related treatment of the latter data. One may test the usefulness of the vital records of certain towns in the same way. We cannot be entirely certain of the accuracy of the earliest census figures but it is unlikely that they are, for the purposes suggested in this paper, dangerously erroneous.

A further possibility for the census records is that they offer direct data for studying population movement and related change in population density. Furthermore these figures may offer a sufficient basis for approximations-by-extrapolation to earlier population sizes for which direct data are not available.

CAUSE OF DEATH

Gravestones are inadequate records of cause of death. Among those erected before 1840 the proportion bearing such information averages somewhat less than five percent, and there is considerable bias as to those causes which *are* recorded on the stones. For example, of the forty two stones (out of about 900) giving cause of death in Plymouth, thirty three are deaths from drowning or from loss at sea, and two more are deaths from lightening. Of the thirteen gravestones recording causes in Lexington eight named smallpox, five of which cases occurred in the same year.

Drowning and loss at sea are bound to occur more often in coastal towns than in-land, and we know that Lexington was a frequented retreat from Boston's epidemics of smallpox. Even so, neither drowning nor smallpox ever approached the high frequencies indicated if we were to use the gravestone records as our sole source of information. Drowning and loss at sea simply were more worthy of incisive re-mark than were more commonplace causes. One must also consider it unlikely that drowning or smallpox were often confused with other causes of death. Perhaps if one were assured that one knew the spe-cific cause of another's demise one was more inclined to say so on his gravestone. Similarly, rare accidental causes were more often stated, and causes from which moral messages might be derived. So we see here that a man was struck by lightening and there that a disobedient child fell from a rooftop.

On the other hand many of the pub-lished volumes of vital records list some sort of "cause" of death in a relatively high proportion of cases. In the vital records of Kingston, Massachusetts, for example, more than half the mortality listings be-fore 1850 include some suggestion as to cause of death. For the same town in the period between 1800 and 1850 about 90% of the mortality entries list cause of death. But in the early nineteenth century there was still much confusion of symptoms with causes in mortality records; hence one finds many individuals dying simply of "fever" or dropsy." Even with this sort of data it should be possible to work out a broadly categorical system by which causes of death in colonial times may statistically be compared with modern day causes. One possibility is to apply the Modern Standard Nomenclature (Plunkett and Hayden, '52) to the causes of death listed before 1850 in Kingston. It is al-ready perfectly clear by inspection of the data that deaths not only from causes as-sociated with childbirth but from acciden-tal causes, particularly drowning, were rel-atively more frequent in colonial times than they are today.

AGE AT DEATH

The average age at death during the eighteenth century for the various grave-yards examined so far ranges from about twenty-nine to forty-five years, the lower figure occurring least frequently. While much of this range may be due to un-known biases in local samples, it is none-the less true that, even as early as the eighteenth century, the age composition of the various towns differed markedly (table 1). Boston, for example, had already be-come heavily urbanized and the data from its largest cemetery show an expectedly low proportion of subadults. On the other hand, Sudbury, being strictly a rural, agri-cultural community, had a higher propor-tion of subadult deaths, no doubt because there were more subadults around, rela-tively speaking.

Infant mortality is probably not as well represented in graveyards as is adult mor-tality. One would expect this to be the case, since gravestones were a source of

TABLE 1

Mortality data for six towns in eastern Massachusetts, 1700–1799

Town	Data Source	n	Subadults [1]	$\overline{A}_d$
			%	
Sudbury	Cemetery	69	37.7	39.1
Boston	Cemetery (Copp's Hill)	182	22.5	39.6
Charlestown	Cemetery (Phipps St.)	111	31.5	37.0
Cambridge	Cemetery	139	25.9	40.5
Lexington	Cemetery	281	22.8	45.0
Hingham	Cemetery	227	—	37.5

[1] Subadults aged 0–19.

some expense. When we turn to written vital records, however, we find, at least in the case of Sudbury, that the estimated true proportion of subadults in the written records is roughly the same as that in the cemetery (table 2). Unfortunately, while age at death is regularly given on the gravestones it is not always given in the vital records. Hence if we look at the proportions of subadults among those deaths actually recorded by age we find a bias in age records that makes the proportion of subadults appear to be 100% higher than it actually is. So far as Sudbury and age at death are concerned, the cemetery sample, although smaller, is without a doubt the more dependable data source.

Sudbury is something of an exceptional case in its contrast between cemetery data and Vital Records. If we look at average age of death in Kingston and Cohasset (table 3), we find that similar problems arise, although not quite so serious. In the written records of these towns age at death is given in most of the mortality listings. But, while the cemeteries increase more

or less regularly in sample size through time, the written records tend to fluctuate more, probably on account of two factors: written records can be lost or destroyed far more easily than gravestones can; written records are kept by single individuals for selected periods of time, so that variations in conscientiousness on the part of different recorders may affect the whole sample.

The huge number of deaths recorded in Cohasset in 1720–1739 is belied by the cemetery representation. Furthermore there are no records of gigantic epidemics or other major causes of death during this period. Chances are there was just a very conscientious town clerk, who listed ages for everyone deceased. For the sample size in this instance (table 3) is not the total number of recorded deaths but only those for which age at death is given. Barring such foreseeable difficulties, one finds a rough agreement among the total figures for these two towns, which were, incidentally, rather similar in size and habitat.

TABLE 2

Characteristics of mortality from vital records, Sudbury, Massachusetts, 1700–1799 (N.E.H.G.S., 1911)

	Subadults		Adults		Total
	n	%	n	%	n
Age given	143	67.2	70	32.8	213
Age not given [1]	68	17.7	317	82.3	385
Total	211	35.3	387	64.7	598

[1] Subadults inferred from family references.

TABLE 3

Average age at death compared for two towns and two data sources

Period	Cemetery		Vital records (N.E.H.G.S., 1911)	
	n	$\bar{A}_d$	n	$\bar{A}_d$
		Kingston, Mass.		
1720–39	47	35.1	52	34.5
1740–59	55	31.2	69	30.2
1760–79	81	27.3	94	29.3
1780–99	120	29.9	218	31.3
1720–1799	303	30.0	433	31.0
		Cohasset, Mass.		
1720–39	15	24.1	174	32.6
1740–59	29	25.6	45	25.9
1760–79	23	34.9	39	46.2
1780–99	32	36.1	62	38.7
1720–1799	99	30.6	320	34.3

Looking at the subadult mortality proportions for the two towns shown in table 4, we again find rough agreement except in the case of Kingston cemetery, the only one so far with the low cemetery proportion one might have expected. Even so it is clear that in these cases the differences may be merely artifacts of sample size.

Finally, if we compare our small sample of cemeteries with data on subadult proportions of modern and various archaeological samples (table 5), it is possible to see a degree of consistency in our colonial samples, especially compared with the Pre-Columbian American data. Also there is some logical defense for the range of colonial subadult proportions, there being an agreeable increase in these proportions with distance away from the urban habitat. It is worth noting again that, for comparative purposes, the Vital Records remain more or less consistent with the grave-

TABLE 4

Proportions of age-recorded subadult deaths [1]

Period	Cemetery		Vital records	
	n	% total d	n	% total d
	Kingston, Mass.			
1720–39	14	56.0	9	39.0
1740–59	12	34.3	14	41.2
1760–79	11	26.2	21	40.4
1780–99	33	36.7	58	47.1
1720–1799	70	36.4	102	44.0
	Cohasset, Mass.			
1720–39	9	64.2	81	46.5
1740–59	15	51.7	24	53.3
1760–79	8	34.8	7	17.9
1780–99	14	43.7	23	32.0
1720–1799	46	46.4	135	42.2

[1] Subadults aged 0–19.

TABLE 5

Proportions of subadult deaths in selected mortality samples

Sample	% Subadults (0–19)	Sample	% Subadults (0–19)
U.S. White Females (1953) [3]	4.2	—	—
U.S. Non-W Males (1953) [3]	7.8	—	—
U.S. Rural Farm (1950) [3]	11.1	—	—
U.S. Reg. Area (1910) [1]	20.0	Boston (1700–79) [8]	22.5
U.S. White Females (1900) [3]	21.0	Lexington (1700–79) [8]	22.8
Texas Indians, to 1700 [1]	27.6	Cambridge (1700–79) [8]	25.9
Italy, Males (1901–10) [1]	31.5	Charlestown (1700–79) [8]	31.5
U.S. Rural Far. (1910) [3]	35.0	Sudbury (1700–79) [7]	35.3
Pecos Pueblo [2]	39.8	Kingston (1720–99) [8]	36.4
U.S. "Negro" Males (1910) [1]	41.8	Sudbury (1700–79) [8]	37.7
Mohave Indians [5]	43.2 ("Subad.")	Cohasset (1720–99) [7]	42.2
Forked Lightening Ruin [2]	44.7 ("Subad.")	Kingston (1720–99) [7]	44.0
Indian Knoll [4]	51.4	Cohasset (1720–99) [8]	46.4
India, Males (1901–10) [1]	56.2	—	—
Bronze age Greece [4]	59.2	—	—
Czech., 9–10th cent. [6]	61.8 ("Subad.")	—	—
Dakota Indians [5]	64.6 ("Subad.")	—	—

[1] Goldstein, 1953.
[2] Kidder, 1958.
[3] Computed from Bogue, 1959.
[4] Derived from Howells, 1960.
[5] Howells, 1960, after Wissler, 1936.
[6] Howells, 1960, after Pavelcik, 1949.
[7] Computed from Vital Records for the towns indicated.
[8] Computed from gravestone data.

yards. Thus the two sets of data for Sudbury, Kingston and Cohasset are both grouped and intermixed.

Having worked through a number of sets of cemetery data and of samples from written mortality records, I think that while infant and child mortality is under-represented and old age is over-repre-sented, this seems to be a relatively uni-form sort of bias compared to the huge variations in the written records. If ap-propriate adjustment factors can be devised the cemeteries should be distinctly supe-rior to written records for most palaeo-demographic purposes.

NUMBER OF DEATHS

A point worth noting here for critical comparison of written vital records with cemetery data is fluctuation through time in the number of deaths recorded. In Kingston, for example (fig. 1), the number of written recorded deaths takes a sharp upswing starting in 1780, and the curve gets even more steep after 1800. The cemetery data increase in a more gradual fashion until 1800 when, for technical reasons, my cemetery data become unde-pendable.

One would anticipate from the written data that there was a tremendous popula-tion increase in Kingston beginning around 1780. In fact, this was not at all the case according to the census figures which show a regular increase from 1765 to 1800 of about 1% per year; so even the ceme-tery figures seem somewhat exaggerated. It is probable that around 1780–1790 town officials became more concerned with the careful maintenance of complete vital rec-ords. Reflective on this increase conscienti-ousness is the fact that the first Federal Census was in 1790 which, incidentally, is when cause of death begins most regu-larly to be recorded. In spite of the pos-sible ravages of the Revolution the death rate should not have increased by a frac-tion as much as the written records indi-cate.

SEX DIFFERENCES IN AGE AT DEATH

Again referring to the Kingston data we can compare the ages at death of males and females, as indicated by the two data sources (fig. 2). We are presented here with a peculiar situation in which the cem-etery data (at the left) are remarkably complete and probably quite representa-tive, up to 1800, shortly after which the sample size is reduced, with an obvious bias toward the aged. On the other hand the written records give a relatively low

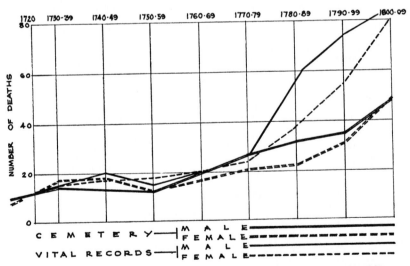

Fig. 1 Recorded deaths per decade, Kingston, Massachusetts, 1720–1809.

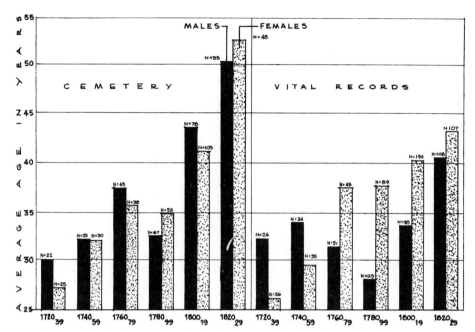

Fig. 2 Average age at death, Kingston, Massachusetts, 1720–1829.

number of ages at death before 1800 and a high proportion afterward probably very near 100%.

The results is that the cemetery data *up to* 1799 match up quite well with the vital records data *after* 1799. This combination could be a more reliable form in which to examine our data: that is, ignore the vital records before 1800, and ignore the cemeteries after that date. The remaining composite indicates that it was around the turn of the nineteenth century, or a little before, that the average length of life for females began to surpass that for males, at least in Kingston. Examination of the data from other cemeteries supports that approximation.

LIVING POPULATIONS COMPARED WITH MORTALITY SAMPLES

Among nearly a hundred colonial graveyards examined in the course of these preliminary studies there have been surprisingly few mentions of Revolutionary War deaths — the number observed is really negligible. At the same time the Vital Records contain even smaller proportions of such references. But comparisons of sample sizes in this and other sets of cemetery and written data indicate substantially more male than female deaths between 1760 and 1799.

A brief glance at the comparative data from some living populations in 1765 and 1790 (table 6), indicates a generally decreasing ratio of subadult to adult males as shown in the first two columns. This could be tested by examination of written records of births vs. deaths. Perhaps families were becoming smaller. The ratios of adult males to adult females in the census populations of 1765, shown in the fourth column, tend to be somewhat smaller than in the cemeteries, an extreme case being Cambridge, which has several other peculiarities.

The ratio of all males to all females shown in the last three columns is generally reduced in the living populations between 1765 and 1790; possibly this too reflects Revolutionary War deaths.

TABLE 6

Some population composition ratios, 1700–1799, comparing census and cemetery populations

Town	Ratio: ♂ Subadults [1]/♂ Adults			♂ Adults/♀ Adults		Total ♂/Total ♀		
	Census		Cemetery	Census	Cemetery	Census		Cemetery
	1765	1790		1765		1765	1790	
Boston	(?)1.39 >	0.78	0.26	0.81	0.83	0.93 >	0.80	0.86
Lexington	0.92 >	0.84	0.22	0.95	1.11	1.02	0.99 <	1.11
Kingston	0.99 >	0.85	0.49	1.00	1.17	1.09	1.05	1.08
Sudbury	0.97 >	0.89	0.25	0.93	0.90	0.97	0.91	0.90
Charlestown	0.76	0.91	0.69	0.75	0.90	0.83	0.93	0.86
Cambridge	0.83	0.85	0.15	0.73	1.46	0.86	0.93 <	1.25
Plymouth	0.92 >	0.86	—	0.88	—	0.95	0.90	—
Cohasset	—	1.13	0.64	—	0.95	—	0.96	1.00
(Vit. Rec.) [2]			(0.61)		(1.16)			(1.19)

[1] "Subadults" all aged 0–16.
[2] Last ratios taken from Cohasset Vital Records (N.E.H.G.S., 1916).

This last set of ratios is reflected in the cemeteries, whose figures for the century correspond quite well with the census ratios. The exceptions are Cambridge and Lexington, which clearly show an improbable preponderance of men, probably for such cultural reasons as could be illustrative of an obscure form of paleodemographic pitfall. In any event these ratios are probably the best test so far of the representativeness of the cemeteries; knowing Cambridge and Lexington as they are today one is tempted to view with suspicion the census figures rather than the cemeteries!

Turning now to seasonal distribution of deaths and ages at death we can again begin with Kingston's data (fig. 3), partly because its written records seem to be exceptionally complete, even though they are far from actual completeness before the nineteenth century. There is a fair correspondence between Vital Records and cemetery data on seasonal distribution of female deaths, but the distributional correspondence is poor for males, although the curves are not opposed at any point on the graph.

If we examine the seasonal differences in average age at death obtained from the

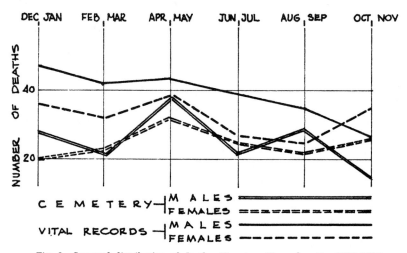

Fig. 3   Seasonal distribution of deaths, Kingston, Massachusetts, 1720–1799.

two data sources (fig. 4), we find a maximum difference of almost 17%, which is a little distressing, especially when we remain uncertain as to which of the data sources is least faulty. But as I pointed out earlier there is good reason to think that it is the written records that seem the more misleading where age at death is concerned.

If we look at four other graveyards with regard for seasonal differences in age at death (fig. 5) we can see a strong tendency for younger deaths to occur in late summer. While older deaths do not show such a clear cut distribution in this broad representation of extreme cases, the impression is given here, and strengthened by other cemeteries, that older people died most frequently in late winter. There are sexual differences, too, in seasonal distribution of ages at death, but discussion of these must be put off until another time.

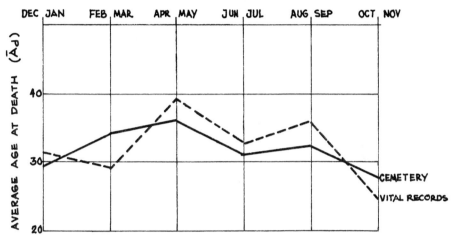

Fig. 4   Seasonal differences in average age at death, Kingston, Massachusetts, 1720–1799.

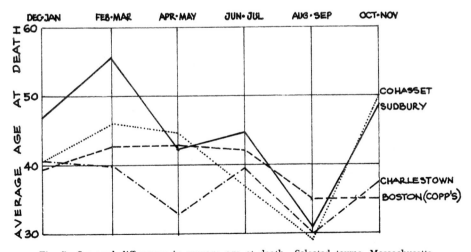

Fig. 5   Seasonal differences in average age at death. Selected towns, Massachusetts.

Of potential interest from a genetical standpoint are the distribution of surnames in various cemeteries through time and distance (fig. 6). So far I have only been able to investigate these matters in a very preliminary way, since distances are complicated both by physiography and by economic relationships. In the long run written records are most useful for studies of speed and direction of population (gene?) flow, since they provide data on marriages and births as well as deaths. But written records do not exist in all instances, nor do

they always adequately represent pre-nineteenth century populations.

A comparison of the numbers of surnames shared with Plymouth, Massachusetts, by the cemeteries of seven nearby towns shows a clear relationship between distance and the sharing of surnames. Of note here is that Weymouth was one of the first outposts of Plymouth, established before most of the other towns existed; hence its initially high proportion of shared surnames. Furthermore it was rather easily accessible from Plymouth by sea, while

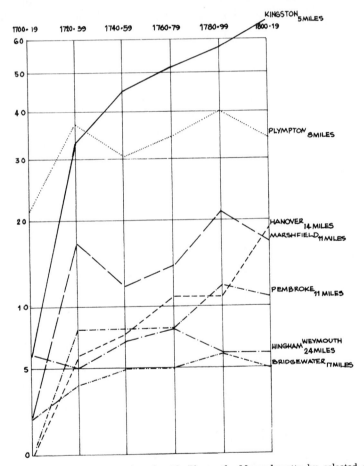

Fig. 6 Number of surnames shared with Plymouth, Massachusetts by selected towns, with linear distances from Plymouth, (cemetery data 1700–1819 corrected for 1790 census populations).

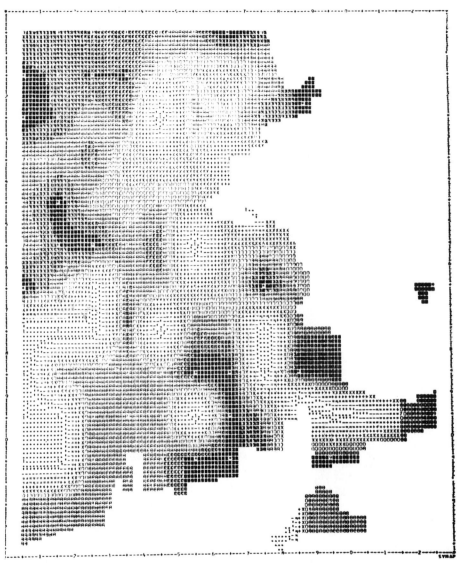

Fig. 7a Computer map of eastern Massachusetts and Rhode Island showing RELATIVE population increase between 1765 and 1790 censuses. Mapped in 10 graded levels between extreme values; left-expanding percentage logarithmic scale. (Grid arbitrary, approximately 50 mile^2 interval). Absolute values applying to each of the levels symbolized:

1	2	3	4	5	6	7	8	9	*
0.0 to 2.0%	2.1 to 3.0%	3.1 to 4.0%	4.1 to 6.0%	6.1 to 10%	11 to 16.0%	16.1 to 26.0%	26.1 to 40%	41 to 64.0%	64.1 to 100%

Fig. 7b Computer map of eastern Massachusetts and Rhode Island showing ABSOLUTE population increase between 1765 and 1790 censuses. Mapped in 10 graded levels between extreme values; left-expanding percentage logarithmic scale. (Grid arbitary, approx. 50 mile² interval.) Absolute values applying to each of the levels symbolized (indiv. per 50 mile² ±):

1	2	3	4	5	6	7	8	9	*
0.0 to 60	61 to 100	101 to 160	161 to 260	261 to 400	401 to 640	641 to 1040	1041 to 1590	1591 to 2550	2551 to 3985

Hanover, Pembroke and Bridgewater were all established later than Weymouth and were only accessible by land.

The *rate* of spatial extension of surnames is vastly more complicated but preliminary studies show encouraging predictability.

POPULATION GROWTH

With reference to the foregoing remarks, the use of computer techniques is essential if any more precise mathematical formulations are to be made. As a side note to that, one technique that is promising is the SYMAP program developed by Dr. Howard Fisher, of Harvard's Urban Planning Department. By plugging 1765 and 1790 census figures into this program I obtained, for example, the maps in figures 7a and 7b, showing areas and degrees of relative and absolute population increase in eastern Massachusetts and Rhode Island between those censuses. Note especially the differences in the two views of population change (relative vs. absolute) in the Boston and Providence areas.

CONCLUSION

The purpose of my remarks has been to describe some sources and limitations of colonial demographic data and, in a preliminary way, to explore a few of their "paleodemographic" potentialities. The data concern people most of whom lived and died while medical thought and practice were still in a relatively benighted state of infancy. For this reason alone these data may be of greater comparative interest than has been suspected.

But in addition the data represent an immigrant population whose growth characteristics have not yet been studied in depth from an anthropological point of view. There are colonial cemeteries in other parts of the world, notably in Australia, but elsewhere as well, containing vital data of other immigrant populations which may not be available in any other form. The fact that New England contains such a variety of records of life and death (I have

hardly mentioned the extensive records of births and marriages) suggests that many of its cemeteries are susceptible to thorough testing of their representativeness. While none of the samples is complete nor entirely accurate in itself the mutual complementarity of kinds of data will surely help to bridge the existing gaps.

The sampling of data in the figures and tables shown above can only hint, for the time being, at some intriguing generalizations that seem to be well worth serious investigation.

ACKNOWLEDGMENTS

I am grateful to Professor James. Deetz, of Brown University, for arranging access to the SYMAP program and for other valuable assistance, to T. S. Avery, of Kingston, for reproducing the maps in figures 7a,b, and to Willard E. Gwilliam, R. A., of Plymouth, for preparing figures 1–6.

LITERATURE CITED

Benton, J. H., Jr. 1905 Early Census Making in Massachusetts. Charles E. Goodspeed, Boston.

Bogue, D. J. 1959 The Population of the United States. The Free Press of Gencoe, Illinois.

Brigham, W. ed. 1836 Laws of the Colony of New Plymouth, Part I. Boston.

Bureau of the Census 1967 A Century of Population Growth. Genealogical Pub. Co., Baltimore.

Goldstein, M. S. 1953 Some Vital Statistics Based on Skeletal Material. Human Biology, 25: 5–12.

Howells, W. W. 1960 Estimating Population Numbers Through Archaeological and Skeletal Remains. In: The Application of Quantitative Methods in Archaeology. R. F. Heizer and S. F. Cook, eds. Viking Fund Publications in Anthropology, 28.

Kidder, A. V. 1958 Pecos, New Mexico: Archaeological Notes. Papers of the Peabody Foundation for Archaeology, 5, Cambridge.

New England Historic Genealogical Society 1911 Vital Records of Sudbury, Massachusetts to the Year 1850. N.E.H.G.S., Boston.

———— 1911 Vital Records of Kingston, Massachusetts to the Year 1850. N.E.H.G.S., Boston.

———— 1919 Vital Records of Cohasset, Massachusetts to the Year 1850. N.E.H.G.S., Boston.

Plunkett, R. J., and A. C. Hayden eds. 1952 Standard Nomenclature of Diseases and Operations (4th ed). The Blakiston Co., New York.

Mortality Rates and Trends in Massachusetts Before 1860

Maris A. Vinovskis

THE study of mortality rates and trends in the United States before 1860 has been rather unsystematic to date. Most scholars have been content to estimate the mortality rate at some point in time and only a few serious efforts have been made to ascertain the long-term trends in mortality. Particularly lacking are efforts to relate estimates of mortality in the seventeenth and eighteenth centuries to those of the nineteenth century. In addition, the few studies that have attempted to discuss long-term trends in American mortality have been forced to rely on estimates of mortality gathered from different sources and based on different techniques of analysis. Unfortunately, almost no efforts have been made to estimate possible biases introduced when comparing mortality data from different types of records.

This paper will attempt to examine mortality rates and trends in one state, Massachusetts. Massachusetts was selected because its mortality data are generally more accurate than those of any other state during this period and because so many of our previous estimates of United States mortality rates are based on studies of Massachusetts. Massachusetts is clearly not a typical state in the Union in that it became more urbanized and industrialized in the early nineteenth century than did the rest of the country. However, the mortality rates from Massachusetts should prove generally useful to economic historians, particularly whenever these rates can be broken down by the type of town, for estimating rates in other states after adjusting for differences in the degree of urbanization and industrialization.

Particular attention will be placed on the sources and the methodology of earlier studies in order to discover how differences in these factors might affect the validity of comparing mortality rates from the various studies. Since economic historians and historical demographers are often forced to use less than perfect mortality data, it

I would like to acknowledge the financial help for computer time from the Harvard Department of History and the Harvard Population Center.

Reprinted from *Journal of Economic History* **32**, No. 1, 184–213. Copyright ©1972 by permission of the publisher.

should be useful to be able to at least have some idea of in which direction are the biases.

Due to limitations of space, no attempt will be made in this paper to discuss the causes or the significance of changes in mortality rates in Massachusetts. Before anyone can explain or analyze the consequences of such changes, we must first try to establish exactly what did happen to mortality rates before 1860.

Finally, it will become obvious that this paper cannot definitively establish or analyze mortality rates or trends even in Massachusetts before 1860. There have been too few detailed studies of mortality in Massachusetts to provide the necessary data for ascertaining with any degree of confidence the trend in mortality rates before 1860. At best this paper will introduce some new mortality data for Massachusetts, re-examine the methodology and the reliability of some of the earlier studies, and provide preliminary guidelines that will facilitate the future investigation of mortality rates in the United States before 1860.

RELIABILITY AND USEFULNESS OF MORTALITY DATA

The determination of death rates in Massachusetts before 1860 is seriously hampered by especially incomplete registration of deaths during the seventeenth and eighteenth centuries.[1] Because death rates are subject to considerable yearly fluctuations, the identification of trends in mortality based upon such fragmentary data is likely to be tentative at best. In attempting to deal with the problem of incomplete registration of deaths, historical demographers have used numerous sources of information on mortality and have analyzed their data in a variety of ways. Unfortunately very little effort has been devoted to investigating the relative accuracy and applicability of the various approaches. As a result, it has been almost impossible for economic historians who need demographic estimates for their projects to evaluate the significance of the growing body of mortality data on early America. This section will examine some of the many techniques and sources and, wherever possible, compare results based on different methods.

---

[1] For a discussion of birth and death registration in seventeenth- and eighteenth-century Massachusetts, see Robert Gutman, "Birth and Death Registration in Massachusetts: The Colonial Background, 1639-1800," *Milbank Memorial Fund Quarterly*, XXXVI, No. 1 (Jan. 1958), 58-74; John B. Blake, "The Early History of Vital Statistics in Massachusetts," *Bulletin of the History of Medicine*, XXIX (1955), 46-54.

The most accurate source of mortality data in Massachusetts before 1860 is the collection of death records assembled by the state
after the passage of the Registration Law of 1842. Though it was
another decade before the new law became really effective, it was
a significant step in the right direction. By 1860 it has been estimated
that, at most, only 8 percent of the deaths in Massachusetts were
unrecorded.[2]

Before the registration law was again revised in 1844, the town
clerks were held responsible for recording all the deaths. Most clerks
did not bother to keep accurate records and there was little incen-
tive for citizens to report all deaths. Consequently, the law was
changed in 1844 to require that sextons or any other person in charge
of a burial ground be required to furnish a list of burials each month
to the town clerk. Though this change helped to make the registration of deaths more thorough, it was not until 1849 when "registrars"
were required in all towns of more than 10,000 persons and a penalty
was introduced for failure to comply with the law that a truly significant improvement occurred. The completeness of death registration jumped from an estimated 65 percent in 1849 to 89 percent in
1855.[3]

Though the registered deaths provide us with relatively good
data after 1855, there are few reliable sources prior to that time.
One source that may have great potential and that has not been
adequately investigated up to now is the bills of mortality collected
(though usually sporadically) in many Massachusetts towns. Many
of the earlier bills of mortality were gathered in a similar manner to
the procedures required by state law after 1849. For example, Salem
collected monthly returns from the various burial grounds and then
issued yearly bills of mortality for the town. These bills of mortality
are often almost as accurate as records gathered during the 1850's
under the new registration system. Salem was an exception to the
pattern of data collection in other Massachusetts towns in that it
kept fairly accurate bills of mortality over a long period of time—
from 1768 to 1843. Most towns did not attempt to collect these bills
for any length of time. In these towns the bills of mortality were
usually collected by the local clergyman or the amateur scientist who
had been encouraged to maintain these records by the American

---

[2] Robert Gutman, "The Accuracy of Vital Statistics in Massachusetts, 1842-1901,"
(unpublished Ph.D. thesis, Columbia University, 1956), pp. 114-231.
[3] *Ibid.*

Academy of Arts and Sciences in Boston.[4] Many of these bills seem reasonably accurate—particularly in small towns where the local clergyman knew everyone. Unfortunately many of the early bills of mortality were kept only for a particular congregation so that it is impossible to calculate death rates as we do not know the size of the population at risk. In addition, the determination of age-specific death rates from the bills of mortality before 1830 is all but impossible because we do not have sufficiently narrow age-categories in the United States censuses from which to calculate these rates. However, these bills of mortality can be used to estimate the crude death rates of the towns whenever accurate estimates of the total population are available. Whenever one uses bills of mortality, it is important to remember that their quality depends on the care exercised by the compiler—and this certainly varied from one community to another. Sometimes the bills of mortality were nothing more than a recapitulation of deaths registered by the local town clerks whose records, as we have already said, were often incomplete.

Probably the most widely used source of mortality data for the seventeenth and eighteenth centuries is the vital records kept by the town clerks. Many of these records are readily available in the series, *Vital Records of the Towns of Massachusetts to 1850*. These printed volumes are more complete than the town records since they include data from family manuscripts, church records, Bibles, newspapers, cemetary and court records, and personal diaries.[5] Several studies have relied very heavily on these printed volumes for mortality data.[6]

Despite the importance of this source of data, very little substantive work has been done to ascertain the reliability of these records

[4] For a discussion of the attempts by the American Academy of Arts and Sciences to collect bills of mortality, see Maris A. Vinovskis, "The 1789 Life Table of Edward Wigglesworth," THE JOURNAL OF ECONOMIC HISTORY, XXXI, No. 3 (Sept. 1971), 570-90. For a general discussion of colonial bills of mortality, see James H. Cassedy, *Demography in Early America: Beginnings of the Statistical Mind, 1600-1800* (Cambridge, Mass.: Harvard University Press, 1969), pp. 117-47, 243-73.

[5] The volumes were compiled and edited by several genealogical societies. Most were done under the guidance of the New England Historic Genealogical Society and the Essex Institute. Whichever group published them, the records generally had the title, *Vital Records of . . . to 1850*. For a discussion of the type of information available in these volumes, see James K. Somerville, "Family Demography and the Published Records: An Analysis of the Vital Statistics of Salem, Massachusetts," *Essex Institute Historical Collections*, CVI, No. 4 (Oct. 1970), 243-51.

[6] For example, Robert Higgs and H. Louis Stettler, III, "Colonial New England Demography: A Sampling Approach," *William and Mary Quarterly*, 3rd Ser., XXVII, No. 2 (April 1970), 282-94; A. J. Jaffe and W. I. Lourie, Jr., "An Abridged Life Table for the White Population of the United States in 1830," *Human Biology*, XIV, No. 3 (Sept. 1942), 352-71.

due to the lack of mortality data from a second source for purposes of comparison. Fortunately, we have two concurrent almost continuous series of independent data—vital records and the bills of mortality for Salem between 1768-1843. By comparing these two series with each other, we can get some idea of their relative reliability.

TABLE 1

COMPARISON OF SALEM DEATHS OF WHITES FROM PRINTED VITAL RECORDS AND BILLS OF MORTALITY: 1768-1843

Year	Percentage Deaths from Vital Records are of Bills of Mortality	Year	Percentage Deaths from Vital Records are of Bills of Mortality
1768	19.5	1804	72.0
1769	9.8	1805	79.1
1770	11.0	1806	78.4
1771	18.6	1807	83.7
1772	16.3	1808	79.1
1773	27.7	1809	75.9
		1810	96.5
1782	28.0	1811	92.7
1783	24.3	1812	90.8
1784	29.3	1813	85.3
1785	55.3		
1786	49.3	1818	109.8
1787	69.1	1819	122.1
1788	55.6	1820	120.4
1789	62.0	1821	138.5
1790	64.3	1822	135.7
1791	45.2	1823	160.5
1792	67.6	1824	118.7
1793	61.9	1825	131.7
		1826	132.4
1795	61.0	1827	131.8
1796	60.6	1828	133.2
		1829	121.9
1798	63.7	1830	119.3
1799	68.4		
1800	74.1	1840	119.4
1801	81.9	1841	123.9
1802	95.1	1842	112.0
1803	79.0	1843	107.9

Source: Calculated from data in Essex Institute, *Vital Records of Salem, Massachusetts to the End of the Year 1849* (Salem, Mass.: Newcomb & Gauss, 1925), V-VI; Joseph B. Felt, *Annals of Salem* (2d ed.; Salem, Mass., 1849), pp. 439-42.

At first glance the results seem puzzling. During the first fifty years, the vital records were under-registered relative to the bills of mortality, while, for the next twenty-five years, the situation was exactly reversed. We can investigate this dilemma in more detail for 1820 because we have the original data that was used in assembling the bill of mortality as well as the vital records for that year.[7]

In 1820 the vital records had 248 deaths whereas the bills of mortality listed only 181 deaths for that year. Of the 181 deaths in the bills, 176 of them also appeared in the vital records. Of the 68 deaths in the vital records that did not appear in the bills of mortality, approximately 28 percent were of Salem residents who died abroad (mostly sailors) and 13 percent who died at the workhouse. Another 16 percent of the deaths unrecorded in the bills of mortality came from one cemetary that had been overlooked and from church records. In other words, the bill of mortality in 1820 omitted approximately 35 deaths due to unrecorded deaths at sea and the workhouse, and unrecorded cemetary and church records. However, the remaining 40 percent of the deaths listed in the vital records but not in the bills were based on entries in family Bibles, family manuscripts, and the newspapers. While some of this 40 percent may be additional deaths omitted from the bill of mortality, a substantial portion of it probably represents an exaggeration of the extent of mortality caused by a tendency on the part of the compilers of the vital records to include entries from family Bibles and papers even though there was no definite evidence that the person actually died or even lived in Salem.

Though it is impossible to know exactly the number of deaths that occurred in Salem in 1820, it is likely that the bill of mortality underestimates them by 10-15 percent and the printed vital records exaggerate them by 5-10 percent for that year. Though this pattern may not be typical of other towns (since Salem was atypical as a commercial seaport with a significant proportion of its population dying at sea), it does suggest the caution that must be exercised in handling such data.

Overall, the bills of mortality are probably a much more accurate source of mortality rates and trends than the vital records. The vital records are so under-registered in the eighteenth century that it is questionable how much one can generalize from them whereas the bills of mortality appear to have been reasonably accurate throughout the entire period.

One further point should be mentioned—the steady increase in the completeness of death registration in the printed vital records. Births

---

[7] The original data used in assembling the bill of mortality for Salem in 1820 is located at the Essex Institute, Salem, Massachusetts.

were usually registered more completely than deaths in seventeenth-
and eighteenth-century America and there was more potential for
improvement of death registration than of birth registration. Some
scholars have attempted to use an index of deaths per birth as a
means of ascertaining changes in the death rate, but the example
of Salem should point out the obvious dangers of such a technique.[8]
If the relative completeness of death to birth registration fluctuates
over time, as it was very likely to do in most early American communities, an index of deaths per birth would not necessarily reflect
real changes in the death rate.

Though we now know that the bills of mortality and the printed
vital records do not yield identical numbers of deaths in Salem, the
question of how much bias this introduces into the calculation of life
expectancies remains. A. J. Jaffe and W. I. Lourie, Jr., used mortality
data from the printed vital records for the years 1826-1835 and assumed that after the age of four years these records were quite accurate.[9] Again we can compare the life tables obtained from these
two sources for Salem whites in 1818-1822. We can also minimize
the differences between them by including only whites who died in
Salem during those years plus the whites who died outside of Salem
in 1821 and 1822 since they were included in the calculations of the
original bills of mortality for those two years. The results are as
follows:

Jaffe and Lourie's assumptions are at least partly validated—female life expectancies from these two sources in 1818-1822 are reasonably close to each other after the first four years of life. However,
there are considerable differences in male life expectancies—particularly during the first thirty years of life. How serious a problem
this introduces when attempting to use these two sources of data
interchangeably in the early nineteenth century is difficult to say.
Unfortunately, we have very little concurrent and continuous independent data from other towns to make similar comparisons. It is
likely that these two sources of data are reasonably interchangeable
and that the differences for Salem males probably reflects the peculiarities of Salem as a commercial seaport and the zealousness of
the compilers of the Salem vital records. Most agricultural towns

---

[8] For example, see Philip Greven, Jr., *Four Generations: Population, Land, and
Family in Colonial Andover, Massachusetts* (Ithaca, N.Y.: Cornell University Press,
1970), p. 188.

[9] Jaffe and Lourie, "An Abridged Life Table . . . ."

TABLE 2

COMPARISON OF SALEM LIFE EXPECTANCIES BASED ON REGISTERED
DEATHS AND ON BILLS OF MORTALITY FOR WHITES FROM 1818-1822

Age Group	Males		Females	
	Registered Deaths	Bills of Mortality	Registered Deaths	Bills of Mortality
Under 5	36.5	42.5	45.9	49.4
5-9	41.2	47.1	51.0	52.4
10-19	37.4	43.2	47.6	49.1
20-29	29.8	35.0	39.7	41.1
30-39	25.4	28.0	33.9	34.9
40-49	22.3	23.5	28.4	29.6
50-59	17.5	18.5	21.6	22.4
60-69	11.9	13.0	14.7	15.5
70-79	7.9	9.2	9.9	11.2
80-89	5.2	6.3	5.5	6.4
90 & Above	1.0	5.0	1.3	1.0

Note: The above life expectancies include those who died abroad in 1821-1822 but exclude them for the years 1818-1820. This procedure was necessary as the original bills of mortality did not permit uniformly including or excluding deaths abroad for this period. As the U.S. census of 1820 did not have an adequate age-distribution break-down to permit construction of life tables, it was assumed that the age-distribution in 1820 was the same as that of 1830.

Source: Calculated from data in Essex Institute, *Vital Records of Salem, Massachusetts to the End of the Year 1849* (Salem, Mass.: Newcomb & Gauss, 1925), V-VI; Joseph B. Felt, *Annals of Salem* (2d ed.; Salem, Mass., 1849); U.S. Censuses for 1820, 1830.

are much more likely to have a pattern of life expectancies similar to that of the Salem females from 1818-1822.

One of the more frustrating aspects of using vital records is that an independent source of reasonably accurate mortality data by which to judge the accuracy of the vital records is rarely available. One way of getting around this dilemma is to use the vital records to reconstitute families and then to calculate the death rates on the basis of these families. This is a very powerful technique and has been employed successfully by many historical demographers. However, there are limitations on the applicability of the results of reconstitution studies because of the sampling biases introduced by the manner in which families to be investigated are chosen.[10]

In order to avoid some of the tedious work involved in family reconstitution, several scholars have relied solely on family genealogies, readily available for most New England towns, to supply the

[10] For a thorough discussion of the techniques and hazards of reconstituting families, see *An Introduction to English Historical Demography*, ed. E. A. Wrigley (New York: Basic Books, Inc., 1966).

MARIS A. VINOVSKIS

reconstituted families.[11] In addition to the obvious question of how accurate is the work of the genealogist, there is the question of how typical of the community as a whole are the individuals included in the genealogies. There is a strong bias in genealogies toward wealthy, married people who produced offspring.

Another frequently used procedure has involved the investigation of a well-defined group such as the New England clergymen or Harvard graduates.[12] Usually very reliable data are obtained since the groups under study generally left more detailed demographic records than the population as a whole. However, it is extremely dangerous to generalize from the experiences of these narrow groups to the population as a whole because they are biased toward wealth, education, and social status—factors which are quite likely to affect fertility and mortality rates.

Most of the recent efforts in reconstituting families have focused on some geographic area—usually a small, agricultural community. The criteria for selecting families for the study varies—sometimes the descendents of the first settlers are used, sometimes a random sample of the names contained in the vital records is employed or, usually, anyone whose demographic experiences can be successfully ascertained is included in the sample. Again various biases are likely to enter into the results, depending on how the data was collected and what criteria were employed to include or exclude cases from the sample.

For example, Susan Norton reconstituted families in Ipswich, Massachusetts, and calculated their mortality rates for the seventeenth and eighteenth centuries.[13] Though Ipswich was a commercial seaport during this period, she surprisingly found mortality rates comparable to more agrarian communities like Andover or Plymouth colony. However, one should note that she used only married adults in calculating her mortality rates.[14] A significant portion of the

[11] George J. Engelmann, "The Increasing Sterility of American Women," *The Journal of the American Medical Association*, XXXVII (Oct. 1901), 891-93; Carl E. Jones, "A Genealogical Study of Population," *Publications of the American Statistical Association*, XVI (Dec. 1918), 201-19.

[12] For example, see P. M. G. Harris, "The Social Origins of American Leaders: The Demographic Foundations," *Perspectives in American History*, III (1969), 157-344.

[13] Susan L. Norton, "Population Growth in Colonial America: A Study of Ipswich, Massachusetts," *Population Studies* (forthcoming).

[14] For an excellent discussion of the various problems in trying to calculate accurate mortality data from reconstituted families, see E. A. Wrigley, "Mortality in Pre-Industrial England: The Example of Colyton, Devon, Over Three Centuries,"

community were seamen, men who were engaged in a particularly hazardous occupation and who were likely to be unmarried. Their exclusion from Miss Norton's study probably means that the mortality rates which she determined for men are lower than for the whole community. This might have been a sizable under-estimation of mortality rates. In Salem we can examine the estimated life tables for white males between 1818-1822, based on the vital records, and see the impact the inclusion of deaths at sea have on the mortality rate for that community.

TABLE 3
LIFE EXPECTANCY OF WHITE MALES IN SALEM FROM 1818-1822
BASED ON REGISTERED DEATHS

Age Group	Excluding those Who Died Abroad	Including those Who Died Abroad
Under 5	39.7	33.9
5-9	45.3	37.8
10-19	41.6	33.9
20-29	33.5	26.5
30-39	27.2	23.5
40-49	23.2	21.3
50-59	17.8	17.2
60-69	11.9	11.9
70-79	7.9	7.9
80-89	5.2	5.2
90 & Above	1.0	1.0

Note: As the U. S. census for 1820 did not have an adequate age-distribution break-down to permit construction of life tables, it was assumed that the age-distribution in 1820 was the same as that of 1830.
Source: Calculated from data in Essex Institute, *Vital Records of Salem, Massachusetts to the End of the Year 1849* (Salem, Mass.: Newcomb & Gauss, 1925), V-VI; U. S. Censuses for 1820, 1830.

The results confirm the importance of deaths abroad in producing higher male mortality rates in seaport towns. This example demonstrates, in a somewhat unusual situation, the significant effect of sampling procedure on the results of studies using reconstituted families.

An interesting and useful study has been made by Edwin Dethlefsen of colonial cemetary records as a source of mortality data. He argues that colonial gravestones may be a more accurate source of mortality data in the seventeenth and eighteenth centuries than the vital records that were haphazardly kept by the town clerks. He

---

Daedalus, XCVII, No. 2 (Spring 1968), 546-80. Wrigley also relied on married adults in order to estimate life expectancies in Colyton.

supports his hypothesis by presenting data for Kingston, Massachusetts, from 1720-1809 from both the gravestones and the vital records.[15] Yet it is likely that both of these sources under-registered deaths during that period so that the relatively high agreement between them does not necessarily mean that either of these records are very complete. In addition there is still the problem of how to use such data as the census tracts before 1830 do not have sufficiently narrow age-categories from which to calculate age-specific death rates. Though one might calculate a stationary life table based on the total number of deaths and the assumption of a closed population, it is really not an adequate substitute.[16] For example, we can examine the life tables for Salem in 1818-1822 to see that there are significant differences between a stationary life table and one based on age-specific rates.

TABLE 4

LIFE EXPECTANCY OF WHITES IN SALEM
FROM 1818-1822 BASED ON REGISTERED DEATHS

	Males		Females	
Age Group	Using Census Age Categories	Using Stationary Population Model	Using Census Age Categories	Using Stationary Population Model
Under 5	39.7	29.5	45.9	34.3
5-9	45.3	38.2	51.0	42.9
10-19	41.6	35.4	47.6	40.3
20-29	33.5	28.1	39.7	33.5
30-39	27.2	23.6	33.9	30.3
40-49	23.2	20.8	28.4	26.4
50-59	17.8	17.0	21.6	20.9
60-69	11.9	12.5	14.7	14.6
70-79	7.9	9.0	9.9	10.0
80-89	5.2	6.0	5.5	6.8
90 & Above	1.0	5.0	1.3	5.0

Note: The above life expectancies do not take into account those who died abroad. As the U. S. census for 1820 did not have an adequate age-distribution break-down to permit construction of life tables, it was assumed that the age-distribution was the same as that of 1830.

Source: Calculated from data in Essex Institute, *Vital Records of Salem, Massachusetts to the End of the Year 1849* (Salem, Mass.: Newcomb & Gauss, 1925), V-VI; U. S. Censuses for 1820, 1830.

The results for Salem again suggest that such a technique involving the substitution of a stationary life table for one based on age-

[15] Edwin S. Dethlefsen, "Colonial Gravestones and Demography," *American Journal of Physical Anthropology*, XXXI, No. 3 (Nov. 1969), 321-33.

[16] For a discussion of the use of stationary life tables, see George W. Barclay, *Techniques of Population Analysis* (New York: John Wiley & Sons, Inc., 1958), pp. 131, 214, 216. For a critique of Wigglesworth's efforts to use a stationary life table model, see Vinovskis, "The 1789 Life Table of Edward Wigglesworth."

specific rates is less than satisfactory as the life expectancies obtained by the two methods are quite dissimilar. The stationary life table simply isn't well suited for an area that is characterized by a changing population and heavy out-migration.

Though much remains to be said and tested about the different sources and techniques used in historical demography, it does appear that one has to be very conscious about the biases introduced by the diversity of sources and techniques of analysis. Consequently all of our generalizations about trends in mortality rates in Massachusetts must be tempered by an awareness of the limitations in the accuracy of our results.

MORTALITY RATES IN SEVENTEENTH- AND EIGHTEENTH-CENTURY MASSACHUSETTS

Sparse data makes discussion of seventeenth- and eighteenth-century Massachusetts mortality highly speculative and any conclusions we reach must be considered only tentative. Definitive analysis is hampered by incomplete death records and poor estimates of town populations during most of this period and the few studies that have been done to date have not been as concerned about mortality rates as we might have wished.[17] While we can anticipate that more demographic studies of colonial Massachusetts will be produced within the next few years, it is necessary for us to review the existing studies and what they say about mortality rates even though some of these efforts lack a rigorous analysis of the mortality data.

In general, seventeenth-century Massachusetts was relatively more healthy than Europe. Once one had survived the rigors of the Atlantic passage and endured the hardships of the first years of settlement, chances of survival were quite favorable. To go further than these general statements and quantify even crude death rates during the seventeenth century is nearly impossible due to the lack of population statistics and incompleteness of death registration. However, Kenneth Lockridge's estimate of twenty-four deaths per thousand in seventeenth-century Dedham is reasonable.[18] In fact, it is likely that in small, agricultural New England towns we will often find death rates equal to or below that figure.

[17] Two studies of mortality in colonial America that have been quite careful from a methodological point are Norton and Greven (see fns. 8, 13).

[18] Kenneth A. Lockridge, "The Population of Dedham, Massachusetts, 1636-1736," *Economic History Review*, 2nd ser., XIX (Aug. 1966), 324-26, 332-39.

Agricultural communities such as Dedham, Andover, and Plymouth experienced low death rates during the seventeenth century, while coastal ports such as Salem and Boston experienced much higher mortality rates—especially among children and young adult males. Though Ipswich, a small seaport north of Salem, displayed a death rate in the seventeenth century comparable to Andover and Plymouth rather than to Boston and Salem, a large part of this apparent discrepancy might be explained by the fact that the Ipswich mortality rates are for married adults. Since a large number of deaths in coastal towns occurred among young, unmarried sailors, their omission from the calculation of mortality rates might account for some of the difference.

Considerable disagreement exists among scholars as to whether death rates increased or decreased from the seventeenth to the eighteenth century. The entire matter suffers from the dearth of studies which even attempt to estimate mortality rates for the entire period. In addition, there is also the question of how conclusively the data demonstrate changes over time.

For example, Greven asserts that there was an increasing death rate in eighteenth century Andover. He cites the increase in the ratio of deaths to births from the town vital records as one indication. He goes on to demonstrate the increase in infant and adult mortality among his reconstituted families in the eighteenth century.[19]

Though I generally agree with Greven's interpretation of mortality trends in Andover, there are some reasons why one might be even more tentative about this conclusion. Though Greven feels that the vital records are reasonably complete for those who survived infancy and remained in Andover, there are some general reasons why one might still suspect an under-registration of deaths in that town. For one thing, most other studies examining vital records have pointed to an under-registration of deaths between 40 and 80 percent—a fact which is supported by contemporaries who lamented the inaccuracy of most death registers.[20] In addition, Greven might even be correct in saying that vital events were adequately registered for his sample of reconstituted families—but the sample is atypical. He investigated the descendents of the first settlers and it is likely

[19] Greven, *Four Generations . . .* , pp. 185-197.
[20] Norton estimated that deaths were under-registered by 59 percent in colonial Ipswich. Lockridge estimated that recorded deaths were only 44 percent of the true total deaths. Lockridge, p. 331. For an estimate of the possible under-registration of deaths in the vital records of Salem, see Table 1.

that they were more conscientious about leaving a full record of their lives than strangers or recent settlers to Andover who had less of a stake in that particular community. These late-comers, who by the eighteenth century make up between one-half and three-fourths of the town's population, are probably not completely represented in the vital records. If the death records for the community as a whole were significantly under-registered there is the danger that a mere increase in completeness of registration might be misinterpreted as an increase in the number of deaths—particularly since deaths were usually more under-registered than births and therefore more likely to show greater improvement in registration. As deaths of children were the most under-registered, there is reason to wonder if the increase in infant mortality and deaths at young ages in the records truly reflects a worsening condition for the young in Andover or simply more attention to the registration of deaths.

When one looks at the death rates of adults in Andover, there is additional reason to question Greven's hypothesis about the increasing death rates in the eighteenth century. If one looked at only the calculated life expectancies from the seventeenth to the eighteenth centuries for males and females, he would find a clear-cut decrease in life expectancy at age twenty (life expectancy for males decreased from 44.6 years to 38.9 years and for females it decreased from 42.1 years to 40.3 years). Yet if we examine this data in smaller groups the trend becomes less clear.

It appears that the cohort born in 1700-1729 was subject to particularly high death rates whereas the ones born in 1730-1759 experienced life expectancies almost as long as their ancestors in the first two cohorts—in fact females in the 1730-1759 cohort who reached the age of twenty lived longer than any of their predecessors. The entire problem is complicated by the fact that we are not investigating current life tables, but generation life tables. Current life tables reflect the mortality rates for the population at that point in time whereas generation life tables reflect the actual experiences of that group over a long period of time.[21] Thus, someone born in 1685 and reaching the age of 30 in 1715 is really subject to death rates that are influenced by the conditions of life in the eighteenth century. Yet because he was born in the seventeenth century, this man's death is

---

[21] For a discussion of current vs. generation life tables, see Louis I. Dublin, Alfred J. Lotka, and Mortimer Spiegelman, *Length of Life: A Study of the Life Table* (New York: Ronald Press, 1949), pp. 174-82.

TABLE 5
LIFE TABLES FOR ADULTS IN SEVENTEENTH-
AND EIGHTEENTH-CENTURY MASSACHUSETTS

	Andover				Plymouth
Age Group	1640-1669 Cohort	1670-1699 Cohort	1700-1729 Cohort	1730-1759 Cohort	Seventeenth Century
	Males				
20-29	44.3	44.8	37.8	41.6	48.2[a]
30-39	40.8	38.7	33.4	36.3	40.0
40-49	32.7	31.4	29.7	28.4	31.2
50-59	23.5	23.5	24.2	24.5	23.7
60-69	16.4	15.2	18.1	17.2	16.3
70-79	10.3	10.2	11.3	10.9	19.9
80-89	6.4	6.7	7.0	7.1	5.1
90 & Above	5.0	5.0	6.4	5.0	
	Females				
20-29	42.1	42.1	39.5	43.1	41.4[a]
30-39	33.8	35.9	36.5	36.5	34.7
40-49	27.7	29.0	31.4	30.9	29.7
50-59	21.3	22.4	25.8	25.0	23.4
60-69	17.6	15.9	19.0	18.8	16.8
70-79	12.1	11.9	14.3	12.0	10.7
80-89	10.0	9.5	8.2	8.3	6.7
90 & Above	5.0	6.2	7.1	5.0	

included in Greven's mortality estimates for the seventeenth century. The numerous individuals whose lives overlap the seventeenth and eighteenth centuries and whose longevity was affected by conditions in both centuries make it more difficult to interpret from Greven's generation life tables how the general healthiness of Andover changed over time.

The most convincing evidence put forth by Greven to demonstrate the increasing unhealthiness of eighteenth-century Andover is his data on infant mortality for the reconstituted families. He found that infant mortality increased from 115 for the cohort born in 1670-1699 to 152 and 156 respectively for the cohorts born in 1700-1729 and 1730-1759.[22] As infant mortality is one of the best indicators of the general social, economic, and health conditions in a community, it is likely that Greven is basically correct in hypothesizing that there was an increased death rate in eighteenth-century Andover for children.

We have very little additional information on how death rates were changing during this period. The data on mortality rates for

[22] Greven, *Four Generations . . .* , p. 189.

| Age Group | Salem | | Ipswich | | Wigglesworth Data |
	Seventeenth Century	Eighteenth Century	Married Before 1700	Married Between 1700-1750	
	Males				*Both Sexes*
20-29	36.1[a]	35.5[a]	45.0[a]	39.9[a]	33.8[a]
30-39	29.2[b]	30.3[b]		32.3	30.2
40-49	24.1[c]	25.3[c]	30.0	25.7	26.0
50-59	19.1[d]	19.6[d]	23.1	19.8	21.2
60-69	14.5[e]	14.5[e]	16.1	14.2	15.5
70-79	10.0[f]	10.0[f]	9.5	11.5	10.1
80-89			6.2	7.3	5.8
90 & Above			5.0	5.0	3.7
	Females				
20-29	21.4[a]	37.0[a]	46.3[a]	36.8[a]	
30-39	20.0[b]	32.6[b]		29.9	
40-49	20.9[c]	26.3[c]	32.9	27.4	
50-59	14.4[d]	21.1[d]	22.9	18.7	
60-69	16.2[e]	16.4[e]	15.8	11.8	
70-79	10.0[f]	10.0[f]	12.7	7.8	
80-89			6.3	5.0	
90 & Above			5.0	0	

[a] Age group 21-30.
[b] Age group 31-40.
[c] Age group 41-50.
[d] Age group 51-60.
[e] Age group 61-70.
[f] As the Salem data was aggregated together after the age of 70, it was necessary to estimate life expectancy at that age in order to construct the rest of the life table. An estimate of 10 years was made.
Source: Calculated from Philip Greven, Jr., *Four Generations: Population, Land, and Family in Colonial Andover, Massachusetts* (Ithaca, N.Y.: Cornell University Press, 1970), pp. 192, 195; John Demos, *A Little Commonwealth: Family Life in Plymouth Colony,* New York: Oxford University Press, 1970), p. 192; James K. Somerville, "A Demographic Profile of the Salem Family, 1660-1770," unpublished paper presented at the Conference on Social History at Stony Brook, New York, October 25, 1969; Susan L. Norton, "Population Growth in Colonial America: A Study of Ipswich, Massachusetts," *Population Studies* (forthcoming); Maris A. Vinovskis, "The 1789 Life Table of Edward Wigglesworth," THE JOURNAL OF ECONOMIC HISTORY, XXXI (Sept. 1971), 570-90.

persons reaching the age of twenty-one in Ipswich point to an even more dramatic decline in life expectancy than the results for the same age-group in Andover.[23] On the other hand, there was no discernible trend in Boston (though it was subject to considerable yearly fluctuations) from 1701-1774—death rates there remained higher than in almost any other Massachusetts town throughout the entire period.[24] Whereas death rates increased or remained the same

[23] Norton, "Population Growth . . . ."
[24] For an analysis of health conditions in Boston during this period, see John B.

MARIS A. VINOVSKIS

in Andover, Ipswich, and Boston, there was a visible improvement in the death rates in Salem, which in the seventeenth century were much higher than Andover, Plymouth, or Ipswich, and in the eighteenth century were much lower, particularly for females.[25] In view of the paucity of evidence and the concomitant contradictory trends, only a tentative conclusion can be offered at this time: that there was a tendency for death rates in different communities to converge.

Useful comparisons can be made between European and American infant mortality rates. The death rates for infants in seventeenth-century Andover and Ipswich were significantly lower than those in Europe, while the infant mortality rates in Salem were comparable to those in Europe. In Colyton, England the infant mortality rates were between 118 and 147 for the period 1650-1699 and between 162 and 203 for the period 1700-1749.[26] In Brittany infant mortality rates ranged from 156 to 285 during the years 1720-1792.[27] Greven calculated infant mortality rates of 115, 152, and 156 respectively for the cohorts born in 1670-1699, 1700-1729, and 1730-1759 in Andover.[28] Norton found even lower rates among Ipswich children born before 1750—112 per thousand live births.[29] However, Somerville determined high infant mortality rates in Salem—313 for females and 202 for males in the seventeenth century and 178 for females and 105 for males in the eighteenth century.[30] The differences between male and female infant mortality rates which Somerville found for Salem suggest that either the collection of the data involved some bias or some social or biological mechanism operated to reduce the chances of a daughter surviving. Even though infant mortality rates rose in eighteenth-century Andover, infant mortality rates in Massachusetts as a whole still were either equal to or less than those in Europe.

Blake, *Public Health in the Town of Boston: 1630-1822* (Cambridge, Mass.: Harvard University Press, 1959).

[25] James K. Somerville, "A Demographic Profile of the Salem Family, 1660-1770," unpublished paper presented at the Conference on Social History at Stony Brook, New York, October 25, 1969. Somerville's general findings are probably correct, but they are based on a relatively small sample size and his age-specific mortality rates for women in the seventeenth century are erratic. My own study of Salem families from 1630-1800 is based on a reconstitution of all families who lived there during those years and should improve Somerville's mortality estimates.

[26] See Wrigley, "Mortality in Pre-Industrial England . . .", pp. 564-72.

[27] Pierre Goubert, "Legitimate Fecundity and Infant Mortality in France During the Eighteenth Century: A Comparison," *Daedalus*, XCVII, No. 2 (Spring 1968), 593-603.

[28] Greven, *Four Generations* . . . , p. 189.

[29] Norton, "Population Growth . . . ."

[30] Somerville, "A Demographic Profile . . . ."

Just as infant mortality rates were equal to or lower in Massachusetts than in Europe, so too were death rates after the age of twenty. In fact, the outstanding feature of the seventeenth-century mortality data is that life expectancies were so high and so similar to each other in Plymouth, Andover, and Ipswich. In these communities there appears to have been no significant difference in mortality rates for men and women during the child-bearing ages. However, the situation in Salem was quite different since life expectancies there were much lower in the seventeenth century than in the other three communities. Furthermore, particularly high death rates among Salem females during their child-bearing ages support the hypothesis that maternal mortality was a significant factor in accounting for the male-female differences in life expectancy at age twenty-one.

In the eighteenth century the life expectancies of adults in Ipswich, Andover, and Salem converged as there was a substantial increase in life expectancy in Salem—particularly among females of child-bearing ages—whereas there was a slight decrease in Andover and a much larger decrease in life expectancy in Ipswich. In fact, in the eighteenth century life expectancies for adults in Salem and Ipswich were almost identical—especially if adult male death rates in Ipswich were under-estimated due to the exclusion of single males from the calculations. Though we do not have comparable age-specific mortality rates for adults in Boston during this period, the high crude death rate in Boston suggests that its mortality rates in the eighteenth century might have been as high as those in Salem in the seventeenth century.

The life expectancies at age twenty are so high in Plymouth, Andover, and Ipswich in the seventeenth century that some scholars have questioned the plausibility of these results. Certainly it is likely that the criteria for a successfully reconstituted family has led to an over-estimation of life expectancies to some degree, but if one compares these life expectancies to those of rural Massachusetts towns in 1826-1835 and 1859-1861, these figures seem quite reasonable after all (see tables 8 and 9).

In this connection, the life table constructed by Edward Wigglesworth in 1789 has been often cited as evidence against accepting the relatively high life expectancies at age twenty in Andover, Plymouth, and Ipswich. This table has been used extensively by demographers and economic historians and was once the basis for computing longevity in annuity cases by the Massachusetts Supreme Court. However, the table is of questionable accuracy.

Wigglesworth's attempt to adjust his stationary population model must be viewed as intelligent guessing at best. His sample was not representative of Maine, Massachusetts, and New Hampshire as a whole. Wigglesworth's sixty-two bills of mortality came from towns that were more urban than the region as a whole. As a result of this bias, it is likely that Wigglesworth's table has exaggerated the extent of mortality and therefore cannot be used as an accurate check on the validity of the findings in Andover, Plymouth, or Ipswich.[31]

MORTALITY RATES AND TRENDS IN ANTE-BELLUM MASSACHUSETTS

Despite the increased interest in and need for mortality rates for the first six decades of the nineteenth century, little effort has been expended to provide additional information on this subject and we remain dependent upon a handful of life tables whose methodological soundness is open to question. These tables are based on data from various parts of the eastern United States but rely heavily on Massachusetts data since they are relatively more accurate than those from other states. Unfortunately, the two most widely used life tables, Jaffe and Lourie's table for 1830 and Elliott's Massachusetts life table of 1855, are both marred by methodological problems that make any direct comparisons between them impracticable.[32] By examining their procedures and reworking their data, it will be possible to make a more reliable estimate of mortality trends in Massachusetts than has hitherto been possible.

The standard interpretation of mortality trends in Massachusetts was set forth by Warren S. Thompson and P. K. Whelpton. They argued that there was a steady improvement in the expectation of life during this period and cited the life tables by Wigglesworth and Elliott as their evidence.[33] As we have already demonstrated, the Wigglesworth table is of questionable utility both from the point of view of the data that was used and the statistical techniques that he employed. In addition, the procedures followed by Elliott in selecting his data also raise serious questions about the validity of his results. Consequently, Thompson and Whelpton's estimate of the trend in

[31] Vinovskis, "The 1789 Life Table . . . ."

[32] Jaffe and Lourie, "An Abridged Life Table . . ."; E. B. Elliott, "On the Law of Human Mortality that Appears to Obtain in Massachusetts, with Tables of Practical Value Deduced Therefrom," *Proceedings of the American Association for the Advancement of Science* (Cambridge, Mass., 1858), pp. 51-81.

[33] Warren S. Thompson and P. K. Whelpton, *Population Trends in the United States* (New York: McGraw-Hill Book Company, 1933), pp. 228-40.

mortality might be inaccurate because Wigglesworth and Elliott's estimates of life expectancy were probably too low.

A more recent interpretation of the direction of mortality rates during this period has been put forth by Yasukichi Yasuba who asserts that death rates were probably increasing just prior to the Civil War. Assembling fragmentary indicators of death rates and speculating on the influence of urbanization and industrialization on mortality rates, he reverses the interpretation of Thompson and Whelpton.[34] However, like his predecessors, Yasuba's argument depends heavily upon scattered data from Massachusetts.

What I shall suggest in this section is that rural-urban differences in mortality rates were probably less pronounced in Massachusetts than indicated in Jaffe and Lourie's work and that mortality rates for most of these towns were more stable in the first half of the nineteenth century than asserted by either Thompson and Whelpton or Yasuba.

One source of information on trends in nineteenth-century Massachusetts is the bills of mortality. These bills of mortality, of varying quality, have been gathered for approximately forty Massachusetts towns.[35] Though most of these bills span only a few years, at least some of them bridge much of the first half of the nineteenth century.[36] Since most bills of mortality give us only the total number of deaths in a given year or for a period of years with no breakdown by age, it is impossible to calculate anything but crude death rates for them. Having made a cursory statistical examination (whose details will not be presented here) of these crude death rates, it can be stated with reasonable assurance that, though there is considerable yearly fluctuation, the crude death rates for these towns remain fairly stable during the first half of the nineteenth century. The only dramatic change in the crude death rates occurred just at the end of the eighteenth and in the early nineteenth centuries when the crude

[34] Yasukichi Yasuba, *Birth Rates of the White Population in the United States, 1800-1860: An Economic Study* (The John Hopkins University Studies in Historical and Political Science, LXXIX, No. 2 [Baltimore: Johns Hopkins Press, 1962]), 86-96.

[35] I am indebted to Professor David H. Fischer of Brandeis University for sharing his collection of Massachusetts bills of mortality with me.

[36] For example, bills of mortality are available for Ashburnham (1770-1859), Bedford (1825-1850), Boston (1811-1841), Brookline (1760-1812), Concord (1779-1828), Dorchester (1749-1803), Edgartown (1761-1793), Hopkinton (1772-1794), Kingston (1781-1814), Lancaster (1810-1822), Marlborough (1760-1849), Salem (1768-1843), Sterling (1779-1825), Warwick (1807-1841), and Worcester (1775-1838).

death rate for Boston dropped drastically. Yet the Boston crude death rates remained relatively stable from 1811-1860. This image of fairly stable death rates is reinforced by an examination of Massachusetts life tables for this period.

Jaffe and Lourie constructed an abridged life table for the white population of the United States in 1830 based largely on data from Massachusetts towns. They used the printed vital records for the years 1826-1835 of 46 rural New England towns (40 of which were from Massachusetts) to compute rural mortality rates. They also gathered similar data from Salem, Massachusetts and New Haven, Connecticut to estimate small city mortality rates. Finally, they used published mortality records for New York, Boston, and Philadelphia to calculate the same rates for large cities. After weighting the results according to the rural-urban distribution of the United States in 1830, Jaffe and Lourie constructed a composite life table for the whole of the United States.[37]

They found a clear-cut relationship between death rates and the degree of urbanization: the age-specific death rates were highest in the large cities of New York, Boston, and Philadelphia and lowest in the 46 rural New England towns. The rates for the two smaller cities fell in between. The differences in death rates among towns in these three categories are dramatic.[38] By calculating the crude death rates from Jaffe and Lourie's data, we find them to be, per thousand, 34.0 for the three largest cities, 17.5 for the two smaller ones, and 14.2 for the rural communities. The difference, then, in crude death rates between the largest cities and the rural communities is 19.8 deaths per thousand.

Even though a large majority of the data used to produce these crude death rates came from Massachusetts towns and cities, the figures give a very misleading picture of mortality when they are applied to Massachusetts. First of all, Boston's crude death rate (21.3 per thousand) was significantly lower than either New York's (32.7 per thousand) or Philadelphia's (43.3). Secondly, the death rates for the 46 rural New England towns are probably based on under-registered deaths. In a previous section we have already discussed the problems of using the printed vital records—particularly since the deaths recorded therein under-estimated the actual number who died. The death rates in the 46 rural towns represent

[37] Jaffe and Lourie, "An Abridged Life Table . . . ," pp. 352-71.
[38] *Ibid.*

various levels of mortality and are reliable to various degrees. Under-registration of deaths was prevalent in rural towns and very low death rates are more likely to mean laxness in record keeping rather than long lives for the towns' inhabitants.[39] Consequently, inclusion of towns with death rates below 10 per thousand in the determination of average crude death rates biases the results toward low values. Of the 46 rural towns used by Jaffe and Lourie, nine had crude death rates below 10 per thousand during the ten-year period under observation.[40] If we recalculate the average crude death rate for the rural towns and exclude those with death rates below 10 per thousand, the crude death rate rises from 14.2 per thousand to 15.0 per thousand.

Jaffe and Lourie's aggregate data suggested a difference of 19.8 deaths per thousand between the largest cities and rural communities. However, the data on Massachusetts, after adjusting for anticipated under-registration of rural deaths, reveals a difference of only 6.3 per thousand. In addition, though Jaffe and Lourie found a difference of 16.5 deaths per thousand between the large and the small cities, the difference between Boston and Salem is only 3.2 deaths per thousand during that decade. Consequently, the significance of the rural-urban differences in mortality rates set forth by Jaffe and Lourie is greatly reduced. In short, if their average crude death rates based chiefly on Massachusetts data, do not represent the probable experiences of Massachusetts, then there is serious doubt as to whether the death rates derived by Jaffe and Lourie can represent the experience of the United States as a whole. Whether this is so must await further research on other parts of the country.

Using Jaffe and Lourie's data for 1830 and adding additional life tables for the next three decades, we can investigate changes in the expectation of life in Boston, Salem, and 40 rural Massachusetts communities.

Rather than relying on Jaffe and Lourie's aggregate mortality rate for Boston, New York, and Philadelphia taken together, we can compute life tables for Boston alone by using bills of mortality for 1826-1835 and 1839-1841 and mortality data from the 1859-1861 state registration reports. While the data from the bills of mortality

---

[39] Some of the results are clearly unreasonable. For example, Jaffe and Lourie's data indicate a crude death rate of 4.8 per thousand in Lynnfield and one of 4.9 in Burlington. Jaffe and Lourie, p. 368.
[40] *Ibid.*

and the registration reports are not strictly comparable, they are sufficiently so to reasonably argue that there was apparently little change in life expectancy in Boston during these three decades.

TABLE 6
EXPECTATION OF LIFE IN BOSTON IN 1830, 1840, AND 1860

Age Group	1826-1835 (both sexes)	1839-1841 (both sexes)	1859-1861 (males)	1859-1861 (females)
Under 5	37.8	38.1	34.8	37.8
5-9	46.8	48.4	47.3	49.6
10-19	43.7	45.4	44.2	46.5
20-29	35.8	37.7	36.6	38.9
30-39	29.2	30.7	30.4	32.9
40-49	24.1	25.1	24.0	26.9
50-59	18.9	19.8	18.5	21.0
60-69	13.7	14.4	13.0	15.2
70-79	8.9	9.9	8.4	9.9
80 & Above	5.5	6.6	4.8	6.8

Source: Calculated from Lemuel Shattuck, *Report to the Committee of the City Council Appointed to Obtain the Census of Boston for the Year 1845* (Boston, 1846), p. 163; Secretary of the Commonwealth, *Registry and Returns of Births, Marriages, and Deaths, in the Commonwealth for the Years Ending December 31, 1859, 1860, and 1861* (Boston, 1861-1863); George Wingate Chase, *Abstract of the Census of Massachusetts, 1860, From the Eighth U. S. Census* (Boston, 1863).

When we analyze Salem's mortality rates from 1820-1860 we can also use bills of mortality for 1818-1822, 1828-1830, and 1840-1842 and the registered deaths for 1859-1861. These tables are less easily compared than those for Boston for several reasons. First of all, as there are no adequate age-distribution breakdowns before 1830, it is necessary to assume that the age-distribution in 1820 was the same as for 1830. Secondly, the Salem bills of mortality did not always include the same categories of people—sometimes including or excluding deaths abroad and at the workhouse. The bills for 1818-1822, 1828-1830, and 1840-1842 represent only white deaths whereas the registered data for 1859-1861 include both whites and blacks. However, since the black population of Salem was so small throughout this period, their inclusion or exclusion does not introduce a serious bias. Thirdly, the bills for 1821-1822 and 1828-1830 include the deaths at sea whereas the bills for 1818-1820 and 1840-1842 do not include deaths at sea. In addition, the bills for 1818-1822 and 1828-1830 include deaths at the almshouse whereas those for 1840-1842 do not. The registration data for 1859-1861 include both deaths abroad and in the almshouse. As a result of these complications as well as our previous conclusion that the Salem bills of mortality in 1820 probably under-estimated deaths by 10-15 percent, it is hazardous to make any guesses about the course of mortality in Salem during these decades. However, if pressed one would suppose that the expectation of life remained the same or decreased only slightly. The death rate in Salem was probably slightly lower than in Boston of 1830 and by 1860 the differences between those two communities became minimal.

TABLE 7
SALEM LIFE TABLES FOR 1820, 1830, 1840, AND 1860

Age Group	1818-1822	1828-1830	1840-1842	1859-1861
	Males			
Under 5	42.5	45.3	44.2	38.2
5-9	47.1	51.7	52.5	49.9
10-19	43.2	48.0	50.1	47.2
20-29	35.0	39.6	42.0	40.1
30-39	28.0	34.1	34.4	34.4
40-49	23.5	28.2	27.0	27.7
50-59	18.5	21.3	20.8	20.4
60-69	13.0	14.0	15.1	14.7
70-79	9.2	8.2	9.0	9.0
80-89	6.3	5.3	6.4	5.4
90 & Above	5.0	2.9	3.0	1.0
	Females			
Under 5	49.4	52.8	41.8	41.4
5-9	52.4	55.8	50.3	52.4
10-19	49.1	51.9	48.2	50.1
20-29	41.1	44.5	40.8	43.2
30-39	34.9	38.0	35.5	37.0
40-49	29.6	31.1	29.8	30.7
50-59	22.4	24.0	22.9	23.8
60-69	15.5	17.2	17.0	16.6
70-79	11.2	10.6	11.2	10.0
80-89	6.4	5.4	7.5	5.8
90 & Above	1.0	1.5	3.9	2.3

Note: The data for 1818-1822, 1828-1830, and 1840-1842 are from Salem bills of mortality and the data from 1859-1861 are from registered deaths. The calculated life expectancies are for whites except for 1859-1861 when both whites and blacks were included. The bills for 1821-1822 and 1828-1830 include deaths abroad whereas the bills for 1818-1820 and 1840-1842 do not include deaths at sea. The bills for 1818-1822 and 1828-1830 include deaths at the almshouse whereas those for 1840-1842 do not. The registered deaths for 1859-1861 include both deaths abroad and in the almshouse. As the U. S. census for 1820 did not have an adequate age-distribution break-down to permit construction of a life table, it was assumed that the age-distribution in 1820 was the same as that of 1830.

Source: Calculated from Joseph B. Felt, *Annals of Salem* (2d ed.; Salem, Mass., 1849), p. 440; U. S. Censuses for 1820, 1830, and 1840; Secretary of the Commonwealth, *Registry and Returns of Births, Marriages, and Deaths, in the Commonwealth for the Years Ending December 31, 1859, 1860, 1861* (Boston, 1861-1863); George Wingate Chase, *Abstract of the Census of Massachusetts, 1860, From the Eighth U. S. Census* (Boston, 1863).

Jaffe and Lourie computed the expectation of life for 46 rural New England towns—forty of these were from Massachusetts, five from New Hampshire, and one from Vermont. Though some of these rural towns probably under-registered their deaths in 1830, it is useful to calculate how much rural mortality rates had changed by 1860. Mortality data for New Hampshire and Vermont being unavailable, it is only possible to compute the expectation of life for the same rural towns in Massachusetts in 1860 as used by Jaffe and Lourie in 1830.

TABLE 8
EXPECTATION OF LIFE IN RURAL COMMUNITIES IN 1830 AND 1860

Age Group	Jaffe & Lourie Data for 1826-1835 (Males & Females)	Rural Massachusetts Towns 1859-1861	
		Males	Females
Under 5		47.6	48.4
5-9	54.6	55.5	54.8
10-14	51.0	52.7	52.3
15-19	46.7	48.7	48.4
20-29	42.9	45.1	45.2
30-39	36.2	38.1	39.0
40-49	29.6	31.3	33.5
50-59	22.5	23.4	25.9
60-69	15.3	16.3	18.4
70-79	8.4	10.2	10.9
80 & Above	1.0	5.3	5.9

Source: Calculated from A. J. Jaffe and W. I. Lourie, Jr., "An Abridged Life Table for the White Population of the United States in 1830," *Human Biology*, XIV, No. 3 (Sept. 1942), 357; Secretary of the Commonwealth, *Registry and Return of Births, Marriages, and Deaths, in the Commonwealth for the Years Ending December 31, 1859, 1860, 1861* (Boston, 1861-1863); George Wingate Chase, *Abstract of the Census of Massachusetts, 1860, From the Eighth U. S. Census* (Boston, 1863).

The results indicate that there was very little change in life expectancy in these rural towns over the three decades despite the fact that the average population of these Massachusetts towns increased from 1037 in 1830 to 1413 in 1860. The rural towns had lower death rates in both 1830 and 1860 than either Boston or Salem though there is much less of a rural-urban difference than originally suggested by Jaffe and Lourie.

One of the major landmarks in the construction of American life tables has been Elliott's table for Massachusetts in 1855.[41] This table has been widely used and quoted and is generally regarded as reasonably accurate. Only recently have there been suggestions that

[41] Elliott, "On the Law of Human Mortality . . . ."

Elliott's procedures in selecting the data to be used in the life tables have seriously impaired his findings.[42]

Elliott argued that deaths were under-registered in 1855 and he therefore tried to establish some criterion for accepting or rejecting mortality data from the 331 towns in the Commonwealth. He assumed that death rates in Massachusetts would follow the pattern of England where death rates below 16 per thousand were from towns having excessive unregistered deaths. For his calculations on Massachusetts, Elliott only used towns whose crude death rates were above 16 per thousand—assuming that towns having death rates below that figure would bias the results due to under-registration of deaths. As a result, his final tally of towns included only 166 of the 331 towns in Massachusetts in 1855.[43]

Elliott's procedure for selecting data can be faulted on several grounds. First, he relied on deaths from only one year, 1855. Yet in many of the smaller towns (particularly those under 1000) death rates varied widely from year to year because of the small base population so that a death rate less than 16 per thousand in a single year did not necessarily mean that the town's deaths were under-registered. Secondly, since Elliott used the crude death rates rather than standardized death rates as the basis for including towns in his analysis, towns whose age-distribution pattern included more people in high death-rate categories were more likely to be included in his sample even though their death registration may have been no more complete than other towns with different age-distributions. Finally, Elliott's assumption that accurate death rates below 16 per thousand were unlikely in Massachusetts towns in 1855 is incorrect. The availability of more complete data, accumulated during the decades following the construction of Elliott's table makes it clear that death rates as low as 10 per thousand were reasonable for many small Massachusetts communities.[44]

Besides these methodological flaws in Elliott's table, its applica-

[42] For an excellent critique of the shortcomings of Elliott's table of 1855, see Robert Gutman, "The Accuracy of Vital Statistics in Massachusetts, 1842-1901", pp. 213-26.

[43] Elliott, "On the Law of Human Mortality . . . ," pp. 51-55.

[44] Gutman chose to use 12 per thousand as a cut-off point, but he admitted that death rates of 10-12 per thousand were quite reasonable for many Massachusetts towns during this period. Robert Gutman, "The Accuracy of Vital Statistics in Massachusetts, 1842-1901," pp. 213-26. I have chosen the cut-off point at 10 per thousand as it seems the most reasonable from my investigation of death rates in Massachusetts. However, my estimates of life expectancies might be slightly biased upward by the inclusion of a few towns with under-registered deaths.

tion has been handicapped by the fact that it provides no break-down by sex. Furthermore, though Elliott hypothesized that there was a rural-urban differential in mortality rates, his life table was for Massachusetts as a whole.

Rather than trying to recalculate Elliott's table for 1855, it seems more useful to construct life tables for Massachusetts towns for 1859-1861. Unlike the Massachusetts Census of 1855 which was used by Elliott, the United States census of 1860 has age break-downs by sex—thus permitting us to calculate separate life tables for males and females. Furthermore, the improvements in the registration system by 1860 permit us to use more Massachusetts data than we would have been able to in 1855 when the registration of deaths was less complete.

Mortality and census material was assembled on 325 Massachusetts towns from 1859-1861. Standardized death rates (based on the age-distribution of Massachusetts in 1860) were calculated for each town, thereby eliminating any bias due to differences in age structure among the towns. Towns whose standardized death rates were below 10 per thousand were eliminated from the sample. The remaining 260 Massachusetts towns used in the construction of the life tables were divided into four sub-samples according to town size so that the effect of rural-urban differences on life expectancies could be more readily assessed.

The results indicate that Elliott's 1855 life table for the whole of Massachusetts under-estimated life expectancy. It appears that the excessive exclusion of small towns, which were genuinely healthy and not guilty of under-registering deaths, contributed most to biasing his results toward low life expectancies. It is interesting to note that there are only small variations in life expectancies among towns with population under 10,000 persons. However between towns having populations under 10,000 and towns having populations exceeding 10,000 larger differences in life expectancies are found. This correlation between life expectancy and town size is in keeping with the notion that mortality was influenced by differences in rural and urban living. Nevertheless, though differences in life expectancies for rural and urban areas can be noted from the life tables, the differences are much less pronounced in Massachusetts than previously suggested by Thompson and Whelpton, Yasuba, and other scholars.

Table 9

EXPECTATION OF LIFE IN MASSACHUSETTS TOWNS IN 1860

Age Group	All Massachusetts Towns (260 towns)	Towns Under 1000 (29 towns)	Towns 1000-2499 (119 towns)	Towns 2500-4999 (69 towns)	Towns 5000-9999 (29 towns)	Towns 10,000 & Above (16 towns)
Males						
Under 1	46.4	46.2	48.2	46.6	46.8	37.2
1-5	53.0	54.0	54.2	53.4	53.3	45.1
5-9	54.6	55.6	55.1	54.9	55.6	49.4
10-14	51.6	52.5	52.1	51.9	52.6	46.7
15-19	47.6	49.0	48.1	47.9	48.4	42.6
20-29	44.0	46.0	44.5	44.1	44.5	39.2
30-39	37.4	39.0	38.0	37.5	37.5	33.0
40-49	30.2	31.9	30.8	29.9	30.6	26.7
50-59	22.9	24.4	23.3	22.5	23.4	20.2
60-69	16.0	17.1	16.5	15.3	16.6	13.8
70-79	9.8	10.6	10.3	8.9	10.8	8.5
80 & Above	6.0	7.1	6.0	6.0	7.1	5.4
Females						
Under 1	47.3	45.6	48.4	47.9	47.3	41.0
1-4	52.3	51.6	53.0	53.2	52.2	47.5
5-9	53.2	52.8	53.4	54.2	53.8	51.3
10-14	50.1	49.5	50.5	50.9	50.5	48.6
15-19	46.2	45.4	47.1	47.0	46.5	44.7
20-29	43.0	42.3	44.0	43.7	43.0	41.5
30-39	37.2	37.1	38.6	37.9	36.5	35.2
40-49	31.0	31.5	32.6	31.5	29.9	29.1
50-59	24.1	24.2	25.8	24.3	22.9	22.7
60-69	16.9	16.9	18.8	17.3	15.6	16.2
70-79	10.4	10.3	12.8	10.6	9.0	10.3
80 & Above	5.5	9.2	9.2	5.9	2.6	5.7

Source: Calculated from Secretary of the Commonwealth, *Registry and Return of Births, Marriages, and Deaths, in the Commonwealth for the Years Ending December 31, 1859, 1860, 1861* (Boston, 1861-1863); George Wingate Chase, *Abstract of the Census of Massachusetts, 1860, From the Eighth U. S. Census* (Boston, 1863).

CONCLUSION

Given the scarcity of mortality data and the problems of comparing results based on different sources and different methods of analysis, it might seem premature to hazard any guesses on the possible mortality trends in Massachusetts before 1860. Nevertheless, if we are to stimulate further research and provide at least some minimal framework within which to analyze future results, some hypotheses, however tentative, should be advanced.

In the seventeenth century, there were significant rural-urban differences in life expectancies. Small agricultural communities such as Dedham, Andover, Plymouth, and even Ipswich had very high life expectancies. However, larger coastal towns such as Boston and Salem experienced much higher death rates during this period. Furthermore, though male-female differences in life expectancy were quite small in Andover, Plymouth, and Ipswich, there were pronounced sex differences in life expectancy in Salem, particularly during the child-bearing ages.

The eighteenth century witnessed the convergence of death rates of rural and urban areas as some of the smaller towns such as Andover and Ipswich experienced an increase in mortality rates while life expectancy rose in Salem, particularly for females. Boston continued to remain relatively unhealthy throughout most of the eighteenth century.

During the last quarter of the eighteenth century and the first quarter of the nineteenth century, there was a further convergence of death rates in Massachusetts as Boston's mortality rates dropped sharply. Thereafter mortality rates remained fairly constant throughout the Commonwealth up to 1860.

The surprising finding in this preliminary investigation of mortality rates is that death rates remained relatively constant throughout the entire period, especially for the smaller agricultural towns. Most of the significant declines in mortality occurred in the larger towns such as Salem and Boston which contained only a fraction of the population of the state as a whole. Furthermore, though rural-urban differences were pronounced in the seventeenth and eighteenth centuries, they were much less important during the first half of the nineteenth century.

Whether the mortality rates and trends in Massachusetts before 1860, as suggested in this paper, are also representative of changes in the rest of the nation must await further research. One can only speculate that though there might have been significant differences in mortality rates among cities such as Boston, New York, and Philadelphia, perhaps Massachusetts mortality rates were actually closer in line with the rest of the nation than previously imagined as the degree of urbanization, one of the major factors that sets Massachusetts apart from other states, did not appear to influence mortality rates as much as earlier scholars had believed.

MARIS A. VINOVSKIS, *Harvard University*

The Virginia Muster of 1624/5
As a Source for Demographic History

Irene W. D. Hecht*

I

Current population problems have aroused keen interest in the mechanisms of demographic growth and in the structure of populations. One consequence of this is that despite the difficulty of gaining historic insight into demographic patterns from documents which were not originally designed for that purpose, students of early American history have begun to trace out the contours of the pre-Revolutionary population. The task is still in its early stage, and more detailed studies are needed before an overall synthesis can be made. Nevertheless, as each new piece is added possibilities for comparison arise. Work done by Peter Laslett on the population of Stuart England furnishes insight into the demographic characteristics of the society from which colonial migration emanated.[1] Portions of the New World context have been established for the New England population by the studies of John Demos, Philip Greven, and Kenneth Lockridge, while Richard Dunn has performed a similar service for Barbados.[2] The existence of a key Virginia document, *The Muster of 1624/5,* makes it possible to fill in more of the

---

* Ms. Hecht is a member of the Department of History, Lewis and Clark College. During the year 1971-1972 she was a fellow of the Charles Warren Center for American Studies and of the Radcliffe Institute.

[1] Peter Laslett and John Harrison, "Clayworth and Cogenhoe," in H. E. Bell and R. L. Ollard, eds., *Historical Essays 1660-1750: Presented to David Ogg* (New York, 1963), 157-184; Peter Laslett, *The World We Have Lost* (New York, 1965); Laslett, "The Study of Social Structure from Listings of Inhabitants," in E. A. Wrigley, ed., *An Introduction to English Historical Demography: From the Sixteenth to the Nineteenth Century* (Cambridge, 1966), 160-208.

[2] John Demos, "Families in Colonial Bristol, Rhode Island: An Exercise in His-

Reprinted from *William and Mary Quarterly,* 3rd Series, **XXX,** 65-92. Copyright © 1973 by permission of the publisher.

colonial picture and to press further some intercolonial comparisons initiated by Dunn.

In the history of North American populations the Virginia *Muster* is a very unusual document. Unlike many of the materials to which demographic historians must resort, the *Muster* was intentionally conceived as an inventory of people and provisions. Executed as a house-to-house survey, the *Muster* constitutes the first comprehensive census made in North America.[3]

The *Muster*[4] was ordered by the crown at the time it took over management from the Virginia Company, which by 1624 had demonstrated its incompetence as a colonizing agency. Intracompany wran-

---

torical Demography," *William and Mary Quarterly*, 3d Ser., XXV (1968), 40-57; Philip J. Greven, Jr., "Family Structure in Seventeenth-Century Andover, Massachusetts," *ibid.*, XXIII (1966), 234-256; Greven, *Four Generations: Population, Land, and Family in Colonial Andover, Massachusetts* (Ithaca, 1970); Kenneth Lockridge, "The Population of Dedham, Massachusetts," *Economic History Review*, 2d Ser., XIX (1966), 318-344; Richard S. Dunn, "The Barbados Census of 1680: Profile of the Richest Colony in English America," *WMQ*, 3d Ser., XXVI (1969), 3-30; Dunn, *Sugar and Slaves: The Rise of the Planter Class in the English West Indies, 1624-1713* (Chapel Hill, 1972).

[3] *A List of Names of the Living and the Dead in Virginia*, compiled in February 1623/4, could also be considered a rudimentary census. However, it is far less useful than the 1624/5 *Muster*. The *List* of 1623/4 was designed purely as a "headcount" of those still alive following the Indian massacre in 1622 and contains only names arranged according to place of residence. It is not possible to tell with any reliability how persons were related or what their ages may have been. See John Camden Hotten, ed., *The Original Lists of Persons of Quality . . . and Others Who Went from Great Britain to the American Plantations 1600-1700* (London, 1874), 169-189.

Historians of French Canada have claimed for New France the honor of making the first modern census in the western world in 1666 and 1667. A. J. Pelletier, "Canadian Censuses of the Seventeenth Century," Canadian Political Science Association, *Papers and Proceedings*, II (1930), 20-34, discusses this issue at length. Without diminishing the importance of the extraordinary French-Canadian census, it should be noted that the Virginia *Muster* of 1624/5 shares key characteristics with the French document insofar as both were the result of a thorough, house-to-house inventory of people and goods. Both, in short, deserve the name "census" in its modern connotation.

[4] The *Muster*, the original of which is now housed in the Public Record Office in London, is available on Virginia Colonial Records Project microfilm and in two modern published editions, Hotten, ed., *Original Lists*, and Annie Lash Jester and Martha Woodruff Hiden, eds., *Adventurers of Purse and Person: Virginia, 1607-1625* (Princeton, 1956). The latter is by far the more reliable version. Hotten's lapses include misreadings of dates and outright omissions. In addition Hotten did not publish the provision lists.

IRENE HECHT

gling, which had been superficially calmed during an administrative re-
organization in 1618, reached an unpleasant public peak following the
Indian massacre in March 1622 that eradicated approximately a quarter
of the colony's population. Ensuing food shortages and an epidemic
further reduced the Virginia population and discredited the Company.[5]
The disaster had been more than the failure of a private venture; it represented a national debacle as well, since the colonization of Virginia
had drawn upon the energy, enthusiasm, money, and people of all segments of English society. However, one positive result for posterity is
that the crisis moved the crown to order a detailed inventory of the
colony.

The easiest way to describe the arrangement of the *Muster* is by il-
lustration, of which the following entry for Thomas Chapman furnishes
a fairly typical example:

> The Muster of Thomas Chapman
> Thomas Chapman arived in the *Tryall* in 1610
> Ann his wife in the *George* 1619
> Thomas his sonn aged 2 yeare
> Ann theire daughter aged 6 weeks
> Provisions:
> > Corne, 5 bushells
> > Fish, ½ hundred
>
> Armes and Munitions:
> > Powder, 1 lb.
> > Leade, 10 lb.
> > Peeces, 1
> > Armour, 1
>
> Cattell and Poultrie:
> > Neat Cattell, 1
> > Poultrie, 14
>
> Houses:
> > House, 1[6]

For the purposes of this paper, only information relevant to the persons has been utilized; no attempt has been made to process the prop-

[5] Wesley Frank Craven, *Dissolution of the Virginia Company: The Failure of a
Colonial Experiment* (New York, 1932), 81, 214-220.

[6] Hotten, ed., *Original Lists,* 212; Jester and Hiden, eds., *Adventurers of Purse
and Person,* 16-17.

erty holdings. By careful handling of the data it is possible in most cases
to derive nine separate pieces of information about each person: name,
age (omitted for Thomas and Ann Chapman but often recorded in
other instances), sex, race, arrival date, place of birth (England, Europe,
or Virginia), place of residence in Virginia (listed in the margin of
the *Muster* sheets), social position (i.e., some titles such as "Mr." are
given), and household or family status. Although the total census is small
—only 1,218 persons are named—the number of pieces of information
usually available for each made it helpful to execute the tabulations by
computer.[7]

The format of the *Muster* lends itself easily to arithmetical analysis,
but there are two problems which preclude attaining numerical perfec-
tion. One is that although the original survey was most probably carried out door-to-door, the document as we now have it is clearly a copy
of whatever notes were originally made by the census taker.[8] This
copying introduces the problems of alterations in or loss of the original
material. The existence of alterations and miscopying can be spotted
on occasion. For example, one small section of the document represents
the copying for a second time of material enumerated earlier.[9] The clerk
seems to have realized his error rather quickly, abruptly dropping the
"muster" on which he was then working. Rather than tearing off or
crossing out the duplicated section, however, the clerk proceeded without any notation of what he had done. Internal contradictions in shipping dates are annoyingly frequent and may also represent clerical
errors.[10]

[7] The system used was *Data Text,* a pre-packaged series of programs developed
by the Department of Social Relations and Sociology at Harvard University. The
accompanying manual is David J. Armor and Arthur S. Crouch, *The Data-Text
Primer: An Introduction to Computerized Social Data Analysis Using the Data-
Text System* (New York, 1971).

[8] Examination of the manuscript on microfilm indicates that the document is
in neat clerk's hand. It is possible that the copy may have been made by one person although it is conceivable that two may have been involved.

[9] This curious flaw in the manuscript has not brought comment from any of
the editors. The duplications occur in Mr. Daniel Gookin's Muster. See Hotten, ed.,
Original Lists, 243, 254; Jester and Hiden, eds., *Adventurers of Purse and Person,*
48, 59.

[10] After careful examination of all the discrepant dates it seemed most appropriate
to handle them as follows: (1) where it was possible to ascribe the difference to
the gap between Old and New Style calendars, the New Style date was used and
no record of error or alteration was entered on the computer cards; (2) where the

That the currently available *Muster* is a copy also raises the problem of possible losses of material. One can attempt to assess the degree of loss by comparing the *Muster* with a *List of the Living and the Dead* drawn up in 1623/4 in the wake of the Indian massacre of March 1622.[11] In terms of gross numbers the *Muster* and the *List* are reasonably harmonious, allowing both for in-migration and mortality. However, Edmund S. Morgan, who has made a name-by-name comparison of the two documents, estimates that the losses from the *List* may run as high as 20 percent while those from the *Muster* may be around 10 percent.[12] Even modern censuses do not achieve total accuracy so that the existence of some loss in a seventeenth-century document cannot be too startling. For the purposes of this analysis these losses are probably of minimal importance, for the objective is not to trace particular individuals but to examine the configuration of a population. The degree of internal consistency within the document makes it highly probable that if we can never know the precise size of the total population, we do know the general proportions of its composition quite accurately.

The second area of difficulty is introduced by the process of analysis itself. Despite the initial appearance of the document as a straightforward list, in transposing data to computer cards one is repeatedly forced to make interpretive decisions. Shipping dates are contradictory within the document, discrepant with Company records, or simply omitted. Marital status, frequently given explicitly, is on other occasions omitted.[13] Interpretive decisions are unavoidable, even at the arithmetic level,

---

date as given in the manuscripts seemed impossible, the "correct" date was entered. However, a "z" was entered before the date to indicate that it was not the date given in the manuscript; (3) there were sections of the *Muster* where ship names were entered, but dates were omitted. If these could be ascertained from other sources, dates were recorded, preceded by an "x" to indicate that the manuscript lacked dating.

[11] Hotten, ed., *Original Lists*, 169-189. The *List* includes 1,292 living persons, the *Muster* 1,218 living and 115 dead since 1624. Approximately 400 persons left England during 1623, and although we do not know the arrival dates, the departure dates listed suggest that many should have landed before the 1624 *List* was compiled. Thus the figures for the *List* and the *Muster* are reasonably harmonious. For estimates of yearly migration to Virginia, see Irene W. D. Hecht, "The Virginia Colony, 1607-1640: A Study in Frontier Growth" (Ph.D. diss., University of Washington, 1969), Appendix II.

[12] Edmund S. Morgan, "The First American Boom: Virginia 1618 to 1630," *WMQ*, 3d Ser., XXVIII (1971), 170, n.4.

[13] See n. 10 for the handling of shipping dates. The problem of marital status

and it is wise to recognize that these could introduce slightly different final results were two different historians to attempt to execute the same task.

II

The first step in analyzing the *Muster* involves tabulating the basic demographic information it contains. The results confirm what one would have guessed: the Jamestown population of 1625 was predominantly male, young, and European-born.

Of the 1,218 persons listed,[14] more than three-fourths were males. By actual count there were 934 males (76.7 percent) and 270 females

---

arose because there were 80 instances (40 pairs) where a male and a female having the same surname appeared sequentially in a given muster without being identified as man and wife. In the 254 other cases there was some indication, explicit or implicit, that the persons listed were married. It seems likely that the discrepancy was produced by the differing methods of the several census takers, since "probable marriages" were not scattered haphazardly through the census, but rather were clumped in the latter sections. It is possible the recorder may have assumed that the marital relationship was so obvious as to make further explanation redundant. Although the probability seems high that these were married couples, it has seemed advisable in the absence of certainty to handle these 80 individuals as a separate category.

[14] The simplest possible operation would seem to be that of making a head count of the number of people in the census, yet this most basic of maneuvers has some decided complications. Wesley Frank Craven, *White, Red, and Black: The Seventeenth-Century Virginian* (Charlottesville, Va., 1971), 30, n.6, gives the figure 1,232. The discrepancy apparently arises from three double counts: (1) "Mr. Alnutt and his servant here Planted reconed before in the Muster of James Cittie," who is indeed listed earlier; (2) "Mr. Burrows and six of his men which are planted heare are reconed, with theire armes etc. at James Cittie," and they are; (3) the duplication of the Gookin Muster, which survived as a complete listing. See Hotten, ed., *Original Lists,* 225, 230, 231, 254, and Jester and Hiden, eds., *Adventurers of Purse and Person,* 59. Even the figure 1,218 which has been arrived at with great care, may be off by 2, for it is highly probable that Edward Bennett was not actually in residence in 1625, and Daniel Gookin definitely was not. In both cases, although these men's names appear as heads of musters, they are not enumerated in the lists which follow. Biographical descriptions given in Jester and Hiden, eds., *Adventurers of Purse and Person,* 90-91, 181-182, suggest that these two men were in England in 1625. In the case of Gookin that speculation is confirmed by Frederick W. Gookin, *Daniel Gookin, 1612-1687* (Chicago, 1912), 49. Percentage calculations, however, are based upon the figure 1,218 unless otherwise specified.

(22.1 percent), plus 14 persons (1.2 percent) unidentifiable by sex because of the omission of a first name. There are two striking features in the pattern of age distribution: the preponderance of young people generally and the unusually large number who were in their twenties. Table I indicates that 76.1 percent of those whose age can be determined were under thirty, while 46.9 percent of the total fell within the decile from twenty to twenty-nine. At the same time the table reveals a marked difference in the age distribution of males and females. The largest group of females falls in the years below fourteen and the next largest between twenty and twenty-four, with females totally unrepresented above the age of thirty-nine.

TABLE I

AGE PROFILE OF VIRGINIA SOCIETY, 1625

Age	Men		Women		Total	
	No.	%	No.	%	No.	%
0–14	72	11.0	59	45.4	131	16.7
15–19	92	14.1	6	4.6	98	12.5
20–24	215	32.9	33	25.4	248	31.6
25–29	105	16.1	15	11.5	120	15.3
30–34	66	10.0	11	8.5	77	9.8
35–39	41	6.3	6	4.6	47	6.0
40–44	48	7.3	0	0	48	6.1
45–49	7	1.1	0	0	7	1.0
50 and Over	8	1.2	0	0	8	1.0
Total	654	100.0	130	100.0	784	100.0

Racially the colony was at this time overwhelmingly white. The twenty-three Negroes and two Indians listed constituted only a minuscule 2.2 percent of the *Muster's* population. The inhabitants were, as one would expect at this early stage of settlement, overwhelmingly non-indigenous. Of the total of 1,218, it is possible to establish that 1,085 (89.1 percent) were of English or European birth, while only 78 (6.4 percent) were children who were certainly born in Virginia. There are, however, 55 cases in which it is impossible to identify the place of birth, though 21 are children who could conceivably have been born in the colony. Even including them among the native-born would make only 99 (8.2 percent) of the white population indigenous. Two Indians and one of two Negro children were also American born, bringing the indigenous population of Jamestown to a possible 102 (8.4 percent).

Of the children fourteen years of age and younger in 1625, however, at least 51.9 percent and possibly as many as 75.5 percent (if the twenty-one children whose birthplace is unclear were actually born in the colony) were Virginians. The implications are twofold. First, if at least half the youngsters were born in the New World, it enhances the probability that families were formed after rather than prior to migration, a conclusion which is highly compatible with what we know about the migratory process itself. Secondly, indigenous reproduction was beginning to establish a nucleus in the colony, although its small size suggests that the transition from an imported to a native population would be slow.

In 1625 Virginia was divided into four areas referred to as "corporations": Henrico, James City, Charles City, and Elizabeth City.[15] With the exception of Henrico each corporation encompassed a number of separate settlements. From Table II one can perceive several facets of population distribution. The Corporation of James City was home for nearly half the inhabitants (44.4 percent). The two settlements with the largest concentration of persons were Elizabeth City with 20.9 percent and James City with 10.3 percent. The larger settlements were concentrated in Charles City and Elizabeth City corporations, whereas James City Corporation had more settlements but, except for James City itself, these were smaller in size.

Probing the *Muster* beyond the data for age, sex, race, and birthplace enables one to penetrate some additional characteristics of early Virginia society. Perhaps most distinctive in 1625 was the existence of three levels of social organization. One was the "muster," an entity which is clearly identified by the use of the word, as for example in the "Muster of Thomas Chapman" cited earlier.[16] The 187 musters varied in size ranging from 34 one-man musters to one that encompassed 70 individuals.

[15] Charles E. Hatch, Jr., *The First Seventeen Years Virginia: 1607-1624* (Williamsburg, Va., 1957), 32-109, provides a very helpful index of settlements and a map.
[16] See above, p. 67.

TABLE II

GEOGRAPHIC DISTRIBUTION OF VIRGINIA'S POPULATION, 1625

Corporation	Settlement	No. of Persons	No. of Persons in Corporation	% of Population
Henrico	College Land	22	22	1.8
Charles City	Charles City	44		
	West and Shirley Hundred	61		
	Jordan's Journey	56		
	Chapelains Choice	17		
	Piersey's Hundred	57		
			235	19.3
James City	Paspahegh	30		
	Governor's Plantation at Paspahegh	11		
	The Main	29		
	Dr. Pott's	8		
	James City	125		(10.3)
	James Island	51		
	Neck of Land, James City	16		
	Archer's Hope	14		
	Burrows Mount	7		
	Paces-Paines	14		
	Smith's Plantation	10		
	Blaney's	15		
	Matthew's Plantation	25		
	Crowder's Plantation	6		
	Treasurer's Plantation	18		
	Treasurer's, Jamestown	22		
	Hogg Island	53		
	Martin's Hundred	26		
	Mulberry Island	29		
	Warrasqueoc	31		
			540	44.4
Elizabeth City	Newport News	20		
	Elizabeth City	255		(20.9)
	Company Land, Elizabeth City	93		
	Eastern Shore	51		
			419	34.5
Total			1,216[a]	100.0

[a] Edward Bennett and Daniel Gookin were omitted. See note 14.

Most musters were headed by one person although there were eight cases where two men shared this responsibility. As one would expect, women rarely figured as muster heads. Four widows and one young woman, aged twenty, were so listed, and a man and a woman jointly headed one muster.

Although the socially privileged were most likely to be muster heads, the majority were indistinguishable from the rest of the colony's population. As Table III indicates, only 46 of 191 muster heads bore a distinguishing social title. These 46, however, represented the bulk of persons with social titles, of whom there were 62 in all. Among the 16 who were titled but not muster heads, 2 were "Mr." Argall Yeardley, aged four, and "Mr." Francis Yeardley, aged one, and 8 women who were married to muster heads. Thus in only 6 cases did the socially titled fail to become muster heads.

TABLE III

SOCIAL TITLES IN TOTAL CENSUS AND FOR MUSTER HEADS

Social Title	No. in Census with Title	No. as a Muster Head
Titles denoting respect (Mr., Rev., Dr.)	26	19
Sgt.	2	2
Sir	2	2
Mrs., Lady	11	3
Capt., Lt., Ensign	21	20
Total	62	46

In some cases the use of the word "muster" is less than transparent. As indicated in the *Oxford English Dictionary* the word is frequently used in reference to military affairs. Appearing as this document does on the heels of a massacre, it may have been intended to have some meaning in terms of defense. In most cases, however, one could substitute "family" or "household" without in any way changing the makeup of the lists. There are seven cases, however, where there is no muster head, and in these cases it seems the muster was primarily a geographic specification, as for example "the Muster of the Inhabitants of the Colledge-Land in Virginia," which included fifteen separate households. On the other hand, there are musters, such as "the Muster of Capt. Roger Smith's Men Over Ye Water," which seem to be economic units, the persons in that muster being included because of their dependent relationship to Smith.[17]

The second level of social organization was the household. In terms of the census a household may best be defined as a group of people sharing in some way a common store of provisions and property. Within the Virginia *Muster* the household groups can be identified on the basis of the inventory of goods that appears following the enumeration of persons. Frequently, as in the Chapman example cited previously, muster and household were one and the same; however, there are also instances where households constituted subdivisions of a muster. Thus the number of households recorded in the census is larger than the number of musters.

Household size in Virginia in 1625 showed considerable variation. (See Table IV.) Although the average size of a household was 3.9 persons, sizes ranged from one to thirty-six, and approximately half the population was located in households of five or less.

About one-third of the households included at least one servant. Table V enumerates servants by type and sex and makes clear that although there were Negro servants as well as female servants, the overwhelming majority in 1625 were white males. It is equally clear that the presence of hired servants was a rarity.

Two features of Table VI which illustrate the distribution of servants among the various households are striking. The first is that half the households which had servants had only one or two. The other is that more than half the servants were concentrated in fourteen house-

---

[17] Hotten, ed., *Original Lists*, 210, 223, and Jester and Hiden, eds., *Adventurers of Purse and Person*, 5, 28.

TABLE IV
HOUSEHOLD SIZE IN VIRGINIA, 1625

No. of Persons per Household	1	2	3	4	5	6	7	8	9	10	12
No. of Households	86	61	47	34	23	9	15	10	5	2	1
Total No. of Individuals	86	122	141	136	115	54	105	80	45	20	12

No. of Persons per Household	13	15	16	18	21	22	25	29	36	Total
No. of Households	3	5	1	1	2	1	1	1	1	309
Total No. of Individuals	39	75	16	18	42	22	25	29	36	1,218

TABLE V
SERVANTS IN VIRGINIA, 1625

	Males	Females	Unknown	Total
Negroes	13	9	1	23
Indians	1			1
Hired Servants	3			3
White Servants	437	43		480
Total	454	52	1	507

holds which represented no more than 4.5 percent of all the households. In other words, the distribution of servants was very uneven.

The propensity of servants to be concentrated among a restricted number of households is even more evident in the case of the Negroes. As we see from Table VII fifteen Negroes (65.2 percent) were divided among two households, while the remainder—eight—were spread through five additional households. It is also noteworthy that with but two exceptions all Negroes were located with heads of households who were among the fourteen with the greatest total number of servants.

TABLE VI
DISTRIBUTION OF SERVANTS IN HOUSEHOLD, 1625

No. of Servants in Household	1	2	3	4	5	6	7	10	12	13
No. of Households	23	23	11	9	6	6	2	2	2	1
Total No. of Servants	23	46	33	36	30	36	14	20	24	13

No. of Servants in Household	14	15	16	17	20	23	36	40	Total
No. of Households	1	1	1	4	1	1	1	1	96
Total No. of Servants	14	15	16	68	20	23	36	40	507

TABLE VII

DISTRIBUTION OF NEGRO SERVANTS OR SLAVES IN VIRGINIA, 1625

Muster	Total No. of Servants	Negro Servants or Slaves			
		Male	Female	Child	Total
A. Piersey	40	4	2	1	7
G. Yeardley	36	3	5	0	8
W. Tucker	18	1	1	1	3
W. Pierce	17	0	1	0	1
E. Bennett	12	1	1	0	2
F. West*	6	1	0	0	1
R. Kingsmill*	4	1	0	0	1
Total	133	11	10	2	23

* Not major servant holders.

A review of biographical information which is available for the major servant-owners reveals that these men either held positions of responsibility in the Company or maintained personally advantageous connections with it. Edward Bennett was a London merchant who owned a fleet of vessels which traded with Virginia. Although in 1625 he was listed with but 12 men, Bennett is said to have sent 120 to Jamestown in 1622. Dr. John Pott, also with 12 servants, was the Company physician. Sir George Yeardley, who had 36 servants, had been governor from 1618 to 1621. Abraham Piersey, listed with 40 servants, was the Company's cape merchant. Daniel Gookin, who ferried cattle from Ireland to Virginia, though not resident in the colony in 1625, had 20 servants at Newport News. George Sandys's connections with the Virginia Company were likewise close. His brother, Sir Edwin, was the Company's treasurer in London, and George was appointed to the same post in Virginia in 1621. At the time of the census he had 16 adult servants at the Treasurer's Plantation. Capt. Samuel Mathews, who arrived in Virginia in 1622, served on the Council from 1623 to 1625. At the time of the census he had 23 servants with him at Jamestown. Capt. William Pierce, with 17 servants, had been Captain of the Guard and

IRENE HECHT

Commander of Jamestown since 1623.[18] Capt. William Tucker's un-savory exploits as Company envoy to the Pamunkeys have been de-scribed by Morgan. Tucker's 17 servants place him statistically among the servant-rich. Of Capt. William Eppes (13 servants), Sgt. William Barry (15 servants), Mr. Edward Blaney (17 servants), and Capt. Roger Smith (14 servants) little is known beyond the fact the first two were Company agents.[19]

The census also gives some interesting insight into some of the or-ganizational aspects of these households with numerous servants. In seven of the fourteen cases described above, servants were located in two places, James City and an outlying plantation.[20] In six of these cases a small group of servants was stationed at James City (where the muster head actually resided), while the majority were located at an outlying plantation. Only Sir George Yeardley reversed that pattern, maintain-ing most of his servants in James City. Modest as it may have been in 1625, James City was nonetheless the colony's social and political hub, its leaders maintaining their residences there complete with maid servants, while the work went on at some greater distance.

In addition the *Muster* reflects a strong measure of social bias in housing. The sequential appearance of Governor Wyatt, ex-Governor

[18] For biographical information on these men, see Jester and Hiden, eds., *Adven-turers of Purse and Person, passim*. In addition to these 14 persons, Morgan included Ralph Hamor in his list of "winners in the servant sweepstake"; see Morgan, "Vir-ginia 1618 to 1630," *WMQ*, 3d Ser., XXVIII (1971), 188. Statistically the total listing of servants divides into two nearly equal parts at 10 servants per household. For this reason Hamor is omitted here.

[19] Morgan, "Virginia 1618 to 1630," *WMQ*, 3d Ser., XXVIII (1971), 189, n. 85, 190. There are also some discrepancies in the numbers of servants cited. For ex-ample, Morgan lists William Pierce with 13, located at Mulberry Island; how-ever, Pierce also had 4 servants in James City, making his total 17. For George Sandys, Morgan lists 37 servants. In the *Muster* only 16 are specifically designated as servants. The rest are listed as "those that live in Mr. Treasurer's Plantation." Morgan's conclusion that these, too, were servants is probably correct. However, in an effort to follow the designation used in the *Muster* these persons have been categorized in this study as "social status undefined." In the case of Yeardley, Morgan arrives at 39 servants by including 3 persons listed as "Dwellers." The figure used here for Yeardley is 36. See Hotten, ed., *Original Lists*, 222, 224, 234-235, 238, 240-241, and Jester and Hiden, eds., *Adventures of Purse and Person*, 27, 29, 39-40, 42-43, 44-45.

[20] This is true for Pott, Pierce, Wyatt, Yeardley, Piersey, Blaney, and Smith.

Yeardley, Dr. John Pott, Capt. Roger Smith, Capt. Ralph Hamor, Capt. William Pierce, Abraham Piersey, and Mr. Edward Blaney reflects quite accurately the actual housing arrangements at Jamestown. The locations of all but Piersey have been established, and it so happens that without exception all lived in "New Town." Indeed some held adjacent properties, as is suggested by the muster arrangement. These affluent residents were not the sole population of New Town (they represent about a half of the identified locations), but it is remarkable to see that without exception these persons lived in the same area of Jamestown.[21]

The third level of social organization reflected in the census is that of the family. Everyone in the census belonged to a muster and to a household. Less than half had family with them in the colony. Of the 1,218 persons listed in the *Muster,* 483 (40 percent) had relatives of some sort, the most frequent relationship being that of husband and wife. A maximum of 334 persons were married, 99 were children who had identifiable relatives, 16 colonists were widowed persons with children, 7 Virginians were adult siblings, and 26 were related in a variety of ways ranging from in-laws to miscellaneous children who may have been related to the adults with whom they lived.[22]

The 334 married persons fall into three groups. There are those who, as far as we know, were married for the first time. These numbered 226 persons. In addition, there were 28 who were partners in marriages which for at least one of the parties represented a second or perhaps even a third marriage. It has been possible to isolate these cases in the musters which have children listed as "His" or "Hers" (as distinct from theirs).

---

[21] Hotten, ed., *Original Lists,* 219-224; Jester and Hiden, eds., *Adventurers of Purse and Person,* 26-29; Henry Chandlee Forman, *Jamestown and St. Mary's: Buried Cities of Romance* (Baltimore, 1938), 63-64; Samuel H. Yonge, *The Site of Old "James Towne," 1607-1698: A Brief Historical and Topographical Sketch of the First American Metropolis* (Richmond, 1907), 56-57.

[22] It should be noted that the widowed are traceable only if they have a child. It is possible and in fact probable that there were others who had lost mates and in the process all family connections in Virginia. Also it should be noted that only male siblings are traceable. If females have the same name, they have been recorded as probable wives. If they lost their maiden names through marriage, the *Muster* furnishes no way of linking adult male-female siblings. Twenty-three "miscellaneous" children who lived with adults could have been orphans whose mothers had remarried.

That this method was not a quaint idiosyncracy of recording is confirmed by the fact that children labeled "Hers" always bear a different surname from the mother, who has quite evidently remarried. Finally, there are 80 persons who were probably married.[23]

The nuclear family—husband, wife, and, on occasion, children—was virtually the sole basis of family life as it existed in Virginia. It is also clear that only a minority of the population had family ties within the colony. Who were the people who were so distinguished? Muster heads were more prone to marry, their nuptiality rate being slightly higher than that of the population in general. Whereas a maximum of 334 persons (30.7 percent) were married out of that part of the population who by age could be considered marriageable (i.e., fifteen and over), 42.2 percent of the male muster heads were married.

With the severe imbalance between the number of males and the number of females one might assume that there would be few single marriageable women, but this is not as uniformly true as one might expect. Forty-three women twenty or older were not married. Recent arrival does not explain their spinsterhood, for thirty-nine had been in the colony since at least 1622. The other four had arrived sometime during 1624. Nine should have been highly marriageable, seven being widows, one an uncategorized female, and one a head of a household. Since four of the widows had lost their spouses at least one year earlier, it seems that women were not necessarily inclined to rush to the altar despite the stresses of frontier existence.

The characteristic the unmarried women shared most frequently was that of being servants. Thirty-four fell in that category, 27 being white and 7 Negro. English social practice of the time assumed that servants did not marry until their period of service was completed.[24] However, in Virginia among the 334 married persons 24 were servants. Not only is that figure a surprise in the context of English practice, but an examination of the 1624 *List* also reveals that 6 of these couples had apparently been married for at least a year. One was a Negro couple,

[23] See n. 13.
[24] Laslett, "The Study of Social Structure," in Wrigley, ed., *An Introduction to English Historical Demography,* 201.

Anthony and Isabel, who by 1625 had a child named William.[25] English custom was certainly violated by these servant marriages, but, in view of the sex ratio, what is surprising is not that Old World traditions were violated, but that they were so frequently observed.

It is perhaps equally surprising to find that social structure and nuptiality do not reflect any clear pattern. Muster heads were married somewhat more frequently than the population at large, but not so frequently that one could assume that if a man was a muster head, he was probably married. Servants could and did marry, but the number of unmarried female servants indicates that English social practice in this case was more often accepted than rejected.

When one makes length of residence the key variable in determining family status, a pattern does emerge. What is striking is that in contrast to the nuptiality rate for all the colony's eligible adults, which was no more than 30.7 percent, 70.3 percent of those who arrived between 1607 and 1616 and who were still living in 1625 were married. (See Table VIII.) The percentages are, of course, calculated with small numbers and are therefore subject to exaggeration. Nevertheless it does appear to be true that the early arrivals were more apt to have married and adopted a family-oriented form of social organization. Insofar as current research reveals that the nuclear family was basic in the organization of English

---

[25] The servant couples listed as married in 1623/4 are Joan and Wassell Rayner, Margaret and Thomas Gray, and Alice and Christopher Lawson; see Hotten, ed., *Original Lists,* 174-176, 226, 228, 232. In addition, though not listed as man and wife in 1623, the following appear in both the 1624 *List* and the 1625 *Muster:* Ann and Roger Thompson, Elizabeth and Richard Arrundell, and Isabel and Anthony (Negro); see *ibid.,* 172-173, 183-184, 222, 244, and Jester and Hiden, eds., *Adventurers of Purse and Person,* 27, 49. Four other servant couples appear in the *Muster* listed as man and wife: Elizabeth and Maximilian Stone, "Wife" and John Day, Ann and Hugh Hughs, and Abigail and Richard Atkins. Two other pairs appear sequentially but are not explicitly identified as man and wife: Mary and John Morris, and Rebecca and Robert Browne. See *ibid.,* 42-44, 49, 57, and Hotten, ed., *Original Lists,* 238, 240, 244, 252. Hugh Hughs, John Morris, and Robert Browne are listed in 1624. It appears possible that Ann Window who is listed in the same grouping with Hugh Hughs might be the Ann Hughs of 1625, and that the Mary Mounday of 1624 may be the Mary Morris of 1625. Elizabeth Stone, although she is said in the census to have arrived in 1621, is not traceable in the 1623/4 *List.* Rebecca Browne did not arrive until 1624.

TABLE VIII
SUMMARY OF ARRIVALS: FAMILY STATUS

Year of Arrival	No. Living in 1625	No. Married	% Married
1607	3	2	66.6
1608	8	5	62.5
1609	7	4	57.1
1610	27	19	70.4
1611	27	23	85.2
1612	3	3	100.0
1613	7	6	85.6
1614	0	0	0
1615	2	0	0
1616	17	9	52.9
Total	101	71	70.3

society,[26] it would appear that what Virginians sought to do, given time, was to resume the social patterns with which they were familiar.

The history of family structure in Virginia had some noteworthy idiosyncracies in 1625. In the first place, it appears that families had little to do with the initial process of peopling the colony. Of the 1,218 listed in the *Muster* only 56 can be identified as having arrived in some sort of a familial group. In 44 cases a husband and wife came together, in 8 they brought a child with them, and in 4 a wife and child travelled together.

Furthermore, when families were formed they still remained small

TABLE IX
NUMBER OF CHILDREN PER FAMILY, 1625

						Total
No. of Children	0	1	2	3	4	122
No. of Families	102	62[a]	17	6	2	189

[a] Two are Negro mothers, one with her husband and the other without.

[26] Laslett and Harrison, "Clayworth and Cogenhoe," in Bell and Ollard, eds., *Historical Essays 1660-1750*, 166-168.

in 1625. As Table IX demonstrates, 102 married or probably married couples were childless, which means 61.1 percent of families presumably prepared to bear children had failed to produce surviving offspring by 1625. Of those who had children, 62 had one, 17 had two, 6 had three, and 2 had four. The small number of children is further emphasized when one notes that of the six families with three children, one had been augmented to that number by two orphaned relatives, and two were families where parents had remarried and had children by their preceding marriages. Similarly, one of the two families with four children was composed of parents with two children of their own and two apparently unrelated youngsters. In other words, it was unusual for a given set of parents to have more than a child or two of their own, and the larger number, in fact, remained childless.

The record of marital relationships, the small family size that still prevailed in 1625, and the striking history of what happened to children in the colony combine to suggest how strong was the tendency toward disruption of the family in the early years of the colony. With 71.4 percent of the adults unmarried, the total number of married persons was in any event small, and of those married at least 46 (13.2 percent) had lost a mate. Thirty of these, however, subsequently remarried. For children the security of hearth and home remained especially precarious. Of 122 persons identified in the census as children, only 54 (44.3 percent) had both parents living. The other 68 (55.7 percent) had all suffered some form of familial disruption. Forty (32.8 percent) had lost one parent, 5 (4.1 percent) had no surviving parents and were living with kin, and 23 (18.8 percent) had no identifiable living relatives at all. The census also reveals another significant feature of the life of the first children of the colony. The count of 122 children excludes 20 youngsters aged ten to fourteen whom we would classify as children but who in the *Muster* were listed simply as servants. Such material suggests that childhood in the seventeenth century was more a social status than a biological stage of development, the very poor or orphaned being expected to bear adult responsibilities at a very early age. If the Virginia data are in any way representative, childhood ended by age ten for the less privileged.[27]

---

[27] For an example of the listing of children with their parents, see "Antoney Negro: Isabell Negro: and William theire child Baptised." Jester and Hiden, eds., *Adventurers of Purse and Person*, 49; Hotten, ed., *Original Lists*, 244. In contrast

IRENE HECHT

III

The information that can be derived from the census is interesting in and of itself; however, the material also has significance within a broader context. What light does it throw on later Virginia history and how does it relate both to the English world from which this population emigrated and to the colonial world of which Virginia was a part? In view of the special limitation of a single census and the peculiarity of the society which it depicted, one needs to assess with care the conclusions that one may draw. When one finds a society in which men so overwhelmingly outnumbered women, where almost half the population was twenty to twenty-nine years old, where the normal life of the family was severely limited, and in which social disruption seems to have been rampant, one is hesitant to see it as any sort of norm. Yet the most recent work by Wesley Frank Craven makes it appear that what we find in the census may be closer to the normal pattern of seventeenth-century Virginia than we might have thought. Using the patent records as a source on seventeenth-century migration, Craven found that men outnumbered women throughout the century.[28] We already knew from materials examined by Mildred Campbell that those who arrived in Virginia continued primarily to be young persons probably in their early twenties.[29] Measured against these data, the long-range implications of the *Muster* grow in importance. If indeed migration continued to be dominated by young male servants we can expect the patterns visible in the *Muster* to be perpetuated through much of the seventeenth century. Sex imbalance would reduce the possibility of family formation, and restrictions on servant marriages would further reduce actual nuptiality. Those who survived and remained in Virginia, assuming the *Muster* pattern held, would in due course marry, settle

---

to servant children, there are a number of instances in which the sons and daughters of persons of higher social status continued to be listed as children beyond the age of 14, which suggests that in the 17th century childhood may have been more a social status than a biological stage of development.

[28] Craven, *White, Red, and Black,* 27,

[29] Mildred Campbell, "Social Origins of Some Early Americans," in James Morton Smith, ed., *Seventeenth-Century America: Essays in Colonial History* (Chapel Hill, 1959), 74.

down, and produce families, probably of modest size.[30] Virginia's population would eventually shift from foreign-born to native-born and from nonfamily to family oriented, but the transformations would be slower than for colonies whose founding populations had a less skewed age and sex structure.[31]

One must also expect these demographic patterns to have implications for the social and political evolution of the colony. It would seem plausible that the particular population structure would enhance the power of a small, dominant elite, drawing its strength either from its status in Virginia based on family or from the prestige of social position brought from England. Indeed this is the very pattern described by Bernard Bailyn.[32] One can now have some sense of the demographic mechanisms which contributed to that pattern.

The lag in the establishment of an indigenous population in Virginia may also have simplified the substitution of black labor for white. If indeed Craven is correct in maintaining that Virginia's population was predominantly nonindigenous throughout the seventeenth century and if that migrant population was mostly made up of young males, one would expect little intracolony opposition to the substitution of one

[30] One faces the problem of determining whether the small number of children is a reflection of the peculiarities of the census or whether it is an indication of a long-term trend in family structure in Virginia. A modest attempt has been made to deal with that problem by looking at the genealogical records provided in the Jester and Hiden edition of the *Muster,* which includes a genealogy of the descendants of the 1625 colony through the fourth generation. Where it has been possible to trace descendants, it is remarkable to see how enduring was the pattern of small family size. Of 77 persons who can be traced into the second generation, 3 had no children, 17 had one, 24 had two, 19 had three, 6 had four, 5 had five, and 3 had six. Again we find a dominance of families with one or two children (in this case half the families are so constituted). The major variation is in the number of families with three children, who now accounted for a quarter of all families. One will need to trace the family histories of subsequent arrivals, for again the immigrants of Virginia's early years may have been an atypical group. However, whatever further work is undertaken in Virginia will need to start with the premise that family structure there was far different from that of New England, and that its characteristic stamp was that of small family size.

[31] For example, the rapidity of indigenous population growth in Massachusetts as traced in a study like Greven's *Four Generations* cannot be contemplated with the skewed sex pyramid of Virginia.

[32] Bernard Bailyn, "Politics and Social Structure in Virginia," in Smith, ed., *Seventeenth-Century America,* 90-115.

form of labor for another. The demographic situation does not furnish a comprehensive explanation of the shift to slave labor, which began before the end of the seventeenth century, but it may indeed be one important component.

The studies that Peter Laslett has made of Clayworth, Cogenhoe, and Ealing provide a basis for comparing Virginia's population with that of the parent society. To be sure, one cannot trace direct derivations since we have no way of knowing whether any of the Virginians in the *Muster* came from any of these particular English communities. What one can do, however, is to compare general patterns. Examination of Laslett's work confirms that Virginia was demographically distinctive. The preponderance of males and the age bulge do not in any way reflect the structure of the parent society.[33] Virginia's patterns existed because the colony drew upon a particular segment of English society. The ensuing rarity of family organization follows from Virginia's demographic idiosyncracies and is in no way a duplication of English practice. Similarly the particular complexities of social organization into family, household, and muster should be seen as an effort of a group of people attempting to cope with a new environment. The vocabulary may have been English, but the reality it represented was created by New World conditions.

On the other hand Laslett's studies also indicate that there is a danger of exaggerating the degree of social disruption experienced in Virginia. One cannot say that England represented social stability and Virginia social chaos, for in some instances the resemblance between Jamestown and Laslett's communities of Clayworth and Cogenhoe are startling. For example, we must find it appalling that more than half of Virginia's children were at least partially orphaned. Yet Laslett found 28 percent of Clayworth's children had lost at least one parent. Marriages were perhaps even more frequently disrupted in Stuart England than in Virginia. Laslett estimates that about one-third of all marriages represented second or subsequent marriages.[34] The *Muster* does not permit

[33] Laslett, "Study of Social Structure," in Wrigley, ed., *An Introduction to English Historical Demography*, Table 25, 194.

[34] Laslett and Harrison, "Clayworth and Cogenhoe," in Bell and Ollard, eds., *Historical Essays 1660-1750*, 165.

a thorough assessment of this issue, but to the degree that remarriages can be tabulated these represented only 12.6 percent of Virginia's couples.

Any temptation to view Virginia as a model for the effects of colonization on Englishmen generally will be dispelled by comparing the colony's experience with that of Bristol, Rhode Island, and Barbados. John Demos's study of Bristol rests on a 1689 census and Richard Dunn's work on Barbados on one that dates from 1680, and hence the stage of colonial development is by no means identical in the three instances.[35] Yet the comparison is useful, not for its statistical precision but for its indication of some general patterns of development.

Demos's findings for Bristol make it possible to compare some aspects of Virginia's population structure and household organization with a seventeenth-century New England experience. Demos found that of the 421 persons in the Bristol community, 226 (53.7 percent) were children.[36] In Virginia, even if one were to count all persons nineteen and under as children, only 229 (29.9 percent of the population) would fall into this category. Actually, as we have seen, only 122 youngsters could in social terms be referred to as "children" living under some sort of family supervision. Although it is not possible to reduce the data to a precisely comparable form, it is clear that while children accounted for more than half the Bristol population, in Virginia they were at most a minority of little more than a quarter of the total. The family in Virginia as of 1625 played a less important role, whether our basis of comparison is old England or New.

Demos's material also provides the basis for some interesting social contrasts. Servants in Bristol accounted for 10.9 percent of the population whereas in Virginia they constituted at least 40.9 percent of the population. In terms of the percent of households with servants the experience of the two colonies is almost identical: 34.3 percent of Virginia's households included servants and 31.4 percent of Bristol's.[37] The distribution of servants was, however, quite different. Only two of Bristol's seventy

[35] Demos, "Families in Colonial Bristol," *WMQ*, 3d Ser., XXV (1968), 40-57; Dunn, "Barbados Census of 1680," *ibid.*, XXVI (1969), 3-30.

[36] Demos, "Families in Colonial Bristol," *ibid.*, XXV (1968), 43-44.

[37] *Ibid.*, 46.

households had a substantial number of servants (one household with eight servants and one with eleven). In Virginia, the fourteen men with the largest number of servants held from twelve to forty.

Household size in Virginia and Bristol was also very different. The most frequent household size for Bristol was four, five, or six persons,[38] while in Virginia it was one, two, or three. Again we find in Virginia a deemphasis of the family, both because of the frequency of bachelor households and also because household and family are not synonymous in Virginia as Demos found them to be in Bristol.

Barbados, however, presents some interesting demographic similarities to Virginia. (See Table X.) For example, although the proportion of childless couples was almost twice as large in Virginia as it was in Bridgetown, Barbados, the proportion of all married couples in these two colonies was almost identical (27.5 percent of the total population in Virginia, and 27.6 percent in Bridgetown).[39] One also finds a close resemblance in the proportion of the population made up of children, the widowed, and single householders. There appears to be a

TABLE X

POPULATION OF VIRGINIA, 1625, AND BARBADOS, 1680

	Virginia		Barbados	
	No.	%	No.	%
Married Couples	86	14.1	231	16.6
Childless Couples	82	13.4	98	7.0
Children	122	10.0	330	11.9
Widowed	16	1.3	31	1.1
Single Householders	34	2.8	89	3.2
Servants and Slaves	499	40.9	1,678	60.2
Unknown	379	17.2	0	0
Total	1,218	100.0	2,786	100.0

[38] Ibid., 44.
[39] Dunn, "Barbados Census of 1689," ibid., XXVI (1969), 22.

TABLE XI

CHILDREN PER FAMILY—BRIDGETOWN, VIRGINIA, BRISTOL

		0	1	2	3	4	5	6	7	8	9	10	Total
351 Families Bridgetown	No.	198	58	52	22	7	11	2	1	0	0	0	330
	%	56.4	16.5	15.1	6.3	2.0	3.1	0.6	0.3	0	0	0	100
189 Families Virginia	No.	102	62	17	6	2	0	0	0	0	0	0	122
	%	54.0	32.8	9.0	3.2	1.0	0	0	0	0	0	0	100
69 Families Bristol	No.	7	10	11	12	9	8	6	4	1	0	1	226
	%	10.1	14.5	15.9	17.4	13.0	11.6	8.7	5.8	1.5	0	1.5	100

wide discrepancy in the proportions of servants and slaves, but in part the difference may be artificial since there is a significant part of the Virginia population in 1625 for which no social identification is provided and who may well have been servants.

Table XI, which provides comparison in the number of children and households in Virginia, Bristol, and Barbados, further emphasizes the similarity between Virginia and Barbados and the differences between them and Bristol. In both Barbados and Virginia childless couples were numerous, while in Bristol they were rare. The number of children per family was slightly greater in Barbados than Virginia, but again the most prominent difference lies between the two southern colonies and Bristol. In Bristol families were about equally likely to have one, two, three, or four children, whereas in Barbados and Virginia there was a marked tendency to have but one or two.

Inferring dynamic social patterns from a census which by its very nature presents a static picture is certainly hazardous. If it is combined with other sources, the hazards of inference are reduced and the static can become in part dynamic. Through the *Muster* one can perceive the implications of demographic patterns for social structure, an interaction of more than momentary interest, since migration patterns apparently continued to be much the same in terms of age, sex, and status. It also furnishes a glimpse of the nature of the changes wrought by migration upon Englishmen. In Virginia, at least, one of the most profound innovations must have been the breakdown of family structure. The disruption caused by mortality *per se* was probably less striking to the seventeenth-century emigrant than it is to us. The shattering of the family, on the other hand, may have been traumatic. As Laslett makes clear,[40] the English family maintained itself even if its individual members perished. This type of continuity seems to have vanished to a large degree in the Virginia of 1625. Restoration of family continuity in that setting would in all likelihood be painful and slow. Nor does the *Muster* permit one to see Virginia demographic developments as either a norm or a flight from a norm. Virginia was as different from New England in 1625 as it was to be at any later stage of colonial history.

---

[40] Laslett and Harrison, "Clayworth and Cogenhoe," in Bell and Ollard, eds., *Historical Essays 1660-1750,* 180.

The resemblances with Barbados on the other hand raise the possibility of a correlation between staple production and particular demographic patterns.[41] Certainly the development of both economic and demographic regional characteristics began very early. In short not only does the *Muster* provide an extraordinarily detailed view of the demographic basis of the social disruption experienced in Jamestown, but also it suggests some perspectives on Virginia's later history, the colony's relationship to England, and its place within the colonial world.

[41] Dunn characterized family life in Barbados as "stunted"; as late as 1680 "broken family life was still the rule." For more information on family life in Barbados, see Dunn, *Sugar and Slaves,* 325-334.

Of Agues and Fevers:
Malaria in the Early Chesapeake

Darrett B. Rutman and Anita H. Rutman

O N Tuesday, April 25, 1758, Landon Carter of Sabine Hall, Virginia, recorded in his diary the imminent death of his daughter Sukey. "Her face, feet and hands are all cold and her pulse quite gone and reduced to the bones and skin that cover them and dying very hard . . . severe stroke indeed to A Man bereft of a Wife and in the decline of life." Sukey was probably about seven; Carter was forty-seven but thought of himself as old, and he had lost three wives in all.[1]

Carter's diary entry records as personal tragedy what historical demography is presenting more formally: the fragility of life in the early Chesapeake. Lifespans were in the main far shorter than today, shorter even than in seventeenth- and eighteenth-century New England; childhood deaths were commonplace; and women in their childbearing years ran a greater risk of death than did their husbands, the latter often being left widowers.[2] What were the roots of that fragility? How may it have affected the mind and form of Chesapeake society? Answers to these questions may emerge from an understanding of the endemic nature of malaria in the region.

A caveat is immediately in order. Any entry into the medical life of the past must be undertaken cautiously. On the one hand, Carter and his contemporaries referred to disease in archaic terms and in the context of an archaic medical paradigm. On the other, the nature of modern symptoma-

Mr. Rutman is a member of the Department of History, University of New Hampshire; Mrs. Rutman is a lecturer on paleography and a bibliographer. The current investigation of community organization and life style in Middlesex County, Virginia, 1650-1750, of which this is an outgrowth, has been supported by the Central University Research Fund of the University of New Hampshire, the American Council of Learned Societies through its Committee for Computer-Oriented Research in the Humanities, and the National Endowment for the Humanities. The authors wish to thank Guy C. Marshall, M. D., and Robert L. Barth, M. D., both of Durham, N. H., who listened patiently to much of the evidence on particular cases, and Wilbur D. Bullock, professor of parasitology, University of New Hampshire, who reviewed the technical description of malaria.

[1] Jack P. Greene, ed., *The Diary of Colonel Landon Carter of Sabine Hall, 1752-1778*, I (Charlottesville, Va., 1965), 221.

[2] Lorena S. Walsh and Russell R. Menard, "Death in the Chesapeake: Two Life Tables for Men in Early Colonial Maryland," *Maryland Historical Magazine*, LXIX (1974), 211-227; Darrett B. and Anita H. Rutman, " 'Now-Wives and Sons-

Reprinted from *William and Mary Quarterly*, 3rd Series, **XXXIII**, 31–60. Copyright © 1976 by permission of the publisher.

FIGURE I

THE LIFE CYCLE OF THE MALARIA PARASITE

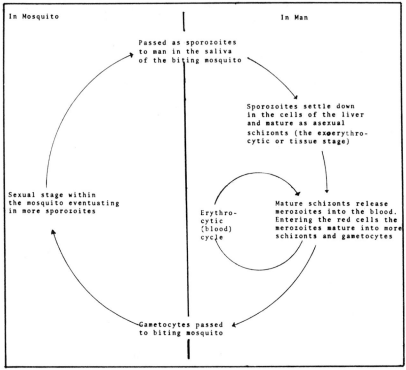

Source:
    Adapted from G. Robert Coatney *et al.*, *The Primate Malarias* (Bethesda, Md., 1971), 30.

tology can delude the historian, for while the clinical and laboratory manifestations of disease are carefully delineated in modern textbooks, the past
had neither the conceptions nor the means to discern the latter, and the
former seldom appeared in pristine form. "Typicality" is vitiated by the
unique circumstances of the particular patient, by the fact that discrete
diseases can combine in unfamiliar manifestations, and by the fact of treatment itself: in the seventeenth century what effect might phlebotomy
(bleeding) have had on the course of a malarial attack? and in the twentieth
century how many physicians have seen an absolutely untreated case of

---

in-Law': Parental Death in a Seventeenth-Century Virginia County," in Thad W.
Tate, ed., *The Chesapeake in the Seventeenth Century: Essays on Its Euramerican
Society and Politics* (Chapel Hill, N. C., forthcoming).

malaria through its full course?[3] In brief, the past, with respect to discrete diseases, is indistinct. Literary references to the maladies and ailments of seventeenth-and eighteenth-century Chesapeake colonists abound in surviving letters, diaries, travelers' accounts, scientific works, and the like, but no single reference points unerringly to malaria as it is described today. Hence historians can only build an inferential case for its prevalence, combining the available literary evidence with a contemporary understanding of the disease so that the two are consonant with each other, then test their case against the known attributes of the society—in the present instance, its demographic attributes.

These cautions lead to a first question: malaria—what is it? Put succinctly, malaria is a febrile disease arising as a reaction of the body to invasion by parasites of the genus *Plasmodium*.[4] The life cycle of the *Plasmodium* forms a complex system involving as hosts a female anopheline mosquito and a vertebrate. In anthropomorphic terms, the human host serves as the nursery within which the parasite spends its asexual "childhood"; its sexual "adulthood" is spent in the mosquito. Figure 1 illustrates this complex system in a more "*Plasmodia*-centric," but still simple, form. A highly idealized clinical reaction in the human host is illustrated in Figure 2. From infection by the bite of the female *Anopheles* mosquito through a tissue stage in the liver the reaction is nil. Only as the parasites enter the blood to attack the red cells do the body's defenses rise to do battle and clinical reactions begin. Headache and general malaise are occasional premonitory symptoms, but the internal battle is most marked by fever paroxysms, with the parasite's cycle setting the tempo. Relatively slight paroxysms follow the first entry into the blood; as the cycle proceeds, wave after wave of parasites are rhythmically released, and the host's fever rises and falls in response. Fever "spikes"

[3] The classic caution was entered by Charles Creighton, *A History of Epidemics in Britain*, II (Cambridge, 1894), 1-2. Donald G. Bates, "Thomas Willis and the Epidemic Fever of 1661: A Commentary," *Bulletin of the History of Medicine*, XXXIX (1965), 393-412, is a brilliant modern restatement and elaboration.

[4] The cumulative nature of scientific writing, with its periodic "position papers," has been our key to an understanding of malaria. As basic references and guides to the pre-1972 literature we have used Forest Ray Moulton, ed., *A Symposium on Human Malaria with Special Reference to North America and the Caribbean Region* (Washington, D. C., 1941); Mark F. Boyd, ed., *Malariology: A Comprehensive Survey of All Aspects of This Group of Diseases from a Global Standpoint* (Philadelphia, 1949); G. Robert Coatney *et al.*, *The Primate Malarias* (Bethesda, Md., 1971); and Robert G. Scholtens and José A. Nájera, eds., *Proceedings of the Inter-American Malaria Research Symposium*, printed as a supplement to the *American Journal of Tropical Medicine and Hygiene*, XXI (1972), 604-851, hereafter cited as *Proceedings*. *Cumulated Index Medicus* (Chicago, 1960-   ) provided entry to the most recent studies.

climb progressively higher, frequently accompanied by antecedent chills and postcedent sweatings. Associated with the paroxysms are secondary symptoms. The host may experience headache (sometimes with an accompanying eye pain), loss of appetite, nausea, generalized aches and pains and specific abdominal pain, and occasional respiratory difficulties, weakness, and vertigo. An observer might discern vomiting, skin eruptions, palpable enlargement of the spleen and liver and a generalized swelling of the limbs, nosebleed, diarrhea, jaundice, and pallor, the last indicative of severe anemia. If the body's defenses ultimately prevail, the cycle is broken and at least the parasites in the blood are destroyed. Remission and recovery follow.

From long association with humans, however, *Plasmodium* has evolved its own defenses against theirs. Defeated in the blood, the parasites can remain ensconced in some manner in the liver.[5] Within eight to ten months after the primary attack they will again enter the blood. The cycle begins anew, and the fever returns, calling forth counter defenses on the part of the host. The initial attack starts a process by which an immunity is acquired, and each successive relapse strengthens the immunity until all outward symptoms disappear. The immunity does not last long—only a few years. But the reintroduction of *Plasmodia* by the bite of a female *Anopheles* brings on enough of an internal reaction to reinvigorate the immunity, even though it may not result in an observable reaction in the host.

Thus far our intent has been to sketch quickly and in idealized terms the principal features of malaria, in order to lay ground for a more complicated discussion. First, our reference has been to genus *Plasmodium*, but genus implies species, and indeed there is a multiplicity of species. Four of these infect humans, two of them commonly: *Plasmodium vivax* and *Plasmodium falciparum*.[6] Between these two species there are clear differences in the reaction of the human host. The patterns of fever spikes vary, reflecting different patterns of parasitic development within the body. The intensity of the disease also varies, *vivax* being the more benign, *falciparum* the more virulent; mortality directly associated with untreated *vivax* is estimated at under 5 percent, while mortality associated with untreated *falciparum* can rise as high as 25 percent.[7] The classic relapse pattern is that of *Plasmodium vivax*, there being little or no relapse associated with *falciparum*.

Acquired immunity likewise varies between species. Immunity to *vivax* is

[5] The relapse mechanism of the parasite is not clearly understood. Coatney *et al.*, *Primate Malarias*, 31-37, succinctly reviews the state of knowledge as of 1971.

[6] *P. malariae* and *P. ovale* have been rarities in North America and hence are omitted here.

[7] Emilio Pampana, *A Textbook of Malaria Eradication*, 2d ed. (London, 1969), 19.

FIGURE 2

HYPOTHETICAL CLINICAL REACTION TO INVASION
BY MALARIA *Plasmodium (vivax)*
(A PRIMARY ATTACK)

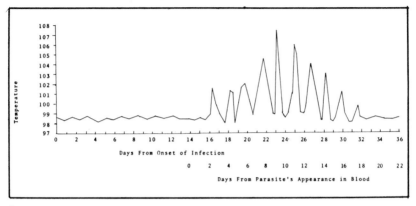

Source:
    Following C. Merrill Whorton *et al.*, "The Chesson Strain of *Plasmodium Vivax* Malaria," Pt. III, "Clinical Aspects," *Journal of Infectious Diseases*, LXXX (1947), 237–249.

rapidly acquired and relatively long-lived (approximately three to five years); that to *falciparum* is more solid but shorter-lived and more dependent on regular reinfection for prolongation. And while there is a pronounced innate immunity to *vivax* among blacks, there seems to be no race-specific immunity to *falciparum*. Whites and blacks are clearly susceptible to infection— indeed, a significant portion of modern research on falciparum malaria takes place in black Africa—but blacks seem to tolerate an attack somewhat better than whites. Among both whites and blacks can be found what is termed the "sickle-cell trait," which seems to confer a resistance to infection, although the interdependence of this genetic trait and malaria on the one hand and the long association of blacks with a malarious Africa on the other have made the trait generally more common among blacks than among Caucasians.[8]

---

[8] Coatney *et al.*, *Primate Malarias*, 283: "There appears to be no racial or innate immunity among Negroes against falciparum malaria as has been observed for vivax malaria. . . . However, the Negro does have a tendency to be able to clinically tolerate falciparum malaria infections better than the Caucasians. The presence of genetic traits which inhibit parasite multiplication or survival, such as sickle cell hemoglobin and enzyme deficiencies, have been reported but are not universally accepted." Cf. Peter H. Wood, *Black Majority: Negroes in Colonial South Carolina from 1670 through the Stono Rebellion* (New York, 1974), 88-89.

Within species, moreover, there are strains—an unknown number, of which only a few have been isolated in the laboratory—and there are clear differences in the reaction of the host to particular strains of the same species. Again, the pattern of fever spikes will vary slightly, but more important with reference to both species and strains is the fact that acquired immunities tend to be species- and strain-specific. A person who is infected by *Plasmodium vivax*, St. Elizabeth Strain, for example, tends to develop resistance only to that strain.

Second, we have referred to the mosquito vector as simply the female anopheline, but this masks a complex reality involving a genus *Anopheles* (within the family Culicidae and tribe Anophelini), six subgenera, and a variety of species and subspecies that vary in range, breeding habitat, and biting characteristics, and also as carriers of the parasite. *Anopheles atropos* and *Anopheles bradleyi*, for example, breed in the saltwater pools and marshes of the coast from Texas to Maryland, but *atropos* prefers water with a high salt content, *bradleyi* a low; and while *bradleyi*, in common with most *Anopheles*, tends to confine its biting to dusk, *atropos* will swarm and bite in bright sunlight. *Anopheles crucians* is a species of the southeastern coastal plain, frequenting fresh to slightly brackish swamps and pools and the margins of ponds and lakes. In the early twentieth century it was suspected as the primary vector in tidewater Virginia, because of its high density in the area and its propensity to enter houses to bite.[9] *Anopheles punctipennis* has the greatest range of any North American species, breeding in shaded springs and pools or along the margins of streams from southern Canada to New Mexico and along the Pacific coast. It bites only outdoors, entering houses in late fall only to hibernate. *Anopheles quadrimaculatus* prefers open sunlit waters for breeding, and although it is one of the *anopheles* most highly susceptible to *Plasmodium* (hence most likely to carry the parasite back to human beings), it seems to have a decided preference for the blood of cows and horses. All of the anopheline mosquitoes share certain characteristics. They are creature of short flight, normally ranging no more than one to two miles from their breeding places. They are highly affected by the weather. Optimal conditions for biting include a bright moonlit night, humidity about 85 percent, and a temperature in the low to mid-eighties. In a temperate climate the onset of cold weather brings on a suspension of all anopheline activity.

Species and strains of *Plasmodium* on the one hand; variety of *Anopheles* on the other—yet we have only touched on some of the many variables

[9] James Stevens Simmons, "The Transmission of Malaria by the Anopheles Mosquitoes of North America," in Moulton, ed., *Symposium on Human Malaria*, 114; Stanley B. Freeborn, "Anophelines of the Nearctic Region," in Boyd, ed., *Malariology*, I, 388.

DARRETT B. RUTMAN AND ANITA H. RUTMAN

involved in what malariologist Mark F. Boyd has described as the most complex and contradictory of disease systems.[10] A third set of complications relates to the behavior of malaria in communities.

In the malarial system the disease manifestation in humans is only one part. *Anopheles* must be infected by a human host, who, in turn, must be infected by *Anopheles*, with the circular transmission dependent on both. An anopheline mosquito must have access to, and must bite, a person (and not a nearby horse or cow) when the blood of that person is carrying the single form of the parasite that will infect the mosquito—in general, during or shortly after a malarial attack. After enough time has elapsed to allow the completion of the parasitic cycle within the mosquito, the mosquito must bite again, passing on the single form of the parasite that will bring about reinfection. To use technical terms, an *Anopheles* with a sporozoite-clear saliva biting a person free of gametocytes will have no more effect than to provoke a swat and a scratch! Within any given malarial community the degree to which the system is established is clearly dependent on the rate of transmission of the parasite from *Anopheles* to human being and back to mosquito through properly timed bites. At the lowest levels of endemicity few infected mosquitoes are abroad, few in the human population play host to the parasite, and transmission is only occasional. At the very highest levels of endemicity—hyperendemicity—virtually all anopheline mosquitoes are infected, and they are so numerous that no member of the human population can avoid being bitten every night. Human infection is then virtually 100 percent, and transmission is virtually constant. Between these extremes lie an indefinite number of levels of endemicity.

To speak of levels of endemicity is not to speak directly of levels of clinical morbidity—that is, the number of persons in the population displaying observable symptoms. Recall that malarial infection results in the human host in a species- and strain-specific immunity, but one of limited duration that is dependent for prolongation on reinfection (although not necessarily morbidity). In a malarial community the development of individual immunities tends to create a degree of group immunity. How effective that group immunity will be depends on the transmission level, or the level of endemicity. In communities of low endemicity individuals will be infected less often and group immunity will be lower than in areas of high endemicity. Clinical morbidity, group immunity, and endemicity levels interact to force a curvilinear relationship between the first and last, as sketched in Figure 3. If we were to measure the endemic and clinical morbidity levels of a number of communities, we would find that morbidity climbs as endemicity rises, since a

[10] Mark F. Boyd, "Epidemiology of Malaria: Factors Related to the Intermediate Host," in Boyd, ed., *Malariology*, I, 552.

greater percentage of infectious bites by *Anopheles* leads to symptomatic malarial attacks. Yet the rate of morbidity will be balanced at some point by the rate of immunities in the population and then will begin to decline until, in a hyperendemic situation, morbidity is largely limited to children, non-immune newcomers to the community, and pregnant women. Moreover, within any given community the level of endemicity (and consequently clinical morbidity) will tend to stabilize at a fixed figure. The figure may rise or fall as the number of anopheline mosquitoes in the area rises or falls, or as the number of the nonimmune changes, or when the onset of a new strain or species makes prior immunities irrelevant, or even as the spatial organization of the society shifts: a trend toward urban clustering, for example, will tend to decrease the proportionate access of mosquitoes to the population and bring a decline in the endemic level. But although the level of endemicity may change, there will invariably be a tendency toward stasis.[11]

Two other aspects of the malarial system in communities must be sketched before we turn to the subject at hand—malaria in the early Chesapeake region. First, whatever the endemic or morbidity level of a population, there is an areal definition to that population. The point is best made by an example. Consider a village located beside a saltwater swamp in which *Anopheles bradleyi* breed. Given the flight and breeding limitations of *bradleyi*, it is clear that even if our exemplifying village is highly endemic, another, four miles away beside a freshwater pond, need not be. The areal boundaries of the malarious population are thus defined by the mosquito. Presume that the pond by our second village is a breeding area for *Anopheles quadrimaculatus*. What then? It will remain malaria-free only if no one laden with gametocytes travels to it from the first village. In this case the areal boundaries are set by levels of population mobility as well as by the mosquito. The example may seem exaggerated, but the abruptness of areal boundaries was clear even in the 1890s when Walter Reed noted that while malaria was endemic among the soldiers of Washington Barracks, on the low flats bordering the Anacostia and Potomac rivers in the District of Columbia, it was significantly less prevalent "among those who live in the more elevated section of the city" away from the flats.[12]

Second, in a temperate climate such as that of the Chesapeake malaria cannot achieve the hyperendemic level that follows from near-constant transmission. As we have noted, the onset of cold weather inhibits anopheline

---

[11] A few malariologists, notably Ronald Ross, and statistician Alfred J. Lotka have attempted to reduce the malarial system to a mathematical model. See Mark F. Boyd, "Epidemiology: Factors Related to the Definitive Host," *ibid.*, 683-687.

[12] Hugh R. Gilmore, Jr., "Malaria at Washington Barracks and Fort Myer: A Survey of Walter Reed," *Bull. Hist. Med.*, XXIX (1955), 348.

FIGURE 3

HYPOTHETIC RELATIONSHIP OF LEVELS OF
MORBIDITY AND ENDEMICITY AMONG
MALARIAL COMMUNITIES

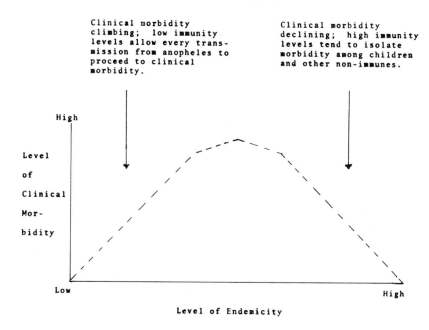

Clinical morbidity
climbing; low immunity
levels allow every trans-
mission from anopheles to
proceed to clinical
morbidity.

Clinical morbidity
declining; high immunity
levels tend to isolate
morbidity among children
and other non-immunes.

High

Level

of

Clinical

Mor-

bidity

Low   High

Level of Endemicity

activity and thus regularly interrupts transmission. In the absence of transmission, morbidity declines, individual immunities diminish, and the non-
immune increase; group immunity thus deteriorates, leaving the population
vulnerable to what is to come. Latent infections will persist over the winter,
and as these bring on a few malarial attacks in the spring, as cases of *vivax*
contracted during the previous fall reappear as relapses, and as mosquitoes
start biting again, transmission restarts and the malarial system is reinvigo-
rated. The endemic level, having declined during the winter, rises again.
Symptomatic morbidity steadily increases through the spring and summer to
a peak in the autumn, then abruptly declines with the coming of another
winter. Figure 4, a seasonal plot of 614 malaria cases treated at The Johns
Hopkins University Hospital in the early 1890s, displays the seasonality of the
two major species of malaria then current in the Chesapeake area.

Was there malaria in the early Chesapeake? Historiographically, the
question has been asked mainly with reference to Virginia, and the answer

has been mixed. Thomas Jefferson Wertenbaker, reflecting a traditional view, wrote in 1914 of the "swarms of mosquitoes" that rose from "the stagnant pools" around Jamestown and attacked the settlers of 1607 "with a sting more deadly than that of the Indian arrow or the Spanish musket ball." In 1930 the tradition was challenged by Wyndham B. Blanton. "No one doubts that there were marshes, mosquitoes and sickness along the James River," but "there is no evidence . . . that malaria was responsible for a preponderating part of the great mortalities." Blanton was rebutted by John Duffy in 1953: with malaria in the Carolina lowcountry to the south and among the French and English to the north, "it is highly improbable that the early settlers in Virginia were exempt." In 1957 Blanton replied that there was no natural habitat around Jamestown for *Anopheles quadrimaculatus* (even if true, Blanton ignored the fact that *quadrimaculatus* is but one of many species). He also contended that malaria was not introduced until late in the century—by which time the colonists, by clearing the forests, had created a habitat for mosquitoes—and that it was brought by slaves from the malaria-infested areas of the west African coast.[13] This mini-debate was in reality a non-debate, for the participants had different frames of reference. Blanton's gaze was fixed on the great mortalities of the years to the mid-1620s, from which he extrapolated forward;[14] Duffy, with a broader view of the whole colonial period, inferred from the whole to the part.

All indications are that malaria was imported into the Americas by Europeans. The disease in its milder form (*vivax*) is thought to have been general in Europe in the sixteenth and seventeenth centuries—Oliver Cromwell seems to have been only one of the more prominent sufferers. The more virulent *falciparum* is thought to have been prevalent in large parts of Africa.

---

[13] Thomas J. Wertenbaker, *Virginia Under the Stuarts, 1607-1688* (Princeton, N. J., 1914), 11; Wyndham B. Blanton, *Medicine in Virginia in the Seventeenth Century* (Richmond, Va., 1930), 54; John Duffy, *Epidemics in Colonial America* (Baton Rouge, La., 1953), 207n. Duffy made good use of St. Julien Ravenel Childs, *Malaria and Colonization in the Carolina Low Country, 1526-1696* (Baltimore, 1940), but to that study must be added Wood, *Black Majority*, Chap. 3, and Wyndham B. Blanton, "Epidemics, Real and Imaginary, and Other Factors Influencing Seventeenth Century Virginia's Population," *Bull. Hist. Med.*, XXXI (1957), 454-462. For a malariologist's answer to the general question of the historical development of malaria in North America see Mark F. Boyd, "An Historical Sketch of the Prevalence of Malaria in North America," *American Journal of Tropical Medicine*, XXI (1941), 223-244.

[14] Hence Blanton could make a part of his chain of evidence for the whole 17th century the "happy, intelligent, and vigorous" nature of the Powhatan Indians of 1607, arguing that they would have been otherwise if malaria had been prevalent, for "malaria notoriously destroys happiness, intelligence and vigor." Blanton, "Epidemics," *Bull. Hist. Med.*, XXXI (1957), 457.

But the Americas appear to have been free of the disease until the arrival of Europeans.[15] G. Robert Coatney and his colleagues find the evidence of pre-Columbian malaria too scant to be convincing, while to Saul Jarcho the existence of the mosquito in pre-contact America is certain, of *Anopheles* probable, and of malaria improbable although not impossible.[16]

FIGURE 4

SEASONAL DISTRIBUTION OF MALARIA CASES TREATED AT
JOHNS HOPKINS HOSPITAL, BALTIMORE, 1889–1894

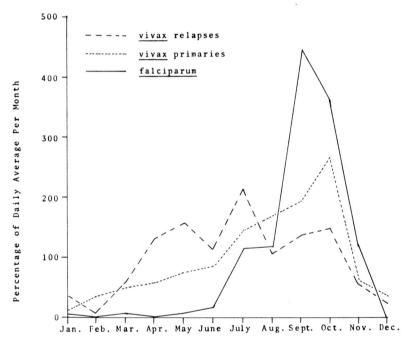

Source and notes:

Adapted from Mark F. Boyd, ed., *Malariology, A Comprehensive Survey of All Aspects of This Group of Diseases From a Global Standpoint* (Philadelphia, 1949), I, 557. The distribution is expressed as the percentage of daily average per month to allow comparison of different sample sizes and to minimize the effect of months of different lengths. The percentage is arrived at by a series of divisions: $[(E_m \div D_m)/(E_v \div 365.25)] \times 100$ where $E_m =$ the events in a month, $D_m =$ the number of days in a month, $E_y =$ the total events in the sample. Feb. is assigned 28.25 days.

[15] Frederick F. Cartwright and Michael D. Biddiso, *Disease and History* (New York, 1972), 138-140.

[16] Coatney *et al.*, *Primate Malarias*, 7; Saul Jarcho, "Some Observations on Disease in Prehistoric North America," *Bull. Hist. Med.*, XXXVIII (1964), 9.

If malaria was not indigenous to the Americas, it could only have been introduced by the entry of infected individuals into areas where *Anopheles* breed. When or from where such persons arrived in Virginia—directly from England or by way of the Caribbean—is irrelevant and certainly indeterminable. Although a variety of strains and perhaps even both major species may have been introduced by diverse carriers at a fairly early date, a more probable model, given the flow of immigration and the prevalence of *vivax* in Europe and *falciparum* in Africa, would have strains of the former entering during the first half of the century, followed by the gradual establishment (perhaps spotty) of areas of stable, low-level endemicity. The shattering of this picture would occur as blacks in numbers began arriving from a variety of African areas, bringing with them new strains of *vivax*, and *falciparum*.[17] In this model, symptomatic morbidity—the number of clinical cases—would rise gradually to about 1650, by which time the occasional, seemingly random cases of the early decades would be giving way to seasonal outbreaks. Through the remainder of the century epidemic-like incidents would mark the entry of each new strain or species, the general level of malaria morbidity rising a bit higher in the aftermath of each such outbreak.[18] The model also suggests that a qualitative change occurred sometime in the second half of the century as *falciparum* entered the colony, precipitating more virulent and wracking attacks, a phenomenon also noted by Peter Wood in his study of South Carolina slavery. The evidence from Carolina suggests to Wood that the benign *vivax* was prevalent in the 1670s but was supplanted by the more virulent *falciparum* in the 1680s.[19]

The literary evidence for Virginia supports this model, although in relating the archaic and imprecise terminology of the sources to the modern symptomatology of the disease we enter on the most treacherous ground of medical history. Blanton, for example, keyed his search for malaria on the word "ague" as referring to the combination of chills and fevers so generally associated in the popular mind with the disease. But chills may accompany fevers other than malarial, and malarial fevers are not always accompanied by chills. In a modern study of 201 paroxysms, 137 were found to be

[17] White susceptibility to diseases prevalent among blacks would be the other side of the coin with regard to Philip D. Curtin's thesis of black susceptibility to diseases prevalent among whites. See Curtin, "Epidemiology and the Slave Trade," *Political Science Quarterly*, LXXXIII (1968), 190-216.

[18] This is the picture drawn by a 100-year simulation based on the mathematics in Boyd, "Definitive Host," in Boyd, ed., *Malariology*, I, 683-687. It has been extended to incorporate elementary shifts in the human population and changes in the immunity level to reflect assumptions as to the sequential introduction of species (*vivax* followed by *falciparum*) and the periodic introduction of new strains.

[19] Wood, *Black Majority*, 87.

unaccompanied by chills, leading the investigators to conclude that "the term 'chills and fevers' inadequately described" a malarial attack.[20] Similarly, the words "intermittent" and "remittent," used in the sources as adjectives for "fever," may or may not refer to the characteristic fever spikes of malaria, as may "quotidian," "tertian," and "quartan" used to describe the timing of the spikes. References to chinchona or its synonyms—Peruvian bark, Jesuit bark, or simply "the bark"—may also be indicative of malaria, for chinchona was introduced into Europe as a specific remedy for what is generally considered to have been malaria. Such references are not infallible, for the bark was sometimes utilized for fevers other than malarial, and its efficacy was widely questioned; hence it was not invariably given.[21] Nevertheless, we must have a measure of confidence: even if many of the references to ague, the varieties of fever, and "the bark" are misapplied, the remainder correctly point to malaria. From the sources it seems clear that the "agues and fevers" that were only occasional in the first fifty years in Virginia became both more general and more severe (reflecting the entry of *falciparum?*) in the second fifty and on into the eighteenth century.

There is no need here to review the occasional evidence for seventeenth-century malaria cited by Blanton.[22] Clearly, by the 1680s the "seasoning"— that period of illness which almost inevitably befell a newcomer to the Chesapeake—was associated with what we can take for malaria. Newcomers might assume any sickness that struck them to be a "seasoning," as Robert Beverley noted in his *History of Virginia* and as George Hume did in 1723. To Hume a whole succession of illnesses—from "a severe flux" to a "now and then" bout with "the fever and ague"—added up to "a most severe" seasoning.[23] But the long-time resident of Virginia was more precise. William Fitzhugh wrote of his newly arrived sister in 1687: she has had "two or

[20] G. Robert Coatney and Martin D. Young, "A Study of the Paroxysms Resulting from Induced Infections of *Plasmodium vivax,*" *American Journal of Hygiene,* XXXV (1942), 141. C. Merrill Whorton *et al.,* "The Chesson Strain of *Plasmodium vivax* Malaria," Pt. III: "Clinical Aspects," *Journal of Infectious Diseases,* LXXX (1947), 241, reported chills in only 46% of 158 primary attacks.

[21] A. W. Haggis, "Fundamental Errors in the Early History of Chinchona," *Bull. Hist. Med.,* X (1941), 417-459, 568-592.

[22] Blanton found 6 references to 1700: *Medicine in the Seventeenth Century,* 52-53; "Epidemics," *Bull. Hist. Med.,* XXXI (1957), 458. A few escaped him, notably John Clayton's. Edmund and Dorothy Smith Berkeley, eds., *The Reverend John Clayton . . . His Scientific Writings and Other Related Papers* (Charlottesville, Va., 1965). To some extent the number of references is a function of the quantity and types of materials extant from the period rather than of the prevalence of the disease.

[23] George Hume to Ninian Hume, June 20, 1723, *Virginia Magazine of History and Biography,* XX (1912), 397-400. Robert Beverley wrote in *The History and Present State of Virginia,* ed. Louis B. Wright (Chapel Hill, N. C., 1947), 306:

three small fits of a feaver and ague, which now has left her, and so consequently her seasoning [is] over." And again, in another letter: "My Sister has had her seasoning . . . two or three fits of a feaver and ague." John Clayton, Virginia's scientific parson, wrote of "Seasonings, which are an intermiting feaver, or rather a continued feaver with quotidian paroxisms," in describing that same year the "distempers" among the English.[24]

By the 1680s sharp geographical differences in levels of health were being noted in the colony. To a French traveler of 1686-1687 the inhabitants of tidewater Gloucester County "looked so sickly that I judged the country to be unhealthy"; those of Stafford and old Rappahannock were obviously healthier, "their complexions clear and lively." The Virginians gave him a reason he considered "quite plausible": "along the seashore and also along the rivers which contain salt, because of the tide, the inhabitants in these places are rarely free from fever during the hot weather; they call this a local sickness; but the salt in the rivers disappears about twenty leagues from the seas, just as one enters the county of Rappahannock, and those who live beyond that point do not suffer from it." Clayton, too, noted the geographic difference, adding a hint of autumnal seasonality: "so far as the Salt Waters reach the Country is deemed less healthy. In the Freshes they more rarely are troubled with Seasonings, and those Endemical Distempers about *September* and *October*."[25] All three phenomena are commensurate with a hypothesis of widespread malaria. As we have seen, autumnal seasonality is inherent in temperate-zone malaria; so too are the susceptibility of newcomers—they must develop immunities to the specific species and strains of *Plasmodia*

"The first sickness that any New-Comer happens to have there, he unfairly calls a Seasoning, be it Fever, Ague, or any thing else, that his own folly, or excesses bring upon him."

[24] William Fitzhugh to Henry Fitzhugh, July 18, 1687, Fitzhugh to Dr. Ralph Smith, July 1, 1687, in Richard Beale Davis, ed., *William Fitzhugh and His Chesapeake World, 1676-1701: The Fitzhugh Letters and Other Documents* (Chapel Hill, N. C., 1963), 229, 230; Dr. Nehemiah Grew to John Clayton, 1687, in Berkeley and Berkeley, eds., *John Clayton*, 26. Richard Harrison Shryock, *Medicine and Society in America, 1660-1860* (New York, 1960), 87, generally associated malaria with the colonial "seasoning"; so did travelers describing the entry of newcomers into the malarious Mississippi Valley of the 19th century. See Michael Owen Jones, "Climate and Disease: The Traveler Describes America," *Bull. Hist. Med.*, XLI (1967), 256.

[25] Gilbert Chinard, ed., *A Huguenot Exile in Virginia, or Voyages of a Frenchman exiled for his Religion with a description of Virginia & Maryland* (New York, 1934), 130, 174; John Clayton to the Royal Society, 1688, in Berkeley and Berkeley, eds., *John Clayton*, 54. Clayton went on to suggest that an investigation of the phenomena might result in "several beneficial Discoveries, not only in relation to those Distempers in *America*, but perhaps take in your *Kentish* Agues." The latter phrase has generally been understood to refer to malaria.

present in an area—and the sharp boundaries between infected and unin-
fected populations, although in this case the boundaries would seem to have
been only temporary. Time would be required to create in newly settled areas
the conditions necessary to maintain the endemic levels that existed in older
areas.[26]

For the eighteenth century the literary evidence is clearer, and there is no
question among historians as to the prevalence of malaria. John Oldmixon,
who presumably drew some of his information from William Byrd II, wrote
at the turn of the century that "the *Seasoning* here, as in other parts of
America, is a Fever or Ague, which the Change of Climate and Diet
generally throws new Comers into; the Bark is in *Virginia* a Sovereign
Remedy to this Disease." Beverley wrote of the Virginians' "Intermitting
Fevers, as well as their Agues," as "very troublesome" and cited "*Cortex
Peruviana*" as a remedy that "seldom or never fails to remove the Fits." Byrd
dosed with the bark his family, himself, and his fellow commissioners of the
North Carolina boundary survey. In 1735 he referred to the shipment of
"infused" bark to Virginia by England's "Drugsters and Apothecarys"—
that is, bark which had been steeped in water, the water being used in
England and the residual bark shipped to the colonies—as "almost as bad as
Murder." Hugh Jones wrote of a people "subject to feavers and agues, which
is the country distemper, a severe fit of which (called a seasoning) most
expect, some time after their arrival." Chinchona was "a perfect catholicon
for that sickness . . . which being taken and repeated in a right manner,
seldom fails of a cure."[27]

[26] In contrast to descriptions of other parts of Virginia, John Banister's descriptions of the falls area of the James make no mention of illness and disease, implying a
relatively disease-free area during the late 17th century. Joseph and Nesta Ewan,
John Banister and His Natural History of Virginia, 1678-1692 (Urbana, Ill., 1970).
At the end of the 18th century Thomas Jefferson wrote that "Richmond was not well
chosen as the place to shake off a fever and ague in the months of Aug. Sep. and Oct.
till frost. All it's inhabitants who can afford it leave it for the upper country during
that season." Wyndham B. Blanton, *Medicine in Virginia in the Eighteenth Century* (Richmond, Va., 1931), 67. In the 19th and 20th centuries no malarial "fall
line" existed as suggested by the earlier distinction between "the salts" and "the
freshes." See the county morbidity and mortality statistics for 1927-1932 in Frederick
L. Hoffman, *Malaria in Virginia, North Carolina and South Carolina* (Newark,
N. J., 1933).
[27] John Oldmixon, *The British Empire in America*, I (London, 1708), 294;
Beverley, *History of Virginia*, ed. Wright, 306; Louis B. Wright and Marion
Tinling, eds., *The Secret Diary of William Byrd of Westover, 1709-1712* (Richmond,
Va., 1941), 232, 372-373, 386-389, 538, 589; Louis B. Wright, ed., *The Prose Works
of William Byrd of Westover: Narratives of a Colonial Virginian* (Cambridge,
Mass., 1966), 102, 130, 189, 340-342, 348; William Byrd to Mrs. Otway, Oct. 2,

Sources from the latter half of the century contain abundant references to what can be construed as malaria, leading Blanton to conclude that "hardly any section . . . escaped the inevitable 'Ague and Fever.' "[28] Indeed, here and there in the literature are such detailed accounts that one is tempted to diagnose individual cases—Landon Carter's Sukey, for example. Autumnal fevers were pronounced in both 1756 and 1757, Carter writing of the fall of the latter year that it was a "very Aguish Season" when nothing "but the barke" would do, and noting that "it has been more usefull this year than common." During the autumn of 1756 Sukey was among the sixty-odd in his family and labor force to take sick. A year later, in the midst of a still worse fever season, Sukey came down again, falling into a monthly pattern of attacks that extended through the autumn and early winter, subsided during the coldest weather, then reappeared in March 1758. In describing his daughter's illnesses Carter noted time and again the secondary symptoms associated with malaria, from nausea and vomiting to pains and pallor. But most telling is his running account of the course of Sukey's fever. In Figure 5 the description of five days of Sukey's first 1757 fever attack in August is superimposed on a modern fever chart of a quotidian (intermittent-remittent type) clinical attack of *Plasmodium falciparum*. Was Sukey's a case of malaria? Diagnosis from such evidence is impossible: all the historian can hope for is consonance between historical evidence and medical understanding. The literary description of Sukey's illness seems entirely consonant with malaria.[29]

Presuming that, from the literary evidence, a circumstantial case can be made for the presence of malaria in the Chesapeake region, or at least in Virginia, in the seventeenth and eighteenth centuries, what demographic effects might follow? Can we discern these effects and substantiate to an extent the literary case already made? In other words, does the hypothesis of malaria fit, perhaps even explain, the empirical evidence? The question requires consideration of as much as possible of the demographic analysis of early America done to date. It requires, too, the drawing of analogies between early America, for which no direct measurement of malaria or its

---

1735, *VMHB*, XXXVI (1928), 121. Byrd in this letter, as Clayton did in 1687 (n. 22), associated the Virginia "distemper" with "your Kentish Distemper." See also Hugh Jones, *The Present State of Virginia*, ed. Richard L. Morton (Chapel Hill, N. C., 1956), 85.

[28] Blanton, *Medicine in the Eighteenth Century*, 67.

[29] Sukey's illness can be followed in Greene, ed., *Diary of Carter*, I, 127, to her death on pp. 221-222. In the case of prominent men even more positive "diagnosis" is common, for example, the diagnosis of Washington as suffering from "chronic malaria" in Blanton, *Medicine in the Eighteenth Century*, 309.

FIGURE 5

EIGHTEENTH-CENTURY FEVER DESCRIPTION SUPERSCRIBED
ON A TWENTIETH-CENTURY FEVER CHART
ARISING FROM AN INFECTION OF *Plasmodium falciparum*

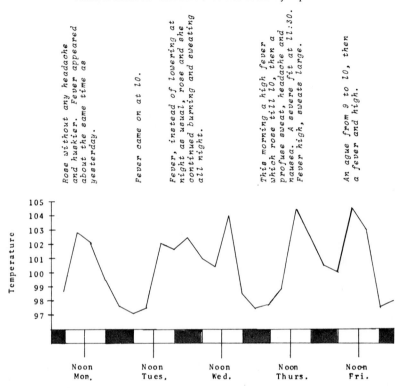

Sources and notes:

Fever description paraphrased from Jack P. Greene, ed., *The Diary of Colonel Landon Carter of Sabine Hall, 1752-1778* (Charlottesville, Va., 1965), I, 165-167; fever chart adapted from S. F. Kitchen, "The Infection in the Intermediate Host: Symptomatology, Falciparum Malaria," in Forest Fay Moulton, ed., *A Symposium on Human Malaria with Special Reference to North America and the Caribbean Region* (Washington, D. C., 1941), 198, Case no. 1164. Mon. was the second day of fever.

effects is available, and malarious areas of the world where measurements have been made during the twentieth century.

Since 1967, when Philip Greven formally introduced early Americanists to the startling possibilities for research opened by the French demographic historians, a great deal of sophisticated demographic work has been done on

TABLE I

COMPARATIVE ADULT LIFE EXPECTANCIES: THE CHESAPEAKE REGION AND NEW ENGLAND

Expected Years Yet to Live

Achieved Age[a]	Andover b.1670-1699		Salem d.17th Cent.		Middlesex b.1650-1710		Salem d.18th Cent.		Andover b.1730-1759	
	Male	Female	Male	Female	Male	Female	Male	Female	Male	Female
15	--	--	--	--	--	24.9	--	--	--	--
20	44.8	42.1	36.1	21.4	28.8	19.8	35.5	37.0	41.6	43.1
25	--	--	--	--	23.7	16.3	--	--	--	--
30	38.7	35.9	29.2	20.0	19.4	13.6	30.3	32.6	36.3	36.5
35	--	--	--	--	15.8	10.7	--	--	--	--
40	31.4	29.0	24.1	20.9	13.0	8.6	25.3	26.3	28.4	30.9
45	--	--	--	--	10.0	9.2	--	--	--	--
50	23.5	22.4	19.1	14.4	7.7	9.3	19.6	21.1	24.5	25.0
55	--	--	--	--	5.8	7.7	--	--	--	--
60	15.2	15.9	14.5	16.2	5.0	7.9	14.5	16.4	17.2	18.8
65	--	--	--	--	3.6	5.0	--	--	--	--
70	10.2	11.9	10.0	10.0	2.9	3.7	10.0	10.0	10.9	12.0
75	--	--	--	--	--	5.2	--	--	--	--
80	6.7	9.5	--	--	--	--	--	--	7.1	8.3
85	--	--	--	--	--	--	--	--	--	--
90+	5.0	6.2	--	--	--	--	--	--	5.0	5.0

Notes and sources:

[a] Achieved age represents the lower inclusive boundary of a group. In the case of Middlesex: 15-19, 20-24, 25-29, etc.; Andover: 20-29, 30-39, 40-49, etc.; but N. B. Salem: 21-30, 31-40, 41-50, etc., with an estimate of 10 inserted for 71-plus. For Andover and Salem see Maris A. Vinovskis, "Mortality Rates and Trends in Massachusetts before 1860," *Journal of Economic History,* XXXII (1972), 198-199 (drawing upon the work of Philip J. Greven, Jr., and James K. Somerville respectively). For Middlesex see Darrett B. and Anita H. Rutman, "'Now Wives and Sons-in-Law': Parental Death in a Seventeenth-Century Virginia County," in Thad Tate, ed., *The Chesapeake in the Seventeenth Century: Essays on Its Euramerican Society and Politics* (Chapel Hill, N. C., forthcoming). The Middlesex table is based upon data for subjects known to have achieved marriageable age and to have chosen to marry. Both sources discuss at length the populations and procedures underlying the tables.

New England and, recently, on the early Chesapeake region.[30] This work has varied in quality and to some extent in methodology. It has been confined for the most part to explorations of particular locales, and for both regions such local studies are few. Investigation has nonetheless advanced to the point where a few basic phenomena seem to be coming into focus—four in particular with regard to mortality. First, radically different mortality schedules seem to have obtained in New England and the Chesapeake region. Men and women in the northern colonies tended to live considerably longer lives than did their contemporaries to the south. Second, in the Chesapeake and in seventeenth-century Salem, Massachusetts (but not apparently in other New England areas studied so far), women fifteen to forty-five years, the child-bearing years, seem to have run a substantially greater risk of death than did males of the same age. The third finding emerges from the second: even within a particular region and time period mortality rates in general, and sex-specific mortality rates in particular, seem to have varied by locality. Finally, in New England at least, mortality rates shifted over time. In the eighteenth century life expectancies rose from seventeenth-century levels in some areas and for some segments of the population and fell in others, the net effect being a tendency toward convergence—the "washing out" of differences. All four of these phenomena can be seen in Table I, drawn from studies of Andover and Salem, Massachusetts, and Middlesex County, Virginia. But Table I also suggests, in its confusion of sample definitions and age groupings, that such cross-study comparisons furnish grounds for only very broad general statements.

Still, the broad statements are enough to prompt questions. Why a difference in mortality between New England and the Chesapeake? Why a shift in mortality over time within New England? Why, in the seventeenth century, a sex-related difference in mortality during the years between fifteen and forty-five? Piecemeal explanations have been offered with respect to the New England data. Rising mortality rates and falling life expectancies between the seventeenth and eighteenth centuries have been attributed to the rise of population density to the point where infectious diseases could be supported. Although this plausible supposition accounts for some of the data, it does not explain those from Salem where mortality rates tended to fall slightly. Maris Vinovskis has related high death rates among Salem's females in the seventeenth century to maternal mortality—but were the conditions of

[30] Philip J. Greven, Jr., "Historical Demography and Colonial America," *William and Mary Quarterly*, 3d Ser., XXIV (1967), 438-454. Maris A. Vinovskis, "Mortality Rates and Trends in Massachusetts Before 1860," *Journal of Economic History*, XXXII (1972), 184-213, is a good introduction to, and critique of, the New England work, particularly that of Greven, Kenneth A. Lockridge, Susan L. Norton, and Vinovskis's own. The Chesapeake work is cited in n. 2 above.

childbirth so very different between Salem and nearby Ipswich where Susan Norton has found "no significant attrition of the female population during the years when . . . married women would be bearing children"?[31] Did the care of women in childbirth improve so greatly in the eighteenth century as to account for the congruence of male and female life expectancies found by Vinovskis in Salem and reflected in Table I? Most importantly, none of the piecemeal answers applies to the sharp contrast between New England and Chespeake mortality.

Does a consideration of malaria suggest a more general answer? The most obvious impact of malaria is on the general level of public health. Malaria is not notorious as a "killer" disease: the 5 and 25 percent mortality rates cited earlier are extremes. It is rather "the great debilitator"; it lowers the level of general health and the ability to resist other diseases. One modern study estimates that for every death ascribed to malaria in an infected population, five additional deaths are actually due to malaria acting in concert with other diseases.[32] Carter's Sukey is a case in point. Weakened by her bouts with a malarial fever, and undoubtedly anemic, she died in the spring of 1758 from what appeared to be a respiratory infection.

That an inverse relationship exists between the degree of malaria morbidity and the death rate is indicated in modern Guatemala. A malaria eradication program was initiated there in 1957, and the death rate declined 20 percent between 1958 and 1963. In Ceylon, where both eradication and a concerted attempt to expand medical facilities began immediately after World War II, the death rate declined by two-thirds between 1946 and 1953, with roughly 23 percent of the decline attributable to the malaria eradication program.[33] Thus a hypothesis of a malarious Chesapeake and a relatively nonmalarious New England might well explain a considerable part of the disparity between New England and Chesapeake mortality rates.

Note, however, that we refer to New England as "relatively" free of malaria. We mean to imply a difference of degree rather than an absolute difference, for there is evidence of malaria in seventeenth-century New

---

[31] Vinovskis, "Mortality Rates," *Jour. Econ. Hist.*, XXXII (1972), 201; Susan L. Norton, "Population Growth in Colonial America: A Study of Ipswich, Massachusetts," *Population Studies*, XXV (1971), 442.

[32] Peter Newman, *Malaria Eradication and Population Growth: With Special Reference to Ceylon and British Guiana* (Ann Arbor, Mich., 1965), 77.

[33] S. A. Meegama, "Malaria Eradication and its Effect on Mortality Levels," *Pop. Stud.*, XXI (1967), 207-208, 232. The effect of eradication on mortality rates is the subject of an intense debate, one largely fought out in the pages of *Pop. Stud.* We have adjusted Meegama's figures to reflect the latest word offered by R. H. Gray, "The Decline of Mortality in Ceylon and the Demographic Effects of Malaria Control," *ibid.*, XXVIII (1974), 226-227.

England. Duffy describes "attacks of pernicious malaria" in Boston in 1658, western Connecticut in 1668, Salem in 1683, and Boston again in 1690. For some reason, however, the northern boundary of malaria shifted in the eighteenth century, leaving New England entirely free of the disease after roughly the mid-century mark.[34]

The whole question of endemic (as distinct from epidemic) disease is undeveloped in early American historiography in general, and for New England specifically,[35] but one can make a calculated guess that malaria had only a marginal foothold in New England even in the seventeenth century and that levels of endemicity varied among the closed populations of the area. Among some, the disease was virtually nonexistent (but the population, lacking immunity, would be susceptible to sudden, short-lived periods of morbidity); among others, malaria was relatively well established.

This view would be consonant with the findings of modern malariologists who break down national malariometric and morbidity rates into regional and even village rates and find enormous variety. It would also be consonant with the diversity of mortality rates being found by historians of New England and—if we assume that Salem was an area of relatively well-ensconced malaria—with the two peculiarities of Salem's mortality schedule presented by Vinovskis. The first is the suggestion that while in other New England towns that have been studied mortality rose in the eighteenth century, Salem's mortality declined—that there was, in effect, a tendency among the towns for mortality to converge. Such a tendency would be very familiar to students of eradication programs;[36] and what was the disappearance of malaria from eighteenth-century New England but a form of natural eradication? The second is the high death rate for women in their childbearing years, which, although unique to Salem among the seventeenth-

[34] Duffy, *Epidemics,* 206-207, 213. Oliver Wendell Holmes's "Dissertation of Intermittent Fever in New England," *Boylston Prize Dissertations* (Boston, 1838), is, from start to finish, a compendium of quotations indicative of malaria in New England.

[35] Richard H. Shryock's complaint in his "Medical Sources and the Social Historian," originally published in the *American Historical Review,* XLI (1935-1936), 458-473, and reprinted in Richard Harrison Shryock, *Medicine in America: Historical Essays* (Baltimore, 1966), is that historians in general, and medical historians specifically, have emphasized the story of medical disasters (epidemics). "It is easier to find records of a sudden 'visitation' than it is to trace obscure, endemic conditions; and once written, the former makes more spectacular reading. Hence the universal attention accorded 'the Black Death.' Hence also the neglect of contemporary endemic diseases, which in the long run were more fatal and perhaps equally significant in their social consequences" (p. 278).

[36] For example, Gray, "Decline of Mortality," *Pop. Stud.,* XXVIII (1974), 226-227.

century New England towns studied, was shared with Middlesex in tidewater Virginia.

Exaggerated maternal mortality can be directly associated with endemic malaria, a relationship intuitively perceived in the malarious South of a half-century ago by country doctors who routinely dosed their pregnant patients with quinine, and more recently demonstrated in a controlled study of 250 pregnant women in urban Nigeria.[37] The nature of the linkage is still undetermined, but the indirect evidence indicates that pregnancy tends to nullify immunities, paving the way for a build-up of parasites, morbidity, and pronounced anemia, with a consequent hazard of abortion, premature labor, and the childbirth death of both mother and infant. Modern medical researchers cannot, of course, measure mortality directly, for of necessity they intervene to stop the course of the disease. Neither can modern medical research duplicate the conditions that exaggerated the hazards in the seventeenth and eighteenth centuries: large households crowded into small houses, exposing anemic, periodically feverish mothers-to-be to contagious ailments; living conditions that can only be described as dirty, with a consequent exposure of the mother to septicemia; and above all, a counterproductive medical practice: the bleeding and stringent dieting that William Byrd imposed on his pregnant and presumably malarious and anemic wife could hardly have been efficacious.[38]

Analogy can, to an extent, supply what the medical research leaves out. Puttalam district, Ceylon, in the late 1930s was an area roughly comparable to Middlesex County, Virginia, in the late seventeenth and early eighteenth centuries. Both were rural; both were devoid of modern medicine; in both, childbirth was managed by traditionally rather than medically oriented midwives; and both (Puttalam district for a certainty and Middlesex for the sake of argument) were malarious. Figure 6 graphs age- and sex-specific death rates for each area. The values are obviously different—for one reason because the figures are based on different statistical populations[39]—but the

---

[37] Warren K. Stratman-Thomas, "The Infection in the Intermediate Host: Symptomatology, *vivax* Malaria," and S. F. Kitchen, "The Infection in the Intermediate Host: Symptomatology, *falciparum* Malaria," in Moulton, ed., *Symposium on Human Malaria*, 187-188, 203-204; H. M. Gilles *et al.*, "Malaria, Anaemia and Pregnancy," *Annals of Tropical Medicine and Parasitology*, LXIII (1969), 245-263. See also P. Tilly, "Anaemia in Parturient Women, with Special Reference to Malaria Infection of the Placenta," *ibid.*, 109-115; C. A. Gill, "The Influence of Malaria on Natality with Special Reference to Ceylon," *Journal of the Malaria Institute of India*, III (1940), 201-252; and R. Menon, "Pregnancy and Malaria," *Medical Journal of Malaysia*, XXVII (1972), 115-119.

[38] For example, Wright and Tinling, eds., *Secret Diary*, 141-142, 344, 364.

[39] Only a very general comparison can be made because of the different age

similarity of the general configuration of the curves is significant. In both areas females in their fertile years ran an exaggerated risk of death in comparison to males. The link between the two areas may well have been malaria, and for the historian who must work from highly tangential evidence the extent to which female deaths exceed male deaths in a given area may well be a rough measure of the hold of malaria on that area. If the suggestion is sound, Middlesex and whatever part of the Chesapeake region it accurately reflects were highly malarious.

What of the social ramifications of malaria? Although disease is biologically defined, it is also to an extent culturally defined. The sickly appearance of Gloucester County men and women in 1687 and the ghostly pallor of those who lived about the Great Dismal Swamp in 1728 invited comment by

FIGURE 6

AGE SPECIFIC DEATH RATES, PUTTALAM DISTRICT,
CEYLON, 1937–1938; SEVENTEENTH- AND EARLY EIGHTEENTH-CENTURY
MIDDLESEX COUNTY, VIRGINIA

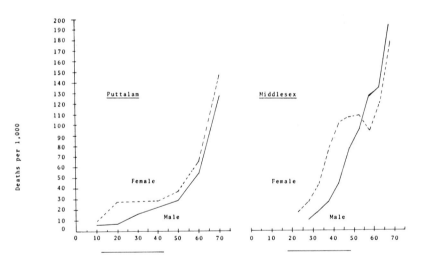

Sources and notes:
For Puttalam see S. A. Meegama, "Malaria Eradication and Its Effects on Mortality Levels," *Population Studies*, XXI (1967), 225; for Middlesex see Darrett B. and Anita H. Rutman, " 'Now-Wives and Sons-in-Law': Parental Death in a Seventeenth-Century Virginia County," in Thad W. Tate, ed., *The Chesapeake in the Seventeenth Century: Essays on Its Euramerican Society and Politics* (Chapel Hill, N. C., forthcoming). High maternity cohorts are underlined. N. B.: The populations at risk varied. See n. 39.

Durand de Dauphine and William Byrd respectively;[40] but did the inhabitants look upon themselves as diseased and sick? Probably not. Even the periodic "agues and fevers" of malaria could be culturally normative rather than culturally exceptional. This is the implication of the almost casual language with which Fitzhugh reported the end of his sister's illness—"and so consequently her seasoning [is] over." Even in Carter's diary most of the seizures are noted in a commonplace way: "Judy's fever left her this day. Lucy her ague and fever at 5 this eve."[41] Only in extreme situations did illness become something more than commonplace, as it did for Carter in the terrible year 1757. "It is necessary that man should be acquainted with affliction," Carter wrote in exasperation toward its end; "and 'tis certainly nothing short of it to be confi ied a whole year in tending one's sick Children. Mine are now never well."[42] It is, perhaps, this cultural definition of illness that underlies the diverse reactions to endemic and epidemic diseases commented on by Richard Shryock: the former are "taken for granted," the latter provoke hysteria.[43]

That said, however, we propose three ways in which endemic malaria, even if matter-of-factly accepted by its victims, conceivably affected their society. What follows can only be quick, tentative, and suggestive. The subject of the interrelationship of disease and society is only now coming into prominence under such rubrics as "medical anthropology," and potentially useful models from contemporary studies are still few and rudimentary.[44] In addition, we have been able to associate the disease only generally with Virginia through literary evidence, and only with regard to one small

---

groups used (Puttalam has been graphed on the basis of the mid-years of the age groups 5-14, 15-24, 25-34, 35-44, 45-54, 55-64, and age 70 for the cohort 65-plus; Middlesex on the basis of smoothed data for the mid-years of 5-year groups), the different species and strains of *plasmodium* prevalent in the two areas, and, above all, the differences in the populations at risk. In Puttalam the entire population of the district, 1937-1938, was at risk; for Middlesex the population at risk is married and widowed adults, the figures being based on the experience of subjects born over the span of years 1650-1710 who both survived to a marriageable age and chose at some time to marry. If the Puttalam population at risk had been so restricted, the resulting "bulge" of female deaths during the fertile years would undoubtedly have been somewhat greater.

[40] Chinard, ed., *Huguenot Exile;* Wright, ed., *Prose Works,* 202.
[41] Davis, ed., *Fitzhugh Letters;* Greene, ed., *Diary of Carter,* I, 203.
[42] Greene, ed., *Diary of Carter,* I, 194.
[43] Shryock, *Medicine and Society,* 93-95.
[44] For example, V. F. P. M. Van Amelsvoort, *Culture, Stone Age and Modern Medicine* (Assen, The Netherlands, 1964). Burton A. Weisbrod *et al., Disease and Economic Development: The Impact of Parasitic Diseases in St. Lucia* (Madison, Wis., 1973), Chap. 2, is a good overview of this literature, but see also Gerald Gordon *et al., Disease, the Individual, and Society* (New Haven, Conn., 1968), Pt. I.

DARRETT B. RUTMAN AND ANITA H. RUTMAN

tidewater area—Middlesex—can we make even a rough statement as to degree. Still, a beginning seems in order.

The most obvious interrelationship between disease and society is that defined by economics. What is the cost to the society of an endemic disease such as malaria? In modern economic scholarship the question has been posed in terms of the economic gain to a society of an eradication program and the answer seems to be coming back as a negative. Robin Barlow has summarized the findings: eradication of malaria brings about a population rise by reducing the death rate and, more important, by raising both the birth rate, as more children are successfully delivered, and the rate of survival through childhood. Moreover, the reduction of mortality, morbidity, and debility increases the quantity and quality of labor output. An immediate economic gain follows, but the society loses in the long run as the added population makes increasing demands on the public sector for services, reduces per capita income, and curtails capital formulation.[45] This econometric approach is cold and impersonal, and it runs counter to the historian's normal prejudice by requiring an "if" proposition—what *if* there had been no malaria in the Chesapeake? But there is some profit in applying it, if only to discount any quick generalization as to malaria and economic backwardness. Without malaria the rate of natural increase in the Chesapeake and the number of people living there would have been greater. This probably would not have resulted in an increased demand for public services, for the concept of public service was weakly defined; yet an increase in a population, dependent on a single cash crop and a finite market, would have resulted in greater production and lower prices—and consequently lower per capita income. Only if receiving lower prices for tobacco had led Virginians to an earlier and more energetic acceptance of economic diversification would the overall economy have improved.[46]

Another approach is perhaps more revealing. The agricultural economy of the Chesapeake region was labor-intensive: in the main a person's economic position depended on the application of labor to land. But disease in

[45] Robin Barlow, "The Economic Effects of Malaria Eradication," *Papers and Proceedings of the Seventy-Ninth Annual Meeting,* in *American Economic Review,* LCII (1967), 130-148. See also Barlow, *The Economic Effects of Malaria Eradication* (Ann Arbor, Mich., 1968); Newman, *Malaria Eradication;* and Gladys N. Conly, "The Impact of Malaria on Economic Development: A Case Study," *Proceedings,* 668-674, a preliminary report on an attempt to measure micro-effects using 300 farm families in eastern Paraguay before and after an eradication program.

[46] John C. Rainbolt, *From Prescription to Persuasion: Manipulation of Seventeenth Century Virginia Economy* (Port Washington, N. Y., 1974), discusses the early and unsuccessful diversification attempts. Avery Odelle Craven, *Soil Exhaustion as a Factor in the Agricultural History of Virginia and Maryland, 1606-1860* (Urbana, Ill., 1926), 69, dates tidewater diversification at about mid-18th century.

general and malaria in particular strike directly at labor.[47] Hence in the Chesapeake one's economic position was constantly jeopardized by disease, as the marquis de Chastellux observed when, with reference to "epidemical disorders" common among the slaves of the Virginians, he reported that "both their property and their revenue" were "extremely precarious."[48] The risk, however, was unevenly spread. The planter who relied on his own labor, with that of his wife and perhaps a single servant or slave, chanced disaster more than did the planter who had built up a labor force of ten or twenty persons. Imagine the small planter struck down by a malaria attack at the moment most appropriate for the transplantation of tobacco seedlings from seedbeds to fields, or when the ripe tobacco leaves had to be cut and housed. A good percentage, perhaps even all, of his year's income might be lost. The intensity of the dependence on labor is illustrated by Peter Mountague of Middlesex County whose one male servant ran away at harvest time in 1701, causing Mountague to complain to the county court in 1702 that he had sustained as a consequence "the whole loss of the last crop."[49] It is true that larger planters could be hard hit. Armistead Churchill of Middlesex lost thirty slaves in one six-month period in 1737.[50] But a large labor force insured against catastrophe. Even at the height of his troubles in 1757 Carter still had laborers in his fields. Moreover, in a society in which working lives were short, the amassment of capital provided defense against the economic effects of death. The short-lived planter, large or small, frequently left orphaned children.[51] But the chances that orphans of the large planter would start their working years with enough capital in the form of labor to protect them from disaster were far greater than those of orphans of the small planter. Generation after generation the latter had to begin their working lives with no

---

[47] Wood, *Black Majority*, 91, argues that in South Carolina the combination of malaria (together with yellow fever), black resistance to both diseases, and the labor-intensive economy "must have done a great deal to reinforce the expanding rationale behind the enslavement of Africans." Wood attempts to demonstrate that South Carolina's whites, from an early date, *thought* of the blacks as more resistant to disease—this in sharp contrast to Winthrop D. Jordan, *White Over Black: American Attitudes Toward the Negro, 1550-1812* (Chapel Hill, N. C., 1968), 259-265. We have found no evidence in Virginia to substantiate Wood's thesis.

[48] Marquis de Chastellux, *Travels in North-America, in the Years 1780, 1781, and 1782*, 2d ed., II (London, 1787), 297.

[49] Middlesex County, Va., MS Order Book, No. 3, 1694-1705, 483, Virginia State Library, Richmond.

[50] *The Parish Register of Christ Church, Middlesex County, Va., from 1653 to 1812* (Richmond, Va., 1897), 275-276. In this case the loss might well have been to yellow fever, a disease then entering the colony.

[51] Rutman and Rutman, " 'Now-Wives and Sons-in-Law,' " in Tate, ed., *The Chesapeake.*

more, and sometimes less, than their fathers had begun with. These in-equalities may well have contributed to economic polarization over time.[52] For the planter who, by virtue of ability, energy, or luck, lived insulated from the economic consequences of disease had a far better chance to improve his economic position and, consequently, still greater insulation.

A consideration of disease and economics has led to one aspect of the structure of Chesapeake society—exaggerated economic polarization. But disease interacts with social structure in other ways as well. Provision must be made for illness. This was in part an individual matter, as it was for Dennis Conyers when he sold one hundred acres on the Piankatank River in Middlesex to Peter Godson on the condition that "the said Pe-ter . . . administer Physick or Physical means to the said Dennis for his own person for the space of one year."[53] For the whole society the provisions for illness take on a more general form. The phenomenon of every planter his own practitioner has long been noted. Equally to the point are the phenom-ena of every claimant to the title "doctor" being engaged as one and, notwithstanding the aspersions of Byrd, the high esteem accorded physicians in the Chesapeake area.[54] On a still higher level of generalization one can suggest that illness and early death were related to the basic social organiza-tion of the Chesapeake. In the continuing study of Middlesex County of which this article is a part, the region is emerging not as an area of isolated plantations and individuals but as a mosaic of close-knit neighborhoods and kinship groups. Few aspects of life reflect this mosaic more clearly than do illness and death. Illness brought visitation, and kin and neighbors clustered about the sickbeds of the county.[55] Death, particularly the death of parents with the consequent orphaning of children, evoked kinship obligations, and

[52] Darrett B. Rutman, "The Social Web: A Prospectus for the Study of the Early American Community," in William L. O'Neill, ed., *Insights and Parallels: Problems and Issues of American Social History* (Minneapolis, 1973), 85, 85n, 112-113, briefly compares polarization in New England and Middlesex.

[53] Lancaster County, Va., MS Deeds, Etc., No. 2, 1654-1702, 116-117, Va. St. Lib.

[54] Philip Alexander Bruce, *Economic History of Virginia in the Seventeenth Century*, II (New York, 1896), 231ff. See Byrd to Sir Hans Sloane, Apr. 20, 1706, *WMQ*, 2d Ser., I (1921), 186: "Here be some men indeed that are call'd Doctors: but they are generally discarded Surgeons of Ships, that know nothing above very common Remedys." Oldmixon, *British Empire*, I, 294, presumably reflecting Byrd, wrote that the Virginians "reckon it among Blessings" that they had few doctors, "fancying the Number of their Diseases would encrease with that of their Physi-cians." These attitudes are in sharp contrast to the social position accorded physicians in Middlesex society.

[55] The phenomenon can be glimpsed in depositions submitted to the county court in cases involving disputed wills—for example, the probate proceedings surrounding

relations (including such relations as godparents) moved to care for the parentless. The effect was a society of open and mixed households. The home was not an isolated castle but a neighborhood focal point. The typical family was not the neat nuclear one of mother-father-children but a mixed affair of parents, stepparents, guardians, natural children, stepchildren, and wards.[56] It could hardly have been otherwise, given the prevalence of illness, the frequency of early death, and the necessity of caring for the sick and orphaned; and it can be argued that in the Chesapeake region the form and strength of the social bonds were direct corollaries of the fragility of life.

Finally, one can suggest an impact of disease on the culture of the Chesapeake, for while culture to an extent defines disease, the relationship is reciprocal. The associations are so tenuously perceived that questions seem more in order than statements. If there is validity in the ideal *mens sana in corpore sano*, then, conversely, the ill do not think clearly. Might this have been related to the low level of intellectual activity in the early Chesapeake, a level frequently contrasted to that of New England? Dr. John Mitchell's biographers, writing of his years in Urbanna, Middlesex, imply as much. "Continuous bouts of malaria . . . left him with little energy and even less *joie de vivre"*; and most of Mitchell's significant work was done after he removed to England.[57] What would be the attitudes of a population that had a relatively high rate of illness and short life expectancy? Richard S. Dunn's comparison of New England and the English Caribbean is provocative, assuming that the Caribbean and Chesapeake were areas of high malarial morbidity. "The Caribbean and New England planters were polar opposites in social expression. . . . The contrast in life style went far beyond the obvious differences in religion, slavery and climate. The sugar planters 'lived fast, spent recklessly, played desperately, and died young.' . . . Their family life was broken, and since the colonists were predominantly young people without effective guidance, they behaved in a freewheeling, devil-may-care fashion."[58]

---

the will of John Burnham in Middlesex County, Va., MS Deeds, Etc., No. 2, 1679-1694, 22, Va. St. Lib. Here and there, too, it can be seen in literary sources— William Byrd, for example, hovering about the sickbed of John Bowman of Henrico County. Wright and Tinling, eds., *Secret Diary,* 89-94.

[56] A point elaborated upon in Rutman and Rutman, " 'Now-Wives and Sons-in-Law,' " in Tate, ed., *The Chesapeake.*

[57] Edmund and Dorothy Smith Berkeley, *Dr. John Mitchell: The Man Who Made the Map of North America* (Chapel Hill, N. C., 1974), 59.

[58] Richard S. Dunn, "The Social History of Early New England," *American Quarterly,* XXIV (1972), 675; Dunn quotes his own *Sugar and Slaves: The Rise of the Planter Class in the English West Indies, 1624-1713* (Chapel Hill, N. C., 1972). See the latter, pp. 302-303, regarding malaria in the English Caribbean.

Applied to Virginia, Dunn's description probably would be an exaggeration, but Virginia can certainly be described, in comparison with New England, as a present-minded society that was more involved, in Wordsworth's phrase, with "getting and spending" than with abstractions or ideals. Do the Virginians' attitudes toward death reflect the fact of frequent illness and early death? Robinson Jeffers's "patient daemon"[59] was much on the minds of colonials north and south, but while the New Englanders seem to have been both enamored of and terrified by death, the Virginians apparently discerned death more as a matter of fact, of "dissolution"—William Fitzhugh's word—and of business, the willing and disposing of property.[60] The comparison can only be highly tentative for little work has been done on the subject, but two vignettes are suggestive. In September 1658 William Price of Lancaster County told of his last conversation with Roger Radford: "I came into the room where Mr. Radford was sitting upon his bed sick. I asked him how he did. 'Pretty well,' he said. 'You are not, I think, a man for this world. Therefore you had best to make your peace with God and set everything to rights with Mr. Cocke.' He answered: 'No, for he is more engaged to me than I to him.' 'What do you give Polly Cole?' [I asked.] 'I give Polly Cole my land.' "[61] The second vignette was recorded by Philip Fithian toward the end of the eighteenth century. The sudden death of a black child "with the Ague and Fever . . . was the Subject of Conversation in the House." "Mr *Carter* observed, that he thought it the most desirable to die of a Short Illness. If he could have his Wish he would not lie longer than two days; be taken with a Fever, which should . . . gradually increase till it affected a Dissolution—He told us that his affairs are in Such a state that he should be able to dictate a Will which might be written in Five Minutes, and contain the disposal of his estate agreeable to his mind—He mentioned to us the Substance."[62]

[59] Jeffers, "The Bed by the Window" (1931):
          We are safe to finish what we have to
finish;
And then it will sound rather like music
When the patient daemon behind the screen of sea-rock
and sky
Thumps with his staff, and calls thrice: "Come, Jeffers."
[60] David E. Stannard, "Death and Dying in Puritan New England," *AHR*, LXXVIII (1973), 1305-1330; W. Fitzhugh to Mrs. Mary Fitzhugh, June 30, 1698, in Davis, ed., *Fitzhugh Letters*, 358.
[61] Lancaster County, MS Deeds, 56-57, Va. St. Lib. The quotation has been modernized.
[62] Hunter Dickinson Parish, ed., *Journal & Letters of Philip Vickers Fithian, 1773-1774: A Plantation Tutor of the Old Dominion*, rev. ed. (Williamsburg, Va., 1957), 182. The deeply religious Fithian continued: "Our School make it [the death]

Economy, social structure, culture—all conceivably bore the imprint of malaria in the early Chesapeake. We do not mean to assert a direct causal association, for the question of the relation of disease to society is far too complex, the variables far too many, and the evidence far too slim. We *do* mean to suggest that malaria was endemic in the early Chesapeake (and relatively absent in New England), and that it is in the nature of societies to adjust to the disease environment in which they exist. These, we argue, should be informing assumptions in early American history, and the processes and consequences of such adjustments, varying by time and place, require the attention of historians.

---

a Subject for continual Speculation; They seem all to be free of any terror at the Prescence of Death; *Harry* in special signified a Wish that his turn may be next." Cf. David E. Stannard, "Death and the Puritan Child," *AQ,* XXVI (1974), 456-476.

The Maryland Slave Population, 1658 to 1730:
A Demographic Profile of Blacks in
Four Counties

Russell R. Menard*

A LTHOUGH historians have written extensively on the origins of slavery, the attitudes of Europeans toward Africans, and the status of blacks in the New World, they have paid scant attention to a wide variety of questions concerning the lives of early Afro-Americans.[1] The surviving evidence limits what can be learned about blacks in Maryland and Virginia in the seventeenth century, but it is possible to move beyond the issues that have preoccupied recent scholarship. This essay utilizes probate inventories to explore the changing character of the slave population in four Maryland counties. While the interpretations advanced are tentative, it is hoped that the data will suggest new questions and provide a useful demographic context for future research.

Slaves were personal property and were listed and appraised along with other possessions in the inventory taken shortly after a slaveowner's death. In the absence of census materials and detailed registers of vital

* Mr. Menard is a Fellow of the Institute of Early American History and Culture and a member of the Department of History, College of William and Mary. Earlier versions of this paper were presented at the St. Mary's City Commission Archaeology Seminar in August 1973 and the Indiana University Economic History Workshop in November 1973. He would like to thank participants in both seminars for their perceptive comments. He also wishes to thank Lois Green Carr, Alan Day, P. M. G. Harris, Allan Kulikoff, Aubrey Land, and Gerald and Martha Mullin for helpful criticism. The National Science Foundation provided funds for the research.

[1] The most recent essays include Alden T. Vaughan, "Blacks in Virginia: A Note on the First Decade," *William and Mary Quarterly*, 3d Ser., XXIX (1972), 469-478, and Warren M. Billings, "The Cases of Fernando and Elizabeth Key: A Note on the Status of Blacks in Seventeenth-Century Virginia," *ibid.*, XXX (1973), 467-474. Vaughan's notes provide a guide to the earlier literature. Wesley Frank Craven, *White, Red, and Black: The Seventeenth-Century Virginian* (Charlottesville, Va., 1971), suggests that the concerns are beginning to shift and expand. Gerald W. Mullin's study, *Flight and Rebellion: Slave Resistance in Eighteenth-Century Virginia* (New York, 1972), demonstrates that seemingly intractable sources can yield a wealth of insight into slavery in the Chesapeake colonies.

Reprinted from *William and Mary Quarterly*, 3rd Series, **XXXII**, 29-54. Copyright © 1975 by permission of the publisher.

events, probate inventories provide an indispensable guide to the demography of slavery. They are perhaps the single most informative source for the history of slavery in the Chesapeake colonies, and they have scarcely been tapped. Inventories yield sensitive price information, data on the distribution of labor and the growth of slavery, evidence on the occupational structure of the slave population, insights into white attitudes toward blacks, a guide to the possibilities for family life among slaves, and a useful index to the incidence of miscegenation. They also furnish data for a sex and age profile of the slave population.

This study is based on the 1,618 slaves listed in inventories taken in Calvert, Charles, Prince George's, and St. Mary's counties, Maryland, between 1658 and 1710,[2] and 1,569 inventoried slaves in Charles and Prince George's for the period 1711-1730. The four counties are situated on Maryland's lower Western Shore and are contiguous. Planters in the region were among the first in Maryland to invest heavily in slavery; in the early eighteenth century more than one-half of the colony's slaves lived in the four counties.[3]

The slave population in the region grew at an extraordinary rate between 1658 and 1710. At most, 100 slaves lived in the four counties at the beginning of the period, perhaps 3 percent of the total population; by 1710, over 3,500 slaves lived there, composing 24 percent of the region's population.[4] Rapid growth began in the middle 1670s, with a sharp ac-

[2] Using funds provided by the National Science Foundation, the staff of the St. Mary's City Commission gathered the data for all four counties for the period 1658 to 1705 as part of a larger study of wealth in inventories in which I have been engaged with Lois Green Carr and P. M. G. Harris. For the years 1706 to 1710, the data on slaves are drawn only from Charles and Prince George's. The inventories are in the following volumes, all at the Maryland Hall of Records, Annapolis: Testamentary Proceedings, I-IV, XVI; Inventories and Accounts, I-XXV; Charles County Court and Land Records, Q#1; Charles County Inventories, 1673-1717; Prince George's County Inventories, BB#1, 1696/7-1720. Lois Green Carr generously supplied the data for Prince George's from 1706 to 1710.

[3] Two thousand two hundred seventy-eight of the 4,475 slaves listed in the 1704 census lived in the 4 counties. William Hand Browne et al., eds., Archives of Maryland . . . (Baltimore, 1883-), XXV, 256, hereafter cited as Md. Arch. Despite the column heading "Slaves young and old," the census lists only taxable slaves, men and women age 16 and over, in at least 5 of Maryland's 11 counties and perhaps in 10. Cf., for examples, the Baltimore County tax list for 1704 or the number of taxables in Prince George's with the census returns. Charles is the only county for which it is reasonably certain that an effort was made to include all slaves. Baltimore County List of Taxables (1699-1705), MS 74, Maryland Historical Society, Baltimore; Prince George's County Court Records, B, 340; Charles County Court and Land Records, B#2, 57, Hall of Records.

[4] The estimate of 100 slaves at the beginning of the period is a projection from

celeration in the 1690s. From 1695 to 1708 at least 4,022 slaves arrived in the province, an average of nearly 300 a year.[5] The adult slaves in Maryland before 1710 were almost all immigrants, a fact of major importance for demographic analysis. Prior to the mid-1690s most slaves came to the province from the West Indies, although there was substantial immigration to the Chesapeake colonies directly from Africa in the middle to late 1670s and again in the mid-1680s. After 1695 most of the new arrivals were African-born, without prior experience in the New World.[6]

Because sex and age were important determinants of value, appraisers usually distinguished male slaves from female slaves and sometimes recorded their ages in years. In most cases when sex is not specifically mentioned, it can be inferred from the 'slave's name. Appraisers often recorded specific ages, but without sufficient frequency or precision to permit a detailed year-by-year analysis. In many inventories appraisers used only broad categories, distinguishing working adults from children and old slaves. Even in those inventories in which specific ages appear, the disproportionate number ending in o (20, 30, 40, etc.) suggests frequent guessing. Moreover, appraisers often recorded the ages of some of the slaves in an estate and then lumped the rest—especially the very young and the old—into residual categories. Because of the lack of precision and consistency, I have placed slaves in only three age groupings: 0 to 15 years, 16 to approximately 50, and old slaves. From the appraiser's description and the value assigned each slave, all but 10 percent of the slaves can be placed in one or another of these categories. Classification requires some educated guesswork. In particular, the divi-

---

the number of blacks found in estate inventories. The figure for 1710 is from the census in *Md. Arch.*, XXV, 258-259.

[5] Margaret Shove Morriss, *Colonial Trade of Maryland, 1689-1715,* The Johns Hopkins University Studies in Historical and Political Science, XXXII (Baltimore, 1914), 77-80; C.O. 5/749/pt. II, Public Records Office Transcripts, Library of Congress; *Md. Arch.*, XXV, 257; Cecil County Judgments, E, 1708-1716, 1-9, Hall of Records. A comparison of the entries in the several lists suggests that they do not include all the slaves brought to Maryland during this period. I have discussed the growth of slavery in "From Servants to Slaves: The Transformation of the Chesapeake Labor System" (paper presented at the annual meeting of the Southern Historical Association, November 1972).

[6] The sources of Chesapeake slaves and the organization of the trade need investigation. Useful comments can be found in Craven, *White, Red, and Black,* 74-109; Philip D. Curtin, *The Atlantic Slave Trade: A Census* (Madison, Wis., 1969), 72-75, 127-162; Morriss, *Colonial Trade of Maryland,* 79-80; and K. G. Davies, *The Royal African Company* (London, 1957). Elizabeth Donnan, *Documents Illustrative of the History of the Slave Trade to America,* 4 vols. (Washington, D. C., 1930-1935), is an invaluable collection.

TABLE I
PROFILE OF SLAVES IN CALVERT, CHARLES, PRINCE GEORGE'S, AND ST. MARY'S COUNTIES, MARYLAND, 1658 TO 1710

	1658-1670	1671-1680	1681-1690	1691-1700	1701-1710	1658-1710
Males 0-15	3	13	21	52	88	177
Females 0-15	5	6	11	42	62	126
Sex ratio	.60	2.167	1.909	1.238	1.419	1.405
Sex unknown 0-15	6	16	25	49	34	130
Total 0-15	14	35	57	143	184	433
Males 16-50	17	48	74	145	241	525
Females 16-50	13	40	54	100	156	363
Sex ratio	1.308	1.200	1.370	1.450	1.545	1.446
Old males	1	2	7	12	19	41
Old females	6	10	15	18	26	75
Sex ratio	.167	.200	.467	.667	.731	.547
Old sex unknown	0	0	0	4	3	7
Total old	7	12	22	34	48	123
Slaves, age, sex unknown	3	22	31	63	55	174
total slaves	54	157	238	485	684	1618
ratio 0-15/16-50	.467	.398	.445	.584	.463	.488
ratio 0-15/females 16-50	1.077	.875	1.056	1.430	1.179	1.193
ratio females 0-15[a]/ females 16-50	.615	.350	.435	.665	.506	.526

[a] Assuming that ½ of the children not identified by sex were females.

sion between working adults and old slaves is imprecise; I may have incorrectly counted as "old" several slaves who were still in their forties. Despite this imprecision at the edges, the results provide a useful profile of the slave population in southern Maryland during the seventeenth century (see Table I).[7]

[7] Throughout this essay I assume that the sex and age profile of the slaves owned by inventoried decedents did not differ in any important respect from that of the slave population as a whole. Unfortunately, the available evidence does not provide an opportunity to test this assumption for the 17th century. However, I did test it against the 1755 census. The sex ratio among adult slaves appearing in Charles County inventories taken in 1755 was 1.22; in the census it was 1.27. The ratio of children to adults in inventories was 1.00; in the census it was 1.10. Charles County Inventories, 4, 1753-1766; *Gentleman's Magazine, and Historical Chronicle*, XXXIV (1764), 261. Allan Kulikoff has compared the sex and age distributions

One striking characteristic was the preponderance of males. Among adults of working age, men outnumbered women by roughly one and one-half to one, with the greatest imbalance occurring at the end of the period when substantial numbers of slaves began to arrive in the Chesapeake colonies directly from Africa. The relative shortage of women reflects the character of the immigrant population. In a tabulation of Virginia headright entries, Wesley Frank Craven found a sex ratio (expressed as the number of men per woman) among black immigrants of 2.464 in the seventeenth century.[8] While Craven was unable to ascertain the sex of a significant proportion of the slaves and therefore suggests caution in the use of this figure, the disparity between the sex ratio calculated from headrights and that found in inventories implies a shorter expectation of life for black men than for women, a hypothesis supported by the fact that among old slaves women outnumbered men by nearly two to one, despite the surplus of males in the other age groups.[9]

The skewed sex ratio apparently reflects the preferences of planters as well as the structure of the immigrant population. The sex ratio among black adults of working age on plantations with ten or more slaves was 1.646, higher than in the slave population as a whole.[10] Even the wealthiest slaveowners—who presumably had some options—did not always provide a wife for each working man on their plantations. This fact supports Craven's suggestion that historians have been too quick to assume that seventeenth-century planters immediately recognized the advantages of a self-perpetuating labor force.[11]

The sex ratio among blacks was similar to that in the white population. Among white immigrants to the Chesapeake colonies in the second half of the seventeenth century, the ratio ranged from 2.5 to 3.5, and was

---

among slaves in Prince George's County inventories to census returns in 1755 and 1776, concluding that inventories do provide a reliable demographic profile. Kulikoff discusses this issue in his dissertation on Prince George's County in the 18th century (Brandeis University, in progress).

[8] Craven, *White, Red, and Black*, 98-100.

[9] There is evidence of higher mortality for male slaves in the West Indies. See Richard S. Dunn, *Sugar and Slaves: The Rise of the Planter Class in the English West Indies, 1624-1713* (Chapel Hill, N. C., 1972), 315-317, and Orlando Patterson, *The Sociology of Slavery: An Analysis of the Origins, Development and Structure of Negro Slave Society in Jamaica* (London, 1967), 99, 107.

[10] Two hundred ninety-nine men and 181 women lived on plantations with 10 or more slaves. Dunn found evidence that large planters in the West Indies attempted to provide mates for each adult slave. *Sugar and Slaves*, 251, 315-316.

[11] Craven, *White, Red, and Black*, 100-101.

even higher before 1650. As late as 1704 the ratio among white adults in the four-county region was 1.807, higher than that of slaves listed in inventories between 1701 and 1710.[12] However, whites had a distinct advantage: they could move about in order to establish as normal a family life as the sexual imbalance in the population permitted. A young white man could also leave the region in search of a wife, thereby bringing the sex ratio among those who remained closer to one. The emigration of young men sharply lowered the sex ratio among whites in the four counties during the first decade of the eighteenth century, from 1.807 in 1704 to 1.348 in 1710.[13] Except for a few runaways, emigration was not an option open to blacks. Nor could a black move about freely within the region in order to establish a family. The restricted freedom of slaves aggravated the sexual imbalance revealed in the aggregate data.

Few planters owned large gangs of slaves in the seventeenth century. Only fifteen of the three hundred slaveowners who left inventories in the four counties between 1658 and 1710 held more than twenty slaves, and only thirty-eight owned more than ten. Nearly half owned only one or two. The slaves on many of the larger plantations, furthermore, were divided into small groups and set to work on outlying plantations or quarters. As a result, many slaves lived on plantations with only a few other blacks, a fact with long-term implications for race relations, the process of assimilation, and the survival of African cultural patterns in the New World. More than one-half of the slaves lived on plantations with ten or fewer blacks, nearly one-third on estates with five or fewer. The pattern of dispersed ownership described in Table II severely restricted the chances for social contact among blacks, making isolation and loneliness a prominent fact of life for Africans in the Chesapeake colonies.[14]

---

[12] *Md. Arch.*, XXV, 256. For sex ratios among white immigrants in the 17th century see Herbert Moller, "Sex Composition and Correlated Culture Patterns of Colonial America," *WMQ*, 3d Ser., II (1945), 113-153, and Craven, *White, Red, and Black*, 26-27.

[13] The emigration can be inferred from the census returns of 1704, 1710, and 1712 in *Md. Arch.*, XXV, 256, 258-259. See also John Seymour to the Board of Trade, June 23, 1708, C.O. 5/716/pt. III, and Edward Lloyd to the Board of Trade, Nov. 4, 1710, C.O. 717/pt. II, P.R.O. Transcripts, Lib. Cong.

[14] Because decedents are older and therefore probably wealthier than the living population, Table II may overstate the concentration of slave ownership. Any adjustment would only strengthen my argument. On the relationship of age and wealth see Alice Hanson Jones, "Wealth Estimates for the American Middle Colonies, 1774," *Economic Development and Cultural Change*, XVIII (1970), 86-97, and Russell R. Menard *et al.*, "Opportunity and Inequality: The Distribution of Wealth on the Lower Western Shore of Maryland, 1638-1705," *Maryland Historical Magazine*, LXIX (1974), 176-178.

TABLE II

DISTRIBUTION OF SLAVES ON MARYLAND'S LOWER WESTERN SHORE, 1658 TO 1710

No. of slaves per estate	No. estates	% estates	Cum. %	No. slaves	% slaves	Cum. %
1-2	145	48.3	48.3	198	12.2	12.2
3-5	70	23.3	71.6	273	16.9	29.1
6-10	47	15.7	87.3	356	22.0	51.1
11-20	23	7.7	95.0	340	21.0	72.1
21+	15	5.0	100.0	451	27.9	100.0
	300	100.0		1618	100.0	

A diversity of tribal origins and the "Babel of Languages" among slaves in Maryland perhaps increased the African's sense of isolation.[15]

The dispersed ownership pattern heightened the imbalance created by the sex ratio among adults. Only 16 percent of the men and 23 percent of the women lived on plantations with an equal sex ratio, while only 41 percent of the men and 53 percent of the women lived on estates where there were fewer than twice as many adults of one sex as the other. One hundred fourteen of the 525 men (22 percent) and 68 of the 363 women (19 percent) lived on plantations with no members of the opposite sex in their age category. The sex ratio in the aggregate population placed definite limits on the opportunities for family life among slaves; the dispersed ownership pattern prevented slaves from taking full advantage of such possibilities for contact with persons of the opposite sex as the sexual imbalance permitted. Together they placed formidable barriers in the way of affectionate relationships between men and women, denying many blacks a fundamental human opportunity.

Some slaves did form families, however, which whites sanctioned or

[15] See the comment of Olaudah Equiano, an African taken to Virginia as a slave in the 18th century, on his response to being unable to talk to other slaves, in John W. Blassingame, *The Slave Community: Plantation Life in the Antebellum South* (New York, 1972), 16. But see also Gov. Alexander Spotswood's warning that the "Babel of Languages" among slaves should not be allowed to lull Virginians into a false sense of security, for "freedom Wears a Cap which Can Without a Tongue, Call Togather all Those who Long to Shake of[f] The Fetters of Slavery," in H. R. McIlwaine and J. P. Kennedy, eds., *Journals of the House of Burgesses of Virginia* (Richmond, Va., 1905-1915), *1710-1712*, 240.

at least recognized. Appraisers occasionally grouped slaves into family units in inventories, giving explicit recognition to the bond between husband, wife, and children.[16] Some masters not only acknowledged the existence of slave families, but granted those families considerable independence. Henry Ridgely, for example, had three outlying quarters run by blacks. The quarters were amply supplied with livestock, bedding, household utensils, and tools, and there is no evidence of direct white supervision. Apparently Mingo, Dick, and Toby, whose names identify the quarters, ran relatively independent operations, often making their own decisions about the organization of work, with some responsibility for the success of the farm and for the maintenance and discipline of their dependents. Their lives perhaps resembled those of poor tenants or of men who farmed shares.[17]

Mingo, Dick, and Toby had acquired a measure of freedom and responsibility. Their positions required judgment and skill as well as strength and stamina, but their experience was hardly typical. The work of the majority of slaves was physically demanding, dull, and repetitive, offering blacks little challenge and only a slight possibility of better employment. Most slaves were kept to the routine tasks of raising tobacco and corn and tending livestock. For variety they could look only to the nearly endless round of menial odd jobs necessary to the operation of any farm. Opportunities for occupational mobility—to move from field hand to house servant or overseer of a quarter, or to learn a trade and work as a cooper, carpenter, or blacksmith—were virtually nonexistent in the seventeenth century. The inventories suggest that perhaps a dozen of the 525 adult males appraised in the four counties before 1710 held positions that paralleled those of Mingo, Dick, and Toby, while only four of the 525 were described as skilled craftsmen.[18] Few masters could afford the luxury of diverting slaves from tobacco to personal service, and few plantations were large enough to require full-time craftsmen or overseers.[19] What supervisory, skilled, and service occupations were avail-

[16] For examples see Testamentary Proceedings, III, 23-24; Inventories and Accounts, II, 128, 305, V, 143-145, 19½A, 28, VIII, 404-406, XA, 10, XIIIA, 122.

[17] Ridgely's inventory is in Inventories and Accounts, XXXIIB, 71. For other examples see Testamentary Proceedings, V, 178-179; Inventories and Accounts, VIIC, 105-107; Prince George's County Inventories, BB#1, 137-141.

[18] See above, n. 17; Prince George's County Inventories, BB#1, 117; Charles County Inventories, 1677-1717, 74, 290.

[19] But see Gov. Francis Nicholson's statement that "most people have some of them as their domestick servants: and the better sort may have 6 or 7 in those

able, furthermore, were awarded to English servants, who spoke their master's language, had often acquired a trade before migrating, and appeared on the plantations of nearly every slaveowner.[20] Seventeenth-century plantation life offered bound laborers few chances for occupational advancement. Given the height of linguistic and cultural barriers and the depth of racial prejudice, unassimilated African slaves could not compete with white indentured servants for the few good jobs that did exist. Plantation work routines did little to alleviate the dreary isolation that slavery forced upon most blacks in the early colonial period.

The isolation of blacks may have been mitigated by visiting in the evening, on Sundays and holidays, or by running away. The literature conveys the impression that slaves had more freedom of movement in the seventeenth century than later, but the evidence is not very firm.[21] There are complaints of blacks wandering about from plantation to plantation on visits, of "continual concourse of Negroes on Sabboth and holy days meeting in great numbers," and of slaves getting "Drunke on the Lords Day beating their Negro Drums by which they call considerable Numbers of Negroes together in some Certaine places." According to Gov. Francis Nicholson, visiting, even at distances of thirty or forty miles, was "common practice."[22] Yet it is impossible to determine, even crudely, how many blacks were able to make social contacts with slaves from other plantations or how frequently such contacts occurred. The wide dispersal of ownership, and in particular the unbalanced sex ratio on most plantations, must have driven blacks to exploit whatever chances

---

circumstances." Nicholson to the Board of Trade, Aug. 20, 1698, *Md. Arch.,* XXIII, 499. Nicholson is usually a reliable witness, but this assertion is clearly an exaggeration.

[20] For servants' skills see Mildred Campbell, "Social Origins of Some Early Americans," in James Morton Smith, ed., *Seventeenth-Century America: Essays in Colonial History* (Chapel Hill, N. C., 1959), 71. Their presence on the estates of most slaveowners is apparent in the inventories.

[21] At least this is the impression conveyed if it is assumed that legislation and case law provide a rough guide to the actual status and privileges of blacks. Despite their disagreements, the participants in the debate over the origins of slavery and race prejudice agree that the law of slavery tended toward increased severity during the late 17th and early 18th centuries. Winthrop D. Jordan, *White Over Black: American Attitudes Toward the Negro, 1550-1812* (Chapel Hill, N. C., 1968), 71-83; Carl N. Degler, "Slavery and the Genesis of American Race Prejudice," *Comparative Studies in Society and History,* II (1959-1960), 49-66; Oscar and Mary F. Handlin, "Origins of the Southern Labor System," *WMQ,* 3d Ser., VII (1950), 199-222.

[22] *Md. Arch.,* XXXVIII, 48; Somerset County Judicials, 1707-1711, I, Hall of Records; Nicholson to the Board of Trade, Aug. 20, 1698, *Md. Arch.,* XXIII, 498.

presented themselves, whether surreptitious or open, whether sanctioned by their masters or forbidden, to relieve the isolation and loneliness that resulted from the demographic conditions of slavery on Maryland's lower Western Shore.

A surplus of males among adults of working age was not the only peculiarity of the slave population. Few children appear in the inventories: appraisers listed less than one slave under age 16 for every two adults between 16 and 50. In addition, the ratio of children to adults shows only the slightest upward tendency through the period under study. The small proportion of children reinforces the impression of a stunted family life for most blacks in early colonial Maryland.

While the difficulty of assessing the impact of immigration on the age structure makes certainty impossible, the small proportion of children does suggest that the slave population did not increase by natural means. Growth depended instead on immigration. Model life tables indicate that in populations with adult life expectancies that approximate those found among whites in Maryland of this period and that are growing by natural means, the ratio of persons under 16 to persons 16 to 50 should approach one.[23] In the West Indies, where it has been established beyond doubt that slaves suffered a net natural decline in the seventeenth and early eighteenth centuries, the black population contained a slightly higher proportion of children than in the four Maryland counties.[24]

The proportion of children in the inventories, furthermore, exaggerates the ability of the slave population to reproduce itself. Between 1658 and 1710 the sex ratio among slave children identifiable by sex was 1.405. Perhaps girls outnumbered boys among those who could not be so identified, or perhaps among children female mortality was much higher than male mortality. More likely, many of the children were not native

[23] For life expectancies among whites see Lorena S. Walsh and Russell R. Menard, "Death in the Chesapeake: Two Life Tables for Men in Early Colonial Maryland," *Md. Hist. Mag.*, LXIX (1974), 211-227. Model life tables are available in Ansley J. Coale and Paul Demeny, *Regional Model Life Tables and Stable Populations* (Princeton, N. J., 1966), and United Nations, Dept. of Social Affairs, Population Branch, *Age and Sex Patterns of Mortality: Model Life-Tables for Under-developed Countries* (New York, 1955). See the comments on their use in T. H. Hollingsworth, *Historical Demography* (Ithaca, N. Y., 1969), esp. 339-353.

[24] Dunn, *Sugar and Slaves*, 316. For a survey of census returns that helps place the proportion of children in the Maryland slave population in context see Robert V. Wells, "Household Size and Composition in the British Colonies in America, 1675-1775," *Journal of Interdisciplinary History*, IV (1973-1974), 543-570.

to the colony but had immigrated. The sexual imbalance probably reflects the predominance of boys among children in the immigrant population.

The apparent failure of the initial slave population to reproduce itself is significant. Much of the recent scholarly literature has been concerned with a comparison of slave systems in the Americas. In particular, historians have debated which of the several forms of slavery was most harsh and dehumanizing, an issue on which there has been more speculation than hard evidence. Most scholars have followed Frank Tannenbaum in arguing that slavery was milder in the Latin colonies than in the regions settled by the English.[25] Yet, as Philip Curtin has pointed out, slaves in British North America enjoyed a rapid rate of natural increase, if the entire colonial period is considered, while in most Latin colonies deaths outnumbered births among blacks. Since the ability to reproduce is a fundamental indicator of well-being, this fact is a powerful criticism of Tannenbaum's hypothesis.[26] While it is clear that by the late eighteenth century the slave population of the United States was growing by natural means, perhaps it had not always done so. The first slaves in Maryland, like blacks elsewhere in the Americas, apparently failed to reproduce themselves fully, a finding that provides support for historians who have been impressed by the similarities of the African experience in the New World.[27]

[25] Frank Tannenbaum, *Slave and Citizen: The Negro in the Americas* (New York, 1946); Stanley M. Elkins, *Slavery: A Problem in American Institutional and Intellectual Life* (Chicago, 1959); Herbert S. Klein, *Slavery in the Americas: A Comparative Study of Virginia and Cuba* (Chicago, 1967). For a dissenting view see Carl N. Degler, *Neither Black Nor White: Slavery and Race Relations in Brazil and the United States* (New York, 1971). On the debate see C. Vann Woodward, *American Counterpoints: Slavery and Racism in the North-South Dialogue* (Boston, 1971), 47-77, and Eugene D. Genovese, "The Treatment of Slaves in Different Countries: Problems in the Applications of the Comparative Method," in Laura Foner and Eugene D. Genovese, eds., *Slavery in the New World: A Reader in Comparative History* (Englewood Cliffs, N. J., 1969), 202-210.

[26] Curtin, *Atlantic Slave Trade*, 92-93.

[27] Maryland was not the only North American region in which slaves experienced an initial natural decline: at times during the 18th century the black populations in South Carolina, Philadelphia, and the province of New York registered an excess of deaths over births. On South Carolina see Peter H. Wood, *Black Majority: Negroes in Colonial South Carolina from 1670 through the Stono Rebellion* (New York, 1974), 153-154, 159-166. On Philadelphia see Gary B. Nash, "Slaves and Slaveowners in Colonial Philadelphia," *WMQ*, 3d Ser., XXX (1973), 232-241. On New York cf. the record of slave imports in U. S. Bureau of the Census, *Historical Statistics of the United States: Colonial Times to 1957* (Washington, D. C., 1960), series Z298-302, with the census returns of 1723 and 1731 in Evarts

Why so few children? The adult sex ratio would seem the most likely culprit, for the number of women of childbearing age in a population is one of the most important determinants of the birth rate. Among Maryland slaves, however, its influence seems relatively minor. If the excess men are excluded, the ratio of children to adults increases to .596, suggesting that even if the sex ratio were equal the population would still have registered a net natural decline, especially if many of the children were immigrants. On plantations with a sex ratio of one, the ratio of children to adults was .500, barely an improvement over that in the aggregate population. Sexual imbalance among adults seems an insufficient explanation of the small proportion of children in the slave population.[28]

Perhaps there were so few children because the slave women found in inventories were recent immigrants who had not been in the colony long enough to bear many children. No doubt this had some depressing effect on the number of children, but, like the sex ratio, it seems a relatively minor influence. In an attempt to obtain a rough estimate of the effect of the number of years slaves had been in Maryland on the proportion of children appearing in inventories, I have examined the biographies of decedents to identify those who had inherited slaves. Thirteen such men were identified. Presumably the 111 adult slaves found in their inventories had been in Maryland longer than most blacks. The ratio of children to adults among these slaves was .580, only slightly higher than that in the aggregate population. Moreover, the sex ratio among children in the inventories of men who had inherited slaves was 2.733, suggesting that the higher proportion of children on their estates resulted more from purchases than from births. This is not an entirely satisfactory test, but it does suggest that the number of years slave women had been in Maryland is of little importance in accounting for the small proportion of children. The profile of the population found in inventories between 1691 and 1700, a period characterized both by heavy black immigration and by a relatively high ratio of children to adults, lends additional weight to this conclusion.[29] The age structure of the slave population in the four-

---

B. Greene and Virginia Harrington, comps., *American Population before the Federal Census of 1790* (New York, 1932), 96-97. In compiling population estimates for *Historical Statistics*, Stella H. Sutherland apparently assumed that Virginia's slave population experienced a natural decline in the early 18th century. Cf. series Z14 with Z294-297.

[28] Roughly equal sex ratios among black adults did not result in natural increase in the West Indies. Dunn, *Sugar and Slaves*, 316.

[29] For slaves brought to Maryland in the 1690s see above, n. 5. If the inter-

county region before 1710 is probably not simply a reflection of the age distribution of immigrants. It reflects as well the failure of Africans to reproduce themselves fully in the New World.

The small number of children may have been a consequence of an extreme alienation among black women. Craven has recently noted that "many comments have been made upon the morbidity, at times expressed in suicide, of the African after reaching America, and the unwillingness of some women to bring a child into the condition of enslavement."[30] Unfortunately, the persuasiveness of this proposition depends almost entirely on the scholar's inclination, for the evidence that could subject it to a test—a survey of the attitudes of imigrant slave women—is unavailable.[31]

Attitudes other than morbidity may have depressed the birth rate. Most West African tribes—the principal home of immigrant slaves in the British colonies—practised polygynous marriage, usually an effective means of birth control. While it seems unlikely that polygyny could withstand the pressures generated by black sex ratios in the Chesapeake, some of the associated attitudes toward child rearing and sexual intercourse may have survived.[32] In particular, West African women usually nursed their children for two or three years and abstained from sexual intercourse until the infant was weaned. Such practice produces an interval between live births of three to four years, much longer than that usually found among European women in the colonies. If widely followed, this practice would severely depress the birth rate among African-born slave women.[33]

---

pretation advanced later in this essay is correct, the rise in the proportion of children in the 1690s reflects an increase in the child/woman ratio among native slaves born in the wake of the first wave of black immigration in the middle and late 1670s.

[30] Craven, *White, Red, and Black*, 101.

[31] See Blassingame, *Slave Community* (esp. Samuel Hall's comment on his mother's reaction to enslavement, quoted p. 22), and Patterson, *Sociology of Slavery*, 106ff.

[32] In the West Indies, where the sex ratio was approximately equal, blacks occasionally practiced polygynous marriage. Dunn, *Sugar and Slaves*, 251; Patterson, *Sociology of Slavery*, 106. According to Edward Kimber, slaves on the Eastern Shore of Maryland practiced polygyny in the mid-1740s. "Eighteenth Century Maryland as Portrayed in the 'Itinerant Observations' of Edward Kimber," *Md. Hist. Mag.*, LI (1956), 327.

[33] Melville J. Herskovits, *Dahomey: An Ancient West African Kingdom*, I (New York, 1938), 239-353; George P. Murdock, *Africa: Its Peoples and Their Cultural History* (New York, 1959); Paul Bohannan, *Africa and Africans* (Garden City, N. Y., 1964), 158-173; Patterson, *Sociology of Slavery*, 110. For birth intervals among European women in the colonies see Robert V. Wells, "Quaker Marriage Patterns in a Colonial Perspective," *WMQ*, 3d Ser., XXIX (1972), 440.

Chronic ill-health and high mortality doubtless limited the reproductive capacity of African-born slave women. Among white male immigrants in Maryland during the seventeenth century, expectation of life at age 20 was only about 23 years.[34] Whether black females died younger or older than white males, it seems safe to assume that their expectation of life was short and that many were afflicted with the chronic ailments that sapped the strength of the white population.[35] In addition, so short an expectation of life among adults indicates a high level of infant and childhood mortality that would lower the proportion of children in the slave population and limit the ability of blacks to reproduce themselves.[36]

Maryland's slave population did not experience a net natural decline throughout the colonial period. At the time of the first federal census, approximately 50 percent more blacks lived in Maryland and Virginia alone than had immigrated to all of British North America before 1790.[37] By 1755 there were more slave children than adults in the four-county region, indicating a substantial rise in the number of births and a rapid natural increase.[38] When did natural increase begin? Why did it occur? Again, data on the age and sex characteristics of the slave population from inventories provide a basis for speculation.

Table III presents a profile of the slave population in Charles and Prince George's counties drawn from inventories taken between 1711 and

---

[34] Walsh and Menard, "Death in the Chesapeake," *Md. Hist. Mag.*, LXIX (1974), 215.

[35] See Philip D. Curtin, "Epidemiology and the Slave Trade," *Political Science Quarterly*, LXXXIII (1968), 190-216, and Patterson's comments on the influence of gynecological problems on the fertility of slave women in Jamaica in *Sociology of Slavery*, 109-110.

[36] On inferring infant and childhood mortality from adult expectation of life see the model life tables cited in n. 23. A word of caution is required here. It is not clear that, given the expectation of life for males at age 20 in the Chesapeake colonies, one can then consult the appropriate model life table to determine the expectation of life at birth. It seems reasonable to assume that infant and childhood mortality in the Chesapeake was high, but whether a model life table based on the experience of late 19th- and 20th-century populations can tell us exactly how high seems an open question. See Hollingsworth, *Historical Demography*, 339-353; Walsh and Menard, "Death in the Chesapeake," *Md. Hist. Mag.*, LXIX (1974), 219-222; and Jack Ericson Eblen, "New Estimates of the Vital Rates of the United States Black Population During the Nineteenth Century," *Demography*, XI (1974), 302.

[37] Greene and Harrington, comps., *American Population*, 133, 155; Curtin, *Atlantic Slave Trade*, 72-75.

[38] *Gentleman's Mag.*, XXXIV (1764), 261. This census understates the number of slave women in Prince George's County by 1,000.

TABLE III

PROFILE OF SLAVES IN CHARLES AND PRINCE GEORGE'S COUNTIES,
MARYLAND, 1711 TO 1730

	1711-1720	1721-1730
Males 0-15	84	185
Females 0-15	78	164
Sex ratio	1.077	1.128
Sex unknown 0-15	20	34
Total 0-15	182	383
Males 16-50	209	287
Females 16-50	120	188
Sex ratio	1.742	1.526
Total 16-50	329	475
Old males	26	53
Old females	21	47
Sex ratio	1.238	1.128
Old sex unknown	3	2
Total old	50	102
Slaves, age, sex unknown	34	14
Total slaves	595	974
ratio 0-15/16-50	.553	.806
ratio 0-15/females 16-50	1.517	2.037
ratio females 0-15[a]/females 16-50	.733	.963

[a] Assuming that ½ of the children not identified by sex were females.

1730.[39] In constructing the table, I have followed the procedures used for Table I. Although it shares the earlier table's imprecision at the edges of each age category and should be used with the same caution, it is adequate for my purpose. Table III describes a slight increase in the proportion of children in the years between 1711 and 1720, and a more substantial gain during the decade beginning in 1721. The increase appears even more pronounced when the relatively equal sex ratio among children is considered. The 1720s, these data suggest, marked a watershed for the slave population on Maryland's lower Western Shore.[40]

[39] Charles County Inventories, 1673-1717; 1717-1735; Prince George's County Inventories, BB#1, 1696/7-1720; TB#1, 1720-1729; PD#1, 1729-1740. Lois Green Carr generously supplied the data for Prince George's from 1711 to 1720.

[40] In 1724 Hugh Jones noted that slaves "are very prolifick among themselves." Jones, *The Present State of Virginia* . . . , ed. Richard L. Morton (Chapel Hill,

Table III also provides some clues to the reasons for the growing number of children. This increase was clearly not the result of a decline in the sex ratio. There was, in fact, a slightly higher proportion of men in the 16 to 50 age category during the 1720s than in the period 1658 to 1710. This suggests that planters had not yet recognized the benefits of natural increase among slaves.[41] Had planter interest in black reproduction suddenly increased, one would expect to find evidence of an effort to eliminate the sexual imbalance. However, on plantations with ten or more slaves, whose owners were usually wealthy enough to adjust sex ratios through purchase, men outnumbered women by nearly two to one in the 1720s.[42]

The high sex ratio suggests that the increase in the number of children occurred despite a continuing high rate of black immigration. Had the rate of immigration declined, one result would have been a movement of the sex ratio toward equality, especially given the apparently higher mortality rate for men and the increasing number of native-born slaves among whom the numbers of men and women were roughly equal. The fact that a sex ratio as high as that of the seventeenth century was maintained despite a growing population of native-born adults and higher male mortality suggests an increase in the rate of black immigration in the 1720s. The number of slaves brought into Virginia in this decade provides support for this argument.[43]

While the sex ratio was fairly stable, the ratio of children to women was not. From 1658 to 1710 appraisers listed just over one child under 16 for each woman aged 16 to 50; by the 1720s this ratio had nearly doubled. Two processes could account for the rise in the child-woman ratio: a decline in the rate of infant and childhood mortality, or an increase in the number of births per woman. Both were probably at work. The expectation of life for white adult males lengthened in the eighteenth century, an improvement doubtless accompanied by an increase in the

---

N. C., 1956), 75. See also Gov. William Gooch to the Council of Trade and Plantations, July 23, 1730, in W. Noel Sainsbury et al., eds., *Calendar of State Papers, Colonial Series: America and West Indies* (London, 1937), *1730*, no. 348.

[41] Dunn attributes the beginnings of natural increase among slaves in the West Indies in the late 18th century to such a recognition. *Sugar and Slaves*, 324-325.

[42] Two hundred one men and 111 women (sex ratio = 1.811) lived on plantations with 10 or more slaves.

[43] *Historical Statistics*, series Z294-297. The record of imports for the late 1720s is probably incomplete. See also the testimony of Mr. Hunt, active in the slave trade, before the Board of Trade, May 4, 1726, "that of late years there are annually imported into Maryland between 500 and 1,000 negroes." *Journal of the Commissioners for Trade and Plantations from January 1722-3 to December 1728* (London, 1928), 254.

RUSSELL R. MENARD

chances of survival beyond infancy and childhood.[44] A similar decline in black mortality would help explain the increase in the proportion of children in the slave population.

There are several reasons to assume an increase in the number of births in the 1720s, all associated with a growing number of native-born women in Maryland's slave population. The slaves who arrived in the four counties during the seventeenth century did not fully reproduce themselves, but they did have some children. By the 1720s natives must have formed a demographically significant proportion of the black population. Perhaps in part because of differences in attitude (presumably, natives were more thoroughly assimilated and less alienated than immigrants[45]), but primarily because their reproductive life in the colony was longer, native women bore more children in Maryland than did their immigrant mothers.

African-born slaves in the New World, Curtin has noted, were "subject to the epidemiological factors that affect all people who move from one disease environment to another. Most important immunities to disease are acquired in childhood. To move into a new disease environment as an adult normally exacts some price in higher rates of morbidity and mortality among the immigrants." As a result, Curtin suggests, African-born slaves died younger and were more often sickly than creoles.[46] Studies of adult expectation of life demonstrate that native-born white men suffered less from chronic ill-health and lived longer than their immigrant parents. Improved health and longevity among native-born black women would result in an extension of the average reproductive life and a rise in the number of births per woman. However, among white males in the seventeenth century, the expectation of life at age 20 was only slightly longer for natives than for immigrants.[47] If the experience of black women was similar to that of white males, improvements in health and longevity are not, by themselves, a sufficient explanation of the increase in the child-woman ratio.

An analogy with Europeans in the Chesapeake suggests not only that the reproductive years were extended by longer expectation of life for

[44] Walsh and Menard, "Death in the Chesapeake," *Md. Hist. Mag.*, LXIX (1974), 218-219.

[45] Mullin, *Flight and Rebellion, passim.*

[46] Curtin, *Atlantic Slave Trade,* 19; Curtin, "Epidemiology and the Slave Trade," *PSQ,* LXXXIII (1968), 190-216.

[47] Walsh and Menard, "Death in the Chesapeake," *Md. Hist. Mag.*, LXIX (1974), 218-219.

THE MARYLAND SLAVE POPULATION, 1658–1730

natives, but that they also began earlier. Most white women who im-migrated to the Chesapeake in the seventeenth century came as indentured servants. They were usually in their early twenties when they arrived and were, bound for a four-year term. Some were purchased by planters as wives, and others had illegitimate children while still servants, but most completed their terms and married before giving birth. Thus the mean age at marriage for immigrant women must have been about 25 years, perhaps higher. For native-born white women the mean age at first marriage in the seventeenth century may have been as low as 16 years, and it was certainly under 20.[48] Perhaps the experience of black women was similar. There seems no reason to assume that native-born slave women bore their first child at a later age than whites, while an average age at arrival of somewhat more than 20 years fits well with what little is known about the ages of slaves purchased by traders in Africa.[49] A recent study of age at marriage among whites in Charles County has found that native-born women, on the average, married seven or eight years younger than had their immigrant mothers.[50] If the age at which black women had their first child in the colony fell as sharply, native fe-males probably had several more children in Maryland than did women born in Africa.

Given the prevailing sex ratio in the 1720s and before, there must have been strong pressure for native-born black women to begin sexual inter-course at an early age. The inventories yield evidence that they were in fact young when they conceived their first child. Twenty inventories filed in Maryland between 1711 and 1730 that associated a woman and her children and listed their ages were discovered. By subtracting the age of

[48] Craven, *White, Red, and Black*, 27-28. Mean age at first marriage for 58 women born in Somerset County, Md., before 1680 was 16.4 years. Calculated from a register of vital events in Somerset County Deeds, IKL, Hall of Records. Mean age at first marriage for women born in Charles County before 1680 was 17.8 years. Calculated by Lorena S. Walsh from a register of vital events in Charles County Court and Land Records, Q#1, P#1. Mean age at first marriage for women born in Prince George's County before 1700 was 17.9 years. Calculated by Allan Kulikoff from published genealogies. For evidence of contemporary recognition of the im-portance of youthful marriages for the rapid growth of both the black and the white populations in the Chesapeake see Gooch to Council of Trade and Planta-tions, July 23, 1730, in Sainsbury *et al.*, eds., *Cal. State Papers, 1730*, no. 348.
[49] Davies, *Royal African Company*, 300. Patterson suggests that slave women were usually between 15 and 25 when purchased in Africa, but introduces little supporting evidence. *Sociology of Slavery*, 109.
[50] Lorena S. Walsh, "Charles County, Maryland, 1658-1705: A Study of Chesapeake Social and Political Structure" (Ph.D. diss., Michigan State University, in progress).

the oldest child plus nine months from the age of the mother, a rough estimate of the age at first conception is possible: 18.7 years on the average for these twenty women. This figure should be considered an upper bound for the mean age at which native-born women initially conceived. The first child of several of the women may have died before the inventory was taken. Furthermore, some of the women may have been immigrants, although appraisers were more likely to record the ages of native than of immigrant slaves. Allan Kulikoff, working with a larger number of observations and in a period when the chances of inflating the result by including immigrants had fallen, has found a mean age at initial conception of just over 17 years for slave women appearing in Prince George's County inventories between 1730 and 1750.[51]

A summary of the argument may prove helpful at this point. The immigrant slave population possessed several characteristics that tended to depress the rate of natural increase. African-born slaves suffered from high rates of mortality and morbidity, an unbalanced sex ratio, and perhaps an extreme alienation expressed in part as an unwillingness to have children. Most important, immigrant women were well advanced in their child-bearing years when they arrived in the colony. As a result, the initial immigrant population failed to reproduce itself. They did have some children, however, and these children transformed the demographic character of slavery in Maryland. The native-born lived longer and were less sickly than their immigrant forebears, they were more thoroughly assimilated, and there was among them a relatively equal ratio of men to women. Most important, native women began their reproductive careers at a much younger age than their immigrant mothers. Creole women had enough children to improve the natural growth rate in the slave population despite a continuing heavy black immigration, a still unbalanced sex ratio, and the apparent failure of their masters to appreciate fully the benefits of a self-perpetuating labor force.[52] Although a good deal of

[51] Kulikoff discusses age at first conception along with other aspects of slave demography in his dissertation. For an example of the nature of the evidence used to estimate age at conception see Inventories and Accounts, XXXVIC, 223. For a similar method applied in different circumstances see Peter Laslett, "Age at Menarche in Europe since the Eighteenth Century," *Jour. Interdisciplinary Hist.*, II (1971-1972), 228-234.

[52] I should emphasize that I am not arguing that fertility necessarily increased, but merely that native-born slave women had opportunity for sexual intercourse in Maryland for a larger proportion of their reproductive lives than did immigrants. A finding of constant age-specific fertility rates for native and immigrant women would not be incompatible with the argument. However, it is likely that

additional evidence is needed before this argument can be more than an interesting hypothesis, it does seem to account for the changing age and sex profile of the slave population. Certainly it is a line of inquiry worth pursuing.

If this interpretation of the demography of slavery is correct, there are some striking parallels between the white and black populations in Maryland. Short life expectancies, high mortality, a surplus of males, and a late age at marriage for women also characterized white immigrants. As a result they suffered a net natural decline. The native-born, however, were healthier, lived longer, married at earlier ages, and had enough children to reverse the direction of reproductive population change.[53]

There are also parallels between the demographic history of slavery in Maryland and the experience of African colonial populations elsewhere in the Americas. Curtin has reported that Africans in the New World usually experienced an initial period of natural population decline. He found the growth of a native-born population the critical process in the transition from a negative to a positive natural growth rate. "As a general tendency," he argues, "the higher the proportion of African-born in any slave population, the lower its rate of natural increase—or, as was more often the case, the higher its rate of natural decrease."[54] In Curtin's view, the improved health and longevity of the creoles and the equal sex ratio

---

age-specific fertility did increase because of declining morbidity and because of attitudinal changes associated with assimilation.

[53] The demography of whites in the colonial Chesapeake is discussed in Craven, *White, Red, and Black*, 1-37; Irene W. D. Hecht, "The Virginia Muster of 1624/5 as a Source for Demographic History," *WMQ*, 3d Ser., XXX (1973), 65-92; and Russell R. Menard, "Immigration to the Chesapeake Colonies in the Seventeenth Century: A Review Essay," *Md. Hist. Mag.,* LXVIII (1973), 323-329. Preliminary investigation suggests that most initial immigrant populations in British colonial North America experienced a period of negative or at least very low natural increase after the first wave of immigration, followed by a rapid increase once native-born adults emerged as a significant proportion of the population. The initial growth rate and the interval between first settlement and the beginnings of rapid natural increase varied widely from region to region, apparently depending on mortality rates, the sex ratio among immigrants, and whether or not the initial settlers were followed by continuous waves of immigration, but the basic demographic mechanism—a fall in age at marriage from immigrant to native-born women—seems to have been nearly universal. I hope to pursue this topic soon. For some suggestive evidence see P. M. G. Harris, "The Social Origins of American Leaders: The Demographic Foundations," *Perspectives in American History*, III (1969), 314; Daniel Scott Smith, "The Demographic History of Colonial New England," *Journal of Economic History*, XXXII (1972), 176-177; and Robert V. Wells, "Quaker Marriage Patterns," *WMQ*, 3d Ser., XXIX (1972), 415-442.

[54] Curtin, *Atlantic Slave Trade,* 28.

among slaves born in the Americas were primarily responsible for the increased growth rate. The experience of slaves in the four counties suggests that Curtin may have overestimated the role of the sex ratio and of mortality and missed the significance of the decline in the age at which women had their first child in the New World. However, the Maryland data do support his belief that the growth of a native-born group of slaves was the key factor in the transition from a naturally declining to a naturally increasing population.

Whether or not these speculations on the changing process of growth in the slave population stand the test of further research, the sharp rise in the proportion of children among blacks in southern Maryland in the 1720s is symptomatic of a series of changes that combined to alleviate the dreary isolation of Africans in the Chesapeake as the eighteenth century progressed. The most important of these changes were rooted in the growth of the black population, an increased concentration of the ownership of slaves, improved sex ratios, and the gradual assimilation of Africans and their offspring into an American colonial culture.

The slave population of the four-county region grew rapidly during the first half of the eighteenth century, from about 3,500 in 1710 to more than 15,000 by 1755, a growth rate of 3.33 percent a year. At that rate, there were approximately 7,000 slaves in the area by 1730. Rapid growth led to a sharp rise in density. During the seventeenth century slaves were thinly spread across the four counties; as late as 1704 there were fewer than one and one-half slaves per square mile in the region. By 1730 this number had increased to about four, by 1755 to over nine.[55]

An increased concentration of ownership accompanied this growth. A comparison of Tables II and IV demonstrates that slaves were more heavily concentrated on large estates in the 1720s than they had been during the seventeenth century. In particular, the proportion of slaves who lived on plantations with only a few other blacks registered a marked decline. Rapid growth, greater density, and the increased concentration of the slave population enlarged the opportunities for social contact among blacks both within and without the plantation.

By the 1720s the proportion of slaves in the region who were natives

[55] Population data for 1710 and 1755 are from *Md. Arch.*, XXV, 258-259, and *Gentleman's Mag.*, XXXIV (1764), 261. The four counties contain 1,662 square miles. Morris L. Radoff and Frank F. White, Jr., comps., *Maryland Manual, 1971-1972* (Annapolis, Md., 1972), 817.

TABLE IV

DISTRIBUTION OF SLAVES IN CHARLES AND PRINCE GEORGE'S COUNTIES,
MARYLAND, 1721 TO 1730

No. of slaves per estate	No. estates	% estates	Cum. %	No. slaves	% slaves	Cum. %
1-2	40	34.2	34.2	57	5.9	5.9
3-5	26	22.2	56.4	105	10.8	16.7
6-10	26	22.2	78.6	188	19.3	36.0
11-20	14	12.0	90.6	198	20.3	56.3
21+	11	9.4	100.0	426	43.7	100.0
	117	100.0		974	100.0	

of Maryland was growing rapidly as blacks born in the wake of the great migration at the turn of the century came of age and had children of their own. Precision is impossible, but it seems likely that by 1730 most slaves were Maryland-born, although among adults Africans may still have predominated. Many of the Africans, furthermore, were by then long-term residents of the province. As a result, the slave population was more thoroughly acculturated than during the seventeenth century. The isolation that resulted from different tribal origins dissolved as English supplanted the variety of languages spoken by Africans upon arrival, as Christianity displaced African religions, and as slaves created a common culture from their diverse backgrounds in the Old World and their shared experience in the New.[56] These relatively acculturated blacks were more sophisticated about slavery than their seventeenth-century predecessors, better able to exploit its weaknesses and to establish and sustain a wider

[56] On the differences in language and religion between African and country-born slaves see the statement by the Virginia House of Burgesses in 1699 "that Negroes borne in this Country are generally baptized and brought up in the Christian Religion but for Negroes Imported hither," among other reasons, "the variety and Strangeness of their Languages . . . renders it in a manner impossible to attain to any Progress in their Conversion." McIlwaine and Kennedy, eds., *Journals of Burgesses, 1695-1696*, 174. See also Jordan, *White Over Black*, 184; Jones, *Present State of Virginia*, ed. Morton, 99; Mullin, *Flight and Rebellion*, 17-19; and Wood, *Black Majority*, 133-142, 167-191. Allan Kulikoff explores the cultural differences between African and native-born blacks in "From African to American: Slave Community Life in Eighteenth-Century Maryland" (paper presented at the Hall of Records Conference on Maryland History, June 1974).

variety of personal relationships despite their bondage and the limitations imposed by the demographic characteristics of the slave population.[57]

The rise of an assimilated native-born slave population combined with the growing concentration of labor on the estates of large planters to make a greater variety of jobs available to blacks within the plantation system. By the 1720s many planters could afford to divert slaves from field work to domestic service, and many plantations were large enough to require the services of supervisory personnel and full-time craftsmen. At the same time, fewer planters owned indentured servants who could compete with blacks for the better positions. Furthermore, the gradual diversification of the Chesapeake economy, particularly the beginnings of local industry and the growth of small urban centers, created more non-farm jobs. As a result, more and more slaves were able to escape the routine drudgery of tobacco and move from field work to more rewarding and challenging (and often more unsettling) jobs as domestics, artisans, industrial workers, and overseers.[58]

Counts based on occupational designations in inventories understate the proportion of artisans in the population because of the occasional failure of appraisers to record a skilled slave's achievement. Nevertheless, inventories provide a useful guide to changes in the jobs held by blacks. Before 1710 only 4 of the 525 adult male slaves who appear in inventories in the four counties were described as craftsmen; from 1711 to 1725 only 3 of 283 men in Charles and Prince George's estates were artisans. In the late 1720s—roughly a generation after the heavy migration at the turn of the century—the number of skilled slaves rose sharply: between 1726 and 1730, 13 of the 213 men (6 percent) in Charles and Prince George's inventories were skilled workmen. Seven were carpenters, two were coopers, one was a blacksmith, one a "tradesman," and two, perhaps representing an elite among black artisans, were skilled in both cooperage and carpentry.[59]

A tax list that survives for Prince George's County in 1733 provides some insight into the proportion of blacks who had attained supervisory positions. Seventy-nine quarters occupied by slaves appear; on thirty-seven no taxable-age white is listed. Ten of the thirty-seven quarters

---

[57] On the increased competence of acculturated slaves see Mullin, *Flight and Rebellion, passim.*

[58] For the often unsettling impact of job mobility see *ibid.,* 72-82, 98-103.

[59] Charles County Inventories, 1717-1735, 290, 291; Prince George's County Inventories, TB#1, 1720-1729, 6, 34, 68, 79, 81, 129, 317, 340. See also Jones, *Present State of Virginia,* ed. Morton, 76.

contained only two taxable slaves; another quarter had only one. On these, the lives of the slaves perhaps paralleled those of poor white tenants. Like Mingo, Dick, and Toby, these slaves apparently operated small family farms away from their master's home plantation. Eleven of the thirty-seven quarters contained three or four adult slaves, while between five and twenty taxable adults lived on the remaining fifteen. Some of the slaves on these larger operations must have enjoyed some measure of responsibility, status, and power.[60] If it is assumed that one black on each of the thirty-seven quarters held a position that approximated that of an overseer, 3 percent of the slave men in the county in 1733 were so employed. To these thirty-seven should be added another handful of slaves who lived either on the home plantations of widows with no resident white man or on estates where adult blacks greatly outnumbered adult whites. In such situations black men probably assumed some of the responsibility for operating the farm and for supervising the work of other slaves.[61]

A firm estimate of the number of slaves engaged in domestic service during the 1720s is impossible, but there can be little doubt that their ranks were swelled as the wealth and labor force of the great planters grew. Nor is it possible to measure the number who found work at the stores and taverns located in the several service centers (most still too small to deserve the name of towns) that were beginning to emerge in the region or in the minor industrial enterprises organized by wealthy planter-merchants.[62] However, when these possibilities are added to the chances to acquire a craft or a supervisory job, it becomes reasonable to suggest

[60] For the freedom and power of men in such positions see the example of Charles Calvert's black overseer who harbored a runaway slave for about a month in the winter of 1728-1729, *Maryland Gazette* (Annapolis), Dec. 24-31, 1728, Jan. 21-28, 1729. See also Mullin, *Flight and Rebellion,* 171-172.

[61] The tax list is in the Black Books, II, 109-124, Hall of Records. Because the list does not distinguish slaves by sex, it has been necessary to estimate the number of black men by applying a sex ratio of 1.500 to the total number of taxable-age slaves.

[62] For examples of blacks in non-farm jobs see the references to the slaves at a copper mine owned by John Digges and at mills owned by John Hoope and William Wilkinson, Prince George's County Tax List, 1733, Black Books, II, 121, and Charles County Inventories, 1717-1735, 208. See also Michael W. Robbins, "The Principio Company: Iron-making in Colonial Maryland, 1720-1781" (Ph.D. diss., George Washington University, 1972), 92-93, 99-101. Mullin, *Flight and Rebellion,* esp. 94-96, reports slaves working at a wide variety of jobs in 18th-century Virginia. On the small urban centers in the region in the 1720s see Allan Kulikoff, "Community Life in an Eighteenth-Century Tobacco County: Prince George's County, Maryland, 1730-1780" (paper presented at the annual meeting of the Eastern Historical Geography Association, October 1973).

that by 1730 as many as 10 to 15 percent of the slave men in the region were able to escape the monotonous work of the field hand. To be sure, the job opportunities for even the most talented, industrious, and competent black men were still severely restricted, but they had expanded since the seventeenth century.

Occupational opportunities for women were even more limited. For them, work as domestics, at the spinning wheel and loom, or caring for slave children, offered almost the only alternatives to agricultural labor. Even the women who did obtain such positions had often spent much of their working lives in the fields, moving to more sedentary tasks after they were, like Edward Lloyd's Bess, "past working in the Ground by Age."[63] Throughout the colonial period it is likely that the proportion of slave women who worked as common field hands was greater than that of men.[64] However, the increasing size of the labor force on the largest plantations and the growth of the proportion of children did permit more women to leave the fields as the eighteenth century advanced.

Sometime after 1730 a rough balance between the sexes was attained. Answers to such questions as when and how the balance was established, whether sudden and dramatic or gradual and little noticed, whether reflecting a decision by planters or simply the result of the growing number of native-born slaves, must await further research. The predominance of males in the black population approached insignificance by 1755, when the sex ratio among adult slaves in the four counties was only 1.105.[65] The near balance between the sexes ended the barracks-like existence forced upon many black men in the early colonial period and made it possible for a larger proportion of slaves to create a more settled and, by English standards if not by African, more nearly normal family life in the New World.[66]

Occupational mobility, cultural assimilation, and, most important, a growing opportunity for social contact, intimate personal relationships, and a stable family life made slavery a less isolating and dehumanizing

[63] Because of her age, Bess "set in the house and spin." Testamentary Papers, Box 25, folder 34, Hall of Records. For examples of younger women working as domestics see Prince George's County Inventories, TB#1, 1720-1729, 81, 129.

[64] Patterson reaches the same conclusion for Jamaica. *Sociology of Slavery,* 157.

[65] The census of 1755 in *Gentleman's Mag.,* XXXIV (1764), 261, understates the number of slave women in Prince George's County by 1,000.

[66] Allan Kulikoff discusses family life among slaves in 18th-century Prince George's County in "From African to American."

experience than it had been in the seventeenth century. It is ironic that, as the law of slavery hardened, as white racism deepened, and as the identification of blacks with bondage became firmly ingrained, demographic processes seldom studied by historians of Africans in the Chesapeake region made slavery more tolerable and slaves better able to cope with their oppression.

NEW ESTIMATES OF THE VITAL RATES OF THE UNITED STATES BLACK POPULATION DURING THE NINETEENTH CENTURY

Jack Ericson Eblen

Population Research Center, University of Chicago, 1126 East 59th Street, Chicago, Illinois 60637, U.S.A. and Population Institute, University of the Philippines, P.O. Box 479, Padre Faura, Manila D-406, Republic of the Philippines

Abstract—The difficulties of obtaining credible estimates of vital rates for the black population throughout the entire nineteenth century are overcome in this study. The methodology employed the notion of deviating networks of mortality rates for each general mortality level, which was taken from the United Nations study *The Concept of a Stable Population.* Period life tables and vital rates for intercensal periods were generated from the new estimates of the black population at each census date. The results of this study are highly compatible both with the life tables for the death-registration states in the twentieth century and the recent Coale and Rives reconstruction for the period from 1880 to 1970 and with several estimates of vital rates previously made for the mid-nineteenth century. This study places the mean life expectancy at birth for the black population during the nineteenth century at about 33.7 years for both sexes. The infant death rate ($1000 \, m_0$) is shown to have varied between 222 and 237 for females and between 266 and 278 for males. The intrinsic crude death rate centered on 30.4 per thousand during the century, while the birth rate declined from 53.2 early in the century to about 43.8 at the end.

Introduction

Previous studies treating the vital rates of the U. S. black population prior to the twentieth century have been piecemeal in coverage and inconclusive. Recent ones by Zelnik (1966), Farley (1965, 1970) and Eblen (1972) provided estimates for specific dates or a part of the century, but the various estimates do not fit together to form a coherent set spanning the century. This is a reflection of the different assumptions and methods used to derive estimates rather than differences in data, for all have used the same kind of data from the same shallow reservoir. The most recent attempts to cope with the paucity of reliable data have used the Coale and Demeny (1966) West model life tables, but the estimates

of vital rates so obtained are not altogether plausible. This paper introduces an alternate methodology which was applied to data for the nineteenth century in order to generate a credible series of mutually compatible estimates of vital rates for the black population covering the period from 1810 to 1900. In so doing the paper illustrates a viable general method of answering some basic questions about populations for which there are few data and points the way toward the further development of this method without sacrificing its fundamental simplicity.

The period from 1810 to 1900 forms something of a distinct unit in the demographic history of the black population. The legal importation of slaves into the

301

Reprinted from *Demography* XI, 301–319.
Copyright © 1974 by permission of the publisher.

United States ended on January 1, 1808, and, from the Census of 1810 on, the United States black population can be treated as demographically closed (see Eblen, 1972, pp. 273–274, 288–289). After 1900 black mortality rates improved rapidly relative to earlier periods, and the period beginning about 1900 is perhaps best considered separately as one of demographic transition. Life tables for the black population, based on death-registration statistics, begin with the year 1900, and the black population of the twentieth century has been subjected to comparatively thorough analysis in recent years. However, it is likely that precise estimates of vital rates for the period prior to 1810 are unobtainable for the whole black population from extant data. This leaves the period from 1810 to 1900 as one for which a comprehensive series of vital rate estimates is needed and for which rather precise estimates of some basic rates can be obtained.

Between the War of 1812 and the outbreak of the Civil War in 1861, slavery flourished as it spread out from the coastal region of the Southeast to envelop the South, all the time keeping pace with the expansion of the nation. As it became more firmly entrenched, it apparently became more harsh, and the domestic slave trade burgeoned. The Civil War ended the institution of slavery, but the black population continued to live, as it had before the War, in an environment full of fear and insecurity created by both the *de jure* and *de facto* denial of fundamental protections and rights. Slavery and the slave trade were replaced by involuntary relocation during the Civil War and Reconstruction, and then by modern forms of racism and segregation, share cropping, tenancy, foreclosure and other kinds of forced removal, and by accelerated voluntary migration to industrial cities in the last decades of the century. Meanwhile, the United States was transformed from a small agricultural nation clinging to the east coast of North America into a major industrial nation of transcontinental dimensions and hemispheric ambitions. The interaction of these historical events and demographic variables is not the subject of this paper, but the new estimates of vital rates below will shed some light on that important subject.

Methodology and Results

The method of successive approximations used in this study starts with the identification of a realm of demographic variables that has to include the values sought. A combination of sex ratios, age distributions, growth rates and survival ratios, from both raw and smoothed census data and from model life tables, are then used to shrink the perimeter of permissible values of that realm until a compatible series of precise estimates are obtained.

The Coale and Demeny (1966) model life tables used previously are inflexible at any given mortality level and do not produce credible results for high mortality situations. In particular, the infant mortality rates associated with the West model at level 5, where the best fit of the *ante bellum* black data occurs, seem excessive in light of the population's growth rate. The most suitable alternative to the Coale and Demeny tables is to be found in the United Nations study *The Concept of a Stable Population*, which provides a range, or network, of mortality characteristics for each sex at each mortality level. The networks were generated by factor analysis, which identified five components of mortality and indicated how they affected the age-specific probabilities of dying $(_nq_x)$.

The U.N. networks are described in terms of downward-deviating, intermediate, and upward-deviating series of model life tables. In the downward-deviating series, the first component of mortality is modified downward, and this produces a life expectancy at birth that is substantially higher than that in the intermediate model. In the upward-deviating series the opposite is done, and between the two extremes there is considerable room for variation in age-specific mortality rates except in the age groups for females where the first mortality component alone is operative. It is to these female age groups, between ages 5 and 35, that the data for a real population are keyed into the networks. If, for example, the female mortality experience for the ages between 5 and 35 is found to fit the U.N. networks at Level 20 (as in this study), it is possible for the life expectancy at birth for both sexes—which is 30.0 for the intermediate model life tables—to be anywhere between 17.0 (the upward-deviating models) and 41.9 (the downward-deviating models) years. At Level 20 the female infant death rate ($1000 \, m_0$) can be as low as 124.8 or as high as 283.4, and the male infant death rate can vary from 139.6 to 316.2.

Thus, unlike the Coale and Demeny models, fitting a population into the United Nations networks at one level does not necessarily produce a single set of results. Instead, it defines the range of variability for every probability of dying ($_n q_x$) at that level, and, as already noted, some of those can vary substantially. This means, of course, that finding the appropriate U.N. level is only one step in obtaining precise estimates of the vital rates of a population. The methodology developed for making the new estimates in this paper is nevertheless relatively simple and straightforward. It could have been used to produce about the same results with fewer data, and some rough estimates could have been made with almost no data. (See Eblen, 1974, which is a study of the Cuban black population from 1775 to 1900 utilizing a similar technique with many fewer data to obtain estimates of vital rates for a population that was not

closed but received substantial annual increments of slaves.)

The available raw census data for the black population were first compiled in uniform age groupings. In order to do this the data from the censuses of 1820, 1830 and 1840 had to be regrouped. (The method of regrouping these data is described in Eblen, 1972, pp. 274, 275. The original census groupings were, for 1820, 0–13, 14–25, 26–44, 45+; and for 1830 and 1840, 0–9, 10–23, 24–35, 36–54, 55–99, and 100+.) There were no age and sex data for the black population in 1810, just a total figure, and there was no published age breakdown for 1880, just a total number of black males and females. Age distributions for 1880 were created by reducing the ones for non-whites by a factor which produced a sum for all ages, for each sex, equal to the published total, but the results for black males are a weak approximation. Unlike the case of the females, other nonwhite males (mainly Oriental) constituted a significant proportion of the total (3.5 percent). They were also heavily concentrated in a few age groups, and their exact age distribution is not known.

The census data are summarized in Table 1 by ten-year age groupings with persons whose age was reported as unknown at each census distributed proportionately among the age groups by sex. These data were smoothed graphically to compensate for the grossest errors of enumeration and adjusted so that the population totals described a relatively smooth growth rate curve. This procedure corrected for differences in methods of reporting ages, age heaping and obvious underenumerations, and it overcame the major problems presented by the notoriously poor Census of 1870. It also had the effect of moving all censuses to the same date, June 1. (For a further description of the smoothing technique, see Eblen, 1972, pp. 275–277. The censuses from 1790 through 1820 were taken as of the first Monday

TABLE 1.—The Black Population of the United States, 1810–1900: Raw Census Data Summarized in Ten-Year Age Groups

Sex and Age Group	Population in Thousands									
	1810	1820	1830	1840	1850	1860	1870	1880	1890	1900
Total, Both Sexes	1,378	1,773	2,329	2,876	3,641	4,443	4,882	6,579	7,489	8,833
Total Females	--	871	1,163	1,442	1,828	2,226	2,487	3,327	3,753	4,447
0- 9	--	*278*	395	477	574	688	723	*1,063*	1,069	1,220
10-19	--	*220*	*272*	*340*	446	554	585	*735*	963	1,057
20-29	--	*159*	*200*	*254*	325	392	470	*611*	673	892
30-39	--	*94*	*159*	*197*	208	255	290	*387*	399	506
40-49	--	*54*	*62*	*80*	131	163	199	*254*	331	348
50-59	--	*35*	*36*	*50*	74	91	114	*151*	158	219
60-69	--	*21*	*26*	*31*	44	53	65	*88*	100	123
70+	--	*10*	*13*	*13*	26	30	41	*58*	60	82
Total Males	--	902	1,166	1,434	1,813	2,217	2,395	3,252	3,736	4,386
0- 9	--	*294*	402	479	566	677	729	*1,034*	1,088	1,212
10-19	--	*224*	*272*	*339*	445	556	581	*721*	955	1,028
20-29	--	*157*	*197*	248	326	397	408	*583*	628	824
30-39	--	*100*	*156*	*190*	202	249	254	*355*	383	498
40-49	--	*56*	*64*	*84*	128	163	187	*239*	309	350
50-59	--	*38*	*39*	*50*	77	94	128	*168*	209	254
60-69	--	*25*	*27*	*31*	45	54	72	*102*	92	143
70+	--	*8*	*9*	*13*	24	27	36	*50*	77	77

Sources: The respective censuses of the United States. The same data also appear in U.S. Bureau of the Census, 1918, pp. 147, 166-167. The figures in italics are ten-year groups derived from the original census age groupings. The derivation for the period 1820-1840 is described in Eblen, 1972, p.274. The 1880 data were derived by proportional reduction of the nonwhite age distribution. Persons of unknown age have been apportioned proportionally among the age groups. Dashes indicate that data are unavailable either by sex or age.

of August. The censuses from 1830 through 1900 were to enumerate the population as of June 1, except in 1890 when June 1 fell on a Sunday and the census date was moved to June 2. However, prior to 1880 the actual enumerations extended over periods of from about six months to more than a year. See Wright, 1900, *passim*.)

Intercensal survival ratios ($_{10}p_x$) were calculated from the smoothed data sets for the period from 1820 to 1900. The most appropriate U.N. networks were selected by comparing these intercensal survival ratios with the corresponding ones in the U.N. model life tables. Every intercensal survival ratio fell within the ranges of the U.N. Level 20 network ratios or just outside of them but much closer to the ratios of the Level 20 networks than to those of the next level.

Having determined that the U.N. net-

works for Level 20 were the correct ones to use, the final age distributions for each sex could be derived from the smoothed data sets. There is a unique age distribution associated with every model life table at any stable growth rate or combination of changing growth characteristics. Similarly, each U.N. network has a limited range of percentage variation for each age group. These percentages and the age-specific survival ratios of the Level 20 networks were used to produce a best fit of the smoothed data and growth characteristics of the black population to the male and female networks at Level 20.

Since the least variability in the U.N. networks occurs among the models for females, a best fit is more easily obtained for females than for males. Consequently the final age distributions for females were derived first. Final male data sets could also be derived from a best fit to the network for males at Level 20, but the more direct method adopted was to obtain them from the final female data sets by using the age-specific sex ratios of the smoothed data in conjunction with those associated with a sex ratio at birth (or secondary sex ratio) of 102 males per 100 females in the U.N. networks for Level 20. (A secondary sex ratio of 102, rather than 103, 104, or 105, was used for this study because it is the one most commonly associated with the data for the black population of the United States.) Since the survival ratios of the resulting male data sets fell within the male network range for each age group, no adjustments were needed, and they could be taken as the final male data sets. The final male and female data sets, raised by almost ten percent to account for all underenumeration, and the cumulative percentages of age distribution are summarized in Tables 2 and 3. The final data sets were raised by nearly ten percent on the assumption that the under-

enumeration of the black population was roughly fifty percent greater than the average estimated underenumeration of whites (see Shryock et al., 1973, p. 109).

Life table values for the total number of years lived from birth by a cohort of 100,000 (T_0) and life expectancies at birth (e_0) were obtained for each sex separately by interpolation within the U.N. networks for Level 20. This was done by using the ratio calculated from the proportion of those persons of each sex who actually survived each intercensal interval (among the final data sets summarized in Table 2) and the proportions who would have survived the same period had the perimeter survival ratios of the networks been valid. Abridged life tables for each sex could then be constructed by finding the $_nL_x$ values (the number of persons who are alive at any moment within the indicated age interval in the stationary population) that, with the survival ratios taken from the final data sets, produced the required T_0 and e_0 values. Two life table functions, the

TABLE 2.—New Estimates of the Black Population of the United States, 1810–1900, Summarized in Ten-Year Age Groups

Sex and Age Group	Population in Thousands									
	1810	1820	1830	1840	1850	1860	1870	1880	1890	1900
Total, Both Sexes	1,629	2,045	2,575	3,227	4,019	4,916	5,961	7,211	8,587	9,875
Total Females	815	1,024	1,288	1,616	2,012	2,460	2,982	3,610	4,299	4,945
0- 9	275	347	437	545	669	794	950	1,140	1,314	1,398
10-19	189	237	298	376	470	572	679	817	981	1,132
20-29	133	166	208	262	331	412	501	596	717	861
30-39	90	113	142	178	224	283	352	428	508	611
40-49	61	77	97	121	151	190	241	299	362	431
50-59	38	48	60	76	94	118	148	189	234	282
60-69	19	24	31	38	48	59	73	93	120	149
70+	10	12	15	20	25	32	38	48	63	81
Total Males	814	1,021	1,287	1,611	2,007	2,456	2,979	3,601	4,288	4,930
0- 9	273	344	434	542	665	790	945	1,133	1,307	1,389
10-19	189	237	299	377	471	573	680	818	983	1,134
20-29	134	168	211	264	335	417	507	601	725	870
30-39	91	115	144	180	227	287	358	434	516	620
40-49	63	78	98	122	152	192	244	303	365	436
50-59	37	47	59	75	92	116	145	185	229	276
60-69	18	22	29	35	44	55	68	86	110	137
70+	9	10	13	16	21	26	32	41	53	68

Source: Calculated from data in Table 1 as explained in text.

TABLE 3.—Cumulative Percentages of Age Distribution of the New Estimates of the Black Population of the United States, 1810–1900, Summarized by Ten-Year Age Intervals

Percentage under the Age of	Year									
	1810	1820	1830	1840	1850	1860	1870	1880	1890	1900
All Females	100.0%	100.0%	100.0%	100.0%	100.0%	100.0%	100.0%	100.0%	100.0%	100.0%
10	33.7	33.9	33.9	33.7	33.3	32.3	31.9	31.6	30.6	28.3
20	56.9	57.0	57.1	57.0	56.6	55.5	54.6	54.2	53.4	51.2
30	73.3	73.2	73.2	73.2	73.1	72.3	71.4	70.7	70.1	68.6
40	84.3	84.3	84.2	84.2	84.2	83.8	83.2	82.6	81.9	80.9
50	91.8	91.8	91.8	91.7	91.7	91.5	91.3	90.9	90.3	89.6
60	96.4	96.5	96.4	96.4	96.4	96.3	96.3	96.1	95.7	95.3
70	98.8	98.8	98.8	98.8	98.8	98.7	98.7	98.7	98.5	98.4
All Males	100.0	100.0	100.0	100.0	100.0	100.0	100.0	100.0	100.0	100.0
10	33.5	33.7	33.7	33.6	33.1	32.2	31.7	31.5	30.5	28.2
20	56.8	56.9	57.0	57.0	56.6	55.5	54.5	54.2	53.4	51.2
30	73.2	73.4	73.3	73.4	73.3	72.5	71.6	70.9	70.3	68.8
40	84.4	84.6	84.5	84.6	84.6	84.2	83.6	82.9	82.3	81.4
50	92.1	92.3	92.1	92.2	92.2	92.0	91.8	91.3	90.9	90.2
60	96.7	96.9	96.7	96.8	96.8	96.7	96.6	96.5	96.2	95.8
70	98.9	99.0	99.0	99.0	99.0	98.9	98.9	98.9	98.8	98.6

Source: Calculated from the data in Table 2.

number of survivors (l_x) and life expectancy (e_x) at exact age x, are given for every tenth year of age in Tables 4 and 5.

Given the new life tables for the black population and the growth rate curve for the total populations of the final data sets, it is a simple matter to estimate the vital rates of the black population. The rates for each intercensal period were taken to be those indicated by interpolation among the relevant models within the U.N. networks for Level 20. In each case, vital rates were interpolated between the intermediate and downward-deviating model life tables and their stable age distributions for the growth rates in question. The principal rates estimated in this manner are presented in Tables 6 and 7 and Figure 1.

Discussion

As can be seen from the foregoing tables, the life expectancy at birth for both sexes fluctuated between 33 and 34 years during the nineteenth century and declined to its lowest points in the decade before the Civil War and during the Civil War and early years of Reconstruction. Most of the fluctuation in life

expectancy was due to changes in the infant and early childhood mortality rates. The infant death rates $(1000 \, m_0)$ of females ranged from about 222 to 237 per thousand while those of males varied between 261 and 278 per thousand. The male and female life expectancies at age 20 (e_{20}) varied only about six months in the period covered, the male expectation centering on 34.0 years and the female on approximately 34.5 years. The gross reproduction rate, which was around 3.6 early in the nineteenth century, began to decline between 1830 and 1840. It fell off sharply after about 1880 and stood at 2.8 in the last decade of the century.

The new estimates reflect a degree of stability which suggests that there were no extreme annual fluctuations in vital rates. According to the estimates in Table 6, the intrinsic death rate (the crude death rate for a stable population) of the black population during the nineteenth century and the expectation of life at birth for both sexes oscillated between only 30 and 31 per thousand and 33 and 34 years, respectively. These figures are in agreement with Farley's earliest estimates (1965, p. 395) for the period 1830

TABLE 4.—Selected *Female* Survivorship Values (l_x) and Life Expectancies (e_x) from the New Period Life Tables for the Black Population of the United States, 1810–1900, and from the Death-Registration States Life Tables for Negroes for the Decade 1901–1910

Exact Age x	Decennial Period of Life Table									
	1810–1820	1820–1830	1830–1840	1840–1850	1850–1860	1860–1870	1870–1880	1880–1890	1890–1900	1901–1910
	Number of Females Alive at Age x of 100,000 Born Alive (l_x)									
0	100,000	100,000	100,000	100,000	100,000	100,000	100,000	100,000	100,000	100,000
10	66,100	66,320	66,130	66,450	64,870	64,970	66,080	65,980	66,330	66,970
20	60,050	60,290	60,100	60,390	59,040	59,100	60,030	59,940	60,250	60,950
30	51,470	51,690	51,520	51,750	50,710	50,730	51,450	51,360	51,620	54,150
40	43,010	43,200	43,050	43,240	42,340	42,340	42,960	42,880	43,130	47,140
50	34,730	34,930	34,800	34,980	34,150	34,060	34,680	34,650	34,900	38,330
60	25,480	25,680	25,610	25,840	25,050	24,840	25,490	25,590	25,890	27,430
70	15,410	15,440	15,450	15,760	15,240	14,990	15,520	15,720	16,010	15,430
	Average Length of Life Remaining to Each Female at Exact Age x (e_x) in Years									
0	34.4	34.6	34.4	34.7	33.6	33.7	34.4	34.4	34.6	35.7
10	41.0	41.1	41.0	41.1	40.7	40.7	41.0	41.0	41.1	42.5
20	34.6	34.7	34.6	34.7	34.2	34.3	34.6	34.5	34.7	36.2
30	29.6	29.7	29.6	29.7	29.2	29.2	29.6	29.5	29.6	30.1
40	24.4	24.5	24.4	24.5	24.1	24.1	24.4	24.3	24.5	23.8
50	18.6	18.7	18.6	18.7	18.3	18.3	18.6	18.6	18.7	18.1
60	12.9	12.9	12.9	13.0	12.8	12.7	12.9	12.9	13.0	13.2
70	8.4	8.4	8.4	8.5	8.3	8.3	8.4	8.4	8.5	9.5

Note: The l_x values are rounded to the nearest ten.
Source: Life table values for the period 1810–1900 are calculated from the data summarized in Table 2 as explained in the text. The figures for the death-registration states life tables are from Glover, 1921, pp. 84–85.

TABLE 5.—Selected *Male* Survivorship Values (l_x) and Life Expectancies (e_x) from the New Period Life Tables for the Black Population of the United States, 1810–1900, and from the Death-Registration States Life Tables for Negroes for the Decade 1901–1910

Exact Age x	Decennial Period of Life Table									
	1810–1820	1820–1830	1830–1840	1840–1850	1850–1860	1860–1870	1870–1880	1880–1890	1890–1900	1901–1910
	Number of Males Alive at Age x of 100,000 Born Alive (l_x)									
0	100,000	100,000	100,000	100,000	100,000	100,000	100,000	100,000	100,000	100,000
10	63,600	64,010	63,260	63,570	62,670	62,440	63,130	63,230	63,430	63,260
20	58,550	58,900	58,170	58,480	57,740	57,480	58,090	58,180	58,340	58,200
30	50,940	51,220	50,630	50,870	50,350	50,090	50,590	50,630	50,760	50,810
40	43,010	43,310	42,780	42,950	42,570	42,280	42,740	42,740	42,900	42,840
50	33,880	34,390	33,810	33,910	33,670	33,330	33,520	33,790	33,980	34,020
60	23,390	24,240	23,470	23,580	23,500	22,880	23,520	23,630	23,900	23,340
70	12,970	13,930	13,170	13,420	13,440	12,830	13,420	13,680	13,920	12,170
	Average Length of Life Remaining to Each Male at Exact Age x (e_x) in Years									
0	33.3	33.6	33.1	33.3	32.6	32.4	33.0	33.0	33.2	32.6
10	41.2	41.4	41.1	41.2	40.8	40.7	41.0	41.1	41.1	40.7
20	34.2	34.4	34.1	34.2	33.9	33.8	34.0	34.1	34.2	33.8
30	28.6	28.8	28.4	28.6	28.3	28.1	28.4	28.4	28.5	28.0
40	22.9	23.1	22.8	22.9	22.7	22.5	22.8	22.8	22.9	22.2
50	17.2	17.4	17.2	17.2	17.1	16.9	17.2	17.2	17.3	16.6
60	11.9	12.2	12.0	12.0	12.0	11.8	12.0	12.0	12.1	11.9
70	7.8	7.9	7.8	7.9	7.9	7.7	7.9	7.9	7.9	8.3

Note: The l_x values are rounded to the nearest ten.
Source: Life table values for the period 1810–1900 are calculated from the data summarized in Table 2 as explained in the text. The figures for the death-registration states life tables are from Glover, 1921, pp. 84–85.

TABLE 6.—New Estimates of the Vital Rates of the Black Population of the United States, 1810–1900: Expectations of Life at Birth for Both Sexes, Annual Rates of Natural Increase, Birth and Death Rates, Approximate Gross Reproduction Rates, and Hypothetical Reproductive Limits of the Black Population during the Nineteenth Century

| | New Estimates of Black Vital Rates | | Annual Intrinsic Rates (per Thousand) | | | | | Hypothetical Crude Birth Rate Limits Derived from[a] | |
| | Expectation of Life at Birth, Both Sexes (in Years) | Gross Reproduction Rate (Circa) | Rate of Natural Increase[b] | + | Crude Death Rate[c] | = | Crude Birth Rate[c] | New Period Life Table nL_x Values: Stationary ($r = 0.0$) Potential | Age Data for Each Census Date from Table 2: "Actual" or Point-in-Time Potential |
Intercensal Interval	e_o	GRR	r	+	CDR	=	CBR		
1810–1820	33.9	3.58	22.7		30.4		53.1	60.7	56.2 (1810)
1820–1830	34.1	3.58	23.0		30.2		53.2	60.5	56.1 (1820)
1830–1840	33.8	3.57	22.6		30.5		53.1	60.9	56.0 (1830)
1840–1850	34.0	3.49	21.9		30.2		52.1	60.9	56.2 (1840)
1850–1860	33.1	3.39	20.2		31.1		51.3	60.5	56.7 (1850)
1860–1870	33.0	3.30	19.3		31.1		50.4	60.8	57.6 (1860)
1870–1880	33.7	3.23	19.0		30.4		49.4	61.0	58.1 (1870)
1880–1890	33.7	3.08	17.5		30.2		47.7	61.1	58.1 (1880)
1890–1900	33.9	2.84	14.0		29.8		43.8	61.1	58.6 (1890)
									60.5 (1900)

a– The sex ratio at birth was assumed to have been 102 males per 100 females for these calculations. It was further assumed that the maximum reproduction at this mortality level occurs when 80 percent of the females are fertile and the childbearing interval is three years.

b– Calculated using the continuous formula: $P_1 \div P_0 = e^{rn}$.

c– Intrinsic death rates are associated with the age distributions in Table 2, derived as explained in the text from the UN stable models used in the study. Birth rates are obtained by adding growth and death rates.

Source: Calculated from data summarized in Tables 2, 4, and 5, as explained in the text.

TABLE 7.—New Estimates of the Infant Mortality Rates of the Black Population of the United States, 1810–1900, and Infant Mortality Rates from the Death-Registration States Life Tables for Negroes, 1900–1911: Probabilities of Dying during the First Year of Life (1000 q_o) and Life Table Death Rates for the First Year of Life (1000 m_o)

Intercensal or Other Interval	Probability of Dying (Proportion of 1,000 Born Alive Who Die) during the First Year of Life 1000 q_o		Life Table Death Rate: Deaths per 1,000 Person-Years Lived during the First Year of Life 1000 m_o	
	Male	Female	Male	Female
1810–1820	215.5	185.3	265.7	223.9
1820–1830	211.9	183.7	261.2	222.0
1830–1840	218.0	185.3	268.9	223.9
1840–1850	215.5	182.6	265.7	220.6
1850–1860	223.3	195.6	275.6	236.6
1860–1870	225.0	194.7	277.7	235.4
1870–1880	219.2	185.3	270.4	223.9
1880–1890	218.4	186.2	269.4	225.1
1890–1900	216.7	183.3	267.2	221.5
1900–1902	253.3	214.8	306.4	250.2
1901–1910 Mean	241.4	206.2	289.3	239.5
1909–1911	219.4	185.1	258.1	212.1

Sources: For 1810–1900, see text. Death-registration states life table rates are from Glover, 1921, pp. 76, 78, 80, 82, 84, 86.

to 1850, and the new estimates of the intrinsic birth rate at mid-century—of 51 to 52 per thousand—are compatible with Zelnik's estimate (1966, p. 82) for 1850. (His birth rate estimate for 1830 is 60–61 per thousand and is well above the limit discussed below.) All of these estimates are much less extreme than the ones obtained from the West models, which put the death rate between 36 and 38 per thousand and the expectation of life at birth for both sexes at less than 29 years during the *ante bellum* period (Eblen, 1972, pp. 284–285). In his more recent study, Farley (1970, p. 67, Table 3-9) used the West models to place female life expectancies at birth as low as 25 years for the late nineteenth and early twentieth centuries, and this implies an intrinsic death rate of about 44! His vari-

ous estimates, however, are inconsistent and contradictory, and they are based on the unwarranted assumption that black mortality rates increased toward the end of the nineteenth century as a result of Emancipation. (Compare Farley's figures [1970, Tables 2-2 and 3-9] and his observations [1965, pp. 396–397].)

The new estimates supersede those derived for the *ante bellum* period from the West models without negating the broad interpretation of the results obtained by using the West models (Eblen, 1972, pp. 288–289). On the contrary, with a single exception, the new estimates serve both to strengthen and to expand that interpretation. For example, within the framework of economic analyses such as the one by Conrad and Meyer (1958), it is more apparent than ever that slavery was

Figure 1. New Estimates of the Vital Rates of the United States Black Population and
Hypothetical Birth Rate Limits, 1810-1900. Data from Tables 6 and 7.

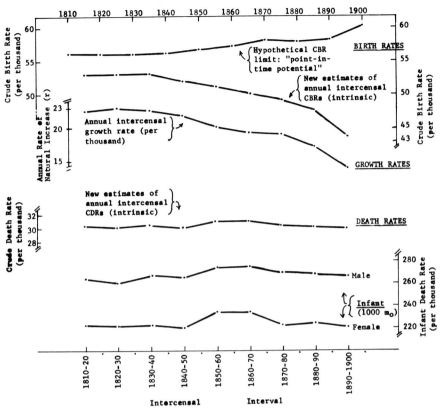

very profitable. However, because the new estimates are less sensational than the earlier ones, they raise some question as to the appropriateness of talking about slave breeding. For one thing, there was no abrupt change in black reproductive rates following the Civil War. In addition, it appears from another recent study (Eblen, 1974) that, when the various rates are standardized to compensate for differing levels of mortality, the black populations of Cuba and the United States were reproducing at about the same percentage of capacity during the nineteenth century. It is even possible that slaves in Cuba were reproducing at a relatively more rapid rate, without widespread encouragement, than were slaves in the United States. In either case, the high gross reproduction rates found for blacks in the United States prior to the Civil War cannot be explained by the fact that slaveholders generally promoted maximum reproduction among slaves.

The new estimates also reinforce the assertion that worsening mortality conditions accompanied the generally increased severity of slavery during the decades immediately before the Civil

War and the gross dislocations and other problems of the first years of Reconstruction. The onset of a secular decline in fertility and the growth rate, and an increase in infant mortality rates, all occurred during the same period, which precedes the urbanization of the black population. The decline in the growth rate and the higher mortality rates can be attributed, at least in part, to changes in the institution of slavery in the era of Sectionalism and Civil War, but mortality rates improved somewhat during the last three decades of the century, so the continued decline in the growth rate after the Civil War is associated only with the secular decline in the birth rate that began before the War. The decline in black fertility roughly paralleled the decline in white fertility during the nineteenth century. Presumably many of the same factors explain the decline in fertility in both populations. What these factors are is open to question, but it is clear that urbanization offers an even less convincing explanation for changes in black fertility than in white.

The viability of the new estimates can be inferred from the hypothetical constructs in the last two columns of Table 6. These columns present crude birth rate "limits" based on the reasonable enough assumption that the maximum birth rate for a high mortality population occurs when about 80 percent of the females of childbearing ages are fertile and bearing children and when the average childbearing interval is approximately three years. When applied to the $_nL_x$ values of the new life tables for the black population during the nineteenth century, these criteria produce the figures in the next to the last column. As can be seen, the maximum birth rate of the life table population is nearly constant at roughly 61 per thousand. The life table birth rate, however, is for a stationary population, that is, one with a stable age distribution whose size is neither increasing nor decreasing.

The figures in the last column are more relevant inasmuch as they reflect the changing growth rates and age distributions of the black population during the nineteenth century. These birth rates are based on the same reproductive criteria as the ones in the next to the last column but are calculated from the final female age distributions and population totals summarized in Table 2. Now the maximum possible crude birth rate is found to have increased from about 56 per thousand at the beginning of the century to almost 61 in 1900. When these limits are compared with the new estimates of the intrinsic birth rate, it is evident that a general decline in fertility set in between 1830 and 1840: at the beginning of the century the birth rate was near the maximum, but it declined to less than three-quarters of the potential by 1900.

The reproductive criteria used to establish maximum birth rates also impose limits on the growth of a population. This is an especially important matter when high mortality conditions prevail. In the case of the United States black population during the nineteenth century, the new estimates of vital rates place a limit of about 24 per thousand on the annual rate of natural increase. Under the higher mortality rates associated with the West models used previously to obtain estimates of vital rates, the same reproductive criteria impose a lower limit on the growth rate. However, the birth rates needed to achieve the growth rates observed and posited were well above the hypothetical birth rate limit, so one cannot avoid the conclusion that the estimates derived from the West models are untenable.

Altogether, this paper provides the first satisfactory estimates of vital rates for the black population that cover the nineteenth century in an empirically rational and comprehensive manner. One indication of this is that, when the differing methods and coverage are taken into account, the survival ratio curves ($_np_x$) of the life tables derived in this study couple nicely with those drawn from the death-registration states life tables which begin in 1900 (Glover, 1921; Hill, 1936; Greville, 1946; U. S. Public Health Service, various dates). In addition, a preliminary analysis of all the census data and life tables of the nineteenth and twentieth centuries indicates that a general improvement in black mortality conditions did not begin until the end of the nineteenth century and that improvements during the early decades of the twentieth occurred primarily by cohort. The youngest, and slightly later the oldest, appear to have experienced the first and the most substantial improvement in mortality rates. This is both a reaffirmation and an extension of the findings recently reported in a study of cohort survivorship in the death-registration states for the period from 1900 to 1968 (Moriyama and Gustavus, 1972). Moreover, when the various estimates of white birth rates (Coale and Zelnik, 1963; Thompson and Whelpton, 1933, summarized in U. S. Bureau of the Census, 1960) are compared with those for the total United States population during the nineteenth century (Sheldon, 1958, derived from the work of Thompson and Whelpton, 1933, and summarized in U. S. Bureau of the Census, 1960) to infer black rates, the results are wildly improbable if the raw census totals for the black population are used. The new population and birth rate estimates presented in this study, however, are compatible: the total United States birth rates appear to be quite reasonable as the product of the white estimates and the new black ones.

The new estimates for the black population in this study are optimum in that the annual growth rates are compatible with the observed ones, and the new population reconstructions and vital rates are compatible with those of the early twentieth century. The last point is confirmed both by the death-registration states life tables and by a reconstruction (Coale and Rives, 1973) of the black population for the period from 1880 to 1970, which was published after this study was completed. The death-registration states life tables are based on data for less than five percent of the black population. Furthermore, the data come from only a few states—all but Indiana and the District of Columbia in the industrial Northeast—where the blacks were largely urbanized; hence the data are to some degree unrepresentative of the total black population. It can be argued that the mortality rates of blacks in the death-registration states were slightly higher overall, but most noticeably in early childhood, than those of the black majority in the rural South. This alone could easily account for the rather small differences in Tables 4, 5, and 7 between the infant mortality rates and life table values of the death-registration states life tables and of the new estimates presented in this study.

The Coale and Rives reconstruction shows that the new estimates are optimum both by its similarities and its differences in the period of overlap, from 1880 to 1900. Although they used different assumptions and employed a more complex method of successive approximations, they arrived at fertility and age distribution estimates that are strikingly similar to the ones derived in this study. Thus the two growth curves dovetail almost perfectly to form a single curve for the period from 1810 to 1970 (see Figure 2). The complementarity of the estimates is apparent whether or not the adjusted Coale and Rives data for the period from 1880 to 1900 are considered (see Tables 8 and 9). Coale and Rives adopted a secondary sex ratio of 103, rather than 102, but their reconstruction differs from the one in this study primarily because they used different models. Their dependence on the West models and death-registration states life tables produced age distributions whose most

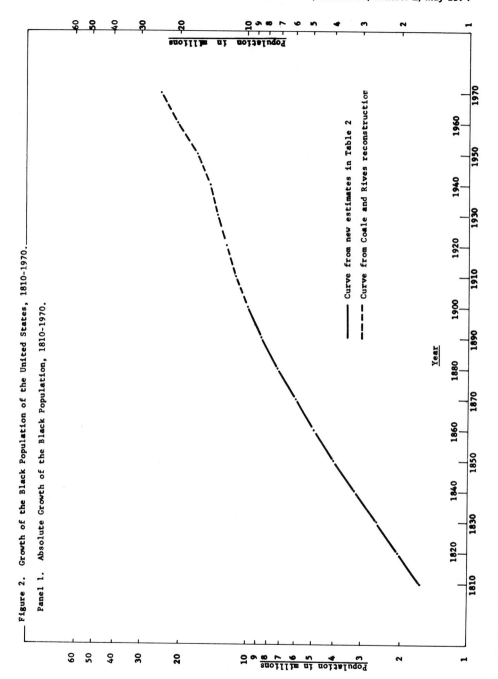

Figure 2. Growth of the Black Population of the United States, 1810-1970.

Panel 1. Absolute Growth of the Black Population, 1810-1970.

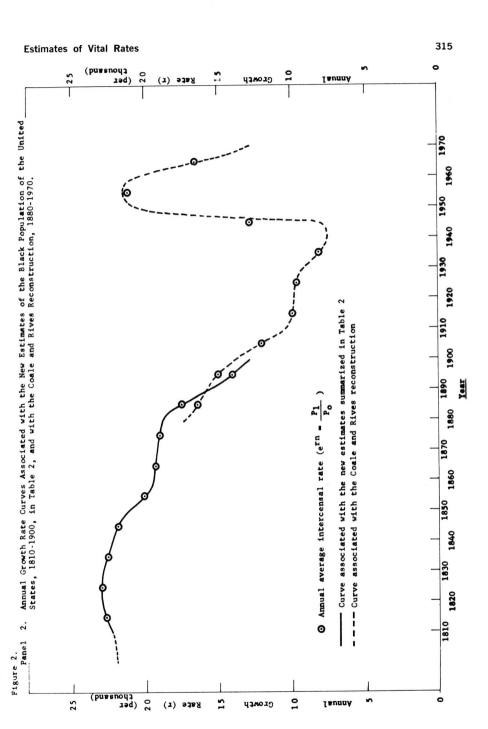

Figure 2.
Panel 2. Annual Growth Rate Curves Associated with the New Estimates of the Black Population of the United
States, 1810-1900, in Table 2, and with the Coale and Rives Reconstruction, 1880-1970.

⊙ Annual average intercensal rate ($e^{rn} = \frac{P_1}{P_0}$)

—— Curve associated with the new estimates summarized in Table 2

--- Curve associated with the Coale and Rives reconstruction

TABLE 8.—Comparison of the New Estimates in Table 2 with the Coale and Rives Reconstruction of the United States Black Population, 1880–1900

Sex and Age Group	1880 Coale and Rives Reconstruction Original	1880 Adjusted	1880 New Estimates from Table 2	1890 Coale and Rives Reconstruction Original	1890 Adjusted	1890 New Estimates from Table 2	1900 Coale and Rives Reconstruction Original	1900 Adjusted	1900 New Estimates from Table 2
Total, Both Sexes	7,241	7,209	7,211	8,535	8,589	8,587	9,921	9,874	9,875
Total Females	3,666	3,609	3,610	4,314	4,300	4,299	5,023	4,944	4,945
0– 9	1,166	1,148	1,140	1,313	1,308	1,314	1,426	1,404	1,398
10–19	807	795	817	998	995	981	1,148	1,130	1,132
20–29	601	592	596	711	709	717	895	881	861
30–39	442	435	428	511	509	508	615	605	611
40–49	299	294	299	364	363	362	429	422	431
50–59	197	194	189	234	233	234	290	285	282
60–69	108	106	93	129	129	120	156	154	149
70+	46	45	48	54	54	63	64	63	81
Total Males	3,575	3,600	3,601	4,221	4,289	4,288	4,898	4,930	4,930
0– 9	1,152	1,160	1,133	1,304	1,325	1,307	1,412	1,421	1,389
10–19	801	807	818	994	1,010	983	1,143	1,150	1,134
20–29	599	603	601	710	721	725	891	897	870
30–39	439	442	434	507	515	516	609	613	620
40–49	288	290	303	351	357	365	411	414	436
50–59	176	177	185	210	213	229	258	260	276
60–69	87	88	86	106	108	110	127	128	137
70+	33	33	41	39	40	53	47	47	68

Source: "Original" reconstruction is from Coale and Rives, 1973, p. 21. The Coale and Rives reconstruction was adjusted to make their total numbers of males and females at each census date equal to the ones in Table 2. The totals are not exactly equal because of rounding.

TABLE 9.—Estimated Net Census Undercounts of the Black Population, by Sex and Ten-Year Age Groups, 1880–1900: Percentages Based on Each of Three Reconstructions as the "True" Black Population

Sex and Age Group	1880 Coale and Rives Reconstruction Original	1880 Coale and Rives Reconstruction Adjusted	1880 New Estimates from Table 2	1890 Coale and Rives Reconstruction Original	1890 Coale and Rives Reconstruction Adjusted	1890 New Estimates from Table 2	1900 Coale and Rives Reconstruction Original	1900 Coale and Rives Reconstruction Adjusted	1900 New Estimates from Table 2
Total, Both Sexes	9.1%	8.7%	8.8%	12.3%	12.8%	12.8%	11.0%	10.5%	10.6%
Total Females	9.2	7.8	7.8	13.0	12.7	12.7	11.5	10.1	10.1
0- 9	8.8	7.4	6.8	18.6	18.3	18.6	14.4	13.1	12.7
10-19	8.9	7.5	10.0	3.5	3.2	1.8	7.9	6.5	6.6
20-29	-1.7	-3.2	-2.5	5.3	5.1	6.1	0.3	-1.2	-3.6
30-39	17.0	15.6	14.3	21.9	21.6	21.5	17.7	16.4	17.2
40-49	15.1	13.6	15.1	9.1	8.8	8.6	18.9	17.5	19.3
50-59	23.4	22.2	20.1	32.5	32.2	32.5	24.5	23.2	22.3
60-69	18.5	17.0	5.4	22.5	22.5	16.7	21.2	20.1	17.4
70+	-26.1	-28.9	-20.8	-11.1	-11.1	4.8	-28.1	-30.2	-1.2
Total Males	9.0	9.7	9.7	11.5	12.9	12.9	10.5	11.0	11.0
0- 9	10.2	10.9	8.7	16.6	17.9	16.8	14.2	14.7	12.7
10-19	10.0	10.7	11.9	3.9	5.4	2.8	10.1	10.6	9.3
20-29	2.7	3.3	3.0	11.5	12.9	13.4	7.5	8.1	5.3
30-39	19.1	19.7	18.2	24.5	25.6	25.8	18.2	18.8	19.7
40-49	17.0	17.6	21.1	12.0	13.4	15.3	14.8	15.5	19.7
50-59	4.5	5.1	9.2	0.5	1.9	8.7	1.6	2.3	8.0
60-69	-17.2	-15.9	-18.6	13.2	14.8	16.4	-12.6	-11.7	-4.4
70+	-51.5	-51.5	-22.0	-97.4	-92.5	-45.3	-63.8	-63.8	-13.2

Source: Calculated from Tables 1 and 8. "Original" reconstruction is from Coale and Rives, 1973, p. 21. The Coale and Rives reconstruction was adjusted to make their total numbers of males and females at each census date equal to the ones in Table 2. The totals are not exactly equal because of rounding.

obvious feature is that they contain many fewer elderly persons than do the distributions of this study. There are also higher death rates associated with the Level 5 West life tables that they appear to have used—a crude rate of around 36 to 37 per thousand and infant death rates ($1000 \, m_0$) of between 307 and 368—and these account for almost all of the differences in birth rate estimates since the growth rates are so nearly the same. Coale and Rives (1973, p. 26) show a decline in the birth rate from 58.6 in the 1850's to about 46.3 in the 1890's, as compared to 51.3 and 43.8, respectively, in this study.

Which set of estimates one picks involves some value judgements, but the ones presented in this study are intuitively more credible and satisfying for several reasons. It can be argued that the estimates of this study best reflect what one would expect to find for a black minority in a white society whose mortality rates were much lower: lower black infant mortality rates than one would predict in a more homogeneous situation where West models were perhaps suitable, somewhat greater survival among the advanced ages, and consequently higher life expectancies than might otherwise be anticipated. In short, it may be supposed that at least the very young and the elderly blacks, free and slave, benefited somewhat—albeit indirectly, unconsciously and incompletely—from living among or in close proximity with the whites.

Life expectancies lower than the ones presented in this study, and closer to those implied by the Coale and Rives reconstruction, could be derived for the nineteenth century by increasing the infant and early childhood mortality rates estimated in this study to improbable and unacceptable levels and by reducing the annual growth rate. This would produce total population estimates at various points in time that would differ from the enumerated totals by more than is

likely. Life expectancies higher than the ones in this study could be obtained within the general context of the observed growth rates by reducing the estimates of infant mortality, but neither the resultant life expectancies nor the infant mortality rates would be plausible. They would be incompatible with data for the twentieth century and would require one to accept the incredible proposition that blacks were significantly better off throughout the nineteenth century than in the early twentieth.

The methodology developed for this study relies primarily upon the interplay of the variability in the percentages of age distribution and in the survival ratios of model life table networks with an annual growth rate curve. Because it depends so heavily on cohort survival, the most reliable fit of data within a network occurs when several cohorts can be followed through the majority of their lives. This does not mean, however, that one must have data that cover all or even most of the period in question for each, or any, cohort. For this reason, the method is equally well suited for interpolation and extrapolation. It is especially adapted to historical analyses and reconstructions, but it can be used just as well to make population projections.

The method could be improved upon by using computers to obtain a best fit within the model life table networks at two or more levels. For the black population of the nineteenth century, it would certainly be appropriate to consider a fit within the U.N. Level 30 networks, and perhaps the Level 40, as well as the Level 20. Because of the overlapping nature of the networks, the reconstructions obtained from two or three successive networks ought to be very similar. One could thus either select from them the results most compatible with the raw data from which the analysis originated, or if all were equally plausible, use them all together to establish bounds for the parameters sought.

ACKNOWLEDGMENTS

This is a revised and updated version of a paper presented at the session on historical demography at the 1973 annual meeting of the Population Association of America in New Orleans. The study was completed during the year 1972–1973, when the author was a National Institute of Child Health and Human Development Special Research Fellow (1 FO3 HD 53486-01) at the Department of Population Dynamics, School of Hygiene and Public Health, Johns Hopkins University. The author wishes to thank all of the people whose thoughtful comments have contributed to the revision of this paper.

REFERENCES

Coale, Ansley J., and Paul Demeny. 1966. Regional Model Life Tables and Stable Populations. Princeton: Princeton University Press.

———, and Norfleet W. Rives, Jr. 1973. A Statistical Reconstruction of the Black Population of the United States 1880–1970: Estimates of True Numbers by Age and Sex, Birth Rates, and Total Fertility. Population Index 39:3–36.

———, and Melvin Zelnik. 1963. New Estimates of Fertility and Population in the United States: A Study of Annual White Births from 1855 to 1960 and of the Completeness of Enumeration in the Censuses from 1880 to 1960. Princeton: Princeton University Press.

Conrad, Alfred H., and John R. Meyer. 1958. The Economics of Slavery in the *ante bellum* South. Journal of Political Economy 66:95–122.

Eblen, Jack E. 1972. Growth of the Black Population in *ante bellum* America, 1820–1860. Population Studies 26:273–289.

———. 1974. On the Natural Increase of Slave Populations: The Example of the Cuban Slave Population, 1775–1900. In Stanley L. Engerman and Eugene D. Genovese (eds.), Slavery and Race in the Western Hemisphere: Quantitative Studies. Princeton: Princeton University Press.

Farley, Reynolds. 1965. The Demographic Rates and Social Institutions of the Nineteenth-Century Negro Population: A Stable Population Analysis. Demography 2:386–398.

———. 1970. Growth of the Black Population: A Study of Demographic Trends. Chicago: Markham Publishing Co.

Glover, James W. 1921. United States Life Tables, 1890, 1901, 1910, and 1901–1910. Washington, D. C.: Government Printing Office.

Greville, Thomas N. E. 1946. Sixteenth Census of the United States: 1940. United States Life Tables and Actuarial Tables, 1939–1941. Washington, D. C.: Government Printing Office.

Hill, Joseph A. 1936. United States Life Tables, 1929 to 1931, 1920 to 1929, 1919 to 1921, 1909 to 1911, 1901 to 1910, 1900 to 1902. Washington, D. C.: Government Printing Office.

Moriyama, Iwao M., and Susan O. Gustavus. 1972. Cohort Mortality and Survivorship: United States Death-Registration States, 1900–1968. National Center for Health Statistics, Series 3, No. 16. Washington, D. C.: Government Printing Office.

Sheldon, Henry D. 1958. The Older Population of the United States. New York: John Wiley and Sons, Inc.

Shryock, Henry S., Jacob S. Siegel, and Associates. 1973. The Methods and Materials of Demography (rev. ed.). Washington, D. C.: Government Printing Office.

Thompson, Warren S., and P. K. Whelpton. 1933. Population Trends in the United States. New York: McGraw-Hill Publishing Co.

U. S. Bureau of the Census. 1918. The Negro Population of the United States, 1790–1915. Washington, D. C.: Government Printing Office.

———. 1960. Historical Statistics of the United States: Colonial Times to 1957. Washington, D. C.: Government Printing Office.

U. S. Public Health Service. Various dates. Life Tables. Vital Statistics of the United States. Washington, D. C.: Government Printing Office.

United Nations. 1968. The Concept of a Stable Population: Application to the Study of Populations of Countries with Incomplete Demographic Statistics. Population Studies, No. 39. New York: United Nations.

Wright, Carrol D. 1900. History and Growth of the United States Census. Washington, D. C.: Government Printing Office.

Zelnik, Melvin. 1966. Fertility of the American Negro in 1830 and 1850. Population Studies 20:77–83.

ELIZABETH H. PLECK

THE TWO-PARENT HOUSEHOLD: BLACK FAMILY STRUCTURE IN LATE NINETEENTH-CENTURY BOSTON

Once the most rural of American ethnic groups, Afro-Americans are now the most urban. Slavery, migration to the city and the adaptation to urban culture have had major effects on black life, yet we know little about the ways in which the most basic unit of black life, the family, was affected by these changes. Through research in the manuscript census schedules of the federal census for 1880 and other largely quantitative materials, I looked for answers to the following questions. What was the effect of migration on the black family? What was the occupational situation of black heads of household? How did urban and rural families differ in their adaptation to life in the city? How did literate and illiterate families differ? What family forms predominated? How frequent was "family disorganization," as reflected in an imbalanced sex ratio, frequent desertions by the head of household and large numbers of female-headed households?

We can learn a great deal about black family life from an examination of Boston in the late nineteenth century. The Hub was a major northern metropolis, with a large and diversified economy, which should have offered opportunities for unskilled but willing black workers. As a result of the long efforts of blacks and whites in the abolitionist movement, the city had no segregated institutions and a widely respected system of free

Ms. Pleck is a graduate student in History of American Civilization at Brandeis University. A Ford Foundation Dissertation Fellowship in Ethnic Studies financed the research cited in this article. The author's ideas about the black family have been greatly influenced by the comments and work of Herbert Gutman, whose forthcoming book on the black family should greatly enlarge our knowledge of the subject. The revision of this paper has benefited from the criticism of Stephan Thernstrom. The author is especially indebted to Joseph Pleck for writing the computer programs employed in this study, and for his aid in data analysis and the use of statistical techniques. Useful comments and suggestions for changes in this article were made by Gordon Fellman, Allan Kulikoff, John Demos, Doug Jones and Peter Knights.

Reprinted from *Journal of Social History* VI, No. 1, 3–31. Copyright © 1972 by permission of the publisher.

public schools. Boston had acquired a reputation among blacks as "the paradise of the Negro," a city of unparalleled freedom and opportunity.[1] Since the black population was so small a percentage of the inhabitants of the city, the racial fears and animosities of the white population appeared, surfaced, but did not explode into major race riots like those in New York and Philadelphia during the Civil War. The large Irish and small black populations lived in an uneasy truce, with the two groups dwelling in close proximity in the west and south ends of the city. Unique in some ways, representative of major Northern cities in others, Boston is an interesting city in which to study many facets of black family life.

The most typical black household in late nineteenth-century Boston included the husband and wife, or husband, wife and children. This predominant household form prevailed among all occupational levels and among families of both urban and rural origins. By enlarging the household to include boarders, families from all occupational strata augmented the family income and provided homes for the large numbers of migrants in the population. This evidence from the manuscript census contradicts the commonly held association between "the tangle of pathology," "family disorganization" and the black family.

Before examining the composition of the black household, I will indicate how inferences were made about the origins and literacy of heads of household and I will discuss three aspects of social life in Boston—the transiency of the population, the depressing occupational position of black heads of household and the physical circumstances of life—which severely constrained family survival.

Comparison of Rural and Urban, Literate
and Illiterate Heads of Household

In the analysis of one- and two-parent households which follows, the foreign-born heads of household were excluded since they offer too few cases for valid comparisons.[2] Comparing the Northern- and Southern-born heads of household, I looked for possible differences in urban and rural family adaptation to life in Boston. Since the manuscript census schedules indicate the state of birth of an individual, but not the city or area where the individual was born or raised, the comparison is imperfect. Although a majority of Northern-born blacks lived most of their lives in urban areas, the Northern-born category also included farmers from New England, townspeople from western Massachusetts and settlers from the free black communities of Ohio. By further separating those born in Massachusetts (mostly natives of Boston) from the rest of the Northern-born, I was able to discern differences between that part of the population which was born in Boston and that portion of the population which migrated into the city.

While most Southern-born blacks were rural folk, that category also includes city-dwellers from Richmond, Baltimore, or Washington, D.C. Even more difficult to distinguish are those Southern-born blacks who were urban in experience, if not in place of birth. But despite these qualifications, it seems useful to perceive the Northern-born as essentially an urban group, and the Southern-born as a rural group.[3]

The distinction between literacy and illiteracy may have been as important as the difference between urban and rural families. Seven out of ten black adults could read a few words and sign their names, the nineteenth-century standard of literacy. Even this minimal knowledge reflected a variety of skills which facilitated successful adaptation to urban life. Those without such skills—the illiterates—were more at a disadvantage than they were on the farm and more noticeable for their deficiency as well. Whole families headed by illiterates faced far greater difficulties in cities than those headed by literate parents.

In the South, illiterates tended to be ex-slaves.[4] (The equation of illiteracy and slave status would have been unneccessary had the Boston census takers directly enumerated the number of freedmen in the black population.) Under slavery, most blacks were not taught to read or write or were prevented from even learning. While there were exceptions, self-educated slaves (Frederick Douglass is the best-known example), the opportunities for literacy were much greater for free blacks than for slaves. But before equating Southern-born illiterates with ex-slaves, two important qualifications must be added. First, even the majority of free blacks like the slaves, was untutored. Second, the number of illiterates was very low, far below any estimate we might make of the number of ex-slaves in the population.[5] Thus, while illiteracy appeared in both Northern- and Southern-born families, its presence among the Southern-born, in addition, reflected the existence of ex-slaves in the population.

Geographic Mobility

From the 3,496 blacks living in Boston in 1870, the population grew ten years later to include 5,873 persons.[6] By 1910, the population had expanded three times to 13,654. In the same forty-year period, the white population grew over two and one-half times, and the foreign-born white population tripled. The metropolis was growing rapidly, and within the city the black population, although small in absolute number and in size relative to the white population—never more than two percent of the total population throughout the period—was growing at a rate faster than that of the foreign-born immigrants.[7]

In the late nineteenth century the black population absorbed a large number of migrants. Though a minority, 42 percent of Boston's blacks in 1880, had been born in the North, a majority were strangers to Northern life; 49 percent of the population was born in the South, while another 9 percent were born in foreign countries. Of the Northern-born population, especially those born in Massachusetts, the majority probably were natives of Boston. Other Northern-born blacks came from neighboring cities in the Northeast and a few were from rural areas in New England. For the foreign-born, their life in Boston was the culmination of the long journey from Nova Scotia, New Brunswick, or other parts of Canada, or the end of a long sea voyage from the West Indies. The largest group in the population, the Southern-born, included migrants from the Upper South, especially Virginia.

These Southern newcomers seem to contradict prevailing theories of migration to cities.[8] Rather than travelling short distances and settling at the first stop along the way, these migrants moved as much as five hundred miles from home, often passing through other urban centers. Why did these men and women make the long journey? The usual explanation of black migration to the North refers to Jim Crow segregation, racism and declining economic opportunities in the South, combined with the expanding economy and promise of a freer life in the North. Pushed out by Southern conditions, pulled to the North, the land of golden streets and busy factories, the combination of push and pull factors explain the Great Migration, the period during and after the First World War. The earlier movement, described by Carter Woodson as the migration of the Talented Tenth, represented a period when blacks were more "pulled" to the North than "pushed" from the South.[9] The absence of two factors—widespread agricultural depression and active recruitment of blacks by Northern employment agents—further distinguished the earlier migration from the Great Migration of World War I. Despite the propaganda of some of their brethren and the appeals of some Southern whites, the black emigrant was above all looking for a better life in the Northern city. One migrant was Ella Beam, a young woman who left the South Carolina Sea Islands for Boston:

She stated that she did not leave home on account of hard times. When she left, her father was doing well on the farm. There were several boys in the family, so she was rarely called upon to go into the fields. She felt, however, that she was not especially needed at home. The fact that she manifested sufficient initiative to take the course at the training school [domestic science] is perhaps indicative of the courage and energy of a young woman who wanted to better her condition. She had been in Boston only one year when she received a simple job caring for children in the home of a Melrose family.[10]

For the most part, the migrants included young adults above the age of twenty, very few of whom came with their families. In households headed by a Southern-born parent, 72.1 percent of the oldest children in the family were born in the North. Among the oldest children of a Canadian parent, 60.7 percent had been born in the North. Six out of seven of the oldest children in West Indian families had been born in the North. Thus the migration from the South and from foreign countries included single individuals or couples, but in very few cases did the whole family make the move.

The story of migration does not end with the arrival of the newcomer in Boston. Instead of settling down, the transient frequently packed up and left. Evidence from several nineteenth-century cities in the Northeast indicates a high rate of black migration, generally higher than that of other groups. But in the South and West the rate of black out-migration was about the same or a little lower than among other groups. Assuming this pattern is substantiated in further research, it indicates the absence of job opportunities for black workers in nearby Southern areas, in contrast to the proximity of many cities in the urban Northeast where the transient could find employment.

An examination of Boston city directories reveals that only 25 percent of adult black males listed in the 1880 census were enumerated in the 1890 city directory, while 64 percent of a representative sample of adult white males in 1880 remained in the city ten years later.[11] The rate of persistence for blacks was very similar among all occupational levels, as Table 1 suggests, while the rate of persistence among white males decreased for lower status workers.[12]

Table 1. Proportion of Adult Male Residents of Boston in 1880 Persisting There to 1890, by Racial Group, Household Status and Occupational Level[a]

	Overall Persistence Rate	White Collar	Skilled	Unskilled and Service	N
White Residents[b]	64%	72%	63%	56%	1,809
All Blacks	25%	26%	25%	25%	1,992
Heads of household	31%	35%	28%	32%	1,066
Sons	21%	25%	33%	15%	63

[a] The white collar category includes professionals, clerical workers, and petty proprietors. Heads of household include black males in single member households, as well as the more prevalent one- and two-parent households. Adult males were defined as those 21 and over. Sons include adult males residing at home. Persistence rates for women were extremely difficult to estimate because of name changes due to marriage and the incomplete city directory coverage given to women who were not heading households. There was no statistically significant relationship between occupational level and persistence for all blacks, nor was there a significant relationship for heads of households or sons.

[b] Data for white residents is from Stephan Thernstrom and Elizabeth H. Pleck, "The Last of the Immigrants? A Comparative Analysis of Immigrant and Black Social Mobility in Late-Nineteenth Century Boston," unpublished paper delivered at the annual meeting of the Organization of American Historians (April, 1970), p. 12.

Among blacks heading households, the rate of persistence was 31 percent, compared with the 25 percent overall figure. Adult sons residing at home, although few in number, were more transient than their fathers, since only 21 percent of them remained in the city for the decade 1880-1890.

High rates of turnover were common in other Northeastern cities. In the depression years of the 1870s black out-migration occurred frequently among Poughkeepsie and Buffalo residents. Only one-third of the black workers in Poughkeepsie in 1870 remained in the city ten years later.[13] In a twenty year trace of black adult males in Buffalo from 1855 to 1875, only 12 percent could be found.[14]

The Northern pattern of high black out-migration and much lower out-migration for other groups is reversed in the South and West. In Atlanta, for example, blacks were much more likely to remain in the city than either foreign-born whites or native whites. Even more remarkable, within all occupational categories, the black departure rate was lower than that of native white and foreign-born immigrants.[15] For Birmingham, Alabama, the much higher rate of black persistence was the result of fewer opportunities elsewhere for black workers.[16] During the depression decade 1870-1880, in San Antonio, blacks, European immigrants and native whites had very similar rates of persistence—36 percent for blacks, 36 percent for European immigrants and 35 percent for native whites—while the Chicano population was the most transient, with only 25 percent of the male population remaining there ten years later.[17] The question remains whether this pattern of Southern black geographic stability was also reflected in long-lasting marriages and continuity of parental care for black children.

Occupational Structure

The occupational position of black heads of household placed a great strain on the black family. While the children of white immigrants moved up the occupational ladder, the black child, like his parent, remained fixed in a world of menial and temporary jobs. Eight occupations—waiter, servant, cook, barber, laborer, porter, laundress and seamstress—accounted for 74 percent of all blacks at work in Boston in 1880. The largest group by far were the 858 servants who worked in white homes, hotels and institutions. Two occupations, laundress and seamstress, were largely the preserve of single women and women heading households. The last hired and the first fired, blacks in late nineteenth-century Boston formed a surplus labor force at the bottom of society.

The concentration of blacks in unskilled and service occupations is demonstrated in Table 2.

Table 2. Occupational Level of Black Male and Female Heads of Household, Black Non-Heads of Household, and Irish, 1880

	Black Heads of Household[a]		Black Non-Heads of Household		All blacks at work	All Irish at work[b]
	Male	Female	Male	Female		
Professional	36	1	25	25	87	562
	3.4%[c]	.6%	2.3%	2.9%	3.2%	1.6%
White Collar	33	2	52	6	93	3,333
	3.1%	1.3%	4.8%	.7%	2.9%	9.6%
Skilled	72	31	54	84	241	6,880
	6.8%	19.4%	5.0%	9.7%	7.2%	19.8%
Unskilled and Service	925	126	950	751	2,752	23,970
	86.8%	78.8%	87.9%	86.7%	86.7%	68.9%
Total	1,066	160	1,081	866	3,173	34,745

[a] heads of household with no occupation were omitted from the head of household group

[b] derived from data in Carroll Wright, *Social, Commerical, and Manufacturing Statistics of the city of Boston* (Boston: Rockwell and Churchill, 1882), pp. 92-116.

[c] Column percentages sometimes do not add up to 100 due to rounding. The relationship between occupational level and household status (head of household vs. non-head of household) is significant at .030 with three degrees of freedom for males, significant at .002 with three degrees of freedom for females.

Overall, 86.7 percent of the total black work force consisted of unskilled and service workers, 7.2 percent of black workers held skilled positions, 2.9 percent performed clerical jobs or owned small shops and 3.2 percent were professionals. Table 2 also includes the percentage of Irish workers in 1880 in each of these occupational status groups. An immigrant group of peasant origins, the Boston Irish were the white ethnic group which ranked lowest in the Boston social order. Except at the top of the occupational structure, where there was a slightly higher percentage of professionals among the black work force than among the Irish, Irish workers had much larger percentages of white-collar

ELIZABETH H. PLECK

and skilled workers and much smaller percentages of unskilled and service workers than the black labor force. While 68.9 percent of the Irish were laborers, teamsters, hostlers and other unskilled and service workers, 86.7 percent of blacks performed this low status work. The classification of menial labor, moreover, tends to obscure the wage differences between the two groups. The black waiter and the Irish cotton mill operative both worked long hours at low pay, but the rewards were somewhat greater for the Irish worker than for his black counterpart.

Of all wage earners, 7.2 percent of the blacks and 19.8 percent of the Irish were skilled workers. Such work, particularly in the building trades, required apprenticeship training which was generally closed to blacks; even buying tools could be an expensive proposition for a black worker. The white-collar group, over three times as large among the Irish as among blacks, owed their jobs to the expansion of record-keeping, paper work and sales in an industrial society. The new jobs in the Boston labor market—office personnel, sales clerks, even telephone and telegraph operators— employed some of the children of Irish parents, while job discrimination and lack of the proper educational qualifications closed this employment to the aspiring black worker. The figures for the white-collar group also reflected the larger proportion of petty proprietors among the Irish than among blacks.

For the black professionals, Boston deserved its reputation as the city of the "Talented Tenth." The relatively large number of black lawyers, doctors and other professionals, compared with the somewhat smaller Irish percentage, was the result of the attractiveness of the city to educated blacks from the South and other parts of the North, as well as the educational opportunities for the black elite in the New England area.

Even so, the black child and the black parent clearly faced more limited job opportunities than even the proletarian Boston Irish. How did the occupational situation of heads of household compare with that of the black worker with no family responsibilities? Although the head of household, in order to support dependents, needed to earn more money than the unattached black worker, Table 2 indicates that there were virtually no differences in occupational situation between blacks heading household and those not heading households. Among unskilled and service workers, one finds 86.8 percent of black heads of household and 87.9 percent of the unattached black workers.

Providing for a family was even more difficult for the widowed or deserted wife. Female-headed households included 22 women with no occupations and 105 women at work, most of them in unskilled and service jobs. The skilled category in Table 2, which includes 18 percent of female workers, is the result of the large number of black seamstresses among females heading households.

Black workers, including male heads of household, female heads of household and workers with no family responsibilities were concentrated in the lowest ranks of the occupational structure. While there were slight differences in occupational level for heads of household as compared with all other workers, heads of household, in general, were no more occupationally diverse than other black workers.

Conditions of Life

In the vast new areas of Boston, large frame houses with plenty of rooms, indoor plumbing and spacious backyards were being built for the middle class. But the streetcar suburbs of late nineteenth-century Boston were restricted to whites. In 1880, about 42 percent of the black population lived in the West End (sometimes referred to as "Nigger Hill"), a conglomeration of tiny alleyways and side streets on the seamy side of Beacon Hill. Tenement commissioners visiting the area described filthy streets, polluted air, overcrowded housing, dirty cellars, unsanitary water closets, poor drainage and unsafe buildings.[18]

At No. – Anderson Street is a little court. Here a single water closet in a small shed, the bowl filled and in abominable condition, was the only accommodation in this line for eight or ten families of colored people, besides the hands in a stable and a couple of little shops.[19]

Since the tenement rooms were crowded, poorly heated and ventilated, children played in the street. Playing stickball in the summer and using Anderson and Phillips streets as ski slopes in the winter, black children made the most of their urban environment.[20] But street play also resulted in children being crushed under the wheels of fast-moving teams of horses.

The poor physical conditions and the inability of parents to provide an adequate family income resulted in sickness and sometimes death for black children. Mission workers from a settlement in the West End found "a young girl, whose only bed was two broken chairs placed between the cooking stove and the door. She was dying with consumption and was left all day with the care of a two year-old child, tied into a chair beside her, while its mother was at work." In the same neighborhood, they found a poor black child "who shared the floor with the rats and mice on a cold winter's night."[21] These cases were probably the most dramatic, not the typical circumstances of black poverty in the West End. The mission workers, no doubt, chose examples which would underline the importance of their work and the need for hospital care for their clients.

Individual human tragedies like the deaths of these two children are hidden in the high death rates in the Boston black community. Although the birth rate for blacks was higher than for whites, the number of deaths was so great that deaths generally exceeded births. In fact, 1905-1910 was the first five-year period since the Civil War when the black birth rate was higher than the death rate.[22] Year after year, the city registrar reported more black deaths than births. In 1884, the registrar speculated that "there can be no question that, so far as the limited field furnished by this city affords the means of judging, were accessions from without to cease, the colored population would, in time, disappear from our community."[23] Arguing that the "colored" race was unsuited to Northern climates, he concluded: "In short, it would not be too much to say, that were all opposing obstacles of every kind, and in every direction, to the entire liberty of the colored race removed, and they were allowed to seek and occupy any position they were qualified to fill, they would instinctively and inevitably gravitate to southern and congenial latitudes as naturally as water seeks its own level."[24]

As a result of poor diet, extremely high rates of infant mortality and deaths for mothers in childbirth and the frequent incidence of tuberculosis and contagious diseases, the mortality rate for the black population in 1886 was 41 per 1000, almost twice the white rate.[25] A black person who grew up in the West End recalled that on Sundays after church his family discussed the number of deaths in the neighborhood and which of the neighbors were dying of consumption.[26] Diseases connected with childbirth accounted for the slightly higher death rate among black females than among black males. In 1890 the death rate per 1000 for white males in Boston was 15.86, for black males, 32. Among white females the mortality rate was 24 out of 1000, while black females died at the rate of 35 for every 1000.[27]

The death rate was highest among children under one year of age, and higher still among male children. But significant reductions in infant mortality for both whites and blacks led to a sharp decline in the death rate in the first decade of the twentieth century. From 1900 to 1910, the white death rate for children under one year of age fell from 189 per 1000 to 185, while the black death rate dropped from 322 to 294.[28] These figures were comparable to the mortality rates in other Northern and Western cities.[29]

The high death rate among adults created a large number of widowed persons. About one-third of women aged 41-50 and a little less than half of women aged 51-60 lost their husbands. Either as a result of migration or in consequence of a higher rate of remarriage, the census takers found only about one-third as many widowers as widows. Some of the widows remarried, others went to live with relatives and the remaining women made up the bulk of one-parent households in the black community.

The death of both parents left about 17 percent of black children homeless in Boston in 1880. These orphans were a much larger part of the population in late nineteenth-century cities than were the one out of ten black youngsters in 1968 who were not living with one or both parents.[30] Homeless black children, in most cases, lived with relatives or friends, for few such children found their way into asylums and homes for foundling children. Discrimination by public institutions combined with the desire of black families to adopt black children meant that few black children without parents became wards of the state.

Family Structure

The high death rate and overcrowded, unsanitary tenements,

the transiency of the population and the low occupational position constitute the kinds of pressures often cited as the causes of family disorganization. But several quantitative indicators—the sex ratio, the small number of one-parent households, the infrequency of desertion and the adaptation of the household to include large numbers of migrants—suggest that the black family structure maintained its organization despite the many depressing aspects of life in Boston.

Several statistics are useful gauges of the nature of family life. One such statistic is the sex ratio, the number of males per one hundred females in the population. A western frontier area, with a ratio of males to females of ten to one, or even higher, would have little family life. For everyone who chose to marry, a stable ratio of males to females would theoretically insure the selection of a mate. Another arrangement of sex ratio, a small male population and a large female population, is said to produce a society with few stable marriages and high rates of illegitimacy, desertion, delinquency and female-headed households. These theoretical possibilities, reasonable in the abstract, have less meaning in concrete historical situations. Even in societies with quite similar sex ratios, great deviations can occur in patterns of sexuality, marriage and family life. Still, for a population on the move, such as the black population over the last one hundred years, the possibility of imbalanced sex ratios due to large numbers of migrants is an important consideration in assessing the framework of family life.[31]

In fact, among blacks in late nineteenth-century Boston, parity of the sexes existed, as the third column of Table 3 discloses.

Table 3. Sex Ratios for Native Whites, Foreign-Born Whites, and Blacks, 1880[a] (Males per 100 Females)

	Native White	Foreign-Born White	Black
All Ages	95.7	79.4	102.9
25 44	95.9	83.8	121.0

[a] derived from data in Carroll Wright, *Social, Commercial, and Manufacturing Statistics*, pp. 94-95.

The overall sex ratio in 1880 was 102.9 though much higher= 121—for the marriageable age group of those 25 to 44. In two other age groups, the very young and the very old, there were more females than males, reflecting the differential mortality of the sexes. The preponderance of males in the 25 to 44 age group stems from the relatively greater economic opportunities drawing adult migrants to the city. Many of these males were "beachhead" migrants, husbands who sent for their wives after they had established themselves in Boston.

When the black sex ratio is contrasted with the sex ratio of the foreign-born and native white populations, we find greater imbalances in the two white groups. For all native whites in 1880 the sex ratio was 95.7, while it was much lower—79.4—for foreign-born whites. Among young adults, Table 3 indicates that there were 96 native white males for every one hundred females, and 83.8 foreign-born white males for every one hundred females. The large number of adult females in the foreign-born white group reflects the presence of adult working women, usually employed as domestic servants and factory workers, some of whom were earning enough money to finance their dowries.

Throughout the last decades of the nineteenth century, there were slightly more males than females in the black population of Boston. Only in 1910 did the census takers find the reverse. Many young adult females, migrants to Boston, created this surplus of females in the population.[32]

The second important statistic for assessing the possibilities of family life is the number of married persons deserted by their spouse. Even though parity in the sex ratio suggests the necessary environment for stable family life, it is still quite possible that a high number of desertions would modify this conclusion. The number of desertions was determined by tabulating all those married persons in the census record who were not living with their spouse. Of those deserted by their spouses, there were 157 females, about 11 percent of all married women, and 167 males, about 13 percent of all married men in this category. The figures for males, as we noted earlier, were probably increased by the large number of men awaiting the arrival of their wives. In a middle-class district of the late nineteenth-century Chicago, where few of the desertions could be explained as the result of large numbers of migrants, about 11 percent of households included a deserted wife or husband.[33]

What seems impressive in these figures for blacks in Boston is the low rate of desertion and separation, given the extremely high rate of out-migration, even among heads of household, and the dismal occupational prospect that blacks faced. W.E.B. DuBois discussed some of the causes of desertion and separation among blacks in Philadelphia.

The economic difficulties arise continually among young waiters and servant girls; away from home and oppressed by the peculiar lonesomeness of a great city, they form chance acquaintances here and there, thoughtlessly marry and soon find that the husband's income cannot alone support a family, then comes a struggle which generally results in desertion or voluntary separation.[34]

As a result of death, desertion or voluntary separation, 18 percent of black households came to be headed by one parent. In nine out of ten instances the one parent was a female. In assessing one- and two-parent households, I included households in which there were no children present as well as those with children. If childless couples were excluded, we would be unable to examine households of young couples, that is, future parents, as well as those households where grown offspring had moved away.

How did one- and two-parent households differ? Without substantial historical evidence it would be foolhardy to apply present-day, widely questioned theories about the "tangle of pathology" associated with one-parent households.[35] Regrettably, I have found no qualitative evidence which bears on the issue of how members of the black community viewed the one-parent household.

Nevertheless, there was an important economic difference between the one- and two-parent household. Although precise income figures are not available for black households, black males enjoyed higher wages than black females. In consequence, a family dependent on a woman's wages almost always lived in poverty. The yearly wage among female domestic servants, for example, was half the wage of male domestic servants.[36] Moreover, given the concentration of female heads of household in the most poorly remunerated occupations, overall income levels between male- and female-headed households were even more disparate. In many two-parent households, the husband's wage was supplemented by his wife's earnings from domestic services or laundry work and the rent money from the boarder. Without these several income sources, the one-parent household was at an even greater disadvantage. Lacking the wages or unpaid labor of a wife, even the one-parent household headed by a male suffered economically.

From an analysis of the manuscript census schedules, three important distinctions emerged among two-parent households in the black community. First, there were proportionately more two-parent households among migrants to Boston than among native Bostonians. Second, the proportion of two-parent households among rural blacks was greater than among urban blacks. Finally, literate blacks headed two-parent households more often than illiterate blacks.

As we observed above, the early movement of blacks to Boston brought persons especially attracted to the advantages of the Northern city. Both those heads of household from the rural South and those Northern heads of household from outside of Massachusetts revealed large and almost identical proportions of two-parent households, 83.3 percent and 83.4 percent respectively, while native Bostonians contributed fewer two-parent households. Given the many theories about the disruptive nature of migration, we might expect a higher percentage of one-parent households among the newcomers to the city than among the long-established urban blacks. But Table 4 reveals that the percentage of two-parent households among the two migrant streams of the population was significantly greater than among black Bostonians.

Table 4. One and Two-Parent Households,
by Place and Birth of the Head of Household[a]

	Born in Massachusetts	Born in another Northern State	Total Northern Born	Born in the South	N
One-Parent	36 27.1%	27 16.6%	63 21.3%	136 16.7%	199 18.0%
Two-Parent	97 72.9%	136 83.4%	233 78.7%	676 83.3%	909 82.0%

[a] This table omits foreign-born heads of household, heads of household with no place of birth, and single-member households. The relationship between place of birth and household status is significant at .02, with two degrees of freedom.

Thus, the stereotype of disruptive migration does not fit the situation of blacks in late nineteenth-century Boston.

The combined effects of rural origins and long-distance movement away from family and friends made Southern-born, rural migrants to Boston a distinctive group. We can compare the effect of rural origins on the household by contrasting rural heads of household (the Southern-born) with urban heads of household (the Northern-born). As we note in Table 4, slightly more two-parent households occurred among rural than among urban heads of household, 83.3 percent as opposed to 78.7 percent. If we assume that a majority of the Southern-born blacks were freedmen, the large number of two-parent households among them is even more remarkable. The common argument, that the abrupt transition from rural to urban life created indelible strains on the black family, does not hold for late nineteenth-century Boston. If anything, we find the reverse of this common proposition. It is clear from column four of Table 4 that households in which both parents were present were more frequent among rural than among urban black heads of household.

Even greater than variations between urban and rural households were variations within these two types of households. Table 5 bears on this issue, differentiating urban and rural blacks according to the literacy of the head of household.

Table 5. One and Two-Parent Households, by Place of Birth and Literacy of the Head of Household, 1880[a]

| | Northern-Born | | | Southern-Born | | | |
	Literate	Illiterate	TOTAL	Literate	Illiterate	TOTAL	N
One-Parent	52	11	63	77	59	136	199
	19.9%	31.4%	21.3%	13.5%	24.3%	16.7%	18.0%
Two-Parent	209	24	233	492	184	676	909
	80.1%	68.6%	78.7%	86.5%	75.7%	83.3%	82.0%
Total	261	35	296	569	243	812	1,108

[a] Table omits foreign-born heads of household, heads of household with no place of birth, and single-member households. The relationship between literacy and household status was significant at .180 with one degree of freedom for the Northern-born, significant at .001 with one degree of freedom for the Southern-born.

For both urban and rural heads of household, a literate black was more likely to head a two-parent household than an illiterate. The percentage of two-parent households dropped from 86.5 percent of Southern-born literates to 75.7 percent among illiterates from the same region, and from 80.1 percent among Northern-born literates to only 68.6 percent among illiterates born in the North. Although these Northern-born illiterate heads of household were a very small group, only eleven persons, nevertheless it is striking that a larger percentage of one-parent households was found among them than among any other group in the population.

If slavery permanently weakened family ties among blacks one would expect to find greater numbers of one-parent households among the ex-slaves. To be sure, there were fewer two-parent households among ex-slaves (Southern-born illiterates) than among Southern-born literates, but the freedmen had two-parent households more often than Northern-born heads of household who were also illiterate. Thus, among both Northern- and Southern-born heads of household, illiteracy was associated with higher proportions of one-parent households.

It is possible that the relationship between illiteracy and one-parent, generally female-headed households, is only a statistical artifact, the consequence of a higher rate of illiteracy among females than males.[37] In order to test whether Table 5 described a spurious relationship, I compared the number of illiterates among two groups of women, female heads of household and those females living with their husbands in two-parent households. If higher rates of illiteracy among one-parent households in both the North and the South were merely the result of the fact that one-parent households were mostly female, we would expect to find roughly similar proportions of illiterates among married women living with their spouses than among females heading households. Instead, female heads of household were much more commonly illiterate than women living with their husbands. Significantly more female heads of household than married females were illiterate; about one-fourth of married women were illiterate, while more than a third of females heading households could not read or write. Among the Southern-born women, most of whom were born into slavery, the rate of illiteracy was much higher. However, the general pattern remained the same; while about one-third of married women were illiterate, almost half of females heading households were illiterate.

ELIZABETH H. PLECK

Whether or not illiterates thought less of themselves than blacks who learned to read or write, the numbers will never tell us. What is clear, however, is that for both urban and rural heads of household there were significantly more one-parent households among the illiterates. Speculation might lead us to conclude that illiteracy was both a real handicap in an urban society and, in addition, a characteristic found among the most disadvantaged adults in the black community.

Migrants and native Bostonians, rural and urban adults, illiterate and literate persons differed significantly in the number of two-parent households they formed. Did differences appear as well in the composition of the household? A single individual, or that person and boarders lived in one out of seven black households in Boston. These solitary adults were excluded from the analysis of household composition. The great majority of black households, as Table 6 indicates, consisted of nuclear families—usually husband and wife, or a husband, wife and children, but occasionally a single parent and child.

Table 6. Nuclear, Extended, and Augmented Households,
by Place of Birth of the Head of Household, 1880[a]

	Born in Massachusetts	Born in another Northern State	Total Northern-Born	Born in the South	N
Nuclear	68	93	161	462	623
	51.2%	57.1%	54.4%	56.1%	56.2%
Extended	16	15	31	80	111
	12.0%	9.2%	10.5%	10.6%	10.0%
Augmented	49	55	104	270	374
	36.8%	33.7%	35.1%	33.3%	33.8%
Total	133	163	296	812	1,108

[a] This table omits foreign-born heads of household, heads of household with no place of birth, and single-member households. The relationship between place of birth and family structure shown in this table is not statistically significant.

Families which added other relatives to the nuclear family, in what it termed an extended household, were 9.7 percent of all black households. Finally, about one out of three black households included boarders, and in a few cases, boarders and relatives, in addition to parents and children. DuBois discovered roughly the same number of augmented households—that is, households with boarders—in late nineteenth-century Philadelphia.[38]

Virtually the same patterns of family composition existed among rural and urban blacks, as columns three and four of Table 6 disclose. In both cases the majority of households were nuclear, although a significant minority—about one-third—included boarders. Only when native Bostonians are separated from the rest of the Northern-born do differences appear in the composition of the household. The household headed by a black person born in Boston was somewhat more likely to mix relatives or boarders in the home than a household headed by a migrant. However, the differences in household composition between blacks born in Massachusetts, other Northern states and the South are not striking. What is important, in fact, is the uniformity of household composition among migrant and stable, urban and rural heads of household.

It might be thought that relatives were more frequent among the poorest families, huddling together because they could not afford to live by themselves. The figures in Table 7 demonstrate that this was not the case.

Table 7. Nuclear, Extended, and Augmented Households,
by Occupational Level of the Head of Household, 1880[a]

	Professional	White Collar	Skilled	Unskilled	N
Nuclear	19 52.8%	16 50.0%	49 57.6%	558 58.8%	642
Extended	7 19.4%	6 18.8%	8 9.4%	84 8.9%	105
Augmented	10 27.8%	10 31.3%	28 32.9%	307 32.3%	355
Total	36	32	85	949	1,102

[a] This table omits persons with no occupation and single-member heads of household. Heads of household from all places of birth are included. The relationship between occupation and family structure is not statistically significant.

Controlling for the occupational level of the head of household, the proportion of relatives increased among higher status heads of household, while the proportion decreased among lower status households. Relatives may have been more welcome to join the family in higher status households which could afford to sustain additional members. The George Ruffins (he was lawyer and judge, she a prominent clubwoman and suffragist) absorbed into their homes Mrs. Ruffin's niece, Daisy Nahar. In other cases, the presence of additional adult family members may have financed the education or supported the family business, which, in turn, resulted in the higher status of the head of household.

Relatives were more common in higher status households, but lodgers appeared more often in lower status households. The number of augmented households, as summarized in line three of Table 7, shows that about one-third of blue-collar households included a boarder, while slightly fewer boarders resided in professional and white-collar homes. Among households headed by unskilled and skilled workers, just as in the female-headed household, the lodger's rent money was often an essential part of the family budget. In response to the influx of Southern migrants, the black family accommodated these lodgers, generally single women and men who worked as servants and waiters. The augmented household was a product of necessity, but it met the housing needs of the lodgers, as well as additional income requirements of black families.

Nineteenth-century observers often described the "demoralizing" influence of lodgers on the household. DuBois exemplified this attitude, fearing that "the privacy and intimacy of home life is destroyed, and elements of danger and demoralization admitted" when the lodger entered the black home.[39] Given the desperate economic circumstances of most black families, the boarder's rent money may have insured family survival rather than destroyed it. Moreover, boarders were common additions to higher status households. The boarder, in many cases, became a "relative" of the family, in function, if not in kinship. Richard Wright recalled that as a boarder he easily became a part of a Memphis home—more so than he liked, since a match-making mother was eager for the boarder to marry her daughter.[40]

Conclusion

This study of the black family in late nineteenth-century Boston views the black family structure at one point in time. Subsequent studies must trace the family over the years in order fully to comprehend changes in the household. If we want to learn about the acculturation of children in the black family, it is particularly important to employ a dynamic perspective. For example, while we know that about seven out of ten black children in Boston in 1880 lived in two-parent households, we do not know how many of these children spent their early years in such a household. Nor, for that matter do we know how the family situation of the minority of children in 1880 who were missing both parents affected their futures, for better or worse. This kind of analysis can only be pursued through the tracing of individuals, a method extremely arduous to undertake, given the mobility of the population.

Any study of black family life largely employing quantitative information represents only a point of departure for further analysis of black families. While the high number of two-parent households, 82 percent of all black households in Boston, indicates the existence of much greater family organization than has been generally assumed, we need evidence about the cultural context in which the urban black family operated. How were one- and two-parent households viewed? Were different values placed on marriage, the family, even desertion in the black community than in other groups? Did the addition of boarders and relatives endanger the intimacy of the home or create additional adult models for black children? Except in the few instances of family diaries and personal accounts, these questions may prove difficult, if not impossible, to answer through literary materials.

While there are limitations to numerical analysis, it does allow for comparisons across time and space. How then did Boston compare with other cities? Perhaps one could argue that, despite the poverty-stricken condition of blacks in Boston, there was still some way in which Boston was, indeed, "the paradise of the Negro," if only because the situation of blacks in the South was so much worse. Although more studies need to be undertaken, overall figures from Southern urban, Southern rural and Northern urban centers in the late nineteenth century demonstrate a striking similarity in the percentages of two-parent households. Theodore Hershberg reports that in both 1880 and 1896 the two-parent household comprised 76 percent of all households among blacks in Philadelphia. He found roughly similar proportions of two-parent households in ante-bellum Philadelphia, where 77 percent of all black households were two-parent. Among a special group of about 87 slaves who had bought their freedom, 91 percent formed two-parent households.[41] From the major work of Herbert Gutman on the black family, the two-parent household in 1880 appeared among 81 percent of Adams County, Mississippi black households and 77 percent of Mobile, Alabama black households.[42] In three urban areas in 1896, Atlanta, Nashville and Cambridge, Massachusetts, Gutman found respectively, 77 percent, 85 percent and 90 percent two-parent households.[43] It would be tempting here to contrast the relative effects on the black household of Southern urban, Southern rural and Northern urban environments. But what we find in the few areas studied is greater variation within a single locale than between locales. All in all, the two-parent household was the prevailing family form in Southern rural, Southern urban and Northern urban areas.

The figures cited above, except in the case of ante-bellum Philadelphia, do not distinguish between native-born city dwellers and rural migrants to the city. Such an analytic strategy is vital to the study of the effects of city and country origins and the migration from one area to another on the black household.

How did migration to the city affect the black family? The standard texts on black history scarcely mention the migration of blacks to Northern cities before the Great Migration of World War I. On the whole, the northward migration was a movement of single individuals or couples; in few cases did the whole family move north. After the migrants from the South or other parts of the North reached Boston, an incredible number of single individuals and families left the city. This movement out of Boston in some cases left behind deserted wives and husbands, but the rate of desertion was rather low given the lack of occupational opportunity for blacks in Boston and the general rootlessness of the black population.

In the work of DuBois and E. Franklin Frazier, migration to the city is viewed as a disruptive factor which weakened the family and produced large numbers of one-parent households. DuBois wrote that "as a whole, it is true that the average of culture and wealth is far lower among immigrants than natives, and that this gives rise to the gravest of the Negro problems."[44] What these writers generally meant by migration was the *transition* from rural to urban culture among Southern migrants to the city. This disruptive transition was said to have been the source of desertion, delinquency and female-headed households. Frazier, in his discussion of the "city of destruction," noted: "Family desertion among Negroes in cities, appears, then, to be one of the inevitable consequences of the impact of urban life on the simple family organization and folk culture which the Negro has evolved in the rural South."[45]

At least for late nineteenth-century Boston, quantitative evidence calls Frazier's thesis into question. Two-parent households were more frequent among both migrant *and* rural black heads of household. Such evidence can be interpreted in two ways. One explanation would reverse the Frazier argument: instead of migration and the transition from rural to urban culture weakening the black family, these influences strengthened it. Persons who had invested so much effort to leave family, friends and familar ways, had a greater stake in establishing households once they were settled in the city. Also, the limited expectations of rural blacks may have meant that city life in the North was, indeed, a significant improvement over life in the rural South. Finally, the special character of this early migration might have distinguished the early newcomers to the city (both in ante-bellum Philadelphia and in Boston about fifty years later) from more recent city-bound blacks.

A second explanation of the differences in the number of two-parent households, offered by Theodore Hershberg, is that neither slavery nor migration but the urban environment produced greater numbers of one-parent households. Tremendous differences in wealth, poor health conditions for blacks in cities, the destructiveness of urban culture—all these are cited as the causes of "family disorganization" among blacks. Without more knowledge of the internal workings of black culture, of the values blacks placed on different family forms, it is impossible to know whether the one-parent, female-headed household was viewed by blacks as "family disorganization." The use of this value-loaded term generally presupposes a hierarchy of family types, with the male-present, nuclear and patriarchal household representing the most-valued family form.[46]

Another danger in substituting one grand interpretation of "family disorganization" in place of another is that it may tend to obscure other important differences in family type and composition which do not appear between rural and urban, ex-slave and free-born blacks. Important differences between city-dwellers and rural blacks must be noted. But in late nineteenth-century Boston the composition of the black household was similar for both rural and urban black heads of household. Moreover, significantly more one-parent households occurred among illiterate blacks from both rural and urban origins. The social meaning of illiteracy for blacks in the city remains enigmatic, but the discovery that the illiteracy of the head of household significantly altered the proportion of two-parent households hints at the existence of other fundamental social characteristics differentiating black households.

While variations in household composition and percentage of two-parent household which are associated with place of birth, illiteracy and migration should be noted and considered, the similarities in two-parent households among diverse groups in the black population are even more striking. The evidence suggests a family pattern of nuclear, two-parent households which prevailed among migrant and rural black heads of household as well as among stable and urban black heads of household. Despite the existence of blacks at the lowest rung of the occupational ladder, most black children lived in homes where both parents were present, and black families generally included husband, wife and children.

The presentation of these raw statistics force us to challenge and revise previous conceptions about the black family. More lies hidden behind a high death rate, a transient population and a poverty-stricken black community than the phrases like "culture of poverty" or "family disorganization" convey. Our vision of the family as an institution which reacts to and reflects changes is oversimplified, while there seems little understanding of the family as an institution which itself produces changes in individuals and institutions. If the black family were merely the image of the social conditions of urban blacks, we would find a rootless, disorganized mosaic of families. Notions of "black matriarchy" and "the tangle of pathology" of the black family have captivated sociologists and historians alike, but now the task before us is to tell the rather different story of the complex organization and continuity of the black household.

FOOTNOTES

1. "Boston as the Paradise of the Negro," *Colored American Magazine*, Vol. VII, no. 5 (May, 1904), 309-17. For a similar view, see also W.E. Burghardt DuBois, *The Black North in 1901: A Social Study* (New York: Arno Press and the New York Times reprint, 1969), 10-19.

2. There were 139 households headed by a black person born in a foreign country. In 28 of the foreign-born households, the head of household was a single individual, living without kin or children. Excluded from all analysis concerning family were those inter-racial couples which included a white husband and a black wife. Inter-racial couples composed of a black husband and a white wife were included.

3. Marriage records, registered by the Division of Vital Statistics of the Commonwealth of Massachusetts, indicated race and exact place of birth for the bride and groom. Of the marriage partners listing Massachusetts as their place of birth in the 1870 vital records, five out of seven were born in Boston. Half of the remaining non-Bostonians were from Newburyport, Worcester, Cambridge, Lynn and Salem. The largest group of Southern-born brides and grooms were natives of Virginia; two out of five were from Petersburg, Richmond and Norfolk. In the period when these brides and grooms were growing up in Virginia, none of these three towns could be considered "urban" by Boston standards. The largest city in Virginia in 1860 was Richmond, which at the time was only one-fifth the size of Boston. James M. McPherson, *The Negro's Civil War: How American Negroes Felt and Acted During the War for the Union* (New York: Vintage Books, 1965), Appendix B, 320.

4. I am indebted to Peter R. Knights for suggesting this use of the literacy category.

5. At first glance, it seems possible to estimate the number of Southern slave migrants to Boston by taking the percentage of slaves in the states of the upper South just before the Civil War. Between one-half and two-thirds of the Southern migrants to Boston in the late nineteenth century were from Virgina, whose population in 1860 consisted for about ten slaves to every free-born black. If black migration operated randomly, the Southern black population in Boston consisted of about ten freedmen for every free-born black. But migration to the North after the Civil War was extremely selective. We cannot assume that freedmen and free blacks migrated in proportion to their numbers in the population.

   If we make the assumption that literacy corresponds to free status for blacks in the South, we arrive at a probability that it was twenty-seven times as likely for a free-born person to move north as it was for an ex-slave. This proportion is derived by taking the proportion of free persons to slaves in the 1860 Virginia population, a ratio of one to nine, multiplied by the proportion of literates to illiterates in the black population of Boston in 1880, a ratio of three to one.

   For the proportions of blacks from the upper South in Boston's black population, see John Daniels, *In Freedom's Birthplace: A Study of the Boston Negroes* (Boston: Houghton Mifflin, 1915), 141, 468. For the number of ex-slaves in the Virginia 1860 population, see U.S. Bureau of the Census, *Negro Population of the United States, 1790-1915* (Washington, D.C.: U.S. Government Printing Office, 1918), Table 6, 57.

6. The statistics used in this paper are based on a total of 5847 individuals found in the

manuscript census schedules for Boston in 1880. The discrepancy between this figure and the official figure, 5873, is due to mistakes I may have made in transcribing the manuscript schedules, as well as errors in the original tabulated figure.

7. Net migration increases indicate only a small part of the actual population turnover. Stephan Thernstrom estimated that nearly 800,000 persons moved into Boston between 1880 and 1890. Since the population streams of in-migrants and out-migrants tended to cancel out each other, the total Boston population only increased from 363,000 in 1880 to 448,000 in 1890. Stephan Thernstrom and Peter R. Knights, "Men in Motion: Some Data and Speculations About Urban Population Mobility in Nineteenth-Century America," Tamara K. Hareven, ed., *Anonymous Americans: Explorations in Nineteenth-Century Social History* (Englewood Cliffs, N.J.: Prentice Hall, 1971), 21, 25.

8. E.G. Ravenstein, "The Laws of Migration," *Journal of the Royal Statistical Society*, XLVIII (1885), 167-227; Samuel A. Stoffer, "Intervening Opportunities: A Theory Relating Mobility and Distance," *American Sociological Review*, V (1940), 845-67.

9. Carter Godwin Woodson, *A Century of Negro Migration* (Washington, D.C.: The Association for the Study of Negro Life and History, 1918), 162-66.

10. Clyde Kiser, *Sea Island to City* (New York: Columbia University Press, 1932), 170.

11. Thernstrom and Knights, "Men in Motion," 22.

12. These four-fold classifications of occupation were based on an eight-scale occupational code devised by Stephan Thernstrom for his study of occupational mobility in Boston. Since there were so few high status black workers, professionals, large-scale proprietors, managers and officials and semi-professionals were collapsed into one category called professionals. The white collar category included clerical and sales personnel, petty proprietors and minor managers and lower level government officials. I maintained a distinctive category of skilled workers as Thernstrom did, but the semi-skilled, service, unskilled and menial service groups were merged into one category called service and unskilled workers. I am indebted to Professor Thernstrom for providing me with this occupational code. For a more detailed explication of the code, see Peter R. Knights, *The Plain People of Boston, 1830-1960: A Study in City Growth* (New York: Oxford University Press, 1971), Appendix E, 149-56.

13. Clyde Griffen, "Making it in America: Social Mobility in Mid-Nineteenth Century Poughkeepsie," *New York History*, Vol. II, no. 5 (October, 1970), Table II, 498.

14. Data cited in Thernstrom and Knights, "Men in Motion," 46.

15. Richard J. Hopkins, "Occupational and Geographic Mobility in Atlanta, 1870-1896," *Journal of Southern History*, XXIV (May, 1968), Table 6, 207.

16. Paul B. Worthman, "Working Class Mobility in Birmingham, Alabama, 1880-1914," Hareven, ed., *Anonymous Americans*, 180-185.

17. Alwyn Barr, "Occupational and Geographic Mobility in San Antonio, 1870-1900," *Social Science Quarterly*, Vol. 51, no. 2 (September, 1970), Table 3, 401.

18. Horace G. Wadlin, *A Tenement House Census of Boston*, Section II (Boston: Wright and Potter, 1893), 89-93.

19. Dwight Porter, *Report upon a Sanitary Inspection of Certain Tenements-House Districts of Boston* (Boston: Rockwell and Churchill, 1889), 37-8.

20. Walter J. Stevens, *Chip on My Shoulder* (Boston: Meador Publishing Company, 1946), 22.

21. *New York Age* (June 15, 1889), 1.

22. Daniels, *In Freedom's Birthplace*, 472.

23. *Boston City Document No. 68* (1884), 7-8.

24. *Ibid.*, 8.

25. *Boston City Document No. 100* (1887), 11.

26. Walter J. Stevens, *Chip on My Shoulder*, 18.

27. Frederick L. Hoffman, *Race Traits and Tendencies of the American Negro* (Publications of the American Economic Association, 1896), 47.

28. U.S. Census Bureau, *Negro Population, 1790-1915*, 32.

29. *Ibid.*

30. U.S. Bureau of the Census, *Current Population Reports*, Series P-20, No. 187, Tables 4 and 9; and *U.S. Census of the Population: 1960, Detailed Characteristics, U.S. Summary*, Tables 181, 182, and 185, as quoted in Paul C. Glick, "Marriage and Marital Stability Among Blacks," *The Millbank Memorial Fund Quarterly*, Vol. XLVIII, no. 2 (April, 1970), Table 8, 113.

31. The sex ratio does more than reflect differing economic opportunities for females and males in the city. Jacquelyne Jackson in a recent article also maintains that the sex ratio is related to the number of female-headed families. In states with high sex ratios in 1970, she found few female-headed families, but in states with low sex ratios, she found large numbers of female-headed families. Massachusetts, with a sex ratio of 88.6 in 1970, had the highest number of black female-headed families of any state in the nation. Jacqueiyne J. Jackson, "But Where are the Men?" *The Black Scholar*, Vol. 3, no. 4 (December, 1971), 30-41.

32. U.S. Census Bureau, *Negro Population, 1790-1915*, 156.

33. Richard Sennett, *Families against the city: Middle Class Homes of Industrial Chicago, 1872-1890* (Cambridge, Massachusetts: Harvard University Press, 1971), 115.

34. W.E.B. DuBois, *The Philadelphia Negro* (New York: Schocken Books, 1967), 67.

35. Robert Staples, "Towards a Sociology of the Black Family: A Theoretical and Methodological Assessment," *Journal of Marriage and the Family*, Vol. 33, no. 1 (February, 1971), 119-30 contains a comprehensive review of current sociological literature on the black family and maintains a critical stance towards views which associate "the tangle of pathology" with the black family.

36. DuBois, *The Philadelphia Negro*, 448. For related income figures, see also the same work, 173-8 and W.E.B. DuBois, *The Negro American Family* (Cambridge, Massachusetts: MIT Press, 1970), 111-13.

37. Carroll D. Wright, *The Social, Commercial, and Manufacturing Statistics of the City of Boston* (Boston: Rockwell and Churchill, 1882), 130-1.

38. DuBois, *The Philadelphia Negro*, 164, 194.

39. *Ibid.*, 194.

40. Richard Wright, *Black Boy: a record of childhood and youth* (New York: Harper, 1937).

41. Theodore Hershberg, "Free Blacks in Ante Bellum Philadelphia: A Study of Ex-Slaves, Free-Born and Socio-Economic Decline," *Journal of Social History* (December, 1971), Table 1, and p. 186. Mr. Hershberg kindly sent me a manuscript copy of this paper.

42. Herbert G. Gutman and Laurence A. Glasco, "The Negro Family, Household, and Occupational Structure, 1855-1925, with special emphasis on Buffalo, New York, but including Comparative Data from New York, New York, Brooklyn, New York, Mobile, Alabama, and Adams County, Mississippi," (unpublished tables presented at the Yale Conference on Nineteenth Century Cities, November, 1968), Table XXI. Figures were computed from this table in order to derive a percentage of one- and two-parent households. Professor Gutman kindly allowed me to quote from his unpublished data.

43. *Ibid.*, Table XXVI. Figures for one- and two-parent households were computed based on data in this table.

44. DuBois, *The Philadelphia Negro*, 80.

45. E. Franklin Frazier, *The Negro Family in the United States* (Chicago: The University of Chicago Press, 1966), 255.

46. For example, these paragraphs can be found in the Moynihan Report. "But there is one truly great discontinuity in family structure in the United States at the present time: that between the white world in general and that of the Negro American. The white family has achieved a high degree of stability and is maintaining that stability. By contrast, the family structure of lower class Negroes is highly unstable, and in many urban centers is approaching complete breakdown." Office of Policy Planning and Research, United States Department of Labor, *The Negro Family: The Case for National Action* (Washington, D.C.: U.S. Government Printing Office, 1965), 5.

Does Human Fertility Adjust to the Environment?*

By Richard A. Easterlin
University of Pennsylvania

From Malthus to Paul Ehrlich, there have been those who see the growth in man's numbers driving him inexorably, like lemmings to the sea, towards misery and death. A basic premise of this view is that human reproductive behavior does not voluntarily respond to environmental conditions. Instead, man, following his natural instincts, will breed without restraint and population will grow until environmental limits force a halt through higher mortality.

Nowhere, I think, is this view called more into doubt than by American historical experience. Here, if anywhere, environmental constraints on population growth at the start of the nineteenth century appeared to be at a minimum. Certainly this is what Thomas R. Malthus himself thought. Writing of "the English North American colonies, now the powerful people of the United States of America," he said:

> To the plenty of good land which they possessed in common with the Spanish and Portuguese settlements, they added a greater degree of liberty and equality. Though not without some restrictions on their foreign commerce, they were allowed a perfect liberty of managing their own internal affairs. The political institutions that prevailed were favourable to the alienation and division of property. . . . There were no tythes in any of the States, and scarcely any taxes. And on account of

the extreme cheapness of good land, a capital could not be more advantageously employed than in agriculture, which at the same time that it supplies the greatest quantity of healthy work, affords much the most valuable produce to the society.
> The consequence of these favourable circumstances united, was a rapidity of increase, probably without parallel in history.[1]

Indeed, American fertility was extremely high. According to Coale and Zelnik, the birth rate at the start of the nineteenth century "was markedly higher than that ever recorded for any European country and is equaled in reliably recorded data only by such unusually fertile populations as the Hutterites and the inhabitants of the Cocos-Keeling Islands."[2] The reproductive performance of a number of today's high-fertility nations is modest by comparison with the early American record.

The astounding thing is that from about 1810 on, American fertility started to decline. And this, shortly after a vast expansion of natural resources had been accomplished through the Louisiana Pur-

* Comments on an earlier draft of this paper by Glen G. Cain, Joseph L. Fisher, Albert Fishlow, Ronald Freedman, William H. Newell, and Almarin Phillips are gratefully acknowledged. This research was supported in part by National Science Foundation grant NSF-GS-1563.

[1] Thomas Robert Malthus, *First Essay on Population 1798* (New York: Augustus M. Kelley, 1965), pp. 104–105.

[2] Ansley J. Coale and Melvin Zelnik, *New Estimates of Fertility and Population in the United States* (Princeton: Princeton University Press, 1963), p. 35. While source references in this paper have been kept to a minimum, a number are given in Lance E. Davis, Richard A. Easterlin, and William N. Parker, eds., *American Economic Growth: An Economist's History of the United States* (New York: Harper & Row, forthcoming 1971), chapter 5, and Richard A. Easterlin, *Population, Labor Force, and Long Swings in Economic Growth* (New York: Columbia University Press, 1968), Part II.

399

Reprinted from *The American Economic Review*
LXI, 399–407. Copyright © 1971 by permission of the publisher.

chase! While the data are not perfect, by 1860, for the white population, the ratio of children under five to women 20–44 years old (the fertility measure most generally available) had fallen by a third from its 1810 level, and by 1910, by over a half. Put differently, in 1790 almost half of the free families contained five or more persons; by 1900, the proportion of families with five or more persons had fallen to less than a third.

How can one reconcile this dramatic reduction in fertility with the seemingly abundant state of natural resources throughout much of this period? In this paper, I shall suggest that, while our state of knowledge is far from adequate, a plausible case can be made that the secular decline in American fertility was a voluntary response to changing environmental conditions. For obvious reasons we need to know much more about the mechanisms involved, but if the line of reasoning here is correct, it refutes the analogy commonly drawn between human population growth and that of fruit flies in a jar.

Theory

The analysis builds on the economic theory of fertility. In this theory, tastes, prices, and income determine the optimal number of children. The optimal number of children, together with infant and child mortality conditions, determines the optimal number of births. Finally, the extent to which actual births exceed optimal births depends on attitudes toward and extent of information about fertility control practices, and the supply conditions of such practices.

The population is subdivided into several component groups, each subject to rather different conditions. For the present discussion, attention is focussed on a classification in terms of location—frontier areas, settled agricultural areas, new urban areas, and old urban areas. The argument is that the basic fertility determinants—in particular, the cost of children, fertility control practices, and factors other than income change influencing tastes—vary among these locations in such a way that fertility tends to be progressively lower as one moves from the first to the fourth of these situations. Since the course of American economic growth in fact involved a population shift in just this direction, the result was a continuing secular pressure toward fertility reduction.

To take up first the matter of tastes, two determinants directly bound up with economic and social development are the progress of education and the introduction and diffusion of new goods. Both tend to alter preferences for goods versus children in a manner adverse to fertility, because they create or strengthen consumption outlets competitive with children as a source of satisfaction. Education creates awareness of new modes of enjoyment and opens access to them. (For example, while children are a recognized source of satisfaction to all, it is usually only persons of higher educational status who consider foreign travel as a serious consumption alternative.) The progress of education during economic development means that a growing number of households experience a widening of consumption alternatives. Considering different locations at a given time, education was typically more advanced, and hence this influence stronger, in older rural areas than on the frontier, in urban areas than rural, and in older urban areas than in newer urban areas.

Much the same type of argument may be made regarding new goods. New products were more available in older rural areas than on the frontier, because the marketing system was more advanced; hence a wider range of items competed with children in the older areas. Similarly, people in urban areas were more exposed to new goods than people in rural areas by virtue of the greater market potential offered by the denser populations, residents of older urban areas being more exposed than those in newer.

As for costs of childbearing, both the outlays on and returns from children tended to create cost differentials among areas with an effect on fertility similar to that of tastes. On the frontier, with its demands for breaking and clearing new land, the potential labor contribution of children was greater than in established agricultural areas. Also, with land relatively abundant, the problem of establishing mature children on farms of their own was less serious. Nevertheless, in the established agricultural areas, the labor contribution of children on family farms was higher than in cities where work possibilities were more restricted. At the same time the costs of raising children were higher in the cities, since food and housing were typically more expensive there than in rural areas. Thus, taking account of both costs and returns, children were increasingly expensive as the situation changed from frontier to settled agriculture to an urban location.

Finally, consider the situation with regard to methods of fertility limitation. In general, knowledge and availability of a variety of fertility control practices were greater in urban areas than in rural. Similarly these conditions were better in settled agricultural areas than on the frontier, which was at the periphery of the communications network.

Putting together these influences— tastes, cost, and fertility control practices —leads one to expect the following ordering of areas from high to low fertility at any given time: frontier, settled agriculture, new urban areas, old urban areas. Also since frontier areas gradually become transformed into settled agriculture and new urban areas into old, one would ex-pect that over time fertility would decline as new areas "age". Moreover, since "new" and "old" are matters of degree, not of kind, one might expect that even in settled agricultural areas and older urban areas, fertility would continue to decline, at least for some time, as "aging" continues.

In urban areas this process of aging is reinforced by the trend in the composition of the population by origin. Initially, the populations in urban areas are dominated by in-migrants from rural areas or abroad who bring with them a high fertility heritage. In the course of time, these first generation urbanites are gradually replaced by second and later generations born and raised in urban areas, and with consequently lower fertility "tastes." Even today fertility among new rural migrants to urban areas exceeds that of persons who originate in urban areas. Thus to the pattern of cross-section differences by location noted above, one can add an expectation of fertility declines through time in all four locations.

Evidence

These expectations are supported by the available evidence, though much more work is needed. In Figure 1, the ratio of children under five to females aged 20–44 is shown for the rural white population in each geographic division from 1800 to 1960; Figure 2 presents similar data for the urban white population. In both figures the United States ratio is depicted by a heavy line. This is the average for the population as a whole, rural and urban combined, and therefore provides a common reference point in the two figures. Unfortunately the rural-urban data are not available from 1850 to 1900; hence the 1840 and 1910 observations for each division are connected with a thin line. The Mountain and Pacific divisions have been omitted, because of the absence of data for the period when they were being

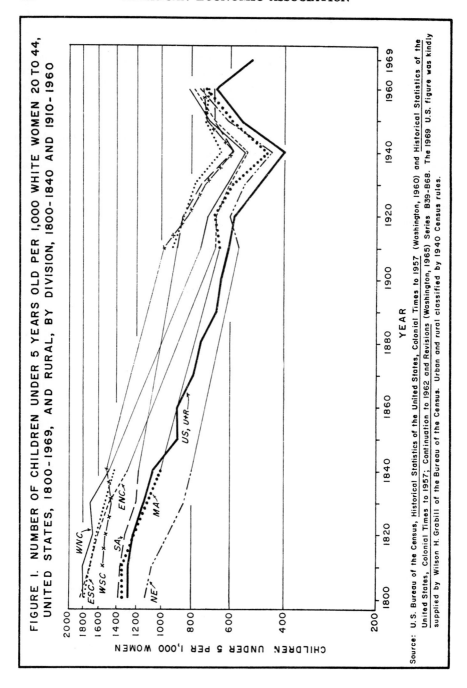

FIGURE I. NUMBER OF CHILDREN UNDER 5 YEARS OLD PER 1,000 WHITE WOMEN 20 TO 44, UNITED STATES, 1800-1969, AND RURAL, BY DIVISION, 1800-1840 AND 1910-1960

Source: U. S. Bureau of the Census, Historical Statistics of the United States, Colonial Times to 1957 (Washington, 1960) and Historical Statistics of the United States, Colonial Times to 1957; Continuation to 1962 and Revisions (Washington, 1965) Series B39-B68. The 1969 U.S. figure was kindly supplied by Wilson H. Grabill of the Bureau of the Census. Urban and rural classified by 1940 Census rules.

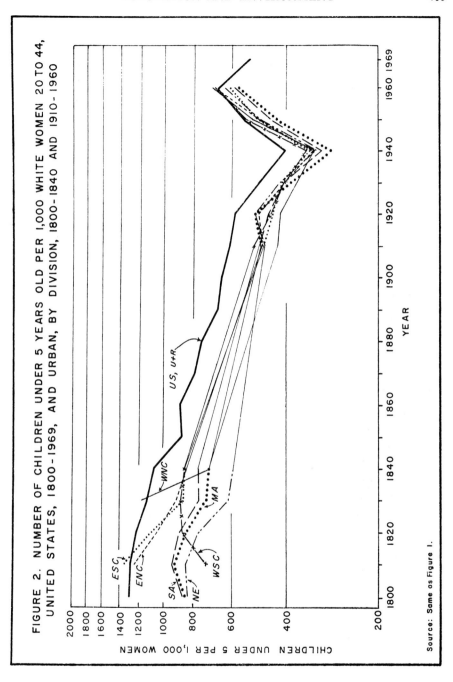

FIGURE 2. NUMBER OF CHILDREN UNDER 5 YEARS OLD PER 1,000 WHITE WOMEN 20 TO 44, UNITED STATES, 1800-1969, AND URBAN, BY DIVISION, 1800-1840 AND 1910-1960

Source: Same as Figure 1.

settled. One would expect these divisions to be somewhat different from the others, however, because of the importance of mining rather than agriculture in their early development. Similarly, the non-white population has been omitted for lack of data. It is the white population, however, which predominantly accounts for the national patterns.

The child-woman ratio used here as a fertility measure typically exceeds the crude birth rate by a factor in the neighborhood of 20 to 25. Analytically, this reflects the fact that the child-woman ratio is computed from (a) a denominator about one-fifth as large as that for the crude birth rate (females aged 20–44 instead of the total population), and (b) a numerator four to five times as large. (Implicitly, birth experience over a five-year period is totalled rather than averaged, and is multiplied by a survival rate on the order of .80 to .95 to exclude those dying before the end of the period.) Although the child-woman ratio is an imperfect measure of fertility, it provides a reasonable basis for a preliminary test of the implications of the foregoing analysis.

Consider first the differentials by location in the early part of the nineteenth century. As shown in Figure 1, among rural areas, fertility was lower in the older settled areas in the East than in those undergoing settlement, the areas west of the Appalachians. This differential between new and old areas existed in both the North and the South. Differences among areas in the age distribution of women of reproductive age, whether due to vital rates or migration, had little to do with this fertility differential. The same differential between newer and older regions holds also for urban areas (Figure 2). Thus it is the three older East Coast divisions which are grouped together at the bottom of Figure 2. Even the seemingly partial exception, the West South Central

division, is not really an exception, because the figures are dominated by Louisiana, an area which was settled early. Finally, within every division, urban fertility is lower than rural fertility. This is quickly seen by comparison with the United States reference line in the two figures. Virtually all of the urban ratios are below the United States average, and except for New England, almost all rural ratios are above. Thus, there is a clear and consistent pattern of fertility in frontier areas exceeding that in older established areas, and of rural fertility generally exceeding urban.

With regard to trends, the United States ratio declines from 1810 on, and this is seen to occur in both rural and urban sections of all geographic divisions, though with some differences in timing. Frontier areas become progressively settled and new urban areas are transformed into old, while within the older rural and urban areas the process of aging continues.

Further evidence consistent with the present interpretation is provided by Yasuba's analysis of the fertility ratios of states for the period 1800–1860. His principal result, which bears particularly on the rural fertility patterns, is that the most important factor associated with fertility differences and trends was population density—the higher the density, the lower the fertility ratio. Yasuba interprets population density as a measure of the availability of land, and argues that:

... [In] a community where the supply of land is limited, the value of children as earning assets is low and hence the demand for children may not be so great as where there is plenty of open land nearby. The increased cost of setting up children as independent farmers and fear of the fragmentation of family farms may further encourage the restriction of family-size in densely populated areas.[8]

[8] Yasukichi Yasuba, *Birth Rates of the White Population in the United States, 1800–1860* (Baltimore, Johns Hopkins Press, 1962), p. 159.

More recently, Colin Forster and G. S. L. Tucker have extended Yasuba's analysis, strengthening and refining the basic finding of inverse association between density and fertility.[4]

Mention should be made of another possible influence in the secular fertility decline, the lowering of infant and child mortality. The child-woman ratio fails for the most part to reflect this influence, since it relates not to births but to surviving children as of the census date. The trend in American mortality for much of the nineteenth century is uncertain. But it is clear that from the late nineteenth century onward, there was a substantial reduction in infant and child mortality, and this probably strengthened the tendency toward fertility decline, since fewer births would be needed to obtain a given number of surviving children.

The question arises whether the growth of per capita income associated with economic development may have exerted a strong counter force tending to raise fertility. The answer to this, in my view, is that income growth is a two-edged sword. On the one hand, it tends to make for higher fertility by augmenting the resources available to a household. On the other, it tends to lower fertility through what might be described as an "intergeneration taste effect." The argument in its simplest form is that in a steadily growing economy successive generations are raised in increasingly affluent households and hence develop successively higher living aspirations in the course of their normal upbringing. Thus, while, on the one hand, each generation on reaching adulthood normally has more resources at its command, on the other, it has greater goods aspirations. If long-term growth is not steady, but fluctuating, temporary dispar-

ities can result between the growth of resources and that of aspirations with consequent swings in fertility, such as the United States has been experiencing in recent decades. Secularly, however, the two influences tend to cancel out in their effect on fertility. Whether they do so completely remains an open and important empirical question. It is clear, however, that if this view is adopted, then the presumption no longer holds that secular per capita income growth tends to raise fertility—the net effect could be positive, negative, or zero.

Another question relates to the possible impact of immigration on native white fertility. The first president of the American Economic Association, Francis Amasa Walker, argued vigorously in an article entitled "Immigration and Degradation" that "as the foreigners began to come in larger numbers, the native population more and more withheld their own increase."[5] In Walker's view:

> The American shrank from the industrial competition thus thrust upon him. He was unwilling himself to engage in the lowest kind of day labor with these new elements of the population; he was even more unwilling to bring sons and daughters into the world to enter into that competition.[6]

The argument that immigration led to lower native fertility is suspect, however, because declines in American fertility occurred in times and places not only where immigration was high, but also where immigration offered little or no competition. Thus, as has been noted, fertility turned down early in the nineteenth century, before any substantial influx of immigrants occurred. Recent studies in colonial demography suggest that in parts of New England such declines occurred even in the eighteenth century. Moreover, fertility

---

[4] Colin Forster and G. S. L. Tucker, *Economic Opportunity and American Fertility Ratios, 1800–1860* (forthcoming).

[5] Francis A. Walker, "Immigration and Degradation," *The Forum*. Vol. 11 (August 1891), p. 638.

[6] *Ibid.*, p. 641.

declines occurred not only in the areas of immigration but in others as well, notably the American South. What seems to be a common feature of many areas where fertility declines set in is not that they were experiencing competition from foreign immigrants, but that the land supply had been largely exhausted and the process of settlement completed.

At issue here is the likely course of the American birth rate had there been no immigration. If one follows the line of reasoning suggested previously, an important consideration is the type of economic activity that the native population would have followed. In the absence of a foreign labor supply in the nineteenth century, it seems plausible to suppose that the workers for American industrial expansion would have been drawn more from rural areas than was actually the case. Correspondingly, the rate of settlement would have been slowed. As a result, over time the native-born population would have been less involved in new settlement and more engaged in urban activities, that is, more exposed to a low than a high fertility environment. This implies that if there had been no immigration, not only is it doubtful that native fertility would have been higher than that actually observed, but it might possibly have been lower.

It is worth noting that the fertility declines of the past were accomplished entirely by voluntary action on the part of the population. To some extent marriage was deferred. But also there were declines in fertility within marriage. These developments took place in a situation where not only was there no public policy to help those interested in fertility limitation, but attitudes, and even laws in many states, were hostile to the practice or even discussion of contraception or other fertility control practices. To emphasize the voluntary nature of this development, however, is not to suggest that there was no need

for family planning policies then or, for that matter, that there is no need today. What historical experience shows is a voluntary decline in fertility, but this is not necessarily the optimal rate of decline from the point of view of social welfare. One can only conjecture how many households suffered from the miseries of unwanted children because of the hostile public environment. Today our evidence on this matter and on the need for intelligent public policy is straightforward.

In the literature on the demographic transition, the secular fertility decline is typically linked to the processes of urbanization and industrialization. But the American experience suggests an additional dimension associated with the transformation of a rural area from frontier to settled agriculture. Nor is this peculiar to the United States. Canada seems to show a similar pattern, while in Europe the association of high fertility and settlement has been noted with regard to parts of Scandinavia, Finland, and Russia in the nineteenth century. Thus, seen very broadly, the American fertility decline reflects not only the processes of urbanization and industrialization but that of settlement as well. This aspect is crucial, because of its implications for today's less developed countries. The traditional view of secular fertility decline has led to emphasis on industrialization in these areas as a prerequisite to a decline. The American experience raises the possibility that, as population increasingly presses against land resources, fertility declines set in within the rural sector itself.

One may, of course, discount the possibility that American experience is relevant to today's less developed countries. This would carry the highly questionable implication that Americans are in some way a distinctive and exceptionally rational species of mankind. Moreover, the historical experience of Europe and Japan shows that elsewhere in the world, as similar pressures for reducing population growth have mounted, similar responses have taken place. It seems reasonable to suppose that history will, in time, record that the same was true of today's less developed nations as well. Indeed, fertility declines are already occurring in some of these areas.

Conclusion

The conclusion to which this discussion points is that both theory and the empirical research done so far on historical American fertility suggest that human fertility responds voluntarily to environmental conditions. If this is so—and it seems hard to ignore the evidence—then the nature of what is called "the population problem" takes on a radically different guise. The question is not one of human beings breeding themselves into growing misery. Rather, the problem is whether the voluntary response of fertility to environmental pressures results in a socially optimal adjustment. In thinking about this, it seems useful to distinguish between the potential for population adjustment and the actual degree of adjustment. The staggering change in American reproductive behavior over the past century and a half clearly demonstrates the immense potential for adjustment. Whether, currently, the degree of adjustment is socially optimal remains a matter for research. Such research requires clarification of the mechanisms through which environmental pressures influence reproductive behavior —a subject to which economic analysis can contribute much more than it has so far. One may add—though this lies outside the scope of the present paper—that further research also requires a deeper understanding of the wants and aspirations of individual families in regard to human welfare. For judgments on the social optimality of adjustment obviously call for a welfare function that takes account of the pervasive human desire to have and raise children. It is to be hoped that such research will go forward promptly, in an atmosphere not of hysterical urgency, but of sensitive concern.

Family Limitation and Age at Marriage: Fertility Decline in Sturbridge, Massachusetts 1730–1850*

NANCY OSTERUD AND JOHN FULTON

The question of the timing of the American fertility decline has recently been re-opened. Until the 1960s historians and demographers had assumed that the long-term decline in American fertility began in the late nineteenth century, with urban areas leading rural ones in both the onset and the magnitude of the decline. This notion was challenged by Coale and Zelnik's 1963 book, *New Estimates of Fertility and Population in the United States*. Using data from the decennial federal census Coale and Zelnik demonstrated that the birth rate began its long-term fall in the first half of the nineteenth century. More recently, both Maris Vinovskis and Richard Easterlin have used census data to challenge the assumption of urban–rural fertility differentials as well. While the aggregate analysis of census data has thus established the fact of an early fertility decline in the United States, and has posed the question of its nature and pace, census data are too limited to yield precise information on the magnitude of that decline or to illuminate the process through which it took place.[1] It is possible, however, to ask these questions of data drawn from the vital registration systems of particular communities. While such a study is necessarily microcosmic, record linkage of nominative data allows the historical demographer to investigate fertility at the family level and to examine the dynamics of change in fertility over time. Absolute levels of fertility undoubtedly varied from community to community, but the demographic mechanisms through which the early fertility decline occurred may be more widely generalizable.

This study examines the fertility behaviour of the population of Sturbridge, Massachusetts, from the founding of the town in the early eighteenth century to the middle of the nineteenth century. The social history of the town during this period is fairly representative of that of rural central New England as a whole. Located in southern Worcester County, the town of Sturbridge was founded in the 1730s by settlers from Medfield, Massachusetts, a town nearer Boston that had been settled in the seventeenth century. Although the soil was of mixed quality, agriculture provided the economic base of the community. Throughout the eighteenth century, in-migrants from more densely populated areas joined the community's residents in establishing farms and practising agriculture-related trades such as blacksmithing, lumbering, and tanning. There were no recognized villages; the population was dispersed across the landscape on 50–150 acre family farms.

After the revolutionary war the town began to send out-migrants to newly settled communities in northern New England and the West; those who migrated into the community later were more often tradesmen and merchants than farmers. But the landscape remained much the same until the turn of the nineteenth century, when the commercialization of the region's

* We wish to thank Richard and Polly Rabinowitz, who began the family reconstitution; former and present staff of Old Sturbridge Village, who have studied the community; Stephens College students participating in a workshop on social history, who first scrutinized the FRFs for evidence of family limitation; John Knodel, who gave useful criticism of the work; William Mosher and Ian Rockett, who studied the age-at-marriage data.

[1] See Ansley J. Coale and Melvin Zelnik, *New Estimates of Fertility and Population in the United States* (Princeton: Princeton University Press, 1963). Maris Vinovskis presented data for Massachusetts in a paper he delivered at the 1974 Berkshire Conference; Richard Easterlin's paper, also delivered in 1974 and unpublished, is based on data for the state of Michigan. Preliminary discussions of their findings are contained in Maris A. Vinovskis, 'Socioeconomic Determinants of Interstate Fertility Differentials in the United States in 1850 and 1860', *Journal of Interdisciplinary History*, **6**, 3 (Winter, 1976), pp. 375–396, and Richard A. Easterlin, 'Does Human Fertility Adjust to the Environment?', *American Economic Association Papers and Proceedings* (1971), pp. 399–407.

481

Reprinted from *Population Studies* XXX, 3,
481–493. Copyright © 1976 by permission of the
publisher.

economy began to affect the economic and social life of the community. Symbolic of this transformation was the building of the Worcester–Stafford Turnpike Road through the town in 1812. Crossing the town common, around which a tentative commercial development had begun in the early years of the century, the turnpike linked the community more closely to other towns and cities, increased the flow of goods and people through the community, and catalysed the development of a true central village. Stores and shops serving both the town itself and the larger region multiplied around the common.

This 'commercial revolution' was quickly followed by an industrial revolution in the economic life of the community. In 1829, a small cotton textile factory was established on the Quinebaug River. Although the mill suffered from unstable profits and ownership (and the mill workers suffered from intermittent unemployment), the factory expanded through the first half of the century. In 1850, just over 200 men, women and children were engaged in tending the machinery and doing general labour in the mill. A separate village, Fiskdale, grew up around the factory; after mid-century, this became the dominant commercial centre of the town. More important to the economic life of the whole population, however, was the spread of wage work in non-mechanized and partially centralized forms. Some work, such as the braiding of palm-leaf hats, was done at home for piece-rate wages. Other industries, especially shoe-making, were carried on both in households and in consolidated workshops. Still others, such as the making of shoe-tools or carriages, were located in manufactories which used hand tools and limited sources of power. While the majority of the population were still engaged in farming, agriculture was changing as well, as farmers assumed a new orientation towards local and regional markets and experimented with new methods of stockbreeding and cultivation.[2]

The social history of the town of Sturbridge in this period, then, consists of the interaction of two processes of change: the settlement process, which occupied the eighteenth century but defined the nineteenth as well, and the development of commercial and industrial capitalism in the early nineteenth century.

The data upon which this study of fertility is based have been drawn from family reconstitution of the vital records of the town for the period from 1730 to 1850.[3] While there are family reconstitution forms (FRFs) for approximately 2,400 marital unions over the 120-year period, the rate of geographical mobility, the underregistration of deaths, and changes in the boundaries of the town greatly reduce the number of FRFs available for analysis. This study relies upon two sub-sets of the data: a set of almost 1,000 cases for which age at first marriage is known, and a set of just under 200 FRFs which represent completed families. The criteria for selecting the cases in which age at first marriage can be determined included: (1) date of birth known; (2) date of marriage or publication of intention to marry known; (3) no evidence that this might be a second marriage.[4] The criteria for determining that a given FRF represented a completed family were: (1) date of marriage or publication of intention to marry known; (2) survival of the marital union intact and under observation until the wife reached age 45, or 30 years had passed since the marriage; (3) no evidence of births occurring outside the town. Because of the underregistration of deaths, it was not possible to determine the date of the end

---

[2] This sketch of the history of Sturbridge is based upon the work of a number of researchers who are or have been associated with Old Sturbridge Village, an outdoor historical museum located in the town. There is also a town history: George Davis, *A Historical Sketch of Sturbridge and Southbridge* (West Brookfield, Massachusetts: O. S. Cooke and Co., 1856).

[3] The vital records of the town, which state law required the elected town clerk to keep, were indexed and published in 1906: *Vital Records of Sturbridge Mass. to the year 1850* (Boston: New England Historic Genealogical Society, 1906). Family reconstitution was performed by Richard and Polly Rabinowitz and by Nancy Osterud, and followed the procedure outlined by E. A. Wrigley in his *Introduction to English Historical Demography* (New York: Basic Books, 1966).

[4] Initial analysis of the age-at-marriage data was performed by William Mosher and Ian Rockett; see their 'A Century of Age at Marriage in Sturbridge, Massachusetts: 1741–1839', read at the annual meeting of the Population Association of America, Montreal, Canada, 1976.

of the marital union for all couples. For FRFs in which this date was unknown to qualify as completed families, they had to meet the following conditions: (1) no evidence of a possible re-marriage for either spouse; (2) evidence of the presence of the family in the town beyond the wife's 45th year, or after 30 years of marriage, as indicated by the marriage of a daughter or the death of a minor child; (3) no evidence of a possible migration of the family.

The group of completed families is obviously not representative of all those who lived in the town at some time before 1850; simply by remaining in the community from the time of their marriage until the end of the childbearing period, these couples differed from the majority. (Most migration, however, was local; some was also artificial, resulting from the setting off of one section of the town into a new political unit in 1816.) It is clear that the group of completed families also excludes families primarily engaged in cotton-factory work, who were extraordinarily mobile, and underrepresents the poorest one-fifth of the population, who were landless labourers. Until a census is linked to the vital records, we will not know if the 'persisters' differed in other respects from the migrants; work is presently under way to link the 1850 federal census with the FRFs.[5] The question of the representativeness of this group of families is not, however, an abstract one. Since the analytical focus of this study is on the interaction between social change and patterns of fertility, it is appropriate that the families we study be those who lived out their reproductive lives under the social–historical conditions we have described.

The most immediately striking feature of the fertility of the completed families over time is the substantial decline in the mean number of children ever born over the 120-year period, a decline of 3·5 children from a high of 8·8 for the 1730–59 marriage cohort to a low of 5·3 for the 1820–39 cohort. Table 1 shows that this decline was a fairly steady one. Just under half the

TABLE 1. *Mean number of children ever born**

Cohort	Children ever born†	Standard deviation	Number of completed families
1730–59	8·83	2·72	23
1760–79	7·32	2·44	56
1780–99	7·32	3·08	43
1800–19	6·02	2·93	42
1820–39	5·30	3·01	33

* Completed families, only.
† Difference among cohorts is statistically significant at the 0·001 level using the F-test. The difference between the first and last cohorts is statistically significant at the 0·1 level, using the t-test.

total decline occurred between the first and second marriage cohorts; after a short period of apparent stability the decline resumed with the cohort married after 1800 and continued to the last cohort studied. The distribution of completed family size over time changed in a similar manner. While the cohorts married in the eighteenth century had a modal family size of eight, those married in the nineteenth century had a modal size of five; the frequency of large families with ten or more children, too, had begun to decline well before the turn of the century. This is illustrated in Figure 1.

How can this early fertility decline be explained? The demographic processes through which the decline took place must be elucidated before the question of causality can be raised.

[5] Under the direction of Nancy Osterud.

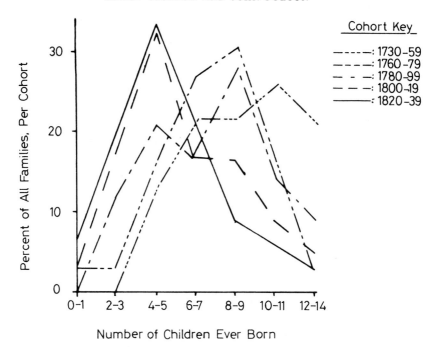

FIGURE 1. Distribution of children ever born, completed families.

TABLE 2. *Mean age at first marriage for females**

Cohort	Mean age at first marriage †	Standard deviation	Number of completed families
1730–59	20·65	3·72	17
1760–79	22·85	4·26	47
1780–99	22·46	3·88	35
1800–19	23·53	4·24	34
1820–39	24·42	4·23	26

* Completed families, for whom woman's date of birth is known, only.
† Difference among cohorts is statistically significant at the 0·05 level using the F-test.

One possibility is that there was an increase in the mean age of women at first marriage. Table 2 reveals that an increase in female age at marriage did occur over the period, from a mean of 20·7 years for the 1730–59 cohort to a mean of 24·4 for the 1820–39 cohort. The timing of this increase parallels that of the decrease in the mean number of children ever born. Half of the increase again took place between the first and second marriage cohorts; after a short period of stability the increase resumed with the cohorts married after 1800.

The larger set of cases for which age at first marriage is known confirms this trend. Mean ages at marriage for men and women in the larger marriage cohorts may be found in Table 3; these means are graphically compared with those for women from the completed families in

TABLE 3. *Mean age at first marriage for females and males**

	Females			Males		
Cohort	Mean age at first marriage†	Standard deviation	Number in cohort	Mean age at first marriage‡	Standard deviation	Number in cohort
1730–59	19·54	2·48	21	24·84	4·62	8
1760–79	21·61	3·61	75	25·51	4·86	65
1780–99	23·62	6·17	153	25·61	4·91	127
1800–19	23·33	4·56	155	26·06	4·54	133
1820–39	25·54	7·62	143	27·63	5·15	121
1840–49	25·50	6·89	34	28·93	7·96	19

* Cf. Mosher and Rockett, *loc. cit.* in footnote 4.

† Difference among cohorts is statistically significant at the 0·001 level using the F-test.

‡ Difference among cohorts is statistically significant at the 0·01 level using the F-test.

FIGURE 2. Mean age at first marriage, Sturbridge, males and females (cf. Mosher and Rockett, *loc. cit.* in footnote 4).

Figure 2.[6] While the difference in mean age at marriage for women between the first and last cohorts is larger among this group than among women belonging to completed families, amounting to almost six years, and while the timing of the change varies somewhat, the pace of the increase in female age at marriage is quite similar.[7] Half the increase occurred before and

[6] Cf. Mosher and Rockett, *loc. cit.* in footnote 4. We would like to thank the authors for re-grouping the data into the periods used in this study.

[7] Much of the difference between mean ages for the two groups of cohorts can be explained by the fact that the numbers in these cohorts are small.

half after the turn of the century; the two periods of increase were separated by a short period of relative stability.

The mean age at marriage for men was rising as well during this period. A significant increase began with the 1800–19 marriage cohort, and continued until the last cohort studied. The overall increase in the mean age at first marriage for males was also somewhat smaller than that for females. Male and female ages at marriage tended toward convergence in the late eighteenth century, but began to diverge again in the nineteenth.

The fact that rates of pre-nuptial conception were changing during this period complicates the situation to some extent. Referring to Table 4 we see that for the larger sample of marriages the proportion of fertile couples who gave birth to a child within seven months of their wedding decreased in the years after 1800 from approximately one-third to less than three per cent. As bridal pregnancy became less common, significant differences emerged between the mean ages of women who were pregnant at first marriage and those who were not. Women who were pregnant at marriage did not participate in the trend toward older marriage ages after the turn of the century; at the same time, they represented a sharply declining proportion of all brides.

Change in the mean age of women at first marriage was a powerful factor in determining change in the mean number of children ever born. The increase in female age at marriage accounts for about half of the decrease in completed family size over the period. Assuming two-year birth intervals, a 3·8-year increase in female age at marriage would account for 1·9 births, just over half of the observed decline in mean completed family size. A more precise measure, based on changes in exposure per woman to the age-specific rates between 15 and 25, suggests that changes in female age at marriage accounted for about half the change in completed family size before the turn of the nineteenth century and for about one-fourth of it after that time.[8] Other powerful factors must have been at work along with the increasing female age at marriage. Age-specific marital fertility rates (which were calculated from the completed families' fertility histories), listed in Table 5 and indexed by level (taking the 20–24 rate for the 1730–59 cohort as 100 and expressing each rate as a percentage of that) in Figure 3, reveal that the cohorts which married in the nineteenth century had lower levels of fertility in all age groups than those married in the eighteenth century. It is this decrease in marital fertility that explains that part of the decline in completed family size not accounted for by the rise in age at marriage.

What was responsible for this decline in marital fertility? While there are a number of involuntary intervening factors that could have affected fertility, it is clear that none of these were changing significantly in ways that might have led to lower fertility. Any change in the level of nutrition in the community in the nineteenth century, for example, would have been in the direction of improvement. Mothers customarily nursed their children for a year, and any

---

[8] This measure was computed as follows:
(Subscripts differentiate cohorts, superscripts differentiate age groups.)

1. $\dfrac{MWY^{15-19}}{Women^{15-19}_1} - \dfrac{MWY^{15-19}}{Women^{15-19}_2} = \Delta MWY^{15-19}_{1-2}$

2. $\dfrac{MWY^{20-24}}{Women^{20-24}_1} - \dfrac{MWY^{20-24}}{Women^{20-24}_2} = \Delta MWY^{20-24}_{1-2}$

3. ΔMWY^{15-19}_{1-2} $ASMFR^{15-19}_{cohort \ with \ greater \ exposure}$ = expected births attributable to difference in exposure$^{15-19}_{1-2}$

4. ΔMWY^{20-24}_{1-2} $ASMFR^{20-24}_{cohort \ with \ greater \ exposure}$ = expected births attributable to difference in exposure$^{20-24}_{1-2}$

5. (result 3) + (result 4) = total expected births attributable to difference in exposure$^{15-24}_{1-2}$

6. $\dfrac{(result\ 5)}{(total\ difference\ in\ CEB)_{1-2}}$

TABLE 4. *Mean age at marriage by pregnancy status at marriage**

Cohort	Not pregnant at time of marriage	Pregnant at time of marriage†	Percentage pregnant‡ in cohort	Number in cohort
1730–59	18·94	18·26	25	12
1760–79	22·76	20·71	33	42
1780–99	22·75	22·71	30	67
1800–19	22·89	21·74	18	89
1820–39	23·76	20·23	3	72
1840–49	24·83	—	0	12

* Based on fertile marriages for which an exact marriage date is known, only.

† Difference among cohorts is statistically significant at the 0·05 level using the F-test.

‡ Pregnant at time of marriage.

TABLE 5. *Age-specific marital fertility rates**

Cohort	Age						
	15–19	20–24	25–29	30–34	35–39	40–44	45–49
1730–59	(0·571)‡	(0·455)	(0·468)	(0·376)	(0·294)	(0·242)	(0·012)
1760–79	(0·167)	0·470	0·386	0·389	0·315	0·128	0·021
1780–99	(0·417)	0·495	0·399	0·376	0·280	0·183	0·034
1800–19	(0·500)	(0·446)	0·383	0·322	0·189	0·100	0·006
1820–39	(0·333)	(0·366)	(0·352)	0·331	0·200	0·024	0·000
1730–99	(0·363)	0·469	0·410	0·391	0·296	0·144	0·026
1800–39	(0·412)	0·435	0·381	0·338	0·210	0·098	0·003
'Natural fertility'†	—	0·435	0·407	0·371	0·298	0·152	0·022

* Completed families, only.

† The natural fertility rates are taken from Louis Henry, and represent the average age-specific legitimate fertility rates for 13 populations in which family limitation was not practised. (See Henry's 'Some data on natural fertility', *Eugenics Quarterly* (June 1961).)

‡ All cohort rates based on less than 100 married woman-years have been enclosed in parentheses.

change would have been in the direction of earlier weaning or supplemental feeding. There was also no apparent change in the level of infant mortality.

Instead, we must investigate the hypothesis that couples married after 1800 were voluntarily engaging in practices that limited the size of their families. One possibility, of course, is that family size decreased because couples were seeking to maximize the health and activity of the woman by increasing the interval between pregnancies. While this cannot be entirely discounted, the shape of the age-specific marital fertility curves argues against this explanation. A careful perusal of Table 5 suggests that age-specific rates decreased more sharply among women over 35 than among younger age groups. In Figure 4, the rates have been indexed to the 20–24 level for each cohort so this can be seen more clearly; note the marked decline in the 30–35 age group with the 1800–19 cohort, and the equally sharp decline in the 40–44 age group in the cohort married after 1820. If couples were merely following a child-spacing strategy, the shape of the curves would not change noticeably over time.

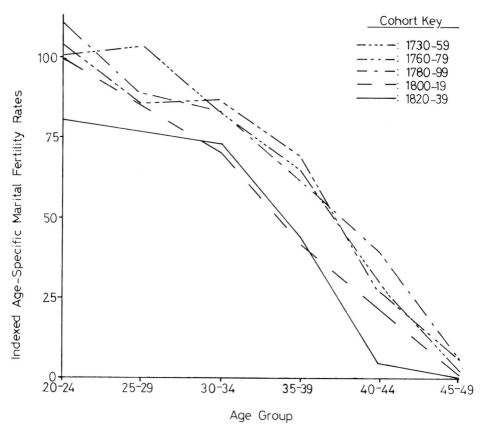

FIGURE 3. Age-specific marital fertility rates, indexed by level of 20–24 rate for the 1730–59 cohort (equivalent to 100), for completed families.

The alternative explanation is deliberate family limitation. While the suggestion that family limitation was beginning to be practised in a rural community among couples who married in the first decades of the nineteenth century is certainly unorthodox, it does fit the data very well. As defined by Louis Henry, family limitation is present if, once a couple have had the number of children they wish to have, they take steps to avoid having more.[9] Because the definition is linked to a desired family size, which is affected by various cultural and socio-economic factors, it is particularly suitable for the study of fertility in historical populations; rather than specifying a level of fertility required for family limitation to be presumed to exist, it describes the characteristics of family-limiting behaviour. The definition suggests a number of simple statistical tests for the presence of family limitation; most are based on the fact that family-limiting behaviour is defined as parity-related. If a population is beginning to practise family limitation, one would expect fertility to decrease in the older age groups after couples had already reached their desired family size. One would also expect the mean age of mothers at the birth of their last child to decrease over time.

Both these things happened in Sturbridge completed families after 1800. Looking first at the mean age of mothers at last birth, which is presented in Table 6, we can see that the mean

[9] Louis Henry, 'Some Data on Natural Fertility', *Eugenics Quarterly* **8,** June 1961.

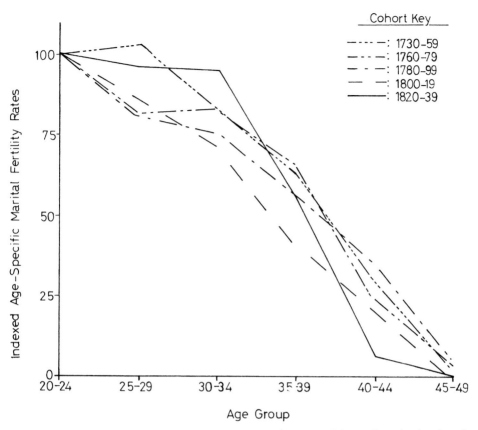

FIGURE 4. Age-specific marital fertility rates, indexed by shape, where the 20–24 rate for each cohort is equivalent to 100, for completed families.

TABLE 6. *Mean age of mother at last birth**

Cohort	Age at last birth†	Standard deviation	Number of completed families
1730–59	38·65	4·55	17·
1760–79	39·47	4·40	45
1780–99	39·34	5·84	35
1800–19	37·82	4·20	33
1820–39	35·71	4·26	24

* Completed families, only.
† Difference among cohorts is statistically significant at the 0·05 level using the F-test.

fell by nearly three years between the first and last marriage cohorts; all of this decline, furthermore, took place after the turn of the century. Figure 5, a distribution of the age of mothers at last birth for the eighteenth- and nineteenth-century cohorts, shows that the modal age of women at the birth of their last child was between 40 and 44 in the eighteenth century, and

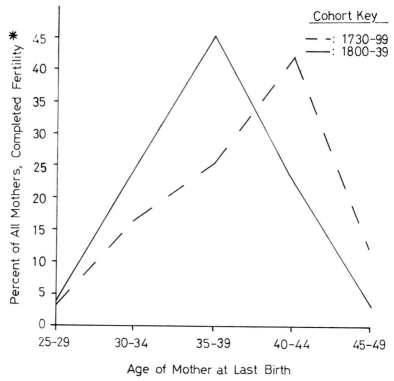

FIGURE 5. Distribution of age of mother at last birth, completed families.
* Per Cohort, i.e., the sum of percentages, each cohort, is equivalent to 1·0.

TABLE 7. *Comparison of Sturbridge fertility rates with natural fertility rates**

	Cohort	Age					
		20–24	25–29	30–34	35–39	40–44	45–49
Indexing	1730–99	100	87	83	63	31	6
by shape†	1800–39	100	88	78	48	23	1
	Natural fertility	100	94	85	69	34	5
By ratio	1730–99	100	94	97	92	87	109
and shape‡	1800–39	100	94	91	70	65	14
	Natural fertility	100	100	100	100	100	100

* Completed families, only.
† 20–24 rate for each cohort equivalent to 100.
‡ These curves have been first expressed as ratios of the indexed natural fertility curve, and these ratios have then been indexed again to the 20–24 ratio, per curve. Thus, if a curve had exactly the same shape as the natural fertility curve, its indexed ratio would be 100 in all age groups.

between 35 and 39 in the nineteenth. This indicator, then, suggests that deliberate family limitation began in Sturbridge with the couples who were married after 1800, and increased in scope and magnitude through the early nineteenth century.

Henry has provided another test for the presence of family limitation by computing average age-specific 'natural fertility' rates from populations which did not control fertility.[10] Table 7 compares these rates with those obtaining in Sturbridge; with few exceptions, they are surprisingly close to those for the earlier cohorts and quite distinct from those for the later cohorts. (The indexed curves have been expressed as ratios of the indexed natural fertility curve, and those ratios have then been indexed again to the 20–24 ratio; if a curve had exactly the same shape as the natural fertility curve, its indexed ratio would be 100 in all age groups.) Figure 6 demonstrates this graphically. When the rates are indexed so that the shape of the

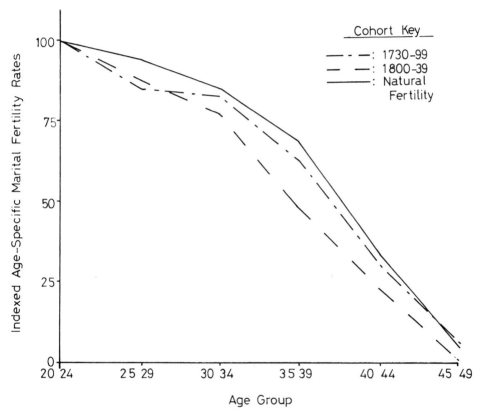

FIGURE 6. Age-specific marital fertility rates, indexed by shape, where the 20–24 rate for each cohort is equivalent to 100, for completed families.

curve, rather than its level, is the basis of comparison (taking the 20–24 rate for each cohort as 100), one finds that the eighteenth-century curve has the same general shape as that for natural fertility; the curve for the nineteenth-century cohort, on the other hand, is quite different, becoming concave rather than convex at the older ages. This is exactly what would be expected if family limitation were beginning to be practised.

[10] Louis Henry, *loc. cit.* in footnote 9.

Given the simultaneous change in rates of pre-marital pregnancy, the relationship between pre-nuptial conception and marital fertility was also investigated. While the average size of families of women who were pregnant at marriage did not fall below seven in the nineteenth-century cohorts, the mean age of these mothers at the birth of their last child was slightly lower than that of women who were not pregnant at marriage. The age-specific marital fertility rates of pre-maritally pregnant women were also higher in the 15–24 age group and lower in the 35–44 age group than those of non-pregnant women. There was, in other words, no discernible association between pre-nuptial pregnancy and uncontrolled fertility at the individual level.[11]

The decline in completed family size in Sturbridge between 1730 and 1840, then, was caused by the interaction of a rising age at first marriage of females and the beginning of deliberate family limitation. For couples married in the eighteenth century the increase in age at marriage was most important; for couples married in the nineteenth century the evidence suggests that family limitation was an equally strong influence in determining lower completed family size. While we cannot fully explain why these demographic shifts took place, it is possible to sketch alternative interpretations and explore some of their implications.

With regard to the rising age at marriage, it is likely that the initial increase in the mean age at first marriage for women in the eighteenth century can be explained by the changing sex ratio in the community. Throughout the first two-thirds of the century, Sturbridge was a newly settled community, and men probably constituted a significant majority of the inhabitants. After that time, however, the sex ratio balanced. (The first census of the town was taken by the federal government in 1790, and showed a fairly even sex ratio.) This would accord with the stabilization in the mean age at marriage observed both among the completed families and in the larger marriage cohorts. The rise in age at marriage that began in the nineteenth century, however, cannot be explained in that way. Men as well as women began marrying at older ages, and any explanation of this trend must account for increases in the mean age at marriage for both sexes.

In an agricultural community characterized by a nuclear family pattern, marriage means the establishment of an independent household and farm. In the earliest years of settlement land was abundant and cheap; many proprietors held enough uncultivated land to provide their children with farms when they married, and it was not difficult for young in-migrants to obtain the necessary capital to purchase land. As the town filled up in the late eighteenth century, however, land prices rose and most family farms had become too small to be profitably sub-divided. The beginning of out-migration to newer communities is one sign of this phenomenon; the rise in the age at marriage may be another. If parents were less able to contribute to the independent establishment of their children, and the capital costs of farming were increas-

11

	Children ever born		Mean age at marriage		Mean age of mother at last birth		Percentage of brides
Cohort	Not pregnant	Pregnant	Not pregnant	Pregnant	Not pregnant	Pregnant	pregnant
1730–59	8·3	11·7	20·8	19·0	38·1	41·5	13·6
1760–79	7·2	6·7	22·5	21·7	40·2	40·8	28·6
1780–99	7·1	7·3	23·0	20·6	39·9	36·3	30·2
1800–19	5·8	7·3	24·3	20·9	37·9	37·4	23·3
1820–39	5·3	7·0	24·4	—	35·7	—	2·9

Age-Specific Marital Fertility Rates

	15–24		25–34		35–44	
Cohort	Not pregnant	Pregnant	Not pregnant	Pregnant	Not pregnant	Pregnant
1730–59	436	583	391	500	234	250
1760–79	449	460	406	373	268	185
1780–99	525	500	418	351	246	170
1800–19	488	519	349	529	146	100
1820–39	362	—	339	—	115	—

ing, then young people would have to spend more time working as labourers in order to amass the resources required for marriage.

The limitation of this argument is that while it is rooted in the specific conditions of a rural agricultural community, it does not take into account the economic changes that began in Sturbridge and similar towns in the early nineteenth century and which had significantly transformed social life by 1850. In a study of a single community it is impossible to separate the effects of these changes from those resulting from the settlement process; comparative studies of communities in which settlement and economic change interacted differently would be required to clarify their interactions. (The commercialization of the economy may also have been substantially related to the culmination of the settlement process; the increase in land prices and in the capitalization of farming are signs of both phenomena.) But it is possible, minimally, to say that the spread of wage labour did not substantially counteract the difficulties that the land–population situation posed to young people seeking to marry. We know from other sources that youths working in factories did not marry at younger ages than those employed in agriculture, and that mean ages at marriage were not lower in industrial villages than in farming communities.[12] The ways in which the expansion of the market economy affected young people, moreover, were mediated by the family system; decisions about work as well as about marriage were made within the context of family relationships and the family economy. Most wage work was done by persons whose families were also engaged in agriculture; which family members worked for wages in or outside of the household, and what was done with the wages they received, was a matter decided by the family.

The practice of deliberate family limitation may be explained, at least in part, by reference to the settlement process. If couples were becoming conscious of the impact of developing land–population pressure on their ability to provide for their children (which would be especially clear to them if they had themselves experienced increasing difficulty in obtaining the resources needed for marriage), they might decide to limit their fertility when they had had as many children as they felt they could reasonably help to get established in life. But while the social control of family formation in response to changing economic conditions was a common feature of the demographic history of rural communities, deliberate control of family size by married couples was not; however rational the choice of this course of action, something else must have been happening to make this response part of the available repertoire of the population.

The question here is not primarily one of ways and means, but rather of an orientation toward the family and economic life that allowed childbearing to become a matter of conscious decision.[13] There was no basis for such an orientation in the life-experience of most families prior to the expansion of the market economy in the early nineteenth century. Although the ways in which participation in the market affected attitudes toward the family's economic future are difficult to trace, it is possible to outline one set of plausible connections. First, however, we must be clear that we are not talking about family planning in the modern sense, nor is any change in the optimal effective family size necessarily involved. Rather, the kind of choices about fertility we are concerned with here were made relatively late in the family life cycle, and had reference to the future of an existing family. The development of commercial and industrial capitalism in the early nineteenth century does not seem to have significantly shifted the relative contributions made by children and adults to the family labour supply or income pool. Contrary to earlier assumptions, early industrialization seems neither to have increased

[12] The first statement can be substantiated from the Sturbridge vital records; the second is based upon Nancy Osterud's unpublished study of the 1850 federal census of Providence County, Rhode Island.

[13] The early decline in marital fertility cannot have been accomplished through mechanical methods of contraception; abstinence and *coitus interruptus* were the only available and effective voluntary methods of fertility control.

nor diminished the amount children's labour could add to the family income. The same seems to hold true for women, although that case is complicated by the difficulty of ascertaining the value of work women did inside the home. The proportion of a family's income that could be earned by family members of a specific age and sex who worked outside the household seems generally to be surprisingly close to the proportion of the family's labour they could perform in a farm household. Furthermore, a decline from an average of eight to five children per family would not have significantly reduced the burden of dependency at any one point in the family life cycle. Assuming two-year intervals between births (and no change in the spacing of children when family limitation began), the oldest child in a five-child family would be doing work of some value by the time the last child was born; a family with eight children could also not have more than four children under the 'useful' age of seven at any one time. Under similar labour income conditions, only families smaller than five would have a reduced dependency burden at any one time.

What the increasing absorption of rural farm families into the capitalist economy did do was to make the family economy itself a matter of conscious awareness and planning. When it was equally possible to set a child to pegging boots and shoes as to weeding the kitchen garden, the money received for the former was a reminder of the economic nature of the child's activity and a measure of the value of his or her labour. When a woman could earn 12 cents per dozen for braiding palm-leaf hats, it was harder to regard her sewing of the family's clothes as merely an expression of her role as wife and mother. When a man could decide whether to plant grass or oats depending upon their anticipated market price rather than on his family's needs, the most customary of a farmer's tasks entered the realm of planning. Whether or not any particular family member engaged in wage labour, and whether or not any particular farm or household product was sold, that possibility affected the way in which life was conducted. Labour became separated from personal character and from interpersonal relations, and became subject to calculation of value and to conscious allocation. Rationalization replaced improvisation in many areas of daily life. Ample evidence of this shift can be found in the flood of manuals published in New England in the 1830s. Ministers, educated women, and popular journalists advised New Englanders on the best methods of conducting a farm, cooking a meal, building a mill, or raising a family. It is not the content, but the existence of this literature that is most important here; it meant that things that were once regarded as situations to be coped with as they arose were now becoming things to be planned for and controlled.

The explanation of family limitation proposed, then, is one that relates fertility behaviour to economic change primarily at the level of *mentalité*, while suggesting that consciousness is produced in the course of people's daily life activities. The specific forms of economic transformation occurring in towns like Sturbridge in the first half of the nineteenth century led parents to think about the future of their families in a new way, and to limit their childbearing at the point when they felt that they had borne as many children as they could acceptably provide for later. While land-population pressure in the rural community made such a response appropriate, the expansion of the market economy made it possible. We should not forget, however, that this response did not occur in isolation. At the same time when married couples began to limit their fertility, the more traditional social controls over family formation were also being employed. The demographic history of Sturbridge in the early nineteenth century thus consists of the interaction of old and new means of fertility control.

JOHN MODELL
University of Minnesota

Family and Fertility on the Indiana Frontier, 1820

IN 1820 THOSE PARTS OF THE STATE OF INDIANA ALREADY SETTLED BY WHITE men were recent additions to agricultural America. Much the largest part of the young state, indeed, was included within three enormous and barely populated northern counties. The state's population of nearly 150,000, or about four persons per square mile overall, represented a sixfold growth since the territorial census of 1810; in 1801, the count had been only 5,641. Indiana's population in 1820, thus, was clearly a new one. It was also a rapidly growing one, and it would double again by 1830. Indiana was the frontier.

Recent inquiries directed toward determining with precision the demographic character of the American frontier have indicated that such common aspects of frontier imagery as the single, unattached frontiersman have been grossly overemphasized. Jack E. Eblen has found, by constructing composite agricultural populations from various United States census reports for the mid-19th century, that although males and the young tended to be somewhat more common in frontier populations than in those of more mature settlements, the self-sufficient frontiersman was indeed numerically rare in these settings. Families, instead, provided the basic element of social structure on the frontier, as elsewhere in American society. This paper will seek to demonstrate that the family passed almost intact to the Old Northwest frontier; besides reaffirming Eblen's important argument about the widespread presence of families on the frontier, it will lay out some of the parameters of their size and composition.[1] Moreover, it will be shown that these parameters scarcely varied with

[1]Jack E. Eblen, "An Analysis of Nineteenth-Century Frontier Populations," *Demography*, 2 (1965), 399–413. One study of the frontier family, lacking, unfortunately, in demographic detail, is Blaine T. Williams' study of a six-county area in central Texas in 1850: "The Frontier Family. Demographic Fact and Historical Myth," in *Essays on the American West*, Harold M. Hollingsworth, ed. (Austin: Univ. of Texas Press, 1969). On cultural patterns of

Reprinted from John Modell, "Family and Fertility on the Indiana Frontier, 1820." *American Quarterly* **XXIII**, No. 5 (1971), published by the University of Pennsylvania. Copyright © 1971, Trustees of the University of Pennsylvania.

population density, and that the most nearly exceptional places were the proto-urban settlements which dotted the American frontier, even minute towns like Rising Sun and Vevay, which, in the words of the historian of "the urban frontier" were "soon forgotten."[2]

From a very early date, sophisticated observers noticed a tendency for birthrates to be higher on the frontier than in the older states. The differential remained even as birthrates, nationally and state-by-state, were declining. Yasukichi Yasuba, in the most detailed account of the subject, has shown that in Indiana (for example) the ratio of children 0–9 years old to women in the fertile ages 16–44—a common proxy for fertility where registration data are lacking—declined from 2.24 in 1820 to 2.14 in 1830 to 1.84 in 1840, as the frontier passed through and beyond the state.[3] At the same dates Ohio, abutting Indiana to the east, had ratios of 2.13, 1.87 and 1.70; while Pennsylvania, one of Ohio's eastern neighbor states, revealed a pattern of decline from 1.75 to 1.54 to 1.46.

Yasuba attempts to prove that before 1830, frontier states permitted higher fertility because they offered cheap farmland to people in the family-formation stage of life. "In a predominately agricultural society," he argues, "land constituted the major, if not the sole, economic opportunity, and its relative scarcity may affect the life of the society profoundly."[4] After about 1830, however, changing economic conditions within households, brought about by incipient industrialization and urbanization, seem to Yasuba to have been more responsible than a shortage of land for fertility decline in long-settled areas. There is more than a little truth in what Yasuba has found. But the following analysis, based on punch-card transcriptions of entries by household in the census enumerators' manuscripts for Indiana in 1820, shows that the simple story of economic-

---

the frontier see Allan G. Bogue, "Social Theory and the Pioneer," *Agricultural History*, 34 (1960), 21–34; and Robert F. Berkhofer Jr., "Space, Time, Culture and the New Frontier," *Agricultural History*, 38 (1964), 21–30.

[2]The quotation is from the introduction to Richard Wade's seminal study, *The Urban Frontier The Rise of Western Cities, 1790–1830* (Cambridge: Harvard Univ. Press, 1959). Wade chooses to ignore the role of such minuscule population nodes as will here be treated as "urban."

[3]The measure will of course be affected by mortality as well, but unless the mortality of children varied far more than one could reasonably expect, fertility variations dominate it. Clyde V. Kiser, Wilson H. Grabill and Arthur A. Campbell, *Trends and Variations in Fertility in the United States* (Cambridge: Harvard Univ. Press, 1968), p. 97; Yasukichi Yasuba, *Birth Rates of the White Population in the United States, 1800–1860* ("Johns Hopkins University Studies in Historical and Political Sciences," Ser. LXXIX, no. 2 [Baltimore: Johns Hopkins Press, 1962]). Wendell H. Bash, "Changing Birth Rates in Developing America: New York State, 1840–1875," *Milbank Memorial Fund Quarterly*, 41 (1963), 161–82, finds for 1855 a fertility decline in townships with a density greater than 37 persons per sq. mi.

[4]Yasuba, *Birth Rates*, pp. 158–59.

demographic interrelationships Yasuba found was not the whole story. The frontier, as historians have begun to learn, was a complex social system, as well as a mobile one.

The 1820 federal census called for deputy marshals, who performed the enumeration, to record for "each dwelling house, or ... head of every family," the following information: name of head of household; number of white males in the household 0–9, 10–15, 16–17, 18–25, 26–44 and 45 or older; number of white females 0–9, 10–17, 18–25, 26–44 and 45 or older; a smaller number of age categories for free black males and free black females, and for male and female slaves; number of Indians not taxed; number of aliens; and number of persons engaged in agriculture, commerce and manufactures. In the 1960s, these data were recorded verbatim on punch cards by the Genealogical Section of the Indiana Historical Society, through whose generosity I obtained the cards.[5]

As in all secondary analyses, assessing the quality of the data to be reexamined was the first order of business. A spot check on the age-sex data for whites, comparing the punch cards with microfilm copies of the original enumerators' manuscripts, was most encouraging, suggesting only about one discrepancy in a thousand entries. The error rate for columns dealing with occupational types, however, was much higher—perhaps 2 or 3 per cent of all entries disagreed with the microfilm original. A certain proportion of the occupation errors, though, was caused by a few systematic errors, and permitted the correction of many cards. The most common keypunch error, however, came in those columns which treated the small black population of the state, which will not be discussed in this paper; here, for some reason, free men were often rendered slaves by the Genealogical Section's keypunchers, with a few manacles being struck off in compensation.

On the whole, the corrected punch cards agreed quite well with the pub-

---

[5]The manner in which the data came to my attention may perhaps be instructive. Quite by accident, in perusing books on a library shelf, I noticed a volume entitled *1820 Federal Census of Indiana* (Willard Heiss, comp.; Indianapolis: Genealogical Section of the Indiana Historical Society, 1966). Genealogists have frequently found it worth their while to publish printed versions of scarcely legible census enumerators' manuscripts, but this volume, upon examination, clearly seemed to be composed of photo-offset computer printout: the compiler, in order to alphabetize names, had wisely chosen to punch each entry on the manuscripts onto an IBM card. Moreover, and what most appealed to me, fixed-column format had been employed for the demographic data, making it easily accessible for "secondary analysis." Given data punched in this fashion, we would be able to reexamine the original census materials for a very large area and create new tables in forms that the census as originally published did not have. The genealogists who had put out the Indiana volume had no further plans for the punch cards and very generously offered to allow me to use the cards for such analytical purposes as I might see fit—a fine argument for a bit more contact between genealogists and historians.

lished census tabulations. The total number of whites recorded in Indiana according to the Genealogical Section cards (which omit Daviess County, for which the manuscript censuses have been lost) was 141,938; the published census counted 142,464 outside of Daviess County. There was, thus, a deficit of 0.3% in the cards. As one might expect, agreement was less nearly perfect in the occupational categories: the cards recorded about 4 per cent too few farmers, 8 per cent too few persons in commerce, and a bare excess of manufacturers. Anyone who has ever worked with old enumerators' manuscripts and old census tabulations will probably join me in my suspicion that the cards are at least as likely to be correct as the official census publication.[6]

In fact, the most important inadequacies of the 1820 Indiana data are not those of the cards, but of the original census. Even if we assume that the assistant marshals who took the census understood perfectly the age and sex categories, they surely had no special reason to know just what the occupational categories meant—especially as they were not carefully instructed about the matter. The enumerators' instructions in 1820 in fact admitted that "the discrimination between persons engaged in agriculture, commerce, and manufactures, will not be without its difficulties." The enumeration of occupations on the 1820 census was a vastly imperfect operation, and was a task which the Census Office would avoid altogether in 1830. A large majority of families with adult males present, however, had at least some occupational entry listed, enabling one to assign all but 9 per cent of the households with white adults present to one of three "chief occupation" categories: agricultural, commercial or manufacturing. For families with more than one occupation listed (a rare difficulty), the occupation with the most members working in it was counted as the "chief" family occupation; in cases with equal numbers in two or more occupations, "commerce" was arbitrarily assigned preference over the other two, while manufactures was preferred to agriculture. Those households for which no occupation was listed were excluded from the following analysis, although an alternative approach might have been to assume these families belonged to the agricultural majority. The assignment of a *single* occupation to each family, and the exclusion of families with no listed occupation permitted a solution to a very obvious problem in the published census materials, for it is there perfectly apparent that while some enumerators had assigned an occupation to each adult male, or to each adult,

---

[6]This faith even survives the somewhat more threatening discrepancies found in a county-by-county comparison of total whites. For 21 counties the cards show a deficit as compared with the published data, and in twelve an excess; in one county there was perfect agreement. In only four counties, however, was the discrepancy between cards and the published report as great as 5 percent: the maximum errors were a deficit of 16.3% in one county, an excess of 10.1% in another.

others had ignored their instructions and listed a maximum of one occupation per family.

The reader must be apprised of one further problem: that at least some households must have been completely ignored by the enumerators. If Daniel Boone fled civilization at the sight of a neighbor's chimney smoke, he presumably also escaped the federal count. The omission of such cases, and others somewhat less extreme, would constitute a systematic bias directly affecting our conclusions about the composition of households. With the caveat, then, that the enumerated Indianians may include only the relatively settled population, these data are presented as an addition to our knowledge in an area where systematic study is slight, and resources surely nowhere superior to those here analyzed.

Table One lists the counties of Indiana in order of population density in 1820.[7] The year of their establishment as counties, in parentheses, does not of course indicate the date of first settlement in the county, since several were subdivided from already-established counties. But a rough parallel between density and "age" does clearly obtain, pointing toward the frontier continuum present in Indiana in 1820.

Household size[8] obviously does vary from county to county. The range is rather narrow, being in all instances between five and seven persons per household, with the vast majority falling between 5.5 and 6.5. By excluding from calculations all households which consisted entirely of one person, this range is reduced considerably. Likewise, an even smaller range of median household size is found when we treat only households in which the oldest female enumerated was 26–44 years old, that is, a probably-married woman almost certainly not yet out of her fertile period.[9] The medians, of course, are higher for these households, since they generally were weighted heavily with families that were well formed, yet not substantially reduced in size by the departure of adult offspring. Students of the cultural patterns of the frontier will recognize that standards of household size

[7]Wabash County, with a minute population, is for that reason omitted from the county-by-county analysis here. County areas were computed by overlaying squares keyed to the scale of the 1820 map. Even if the absolute density figures thus created are imperfect, their relative values will be approximately correct.

[8]Median rather than mean household size is employed to prevent boarding houses and other large nonfamily dwelling units from biasing the results upward.

[9]This type of "controlling," common in studies of recent populations, would have represented an unthinkable amount of work in the distant pre-computer days of 1820, and certainly permits additions to what we know about early American families. Yet the method is full of imperfections for serving as an indicator of "normal" or "complete" household size. The excessive range of the "mature female" category, the uncertainty that she is actually the wife or widow of the head of the household, the uncertain inclusiveness of the household itself, and the possibility that young adult offspring may have moved away should make one wary of the exact values presented in this paper.

(and, by inference, family structure) quite apparently had been transmitted intact there. For all types of households, what variation we do find is quite unrelated to population density. (Uncollapsed household-by-size data for counties are presented in Appendix A for readers who may wish to pursue further the nature of variations implied by the medians. Data from the first federal census of 1790 have been presented elsewhere in similar form.[10] At that time in Pennsylvania, a state straddling the frontier, the range of median household size by county was like that for Indiana 30 years later—5.52 to 6.38—and bore no systematic relationship to the frontier.)

Table One also presents values for three characteristics of households in Indiana which might be expected to show a systematic relationship to population density. The figures do show a great deal more county-to-county variation than those for household size. But, except for a slight tendency for fewer households lacking adult males to be found in the least dense counties—perhaps those widowed at the margin of civilization sensibly retreated to more populated areas—there is no clear connection to density.[11] "Widowhood," being relatively nonvolitional, was also comparatively stable county-to-county. Households with only one member, or with more than two persons 26 years or older, varied somewhat more widely. But neither was regularly a function of density. To a great extent Indiana family size was determined basically by a cultural definition of family practices that was more or less consistent throughout the state: a shunning of "incomplete" family structures and a tendency to avoid households with more than two adults. "Normal" families in Indiana in 1820, therefore, were like "normal" American families now: nuclear families with both spouses present, and their minor children. Deviance from this pattern was unrelated to how close the family was to the frontier.

Demographically, the most important variable affecting family size in a situation in which "completeness" and "nuclearity" dominate is fertility. Did fertility have any relationship to the frontier in newly-settled Indiana, as Yasuba's state findings would lead us to expect? Table One further reveals that there was *no* clear-cut relationship between fertility (measured by a child/woman ratio like Yasuba's) and population density. There was a fair range in fertility, which, as mapping would indicate, was "regional" rather than randomly scattered through the state. But "frontierness," or at any rate population density, cannot explain it.

It further appears from Table One, however, that what Yasuba calls

[10]W. S. Rossiter, ed., *A Century of Population Growth* (Washington: Government Printing Office, 1909).

[11]Households which were listed under an obviously female name showed a pattern generally similar, though different in detail, to that of the "no adult male" approach to a measurement of "widowhood."

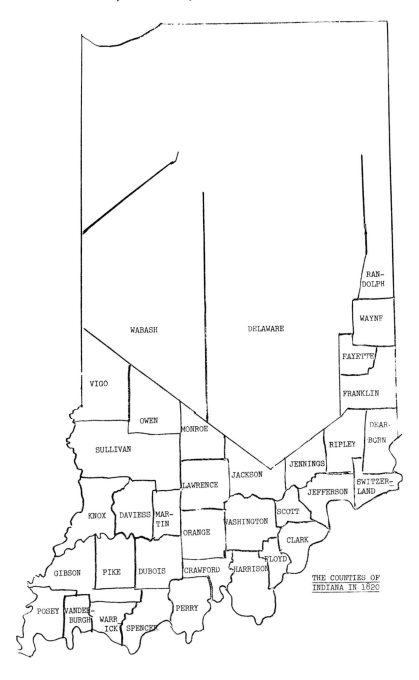

RAN-
DOLPH

WAYNE

FAYETTE

FRANKLIN

WABASH

DELAWARE

VIGO

OWEN

MONROE

DEAR-
BORN

SULLIVAN

RIPLEY

JENNINGS

JACKSON

LAWRENCE

SWITZER-
LAND

JEFFERSON

KNOX

DAVIESS

MAR-
TIN

SCOTT

WASHINGTON

ORANGE

CLARK

GIBSON

PIKE

DUBOIS

CRAWFORD

HARRISON

FLOYD

THE COUNTIES OF
INDIANA IN 1820

POSEY

VANDER-
BURGH

WARR
ICK

SPENCER

PERRY

TABLE ONE

Demographic and Household Characteristics by County, Indiana, 1820
(Listed in Order of Population Density)

County (with year of establishment)	Median Size: All households	Median Size: Multiple-person households	Households in which oldest female is 26–44 yrs.	Proportion of Households With: No male 18 yrs. or older	Only one member	More than two adults aged 26 or older	Fertility ratio [a]	Propensity to "headship" of women 16–25 yrs [b]
Dearborn (1811)	6.16	6.25	7.38	2.0	2.0	9.6	2.16	51.5
Fayette (1819)	6.27	6.30	7.74	1.8	0.8	11.0	2.28	57.7
Wayne (1796)	6.15	6.20	7.65	3.0	0.8	6.5	2.38	55.5
Floyd (1819)	5.61	7.02	6.94	3.7	3.7	9.6	2.02	55.1
Jefferson (1811)	6.43	6.55	7.69	2.8	1.7	13.2	2.09	47.0
Franklin (1811)	6.45	6.55	7.58	2.8	2.0	8.6	2.37	45.0
Washington (1813)	6.55	6.63	7.81	2.8	1.0	10.5	2.29	51.2
Clark (1801)	6.37	6.51	7.75	4.3	1.9	14.1	2.03	45.4
Switzerland (1814)	5.92	6.03	7.47	2.6	2.2	5.6	2.58	61.3
Harrison (1808)	6.76	6.85	7.75	3.2	0.8	9.7	2.46	46.2
Scott (1820)	5.96	6.01	8.13	2.1	1.4	10.9	2.29	66.1
Knox (1790)	5.15	6.19	7.12	5.0	22.4	12.3	1.75	43.8
Posey (1814)	5.89	5.90	7.36	3.2	0.3	17.9	1.85	47.4

Orange (1816)	6.35	6.45	7.72	4.4	1.0	9.8	2.30	56.5
Crawford (1818)	6.56	6.59	7.82	4.7	0.8	11.8	2.39	50.1
Lawrence (1818)	5.90	5.93	7.20	2.0	0.9	8.5	2.41	61.3
Warrick (1811)	6.48	6.55	7.74	3.6	2.1	8.6	2.49	57.5
Vanderburgh (1818)	5.28	5.79	7.45	2.1	11.2	7.2	2.00	52.6
Gibson (1811)	6.24	6.51	7.76	3.8	3.0	10.0	2.01	48.5
Jennings (1817)	5.86	5.93	6.91	0.9	2.4	12.0	2.23	54.3
Perry (1814)	6.07	6.14	7.42	7.0	1.8	8.6	2.32	55.6
Pike (1817)	6.18	6.34	8.03	1.7	2.1	12.7	2.64	58.8
Monroe (1818)	6.35	6.36	7.63	1.9	0.2	11.5	2.35	60.1
Jackson (1815)	6.15	6.17	8.00	1.9	0.3	9.3	2.28	60.5
Spencer (1818)	6.26	6.34	7.32	1.6	2.3	8.8	2.47	54.2
Ripley (1817)	5.68	5.81	7.32	0.3	3.7	7.3	2.07	60.8
Vigo (1818)	6.45	6.53	7.73	2.0	1.7	18.1	2.06	58.9
Sullivan (1817)	6.38	6.41	7.71	2.1	0.5	14.5	2.10	50.0
Dubois (1818)	6.12	6.24	7.68	5.0	3.0	8.3	2.24	58.3
Martin (1820)	6.16	6.23	7.93	1.9	1.2	10.7	1.94	62.0
Owen (1819)	6.73	6.73	8.25	0.9	0	18.8	2.37	49.3
Randolph (1818)	5.84	6.02	7.56	2.7	4.3	8.1	2.30	66.7
Delaware (1820)	5.92	6.23	7.64	3.0	7.4	6.8	2.46	61.6

[a] Ratio of number of children 0–9 to number of women 16–44.
[b] Ratio of households in which the oldest woman was 16–25 to total number of women 16–25.

"marriage customs" did somewhat favor frontier fertility, for there was a slight tendency on the frontier for women in the 16–25 age category to be the oldest women in their households, probably a fair indication of being married to the household head (or, less commonly, of being a widow). This tendency, though by no means showing a direct relationship with density, may reveal one reason why frontier states might have had a higher ratio of children to fertile-aged women, as Yasuba found. The simple relationship in Indiana between county child/woman ratio and the headship proportion of 16–25-year-old females is quite weak, with an insignificant Spearman rank-order correlation of only +0.27. Obviously, other factors than frontier "marriage customs" were at work. Density per se explains little about family structure in the young American west.

Table Two, which examines five groups of counties, aggregated by population density, repeats some of the measures shown in the previous table.[12] Here, the unimportance of density as a category affecting the

TABLE TWO
Characteristics of White Households, by County
Population Density, Indiana, 1820

	Densest Counties	Second Densest	Third Densest	Fourth Densest	Least Dense Counties
Median household size	6.16	6.18	6.08	6.17	6.14
Households with no adult male (%)	2.0	2.5	2.3	1.6	1.8
Households with more than two adults (%)	8.2	9.2	9.3	9.2	10.0
Fertility ratio	2.25	2.15	2.12	2.26	2.22
Propensity to headship of women 16–25 (%)	52.2	48.9	54.8	55.4	57.7
Households with only one member (%)	1.5	6.0	2.0	1.9	3.2

[12]Density is treated, properly in view of the present state of our knowledge of its effects, as a continuum, with breaking-points between counties for purposes of Table Two assigned merely on the basis of statistical convenience, and with no theoretical justification for making the particular divisions that were made. They are, between Washington (20.1 persons per

more important demographic measures—household size and fertility ratio is once again made clear, as is also its relatively minor importance, even to those family measures which to some extent varied with it. We find, for example, that though widowhood was somewhat less common on the frontier, it was irregularly so; that there was a weak inverse relationship between density and tendency to live in what were perhaps extended families (or at least households large enough to accommodate more than the usual component of two adults), but that the absolute magnitude of this characteristic was nowhere great; and that tendency toward earlier family formation on the frontier, too, was of little absolute importance, even though it does seem to point to somewhat different frontier marriage customs. We are led once again to ask whether indeed the frontier did differ from areas to the east in any basic way other than in age and sex structure, and to what extent the common finding of greater human fertility at the margin of European society may have been a result merely of this different age structure.

Despite weaknesses in the occupational measure, child/woman ratios for the families with the several occupational specializations were significantly different. Agricultural families had, statewide, an average of 2.28 children per woman; the corresponding figure for manufacturing families was 2.02; for commercial families it was 1.49. Although there was a slight tendency for older families to be farmers, this fact does not wholly explain the observed differences in the child/woman ratio. Evidently, in some way, involvement with trade on a regular basis affected family size. The finding that differential fertility obtained in America, with farmers the most fertile occupational group, is hardly a surprising one: but to find it in a frontier state in 1820 means that factors other than Yasuba's notions about free or inexpensive land were important. Inexpensive land was, after all, available to farm families and nonfarm families alike.

We can also examine the effect of occupational differences by computing a rank-order correlation between the proportion of families in each county engaged in agriculture and the child/woman ratio. We earlier found no relationship between density and fertility, but we now find a distinct relationship, with a Spearman rank-order correlation of $+0.67$, between proportion of families agricultural and fertility ratio for all families. Thus, on the state level, which Yasuba examined, density may well have stood as a proxy for agricultural concentration; but within Indiana, on a county-by-county basis, it did not.

---

sq. mi.) and Clark (18.3); Knox (10.1) and Posey (9.7); Vanderburg (7.1) and Gibson (6.8); Ripley (4.8) and Vigo (3.6). I have tried to make the groups of more or less equal numbers of counties, but respected those clusterings that inhered in the data.

To decide whether from the point of view of human fertility the frontier meant nothing more than a concentration of farmers, the effects of individual occupation must be separated from the general *context* of frontier farm concentration. The question is an important one, for frontier as context has long been a central theme of American history. In answering this question our data have unique value, and indicate distinctly that *both* individual and contextual factors were operative upon Indiana fertility in 1820. Not only, that is, did farmers as such have more children, finding them perhaps economically beneficial, they also were more fertile because they lived in a milieu in which agrarian values predominated. That this is so is demonstrated at the top of Table Three, where counties are grouped according to occupational enumeration into five levels of concentration in agriculture,[13] with families further divided into agricultural and non-agricultural. At all levels of county agricultural concentration, farmers had more children than nonfarmers, while both agricultural and nonagricultural families were more fertile in highly agricultural counties. A middling fertility characterized both farmers in areas with relatively high levels of nonagricultural employment and nonfarmers located in the more purely agricultural areas.

TABLE THREE

Fertility Ratio for Agricultural and Nonagricultural Households, Indiana, 1820, by Level of County Agricultural Concentration, and by Degree of County "Urbanization."

	Level of Agricultural Concentration				
	High	2	3	4	Low
Agricultural households	2.32	2.38	2.34	2.12	2.11
Nonagricultural households	2.05	2.15	2.11	1.87	1.80

	Level of "Urbanization"			
	Quite Unurb.	Minimal Urbaniz.	Incipient Urbaniz.	Relatively Urbanized
Agricultural households	2.27	2.44	2.26	2.12
Nonagricultural households	1.86	2.27	2.21	1.81

[13]The cutting points, again arbitrary incisions into a presumed continuum, are between Fayette (21.2% nonagricultural) and Posey (18.1); Gibson 16.8) and Franklin (14.9); Switzerland (12.8) and Owen (12.0); and Sullivan (7.8) and Crawford (6.8).

A final word on this part of Table Three must be a puzzled one: the step-wise movement of fertility ratios, with a big spread between levels three and four, indicates either a statistical quirk or some critical level of non-agricultural activity at which fertility was often reduced. Were there such a critical level, these data would seem to suggest that it was around 15 or 16 per cent of all families engaged in nonagricultural pursuits, but the data also provide several exceptions. Although the farm/nonfarm dimension is one deeply and doubly involved in determining the fertility (and thereby the family size) of Indiana people in 1820, the factor cannot by any means explain all county-to-county differences.

Although the very spare data of the 1820 census do not permit deep understanding of the relationship of urbanization to fertility, we can approximate a measure of its effect. Two approaches were available, and both point to an urbanization process which, though rudimentary, was also central to whatever systematic demographic variation, outside of age and sex structure, was present in frontier Indiana.

The first test involves ranking the Indiana counties, the smallest units for which data were published, by their estimated level of urbanization in 1820, basing the ranking on roughly contemporary noncensus materials.[14] The resulting typology, which is manifestly unreliable but seems the best attainable independent of the occupational data from the census itself and from other materials from the manuscript census, divides counties into four categories: 1) those with one well-established town or several growing ones; 2) those with at least one growing town, even if not much developed; 3) counties displaying any other reported sign of nucleated development, which would seem to have contained as many as 100 persons; 4) counties where no nucleated development had been noticed.[15]

Table Three at the bottom displays child/woman ratios for all families, chiefly engaged in agriculture and otherwise, by the degree of "urbanization" of the counties in which they lived. The results are substantially similar to those in which agricultural concentration of counties defines the

[14]Works employed to create the "urbanization" typology were the travel accounts of Samuel R. Brown, Edmund Dana and Timothy Flint, in Harlow Lindley, ed., *Indiana as Seen by Early Travelers* (Indiana Historical Society *Collections*, 3 [1916]), and *Indiana Gazetteer* (Indiana Historical Society *Publications*, 18, 1 [1954]).

[15]Because the choice by enumerators whether to record their data by minor civil divisions or not often appeared to follow no clear logic, the "urbanization" typology did *not* employ the 1820 manuscript census. Too, census occupational statistics were ignored in order to keep the "urbanization" typology independent of the one based on agricultural concentration. According to the typology as derived, the following counties are classed as relatively urbanized: Clark, Dearborn, Floyd, Jefferson, Knox, Switzerland; as slightly urbanized: Fayette, Franklin, Posey, Washington; as minimally urbanized: Harrison, Jackson, Jennings, Perry, Ripley, Vigo, Wayne; as quite unurbanized: Crawford, Dubois, Delaware, Gibson, Lawrence, Martin, Monroe, Orange, Pike, Scott, Spencer, Randolph, Sullivan, Owen, Vanderburgh, Warrick.

typology.[16] The urbanization typology, although composed of only four categories, produces quite nearly the same "spread" between minimum and maximum fertility as did the agricultural concentration typology. There is, moreover, for both agricultural and nonagricultural families something like the same discontinuity between the most urban category and all others, as seen between the second and third categories of the agricultural concentration typology. When we recall that the largest town in the "relatively urbanized" category was Vincennes, with a white population of 1,250, and that Vincennes was much more populated than any other town in the state, we are again led to conceive of the effects of "urbanism" extending far down the scale into areas usually considered basically rural. But it is equally clear that its effects do stop *somewhere*.[17]

Although not *reported* by town, certain of the Indiana census data for 1820 were so *collected*. As a result, one can in some but not all instances

[16]There is of course considerable overlap among the three sets of county typologies. The overlap, however, is far from total, as is indicated by the tables below, which justify the use of the typologies as empirically as well as theoretically independent measures. The figures shown are numbers of counties falling into the cell in question. The three counties for which no data on agricultural concentration are available are omitted here.

1. Density by Agricultural Concentration

Density	Ag. Concentration				
	Most	2nd	3rd	4th	Least
Most	3	1	1	2	0
2nd	2	0	2	1	0
3rd	1	1	0	1	1
4th	0	1	3	1	2
Least	0	1	1	3	2

2. Density by "Urbanization"

Density	"Urbanization"			
	Most	2nd	3rd	Least
Most	3	3	1	0
2nd	3	0	1	1
3rd	0	1	0	5
4th	0	0	4	4
Least	0	0	1	6

3. Agricultural Concentration by "Urbanization."

Ag. concent.	"Urbanization"			
	Most	2nd	3rd	Least
Most	4	1	0	1
2nd	1	1	0	2
3rd	1	1	3	2
4th	0	1	3	4
Least	0	0	1	4

[17]Where the effect of the city stops is of course an argument among American rural sociologists, as the debate among Leo Schnore and others (*Rural Sociology*, 31 [1966], 131–55) indicates.

JOHN MODELL

reconstitute town data from the census manuscripts, and, less often, extract from among the Genealogical Section punch cards those families who lived within certain of these cities, including the largest, Vincennes. Table Four presents child/woman ratios for five rather sizable towns

TABLE FOUR

Fertility Ratios of Selected Towns, Their Immediate and
Less Immediate Environs, Indiana, 1820

County	Place (s)	Incorporated White Population	Fertility ratio
Dearborn	Lawrenceburg town	601	1.72
	Neighboring towns	265	2.08
	Balance, Lawrenceburg twp.		2.14
	Rising Sun Town	403	1.59
	Balance, Randolph twp.		2.14
	Balance, Dearborn County		2.14
Fayette	Connersville town	403	1.75
	Balance, Connersville twp.		2.44
	Balance, Fayette Co.		2.28
Knox	Vincennes town	1250	1.59
	Balance, Vincennes twp.		1.79
	Balance, Knox County		1.80
Switzerland	Vevay town	438	1.96
	Balance, Jefferson twp.		2.40
	Balance, Switzerland County		2.41

in four Indiana counties, three of them in my "most urbanized" category, the fourth in the "slightly urbanized" category. Similar calculations were made for the balance of each of the townships in which the incorporated towns were located, and for the balance of the county, outside the township or townships in question. The findings, although not fully representative of Indiana in 1820, do point to the same kind of yes-or-no situation suggested by the discontinuity found in our typologies. The towns with one partial exception had quite low child/woman ratios—lower, in fact, than for nonagricultural families in nonagricultural and in urbanized counties. Although Vincennes had a population three times that of Rising Sun, its child-to-woman ratio was no lower; and Connersville and Lawrenceburg were only slightly more fertile. Town life per se, at least at the level of 400 persons or more, seems in more-or-less uniform fashion to have inhibited fertility,[18] although mere proximity to a town did not. Even the small incorporated towns near Lawrenceburg had a fertility ratio much more like the environing rural area than their big neighbor.[19]

On the other hand, Knox County, containing the state's chief city, displayed quite a reduced fertility overall, although Vincennes represented only about a quarter of Knox's total population; and the county-by-county relationship to urbanization, as we saw, was quite pronounced. Whether or not the "urban" factor in frontier demography can be held literally to be "pervasive" on the basis of these data is not certain; that it is a factor that must be considered in studies of frontier culture and demography is, on the other hand, clear.

Our data permit a preliminary consideration of the relationship of "urbanization" to certain household characteristics. Table Five presents statistics on median family size, households with no adult male, "singleton" households, households with more than two adults, and propensity to headship by young women, for Vincennes (whose characteristics were somewhat peculiar), for all other incorporated areas for which family data can be isolated, for the unincorporated areas in the counties surrounding these urban places, as well as for the county "urbanization" typology. We are hardly in a position to speak with confidence on the basis of so few data, but Table Five suggests that apart from smaller median household size in towns, relatively urbanized areas may have permitted a slightly larger concentration of "deviant" household patterns than did other areas. The Vincennes figures for singleton households and for households with no male head point to this possibility, although those for the aggregation of smaller incorporated places certainly do not show the same pattern.

Moreover, when we seek to discover whether or not frontier "urbanization" is reflected systematically in the county figures, we find only a slight excess of widows in the *un*urbanized counties, along with a clearly greater propensity there to headship by young women. These two factors, it seems, overcome the higher fertility characteristic of the nonurban areas to produce smaller median households there. But the reverse was the case both in Vincennes and in the other incorporated places, where the urban areas

---

[18]The 1801 and 1810 territorial censuses indicate a relatively low fertility in Vincennes town, even in the former year. At that date, the local child/woman ratio was 1.77, as compared to 2.05 for the "neighborhood of St. Vincennes." In 1810, the figures were 1.83 and 1.90. Note a decline in both town and vicinity fertility ratios by 1820, along with the maintenance of the urban/rural differential.

[19]Several tiny incorporated towns in Laughery township, Dearborn County, however, with a combined population of 343, had a child-to-woman ratio of 1.95, as compared with 2.26 for the unincorporated part of the township, so that the data leave the question of the vanishing point of the effect of urbanization up in the air.

TABLE FIVE
Characteristics of Households in Selected Urban Places and Their Environs, and by Degree of County "Urbanization"

	Median household size	Med. hh. size (single-tons exclu.)	Households with no male 18 or older (per cent)	Households with only one member (per cent)	Households with more than two adults (per cent)	Propensity to headship of women 16–25 (per cent)
Vincennes	3.33	5.89	8.2	44.0	9.6	53.4
"Incorp. places."	5.64	5.74	2.0	2.4	9.7	56.6
Knox Co. outside Vincennes	6.03	6.49	3.3	9.9	11.4	41.2
Unincorp. Dearborn & Fayette Co.	6.25	6.31	1.8	1.5	8.6	53.2
Quite unurbanized counties	5.76	5.87	5.3	2.9	9.3	57.7
Minimally urbanized counties	6.24	6.34	5.1	1.2	7.1	55.6
Incipiently urbanized counties	6.37	6.41	4.5	1.2	9.5	49.9
Relatively urbanized counties	6.02	6.56	3.3	5.2	9.7	49.5

had substantially smaller households, even excluding singletons, than did their rural environs. The pattern is, at this point, paradoxical.

Once again, however, the chief finding may be in the column showing the proportion of households with more than two adults: the nuclear household was uniformly the rule. If the frontiersman's fertility behavior was a function of the particular part of the frontier he lived in and of his occupation, he clearly took his ideas about family structure to the frontier with him. Yet, while this picture holds true in general, the exceptions to it are frequent enough to remain intriguing. "Commercial" households, for example, were much more likely to have an extended-family structure (18.3 per cent with more than two adults) than either manufacturing or agricultural (10.9 per cent and 8.7 per cent). And the reader is reminded that despite the regularity of "doubling up" in Table Five, Table One showed a very substantial though irregular county-to-county variation in this characteristic.

The findings of this paper cannot claim to be definitive, but do establish three basic points of considerable importance. 1) The notion of "urbanization" has a meaning for the agricultural frontier that extends to quite small places, but its meaning is far from completely understood. 2) While fertility at the state level varied rather regularly with the frontier, as Yasuba found, on a lower level it was subject to a variety of factors related complexly to the frontier, notably age at family formation, economic context—both personal and regional—and degree of urbanization. 3) Family structure was overwhelmingly nuclear in all areas on the Indiana frontier. What differences did exist do not seem to have been systematically related to the "frontier" variables.

We have long known that we must examine the American agricultural frontier as part of a continuum with the rest of the society. This paper is one effort to explore in detail some of the complexities implied by recognition of this fact.

JOHN MODELL

APPENDIX A

Number of White Households, by Size, by County, Indiana, 1820

(Listed in Order of Population Density)

County	1	2	3	4	5	6	7	8	9	10	11	12	13+	Total White Families
Dearborn	38	147	237	252	252	252	208	192	142	108	60	29	15	1932
Fayette	8	78	94	135	140	120	102	89	86	59	31	15	16	973
Wayne	16	159	259	255	267	264	219	194	171	90	53	19	26	1992
Floyd	18	49	68	68	66	50	48	30	32	25	17	7	8	486
Jefferson	22	80	127	160	166	179	126	125	87	83	58	31	20	1264
Franklin	34	124	184	199	219	244	197	161	149	116	55	38	22	1742
Washington	15	90	149	191	173	177	169	151	109	104	53	34	17	1432
Clark	27	107	160	174	163	173	153	127	104	73	64	33	31	1389
Switzerland	15	67	93	83	99	81	74	69	53	26	19	9	9	697
Harrison	10	58	133	145	156	131	146	118	127	79	44	22	34	1203
Scott	6	34	60	50	69	38	57	43	27	23	9	9	8	433
Knox	231	62	96	111	110	113	93	68	58	36	25	15	12	1030
Posey	2	34	77	127	105	81	71	49	45	30	21	13	11	666
Orange	9	73	90	120	113	97	116	88	65	45	39	11	12	878
Crawford	3	30	42	54	37	43	54	37	28	23	12	12	5	380
Lawrence	6	61	91	103	92	83	71	51	60	34	23	8	5	688
Warrick	6	26	23	41	25	40	35	30	22	13	9	5	5	280
Vanderburgh	38	26	44	51	38	30	42	28	18	9	8	3	4	339
Gibson	19	47	71	86	79	81	77	62	50	33	20	10	8	643
Jennings	8	28	33	50	57	40	33	21	24	20	12	4	6	336
Perry	7	39	35	51	57	48	54	26	20	19	14	11	4	385

APPENDIX A (*continued*)

County	1	2	3	4	5	6	7	8	9	10	11	12	13+	Total White Families
Pike	7	14	26	36	33	25	25	20	24	19	8	2	2	241
Monroe	1	32	46	57	56	63	41	37	39	17	22	4	4	428
Jackson	2	60	100	86	77	72	66	75	55	37	20	14	8	672
Spencer	7	19	28	51	37	43	35	33	22	12	8	6	5	306
Ripley	12	21	41	55	49	43	29	26	15	17	8	6	3	325
Vigo	9	41	60	61	69	71	66	61	33	29	13	16	15	560
Sullivan	3	37	58	75	81	69	62	56	44	23	26	13	13	544
Dubois	6	21	20	29	22	25	27	14	19	8	6	4	1	202
Martin	2	10	23	25	18	15	19	12	14	8	7	3	5	161
Owen	0	7	11	13	19	11	15	9	10	5	8	4	4	116
Randolph	14	27	42	47	37	42	31	29	20	20	9	3	1	322
Delaware	49	41	75	90	83	79	58	54	40	38	24	14	18	663
Total	650	1749	2696	3131	3064	2923	2619	2185	1812	1281	805	427	366	23708

(Daviess and Wabash Counties are excluded)

DIFFERENTIAL FERTILITY IN MADISON COUNTY, NEW YORK, 1865

WENDELL H. BASH[1]

THE hypothesis that the "normal" pattern of differential fertility in a population is that of a "J" shaped curve rather than a straight line inverse relationship between birth rates and social status has gained increasing acceptance in recent years. According to the interpretation of the history of these patterns, the straight line inverse relationship is a product of the diffusion of contraceptive information through a population, beginning in the upper classes and in the urban centers and spreading downward and outward. Most of our reliable information about differential fertility falls into the period of this transition, and actually toward the end of it as we can make out the cycle.[2] Verification of the "J" hypothesis depends upon the most recent census information in the United States and Europe,[3] and this is necessarily incomplete. The surge in the birth rate of these nations during the 1940's and early 1950's is closely related to the rapidly rising marriage rate and consequent speeding up of family formation. Not until reproductive histories of this generation of wives is more complete can we be certain, even though there are many indications in census materials,[4] of some real change in family size.

Another source of materials for the verification of the "J" hypothesis can be in the historical period before the beginning of this transitional period. Unfortunately, Western nations in this stage of the cycle rarely collected census information usable for this analysis, and this has also been true of those non-West-

[1] From the Department of Sociology, Colgate University. This study was made possible by assistance from the Milbank Memorial Fund and by the friendly advice and counsel of Clyde V. Kiser.

[2] For an exception, see Jaffe, A. J.: Fertility Differentials in the White Population in Early America. *Journal of Heredity*, 31, No. 9, September, 1940, pp. 407–411.

[3] Edin, K. A. and Hutchinson, E. P.: STUDIES OF DIFFERENTIAL FERTILITY IN SWEDEN. London, P. S. King & Son, Ltd., 1935; Innes, John W.: CLASS FERTILITY TRENDS IN ENGLAND AND WALES, 1876–1934. Princeton University Press, 1938. Also, the entire "Indianapolis Study" is related to this problem.

[4] Whelpton, P. K.: COHORT FERTILITY. Princeton University Press, 1954.

Reprinted from *Milbank Memorial Fund Quarterly* XXXIII, No. 1, 161–186. Copyright © 1955 by permission of the publisher.

ern nations which today fall into the early stage of demographic development.[5] Nevertheless, we can help to extend the time span within which we have substantially reliable information by referring to manuscript copies of some censuses.[6] Published data help to provide a context for special studies.

The Census of the State of New York in 1865 is one such source inasmuch as it included a question on completed fertility. The published volume provided only a tabulation of the number of women who had had specified numbers of children, by county and for the native and foreign-born population, but the manuscript copies located in most of the court houses in the State make possible detailed tabulations by occupation and other measures of social status with age and marital condition controlled.

This study is concerned with 5,343 women in Madison County in 1865 with special attention to 4,300 of these women who were native white. Cards were prepared only for couples who had been married only once, thus omitting plural marriages for either spouse, widows, and women who were listed as married but with no husband listed on the household schedule.[7]

MADISON COUNTY IN RELATION TO OTHER COUNTIES

The editors of the New York State Census of 1865 expressed a faith that the returns were reasonably accurate on cumulative fertility. Instructions to the census takers were as follows:

> 11. *Of how many children the parent.*—This inquiry is to be made only of adult *females,* and usually of wives or widows. It should, in all cases, include the number of living children the woman has borne, *whether now living or dead,* and *whether present or absent* from the family. These children may perhaps be

[5] Chen, Ta: Population in Modern China. *American Journal of Sociology,* LII, No. 1, Part 2, July, 1946.

[6] Sydenstricker, Edgar and Notestein, Frank W.: Differential Fertility According to Social Class. *Journal of the American Statistical Association.* 25 (NS) 169: 9–32, March, 1930; Sydenstricker, Edgar: A Study of the Fertility of Native White Women in a Rural Area of Western New York. Milbank Memorial Fund *Quarterly Bulletin.* 10: 17–32, January, 1932.

[7] In one tally of 3,453 married women, some 14 per cent were widowed, and 2 per cent were listed as married with no husband in the household.

themselves the heads of families, and residents of another state, or they may have died in childhood. The object of the inquiry is to obtain data for determining the natural increase of the population in this state among the various classes, and it should be taken fully and uniformly to possess value. Be careful to note in this column the number of children borne by females now aged, as well as that of those now surrounded by their families. We can thus determine the relative rate of increase of a former age, for comparison with the present.[8]

No detailed check of the completeness of this enumeration is possible on a statewide basis, since the published data included nothing on age or marital condition. Nevertheless, the editors' guess that the census was reasonably complete seems to be justified since the tables derived from the manuscript copies of the census include only eighteen wives for whom no information about fertility was obtained.

The published data on completed fertility indicate a generally negative relationship between the birth rate and urbanization and industrialization. The number of children ever born per 100 women was calculated for each county and for native and

Table 1. Correlations between native and foreign birth rates by counties and indexes of urbanization, New York, 1865.

	CHILDREN EVER BORN PER 100 NATIVE WHITE WOMEN	CHILDREN EVER BORN PER 100 FOREIGN-BORN WHITE WOMEN	PER CENT POPULATION FOREIGN BORN	NUMBER UNABLE TO READ AND WRITE PER 1,000 POPULATION	NUMBER OF PERSONS EMPLOYED PER 1,000 POPULATION
Population per Square Mile	−0.44[a]	−0.57[a]	0.72[a]	*	0.42[a]
Number of Persons Employed per 1,000 Population	0.10	−0.24	0.34	0.38	
Number Unable to Read and Write per 1,000 Population	0.13	0.30	0.38		
Per Cent Population Foreign Born	−0.50	−0.24			
Children Ever Born per 100 Foreign-Born White Women	0.48				

* Less than 0.01.
[a] Calculated without Kings, New York, and Richmond Counties because of their extreme departure from the density of other counties.

[8] Instructions for taking the Census of the State of New York, in the year 1865, Albany, Weed, Parsons & Co., 1865, p. 18.

foreign-born white women. These were then correlated with (1) the population per square mile, (2) the number of persons employed per 1,000 population, (3) the number unable to read and write per 1,000 population, and (4) the per cent of the population foreign born.

The inter-correlations between these factors (*see* Table 1.) show population density as being the most important single factor. Birth rates of native and foreign-born white women were positively related (0.48) and both of them were lowest in areas of high density with correlations of – 0.44 and – 0.57 respectively.

The geographical differentials in birth rates in 1865 can be compared with Anderson's[9] data for 1930 with profit. The mountainous and hilly sections of the State had high birth rates, and these were generally isolated and rural. But a broad band through the central part of the State, the "David Harum"

Table 2. Cumulative birth rates for native and foreign-born white women living in New York State in 1865.

	TOTAL	NATIVE	FOREIGN BORN
New York State[1]			
Number Women Reporting	842,560	520,250	322,320
Number Live Births	3,088,233	1,857,151	1,231,082
Births per 100 Women	367	357	382
Eight Counties[2]			
Number Women Reporting	81,847	67,939	13,908
Number Live Births	298,100	236,125	61,975
Births per 100 Women	364	348	446
Madison County			
Number Women Reporting	10,444	9,057	1,387
Number Live Births	36,201	30,126	6,075
Births per 100 Women	347	333	438
Nine Townships[3]			
Number Women Reporting	5,301	4,522	779
Number Live Births	18,038	14,659	3,379
Births per 100 Wives	340	324	435

[1] Derived from pp 66–67, New York Census, 1865.
[2] Chenango, Genesee, Ontario, Orleans, Oswego, Otsego, Tompkins, Wayne.
[3] Both husband and wife married only once, husband present. These rates are lower than the rest of the County because widows are not included, most of whom are in the older age brackets.

[9] Anderson, W. A.: NATURAL INCREASE IN THE POPULATION OF NEW YORK STATE. Cornell University Agricultural Experiment Station Bulletin 733. Ithaca, N. Y., 1940.

part, was also prevailingly agrarian and had low birth rates. Among the counties in the lowest quartile of cumulative birth rates for native women in 1865 were the following near neighbors of Madison county: Otsego, Chenango, Tompkins, Ontario, Genesee, Orleans, Wayne, and Oswego, with only the last having a city of over 10,000 inhabitants. (*See* Table 2.)

If one accepts the hypothesis of urbanization and industrialization as being related to falling birth rates, then he must assume that low birth rates in these relatively prosperous, but fundamentally rural, counties are the product of early diffusion. The possibility that the analysis must be even more complicated may be indicated by the study of differentials according to nativity in the next section.

NATIVITY

In the Madison County sample wives born in Madison County had the lowest birth rate at all ages except under 25, and foreign born wives the highest. (*See* Table 3 and Figure 1.) Native women from New York and other states fell in between. When standardized by age the cumulative birth rates of these groups of white women were as follows: native to Madison County 289, born in New York State outside Madison County 315, born in the United States outside New York State 321, foreign born 418. Recognizing that birth rates of all three native groups were close at most ages, the fact that the Madison County wives were least fertile on all counts is considered significant. They have the highest percentage of childlessness and the lowest birth rate.[10]

Madison County was not selected for this study because it was considered representative of the upstate farming areas, but it is not far from it. The County was settled after 1790, largely by migrants from New England and the eastern counties. It has some good and some poor farm land. It has never been highly urbanized; but it has never been too isolated. The

[10] Birth rates were also computed for mothers only. These come out as one would expect when the proportion childless is recognized. The tables are not reproduced here because they offer relatively little additional information.

AGE OF WIFE AND VARIABLE CONSIDERED	NATIVITY OF WIFE			
	Madison County	New York not Madison County	United States not New York	Foreign Born
Number of Wives				
Total Under 65	2,094	1,775	430	757
Under 25	369	266	22	68
25–34	708	536	58	275
35–44	547	414	83	229
45–54	326	347	130	134
55–64	144	212	137	51
Children per 100 Wives				
Total Under 65 (Not Standardized)	273	323	422	427
Under 25	95	87	105	122
25–34	199	213	224	315
35–44	343	362	390	534
45–54	430	472	448	539
55–64	469	579	551	671
Standardixed Rate	289	315	321	418
Median Age of Wife	34.1	36.6	48.5	36.1
Per Cent Childless 45–54	10	7	10	6

Table 3. Cumulative birth rates by nativity of wife, Madison County, 1865.

Cherry Valley Turnpike pushed west across the middle of the County in 1806 and the Erie Canal later crossed the upper townships. By 1865 the Chenango Canal (Binghamton-Utica), the Seneca Turnpike, the Skaneateles Turnpike, and the New York Central Railroad provided other transportation.

Over half of the native-white population of Madison County was in agriculture, and among the native families the smallest ones were those most characteristic of the early life of the area, the two thousand wives native to Madison County. Clearly, the birth rate of this segment of the population was never very high, or the decline began very early. Compare, for example, the 1865 completed family (4.3 to 4.7 children) of the women native to Madison County with that for native white women in

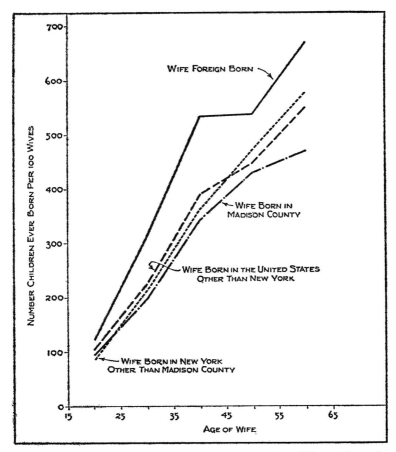

Fig. 1. Cumulative birth rates of married women by wife's nativity and by age.

the Northeastern Region in 1910 when the average woman of completed fertility had four children.[11]

One may assume that New York State birth rates were somewhat depressed by the Civil War as they were in New England.[12] The nature of the data presented in this study demon-

[11] U. S. Bureau of the Census: DIFFERENTIAL FERTILITY, 1940 AND 1910, WOMEN BY NUMBER OF CHILDREN EVER BORN. Washington, Government Printing Office, 1945, Table 81.

[12] Spengler, J. J.: The Fecundity of Native and Foreign-born Women in New England. Brookings Institution, Pamphlet Series, Vol. II, No. 1, 1930.

Occupation of the Husband	Wife Native White	Wife Foreign-Born White
Total	4,524	779
Per Cent	100.0	100.0
White Collar	10.8	2.5
Skilled and Semiskilled	19.5	15.2
Unskilled	8.2	35.6
Farm Owner	41.0	26.3
Farm Tenant and Laborer	15.9	15.8
None	1.1	0.5
Unknown	3.5	4.1

Table 4. Percentage distribution of native and foreign-born white wives, by occupation of husband.

strates, however, that this can have had no pronounced effect.

The early decline in the birth rate in this area is also inferred from the fact that the birth rates of women over age 45 continue to increase with each age group. Beginning with those aged 45–49 and increasing in age by five-year groups to 75 and over, the cumulative birth rates are as follows for all native white women: 429, 480, 523, 561, 613, 653, and 659. Of course, the ages given are for women at the time of the census in 1865, and these rates are for different cohorts of women. Thus, one hundred women aged 65–69 in 1865 had had 613 children at the time they completed their families in 1845 as compared to 100 women aged 45–49 in 1865 who had had 429 children.

Some fraction of these differentials according to age groups may well be attributed to a relationship between high birth rates and longevity. Dorn and McDowell found in the Australian statistics that the difference between the birth rates of women who died at advanced age and those who died in middle age could often amount to as much as twenty per cent.[13] If the birth rate of native women aged 45–49 in 1865 is 100, then the rates of the older age groups in Madison County is as follows: 112, 122, 131, 143, 152, 154.

The birth rates of Dorn and McDowell are computed for

[13] Dorn, Harold F. and McDowell, Arthur J.: The Relationship of Fertility and Longevity. *American Sociological Review*, 4: 234–246, April, 1939.

OCCUPATIONAL CLASS OF HUSBAND AND NATIVITY OF THE HUSBAND AND WIFE	AGE OF WIFE		
	25–34	35–44	45–54
	CHILDREN EVER BORN PER 100 WIVES		
Skilled and Semiskilled			
Native	216	349	
Foreign Born	324	550	
Unskilled			
Native	231	462	541
Foreign Born	342	553	560
Farm Owner			
Native	203	348	449
Foreign Born	367	537	561
Farm Tenant and Farm Laborer			
Native	190	403	
Foreign Born	327	511	
	RATIOS OF RATES OF FOREIGN BORN TO THOSE OF NATIVE WHITES		
Skilled and Semiskilled	150	158	
Unskilled	148	120	104
Farm Owner	181	154	125
Farm Tenant and Farm Laborer	172	127	

Table 5. Cumulative birth rates of native[1] and foreign-born white[2] couples of specified occupational class of the husband.

[1] Both husband and wife native white.
[2] Both husband and wife foreign-born white.

women dying in a five-year period, while these data are for women still living by five-year age groups. Also date of marriage and age of marriage are not available for Madison County women. Thus, the two series can not be compared directly. Nevertheless, the conclusion seems warranted that the age differentials reflect much more than a factor of longevity.

The birth rate in Madison County in 1865 was not far above that for Cattaraugus County a generation or two later. The standardized birth rate for all native families of 315 may be compared with Sydenstricker's rate of 285 for Cattaraugus County in 1900.[14] In the latter county the rate was 269 in 1910 and 298 in 1929. The unstandardized rates for these two coun-

[14] Sydenstricker, Edgar: *op cit.*

Table 6. Percentage age distribution of wives by occupational class of the husband.

| Occupational Class of the Husband | Number | Per Cent | Age of Wife | | | | | | | Median Age | Median Value Dwelling |
			15–24	25–34	35–44	45–54	55–64	65+		
Professional	148	100.0	14.8	27.7	27.0	16.3	10.1	4.1	36.9	$1,282
Proprietor	243	99.8	13.1	31.7	30.0	16.8	7.4	0.8	36.2	Over 1,500
Clerical	77	100.1	20.8	39.0	20.8	10.4	6.5	2.6	31.6	1,346
Skilled	581	100.1	11.0	30.3	24.6	19.2	11.4	3.6	37.5	645
Semiskilled	245	99.9	15.5	35.1	21.6	15.5	6.5	5.7	34.3	614
Unskilled	328	100.0	26.8	29.6	16.8	14.0	8.0	4.8	31.9	316
Farm Owner	1,803	100.0	7.3	23.4	25.6	22.7	15.2	5.8	42.0	616
Farm Tenant	645	100.1	25.1	35.7	18.7	10.6	5.9	4.1	30.5	352
Farm Laborer	45	99.9	31.1	31.1	20.0	13.3	2.2	2.2	28.9	275
None	51	99.9	9.8	15.7	11.8	15.7	15.7	31.3	49.1	1,437
Unknown	149	99.9	24.1	26.8	16.8	14.8	10.0	7.4	33.9	545

Both husband and wife native white, husband present.

ties in 1865 were 391 and 333 for native wives. Thus, the birth rate for Madison County was probably below its more western, southern tier neighbor in 1865.

The higher birth rate of the foreign-born women is in part a product of their husbands' occupation and income. The foreign born performed a great many menial tasks, over a third of them being unskilled laborers as against one-twelfth of the native group. (*See* Table 4.)

The number of foreign born is too small to provide many meaningful comparisons, but Table 5 gives the data for those occupational and age classes with at least 20 wives. Foreign-born wives generally had a birth rate fifty per cent higher than native wives whose husbands were in similar occupational categories. There may also be a tendency for these differentials to decrease with advancing age.

Occupation

The predominant impression from the study of occupation in relation to fertility in 1865 is that economic factors were of great importance. (*See* Table 7.) White collar groups had the lowest birth rate, especially over the age of 45, and unskilled workers had the highest birth rate at all ages. Second highest were the farm tenants and farm laborers with two classes, the skilled and semiskilled and the farm owners, coming third with almost identical rates. The median value of the dwelling for these groups, reading from high birth rates to low birth rates, was $316, $344, $637, $616, and $1,445.

For this study occupations were coded generally according to the 1940 Index of Occupations and Industries of the Bureau of the Census with some few modifications for differing circumstances and functions. Since the area involved in the study was so strongly agrarian, some problems of classification of occupations did not emerge as they might in an urban setting. The final grouping of occupations into five categories was partly the product of necessity in obtaining numbers for analysis and partly the combining of apparently related classes. White collar is composed of professional, proprietor, and clerical occupations (respectively V, 1, and 2 as the first digit of the occupation code). These compose a rather homogeneous group economically, though the wives of clerical workers were substantially younger. (*See* Table 6.) The skilled and semiskilled group (coded 3, 4, or 7) were similarly differentiated slightly in the median value of the dwellings and in the age of the wives, but their combination seemed reasonable. Unskilled workers were much younger and lived in cheaper houses. As far as they could be derived, the birth rates of skilled and semiskilled workers seemed to be similar, as against those of the unskilled.

Some skepticism is appropriate about the denotation of farmer and laborer in this census, and some reasons must be advanced for the classifications used. It may be that farmer, laborer, and farm laborer were used indiscriminately by some enumerators, with only one little mark in the proper column (owner of land) separating farm owners and farm renters. Farm laborer was used for only 64 husbands in the sample, 45 of them native, and only five out of twenty-four enumeration districts listed anyone as a farm laborer. Certainly some of the farm tenants are younger sons who will some day own the land, and some may be fathers who have already passed title to their sons. Confirming the family pattern, perhaps, is the fact that wives of farm tenants averaged twelve years younger than farm owners' wives.

Farm tenants and farm laborers are grouped together, however, because they seemed to be more closely related to each other than to any other groups. They are comparable in age and value of dwelling and significantly different from farm owners. (*See* Table 6.)

Laborer is largely a town occupation as these men are found in large numbers in a few enumeration districts which are primarily non-agricultural.

In most of the recent studies of differential fertility the people in rural occupations have birth rates higher than those in the urban occupations. In the 1865 Madison County sample, however, the skilled and semiskilled workers in the towns and villages had almost exactly the same birth rate as the farm owners, and the unskilled laborer group was above the farm tenant-farm laborer group. (*See* Table 7 and Figure 2.) Within the town and rural categories, the occupations followed an inverse relationship with skill and economic condition. One also notes that regardless of residence the occupations are located rather precisely in an apparent economic hierarchy.

There is some possibility that the higher rate of unskilled workers is also related to nativity; these may be (at least in significant proportion) the native children of foreign parents, since there were 656,000 foreign born in a population of slightly over 3,000,000 in New York State in 1850. Yet, in spite of this large number of foreign born in the State as early as 1850, it is

Table 7. Cumulative birth rates of native white families by occupational class of husband and age of wife.

		OCCUPATIONAL CLASS OF HUSBAND			
	WHITE COLLAR	Skilled and Semi-skilled	Unskilled	Farm Owner	Farm Tenant and Farm Laborer
Number of Wives					
Total Under 65	458	790	312	1,691	662
Under 25	70	102	88	132	175
25–34	148	262	97	419	244
35–44	129	196	55	459	130
45–54	73	148	46	407	74
55–64	38	82	26	274	39
Children per 100 Wives					
Total Under 65 (Not Standardized)	242	311	325	348	258
Under 25	86	99	116	92	70
25–34	180	216	231	203	190
35–44	288	349	462	348	403
45–54	364	443	541	449	504
55–64	382	548	708	544	580
Standardized Rate	247	306	375	301	321
Median Age of Wife	35.4	36.1	31.5	40.9	30.9
Per Cent Childless 45–54	10	9	4	9	8
Median Value of Dwelling	$1,445	$637	$316	$616	$344

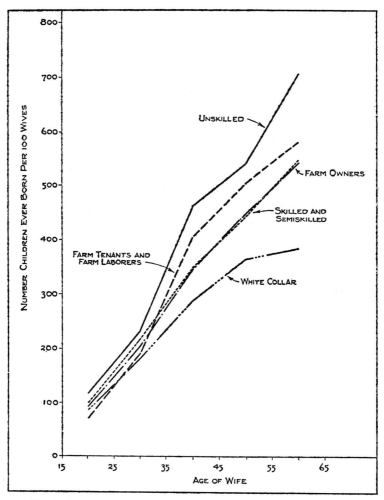

Fig. 2. Cumulative birth rate of married women by husband's occupation and age of wife (both native white).

doubtful if there were very many native women of foreign parentage in the child-bearing ages in 1865. The national record shows, during the decade preceding 1850, 1,415,000 immigrants, but only 409,000 of these came in the first five years; and there were just over 500,000 in the decade of the '30's.[15] Thus the

[15] Thompson, Warren S. and Whelpton, P. K.: POPULATION TRENDS IN THE UNITED STATES. New York, McGraw-Hill, 1933, p. 294.

annual rate of immigration was fairly low before 1845, and only from this group could one expect native women of foreign parentage in the child-bearing ages in 1865.

Although the difference between the standardized rates of the unskilled laborers (375) at one extreme and of the white collar group (247) at the other is substantial, it is not unduly large. For example, Sydenstricker and Notestein found cumulative birth rates in 1910 ranging from 129 for professional wives under 45 to 299 for farm laborers' wives.[16] Relatively and absolutely these 1910 differentials are greater than those for 1865.

One other comparison with the 1910 data is fruitful. Wives of "urban" occupational groups in 1865 have rather substantially higher cumulative birth rates at nearly every age up to 45 than comparable occupational groups in 1910, but farmers' wives in the two censuses were very nearly alike, with any possible difference being in the direction of a higher rate for 1910. (*See* Table 8.) Since the urban data in the study by Sydenstricker and Notestein came from cities of over 100,000 the

Table 8. Comparison of cumulative birth rates in 1865 and 1910 by age of wife and occupational class.

OCCUPATIONAL CLASS	AGE OF THE WIFE AT CENSUS OF 1910 OR 1865					
	15–19	20–24	25–29	30–34	35–39	40–44
White Collar	*	89	148	209	231	345
Professional[1]	35	59	89	133	177	211
Business[1]	37	66	104	147	184	224
Skilled and Semiskilled	*	113	183	251	332	371
Skilled Workers[1]	45	93	137	185	235	277
Unskilled	56	140	172	315	448	479
Unskilled Laborers[1]	59	113	175	229	296	334
Farm Owner	*	98	157	244	328	369
Farm Owners[1]	50	122	188	265	325	376
Farm Tenant & Laborer	29	80	154	251	376	452
Farm Renters[1]	52	113	195	284	367	467
Farm Laborers[1]	59	126	221	320	405	471

* Less than 20 wives.
[1] From Sydenstricker, Edgar and Notestein, Frank W., *Differential Fertility According to Social Class. Journal of the American Statistical Association*, xxv, (N. S. No. 169), p 25.

16 *Op cit.*, p. 25.

comparison is more interesting than enlightening. If it has any meaning, the comparison demonstrates again that the decline in the birth rate in this part of New York State began very early, and that the farm population did not necessarily lag in this movement.

This discussion of occupational differentials has emphasized most strongly the broad pattern, because safety seemed to lie in numbers. The standardized birth rates show a fairly clear ranking, rather consistently related to assumed economic position as measured by the value of the dwelling. And farmers' birth rates, rather than being higher than those of town residents, are often lower; unskilled laborers' rates are higher than those of farm laborers and farm tenants, and farm owners' rates are very nearly the same as the rates for the skilled and semi-skilled group. The relatively low birth rates of the farm tenant and farm laborer class in the younger ages is worthy of note, however; in the standardized rate they rank second, but they rank fifth and fourth in the two younger age groups where two-thirds of these wives are found.

The numbers of foreign born are so small in this sample that little has been done with them in connection with occupational analysis. Nonetheless, the data in Table 5 are of interest, since they reveal almost no significant occupational differentials.

Table 9. Ratios of birth rates of other occupational classes to unskilled laborers by age of the wife and nativity.

Nativity of Couple and Occupational Class of the Husband	Age of Wife		
	25–34	35–44	45–54
Both Husband and Wife Native White			
Skilled and Semiskilled	94	76	82
Unskilled	100	100	100
Farm Owner	88	75	83
Farm Tenant and Farm Laborer	82	87	93
Both Husband and Wife Foreign-Born White			
Skilled and Semiskilled	95	99	
Unskilled	100	100	100
Farm Owner	107	97	100
Farm Tenant and Farm Laborer	96	92	

Table 9 provides a comparison of the birth rates for several occupations and age groups by nativity, using data from Table 5 and Table 7. Note that if the birth rate of the unskilled group is 100, then the birth rate of farm owners is 107 at ages 25–34, and 97 and 100 in the next higher age groups. Among native families these ratios are 88, 75, and 83, respectively. Similarly, the differentials for other occupational groups among the foreign born are essentially flat.

VALUE OF THE DWELLING

Evaluations placed by the census enumerators on the dwellings were assumed to be one index of an economic character which could be independent of other measures of social position. Because of its subjective character, this index was used with some diffidence; but experience with it indicates that the interviewers must have used a fair discrimination. Individual homes were valued from $50 for some log houses to over $15,000, and the average value of dwellings has been noted as being significantly related to occupation.

In 3,049 households there was only one marital couple per household; an additional 1,045 families were doubled up, 419 of them being considered as the principal family (being listed first in the household) and 626 as secondary families. The difference between the last two categories is due to the fact that occasionally there were two or more secondary families in a household. Then, too, many principal families were not qualified for inclusion in the study due to plural marriages on the part of one spouse, or due to widowhood. Normally widowed parents were not listed first in the household; but when they were they were counted as the principal family.

Crowding was closely related to the size of the family except at the oldest ages. Secondary families were smallest at all ages, and families living alone tended to be slightly larger than either of the "doubled up" types except over the age of 45, where they were slightly smaller than "principal families." (*See* Table 10.) No economic differential is evident here, except what one would expect, in that the median value of "only one couple" dwellings is $586 and of dwellings with two or more families $785. There is a substantial difference in the ages represented; "principal families" average 44 years for the wife and "secondary families" have a median of 27 years. "Only one couple" families fall in between with a median age of 38 years for the wife.

Cumulative birth rates per hundred mothers are also given in Table 10 because secondary families include a substantial number of childless marriages. Differentials for mothers are reduced somewhat, but they are by no means eliminated.

Analysis of families living alone indicates a weak relationship

Table 10. Cumulative birth rates per 100 wives and per 100 mothers by housing status and by age of wife or mother.

AGE	ONLY ONE COUPLE	MORE THAN ONE COUPLE	
		Principal Family	Secondary Family
Number of Wives	3,049	419	626
	CHILDREN EVER BORN PER 100 WIVES		
Total Under 65	331	381	143
15–24	102	100	65
25–34	219	211	134
35–44	364	332	205
45–54	451	458	335
55–64	533	599	460
Median Age	38.2	44.3	27.4
Median Value Dwelling	$586	$785	
Per Cent Childless 45–54	9	5	19
Number of Mothers	2,681	383	391
	CHILDREN EVER BORN PER 100 MOTHERS		
Total Under 65	377	416	228
15–24	161	156	136
25–34	251	229	203
35–44	385	365	413
45–54	494	484	413
55–64	586	605	493

WENDELL H. BASH

between the birth rate and the value of the dwelling. (*See* Table 11 and Figure 3.) When standardized by age the cumulative birth rates range from lowest value of dwelling to highest as follows: 370, 322, 284, 282, and 282; but only at ages 55–64 is the relationship inverse. At other ages there are variations in the rank order of the categories. Especially is there variation in the three categories above $600, and almost half of the number of families with known valuations fall into these three. The very slight difference in standardized rates for these three categories and the apparently random variations in specific age groups suggests that no significant differentiation can be made here. Value of the dwelling *per se* has slight relation to the birth rate except in so far as only the extremes are considered, and even then the magnitude of the differentials is not great.

Table 11. Differentials in cumulative birth rates by value of dwelling and age of wife.

	VALUE OF DWELLING					
	Under $300	$300–599	$600–999	$1,000–1,499	$1,500 & Over	Unknown
Wives						
Total Under 65	668	778	578	399	401	213
Under 25	117	91	60	18	22	22
25–34	222	225	167	111	98	56
35–44	168	228	145	120	113	70
45–54	95	154	126	95	117	40
55–64	66	80	80	55	51	25
Children per 100 Wives						
Total Under 65 (Not Standardized)	354	338	308	327	322	345
Under 25	110	101	93	*	118	96
25–34	254	223	205	198	204	184
35–44	442	385	334	313	325	331
45–54	566	454	383	444	406	578
55–64	588	573	519	495	439	588
Standardized Rate	370	322	284	282	282	318
Median Age of Wife	34.3	37.7	38.8	40.4	41.6	38.6
Per Cent Childless 45–54	5	12	11	11	5	5

* Under 20 wives.

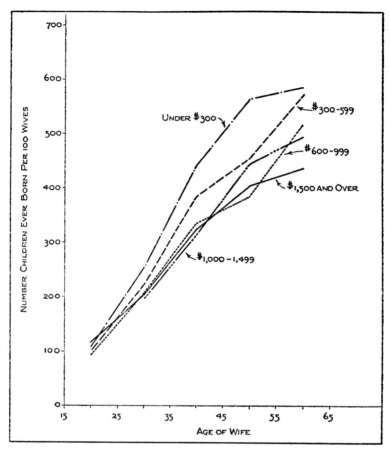

Fig. 3. Cumulative birth rate of married women by value of dwelling and age of wife (both native white, only one married couple in the household).

Slight as the differences are between these economic levels, some of them are related to childlessness, since the proportion of married women who were childless increased on the higher economic levels. An exception to this appeared among those in the $1,500 and over bracket where the proportion childless was low.

Cash Value of the Farm

The fact that broad occupational categories often conceal within averages some very substantial internal differences has often been noted, and an economic analysis within an occupational group sometimes demonstrates a relationship with fertility that is different from the one that is otherwise discernible. For these reasons the farm owners were given particular attention, since the agricultural section of the census provided additional information about each farm. In the coding process the name of each farmer was recorded in order to find his listing in the other section for the cash value of the farm and the value of tools and machinery. Other farm variables were as easily obtained, but these two were selected, the first to obtain an overall indication of general worth, and the second as a presumed index of "modernization." Cash value of the farm ranged from less than $500 to over $15,000, and value of tools and machinery from less than $10 to over $500. Among 1,797 wives of

Table 12. Cumulative birth rates of farm owners wives by cash value of the farm and age of the wife.

	Cash Value of the Farm				
	Under $3,000	$3,000–4,999	$5,000–6,999	$7,000 and Over	Unknown
Wives					
Total Under 65	477	411	263	321	219
Under 25	39	34	25	10	24
25–34	115	115	61	62	66
35–44	153	97	67	86	56
45–54	98	100	74	100	35
55–64	72	65	36	63	38
Children per 100 Wives					
Total Under 65 (Not Standardized)	369	297	330	417	321
Under 25	100	88	92	*	96
25–34	220	176	192	232	206
35–44	372	308	313	393	327
45–54	536	387	427	467	383
55–64	521	466	561	608	600
Standardized Rate	328	263	286	328	
Median Age of Wife	40.0	40.3	41.3	44.8	38.0
Per Cent Childless 45–54	7	14	7	7	6

* Under 20 wives.

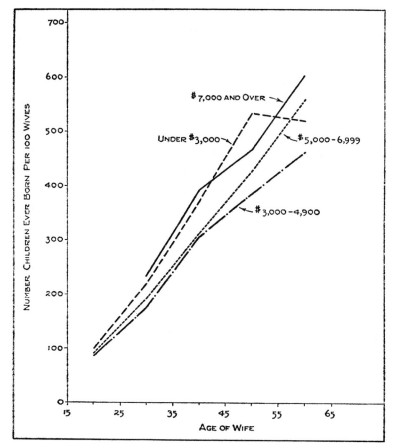

Fig. 4. Cumulative birth rates of farm owners' wives by cash value of farm and age of wife (both native).

farm owners there were 219 for whom data were not obtainable on the value of the farm and 307 on the value of tools and machinery. The remainder were divided into four categories of approximately equal sizes.

These two economic variables were related significantly. Though the mathematical value of the relationship was not calculated, inspection of a scattergram for a substantial proportion of the farm owners showed a positive correlation but with considerable spread.

The cumulative birth rates for wives of farm owners on four different levels of farm value lead to two propositions: (1) differentials between economic levels are quite moderate, and (2) the birth rate is positively related to farm worth except for the poorest group. (*See* Table 12 and Figure 4.)

At all ages the cumulative birth rates of the three upper economic groups are ranked in positive order, the highest birth rates being found among the most prosperous farmers. The birth rates of the poorest farmers are very similar to the ones for the top group. Standardized birth rates for these groups, reading from the poorest to the prosperous are 328, 263, 286, and 328.

Some progression upward in an economic hierarchy with advancing age was noted in connection with the data on value of the dwelling. This re-appears here with the wives of the most prosperous farmers being about four years older than the others.

Table 13. Cumulative birth rates of farm owners wives by value of tools and machinery and age of wife.

	VALUE OF TOOLS AND MACHINERY				
	Under $100	$100–199	$200–299	$300 and Over	Unknown
Wives					
Total Under 65	375	464	293	252	307
Under 25	37	36	12	13	34
25–34	93	119	59	56	92
35–44	93	126	89	67	84
45–54	89	115	80	75	48
55–64	63	68	53	41	49
Children per 100 Wives					
Total Under 65	332	331	383	396	322
Under 25	103	69	*	*	94
25–34	215	194	190	211	208
35–44	354	326	336	382	362
45–54	434	437	476	495	394
55–64	465	543	604	576	557
Median Age of Wife	40.7	40.6	43.0	43.0	37.8
Per Cent Childless 45–54	17	9	5	4	6

* Under 20 wives.

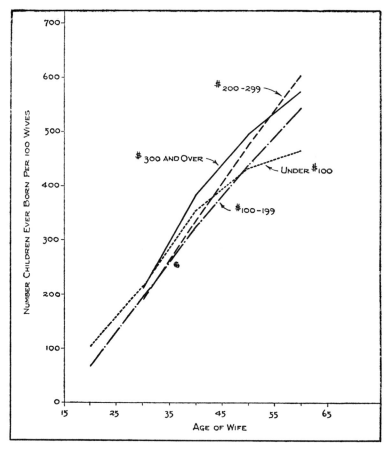

Fig. 5. Cumulative birth rates of farm owners' wives by value of tools and machinery and age of wife (both native white).

VALUE OF TOOLS AND MACHINERY

Differentials in birth rates according to the value of tools and machinery are less pronounced than according to the cash value of the farm. (*See* Table 13 and Figure 5.) Except at age 55–64 one is likely to conclude that most of the differences observed can be attributed to chance factors—that there are no significant differentials present. It is true that the rank order of the groups is similar with the most prosperous group tending to have the highest birth rates, but the poorest group here comes out with a middling or low birth rate rather than a high one. And here one particularly interesting fact comes out, namely, that childlessness for those women over the age of 45 tends to decrease in the higher economic positions. Some 17 per cent of the wives over 45 in the poorest economic group had had no children as against 9 per cent, 5 per cent, and 4 per cent for the other groups on a rising scale.

In this section of the study one is reminded of the stereotype of the old fashioned American farm family in which fertility was supposed to be directly related to success; the more sons a family had the better it could live and prosper.

Conclusions

This study of some four thousand native-white families and an additional thousand foreign-white families in New York State in 1865 can hardly be used to support the "J" hypothesis except insofar as one confines himself to the economic differentials within the farm group. There the top and the bottom groups had higher birth rates than those in between. When one examines nativity, occupation, and value of the dwelling, he finds that the differentials tend to go in the "expected modern" direction, *i. e.*, they are inversely related to economic position.

Relatively, the differences between classes were not large. Possibly this may be due to the fact that the birth rate was already quite low. The standardized birth rate for all native-white couples was 315, which may be compared with a standardized birth rate of 285 in 1900 in Cattaraugus County, and 269 in 1910 and 298 in 1929. The birth rate was also low in some unexpected segments of the County's population. Birth rates were higher for some "town" occupations than for some "rural" occupations. Since Madison County belongs to a group of rural counties which fall in the lowest quartile of the State's counties in 1865 in the birth rate of native-white women, one wonders whether this same phenomenon would be found in a comparable county in the top quartile.

Increasingly higher birth rates for women over forty-five, low birth rates for women native to Madison County, higher birth rates for some town occupations—all these tend to reinforce the conclusion that the decline in the birth rate in Madison County began very early. And it may have begun among farm families as early as among town families.

If these data do not clearly support a "J" hypothesis for Madison County for 1865, neither do they clearly support the earlier analysis of the diffusion of the small family type. Although for the State as a whole there is a negative relationship between urbanization and industrialization and the birth rate, nevertheless, Madison County fails to fit the pattern. This is true in terms of the County's position as a unit, and it is true when one examines the differences within the County in more detail. If the diffusion of the small family pattern began in the cities in some areas of the country, then it may have come very early in the farming areas in Madison County.

Maris A. Vinovskis

Socioeconomic Determinants of
Interstate Fertility Differentials
in the United States in 1850 and 1860   Recent efforts
to explain fertility patterns in America in the first half of the
nineteenth century have focused on the possible effects of land scarcity
and urbanization. The conclusion of most economic historians who
have analyzed fertility during that period is that the relative availability of farm land rather than urban or industrial development accounted for fertility differentials and trends.

    The major work on fertility in the first half of the nineteenth
century is Yasuba's analysis of the fertility ratios of the white population
of the United States between 1800 and 1860. He argued that the
steadily decreasing supply of farm land is the best explanation of the
differentials and trends in the white fertility ratios—particularly in the
period before 1830.[1] Recent work has challenged many of Yasuba's
points. For example, his work has been criticized for its use of state
rather than county or township data; its reliance on rank correlation
techniques of analysis rather than the multiple regression procedures
which would have permitted him to examine simultaneously the effects
of several variables on fertility, and its use of cropland in 1949 as an
index of land availability in the nineteenth century.[2] However, most

Maris A. Vinovskis is Assistant Professor of History and Faculty Associate in the Center
for Political Studies of the Institute for Social Research at the University of Michigan.
This article was written while the author was the Rockefeller Fellow in the History
of the Family Project at the American Antiquarian Society and Clark University.

    The author would like to thank Allan Bogue, Richard Easterlin, Tamara Haraven,
Don Leets, Peter Lindert, R. Marvin McInnis, Morton Rothstein, and James Sweet
for their comments on an earlier version of this paper; and the Spencer Foundation and
the School of Education at the University of Wisconsin for financial assistance.

1 Yasukichi Yasuba, *Birth Rates of the White Population in the United States, 1800–1860:
An Economic Study*, (Baltimore, 1962).

2 Susan E. Bloomberg, Mary Frank Fox, Robert M. Warner, and Sam Bass Warner,
Jr., "A Census Probe into Nineteenth-Century Family History: Southern Michigan,
1850–1880," *Journal of Social History*, V (1971), 26–45; Richard A. Easterlin, "Does
Human Fertility Adjust to the Environment?" *American Economic Association Papers
and Proceedings*, LXI (1971), 399–407; John Modell, "Family and Fertility on the Indiana
Frontier, 1820," *American Quarterly*, XXIII (1971), 615–634; Francis Notzon, "Fertility
and Farmland in Weston, Massachusetts: 1800–1820," unpub. M.S. thesis (University
of Wisconsin, 1973); Maris A. Vinovskis, "A Multivariate Regression Analysis of Fertility
Differentials Among Massachusetts Towns and Regions in 1860," forthcoming.

Reprinted from *The Journal of Interdisciplinary
History* **VI**, 375–396 (1976). By permission of The
Journal of Interdisciplinary History and The
M.I.T. Press, Cambridge, Massachusetts.

of these criticisms have raised questions about certain procedures involved in his analysis rather than challenged the validity of his findings. In fact, the most recent, comprehensive reevaluation by Forster and Tucker of Yasuba's land scarcity thesis strongly supports Yasuba's findings while improving upon many of the shortcomings of the earlier study.[3]

Despite the addition of recent work supporting Yasuba's land scarcity thesis, there is a need to reexamine the entire problem. First, there is the definition of land availability in the nineteenth century. Though Forster and Tucker have improved upon Yasuba's measure by calculating the number of white adults per farm (adult-farm ratio), their measure also lacks conceptual clarity. Secondly, all of the economic historians who have analyzed this issue have ignored such potentially important factors as the educational level of the population. Finally, though the use of multiple regression analysis by Forster and Tucker is a significant improvement on the statistical techniques employed by Yasuba, by restricting themselves to only three independent variables they do not make full use of its potential. In addition, the particular measures of land availability and urbanization that Forster and Tucker have used raise the possibility of multicollinearity in their regression analysis.

In order to reexamine fertility differentials in more detail than has been hitherto attempted, this analysis will be confined to 1850 and 1860, for which we have more detailed census data available than in the early decades of the nineteenth century. The study is based on all states in the New England, Middle Atlantic, North Central, South Atlantic, and South Central census divisions.[4]

DEFINITION OF VARIABLES   The difficulty in analyzing fertility differentials in 1850 and 1860 was to decide how many and which variables to include in this investigation. On the one hand, it seemed necessary

---

3   Colin Forster and G. S. L. Tucker, *Economic Opportunity and White American Fertility Ratios: 1800–1860* (New Haven, 1972).
4   Regression runs were also made including the territories in 1850 and 1860. However, the territories were omitted in the final regression equations in order to avoid biasing the results by including such unsettled areas as the Dakota territory, which had a white population of only 2,576 in 1860. If the territories had been included, the results would have been very similar in 1850 but not in 1860 because the Dakota territory had a very low white refined fertility ratio (1,157) and an unusually high white sex ratio (1,710). Rather than have the entire analysis distorted by such an extreme case, all the territories in those regions were omitted from the analysis (Minnesota territory in 1850 and the Nebraska and Dakota territories in 1860).

to include as many variables as possible in order to explore the effects of the socioeconomic factors on fertility differentials. On the other hand, it was necessary to limit the number of variables in the final regression equations due to the small number of cases (30 in 1850 and 32 in 1860) and the problem of high correlations among many of the proposed independent variables. As a result, the final regression equations were based on five independent variables though others were included in preliminary runs.

Table 1 Variables used in multiple regression analysis of fertility differentials in the United States in 1850 and 1860

I. INDEX OF FERTILITY
    Y   The number of white children under 10 years old per 1000 white women aged 16–44

II. SEX RATIO OF POPULATION
    $X(1)$ The number of white males aged 15–49 per 1000 white females aged 15–49

III. EXTENT OF FOREIGN-BORN
    $X(2)$ The percentage of the free population that is foreign-born

IV. AGRICULTURAL DEVELOPMENT
    $X(3)$ Value of the average farm

V. DEGREE OF URBANIZATION
    $X(4)$ The percentage of the population living in towns over 2500

VI. EDUCATIONAL LEVEL OF POPULATION
    $X(5)$ The percentage of the white population over 20 which cannot read and write

---

The index of fertility used was the ratio of white children under ten years of age to white women between the ages of sixteen and forty-four. This data had already been calculated by Yasuba from the 1850 and 1860 censuses. By using the white refined fertility ratio rather than a crude one based on the size of the total population, we can minimize some of the differences in fertility due to variations in the age structures among the states. Although it would have been desirable to use a white refined birth rate rather than a white refined fertility ratio, it was impossible due to the lack of accurate information on the number of births during these years. However, the use of white refined fertility ratios probably does not introduce any serious distortions into the analysis as the measures are usually highly correlated.[5]

5 The white refined fertility ratios used in this analysis are based on Yasuba's calculations. These ratios are not standardized for the age-distribution of the women in the

The sex ratio of the population was calculated as the number of white males between fifteen and forty-nine per 1000 white females between fifteen and forty-nine. This variable was included as an indirect measure of the differences in marriage behavior among the states and territories due to the surplus of men over women in the newly settled areas. T'ien has pointed to the significance of this factor in accounting for fertility differentials in 1850 and 1860, though his interpretation has been strongly questioned by Yasuba and others.[6] Ideally, one would have liked to use the median age at first marriage and the proportion ever married, but unfortunately that data was not available in 1850 and 1860. As a result, it was necessary to rely on the crude approximation offered by the sex ratio of the white population.

Debate has often focused on the differentials in fertility between foreign-born and native-born persons in the United States. Therefore, it seemed logical to include a variable on the percentage of the free population that was foreign-born. Although it is possible to differentiate among the national origins of the foreign-born population, this exercise was not carried out in the final regression runs, although a distinction was made between the Irish and German immigrants in the preliminary runs.

Much analysis of nineteenth-century fertility has focused on the relative opportunity to establish farm households. Unfortunately, the connections between the availability of opportunities in farming and changes in fertility at the household level have not yet been fully or carefully delineated. Furthermore, there is little agreement among historians on the proper measure of agricultural development. This is partly because not much data are available on agriculture during most of the first half of the nineteenth century. Only in 1850 and 1860 do the federal censuses begin to provide more detailed agricultural data.

---

child-bearing ages. Yasuba's effort, however, to standardize these ratios for the age-distribution of the women revealed that the effect of the differences among the states in the age-distribution of their women was only minor. Yasuba, *Birth Rates of the White Population*, 61, 128–131.

For an analysis of the reliability of fertility ratio measures, *ibid.*, 23–37; Donald J. Bogue and James A. Palmore, "Some Empirical and Analytical Relations Among Demographic Fertility Measures with Regression Models for Fertility Estimation," *Demography*, I (1964) 313–338; Wilson H. Grabill and Lee Jay Cho, "Methodology for the Measurement of Current Fertility from Population Data on Young Children," *Demography*, II (1965), 50–73; Tamara K. Hareven and Maris A. Vinovskis, "Marital Fertility, Ethnicity and Occupation in Urban Families: An Analysis of South Boston and the South End in 1880," *Journal of Social History* (forthcoming).

6 H. Yuan T'ien, "A Demographic Aspect of Interstate Variation in American Fertility, 1800–1860," *Milbank Memorial Fund Quarterly*, XXXVII (1959), 49–59.

Some scholars such as Modell have used population density as the measure of agricultural opportunity. However, this is an inadequate measure of agricultural opportunity because it does not take into account the quality of the land and the degree of agricultural development of the area. It is a reflection of village and town populations as well as those living on farms.[7]

Yasuba tried to avoid this problem by calculating the number of persons per 1000 arable acres.[8] But his index was based on the cropland in 1949 and properly has been criticized for reflecting the levels of twentieth-century farming technology and practices rather than nineteenth-century agricultural potential.

The most recent effort by Forster and Tucker calculates the number of white adults per farm, using the white adult population in the census year under investigation and the number of farms in 1850, 1860, and 1880.[9] Their index has the advantage of reflecting nineteenth-century farming conditions and practices more accurately than Modell or Yasuba's measures.

However, even Forster and Tucker's index of land availability leaves much to be desired. At the state level, an index of white adults per farm is highly correlated with the percentage of the population engaged in nonagricultural occupations and with the percentage of the population in urban areas.[10] Therefore, we cannot be sure whether the high correlation between the white adult-farm ratio and the white refined fertility ratio is due to the availability of farms, to the percentage of the population in nonagricultural occupations, or to the percentage of the population living in urban areas. Furthermore, because of the high correlations among these variables, if any two of them are included in the same regression equation, the results might be misleading due to multicollinearity.

The number of white adults per farm is not only an ambiguous measure of land availability in terms of being highly correlated with other indices, but it is also conceptually weak in that it does not reflect the relative cost of establishing a farm household. When economists speak of the availability of farms, they are in effect considering the

---

7 Modell, "Family and Fertility on the Indiana Frontier, 1820."
8 Yasuba, *Birth Rates of the White Population*, 158–169.
9 Forster and Tucker, *Economic Opportunity*, 19–42.
10 For example, in 1850 the correlation between the white adult-farm ratio and the percentage of the population in urban areas was .615, and with the percentage of persons in nonagricultural occupations it was .815. Similarly, the correlation between the white adult-farm ratio and the percentage of the population urban in 1860 was .886.

relative costs of establishing a farm. Forster and Tucker's measure of agricultural opportunity implicitly treats all farms as equally priced, though in reality there were wide differences in the cost of farms in ante-bellum America. Thus, to take an extreme example, the average value of a farm in 1860 in Kansas was $1,179, whereas the average value of a farm in Louisiana was $11,818 in that same year. Surely it was more difficult for a young man to purchase a farm in a state such as Louisiana than in Kansas.[11]

In order to reduce these difficulties, the average value of the farm was used as an index of agricultural opportunity. This index has the advantage of measuring the relative cost of obtaining a farm. Ideally we would like to have data on the cost of establishing a new farm rather than the average value of all farms. However, although these data are unavailable in 1850 and 1860, it probably does not introduce a serious bias as the two measures probably are highly correlated.[12]

Measuring the degree of urbanization is also difficult as few scholars are able to agree upon any single definition of urbanization. Often the term is used as a broad category which includes such factors as industrialization and commercialization of the economy as well as population concentration. However, in order to make the results of this analysis as comparable as possible to the works of earlier scholars,

11 Yasuba also discussed the ability of farmers to assist their children in establishing their own households. He reasoned that to do so was easier when land was readily available and harder when an area became developed. However, there is another aspect of this process that he might have considered. Though farm land becomes more expensive as an area is developed, the value of the farmer's own property also increases. Hence, the farmer is more able to assist his children than previously though the rising cost of farmland in that area might encourage his children to migrate once they receive their inheritance. Again, the relative ability of parents to help their children financially would be better measured by the relative value of the farms than the white adult-farm ratios.

The possible impact of inheritance on fertility has not been resolved. Philip Greven found that the age at marriage for sons was postponed in seventeenth-century Andover, Mass. by the practice of fathers delaying legal transfer of their grants of land to their children. Philip S. Greven, Jr., *Four Generations, Land and Family in Colonial Andover, Massachusetts* (Ithaca, 1970). For a critique of that interpretation, see Vinovskis, "American Historical Demography: A Review Essay," *Historical Methods Newsletter,* IV (1971), 141–148; Vinovskis, "The Field of Early American Family History: A Methodological Critique," *The Family in Historical Perspective,* VII (1974), 2–8.

Notzon's analysis of fertility differentials at the household level in Weston, Mass. from 1800 to 1820 found no statistically significant relationship between the amount of land and the level of fertility. Notzon, "Fertility and Farmland in Weston."

12 For a discussion of the measurement of the value of the average farm see Thomas J. Pressly and William H. Scofield, *Farm Real Estate Values in the United States by Counties, 1855–1959* (Seattle, 1965), 3–11.

the degree of urbanization will be simply defined as the percentage of the population living in towns over 2,500.

Finally, the educational level of the population might also be measured in a variety of ways. For example, one might calculate the percentage of the white population between five and nineteen attending school during the year. However, this index would reflect the future educational level of the population rather than the current level. Therefore, the level of education was measured by the percentage of the white population over twenty who could not read and write according to the census.[13]

STATISTICAL PROCEDURES EMPLOYED   Multiple regression analysis allows one to study the linear relationship between any of the independent variables, $X(1)$ to $X(5)$, and a dependent variable, Y, while taking into consideration the effect of each of the remaining independent variables on the dependent variable. Multiple regression analysis attempts to produce a linear combination of independent variables which will correlate as highly as possible with the dependent variable. The underlying mathematical procedure is the use of the linear least-squares method which produces the smallest possible residual between the predicted value of the dependent variable from the regression equation and its actual value. In addition, multiple regression analysis minimizes any problems due to ratio correlation.[14]

The relationship between two variables is not always linear. Thus, even though the coefficient of linear correlation between two items may be low, it does not necessarily mean there is little or no association between them, as that relationship might be curvilinear rather than linear. To investigate this possibility, each of the independent variables was plotted against the dependent variable and examined for non-linearity. In addition, each independent variable was transformed into Log_{10} and then correlated with the white refined fertility ratio to see if it provided a better fit. On the basis of this investigation, it was discovered that the independent variables $X(1)$, $X(2)$, $X(3)$, and $X(5)$ should be converted to Log_{10}.

13 For an analysis of the extent and importance of illiteracy in the United States during these years, see Richard M. Bernard and Vinovskis, "Women and Education in Ante-Bellum America," unpub. paper presented at the Berkshire Conference on Women in History, 1974.
14 N. R. Draper and H. Smith, *Applied Regression Analysis* (New York, 1966); William L. Hays, *Statistics* (New York, 1963), 490–577; Edwin Kuh and John R. Meyer, "Correlation and Regression Estimates When the Data are Ratios," *Econometrica*, XXIII (1955), 400–416.

Due to the small number of cases involved, there was always the danger that two or more of the independent variables would be highly correlated with each other. As multiple regression analysis is based on the assumption that no linear dependence exists between the explanatory variables, the existence of multicollinearity among the variables would invalidate our results. Therefore, care was taken not to include any independent variables which were highly correlated with each other.[15]

In an effort to test the relative contribution of each independent variable to the explanation of the white refined fertility ratio, a series of stepwise regressions was run with each of the independent variables individually omitted while the remaining variables were regressed against the white refined fertility ratio. The resultant changes in R^2 due to the omission of each independent variable give us another indication of the relative importance of these variables in accounting for differentials in the white refined fertility ratios among the states.

RESULTS   The mean and standard deviations of each variable are displayed in Table 2.

Table 2 Mean and Standard Deviations of Variables

	1850		1860	
	MEAN	STANDARD DEVIATION	MEAN	STANDARD DEVIATION
White refined fertility ratio under ten	1,406.2	285.8	1,356.4	249.1
Number of white males aged 15–49 per 1000 white females aged 15–49	1,082.9	119.3	1,072.2	114.7
Percentage of the free population that is foreign-born	9.9	8.2	12.4	9.3
Value of the average farm ($)	2,277.2	1,192.9	3,410.0	1,955.7
Percentage of population living in towns over 2500	13.2	13.8	16.9	15.6
Percentage of the white population over 20 which cannot read and write	11.8	7.6	9.5	5.6

15 J. Johnston, *Econometric Methods* (New York, 1972, 2nd ed.), 159–168; Hubert M. Blalock, Jr., "Correlated Independent Variables: The Problem of Multicollinearity," *Social Forces*, LXII (1963), 233–238.

In order to ascertain the relationships between the white refined fertility ratio and the independent variables, simple correlation coefficients were calculated.

Table 3 Correlation Matrices

	Y	X_1	X_2	X_3	X_4	X_5
			1850			
Y	1.000					
X_1	.577	1.000				
X_2	−.409	.273	1.000			
X_3	−.642	−3.05	.444	1.000		
X_4	−.746	−.318	.530	.637	1.000	
X_5	.725	.267	−.550	−.256	−.439	1.000
	Y	X_1	X_2	X_3	X_4	X_5
			1860			
Y	1.000					
X_1	.755	1.000				
X_2	−.285	.153	1.000			
X_3	−.317	−.374	.123	1.000		
X_4	−.733	−.509	.559	.389	1.000	
X_5	.543	.123	−.672	.146	−.419	1.000

The results indicate a positive correlation between the white refined fertility ratio and both the white sex ratio and the percentage of illiterate white adults. The correlation coefficients of the white refined fertility ratio and the percentage foreign-born, the farm value, and the percentage of the population urban are negative. In 1850 the correlations with the farm values, the urban population, and the illiterate white population were particularly strong, though the farm value declines in strength in 1860. Except for the white sex ratio, the correlation coefficients between the white refined fertility ratio and the other variables are weaker in 1860 than in 1850.

Though correlation coefficients are useful in establishing the relationship between two variables, they are handicapped because the relationship may really be caused by a third factor which has not been considered. One way to minimize this danger is to use multiple regression analysis, which allows us to see the relationship between the dependent variable and any independent variable after controlling for the influence of the remaining independent variables on the dependent one. Therefore, regression equations were calculated for 1850 and 1860 in the form:

$$Y = a + b_1 \log_{10} X(1) + b_2 \log_{10} X(2) + b_3 \log_{10} X(3) \\ + b_4 X(4) + b_5 \log_{10} X(5)$$

where Y is the white refined fertility ratio, a is a constant, $X(1)X \cdots (5)$ are the independent variables, and $b_1 \cdots b_5$ are the regression coefficients.

The results of the regression equations for 1850 and 1860 are summarized below in Table 4.

Table 4 Regression Coefficients

	1850	1860
Constant	$-1,729.426$	$-5,981.614$
Log$_{10}$ of the number of white males aged 15–49 per 1000 white females aged 15–49	1,330.260	2,430.668
Log$_{10}$ of the percentage of the free population that is foreign-born	69.795	104.157
Log$_{10}$ of the value of the average farm	-385.386	-119.687
Percentage of the population living in towns over 2500	6.882	-6.070
Log$_{10}$ of the percentage of the white population over 20 which cannot read and write	427.131	443.336

Though the regression coefficients indicate the effect of each of the independent variables on the dependent one, it is impossible to evaluate the relative importance of each variable on the basis of regression coefficients since the independent variables are measured in different units. Therefore, it is necessary to calculate standardized regression coefficients (*beta* coefficients) as they indicate the relative importance of the independent variables.

Table 5 Beta Coefficients

	1850	1860
Log$_{10}$ of the number of white males aged 15–49 per 100 white females aged 15–49	.2140	.4391*
Log$_{10}$ of the percentage of the free population that is foreign-born	.1186	.1880
Log$_{10}$ of the value of the average farm	$-.2861$*	$-.0973$
Percentage of the population living in towns over 2500	$-.3325$*	$-.3793$*
Log$_{10}$ of the percentage of the white population over 20 which cannot read and write	.5143*	.4703*

*=significant at the .01 level

Examining the signs of the correlation coefficients and the *beta* coefficients, we see that there are significant differences. Whereas the relationship between the white refined fertility ratio and the percentage of the free population foreign-born was negative before, it now becomes positive when taking into account the effects of the other independent variables. In other words, the foreign-born population was concentrated in low fertility states so that a simple correlation coefficient revealed the relationship as negative. However, once we controlled for the white sex ratio, the degree of urbanization, the extent of white adult illiteracy, and the value of the average farm, it turns out that the percentage of the free population foreign-born and the white refined fertility ratio are really positively related.

On the basis of the *beta* coefficients, we discover that the value of the average farm and the percentage of the population urban are negatively related to the white refined fertility ratio while the white sex ratio, the percentage of the free population foreign-born, and the illiterate white adult population are positively related.

In terms of the relative ability of the independent variables to account for the fertility differentials, the percentage of the population urban and the percentage of white adults who were illiterate stand out in both 1850 and 1860. The value of the average farm was important in 1850 but became quite insignificant in 1860. The white sex ratio was moderately important in 1850 and became even more important in 1860. The percentage of the free population foreign-born was not very significant in either period.

Besides examining the *beta* coefficients in order to judge the relative significance of the independent variables, we can also examine changes in R^2 when each of the independent variables is removed while the rest of them remain in the regression equation.

In most instances there is a loss in R^2 when any independent variable is removed. However, when the percentage of the free population in 1850 or the value of the average farm in 1860 is omitted there is an increase in R^2 because the loss in R^2 caused by the removal of that variable is more than made up by the gain in an additional degree of freedom in calculating our results. In other words, if we had been interested simply in finding the least number of independent variables needed to predict fertility levels rather than in examining the relative importance of the variables we chose to examine initially, we might have omitted the percentage of the free population foreign-born in 1850 and the value of the average farm in 1860.

The results of this analysis basically confirm our findings from the

Table 6 Change in R^2 due to Removal of each Variable from Regression Equation while the Rest of the Variables are Retained

VARIABLE REMOVED	CHANGE IN R^2	
	1850	1860
Log_{10} of the number of white males aged 15–49 per 1000 white females aged 15–49	−.0154	−.0685
Log_{10} of the percentage of the free population that is foreign-born	.0015	−.0018
Log_{10} of the value of the average farm	−.0401	.0002
Percentage of the population living in towns over 2500	−.0492	−.0437
Log_{10} of the percentage of the white population over 20 which cannot read and write	−.1338	−.0843
R^2 with all variables in equation	.8544	.8117

investigation of the *beta* coefficients. Again the percentage of the population urban and the percentage of white adults who were illiterate were important in both 1850 and 1860. The value of the average farm was important in 1850 but not in 1860, whereas the reverse was true for the white sex ratio. In neither year was the percentage of the free population foreign-born significant.

Though the use of correlation coefficients, *beta* coefficients, and changes in R^2 have given us a good indication of the relative importance of individual variables, we also need to look at the overall effectiveness of the resultant regression equations in explaining the dependent variable. Probably the most useful measure of this is R^2— the ratio between the variance of the dependent variable explained by the independent variables and the total variance of the dependent variable. Thus, if the independent variables perfectly predict the values of the dependent variable, R^2 would be equal to one. On the other hand, if the independent variables have no relationship to the dependent variable and therefore are not helpful in predicting values of the dependent variable, R^2 would be equal to zero.

For the states analyzed in 1850, R^2 is .8544. In other words, approximately 85 percent of the variance in the white refined fertility ratio can be explained by the five independent variables in 1850. The explanatory ability of the same five variables in 1860 is .8117.

DISCUSSION OF RESULTS   The results of this study confirmed the value of including more independent variables in the analysis. Yasuba's and Forster and Tucker's investigations confined themselves mainly to examining the effects of urbanization and land availability, ignoring such potentially important factors as education. In fact, this analysis discovered that the percentage of white adults who were illiterate was the best predictor of fertility differentials in 1850 and 1860.

Another general finding of this study is the need for an awareness of the limitations of analyzing fertility differentials at the state level only. Due to the small number of cases available, we are faced with the problem of high correlations among the independent variables. Although the strictly statistical problem of multicollinearity can be avoided by carefully selecting variables for the regression equations that are not highly correlated amongst themselves, it is still very difficult to interpret the meaning of some of these variables. For example, the percentage of the population living in urban areas was used as an independent variable in order to test whether or not the degree of urbanization of a state affected its level of fertility. Though the results strongly suggest that it does, we cannot be certain that we have really measured the effects of urbanization rather than the effects of the percentage of persons in nonagricultural pursuits, as these two variables are highly correlated with each other. Similar problems exist in interpreting the meaning of Yasuba's and Forster and Tucker's measures of land availability. Furthermore, as there are often significant socioeconomic differences within each of the states, any analysis that in effect treats each state as a demographically homogeneous unit may be quite misleading. Therefore, more research will have to be done at the county, township, and household levels. This is not to suggest that further research at the state level would be unproductive—we clearly need more sophisticated analysis than has been available so far. But it does imply that any general models of fertility that we derive from such analyses will have to be tested and refined using smaller units than states.[16]

We now turn to a discussion of the independent variables in this

16 Forster and Tucker did attempt to analyze New York and Virginia at the county level, but they did not apply the same level of statistical sophistication at the county level as they did at the state level. Forster and Tucker, *Economic Opportunity*, 43–48; Don R. Leet has undertaken an investigation of fertility and agricultural opportunities in Ohio counties from 1810 to 1860 and Vinovskis is analyzing fertility differentials for all counties in the United States in 1850. At the township level, Bash studied fertility differentials in New York, but his analysis was limited by the small number of socioeconomic variables that he used, as well as the statistical procedures he employed. Wendall H. Bash, "Changing Birth Rates in Developing America: New York State, 1840–1875," *Millbank Memorial Fund Quarterly*, XLI (1963), 161–182; Vinovskis is completing an analysis of fertility differentials and trends among Massachusetts townships from 1765 to 1860.

analysis—the white sex ratio, the percentage of the free population foreign-born, the value of the average farm, the degree of urbanization, and the percentage of the white adults who are illiterate.

One area of controversy has been the importance of the sex ratio affecting fertility differentials and trends in the ante-bellum period. T'ien has argued that sex ratio differences were very important as they indirectly affected fertility ratios by altering the likelihood of women marrying. Areas where women were outnumbered by men would probably have a higher proportion of women married than areas where the reverse situation existed.[17]

Yasuba disagreed with T'ien's analysis and minimized the significance of sex ratios. Yasuba argued that the high correlation between the white refined fertility ratio and the white sex ratio was spurious— if T'ien had included other factors, such as urbanization or land availability, the importance of the sex ratio variable would disappear. Furthermore, Yasuba demonstrated that the shifts in the sex ratio from 1800 to 1860 could not account for the drop in fertility over that period.[18]

This analysis suggests that the white sex ratio is an important explanatory variable in accounting for fertility differentials in 1850 and 1860 even after controlling for the other four independent variables. In fact, for 1860 the sex ratio is the second best predictor of fertility differentials, being surpassed only by the percentage of white adults who were illiterate. Furthermore, the analysis of fertility differentials among Massachusetts towns and regions in 1860 confirms the importance of the sex ratio variable.[19] Nevertheless, though Yasuba was too hasty in dismissing the importance of the sex ratio variable in terms of cross-sectional analysis, his critique of its ability to account for the overall decline in fertility from 1800 to 1860 appears to be valid.

Another issue is the role of immigration in determining fertility levels, and in particular whether immigrants had higher fertility rates than the native-born population. This problem is extremely complex and the results so far are not at all clear.

Traditionally, demographers have stressed that the fertility of immigrants was significantly higher than that of the native-born population. However, most of that literature refers to the period in the

17 T'ien, "Demographic Aspect."
18 Yasuba, *Birth Rates of the White Population*, 125–128.
19 Vinovskis, "Regression Analysis of Fertility."

late nineteenth and early twentieth centuries when immigration was from high fertility cultures in southern and eastern Europe. Forster and Tucker reexamined the entire question in the period before the Civil War and concluded that immigrants to America came from areas in Europe where the fertility rates were actually lower than in the United States at that time.[20]

In order to investigate the possible significance of this factor, the percentage of the free population that was foreign-born was included as an independent variable. The results suggest that the relationship between the white refined fertility ratio and the percentage foreign-born was relatively weak and positive. To gain another perspective on this question, the percentage of the population that was Irish and the percentage that was German were substituted in the 1860 regression for the foreign-born variable. The results of this refinement were that the percentage of Irish was moderately negatively related to fertility while the percentage German was positive and much stronger. Whether these differences actually reflect differences in the fertility of the foreign-born population or merely that more Irish than Germans happened to immigrate to states with lower fertility cannot be determined on the basis of this analysis. It is interesting to note that the relationship between the percentage of Irish and the white refined fertility ratio among Massachusetts towns in 1860 was positive, though not very strongly so—exactly the opposite of our findings at the state level.[21] Again, any definitive statement on this issue must await more detailed analysis, particularly at the household level.

Agricultural opportunity has been the focus of most of the earlier works on nineteenth-century fertility. However, as we have already noted, their measures of agricultural opportunity have not been satisfactory and therefore we have used the value of the average farm instead. Although even this measure has its shortcomings, it does seem better able to measure the relative costs of establishing a farm household than earlier measures.

The results show that in 1850 the value of the farm was strongly negatively related to the white refined fertility ratio, though it was less important than the percentage of the population in urban areas or the percentage of the white adults who were illiterate. In 1860 the value of the farm remains negatively related to fertility, but it becomes quite unimportant in terms of strength. In fact, when the value of the

20 Forster and Tucker, *Economic Opportunity*, 70–86.
21 Vinovskis, "Regression Analysis of Fertility."

farm is removed from the 1860 regression equation, there is an increase in R^2 as the loss of this variable from the equation is offset by the gain in an additional degree of freedom in the computation of the results.

The .relative weakness of the value of the farm in 1860 is quite different from the results obtained by Yasuba or Forster and Tucker. Although they acknowledged that the relationship between land availability and the white refined fertility ratio was strongest in the first three decades of the nineteenth century rather than in the period 1850 to 1860, their measures of land availability suggested a much stronger relationship in 1850 and 1860 than found in this analysis. Furthermore, that the degree of illiteracy of the white adult population was much stronger than the value of farms in both 1850 and 1860 suggests that perhaps the particular significance of land availability has been overstated by scholars.

An analysis of Massachusetts townships in 1790 and 1840 using more refined measures of land availability at the state level for those years than were available to Yasuba or Forster and Tucker suggests that land availability was indeed positively related to fertility levels, but that the relationship was much weaker than previously suggested once other factors, such as the level of wealth of an area, were also considered.

Again, there is no intention or illusion of settling the issue of land availability in this paper, especially since this analysis is confined to the period after 1850. However, the results here indicate that future work on this topic should try to develop measures of land availability that take into account relative prices. Furthermore, much more effort must be directed toward clearly delineating the variety of effects that land availability may have on fertility at the household level. One receives the impression that the high correlations between measures of land availability and the white refined fertility ratio found by previous scholars confirm Yasuba's hypothesis, so that little additional work has been done in exploring the actual mechanisms that might be involved.[22] The demographic experiences of farm populations ap-

---

22 Economists are now developing much more sophisticated models of household fertility. For example, see the proceedings of the Conference on New Economic Approaches to Fertility in the *Journal of Political Economy*, LXXXI (1973) S1–S299. Some very promising efforts currently in progress on the use of the analysis of household fertility for explaining American demographic development historically are by Richard A. Easterlin, Peter H. Lindert, and R. Marvin McInnis. For an attempt to use fertility ratios at the household level to test for rural-urban differences in fertility, see Hareven and Vinovskis, "Rural-Urban Differences in Fertility: An Analysis of Marital

pear to have been much more complex and less dependent upon land availability than suggested by Yasuba and others. Unfortunately, almost no work has been done so far on the determinants of rural fertility at the household level for the first half of the nineteenth cetntury.[23]

The impact of urbanization on fertility has been a major theme of modern demographers. However, the significance of urbanization in explaining fertility differentials or decline in the first half of the nineteenth century has been minimized—largely because the United States was still basically a rural rather than urban society throughout these years. Furthermore, the statistical analysis of the relative importance of the degree of urbanization and land availability by Yasuba or Forster and Tucker have pointed to the importance of the latter factor. However, as we have previously noted, their measures of land availability were highly negatively correlated with the degree of urbanization, so that it is not clear exactly what socioeconomic factors they were measuring by their indices.

The results indicate that the degree of urbanization was strongly negatively related to the white refined fertility ratio in 1850 and in 1860. In both of those years, the degree of urbanization was more strongly correlated with the fertility ratio than was the value of the average farm.

However, again we must remind ourselves of the possible ambiguities in our measure of urbanization. Though the strong inverse relationship between urbanization and earlier measures of land availability was avoided by using the value of the average farm, the extent of urbanization was still highly correlated with other variables such as

---

Fertility, Ethnicity, Occupation, and Literacy in Five Essex County Towns in 1880," paper presented at the American Historical Association meeting in Chicago, 1974.

23 Despite Modell's use of population density as his index of agricultural opportunity, his article is a significant step in the right direction because he attempts to relate fertility differentials at the household level to the characteristics of the family and county. His conclusion is that Yasuba's analysis does not take into account the complexity of factors affecting rural fertility in an area such as Indiana. Modell, "Family and Fertility on the Indiana Frontier, 1820." Bloomberg et al. analyzed fertility changes in southern Michigan between 1850 and 1880 at the household level and also attempted to relate it to the characteristics of the household and the community. However, the results of that study must be cautiously interpreted because of the very small sample size of the 1850 data (used without due consideration of the problems of sampling errors). Bloomberg et al., "A Census Probe."

the percentage of the population in nonagricultural occupations.[24] Therefore, it is difficult to separate these factor at the state level of analysis. Perhaps the degree of urbanization as used in this study is only a proxy for a much more complex phenomenon than suggested by the presence of persons in towns having populations over 2500 persons.

The analysis of Massachusetts townships in 1860 suggested that urbanization, as measured by the number of persons in each of the towns, was not particularly useful in predicting fertility differentials. Instead, the index of commercialization proved to be a much more useful variable in accounting for the fertility differentials.[25] Though it was possible to separate to some degree the effects of commercialization from the effects of the size of towns at the township level, it is virtually impossible to do so at the state level. As a result, though the relationship between urbanization and fertility appears to be quite strong in this investigation, we do not necessarily place much credence on its importance until further work can be done at the county or township levels, where the variety of factors that scholars commonly associate with urbanization can be separated out for more detailed analysis.

Though demographers have frequently pointed to the importance of education in determining the fertility of the population, historical demographers have not seriously analyzed this factor. Although some of the earlier scholars, such as Yasuba, have suggested that education should be investigated as a possible influence on fertility, none of the subsequent research on nineteenth century fertility has attempted to utilize this variable. This failure has been partly because of the general reluctance of economic historians to study until recently the impact of education on American society and partly because the data are unavailable for most states before 1840.[26]

24 For example, the correlation between the percentage of persons in nonagricultural occupations and the percent urban in 1850 was .751.
25 Vinovskis, "Regression Analysis of Fertility."
26 On the recent efforts by economic historians to analyze the role of education in the first half of the nineteenth century, see Albert Fishlow, "The American Common School Revival: Fact or Fancy?" in Henry Rosovsky (ed.), *Industrialization in Two Systems: Essays in Honor of Alexander Gershenkron* (New York, 1966), 40-67; Vinovskis, "Horace Mann on the Economic Productivity of Education," *New England Quarterly*, XLIII (1970), 550-571; Vinovskis, "Trends in Massachusetts Education, 1826-1860," *History of Education Quarterly*, XII (1972), 501-529. For a summary of the type of problems encountered in studying the role of education in economic development from a historical point of view, see Stanley L. Engerman, "Human Capital, Education, and Economic Growth," Robert W. Fogel and Stanley L. Engerman (eds.), *The Reinterpretation of American Economic History*, (New York, 1971), 241-256.

One of the major reasons for undertaking this research was to test for the possible impact of education on the fertility of the population. Therefore, the percentage of whites over twenty who were unable to read and write was included as one of the independent variables. The results were striking—the educational level of the white population was the single best predictor of fertility differentials among the states in 1850 and 1860. Furthermore, when a similar regression equation was calculated for 1840 (though the value of farms was unavailable and therefore excluded), the importance of the educational level of the white population remained strong.

In order to gain another perspective, the percentages of the white population aged five to nineteen attending school in 1840, 1850, and 1860 were also calculated and substituted in the regression equations for the educational variable. Again the importance of an index of education was confirmed.

Finally, in 1850 the percentage of the white population aged five to nineteen attending school and the percentage of white adults who were illiterate were separated by sex and the results were individually run as the educational variable in a series of regression equations. The results were the same—the educational variable continued to be strongly related to the white refined fertility ratio.

In the analysis of Massachusetts townships in 1860, two measures of education were used—the percentage of the population under twenty attending school and the amount of money spent per public school student in each town. The educational factors were consistently negative for the state as a whole as well as for the three subdivisions, and were important factors in terms of their contribution to the explanation of the differences in the white refined fertility ratios among the towns.[27]

The implications of these findings are very important as they suggest that demographic historians should pay more attention to factors such as education in understanding fertility differentials and trends in nineteenth-century America. Considerable time and effort has already been devoted to urbanization and land availability in an attempt to account for fertility differentials and trends, but too little attention has been paid to the role of educational and cultural factors.[28]

27 Vinovskis, "Regression Analysis of Fertility."
28 The use of literacy data in our analysis of fertility differentials in the United States in 1850 and 1860 was adequate because these rates probably do reflect roughly the state variations in the educational level of the population. However, for studies which focus

Fig. 1 Number of White Children under 5 Years Old per 1000 White Women 20–44 Years Old, Rural and Urban, by Census Division 1800–1840

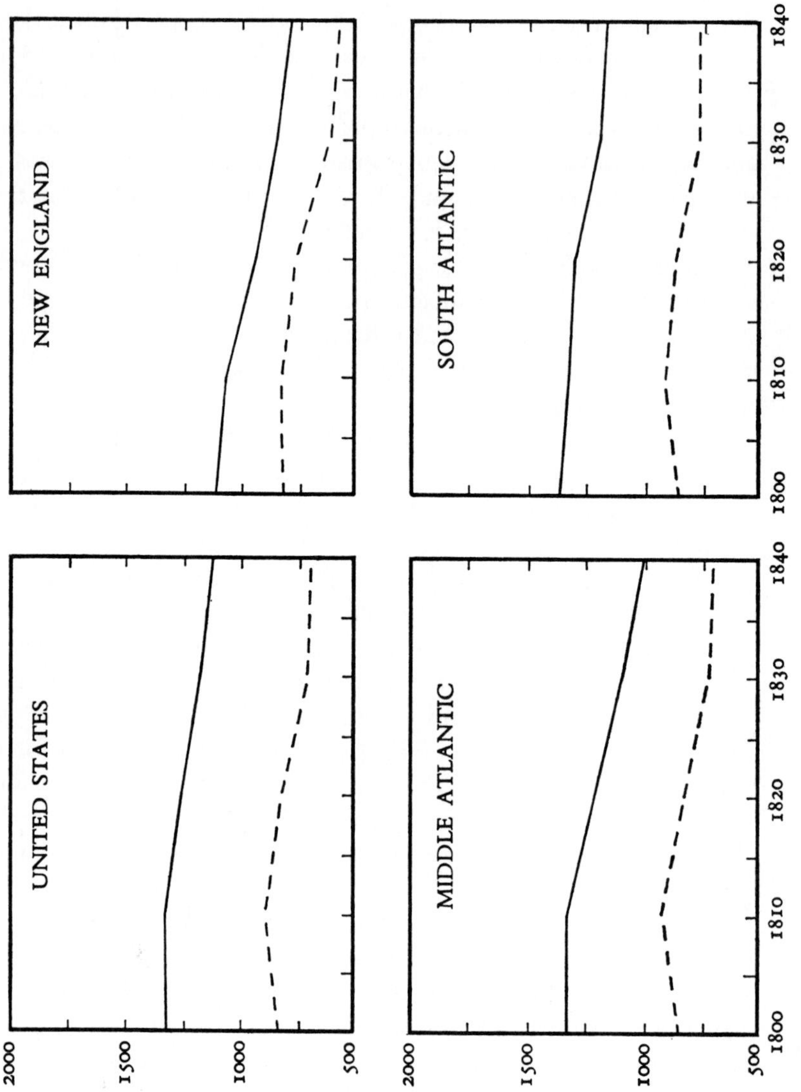

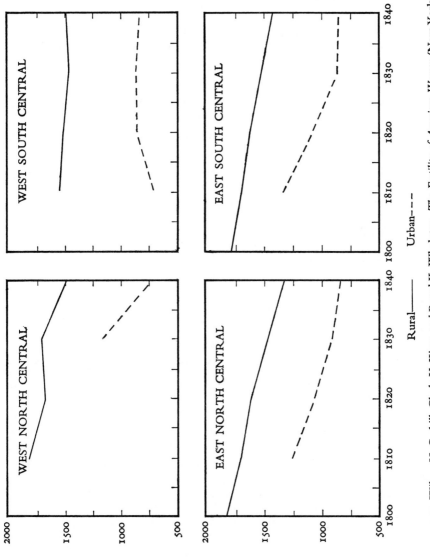

WEST SOUTH CENTRAL

EAST SOUTH CENTRAL

WEST NORTH CENTRAL

EAST NORTH CENTRAL

Rural——— Urban- - -

SOURCE: Wilson H. Grabill, Clyde V. Kiser, and Pascal K. Whelpton, *The Fertility of American Women* (New York, 1958), 17.

One final point should be made. Though this study has focused on fertility differentials rather than trends, many of the same criticisms could be applied to the analysis of changes in nineteenth-century fertility. The debate on the case of the decline in fertility in the first half of the nineteenth century has been focused on rural vs. urban explanations. Yet perhaps the fertility differentials between rural and urban areas persisted because there was a steady decline in fertility in both areas. So much time and effort has been spent on examining the particular causes of declines in rural or urban fertility that demographic historians have not noticed that the declines in both areas may have paralleled each other and both may have been influenced by broad change within American society during those years.

Fortunately, we do have some data on this question for 1800 to 1840 for the United States and for seven of its subregions (see Fig. 1).

It is interesting that the fertility declines in rural and urban areas of the United States and its regions generally parallel each other throughout this period. Similar results were found at the township level in Massachusetts in the period 1765 to 1860.

Perhaps we need to escape from the rural-urban debate long enough to check whether there might not have been some other developments in American society in the first half of the nineteenth century that may partly account for both the rural and urban declines in fertility. That is, though some of the causes of fertility decline in rural areas undoubtedly were different from those for urban areas, we must also entertain the possibility that both rural and urban areas were reacting to the same general changes in American society during the first half of the nineteenth century. Though this paper has not solved this dilemma, preliminary research on this issue suggests that broad attitudinal changes, often preceding rather than being caused by urbanization and industrialization, are probably as significant in accounting for the fertility decline in America as the shifts in economic factors that have dominated the analysis of fertility up to now.[29]

---

on more homogeneous populations, such as an analysis of a particular state or a group of native-born farmers, the variations in adult literacy may be too small to reflect properly the actual differences in their level of educational achievement. Instead, we would like to have the number of years of education each person has obtained. Unfortunately, this type of information is very difficult to find for nineteenth-century America since such data were not often collected.

29   For an analysis of this possibility, see Vinovskis, "Demographic Changes in America From the Revolution to the Civil War: An Analysis of the Socio-Economic Determinants of Fertility Differentials and Trends in Massachusetts from 1765 to 1860," unpub. Ph.D. thesis (Harvard University, 1975).

MARITAL FERTILITY, ETHNICITY, AND OCCUPATION IN URBAN FAMILIES: AN ANALYSIS OF SOUTH BOSTON AND THE SOUTH END IN 1880

Tamara K. Hareven and Maris A. Vinovskis

Introduction

The fertility pattern of urban populations in the second half of the nine-teenth century is one of the great unknowns in historical demography and family history. Yet the analysis of the determinants of fertility is critical for the study of nineteenth-century behavior. It is particularly significant to the understanding of the individual and family life cycles of various groups in the population and to the study of the relationship of women's childbirth cycles and their occupational careers. Fertility is also a crucial variable in the study of differences among the various ethnic and socioeconomic groups within nineteenth-century society.

An exploration of fertility on the household level is particularly important because it provides the link between aggregate demographic behavior in the larger society and family behavior on the household level. While aggregate demographic data reveal general patterns, analysis on the household level pro-vides insight into the relationship between family structure and demographic behavior. As Irene Tauber has pointed out, "the changes that influence the demographic variable do so largely through the intermediation of the family. Marriage practices, family formation and family limitation practices are all essential determinants of fertility patterns and demographic transitions, and must be brought to bear on each other."[1]

Studies of nineteenth-century historical demography and the history of the family have been developing along diverse lines. While demographers have studied trends based on aggregate behavior, family historians have looked at the structural aspects of the individual household units. The dividing line be-tween demographic and family research also stretches along chronological boundaries. While most studies of fertility and mortality are focused in the preindustrial period and end before the Civil War, studies of the family struc-ture commence around 1850 and run through 1880.[2]

One reason for this disparity is that most social historians have been un-able to construct an adequate index of fertility at the household level from the federal censuses. A demographic technique used on contemporary U.S. censuses, however, has suggested the possibility of constructing an index of fertility at the household level whenever the number of children under five and the age of their mother are available. We believe that the use of a child-woman ratio (usually referred to as a fertility ratio) as the index of fertility

69

Reprinted from *Journal of Social History*, March 1975. Copyright © 1975 by permission of the publisher.

will make possible a much more extensive use of the federal manuscript censuses for the nineteenth century.

We have selected two wards in Boston in 1880 as the testing area for this technique because of the availability of data from an earlier study. These two areas were chosen because of the difference in their location in the city and their particular ethnic and occupational composition.[3] South Boston (Ward 13) was a predominantly Irish neighborhood – an area where 30.5 percent of its inhabitants were first-generation immigrants from Ireland (and were 71.6 percent of all foreign-born in that ward) and another 38.6 percent were second-generation Irish. In contrast, the South End (Ward 16) was a more cosmopolitan section in the center of the city. Its population consisted of native Americans (many of whom were newcomers from New England), Irish, Canadians from the maritime provinces, and Germans. As one of the city's major depositories for newly arrived immigrants and rural migrants, the South End was also characterized by a large percentage of unmarried individuals, professionals and semiprofessionals, who were boarding and lodging with families or in the commercial boarding houses.

The South End contained a larger percentage of highly skilled white-collar workers than South Boston as well as a higher concentration of skilled women workers. Since both areas had a high concentration of Irish, we can compare the behavior of immigrants of the same origin in two different locations in the city. Underlying our choice of wards was the hypothesis that location in the city is a significant variable in affecting family and demographic behavior. The differences between these two distinct areas of the city have already been documented in a study of family structure in four Boston wards in 1880 as well as in an analysis of patterns of boarding and lodging in those areas.[4]

Our analysis of fertility differentials in these two wards is based on a 23 percent sample of all the white households. In this article we are only interested in analyzing marital fertility of women whose husbands were present in the household in 1880. Therefore, the total number of households used in this analysis from South Boston was 654 and from the South End 422.[5] Furthermore, though many different aspects of the demographic behavior of families can be analyzed from our data, in this essay we will focus only on the relationship between fertility, ethnicity, and occupation.

The Use of Fertility Ratios at the Household Level

In recent years there has been a rapid increase in the number of household studies based on the 1850 to 1880 federal censuses. Most of these efforts have analyzed either patterns of geographic and social mobility or household and family structure.[6] Surprisingly, very little effort has been made to utilize the same data to analyze fertility differentials at the household level. As most states did not institute accurate birth registration systems before 1900, it has

70

been impossible to calculate directly the birth rates for the various socio-economic groups in the population.

It is possible, however, to estimate fertility levels from the federal censuses. Scholars such as Yasukichi Yasuba have used these censuses to analyze fertility at the aggregate level by calculating child-woman ratios and a very similar procedure could be used to analyze fertility at the household level.[7] One of the great advantages of analyzing fertility ratios at the household rather than the aggregate level is that it permits the researcher to analyze relationships between fertility and other socioeconomic variables that are not otherwise available from the aggregate data in the printed census volumes. Most social historians have not studied fertility differentials and trends at the household level because they have not been able to develop an adequate index of fertility based solely on the federal censuses, which have served as the only major source for nineteenth-century family studies.

There have been two major attempts to study fertility differentials and trends at the household level in the period 1850 to 1880. One is an investigation of family characteristics in southern Michigan from 1850 to 1880, and the other is an analysis of fertility differentials in Madison County, New York in 1865.[8] Though both of these studies are valuable pioneering efforts in this field, they do not provide adequate guidance for the construction of fertility indices from the federal censuses.

The southern Michigan study used the number of children in the household as the index of fertility. The problem lies in its definition of children — it seems to include all children living in the household regardless of age. Since the age-specific rate of children leaving home may vary by the ethnic and socioeconomic characteristics of the family, the total number of children is not a very good index of fertility. Furthermore, in analyzing fertility differentials and trends among the various groups and communities, no effort was made to standardize the results for variations in the age-composition of the female population.[9]

The analysis of fertility differentials in Madison County, New York is based on the state census of 1865, which provides information on the number of children ever-born per woman. The federal census does not include such information until 1890. Therefore, although the analysis of Madison County is a valuable contribution to the analysis of fertility differentials in nineteenth-century America, its methodology cannot serve as a guide for the study of fertility at the household level based on the federal censuses of 1850 to 1880.[10]

An alternative method of constructing an index of fertility from the federal censuses is computation of the ratio of children under 5 per 1000 women aged 20 to 49. Though this method has been used extensively by demographers, only recently has its full potential been developed by Lee-Jay Cho, Wilson H. Grabill, and Donald J. Bogue in their analysis of the 1960 census.[11] We believe that the use of this child-woman ratio will permit social

71

historians to greatly expand our knowledge of nineteenth-century fertility at the household level.

There are several different ways of computing the child-woman ratio from the federal censuses.[12] We prefer to use the number of children under 5 per 1000 women aged 20-49. The use of children under 5 rather than under 10 gives us a closer approximation to current fertility, as the former is based on the number of births in the last five years rather than the last ten years. The use of women aged 20-49 in the denominator eliminates the need for estimating the proportion of women aged 16-19 from the aggregate compilations of the censuses. The extension of fertility analysis to women aged 49 permits a more comprehensive picture of fertility behavior as there is a significant proportion of women aged 45-49 who continue to bear children. Furthermore, the use of this ratio will facilitate comparisons between historical works and the analysis of recent censuses.[13]

One of the problems of using child-woman ratios as an estimate of fertility is that this index reflects not only birth rates, but also death rates. The number of children under 5 in any given census year is composed of the number of children born during the preceding 5 years who managed to survive the perils of early childhood. Ideally, we would like to adjust our data to take into account the differences in mortality among the various socioeconomic and ethnic groups in the period 1850-1880. It is impossible, however, to make this refinement at the present time because we do not have life tables by occupation and ethnicity. The amount of distortion of our results due to differential mortality is minimized by the fact that the differences in death rates among the various socioeconomic and ethnic groups probably was not very large in the mid-nineteenth century, especially when we are dealing only with the white population.[14]

Our child-woman ratio is based on the number of children under 5 each married woman had living with her. This means that there is the possibility of underestimating the number of own children per married woman because some children under 5 may not have been living with their mothers. This might be a serious problem in situations where households are not very stable. For example, in the United States a considerable proportion of nonwhite children under 5 do not live with their mothers (about 21.9 percent in urban areas in 1910). This is largely due to the higher rate of illegitimacy among nonwhites, and the tendency for an unmarried mother to place her children with relatives while she lives and works elsewhere. This is less of a problem for our data as rates of illegitimacy were lower for the native and foreign-born than the nonwhite population. In addition, as our study is based only on married women with husbands present, it is less likely that any of the children under 5 were living elsewhere. The percentage of white children under 5 who were not living with their mothers in urban areas in 1910 was only 5.4.[15]

Another problem is the distortion due to any systematic differences in the

72

undercounting of young children among the various ethnic and socioeconomic groups. Censuses normally miss a small proportion of the population, and the percentage missing varies by age, color, and other characteristics. If both children under 5 and their mothers were missing in proportionate numbers, our fertility ratios would not be affected. The problem of the undercounting of young children has already been investigated. It was discovered that the rates of underestimation of children under 5 were not very high — particularly for the white population. Furthermore, as our analysis is not affected extensively by the underreporting of both young children and their mothers, this issue becomes less problematic.[16]

In order to compare fertility differentials among and within various subgroups of the population in more detail, we have calculated age-specific fertility ratios by five-year intervals (based on married women aged 20-24, 25-29, 30-34, 35-39, 40-44, and 45-49). It is important to recognize that the reliability of these age-specific ratios suffers if they are based on a very small number of cases. To avoid possible distortions from erratic patterns of fertility ratios due to the small number of units in each age-group, it is often advisable to combine two or three five-year intervals into a single ten- or fifteen-year age-group.

In addition to analyzing age-specific fertility ratios, it is often useful to have a summary measure of fertility over the entire reproductive span of married women. There are several different indices of fertility available which summarize the data. Historians should select among these alternative measures the one most appropriate to the particular questions they are trying to answer.

The most commonly used index of fertility is simply the number of children under 5 per thousand married women aged 20-49. The advantage of this measure is that it is often easy to calculate from aggregate as well as household census data and because it does not subdivide the data into age-specific categories, each of which are based upon a smaller number of cases and therefore less reliable, it may well give more trustworthy figures where cases are few. This fertility measure gives us an indication of the total number of children per married women in the reproductive ages without adjusting for differences in the age-distribution of married women among the various subgroups in the population (being based on the actual age-distribution of married women within that particular group). This unstandardized measure of the number of children under 5 per thousand married women aged 20-49 probably reflects the image most casual observers had at the time of the extent of fertility among the different subgroups of the population. If one is interested in the overall impact of fertility behavior on socioeconomic conditions (such as the perspective demand for children's clothing), the unstandardized fertility ratio is preferable.

While differences among the various ethnic and socioeconomic groups in mortality, in the percentage of children under 5 living away from their

73

Graph 1   Distribution of Married Women Aged 20-49 in both Wards in
           1880 by Ethnic Origin

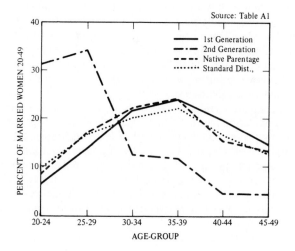

Graph 2   Comparison of Standard Age Distribution to Massachusetts
           Pattern in 1885 of Married Women Aged 20-49

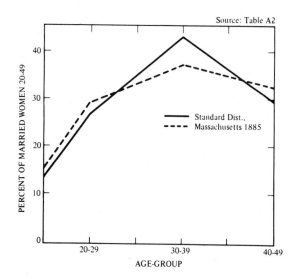

74

mothers, and in the underenumeration of young children probably will not seriously distort most of our results based on the child-woman ratio, differences in the age distribution of married women will affect the overall fertility ratios of our sample. For example, the age-distribution of married women in South Boston and the South End varies by ethnic background (see Graph 1). The distribution of married foreign-born women is very similar to that of married women of native parentage. But the pattern for married second-generation American women is very different. In the latter group, there is a much higher proportion of married women in the age-group 20-24 and 25-29 — reflecting the recency of immigration and childbearing of their parents.

As age-specific fertility ratios vary considerably, it is often desirable to standardize our data by age in order to eliminate differences in the overall fertility ratios among our groups solely due to the concentrations of married women in particularly high fertility age-groups. It is necessary, therefore, to adopt a standard age-distribution for married women aged 20-49 and adjust all of our results according to this hypothetical marriage pattern. In the absence of detailed age-specific marriage data in the 1880 U.S. census, we have decided to use the distribution of marriages from our combined samples in the South End and South Boston (see Graph 1).

The marriage pattern we have selected as our standard is a reasonable approximation of the actual marriage pattern in that period. We can compare our standard with the distribution of married women from the Massachusetts Census of 1885 (see Graph 2). The two patterns are very similar at ten-year intervals with our distribution being more concentrated in the age-group 30-39 than the state as a whole.

The method of weighting our results to eliminate differences in overall fertility ratios due to variations in the age-distribution of married women is as follows:

Table 1   Method of Standardizing Fertility Ratios for Age-Distribution of Married Women

$$Y = .10X_{20-24} + .17X_{25-29} + .21X_{30-34} + .22X_{35-39} + .17X_{40-44} + .13X_{45-49} *$$

Where:
Y is the age-standardized fertility ratio per 1000 married women aged 20-49 to be calculated

X_{20-24} is the number of children under 5 per 1000 married women aged 20-24

    •
    •
    •

X_{45-49} is the number of children under 5 per 1000 married women aged 45-49.

*   The coefficients .10, .17, .21, .22, .17, and .13 are the percentages that the married women of each of these age-groups are of all married women aged 20-49 of the population which we are using as the standard.

75

We hope that future studies of fertility differentials at the household level using the censuses will follow the same weighting procedure for age-standardization in order to make all of the results more comparable. At the present time, several other social historians are already adopting the same weighting system for analyzing their data.[17]

The age-standardization of the overall fertility ratios eliminates differences among groups attributable to variations in the concentration of married women in certain age-groups. Many different ways of weighting the married population could have been selected. The advantage of the particular standard that we have chosen is that it probably approximates closely the age-distribution of married women in the United States in 1880.[18]

Finally, we may also want some indication of the number of children the average woman can expect to have during her lifetime if the current fertility rates were to persist throughout her reproductive years. This completed fertility ratio can be calculated by adding the five-year age-specific ratios for married women aged 20-49. This index indicates the average number of children a woman aged 20 could have expected to have if the current age-specific fertility ratios were to have continued for the next 30 years of her life.[19]

Fertility Patterns in South Boston and the South End

Our data indicate that ethnicity was a major variable in accounting for fertility differentials. In the combined sample of the South End and South Boston, foreign-born women always had higher age-specific marital fertility ratios than native-born women (see Graph 3). This difference was especially pronounced for the age-group 30-34. Overall, the age-standardized marital fertility ratio of foreign-born women was 63.9 percent higher than that of native women. This conforms with the general pattern for the United States population derived from the aggregate censuses for the late nineteenth and early twentieth century.[20]

Foreign-born women generally had higher marital fertility rates than native women for all age-groups in each of the two wards. But the differences in marital fertility between these two ethnic groups varied greatly in the two areas. In the combined sample the age-standardized marital fertility of foreign-born women was 63.9 percent higher than that of native women while in the South End it was 102.3 percent, and in South Boston only 26.6 percent higher. Furthermore, the age-standardized marital fertility ratio for both the foreign-born and native women was higher in South Boston than in the South End.

We can investigate differences in fertility ratios among the ethnic groups in more detail by subdividing foreign-born women into those born in Ireland, Canada, and elsewhere (see Graph 4). The Irish women had the highest age-standardized fertility ratio and the Canadians the lowest among these three foreign-born groups. In most age-groups the three divisions of foreign-born

76

Graph 3   Number of Children under 5 years old per 1000 Married Women
Aged 20-49 in both Wards in 1880 by Nativity

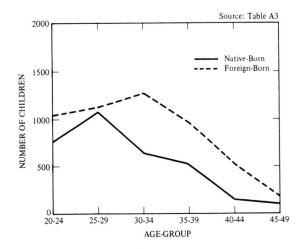

Graph 4   Number of Children under 5 years old per 1000 Married Women
Aged 20-49 in both Wards in 1880 by Nativity

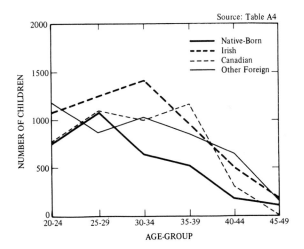

77

women had higher fertility ratios than the native women. The difference between Irish and native fertility ratios was particularly high in the age-group 30-34 whereas for Canadians it was at ages 35-39.

Our results generally fit the pattern of cumulative fertility found among these ethnic groups in the 1910 census. Foreign-born women who in 1910 were aged 45-74, with the exception of the English-speaking Canadians, had higher cumulative fertility than native American women. The higher fertility ratios of first-generation Irish in our sample parallel the high cumulative fertility of the Irish in the 1910 census. The 5,428 children ever born per 1,000 Irish married women aged 45-74 in 1910 was surpassed only by the French-Canadians, who had 7,382 children.[21] In our sample the Canadian women had low fertility ratios — mainly because most of them were English-speaking, primarily from the maritime provinces. To what extent length of stay in the country for foreign women affected fertility behavior cannot be measured from our 1880 census data. An analysis of the 1910 retrospective study suggests, however, that recency of migration did not significantly affect the fertility of foreign-born women.[22]

At the ward level, the pattern of fertility differentials among the various ethnic groups was basically the same as in our combined sample. Again, the fertility ratios of all ethnic groups were higher in South Boston than in the South End.

Were there pronounced differences in the pattern of second-generation foreign-born? Fertility ratios of natives of foreign parentage were closer to those of immigrants than to Americans of native parentage and were higher than the latter in almost all age-groups (see Graph 5). The gap between second-generation immigrants and native Americans was particularly high in the age-groups 35-39 and 40-44, while the difference between natives and first-generation immigrants was highest in the age-groups 30-34 and 35-39.

Previous studies based on aggregate retrospective data for the United States in 1910 have found that second-generation women usually have higher cumulative fertility than American women of native parentage but lower than that of first-generation women.[23] Our findings suggest that in the two wards we have investigated, the fertility ratios of second-generation women were only slightly lower than that of foreign-born women (6.7 percent lower). A major reason for this difference in the age-standardized fertility ratios is that the age-specific fertility ratios of second-generation women were considerably higher than those of foreign-born women at ages over 40.

At the ward level, the differences between first-generation, second-generation, and women of native parentage were similar. In both wards the second-generation women had lower age-standardized fertility than the foreign-born women but higher age-standardized fertility than the women of native parentage. The age-specific fertility ratios for all groups were higher in South Boston than in the South End.

In our entire sample, the high fertility ratios of native women of foreign

78

Graph 5

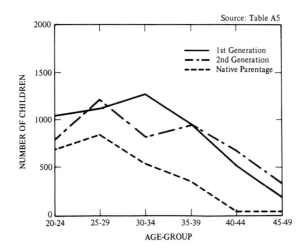

parentage suggests the persistence of premigration customs and values among
second-generation immigrants. Perhaps the high fertility ratios for second-
generation women is partly the result of the high fertility norms acquired
from their parents and the increased economic prosperity in the United States
which made it possible to support a large family.

The data for both Boston wards studied indicate that there were major
ethnic differences in fertility. The difference between foreign-born and native
women became even larger after we removed women of foreign parentage
from our native sample. Finally, there was a consistent pattern of women in
South Boston having higher fertility ratios than those in the South End —
even after examining ethnic origins by more detailed subgroups.

There is a curvilinear relationship between fertility and occupation in our
combined sample of the two Boston wards (see Graph 6).[24] Women whose
husbands were in high occupations had lower fertility than those whose husbands were in middle or low occupations. Women from the high occupational
group generally had a lower fertility ratio at all ages. The age-specific fertility
ratio for middle and low occupational groups is more erratic, but the age-
standardized fertility ratio is higher for the middle occupations than the low
ones.[25]

79

Graph 6   Number of Children under 5 years old per 1000 Married Women Aged 20-49 in both Wards in 1880 by Occupation

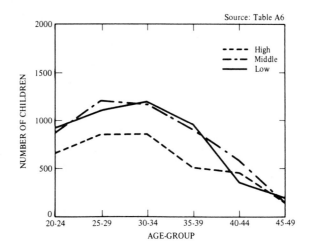

At the ward level, an inverse pattern of fertility and occupation exists for the South End but not for South Boston where women whose husbands were in low occupations had less children than those whose husbands were in the middle occupational group. Again, women in South Boston tended to have more children than those in the South End in all three occupation groups.

We have found significant differences in fertility patterns along ethnic as well as occupational lines in both neighborhoods analyzed. The obvious next question is whether the relationship between ethnicity and fertility exists after controlling for the effects of occupations. As our sample size is rapidly depleted by introducing any controls, we will confine our analysis only to the combined data for the two wards.

Foreign-born women had a higher fertility ratio than native women. When we control for the effects of occupation, that relationship remains the same (see Table 2). The differences in fertility, however, between foreign-born and native women diminish slightly for the low occupational group and remain about the same for the middle and high occupations.

The differences in the age-standardized fertility ratios among native-born women is not very large after subdividing them by the occupation of the husband (the fertility ratio of women whose husbands are in the low occupational category is only 19.7 percent above that of women whose husbands are in

80

Table 2 Number of Children under 5 years old per 1000 Married Women
Aged 20-49 in both Wards in 1880 by Nativity and Occupation

Occupation	Native	Foreign-Born
High	541	723
	497*	760*
	(n = 61)	(n = 65)
Middle	717	950
	571*	957*
	(n = 159)	(n = 279)
Low	659	828
	595*	882*
	(n = 85)	(n = 372)
Total	633	849
	537*	880*
	(n = 324)	(n = 746)

* Standardized for age-distribution (see Table 1).

Source: Manuscript of the *Tenth Census of the United States, 1880: Population of the United States.*

the high occupational group). A similar pattern is true for foreign-born women (the fertility ratio of women whose husbands are in the middle occupations is 25.9 percent higher than that of women whose husbands are in the low occupational group).

We can examine in more detail the relationship between fertility and ethnicity after controlling for occupation by subdividing foreign-born women into those born in Ireland, Canada, and elsewhere (see Table 3). Among the Canadian women, fertility was highest for women whose husbands had high occupations and much lower for the other two groups. Irish women at all levels of occupation generally had higher fertility than either the Canadian or other foreign-born women.

We can further refine our analysis by separating native women by the origin of their parents (see Table 4). The results generally confirm our previous analysis — second-generation women have higher fertility than women of native parentage but lower fertility than foreign-born women for the middle and low occupations. One interesting change is that whereas *native-born*

81

Table 3 Number of Children under 5 years old per 1000 Married Women Aged 20-49 in both Wards in1880 by Nativity and Occupation*

Occupation	Native	Irish	Canadian	Other Foreign
High	541	718	1333	412
	497*	758*	1240*	453*
	(n = 61)	(n = 39)	(n = 9)	(n = 17)
Middle	717	974	889	939
	571*	1070*	679*	927*
	(n = 159)	(n = 152)	(n = 45)	(n = 82)
Low	659	824	788	895
	595*	909*	707*	745*
	(n = 85)	(n = 301)	(n = 33)	(n = 38)
Total:	633	847	890	817
	537*	932*	781*	813*
	(n = 324)	(n = 504)	(n = 91)	(n = 151)

* Standardized for age-distribution (see Table 1).

Source: Manuscript of the *Tenth Census of the United States, 1880: Population of the U.S*

Table 4   Number of Children under 5 years old per 1000 Married Women Aged 20-49 in both Wards in 1880 by Ethnic Origin and Occupation*

Occupation	First Generation Foreign	Second Generation Foreign	Native Parentage
High	723	875	422
	760*	853*	427*
	(n = 65)	(n = 16)	(n = 45)
Middle	950	1029	472
	957*	830*	471*
	(n = 279)	(n = 70)	(n = 89)
Low	828	844	450
	882*	790*	406*
	(n = 372)	(n = 45)	(n = 40)
Total:	849	933	418
	880*	821*	417*
	(n = 746)	(n = 135)	(n = 189)

* Standardized for age-distribution (see Table 1).

Source: Manuscript of the *Tenth Census of the United States, 1880: Population of the U.S.*

women had the highest fertility if their husbands were in the low occupational group, women of *native parentage* had very low fertility if their husbands were in the low occupation group.

The results of our analysis of the relationship between fertility and ethnicity after controlling for occupation suggests that ethnicity was a major determinant of fertility differentials at the household level. Differences in occupational groups also had a major impact on the fertility ratios of American women though the direction and strength of that relationship varied for the different ethnic groups.

Location in the city was also an important determinant of fertility. Women in the center city area of the South End in this study had lower marital fertility than women in South Boston, which was a more peripheral neighborhood. Even members of the same ethnic group were behaving differently in the two wards. Thus, the Irish in the South End had lower fertility than those in South Boston. The difference in fertility between these two areas suggests that scholars should not treat urban areas as homogeneous entities.[26]

In this instance, the South End is typical of a central city area, which because of its proximity to the central business district was less suitable for raising children. This pattern also fits the conclusions of a national fertility study by Grabill, Kiser, and Whelpton which found significant differences in fertility patterns among different sections within major American cities. They found that housing density also had a significant impact on fertility ratios. Dwellers in large apartment houses with multiple dwelling units had lower fertility than residents in one- or two-family houses.[27] While the residents of the section of the South End studied here were living in buildings with multiple dwelling units or in town houses that had been converted into crowded boarding houses, the residents of South Boston were concentrated primarily in one- or two-family dwellings. What the cause and effect relationship between fertility and location was cannot be determined on the basis of only the 1880 census data. Did the South End attract individuals who tended to have lower fertility or did life in the South End depress their previous fertility pattern?

What are the implications of this analysis for the understanding of the family and the household in nineteenth-century society? Historians of the family who have focused on household structure as the most important variable in family behavior have missed other crucial aspects such as the stages of the family cycle or fertility.[28] Though an examination of household structure alone often does not reveal profound differences between ethnic and occupational groups, there may be important variations for other factors. For example, our data suggest that a major difference in family behavior in nineteenth-century American urban populations was fertility. Though this fact has been readily apparent to contemporary demographers, it has apparently eluded the attention of historians of the family.

Now that it is possible to delineate fertility patterns on the household

84

level, one can go on from here to relate fertility to family and household structure, and to distinguish more meaningful patterns in the interaction among them. Particular effort should be made in the future to investigate the relationship between fertility and women's work because the two variables are highly correlated today. Finally, much more effort has to be made in subsequent studies to include other important determinants of fertility such as the level of education, religion, and income.[29]

Tamara K. Hareven
Clark University
and Maris A. Vinovskis
University of Michigan

APPENDIX

Table A1   Distribution of Married Women in both Wards in 1880 by Ethnic Origin

| | Percent of Married Women Aged 20-49 | | | |
Age-Group	First Generation	Second Generation	Native Parentage	Standard Distribution
20-24	6.3	31.2	8.5	10.0
25-29	13.6	34.1	16.9	17.0
30-34	21.5	12.3	22.2	21.0
35-39	24.0	11.6	23.8	22.0
40-44	19.6	4.3	15.3	17.0
45-49	14.6	4.3	13.2	13.0

Source: Manuscript of the *Tenth Census of the United States, 1880: Population of the United States.*

85

Table A2 Comparison of Age Distribution to Massachusetts Pattern in 1885 of Married Women

	Percent of Married Women aged 20-49	
Age-Group	Standard Distribution	Massachusetts 1885
20-29	27.0	29.0
30-39	43.0	37.3
40-49	30.0	32.3

Source: Manuscript of the *Tenth Census of the United States, 1880: Population of the United States; Massachusetts Census of 1885: Population and Social Statistics*, part 2, p. 1173.

Table A3 Number of Children under 5 years old per 1000 Married Women Aged 20-49 in 1880 by Nativity

	Both Wards Combined	
Age-Group	Native-Born (n = 324)	Foreign-Born (n = 746)
20-24	763	1043
25-29	1063	1118
30-34	627	1267
35-39	508	950
40-44	143	510
45-49	97	183
20-49	633	849
	537*	880*

Ward	Each Ward	
	Native-Born	Foreign-Born
	901	922
South Boston (ages 20-49)	766*	970*
	(n = 151)	(n = 502)
	399	697
South End (ages 20-49)	354*	716*
	(n = 173)	(n = 244)

* Standardized for age-distribution (see Table 1).

Source: Manuscript of the *Tenth Census of the United States, 1880: Population of the United States.*

86

Table A4   Number of Children under 5 years old per 1000 Married Women Aged 20-49 in 1880 by Nativity

Age-Group	Both Wards Combined			
	Native-Born (n = 324)	Irish (n = 504)	Canadian (n = 91)	Other Foreign (n = 151)
20-24	763	1080	800	1167
25-29	1063	1236	1087	875
30-34	627	1420	1000	1026
35-39	508	945	1158	853
40-44	143	495	300	643
45-49	97	182	0	267
20-49	633	847	890	817
	537*	932*	781*	813*

Ward	Each Ward			
	Native-Born	Irish	Canadian	Other Foreign
South Boston (ages 20-49)	901	880	1118	1000
	766*	965*	975*	951*
	(n = 151)	(n = 375)	(n = 51)	(n = 76)
South End (ages 20-49)	399	752	600	653
	354*	835*	509*	651*
	(n = 173)	(n = 129)	(n = 40)	(n = 75)

* Standardized for age-distribution (see Table 1).

Source: Manuscript of the *Tenth Census of the United States, 1880: Population of the United States*

87

Table A5 Number of Children under 5 years old per 1000 Married Women Aged 20-49 in 1880 by Ethnic Origin

Age-Group	First Generation (n = 746)	Second Generation (n = 135)	Native Parentage (n = 189)
20-24	1043	791	688
25-29	1118	1213	844
30-34	1267	824	548
35-39	950	938	356
40-44	510	667	34
45-49	183	333	40
20-49	849	933	418
	880*	821*	417*

Each Ward

Ward	First Generation	Second Generation	Native Parentage
South Boston (ages 20-49)	922	1030	654
	970*	940*	636*
	(n = 502)	(n = 99)	(n = 52)
South End (ages 20-49)	697	667	328
	716*	452*	325*
	(n = 244)	(n = 36)	(n = 137)

* Standardized for age-distribution (see Table 1)

Source: Manuscript of the *Tenth Census of the United States, 1880: Population of the United States.*

88

Number of Children under 5 years old per 1000 Married Women
Aged 20-49 in 1880 by Occupation

Age-Group	Both Wards Combined		
	High (n = 126)	Middle (n = 438)	Low (n = 457)
20-24	667	887	927
25-29	852	1215	1103
30-34	852	1161	1188
35-39	500	900	949
40-44	450	576	357
45-49	273	132	188
20-49	635	865	790
	612*	852*	824*

Ward	Each Ward		
	High	Middle	Low
South Boston (ages 20-49)	891	1008	857
	742*	1003*	878*
	(n = 64)	(n = 258)	(n = 321)
South End (ages 20-49)	371	661	654
	301*	642*	704*
	(n = 62)	(n = 180)	(n = 136)

* Standardized for age-distribution (see Table 1).

Source: Manuscript of the *Tenth Census of the United States, 1880: Population of the United States.*

89

NOTES

The Boston data from the U.S. 1880 Federal Census Manuscript Schedules have been gathered and coded under a grant from the Clark University Graduate Research Fund. Computer analysis was supported by the Clark University Computer Fund. We are indebted to Stephen Shedd for programming the data for the computer and to Howard Chudacoff, Richard Easterlin, Stanley Engerman, Laurence Glasco, John Modell, and Roger Revelle for reading an earlier version of this article and making useful suggestions, but we are solely responsible for any errors of fact or judgement.

1.   Irene Tauber, "Continuity, Change, and Transition in Population and Family: Interrelations and Priorities in Research," in National Institute of Health, *The Family in Transition* (Washington, D.C., 1969), p. 317.

2.   On the state of the field of family history, see Tamara K. Hareven, "The History of the Family as an Interdisciplinary Field," *Journal of Interdisciplinary History* II (1970): 400-14. For a review of the current efforts in nineteenth-century historical demography, see Maris A. Vinovskis, "Mortality Rates and Trends in Massachusetts before 1860," *Journal of Economic History* XXXII (1972): 184-213, and Maris A. Vinovskis, "Socio-Economic Determinants of Inter-State Fertility Differentials in the United States in 1850 and 1860," *Journal of Interdisciplinary History* (forthcoming).

3.   The two Boston wards chosen for this study are part of the four areas sampled from the 1880 Census of Boston. The other two wards included in the general study but not in our analysis are the Back Bay and Dorchester. The larger project consists of an analysis of household structure and the stages of the family cycle. For a description of the other aspects of the larger project, see Tamara K. Hareven, "Family Structure in Nineteenth-Century Boston Neighborhoods" (Paper presented at the Conference on the Family, Social Structure, and Social Change, Clark University, 1972), forthcoming, *Journal of Urban History* (May 1975), and John Modell and Tamara K. Hareven, "Urbanization and the Malleable Household, Boarding and Lodging with Nineteenth-Century Families," *Journal of Marriage and the Family* 35 (1973): 467-79.

4.   The total population of South Boston (Ward 13) in 1880 was 21,462. Of these, 12,316 were native and 9,146 foreign-born. Among the foreign-born there were 6,550 Irish and 1,103 English-speaking Canadians. The immigrant composition of this ward is much more dramatic if one takes into consideration the fact that of the 21,462 population of the ward only 1,993 were native Americans of native parentage. The remaining 10,325 native-born were descendants of foreign or mixed foreign-native parentage. The "Irish" character of the neighborhood is especially evident in the 7,211 native Americans whose fathers and mothers were natives of Ireland and another 1,076 native-born of mixed parentage, where one of the parents was a native of Ireland.

In the South End (Ward 16) the total population was 15,184, of whom there were 9,895 native and 5,289 foreign-born. The population contained 2,857 Irish who constituted 18.8 percent of the foreign-born, 1,103 English-speaking Canadians, and 714 Germans. Second-generation Irish constituted 19.4 percent of the entire population. Of the 9,895 natives, however, 4,686 were of foreign parentage. Of these 2,506 were of complete Irish parentage, and another 441 were of mixed descent with one Irish parent. In addition to their ethnic composition, there was a significant difference in the literacy rates between the two wards: in South Boston, 8 percent of all males were reported as unable to write as opposed to the South End, where those unable to write constituted only 1.4 percent of the male population. The difference was less dramatic among females: 9.3 percent of all females in South Boston were unable to write as opposed to 6.3 percent of all females in the South End. The percentages of the South End in each case are closer to those for the entire city (6.6 percent for males and 4.5 percent for

90

females). These data were compiled from the summary tabulations for Boston from the 1880 Census: Carroll D. Wright, *The Social, Commercial and Manufacturing Statistics of the City of Boston* (Boston, 1882).

5.   This study does not include married women who are living in someone else's household; since they constitute a small proportion of married women, their exclusion is not a serious problem.

6.   For examples of leading work in this area see Stephan Thernstrom, *Poverty and Progress in a Nineteenth-Century City* (Cambridge, Mass., 1965) and *The Other Bostonians: Poverty and Progress in the American Metropolis, 1880-1970* (Cambridge, Mass., 1973), and Stephan Thernstrom and Richard Sennett, eds., *Nineteenth-Century Cities* (New Haven, 1969). Examples of studies of family structure in nineteenth-century society, based on the U.S. Federal Census are in: Richard Sennett, *Families Against the City* (Cambridge, Mass., 1970), and Stuart Blumin, "Family Structure in the Hudson Valley," Laurence Glasco, "Ethnicity and Family Structure in Nineteenth-Century Buffalo," and Tamara K. Hareven, "Family Structure in Nineteenth-Century Boston Neighborhoods," (Papers presented at the Conference on the Family, Social Structure, and Social Change, Clark University, 1972), forthcoming, *Journal of Urban History* (May 1975). For an effort to utilize the nineteenth-century census for the study of the family cycle, see Modell and Hareven, "Urbanization and the Malleable Household," and Hareven, "The Family as Process: The Historical Study of the Family Cycle," *Journal of Social History* (1974). The latter also contains a critique of the current methods of utilization of the census for the study of the family structure. For studies of household and family structure of the black population, see Elizabeth Pleck, "The Two-Parent Black Household: Black Family Structure in Late Nineteenth-Century Boston," *Journal of Social History* 6 (1972): 3-31. For a comprehensive comparative collection of household and family studies, see Peter Laslett and Richard Wall, eds., *Family and Household in Past Time* (Cambridge, England, 1972).

7.   On the use of aggregate data from the federal censuses to study nineteenth-century fertility, see Yasukichi Yasuba, *Birth Rates of the White Population in the United States, 1800-1860: An Economic Study*, The Johns Hopkins University Studies in Historical and Political Science LXXIX, No. 2 (Baltimore, 1962); Colin Forster and G. S. L. Tucker, *Economic Opportunity and White American Fertility Ratios: 1800-1860* (New Haven, 1972); Maris A. Vinovskis, "A Multivariate Regression Analysis of Fertility Differentials among Massachusetts Towns and Regions in 1860" (Paper presented at the Conference on Early Industrialization, Shifts in Fertility, and Changes in the Family Structure, Princeton University, June 18-July 10, 1972; forthcoming in a volume of the conference proceedings edited by Charles Tilly); and Richard A. Easterlin, "Does Human Fertility Adjust to the Environment?" American Economic Association, *Papers and Proceedings* LXI (1971), pp. 399-407.

For imaginative attempts to study fertility at the household level in the early nineteenth century, see John Modell, "Family and Fertility on the Indiana Frontier, 1820," *American Quarterly* XXIII (1971): 615-634; Francis Notzon, "Fertility and Farmland in Weston, Massachusetts: 1800-1820" (MS thesis in sociology, the University of Wisconsin, 1973). Unfortunately, their studies are based on federal census data which do not provide the detailed family information that is available for the 1850 to 1880 censuses.

8.   Susan E. Bloomberg, Mary Frank Fox, Robert M. Warner, and Sam Bass Warner, Jr., "A Census Probe into Nineteenth-Century Family History: Southern Michigan, 1850-1880," *Journal of Social History* 5 (1971): 26-45; Wendell H. Bash, "Differential Fertility in Madison County, New York, 1865," *Milbank Memorial Fund Quarterly* XXXIII (1955): 161-86.

9.   Bloomberg, et al., "A Census Probe."

10.   Bash, "Differential Fertility."

11.   Lee-Jay Cho, Wilson H. Grabill, and Donald J. Bogue, *Differential Current*

91

Fertility in the United States (Chicago, 1970). We are heavily indebted to many of the suggestions and techniques in this study in constructing our index of fertility.

12.   For example, Yasuba's aggregate analysis of the fertility ratios of the white population from 1800 to 1860 is based on the number of white children under 10 per 1000 white women aged 16-44. He used this ratio because of the particular age-subdivisions in the U.S. censuses of 1800, 1810, and 1820. The problem with this ratio is that information is not available in the printed census columns on the number of women aged 16-19 or 40-44 in the later censuses. Therefore, Yasuba was forced to make estimates of those age-groups on the basis of the pattern of the age-distribution of the population in 1880. Yasuba, *Birth Rates of the White Population*, pp. 23-37.

13.   Ideally, we would have liked to use the number of women aged 15-49 in our denominator to make it more comparable to the analyses of the recent censuses. However, the number of cases of married women aged 15-19 is usually so small that their inclusion would give us very biased results when we weight our age-specific findings to obtain an overall index of marital fertility.

14.   On the availability and reliability of using mid-nineteenth-century mortality data, see Vinovskis, "Mortality Rates and Trends." On the problem of mortality rates affecting fertility ratios, see Cho, *Differential Current Fertility*, pp. 316-18.

15.   Wilson H. Grabill, Clyde V. Kiser, and Pascal W. Whelpton, *The Fertility of American Women* (New York, 1958), pp. 404-06; Cho, *Differential Current Fertility*, pp. 309-11, 318-21.

16.   Grabill et al., *The Fertility of American Women*, pp. 406-13; Cho, *Differential Current Fertility*, pp. 322-25.

17.   Our age-standardization model is based upon the distribution of married women; therefore, studies of marital fertility should try to use the same method of age-standardization. Studies of the fertility of all women, married or unmarried, should use a different standard age-distribution which more closely approximates the population as a whole. We would suggest that these studies should use the age-distribution of all women ages 20-49 in the U.S. in 1880 as their standard.

18.   One of the problems in the use of any standardization procedure is that it requires the data to be subdivided. This increases the likelihood of errors due to the erratic pattern of fertility ratios when there are only a few cases for each subdivision. For a discussion of the sensitivity of age-standardization procedures to errors in various subdivisions of the data, see Tamara K. Hareve and Maris A. Vinovskis, "Socio-Economic Determinants of Household Fertility Differentials in Essex County, Mass., in 1880" (Paper presented at the seminar on the "Family in the Process of Urbanization" at Williams College, July, 1974).

In order to minimize problems of the small number of cases wherever the data are standardized for the age of the woman, the overall unstandardized fertility ratios are also given. This permits a rough check on the reliability of our results. However, the reader is cautioned that in some instances, such as the number of married Canadian women whose husbands are in high occupations, even the number of overall cases is so small that very little confidence can be attached to the exact level of fertility. It was decided to publish all of the results of the analysis (even where the number of cases is very small) in order to give the reader an opportunity to ascertain the general level of fertility for that subpopulation.

19.   It is important to remember that our suggested index of completed fertility does not represent the number of children ever-born to these women. This measure is based on the age-specific ratios of the number of surviving children under 5 per 1000 women in the various age-categories. Therefore, our index of completed fertility ratios for any group of women would be less than the number of children ever-born using the current age-specific fertility rates.

20.   The data for our analysis are presented in the tables for this article.

92

21. Grabill, *The Fertility of American Women*, pp. 106-07.

22. *Ibid.*, pp. 107-08. See also J. Hill, "Fecundity of Immigrant Women," U.S. Congress, Immigration Commission, Reports of the Immigration Commission, Vol. 28, *Occupations of First and Second Generations of Immigrants in the United States – Fecundity of Immigrant Women*. Senate Doc. No. 282, 61st Cong., 2nd Session (Washington, D.C., 1911).

23. Grabill et al., *The Fertility of American Women*, pp. 107-08; Hill, "Fecundity," pp. 743-57.

24. We classified the occupations in three categories: high, middle, and low. The categories employed for each occupation are based on Stuart Blumin's classification. We are indebted to Professor Blumin for making his classification available to us. See Blumin, "Family Structure in the Hudson Valley."

25. The 1910-1940 data suggest an inverse relationship between fertility and occupation. Grabill et al., *The Fertility of American Women*, pp. 129-36. For an analysis of the relationship between fertility and various occupational categories in the 1910 census, see Xanifa Sallume and Frank W. Notestein, "Trends in the Size of Families Completed Prior to 1910 in Various Social Classes," *The American Journal of Sociology* 38 (1932): 406-07.

26. To what extent location in the city had an impact on demographic behavior is an unexplored question. Most studies of urban demography address themselves to rural-urban differences, but pay no attention to historical studies of the difference between various sections within the city. While historians are rejecting the Chicago School's model of social breakdown, it is important to test on the level of the family whether location in the city had an impact on family structure and behavior. In this essay we pay attention to fertility in this context. The longer Boston study by Hareven subjects all variables to this analysis. The only historical study addressed to this question was Richard Sennett, *Families Against The City*, but he concentrates on one suburb, without any comparisons and controls.

27. Grabill et al., *The Fertility of American Women*, pp. 94-95.

28. Hareven, "The Family as Process."

29. To explore these questions along rural-urban differences, Hareven and Vinovskis have embarked on an analysis of population samples from five select towns in Essex County, Massachusetts, drawn from the 1880 census. The towns are Lawrence, Lynn, Salem, Boxford, and Lynnfield. This study was prepared for an intensive seminar on the Family in the Process of Urbanization, which was sponsored by the Mathematics Social Science Board of the National Science Foundation, and which was held at Williams College in July, 1974. At this seminar fertility on the household level was also analyzed by Richard Easterlin for rural America in 1860 and by Laurence Glasco for Buffalo, N.Y. in 1855-1865.

93

A Study of Cohort Life Cycles:
Cohorts of Native Born Massachusetts Women, 1830–1920

PETER R. UHLENBERG

The normatively sanctioned life cycle that a baby born into American society is expected to follow as he moves from birth to death has remained remarkably stable during the past century. Although the phases of the life cycle often overlap and the transition from one to another is often blurred, the various stages can be rather clearly differentiated. The initial phase for a 'typical' individual is a pre-school period in which training is received in the home. This is followed by the formal educational phase in which the child attends school while living at home. Sex becomes an important factor in the life cycle after the basic educational phase (and perhaps earlier), and the discussion in this paper will concentrate on the life cycles of females. The woman may obtain employment or go on for further education while remaining single for a time, or she may marry very soon after the end of her basic educational period of life. Following marriage there is normally a phase of childbearing, followed by a phase of childrearing. Finally there is the phase of the children marrying and leaving home, of married life together with the spouse after the children are no longer present, and, if the husband dies first, a period of widowhood for the woman.

In every cohort of females, however, there are many who do not experience this 'typical' life cycle with each of its phases. Figure 1 illustrates six different possible types of life cycles that females can experience, depending upon what path they follow at different junctions in their life. The first category consists of those women who do not survive to their twentieth birthday. Second are those who survive to twenty but never subsequently marry. Third are those who marry but remain childless. Fourth are women who marry and become mothers, but die before they reach age 55. This group is further divided into those whose husbands also die before they reach 57, thus producing orphans, and those whose husbands survive to age 57. Fifth are mothers who survive to 55 but are widowed before that age. And finally, there are those women who follow the typical life cycle of marrying, having children and surviving jointly with their husbands to age 55.[1] The particular life cycle of an individual woman is of negligible interest, but the life cycle experience of whole birth cohorts of women is of considerable social and demographic consequence. In response to demographic and social changes, the number of females in a cohort who follow any one type of life cycle may be expected to vary considerably over time. By looking at several cohorts of women born in Massachusetts between 1830 and 1920, this paper will attempt to determine the historical trends in female life cycles, and some of the causes and consequences of these changes.

[1] More types of life cycles can easily be constructed by introducing variables such as divorce and re-marriage. Because of the lack of data and the complications of including other life cycles, the analysis here is limited to these basic six types which are thought to have major theoretical importance and within which all the women included in a cohort can be located, even if they are divorced or re-married.

407

Reprinted from *Population Studies* **XXIII**, 407–420. Copyright © 1969 by permission of the publisher.

Previous studies of life cycles, primarily conducted by Paul Glick, have been limited to the life cycle of the family.[2] All but the latest study by Glick have used census data to determine family cycle data for the cross section of population represented in the census. Main attention has been focused on median ages of men and women at time of first marriage, median ages at the birth of the last child, median ages when the last child leaves home, and ages at the dissolution of the family due to death. For the latest dates, attention has also been given to numbers of children aged under 18 living at home, residential mobility, labour force participation and family income for the different age groups. While this information is interesting, there is much information that it fails to yield. By concentrating on median and mean ages at events, it does not indicate the distribution of women on these variables nor the proportion of women who actually experience such a family cycle. It is quite possible that very few women in fact follow the pattern that is described by the averages. Also, this approach gives no information on women who never enter into a family relationship due to early death or failure to marry. Further, the information refers not to a real cohort, but gives a cross-sectional view of different cohorts at the same point in time. By including all women in the United States, no allowance is made for the changing proportion of women who are foreign-born and who may be expected to follow quite different patterns from the native-born, and variations between smaller regions are concealed.

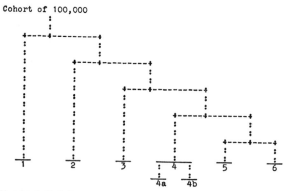

Type 1 life cycle: *Abbreviated*; die before age 20.
Type 2 life cycle: *Spinster*; survive to 20, never marry.
Type 3 life cycle: *Barren*; marry, remain childless.
Type 4 life cycle: *Dying mother*; have children, die before age 55.
Type 4a life cycle: *Motherless-child producing*; husband survives to 57.
Type 4b life cycle: *Orphan producing*; husband dies before he is 57.
Type 5 life cycle: *Widowed mother*; have children, survive to 55, husband dies before he is 57.
Type 6 life cycle: *Typical*; survive to 20, marry, have children, survive with husband alive to age 55.

FIGURE I

[2] Paul C. Glick, *American Families* (New York, 1957), Chapters 3–5; Paul C. Glick, 'The family cycle', *American Sociological Review*, 12 (April 1947), pp. 164–174; Paul C. Glick, 'The life cycle of the family', *Marriage and Family Living*, 18 (February 1955), pp. 3–9; Paul C. Glick et al., 'Family formation and family composition: Trends and prospects', in *Sourcebook in Marriage and the Family* (Marvin B. Sussmann, Ed.) (Boston, 1963), pp. 37–40; Paul C. Glick and Robert Parke, 'New approaches in studying the life cycle of the family', *Demography*, 2 (1965), pp. 187–202.

To correct for some of these weaknesses, a more recent study has considered the family cycle of cohorts of women.[3] The cohort approach is superior to the calendar year approach for the study of family cycles because it refers to real groups of women and thereby takes into account changing patterns of mortality, marriage and fertility. By continuing to emphasize median ages at selected events as the important variable to compare over time, this cohort study by Glick still fails to indicate the number who never marry, never have children, die before their children are married, etc. The information revealed is summarized by this conclusion from the study:

'The youngest women for whom data are available compare as follows, on the average, with the women who are forty to sixty years older: the youngest women marry one to two years younger and complete their childbearing two to three years younger; their age at the marriage of their last child is four to five years younger, and their length of married life is about nine years longer'.[4]

In order to determine the distribution of women according to type of life cycle experienced, which may be of greater social and demographic significance than the results of the studies mentioned above, this paper will calculate the number of women out of selected cohorts of 100,000 who fall into each of the six possible types of life cycles. This study includes all females who are members of the birth cohort, not only those who marry. Also, this study is limited to native-born women in order to eliminate differences due solely to the changing proportion of foreign-born in the cohort, and the analysis goes further back into the nineteenth century than did previous studies.

The data used come from four sources: Massachusetts censuses of 1885 and 1895, United States censuses from 1890 through 1960, Massachusetts Vital Registration Reports, and cohort life tables calculated by Jacobson.[5] The cohort life tables are based upon data from Massachusetts up to 1900, and thereafter upon data from the Death Registration Area, and so quite accurately reflect the experience of the Massachusetts cohorts included in this study. The data from the censuses and vital registration figures likewise appear to be sufficiently accurate to serve the purposes of this study. Due to necessary assumptions (discussed below) and imperfections in the data, a high degree of accuracy is not claimed. Nevertheless, even if the results are off by as much as 5% or more in either direction, the conclusions regarding the trend and relative magnitudes would not be invalidated. Each of the six types of life cycle must now be examined more carefully.

TYPE I. THE ABBREVIATED LIFE CYCLE

The abbreviated life cycle is experienced by all those females who die before they reach age 20. More than 95% of the women in each cohort were single when they reached age 20, so those who died before this age were in general not exposed to the risk of marriage and childbearing. Of those dying before their twentieth birthday, at least 80% died before they reached age 5 for each cohort. Given the cohort life tables (Appendix, Table 1), the number of females dying before age 20 is calculated simply by subtracting the number alive at age 20 from the original number in the cohort, 100,000.

---

[3] Glick and Parke, *loc. cit.*
[4] *Ibid.*
[5] Paul Jacobson, 'Cohort survival for generations since 1840', *Milbank Memorial Fund Quarterly*, 42 (July 1964), pp. 36–53.

The number of females in each cohort of 100,000 who experienced an abbreviated life cycle is given in the following table:

Cohort of:	1830	1850	1870	1890	1920
Type 1. Abbreviated life cycle:	35,600	31,400	30,900	26,300	10,800

The change in mortality over this 90-year period is striking. In the cohort of 1920 only one-third of the number died before age 20 as in the cohort of 1830. Quite obviously a change of this magnitude has significant demographic and social implications. The greatest declines in mortality were experienced by cohorts after 1870, although there was a continuous decline throughout the whole period. Resources spent on children who die before they are themselves economically productive are wasted from an economic point of view. From a demographic viewpoint those who die before they produce children of their own are of no value in replacing the population. When it is seen that over one-third of the females born in 1830 never reached age 20, it becomes apparent that later cohorts invested fewer resources in children who would not survive to adulthood, and later cohorts could replace themselves at a substantially lower fertility level.

TYPE 2. THE SPINSTER LIFE CYCLE

Women who survive to age 20 but never subsequently marry fall into the spinster type of life cycle. In contrast to the abbreviated life cycle, these women are exposed to the risk of marriage, but do not succumb. In order to calculate the number of women in this category it was necessary to make several assumptions. First, it was assumed that mortality rates were the same for married and single women at ages between 20 and 50. Various studies of mortality have indicated that age-specific death rates for unmarried women are higher than those for married women. No data on this differential are available for most of the cohorts studied in this paper. The assumption of equal mortality, however, may not be very unrealistic. The negative selection of the single leading to their higher mortality was counteracted in earlier cohorts by the risk of mortality related to pregnancy and child-bearing which the unmarried women did not encounter. For cohorts prior to 1890 the probability of a woman dying between the ages of 25 and 45 was higher than the probability of a man dying between these ages, indicating that the influence of deaths related to pregnancy may have been significantly large. The 1867 Massachusetts Vital Registration Report attributes about 10% of female deaths directly to childbearing,[6] and it is likely that more were indirectly related to this.

A second assumption is that the 1830 and 1850 cohorts had marital patterns at their younger ages similar to those recorded for women in the 1890 census. Since earlier data on marital status are not available, no other assumption seems preferable. Mean ages at marriage for females, as calculated from vital statistics, do not show large variations (less than one year) between 1850 and 1890, indicating that it is unlikely that major changes in marital patterns occurred.[7] Other cohort marital

[6] *Massachusetts Vital Registration Report, 1867,* pp. lxxii–lxxxvii.
[7] Thomas P. Monahan, *The Pattern of Age at Marriage in the United States* (Philadelphia, 1951).

patterns are based on the results of decennial censuses and more accurately reflect the cohort experience. A final assumption is that no single women marry after age 50, which is reasonable since vital statistics indicate that the number who do marry after they are 50 is wholly insignificant.

The number of women experiencing this second type of life cycle may be calculated by adding the number of single women who die before age 50 and the number who are alive and single at age 50. The number single at 50 is equal to the product of the proportion single at 50 for the cohort and the number of women surviving to 50. The number of single women who die at any age between 20 and 50 is obtained by multiplying the total number of deaths to women during the age period by the ratio of years lived single to total years lived by the cohort during that period.[8] The proportion of years lived single between ages x and $x+5$ by a cohort is approximated by the census figure of the proportion single in the age group x to $x+5$ which includes the cohort.[9] For the 1890 cohort between ages 20 and 25 this comes to 71·3%. The total number of women in the 1890 cohort who die between 20 and 25 is 1,622, so the number of women dying single between 20 and 25 equals 0·713 × 1,622 = 1,156. Summing the number who die in each age group from 20 to 50 gives the number who die single before age 50. (The data used to make these calculations are shown in Tables 1 and 2 in the Appendix.)

The number of women from each cohort who fall into the spinster category is:

Cohort of:	1830	1850	1870	1890	1920
Die single before 50	6,200	6,100	5,400	3,900	1,500
Single at 50	6,700	8,100	12,400	13,900	9,100
Type 2. Total number of spinsters	12,900	14,200	17,800	17,800	10,600

Although the number of unmarried women dying before their fiftieth birthday declined continuously from 1830 onward, the number of women who never married increased from 1830 to 1890, and then declined sharply for the 1920 cohort. The reason for this pattern was primarily the rise in proportion single at age 50 from 14·6 to 22·3 between the 1830 and the 1890 cohorts, and then an abrupt decline to 10·7% for the 1920 cohort. In addition to changing economic and social conditions during this period, which influence age at marriage and proportion who ever marry, there was a significant change in the composition of the population. There was an increase in the proportion of women with foreign-born parents from less than 10 for the 1830 cohort to 47 for the 1870 cohort. Among women with foreign-born parents in the 1870 cohort, 26·9% remained unmarried at age 50, in contrast to 19·1% for the native-born with native parents. Thus the large increase in women with foreign-born parents in the cohorts of 1870 and 1890 was responsible for much of the increase in the proportion never marrying.

[8] This assumes that age–specific death rates are constant within each five-year age group from 20 to 55, which is a reasonably accurate assumption.

[9] The proportion single in the age group x to $x+5$ in the census is the weighted average of the proportion single at each age between x and $x+5$, where the weights are the number at each age. Provided there are no large differences in the number at each age and the marital patterns do not change rapidly over a five-year interval, this is a good approximation of the proportion of time lived single by the cohort as it moves through these ages.

TYPE 3. THE BARREN LIFE CYCLE

Women who marry but never become mothers do not contribute to the replacement of the population. These women compose the third type of life cycle under consideration. The number of childless wives is equal to the sum of the number of ever-married women at age 50 who are childless, plus the number of married women who die childless before age 50. The assumption is made that married women who are childless experience the same mortality rates as those who have children. Again, there are the opposing biases of deaths from childbirth and the selectivity of the less healthy to remain childless, which are assumed roughly to balance each other. (Tables 1 and 3 in the Appendix give the data from which these calculations were made.)

The following table presents the number of childless wives for each cohort:

Cohort of:	1830	1850	1870	1890	1920
Die childless under 50	2,600	2,500	2,300	1,900	500
Childless at 50	6,900	7,500	9,100	10,300	8,500
Type 3. Total number barren	9,500	10,000	11,400	12,200	9,000

The total number of women in this category increases for each cohort up to 1890 and then drops sharply for the 1920 cohort. Each cohort had fewer wives dying childless before age 50 than the previous cohort due to declining mortality and, up to the 1870 cohort, due also to fewer women marrying. The number of women reaching age 50 and still childless rose continuously up to the 1890 cohort, and then declined for the 1920 cohort. The proportion of married women reaching 50 who remained childless reached its peak for the cohort of 1870 when more than one-fifth were in this category. The proportion childless for the 1920 cohort was only slightly more than half that for the 1890 cohort, a significant change to occur in only 30 years.

TYPE 4. DYING MOTHER LIFE CYCLE

A woman is considered to follow a dying-mother life cycle if she is a mother who dies before age 55. Age 55 is chosen as an approximate average age of mothers when their last child leaves home or marries. It may be preferable to calculate this average age for each cohort separately since it varies, but data on age at birth of last child are not available for most of the cohorts. Therefore age 55 was chosen as a reasonable average age, and was used for each cohort. This is about the same age as Glick and Parke have determined for United States cohorts of women born between 1880 and 1900.[10] For the earlier cohorts, age 55 appears to be rather conservative since Hajnal's singulate mean age at marriage for the 1850 cohort was 25·2 years and the average number of children ever born for mothers in this cohort was about 3·5 (Table 1). Allowing one year between marriage and the birth of the first child and two years between subsequent births gives an average age at birth of last child of about 31. Since the mean age at marriage for females born at this time was also close to 25 years, women would on the average be 56 years old or more at the time of marriage of their last child. For the purposes of this paper, however, age 55 appears to be a good approximation for all of the cohorts.

[10] Glick and Parke, *loc. cit.*, p. 190.

Table I. *Distribution of women according to children ever born for selected Massachusetts cohorts, 1830–1920*

Cohort	Number of children				Number of children per woman
	0	1–3	4–6	7+	
1830 (50–59 in 1885C)					
Total ever married	12·5%	35·1%	27·9%	24·5%	4·3
Foreign born	9·3	20·5	28·1	41·8	5·7
Native born	14·8	45·6	27·8	11·8	3·3
Native-born mothers		53·5	32·6	13·9	3·8
1850 (55–64 in 1910C)					
Total ever married	14·6	41·4	20·4	23·5	3·8
Foreign born	8·3	23·5	28·9	39·3	5·2
Native born	18·9	54·0	14·5	12·5	2·8
Native-born mothers		66·6	17·9	15·4	3·4
1870 (40–45 in 1910C)					
Total ever married	16·2	41·0	24·1	18·6	3·6
Foreign born	9·9	29·7	29·7	29·6	4·7
Native born	21·5	50·6	18·6	9·3	2·7
Native-born mothers		64·5	23·7	11·8	3·4
1890 (45–54 in 1940C)					
Total ever married	16·6	51·8	22·7	9·0	2·9
Foreign born	10·4	46·4	29·8	13·4	3·5
Native born	21·2	55·9	17·3	5·6	2·4
Native-born mothers		70·9	22·0	7·1	3·0
1920 (35–45 in 1960C)					
Total ever married	11·2	64·8	21·1	2·9	2·5
Native born	11·2	64·8	21·1	2·9	2·5
Native-born mothers		73·0	23·8	3·3	2·9

SOURCE: Derived from: *Massachusetts Census of 1885*, Vol. II; *U.S. Census*, 1940, 'Population: Differential Fertility, 1940 and 1910'; *U.S. Census*, 1960.

The number of mothers who die before they are 55 years old is simply the residual of all women who die before that age who do not fit any of the previous types. These mothers who do not survive to age 55 can further be divided according to whether their deaths result in their children being left orphans, or whether the father survives. Assuming that the likelihood of the father dying is independent of the likelihood of the mother dying, the number of mothers whose death results in orphanhood of children is equal to the proportion of mothers who die before 55 times the total number of fathers who die before their wife is 55. In order to calculate the number of fathers who die, the assumption that mortality rates for married and unmarried are equal was made, and, as indicated by vital statistics data,[11] husbands were assumed to be on the average two years older than their wives. Further analysis of life cycles should attempt to determine more accurately the differential mortality of married and unmarried persons and the probability of joint deaths of husband and wife, but in the absence of any data on this for the cohorts in this study the above approximations are used.

[11] Monahan, *op. cit.*

2 D

The number of women following the orphan-producing and motherless-child-producing life cycles are given in the following table:

Cohort of:	1830	1850	1870	1890	1920
Type 4. Dying mother	11,900	11,700	8,700	7,800	4,000
Type 4 (a). Motherless-child producing	8,100	8,400	6,300	6,000	3,500
Type 4 (b). Orphan producing	3,800	3,300	2,400	1,800	500

A substantial decline in the number experiencing these life cycles is evident for the more recent cohorts. The decline from 11,900 premature deaths to mothers for the 1830 cohort to 4,000 for the 1920 cohort is even more remarkable when we take into account that the number of women who ever became mothers increased from 42,000 to 69,700. This means that the probability of a mother dying before her last child left home or married declined from 31% for the 1830 cohort to 5·6% for the 1920 cohort. More serious social problems were produced by women leaving orphans than those leaving children with a living father who could support the children and establish a new family by re-marrying. As shown above, the number of women who left orphans declined by 87% over this period, and the drop in the proportion of mothers who left orphans was even more striking. The social problem associated with orphanhood and the social institutions required to care for orphans were greatly altered as a consequence of the demographic changes relative to fewer deaths of mothers with dependent children.

TYPE 5. WIDOWED MOTHER

A woman who becomes a mother and survives to 55 is considered to follow the widowed mother life cycle if her first husband dies before she reaches this age. The following table indicates little change in the total number of mothers reaching age 55 who have been widowed:

Cohort of:	1830	1850	1870	1890	1920
Type 5. Number of widowed mothers	9,100	9,800	8,600	8,500	8,500

The probability that a woman reaching age 55 had been widowed, however, shows the expected sharp decline for later cohorts. About 30% of the mothers living to age 55 in the 1830 cohort had been widowed, while this was the case for 24% of surviving mothers in the 1890 cohort and only 13% in the 1920 cohort. One significant consequence of this demographic change was a reduction in social problems related to families without a male head.

TYPE 6. THE TYPICAL LIFE CYCLE

Finally we arrive at the 'typical' life cycle, that is, the life cycle of the woman who marries, has children and survives jointly with her husband until her last child marries. This pattern is denoted as typical because it is the pattern that one generally expects a new-born baby girl to follow during her life time. For each cohort studied here it was more likely that a female would survive to 20 than die before she reached her twentieth birthday, it was more likely that a woman reaching age 20 would marry than that she would remain single, having married it was more likely that she would become a mother than that she would remain childless, it was more likely that a mother would survive to 55 than die before that age, and having survived to 55 it was more likely than not that her husband was also alive. Nevertheless, as indicated by the following table, only one female in five born into the 1830 cohort of native born Massachusetts females followed the typical life cycle:

Cohort of:	1830	1850	1870	1890	1920
Type 6. Typical	20,900	23,000	22,600	27,400	57,100

Because of decreasing mortality for men and women, decreasing rates of childlessness, and increasing marriage rates, nearly three times as many women in the 1920 cohort were included in the typical life cycle category. Figure 2 demonstrates the great reduction in the number of women who experience life cycles other than the typical one. The 1920 cohort had fewer women in each type of life cycle other than the typical than any previous cohort, indicating a standardization of demographic behaviour. Due to the continuation of these same trends, it appears that there has been even greater uniformity of life cycle among women in more recent cohorts.

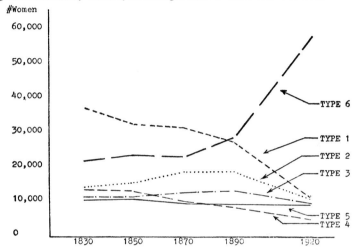

FIGURE 2. *Number of women in each cohort who experience various life cycles*

DISCUSSION OF CHANGING LIFE CYCLE PATTERNS

Increasing uniformity of demographic behaviour since the mid-nineteenth century also appears in the increasing concentration of marriages within the age period 20 to 30 (Appendix, Table 2), and the concentration of number of children ever born within the range 1 to 3 (Table 1). Nearly three-fourths of the native-born mothers in the 1920 cohort had between one and three children, compared to about half the mothers in the 1830 cohort. Another indicator of increased uniformity is shown by the fact that although ever married native-born women in the cohorts of 1890 and 1920 had almost the same number of children per woman, only half as many women in 1920 had either no children or seven or more. In general, fertility of married women declined from the 1830 cohort to the 1890 one, and then remained at the same level for the 1920 cohort.

Noting the rather low fertility even for the early cohorts, the question arises – what level of fertility would have been required of women who became mothers in each cohort in order for the cohort to replace itself, and were they in fact replacing themselves? Assuming a sex ratio at birth of 105 males per 100 females, it would be necessary for each cohort of women to produce 205,000 live births to replace itself. The number of live births per mother required is 205,000 divided by the number of women who became mothers. The number required for each cohort is given in Table 2 along with number actually ever born to mothers surviving to the end of their reproductive period and the ratio of the actual to the required. It is interesting to note that with the mortality and marital conditions prevailing in the nineteenth century, the fertility patterns of the cohorts in that century led to substantial failure of the cohorts to replace themselves. This phenomenon would not have appeared if the cohorts had included foreign-born women with their much higher fertility.

TABLE 2. *Actual number of births per mother and number required for cohorts to replace themselves*

	1830	1850	Cohort of 1870	1890	1920
Number of births per mother	3·8	3·4	3·4	3·0	2·9
Number required for replacement	4·9	4·6	5·1	4·7	2·9
Actual/required	0·78	0·73	0·67	0·64	1·00

The changes in life cycles noted thus far raise two basic types of questions – what produced these changes and what consequences did these changes have upon other demographic and social variables? Several social consequences have already been indicated – decreased wastage of resources spent on children who do not survive to become productive, decreased problems associated with orphanhood, and decreased likelihood of early widowhood. The important demographic consequence of the effect of changed patterns of life cycles upon population growth was also mentioned above. One further change was a very significant increase in the number of women who survive to spend a large part of their married life together with their husband after the last child has left home. Together with the widening gap in mortality rates between the sexes, this has resulted in a large increase in older widows who are dependent either upon their children or upon welfare. This increase is reflected in the expanded system of social security for the old that has developed since the beginning of this century.

The immediate cause of the observed changes in number of women experiencing the various types of life cycles are changes in mortality, percentage marrying and percentage having children. The best understood of these changes is the declining mortality throughout this 90-year period. Table 3 shows the decline in deaths from selected causes from the beginning of this period to the end. The control of contagious and infectious diseases, above all tuberculosis, through improved sanitation, better living conditions, public health efforts and medical advances led to the very different survival patterns recorded for the different cohorts in Table 1 of the Appendix. The improvement in female survival was substantially greater than that for males. The probability of a man surviving to age 50 in the 1830 cohort was 98% of that of a woman surviving to 50; for the 1920 cohort the ratio was reduced to 68%. The superior improvement for women is indicated by the much greater decline in the number of women following the dying-mother life cycle than the widowed-mother type.

In order to trace some of the forces producing the change in proportion marrying and having children, it is helpful to look more closely at the cohorts of 1870 and 1920. Since the possibility of marriage for women will be limited if there are no available single men, the first hypothesis that must be examined is that the sex ratio was more favourable for marriage by women in the 1920 cohort. In order to determine the situation at the time when each cohort became liable to the risk of marriage, the sex ratio of single men aged 15 to 45 to single women of the same age was calculated for the year when each cohort reached age 20. For the 1870 cohort this ratio was 1·04; for the 1920 cohort it was 1·08. Thus there was no significant change between the two cohorts, and for each there were more single men between the ages of 15 and 45 than single women.

TABLE 3. *Changes in mortality from selected causes; Massachusetts, 1856–1865 and 1945*

Cause of death	Death rate per 100,000		Percentage decline
	1856–65	1945	
All causes	1,794·7[1]	1,222·3	31·9
Typhoid and paratyphoid fever	92·5	0·1	99·9
Diphtheria	86·1	0·3	99·7
Measles	17·1	0·2	98·8
Scarlet fever	101·3	0·2	99·8
Whooping cough	23·8	0·5	97·9
Smallpox	11·0	0·0	100·0
Diarrhoea and enteritis	165·9[1]	4·3	97·4
Tuberculosis	446·4	39·3	91·2
Pneumonia	107·4	48·7	54·7
Infant mortality rate	174·2[2]	31·6	81·9

NOTES: (1) Death rate for 1856–60.
(2) This rate for the city of Boston, 1849–50.
SOURCE: Dublin *et al.*, *Length of Life*, p. 164.

As noted earlier, the proportion of native-born women with foreign-born parents was not significantly different for the 1870 and 1920 cohorts. Table 4 shows, however, that there was an almost total shift between the native-born with foreign parents in the two cohorts with respect to area of origin of their parents. The proportion of native-born women with Irish parents declined from 32·1 to 5·5% while that with Italian parents rose from 0·7 to 28·5%. Overall, the ratio of women with parents born in Southern or Eastern Europe to all those with parents born in Europe rose from 3·5 for the 1870 cohort to 80·0 for the 1920 cohort. Women born in Southern and Eastern Europe were characterized by earlier marriages and higher fertility than women born in Western Europe, and the same differences existed between the descendants of these two groups in the United States. Since native-born with foreign parents comprised nearly half the native-born in each cohort, the change in national origin of parents can account for much of the change in marriage and childbearing patterns.

TABLE 4. *Percentage of parents of native-born women with foreign-born parents in 1870 and 1920 cohorts who came from selected areas*

Country or region	Cohort of 1870	1920
Ireland	32·1	5·5
England and Wales	13·7	3·4
Germany	28·3	3·6
Italy	0·7	28·5
Canada	8·9	7·0
Western Europe	86·6	17·1
Southern and Eastern Europe	3·5	72·8

SOURCE: *U.S. Census of Population*, 1940, 'Parentage of Native Born with Foreign Parents, p. 92.

Another factor which seems related to the different distribution of women according to type of life cycle for the two cohorts was the change in economic conditions during their periods of marriage and childbearing. The period when decisions concerning marriage and childbearing were made by the 1870 cohort was 1890 to 1910, a time of very rapid industrialization and very poor working conditions. Table 5 shows that 54% of the women aged 15 to 25 in 1890 were employed, and 58% of those employed worked in manufacturing. By 1940, 35% of the women between 15 and 25 were employed and 35% of these worked in manufacturing, while nearly half had white-collar jobs. The period from 1940 to 1960, when the 1920 cohort was making decisions about marriage and childbearing, was a time of economic prosperity and greatly improved working conditions. There is a need for this and other plausible hypotheses to be further examined in order to determine the causes of the observed changes.

TABLE 5. *Employment of females 15–24 in 1890 and 1940, according to occupation*

	1890		1940	
	Total	Percentage	Total	Percentage
Females aged 15–24	237,667		382,071	
Employed	128,428	54·0	135,071	35·4
White-collar	18,313	14·3	60,520	44·8
Domestic Service	35,586	27·7	23,425	17·3
Manufacturing	74,433	58·0	45,416	33·6
Other			5,710	4·2

SOURCE: *U.S. Census of Population*, 1890, Vol. 1 : 2, pp. 360–371; 1940, Vol. 3 : 3, p. 485.

In conclusion, this approach to the study of cohort life cycles rather clearly traces out what happens demographically in the lives of groups of women beginning life at different periods of time, and suggests that historical changes have been very interesting. Further refinement could specify additional types of life cycles, making each one more homogeneous. This approach enables one to specify what factors were directly responsible for changing life cycle patterns over time, and hence to focus on the social and demographic changes that impinge upon the life cycle. Also, the distribution of women according to type of life cycle followed for different cohorts is of help in understanding other social changes. Basically what this life cycle approach attempts to do is determine the social and demographic consequences of the interaction of several demographic variables which can move more or less independently of one another.

ACKNOWLEDGEMENT

This research has been supported by training grants to the Department of Demography from the National Institute of General Medical Sciences (5 TO1 GMO1240) and the Ford Foundation. I am grateful to Professors Kingsley Davis, Nathan Keyfitz and Judith Davis for their comments on an earlier draft of this paper.

APPENDIX

TABLE A 1. *Number surviving to specified ages for selected cohorts of 100,000 native-born white Massachusetts females and males, 1830–1920*

Age	Females 1830[1]	1850	1870	1890	1920
0	100,000	100,000	100,000	100,000	100,000
5	71,369	75,021	75,957	77,509	91,131
10	68,594	72,519	72,702	76,025	90,305
15	66,434	70,980	71,324	75,049	89,801
20	64,412	68,641	69,140	73,708	89,156
25	61,113	65,099	66,606	72,086	88,516
30	58,065	62,385	64,417	69,842	87,977
35	54,847	59,118	61,931	68,141	87,451
40	52,322	56,022	59,583	66,434	86,797
45	49,372	52,917	57,209	64,621	85,812
50	46,151	50,110	54,537	62,472	84,738
55	42,645	46,444	51,462	59,862	82,953
60	38,579	41,879	47,334	56,681	81,105
65	33,254	36,469	41,954	52,438	77,971

Age	Males 1830[1]	1850	1870	1890	1920
0	100,000	100,000	100,000	100,000	100,000
5	67,528	71,894	73,980	75,561	89,237
10	64,393	69,000	71,088	74,024	88,242
15	62,086	67,671	69,874	73,030	87,573
20	61,393	65,877	67,864	71,581	86,718
25	58,798	63,086	65,199	69,768	84,459
30	56,233	60,780	62,980	66,976	83,391
35	53,477	57,965	60,385	65,272	82,553
40	51,134	54,885	57,536	63,350	81,493
45	48,236	51,639	54,589	61,053	79,820
50	44,839	48,412	51,402	58,066	77,648
55	40,842	44,331	48,019	54,207	74,086
60	36,442	39,151	43,197	49,239	69,971
65	30,684	33,100	36,964	42,772	64,114

NOTE: (1) Assumes same mortality for 1830 cohort as recorded for 1840 cohort.
SOURCE: Jacobson, *Cohort Survival for Generations Since 1840.*

TABLE A 2. *Percentage single for cohorts of native-born women in Massachusetts, by age*

Age	1830[1]	1805[1]	1870	1890	1920
20–24	70·8	70·8	70·8	71·3	67·5
25–29	43·9	43·9	46·8		22·5
30–34	29·1	29·1	32·3	37·5	15·7
35–44	19·9	19·9	25·6	22·5	10·7
45–54	14·6	16·9	22·6	22·3	10·7[2]

NOTES: (1) Where data are not available for younger age periods, these cohorts were assumed to follow the pattern recorded in the 1890 Census.

(2) If no change occurs between age periods 35–44 and 45–54.

SOURCES: *U.S. Census of Population*, 1890, Vol. 1 : 1, p. 851; 1900, Vol. 2, p. 279; 1910, Vol. 1, p. 557; 1920, Vol. 2, p. 429; 1930, Vol. 2, p. 867; 1940, Vol. 4 : 3, p. 104; 1950, Vol. 2 : 21, p. 119; 1960, Vol. 1 : 23, pp. 306–7.

TABLE A 3. *Percentage childless for cohorts of native-born Massachusetts women who ever married, by age*

Age	1830[1]	1850[1]	1870	1890	1920
20–29	31·9	31·9	31·9	36·1	25·1
30–39	20·2	20·2	26·1	26·1	13·1
40–49	17·4	17·4	21·6	21·2	11·2

NOTE: (1) See footnote 1, Table 2 in appendix.

SOURCES: *Massachusetts Census of 1885*, Vol. 2, pp. 1174–1175; U.S. Census of 1940, *Differential Fertility, 1940 and 1910: Women by Number of Children ever Born*, pp. 30, 39, 109, 119; U.S. Census of 1940, *Differential Fertility, 1940 and 1910: Fertility for States and Large Cities*, pp. 206–208.

Robert V. Wells

Demographic Change and the
Life Cycle of American Families
Between the eighteenth and the twentieth centuries, major changes occurred in the patterns of birth and death of the American population. The birth rate declined by over 50 per cent, from around 50 per 1,000 in 1800 to less than 20 per 1,000 today.[1] Although the evidence on mortality is less clear, there can be no doubt that substantial improvements in life expectancy occurred during this period. The best estimates indicate that life expectancy at birth came close to doubling between about 1800 and 1970.[2] In view of the magnitude of these changes, it is surprising to find that so little is known of their impact on American social institutions.

How did these major demographic changes affect one of the fundamental parts of our society—the family? In particular, how did the decline in both fertility and mortality alter the life cycle of the American family in the two centuries since the American Revolution?[3]

Glick, who has played an important role in the study of American families in the twentieth century, has described the life cycle of the family:

> Between formation and dissolution, families go through a series of characteristic stages which lend themselves to demographic analysis. These stages include marriage, the establishment of a household, bearing and rearing children, marriage of the children, and the later years before the family is finally dissolved. Successive readjustments of behavior patterns are required as the adult members shift their roles from

Robert V. Wells is Assistant Professor of History at Union College. He is the author of "Family Size and Fertility Control in Eighteenth Century America: A Study of Quaker Families," *Population Studies*, XXV (1971). An earlier version of this paper was delivered at the 1971 meeting of the Population Association of America.

1 For estimates of the birth rate in 1800, see Ansley J. Coale and Melvin Zelnik, *New Estimates of Fertility and Population in the United States* (Princeton, 1963), 39; W. S. Thompson and P. K. Whelpton, *Population Trends in the United States* (New York, 1933), 263.

2 The standard estimate for life expectancy at birth for before 1800 is about 35 years; see Thompson and Whelpton, *Population Trends*, 239. My own work has indicated that this figure may be slightly low, but not by more than five years.

3 Compare the approach and findings of this study with Peter R. Uhlenberg, "A Study of Cohort Life Cycles: Cohorts of Native Born Massachusetts Women, 1830–1920," *Population Studies*, XXIII (1969), 407–420.

Reprinted from *The Journal of Interdisciplinary History* II 273–282 (1971). By permission of The Journal of Interdisciplinary History and The M.I.T. Press, Cambridge, Massachusetts.

newly wedded persons to parents of small children, parents of older children, older couples without children at home, and surviving widows or widowers.[4]

By comparing the patterns of marriage, childbearing, and death of adults of the eighteenth and twentieth centuries, it should be possible to determine those aspects of family life which have remained relatively stable over time, as well as the ways in which the life of the family has changed in the last 200 years.

Two studies provide the basic evidence for this paper. My own work provides data on 276 Quaker families in which the wife was born before 1786. These families lived in New York, New Jersey, and Pennsylvania in the eighteenth and early nineteenth centuries. As most of the data come from before 1800, these will be referred to as eighteenth-century families. These Quakers cannot be assumed to represent the American population as a whole before 1800, but there is evidence to suggest that their life cycle was much the same as that of their contemporaries. Figures for American families in general in the nineteenth and twentieth centuries have been taken from the study by Glick and Parke, "New Approaches in Studying the Life Cycle of the Family."[5] This study was the first attempt to examine the family life cycle by cohort analysis, and, as such, is more comparable to the Quaker data than Glick's earlier work.[6] In all, Glick and Parke consider the family life cycle of six different cohorts of women (defined by the year of birth), but only two of these groups have been selected for consideration here. The first includes families in which the wives were born between 1880 and 1889; this is the earliest group for which the authors present data. The second group of families is defined by wives born between 1920 and 1929; they are selected for study here

---

4 Paul C. Glick, *American Families* (New York, 1957), 53.

5 See Paul C. Glick and Robert Parke, Jr., *Demography*, II (1965), 187–202; for a listing of Glick's earlier writings, see 187. It should be noted that, although the subjects of Glick's figures are still alive, he has predicted aggregate demographic characteristics on the basis of current mortality trends. Historians who wish to incorporate the family life cycle concept into their own work should consult the article by John B. Lansing and Leslie Kish, "Family Life Cycle as an Independent Variable," *American Sociological Review*, XXII (1957), 512–519. The importance of this study lies in the suggestion that behavior patterns of adults are likely to change as people move from one stage of the life cycle of the family to another.

6 Cohort analysis groups persons under study by events which they all experience at the same time. The two most common events used to define a group (i.e., a cohort) are the year of birth and the year of marriage. The cohorts are then followed over time, for as long as the study requires, to see when, or at what age, other events occur.

because they are the most recent group for which the figures are relatively complete.

Three other points need to be mentioned before proceeding to the analysis of change in family life cycles. First, the following information is for first marriages only. It raises several questions which will be considered at the end of the paper. Second, the discussion concentrates on the experience of the wives. In part this is because the data for the Quaker women of this study are better than that for their husbands, but it is also true that the figures for the men are virtually the same except for the fact that they married later than the women, and hence reached each successive stage of the family at a correspondingly older age. Third, this study concentrates on the experience of the adult members of a family. It would be of obvious interest to know how children were affected by changing fertility and mortality, but the lack of both data and space prevent an exploration of this subject here.

Since the life of a family begins with marriage, let us look first at the changes in the age at first marriage between the eighteenth and twentieth centuries. As seen in my study of the Quakers, the median age at first marriage was 20.5 for the women.[7] Studies of genealogies and New England town records suggest that, in this regard, they were much like other eighteenth-century Americans.[8] Among wives born between 1880 and 1889, however, families were formed somewhat later in the life of the bride as the median age at first marriage had increased to 21.6 among women. This increase is not surprising, for the age at first marriage among women appears to have been on the rise throughout the eighteenth century.[9] The twentieth century brought a reversal to this long-term trend, for women born between 1920 and 1929 were marrying at a median age of 20.8 years, much the same as in the colonial period. Certainly marriage patterns varied, but the difference between the highest and the lowest figures of just over one year among the women suggests that marriages were formed at much the same point in life throughout the last two centuries.

In most cases, marriage was followed within a year or two by a first child, whether the couple lived in the eighteenth or twentieth

7 These figures, and those which follow, have been summarized in Tables 1 and 2 in the Appendix. The sources for the data and the way in which the figures were calculated are described there.
8 This evidence has been collected in Robert V. Wells, "Quaker Marriage Patterns in a Colonial Perspective," unpublished paper.
9 *Ibid.*

centuries. But there the similarity in childbearing patterns ends. According to Glick and Parke, the median age of mothers at the birth of their last child was 30.5 for women born in the 1920s. Thus, for these wives, the median length of time spent between marriage and the end of the childbearing stage of life was only 9.7 years. This figure contrasts sharply with the 17.4 years which one of the Quaker women of the eighteenth century might expect to spend bearing children. Among the Friends studied here, the median age of mothers at the birth of the last child was 37.9 years.[10] I have suggested elsewhere that these Quakers were among the first Americans deliberately to limit the size of their families.[11] As a result, their families were, in all probability, smaller than the average for eighteenth-century America, and their childbearing presumably ended at an earlier age. Thus, if anything, the decline in length of the childbearing period between the late-eighteenth and the mid-twentieth centuries is understated. It is of interest to note that among wives born between 1880 and 1889, the median length of the childbearing period was 11.3 years, considerably shorter than that of the eighteenth-century families. Apparently, the decline in fertility was well underway by the end of the nineteenth century and, among groups like these Quakers, this trend may date back to the era of the American Revolution.

Because of the longer time spent in childbearing, parents of the eighteenth century also spent more of their life rearing their children than did parents in later years. Among the Quakers of this study, the last child married and left home when the mother was of a median age of 60.2. Wives born between 1880 and 1889 were of a median age of 56.2 when their last child left home. They were only slightly younger than the eighteenth-century women in this regard, because the rise in the age at marriage had partially offset the effects of the reduced childbearing period. But, by the mid-twentieth century, earlier marriages and a shorter time spent bearing children combined to free parents of their children at an earlier age. The median age among the last group of wives when their children were finally married and gone was 52.0, almost ten years less than the corresponding figure among the Quakers. Almost forty years passed between the formation of an eighteenth-century family and the time when child-rearing was finished. By the end of the nineteenth century, however, the effects of the

10 This figure is for all women married before the age of forty-five.
11 Robert V. Wells, "Family Size and Fertility Control in Eighteenth Century America: A Study of Quaker Families," *Population Studies*, XXV (1971), 173–182.

gradual decline in fertility were beginning to show. Families in which the wife was born between 1880 and 1889, and whose childbearing held to the average, were spending only thirty-five years in the child-rearing stage; among couples where the wife was born between 1920 and 1929, the median interval between the formation of a family and the departure of the last child was only thirty-one years.

In addition to spending less of their life rearing children, the evidence suggests that parents in the twentieth century experienced a more stable family situation. As Glick has pointed out, once modern parents stopped childbearing, their family was normally of a constant size until their children began to marry and leave home.[12] Families of the late eighteenth century, however, were subjected to growth for a much longer period and high mortality continually threatened the family with the death of parents and children. The stability of twentieth-century families is emphasized by the fact that only 31 per cent of the total time spent rearing children was devoted to childbearing by wives born between 1920 and 1929. The comparable figures are 33 per cent for wives born between 1880 and 1889, and 44 per cent for the wives born before 1786. Undoubtedly women benefited from this change, not only because they had fewer children to raise, but also because the burden of pregnancy less frequently interfered with their ability to rear their children.

In addition to the changes in the life cycle of the family introduced by the long-term decline in fertility, improving conditions of mortality also had a recognizable impact on the family. However, the effects of increased life expectancy were felt predominantly in the twentieth century, for, until about 1890, conditions of mortality improved slowly, if at all.

The most fundamental change wrought by the decline in mortality has been an increase in the length of marriage. Among the Quakers studied here, the median duration of marriage was 30.4 years. Although other information on mortality before 1800 is scarce, studies of Andover and Plymouth in Massachusetts suggest that the life chances of these Quakers were not unusually good in the context of the colonial period.[13] It is important to note, however, that the median duration of marriage is somewhat deceptive regarding mortality conditions. A

---

12 Glick, *American Families*, 67.
13 Philip J. Greven, Jr., *Four Generations: Population, Land, and Family in Colonial Andover, Massachusetts* (Ithaca, 1970), 192, 195; John Demos, *A Little Commonwealth: Family Life in Plymouth Colony* (New York, 1970), 192–193.

surprisingly high proportion of these Quaker unions ended relatively quickly. Although only 1.9 per cent of the marriages lasted less than a year, almost a fifth (18.8 per cent) had been dissolved by the death of one partner before the fifteenth anniversary had been reached; after twenty-five years, 38.4 per cent of the unions once formed no longer existed. Couples who lived at the end of the 1800s could hope for but a little more time together than had these Quakers. Wives born between 1880 and 1889 had a median duration of marriage of 35.4 years, an increase of just over five years in about a century. In the next forty years, however, medical and sanitary improvements had a striking effect on the family, the median length of married life increasing to 43.6 years among the last group of wives.[14]

The fact that husbands and wives could expect a longer life together after about 1900 is, in itself, important. It is especially important, however, when one recalls the reduction in the length of child-rearing which had occurred by that period. Couples who married in the twentieth century were among the first who could reasonably expect a life together after their children had left home. By subtracting the median figure for the length of the child-rearing stage of life from that of the duration of marriage, it is apparent that couples in which the wife was born between 1920 and 1929 could expect 12.4 years of married life after their children had left home. In contrast, half of the marriages involving a wife born between 1880 and 1889 were broken by the death of one partner less than a year after the last child departed. Even more startling is the situation among the families of the eighteenth century. Fully 69 per cent of all the Quaker marriages studied were of shorter duration than the median length of child-rearing among that group. In fact, a Quaker widow or widower, whose experience held to the median, could expect to have children to take care of for 9.3 years after the death of his or her first spouse. Thus, by the twentieth century, longer marriages combined with a continuing decline in fertility to produce a situation in which, for the first time, couples could *expect* a life together after their children were gone. Companionship was beginning to join reproduction as an important expectation of marriage.

The relative decrease in the importance of children in the life of twentieth-century families is further illustrated by the increased duration between the marriage of the last child and the death of the last

14 This figure is based on the estimates of mortality trends among the cohort born between 1920 and 1929 in Glick and Parke, "New Approaches," 194–195, and Table 1.

parent to die. Among the Quakers who lived in the late 1700s, marriage was virtually synonymous with children. We have already seen that one spouse could expect to die before the children were completely reared; of equal importance is the fact that the surviving partner could expect to die less than five years after the last child married. Old age, without family, was not common before 1800. This situation had clearly changed by the twentieth century, as the experience of the wives born from 1880 to 1889 indicates. Among this group of families, wives who outlived their husbands died almost twenty years after their last child had left home; among the men of this group who survived their wives, the corresponding figure was fifteen years. Obviously, similar figures for the families in which the wife was born between 1920 and 1929 are not available. But unless life chances are sharply reduced, the trend toward a longer life after the children have left home should continue. Apparently, old age with no children present is largely a phenomenon of the modern world; the nation's founders seldom had to face the problem.

The last stage of the life cycle of the family which concerns us here is the length of widowhood, that is, the time between the death of one spouse and the death of the second. Here, too, improvements in life expectancy have had their effects. The Quaker widows of the 1700s survived for an average of 13.7 years after the death of their husbands. This figure is considerably below the median length of widowhood of 18.7 years for the wives born between 1880 and 1889. The corresponding increase in the length of widowhood among the men was much less. While the Quaker widowers of this study lived for 12.5 years after their wives had died, the figure for men whose wives were born between 1880 and 1889 was 14.2, an increase of almost two years. In addition to living longer after their children have left home, parents of the twentieth century are faced with an increased amount of time in their old age with none of their family around. In a very real sense, the reductions in fertility and mortality have increased the possibility of loneliness in old age.

This analysis of changes in the life cycle of the family has been carried out on first marriages only. It is, therefore, desirable to examine how typical these patterns are of the experience of all families in the various periods under consideration. Among the Quakers studied here, fully 88 per cent of all marriages were the first for both partners. Furthermore, of the wives, 97.5 per cent had never been married before; among the husbands, the proportion marrying for the first time was 88.8 per cent. Remarriage among these Quakers was rare, and there is evidence to suggest that other eighteenth-century American populations shared this pattern of behavior.[15] While the proportion of first marriages to all marriages is rather high, a surprisingly large number of these Quakers never wed. Perhaps as many as half of the Quaker children born before 1800 never married at all. Of course, most of those who did not marry died before they had the opportunity to wed. But, between 12 and 15 per cent of these Quakers who lived to the age of fifty died without marrying.

Depending upon one's perspective, first marriages were both more and less typical in 1950 than they were before 1800. The proportion of marriages which were the first for both husband and wife had fallen from 88 per cent before 1800 to 67 per cent by 1950.[16] Likewise, while 97.5 per cent of the Quaker wives were marrying for the first time, only 74.4 per cent of the brides in 1950 had never been married before. The corresponding figures for the men show a decline in the proportion marrying for the first time from 88.8 per cent to 75.5 per cent. While first marriages were less typical of all marriages in the twentieth century than they had been earlier, there can be little doubt that a higher proportion of the population took a spouse at least once. The proportion never married in 1950 of 7 to 8 per cent was approximately half that found among the Quakers. The percentage of children who died before marrying was clearly less, too. Perhaps 80 to 85 per cent of all children born in the middle of the twentieth century could expect to marry, compared to about 50 per cent among these Quakers.[17]

One last difference between the Quaker families of the eighteenth century and those of Americans in the mid-twentieth century deserves mention. Once a Quaker couple married they remained united until one spouse died. Divorce was extremely rare among the Friends, and among their contemporaries as well.[18] Among Americans in 1950, however, about 16 per cent of all marriages involved one partner who had been married, but who had divorced his previous spouse.[19] In fact, much of the increase in remarriage between 1800 and 1950 may

15 See Wells, "Quaker Marriage Patterns."
16 Glick, *American Families*, 142.
17 *Ibid.*, 140.
18 George E. Howard, *A History of Matrimonial Institutions* (Chicago, 1904), II, last part.
19 Glick, *American Families*, 142.

be the result of a rising number of divorces which were followed by a new marriage for one or both partners. From the point of view of the children, the increased family stability which resulted from parents being assured of a longer life together has been offset, to some extent, by a willingness of couples voluntarily to end their unions.

When the life cycle of these Quaker families (who do not seem to have been greatly different from their contemporaries) is compared to that of modern families, it seems apparent that, in the course of the last two centuries, the life cycle of most American families has become significantly more complex. From an almost exclusive concern with childbearing and child-rearing before 1800, the emphasis within a family has gradually shifted until now the life of the parents after their children have left home has become a major part of family living. This change can only partially be explained by the improved mortality conditions in modern America. The long-term decline in fertility, which may have started about the time of the American Revolution, also reduced the emphasis on the childbearing aspects of marriage. Thus, the life cycle of the family in the mid-twentieth century reflects both an intimate relationship to the modern world, and has roots which extend back to the founding of the nation.

APPENDIX

Table 1   Median Age of Wives at Stages of the Life Cycle of the Family

STAGE OF THE LIFE CYCLE OF THE FAMILY	WIVES BORN		
	BEFORE 1786 (QUAKERS)	1880–1889	1920–1929
A. First marriage	20.5[a]	21.6	20.8
B. Birth of last child	37.9	32.9	30.5
C. Marriage of last child	60.2	56.2	52.0
D. Death of first spouse to die	50.9	57.0	64.4

a   As measured by the interquartile range, the distribution around the median of the age at first marriage, the age of the mother at the birth of her last child, and the duration of marriage seem to have been much the same from one group to another.

Sources: The data for wives born before 1786 are my own. The information for the other wives is from Glick and Parke, "New Approaches", 190, Table 1.

Table 2 Median Length of Selected Stages of the Life Cycle of the Family (in Years)

STAGE OF THE LIFE CYCLE OF THE FAMILY	WIVES BORN		
	BEFORE 1786 (QUAKERS)	1880–1889	1920–1929
1. Childbearing	17.4	11.3	9.7
2. Child-rearing	39.7	34.6	31.2
3. Duration of Marriage	30.4	35.4	43.6
4. Old Age Together	− 9.3	0.8	12.4
5. Widowhood			
Female	13.7	18.7	—
Male	12.5	14.2	—
6. Marriage of last child to death of last spouse, when last is			
Female	4.4	19.5	—
Male	3.2	15.0	—

Source: The above table was derived as follows:

Table 2

Line 1 = Line B − Line A ⎫
Line 2 = Line C − Line A ⎬ From Table 1
Line 3 = Line D − Line A ⎪
Line 4 = Line D − Line C ⎭

Line 5 = The figures for the husbands and wives born before 1786 were calculated directly from my data. For the others, see Glick and Parke, "New Approaches," 195.

Line 6 = Line 4 + Line 5